ROBERT FROST
THE YEARS OF TRIUMPH

ROBERT FROST
THE YEARS OF TRIUMPH

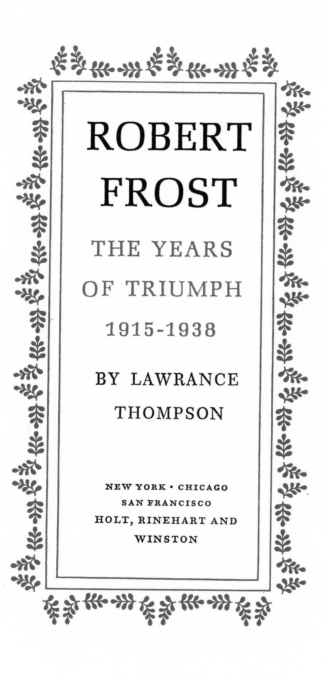

ROBERT FROST

THE YEARS OF TRIUMPH

1915-1938

BY LAWRANCE THOMPSON

NEW YORK · CHICAGO
SAN FRANCISCO
HOLT, RINEHART AND
WINSTON

Grateful acknowledgment is made to the following for permission to reprint excerpts from their publications:
Holt, Rinehart and Winston, Inc., for excerpts from *The Poetry of Robert Frost,* copyright © 1969 by Holt, Rinehart and Winston, Inc., copyright 1916, 1923, 1928, 1930, 1934, 1939, 1943, 1945, 1947, 1949, © 1967, by Holt, Rinehart and Winston, Inc.; copyright 1936, 1942, 1944, 1945, 1947, 1948, 1950, 1951, 1952, 1953, 1954, © 1955, 1956, 1958, 1959, 1960, 1961, 1962 by Robert Frost; copyright © 1964, 1967, 1970 by Lesley Frost Ballantine. For excerpts from *Selected Letters of Robert Frost,* edited by Lawrance Thompson; copyright © 1964 by Holt, Rinehart and Winston, Inc. For excerpts from *Robert Frost and John Bartlett* by Margaret Bartlett Anderson; copyright © 1963 by Margaret Bartlett Anderson. For excerpts from *The Letters of Robert Frost to Louis Untermeyer;* copyright © 1963 by Holt, Rinehart and Winston, Inc.
The Macmillan Company, New York, New York, for the sonnet entitled "New England" by Edwin Arlington Robinson, copyright 1925, © 1951 by The Macmillan Company.
Yale University Press for the sonnet entitled "Old Voices" and for excerpts from other poems in *The Dark Hills Under,* by Shirley Barker, The Yale Series of Younger Poets, copyright © 1933 by Yale University Press.
A special acknowledgment is made to Mr. Alfred C. Edwards, sole executor of the estate of Robert Frost, and former chairman and chief executive officer of Holt, Rinehart and Winston, Inc., for permission to quote the following three poems by Robert Frost which are either uncollected or hitherto unpublished: "Fish-Leap Fall," "Lowes Took the Obvious Position," and "Pride of Ancestry."

To

EDWARD CONNERY LATHEM
in friendship and
gratitude

CONTENTS

	Introduction	xi
	Acknowledgments	xxi
1.	Homecoming	1
2.	From Nowhere up to Somewhere	10
3.	My Own Strategic Retreat	23
4.	Return to Boston	30
5.	Making Friends—and Enemies	47
6.	My Voice and Manner	66
7.	Death of a Soldier-Poet	87
8.	The Amherst Idea	97
9.	Jeanie	123
10.	Trouble in Franconia	135
11.	Transplanted: A New Start	146
12.	Explorations	158
13.	The Michigan Fellowship	174
14.	The Long Trail	188
15.	A Round of Readings	202
16.	The Pulls on Me	215
17.	Yes I Suppose I Am a Puritan	230
18.	In the Councils of the Bold	249
19.	Freed from Obligation	268
20.	Sickness and Scatteration	282
21.	Speaking of Contraries	298
22.	Helping to Shape an Image	316
23.	To Europe for Health	328
24.	Good Old Folkways	344
25.	Encouraging Younger Poets	353
26.	A Farm for Myself	366
27.	Friendship Means Favor	375
28.	No Artist Should Have a Family	390
29.	Things in Pairs Ordained	409
30.	A Further Range	423
31.	A Harvard Year	444
32.	Pride of Ancestry	465
33.	Strike That Blow for Me	476
34.	And I the Last . . .	493
	Notes	513
	Index	705

ILLUSTRATIONS

❧❧❧

FOLLOWING PAGE 298

"New England's New Poet" in 1915
  Dartmouth College Library

The poet using his homemade writing board
  Plymouth State College Library

The Frost family in 1915
  Plymouth State College Library

The strolling bard in Troy, N.Y., 1921
  Louie M. Miner; The Jones Library, Amherst, Mass.

The Stone Cottage in South Shaftsbury, Vt., 1921
  Corinne Tennyson Davids

The farmer-poet at the Stone Cottage, 1921
  Yankee *magazine, Dublin, N.H.*

Fellow in Letters at Michigan in 1925

American visitor, Imperial Hotel, London, 1928
  Wade Van Dore
  World-Wide Photo

The Gully farmhouse, South Shaftsbury, Vt., 1929
  Corinne Tennyson Davids

At Bread Loaf School of English in 1935
  Bernard DeVoto; Dartmouth College Library

The Frost home in Amherst from 1931 to 1938
  The Jones Library, Amherst, Mass.

INTRODUCTION

NO ONE was at the pier in New York City to welcome Robert
Frost when he returned from England with his family in
February of 1915. He expected no one. At home, almost no attention had been given the small and yet important literary
triumph he had achieved in London during the two previous
years. The American edition of *North of Boston,* published only
a few days before he landed in New York, carried no blurb, no
hint that the poet's long struggle for literary recognition in
America was entering what seemed to him a desperately crucial
phase. He knew that if critics or reviewers asked his American
publisher for information about him they would learn practically nothing: no one in the office of Henry Holt and Company
had ever met or even corresponded with him. As it happened,
at least one reviewer was indeed so perplexed that he asked
in print, "Who is Robert Frost?"[1]

For years, the poet had been asking himself the same question, and in England he had wryly answered that he was one
who had the power to consist of the inconsistent, the power to
hold in unity the ultimate irreconcilables, the power to be a
bursting unity of opposites, and the power to make poetry out
of these opposites,[2] but that no one in America seemed to care
enough about him or his poetry. Having gone to England at the
age of thirty-eight, inured to failure, he might have relinquished
his persistent struggle for recognition. His early disappointments had caused him to become self-protectively arrogant,
and scornful of all scorners. A rebel, named after a rebel, he
had given his enemies plenty of chances to mock him for his
inability to succeed at the one thing he considered important.
What remained, however, was the fiercely driving ambition
which made him carry the manuscript of *A Boy's Will* into the
office of a London publisher, without any letters of introduction, soon after he reached England. The same urgency also
made him decide, when the manuscript was accepted, that he
would not sit back and wait to see what the reviewers might say
about his first book. Shrewdly, and among total strangers, he

had begun a campaign on behalf of *A Boy's Will,* and his moves were so skillful that they helped to win the friendship of several influential poets and critics. Now, returning home, he was ready to start a new phase of campaigning, again among strangers.

The results were surprising to everyone, including Robert Frost. A few days after he landed in New York, he went alone to Boston and made a few exploratory gestures. Almost immediately, however, he was acclaimed in print as "Boston's literary sensation of the day," as "a most agreeable personality," and as "one of the most loveable men in the world."[3] The attractiveness of his personality heightened the appeal made by the deceptive simplicity of his poetic idiom, and not long after he had discovered himself in Boston he began to accept invitations to read his poems in public.

On stage, he charmed his listeners with his humorous platform manner, his witty turns of phrase, and a New England accent which gave no hint he had spent the last three years abroad. Further testing his power to consist of the inconsistent, he managed to conceal from his audiences all the hurts and humiliations caused by the previous years of neglect. He also concealed his armor of scorn and arrogance, no longer needed. Deliberately, he created for himself the image of just a "plain New Hampshire farmer" whose theory and practice of poetry was down to earth. The poems he read to his listeners gave support to this image by expressing his genuinely sympathetic admiration for the virtues of back-country people who triumphed over hardship and gloried in the often overlooked attractiveness of ordinary rural experiences. His manner so convincingly dramatized his ideal of nicely balanced detachment and involvement that few if any of his listeners guessed the self-contradictions beneath the surface of this newly discovered poet. And he seemed to be modestly casual about the enormous change which had suddenly occurred in his life.

The persistent quality of this change from failure to triumph was evidenced by the steady flow of honors. Within a few months after the return from England, *North of Boston* became a best-seller. Shortly before the publication of his next book, *Mountain Interval,* he was elected to membership in the National Institute of Arts and Letters. A reading given at Amherst College brought an invitation to join the faculty there, and he accepted. Before long, the University of Michigan began to compete with Amherst for this "poet in residence," and the two academic years he spent in Ann Arbor, from 1921 to 1923, greatly elevated his national standing. His fourth book, *New Hampshire*, was awarded a Pulitzer Prize, and soon after the publication of his *Collected Poems* in 1930 (another Pulitzer Prize winner) he was elected to membership in the American Academy of Arts and Letters. During the next few years, he became the best-known and the best-loved poet in America, praised at home and abroad as one whose poetry had already won him a lasting place as a major American literary figure. He had reason to be elated, and after one exceptionally successful public performance he walked offstage triumphantly singing,

> *"I wish my mother could see me now,*
> *With a fence-post under my arm."*[4]

If his poetry-writing mother had lived to share the excitement of all these triumphs, she might have understood, even better than he, some of the complicated relationships between his earliest humiliations and his consequent craving for glory. She knew how deeply he had been hurt and confused throughout his childhood by family difficulties and the marital estrangements of his parents; difficulties which had made the home in San Francisco more nearly a battleground than a place where a child might acquire a sense of security. Although the boy's father had rebelled against the austere puritanism of his own New England upbringing, the man had clung to a belief in the biblical precept that he who spareth the rod hateth his son, and in his attempt to be a good father he had cast the fury of his impatience on Robbie through frequent whippings, some of which caused lasting scars.

The boy's mother, shocked by the brutality of these punishments, often fled in tears to her bedroom and prayed for mercy while the whippings were being administered. Trying to make amends, she taught her son and her younger child, Jeanie, the consolations of religious belief. The children were made to understand that while the ways of God are indeed mysterious and beyond finding out, they are ultimately just. She also explained that if her children bravely accepted God's ways of testing them in this world, they would be rewarded with life everlasting in the perfect world to come. Mrs. Frost read Bible stories to her children and helped them fashion their ideals around the achievements of heroes and heroines who overcame all painful hardships through actions which reflected courage, skill, cunning, wit, nobility, compassion, and persistent striving for glory.[5]

Perhaps, during his boyhood, Robert Frost became so nervously upset that he confused the ideas of heavenly and earthly punishment. If God could punish by striking back at those who offended him, then there seemed to be divine justification for any man or boy to punish his enemies by striking back. These earliest hurts merely took new forms after the boy's father died; after the widowed mother moved from San Francisco to New England with her two children. Mrs. Frost, trying to earn a living as a public school teacher in Salem, New Hampshire, failed so completely that some of the students and townspeople insulted her and her children until she was forced to resign. The night before the Frosts moved from Salem, the boy said through furious tears, "You wait. Some day I'll come back . . . and show them."[6]

He was determined that some day, somehow, he would be able to strike back, in self-vindication, and beneath all of his later ambition to triumph as a poet was at least the subconscious desire to make amends by retaliating against those who had humiliated him—and his mother. She had indeed made him want to achieve honor and glory based on heroic accomplishment, and this ideal became inextricably bound up with his desire to retaliate. Throughout his boyhood, he kept telling himself that some day he would lift himself above and apart from others, in a way which would let him triumph over all who had hurt him.

For years, these longings for vengeance could be satisfied only through comforting fantasies. Repeatedly he recalled his San Francisco dream of how he had once escaped from his tormentors and had climbed high among mountain peaks to discover a secret pass into a happy valley where a tribe of Indian warriors welcomed him; of how he and these Indian braves made retaliatory raids against their enemies outside their happy valley. The imagined forms of retaliation kept changing, even as the actual forms of humiliation changed. In

Salem, when he became the best pitcher on his grammar school team, he dreamed he would some day achieve renown as a hero in the major league of his choice—and even a baseball could serve as a lethal weapon if carefully aimed at the head of an enemy batter. Later, in high school, where his baseball dreams were spoiled, he achieved excellence as a scholar, and thus found a successful way of scornfully triumphing over those who were better than he at baseball. As soon as he began publishing poems in the high school literary magazine, he began to dream that some day his reputation as a literary hero would provide him with another way of triumphing over his enemies.

His confidence in himself and in his dreams was severely injured by events which occurred not long after his graduation from high school. The most injurious of these was his long and temporarily unsuccessful courtship with the girl he eventually married: Elinor White. During the worst phase of the courtship, when he convinced himself that he had lost out to another suitor, he was so upset that he threatened to kill himself—and unsuccessfully attempted to get himself killed in the Dismal Swamp. Although he returned from the adventure outwardly unscathed, he never completely recovered from the inner wounds suffered at that time. Grimly continuing his courtship until he overcame Elinor White's reluctance, he carried into their marriage the conviction that his beloved must be punished for having hurt him so dreadfully.

In the beginning of that marriage, Frost's pride and self-confidence were further hurt by his recurrent fears that Elinor did not love him as much as he loved her. Those fears, and his increasing lack of confidence in himself, were inseparable from the recurrent illnesses which plagued him during the next few years. When these illnesses were at their worst, his puzzled doctor made the guess that he might be suffering from tuberculosis, and he turned to farming at the suggestion of his doctor.

After he had established himself on the farm in Derry, however, he failed to find in the rural life any power of healing his sickness. One of the few poems he wrote during this desperate period was a study in suicide entitled "Despair."

In retrospect, Frost was never able to explain how or why he gradually recovered enough self-confidence and enough interest in life to go on with his duties from day to day on the

Derry farm. The return of spring after the first hard winter may have had more to do with it than anything else, and it was in the writing of spring poems that he recovered his desire to succeed as a poet, some day. As his family increased to four children, and as he worried about how he was going to overcome his laziness enough to earn a living on the farm, he was beset with new fears. When he turned to teaching at Pinkerton Academy, he was ready to admit his failure as a farmer. But even while his success as a teacher helped to re-establish his confidence in himself, he kept dreaming that somehow he could get away from the farm and from teaching long enough to devote all of his energies to writing. That possibility was made available to him by the terms of his grandfather's will, and as soon as he had a sufficient sum of money from the annuities, he took his family to England, gladly turning his back on farming and teaching.

He brought back from England all the hopes and fears he had taken with him. At the beginning of his triumph in America, he became depressed by a lack of confidence in his ability to continue writing poetry. In one mood of depression he hinted that his immediate poetic concern was with nothing except darkness. Half seriously and half playfully he once claimed he had nearly completed two books of verse, one to be called "Melanism" and the other "The Sense of Wrong."[7] At another time he said, insinuatively, that "Pitchblende" was the title of a manuscript he had completed.[8] These typically cryptic remarks are enough to illuminate a stanza of his poem, "Afterflakes":

> *If I shed such a darkness,*
> *If the reason was in me,*
> *That shadow of mine should show in form*
> *Against the shapeless shadow of storm,*
> *How swarthy I must be.*[9]

Sometimes, in these moods of darkness, when the sense of wrongs done to him was intermingled with the sense of his inability to carry on as a successful poet, his lack of confidence expressed itself in jealous fears. At the time of his return from England, Frost knew that the most highly praised New England poet was Edwin Arlington Robinson, and his jealousy of

Robinson was caused largely by his fear that he might never be able to match Robinson's literary achievement. He felt that another serious competitor, in 1915, was the Imagist poet Amy Lowell, and he initially cultivated her friendship. As soon as he acquired more literary stature than she, however, he began to confide that he would soon "throw off the light mask" he wore when speaking of her in public. Some day he would expose her "for a fool as well as a fraud."[10] Just before Amy Lowell died in 1925, Frost felt that he had managed to triumph over her, in a way which satisfied him. Edgar Lee Masters was another competitor who aroused Frost's jealousy for a time, but he was relieved—and even delighted—when the reputation of Masters began to slip. Sandburg threatened to become the most dangerous rival for popularity, and as a result Frost gradually intensified the harshness of his jealous remarks about Sandburg. Later, an attractive competitor for honors was young Edna St. Vincent Millay, whose vividly successful appeal to college audiences infuriated Frost. When he was elected to membership in the American Academy, in 1930, he privately confessed that he took an "evil pleasure" in this triumph over her. Beneath all these fears and jealousies was his lack of confidence in himself, inseparably tied in with his uncontrollable ambition to triumph over all rivals, and he justified his attitude by drawing one analogy from prizefighting: "There can be only one heavyweight champion at a time."[11]

His fears, jealousies, and lack of confidence also found expression in gossip, which provided what he viewed as another means of triumphing over his enemies. And when he used gossip as a bladelike weapon, he did not hesitate to sharpen it by altering the facts. Of course there were times when his gossiping was reported back to the person thus assaulted, and many of his possible or actual friendships came to an end in this way. Soon after he received complaints from Wallace Stevens, for malicious gossiping, and a reprimand from Ezra Pound, Frost was indignant: "I suspect the same dirty sychophant of having reported me to him [Pound] as reported me to Wallace Stevens."[12] Of no importance to Frost was the question whether he had added falsehood to gossip. What came first was his need to belittle and thus triumph over anyone who seemed to endanger his position as champion.

The alterations of fact, as used by Frost in his gossiping,

were not unrelated to those he made in his improved versions of his own life story. Even as his platform manner dramatized his ideal image of how he wanted to be viewed, so his accounts of his early experiences fulfilled his ideal of what he wished the story of his life to become. Although he tried to make the story distinct from any other in its uniqueness and originality, he often made it sound similar to one of Horatio Alger's accounts of how Ragged Dick or Tattered Tom, battling poverty and humiliation, grew up to win honor and glory—and wealth. Repeatedly claiming that he seemed to be doomed from the start, Frost liked to tell of how he had sold newspapers for pennies on the streets of San Francisco, and of how his father's great promise had been wasted in gambling and drunkenness. He always described his mother as an aristocratic Scots lady, defeated by her marital misfortunes, and subsequently humiliated by cruel circumstances, while the wealthy relatives who might have helped her turned their backs. Later, Frost said, these wealthy relatives turned against him simply because he wanted to be a poet instead of a lawyer. Although the facts do not support these claims, he seemed to convince himself that he was telling the truth most of the time. And in rounding out his mythic autobiography he usually stressed the point that in spite of seemingly insurmountable hindrances he had managed to achieve his goal in a way which was a complete triumph over all his enemies.

There were times when Frost did acknowledge the discrepancies between autobiographical facts and fictions. On one occasion he said in public, "Don't trust me too far. I'm liable to tell you anything. Trust me on the poetry, but don't trust me on my life. Check up on me some."[13] This warning to others may have indicated some of the warnings he also tried to give himself. Earlier, as a teacher of psychology, he had used a text in which William James divided "the self" into "the Me" and "the I" to represent a dangerous aspect of inner conflict. James may have heightened Frost's awareness of the perpetual clash between his idealizing and his realizing responses.

An even more vivid warning, in his own family, caused him to try to reconcile these opposing drives. Over the years, he became increasingly frightened by what he saw happening to his younger sister Jeanie. She found her own ways of coping with her hurts and humiliations: more and more she withdrew into fantasies until she had to be placed in a mental institution, where she spent the remainder of her life. Before and after Jeanie's collapse, her brother warned others about similar dangers confronting anyone who became too self-indulgent in making retreats from realities. Repeatedly he referred to occasions in the past when he had felt himself standing on the edge of an abyss into which he might have fallen if he had not taken firm action to save himself.[14]

One saving action, for Frost, was the writing of poetry, and he repeatedly said his art gave him a way of dealing with confusions which intermittently threatened to overwhelm him. When in an ugly mood, he could not resist using poems as weapons for striking back at those who had perhaps unconsciously and unintentionally injured him. Even in these cases, he was inclined to conceal his purpose by intermingling seriousness with playfulness, to such an extent that his ambiguous meanings left his readers in doubt. Usually, however, he made his poetry dramatize and try to resolve the conflicts between the opposing sides of his consciousness—conflicts between affirming and denying, between hope and fear, between loving and hating.[15]

It might seem that only those who knew Robert Frost well could understand and admire the hard-earned and always precarious triumph he gained over the constant threat of inner chaos. If so, however, he would not have won such widespread and continuous public response with his poetry. Perhaps the major reason why he remains the best-known and best-loved American poet, at home and abroad, is that no themes are more universal and attractive than those which try to offer affirmative resolutions for the conflicts dramatized in his life and in his poetry. Readers old and young, waging their own struggles against the constant threat of chaos, seem to find comfort and encouragement in many of his aphoristic lines which are so cherished that they have become familiar quotations: "Earth's the right place for love: I don't know where it's likely to go better." "The utmost reward of daring should be still to dare." "Ah, when to the heart of man was it ever less than a treason, to go with the drift of things?" "Something there is that doesn't love a wall, that wants it down." "Good fences make good neighbors." "But oh, the agitated heart till someone really find us out."

INTRODUCTION

In trying to represent the many different facets of this man and poet who did indeed have the power to be a bursting unity of opposites, the present writer continues the attempt made in the first volume: to offer a balanced delineation which mingles sympathy with critical detachment, in the narration and in the interpretation. The primary method again employed is to select major and minor episodes of inner and outer experiences which dramatize the complexities of Robert Frost's responses to experience. The secondary method of analytical interpretation is largely relegated to the Notes.

Lawrance Thompson

Princeton University

FAIR WARNING: Robert Frost prided himself so much on his ability to arrange words meaningfully that he felt he could omit some of the conventional uses of punctuation. A more serious problem has been created in the letters here quoted by his acknowledged weakness as a speller. At times, and only to avoid confusion on the part of the reader, bracketed punctuation marks or corrected spellings have been added. L. T.

ACKNOWLEDGMENTS

I TAKE much pleasure in expressing my gratitude and indebtedness to all who have helped me during the various stages of my work on the manuscript of *Robert Frost: The Years of Triumph*. My first thanks go to those members of the Frost family who have continuously provided sympathetic assistance: Mrs. Lesley Frost Ballantine, Mrs. Lillian LaBatt Frost, William Prescott Frost, and Willard E. Fraser.

Each of the following has been helpful in important ways, often by making available to me copies of Frost letters and manuscripts: Frederick B. Adams, Jr., George K. Anderson, Mrs. Margaret Bartlett Anderson, Carlos Baker, Clifton Waller Barrett, Mrs. Edna Hanley Byers, Mrs. Marguerite Cohn, H. Bacon Collamore, R. P. T. Coffin, Mary E. Cooley, Mrs. Jane Monroe Curcuruto, Mrs. Corinne Tennyson Davids, Edward Davison, Alfred C. Edwards, G. Roy Elliott, Thomas Hornsby Ferril, Charles R. Green, John W. Haines, Anson S. Hawkins, Granville Hicks, Mrs. Gwendolyn Lewis Hoitt, Raymond Holden, John S. Van E. Kohn, Julius Bartlett Lankes, Julius J. Lankes, Edward Connery Lathem, Helen Browning Lawrie, Ruth Lechlitner, Lincoln MacVeagh, Mrs. Margaret Dole McCall, Charles A. Madison, Newton F. McKeon, Thomas E. F. McNamara, Merrill Moore, Mrs. Kathleen Johnston Morrison, Mildred E. Morrison, Theodore Morrison, Gorham B. Munson, Ferner Nuhn, Mrs. Ellen C. Richardson, Wilbur E. Rowell, Victor E. Reichert, Mrs. Elizabeth Monroe Riley, Thomas P. Roche, Howard G. Schmitt, Burrhus Frederic Skinner, Wilbert Snow, William E. Stockhausen, Dorothy Tyler, Louis Untermeyer, Wade Van Dore, and Carl Zigrosser. More specific acknowledgments are made in the Notes.

Sincere and heartfelt thanks are also given to Princeton University for several leaves of absence from teaching, for several grants of aid from the Research Fund, and for a McCosh Fellowship in 1965.

The dedication of this volume is intended to serve as a special reminder of my exceptional gratitude to Edward Connery Lathem, Librarian of Dartmouth College, for the extraordinarily generous ways in which he has continued to share with

ACKNOWLEDGMENTS

me so many findings he has made through his own independent researches on biographical and bibliographical matters which relate to Robert Frost. With enormous patience, he gave a meticulously thorough first-reading to the manuscript of this second volume, in an early stage, even as he had done with the first volume, and again he offered extremely helpful suggestions for revision. Here also, the recurrence of his name in so many of my notes is further indication of my indebtedness to him.

L. T.

ROBERT FROST

THE YEARS OF TRIUMPH

HOMECOMING

"Home," he mocked gently.
"Yes, what else but home?
It all depends on what you mean by home."[1]

DURING the slow voyage across the Atlantic from Liverpool to New York City in February of 1915, Robert Frost was worried less by the danger of German submarines than by his own difficulty in choosing where he would make a home for his wife and children. It would be somewhere in New England, of course, and yet there were reasons against going back to any of the places they had previously lived. All of the Frosts, during their stay in England, had often talked of home so wistfully that they seemed to forget they would be homeless when they got back. While abroad, the Frost children had often been encouraged by their parents to write little stories based on their memories of home, and they had always written of incidents on the New Hampshire farm in Derry where three of the four children had been born. Lesley, now almost sixteen, had moved to the Derry farm with her parents in 1900, when she had been too young to remember the event. Her brother Carol was now almost thirteen, Irma was almost twelve, and Marjorie almost ten. They could remember the circumstances under which the farm had been sold, but it was still home to them, and the next best thing would be another farm as much like it as possible.

Fortunately, there was one place where the homeless family knew they would always be welcomed: the White Mountain farm owned by John Lynch on the South Road between Bethlehem and Franconia, New Hampshire. The warm Irish affection shown them by the elderly John Lynch and his wife Margaret, during summer vacations the Frosts had spent with them, had given a special aura to this rural hideaway. When Frost suggested that it might be possible to rent rooms at the Lynch farm, as soon as they got to America, so that they could use it as a temporary base while he searched for a Derry-like farm they might purchase in that region, the children and their mother were delighted. Frost had been thinking along related lines ever since he had written to a friend from Beaconsfield, "My dream would be to get the thing started in London and then do the rest of it from a farm in New England where I could live cheap and get Yankier and Yankier."[2] Long before the SS *St. Paul* entered New York Harbor, plans had been made to get in touch with the Lynches by telephone soon after they landed. If there was no hitch, their father told the children, they might all be in Bethlehem, New Hampshire, within twenty-four hours after they reached New York.

There was a hitch, caused by unexpected hindrances at Ellis Island. No immigration difficulties had been foreseen when the Frosts had volunteered to serve as traveling companions and guardians for fifteen-year-old Mervyn Thomas. The boy's father, Edward Thomas, had wanted to get him out of England during the war and had arranged for him to live with friends in Alstead, New Hampshire. At Ellis Island, however, soon after the SS *St. Paul* made the routine stop there, in full view of the castled New York City skyline, on the morning of Washington's Birthday, 1915, the United States immigration officers frightened Mervyn and his protectors by quoting the law: No alien under the age of sixteen could be admitted to the United States unless met at the immigration office by at least one parent—or by a suitable sponsor who could offer acceptable evidence of financial means which would keep such an alien from becoming a public charge.

The pronouncement was made with such arrogance that Robert Frost was enraged. Wasn't it clear enough that Frost himself was qualified to be sponsor and guardian? No, because he had already admitted that he had neither a remunerative position nor a sufficient income. Brusquely, the immigration officer explained that under the circumstances the case would be referred to a judiciary board which would meet at Ellis Island on the following day: the boy must be detained in a cell at Ellis Island until that time. Frost would be allowed to produce whatever appeals he could muster. The younger Frosts, bewildered, said tearful good-byes to Mervyn, while their parents tried to reassure him that this unforeseen technicality could be straightened out. Frost would return to Ellis Island the next day with enough evidence to satisfy the authorities. Nevertheless, all the Frosts were so upset that they could talk of nothing else while the steamer moved across New York Harbor and was warped to her East River pier at the foot of Forty-second Street.

There was no reception committee: the few friends who knew that the Frosts were coming home on the *St. Paul* were too far away to make an occasion of their arrival. If America knew that Frost had scored a literary triumph in England and that both of his books had been accepted for publication by the firm of Henry Holt and Company in New York City, there seemed to be no sign that anyone cared. Frost did not even know whether either one of his books had yet been published in America. He did find a sort of greeting, in print, however, soon after he had shepherded his family through customs and had made arrangements for baggage and furniture[3] to be held for a few hours until he knew for certain where they were going. As he walked up Forty-second Street toward Grand Central Station with his family, he stopped at a newsstand to buy a paper, casually lifted the cover of the current issue of the *New Republic*, on the stand, and found on the first page a table of contents which listed a review of *North of Boston*. He stopped his little parade long enough to let him buy a copy and scan the review, written by Amy Lowell—the Imagist poet whom he had declined to meet in London when Ezra Pound had given him the chance.[4] Although it was exciting to find that Miss Lowell viewed "this modest little green-covered book" as "certainly the most American volume of poetry which has appeared for some time," some of the comments which followed were annoying:

"The thing which makes Mr. Frost's work remarkable is the fact that he has chosen to write it as verse. We have been flooded for twenty years with New England stories in prose. The finest and most discerning are the little masterpieces of Alice Brown. She too is a poet in her descriptions, she too has caught the desolation and 'dourness' of lonely New England farms, but unlike Mr. Frost she has a rare sense of humor, and that, too, is of New England, although no hint of it appears in 'North of Boston.' And just because of the lack of it, just because its place is taken by irony, sardonic and grim, Mr. Frost's book reveals a disease which is eating into the vitals of our New England life, at least in its rural communities. What is there in the hard vigorous climate of these states which plants the seeds of degeneration? Is the violence and ugliness of their religious belief the cause of these twisted and tortured lives? Have the sane, full-blooded men all been drafted away to the cities, or the West, leaving behind only feeble reminders of a once fine stock? The question again demands an answer after the reading of Mr. Frost's book."[5]

It was plain that the city-bred sister of the president of Harvard College did not entirely understand the poetry of Robert Frost. How could she be so ignorant concerning those persistent virtues he had poetically honored in the back-country people of Miss Lowell's native New England? At least he was pleased that she had liked *North of Boston* well enough to give it three full columns of review.[6]

At Grand Central Station, Frost found seats for his family and immediately made two long-distance telephone calls. The first, to the farm of John Lynch in Bethlehem, New Hampshire, resulted in assurance that the Lynches would be glad to welcome the Frosts as paying guests, and would be ready for their arrival the next day. The second was to Russell Scott, in Alstead, New Hampshire, to explain the immigration difficulties which were holding Mervyn Thomas on Ellis Island, and to ask for help. Scott, an Englishman, had assured Edward Thomas that the boy could stay with him indefinitely, but there were delicate reasons why Scott did not want to be named, formally, as Mervyn's sponsor. Scott did, however, have a brother, Arthur, living in New York and married to an American girl who had influential friends. She could be of help if Frost would ask her assistance. Mrs. Arthur Scott, when reached by telephone, showed immediate sympathy. If Mr. Frost would come directly to the midtown apartment where she and her husband were living she would explain the hesitancy of Russell Scott to serve as formal sponsor for Mervyn, and would also try to get in touch with someone who could solve the difficulty.

As soon as Frost had bought tickets for the rest of his family, and had made arrangements for them to depart from

Grand Central Station, by train, en route to New Hampshire, he continued his campaign on Mervyn's behalf. During his brief visit with Mrs. Scott, he learned far more about these brothers, Russell and Arthur, than Edward Thomas had told him. They were members of a family which for years had been prominently associated with the success of the Manchester *Guardian*. Arthur, since coming to the United States, had continued his career as a journalist. His brother Russell had been a master at a school in England until he abandoned his wife and four children so that he could elope with his wife's half-sister, with whom he was now living in Alstead, New Hampshire, where he was a blacksmith. Obviously, Russell had reasons for not wanting to become involved with immigration officials; but Mrs. Arthur Scott felt certain that a friend of hers, the prominent New York lawyer Charles Burlingham, would be willing to corroborate Frost's statement that he was financially able to serve as sponsor for Mervyn. She was correct. Burlingham, when approached, telephoned the Commissioner of Immigration, Frederic C. Howe, who said he would advise the Ellis Island authorities that Robert Frost was acceptable as the sponsor.[7] Assurances were given that all would be in order by the time Frost returned to Ellis Island, the next day, for the formal hearing.

Free to spend the intervening time as he liked, Frost immediately decided to make a brief visit to his American publisher, Henry Holt and Company, not far away, at 34 West Thirty-third Street, between Fifth and Sixth avenues. When he reached the Holt office, he was received far more cordially than he had expected. Alfred Harcourt, head of the trade department, said Frost must hear the whole story[8] of how Holt had become the American publisher of *North of Boston*. During the previous summer, Florence Taber Holt, the publisher's wife, had somehow acquired a copy of the English edition of *North of Boston* and had liked it so much she had urged her husband to print an American edition. Henry Holt's favorite on his list of authors was Dorothy Canfield Fisher, who was asked to give her opinion.[9] It was extremely favorable, but the decision was made to proceed cautiously by importing from David Nutt and Company only 150 sets of unbound sheets. Although this request had been sent to Nutt early in September 1914, the sheets had not arrived until January 1915. Publication date had been set for February

20, the sheets had been attractively bound, and Holt's trade salesman August H. Gehrs had begun to take orders in the Boston area.

Prior to publication date, Gehrs acquired enough orders to exhaust the small edition, and he had wired the news to Harcourt. Harcourt had immediately sent a cable to Nutt ordering 200 more sheets, but weeks would pass before that new supply of sheets could arrive. The situation was absurd. Orders were coming in steadily for the newly published *North of Boston*, and no copies were available. If Nutt delayed too long, Holt might be forced to print its own edition.

Harcourt had one other bit of news for Frost. Well in advance of the publication date, Harcourt had sold to the *New Republic* the poem entitled "The Death of the Hired Man," and it had appeared in the issue for February 6. At this point in his account, Harcourt took from his desk the *New Republic* check for $40 in payment for the poem, and presented it to Frost.[10]

(A few days later, Frost learned that Amy Lowell had tried to find a publisher for *North of Boston* before it had been taken by Holt. In England, during the summer of 1914, she had bought a copy of the book in Harold Monro's Poetry Bookshop and had been so pleased with it that after her return to the United States she unsuccessfully urged Houghton Mifflin to publish it. When she learned Holt was to bring it out, she wrote to the *New Republic* and asked for permission to review it.)[11]

Harcourt told Frost that, for business reasons, the newly returned poet should remain in New York City for at least a few days. It might be advantageous to let Harcourt take Frost to lunch with the editors of the *New Republic*, who had already demonstrated they paid well for individual poems. Harcourt expressed regret that Henry Holt was not at the moment in the city, but Mrs. Holt was nearby and would be delighted to meet this author whom she had discovered for the firm. In addition, Frost should attend the meeting of the Poetry Society of America scheduled for the very next night. If he would stay, Harcourt could easily arrange to have him escorted to the meeting by a fellow poet. Ready to participate in any campaign strategies and tactics which might advance his reputation, and held by his obligation to Mervyn Thomas, Frost accepted all of these proposals.

The next morning, when he returned to Ellis Island, matters did not go as easily as Mrs. Scott and Mr. Burlingham had promised. The poet was led into a courtroom where Mervyn was waiting his turn to have someone plead his case. No word had yet been received from the commissioner of immigration, and Frost was caught up in the red tape of court routine. A three-man board of lawyers, listening to one case after another, finally invited Mervyn's sponsor to answer questions. If Frost were to serve as guardian for this under-age alien, how did he plan to earn a living? Well, he was a teacher and a poet. Did he have a position now as teacher? No, but he was sure he could get one. Until he did, would he be able to support himself, his family, and this boy on the earnings from his poetry? Perhaps. He had recently published two books in England and one of these books had just been republished in the United States. How much money had he received for these books so far? Well, none so far, but . . . The three men were amused, and Frost was infuriated by their smiles. Desperately, he went on to say he had explained his case to friends, a lawyer named Charles Burlingham had vouched for him as sponsor, and Mr. Burlingham's word had been accepted by Mr. Frederic C. Howe, the Commissioner of Immigration. The three men conferred and announced they had received no word from the commissioner. Then Mervyn was asked if he had anything to say in his own behalf concerning why he should not be sent back to England. Bewildered and frightened, the boy glanced at Frost, whose rage had been mounting steadily. Now disgusted, he answered Mervyn's mute plea by shouting, "Tell them you wouldn't *stay* in a country where they treat people like this!" The case was deferred until after lunch, so that some test could be made of the assertion that the commissioner of immigration knew about the case. Fortunately, the message from the commissioner was found, and Frost was given papers certifying that he was authorized to serve as Mervyn's sponsor. A few hours later, Frost put the boy on a northbound train, with instructions for changes which would take him to Alstead, New Hampshire, as planned, to be met there by Russell Scott.

Alfred Harcourt had been told about the Ellis Island difficulties, and he may have had them in mind when he secured Robert Haven Schauffler to serve as companion and host for

Robert Frost at the February meeting of the Poetry Society of America that night. Schauffler's humanitarian poem "Scum o' the Earth," which dealt with various hardships suffered by enterprising immigrants, had attracted much praise when it had appeared, a few years earlier. What Harcourt did not know, when he made this arrangement, was that the traditionally conservative tastes of the ruling powers in the Poetry Society had been reflected in harsh comments aimed at two of Robert Frost's *North of Boston* poems which had been read aloud at the December meeting. The recording secretary, summarizing those comments, had concluded her account very tartly: "Mr. Frost has been greatly acclaimed by prophets of new poetic cults in England, but his work could hardly be said to have found sympathizers in the Poetry Society."[12] If he had known how his name and his poetry had been abused by the Society two months before, he might have refused to attend the February meeting. But the crowd of nearly two hundred poets was large enough for him to hide in, and he insisted to Schauffler that this first visit should not be marred by any formal presentation. The subject under discussion was free verse, and the visitor himself was conservative enough to enjoy hearing various members of the Society heap condemnations on this so-called new art-form.

Less enjoyable was Harcourt's promotional campaign with the editors of the *New Republic*. At the planned luncheon, a day or so after the meeting of the Poetry Society, Frost became acquainted with Francis Hackett, Philip Littell, Walter Lippmann, and Herbert Croly. If each of these editors projected his own socialistic and humanitarian prejudices into his reading of "The Death of the Hired Man," either before or after it appeared in the *New Republic*, and if each had failed therefore to guess at the unreconstructed political or social conservatism of its author, one luncheon with him may have been enough to reveal his hostility to their liberalism. To be sure, he had urged John Bartlett to "emphasize the social values" in writing journalistic newspaper sketches.[13] Nevertheless, his own basic concern in his art and in his life was for individuals rather than for relationships of individuals within social groups. The editors of the *New Republic* may even have decided, before their luncheon was completed, that he was not likely to offer them many poems fit for their purposes. Indeed, no other poem of his appeared in the *New*

Republic until the poet Ridgely Torrence became one of its editors.

During this unexpected lingering in New York City, Frost did call on Mrs. Henry Holt, who had been the first stranger in America to send him a letter of praise for *North of Boston.* Writing to him in England from her mother's home in Stowe, Vermont, she had asked, "Do you live in Vermont? My mother knows the people about here better than I do, & she finds many similar to them in your verses: certainly you have New England in them."[14] He had answered her letter without even suspecting that she might be the wife of the celebrated publisher. When she learned, during Frost's visit with her, that he had just returned from England and that he hoped to buy a small farm in northern New England, she insisted he should reach no decision until he had explored possibilities in the Green Mountains, around the village of Stowe. She was so persuasive in describing the attractions of Vermont that he did later extend his search to the Stowe region before he decided to settle in the White Mountains.[15] Mrs. Holt had another reason for being pleased to meet Robert Frost. She confided to him that she herself had been writing poetry for years and was preparing a manuscript for publication. She read some of her poems aloud to him, and perhaps she misinterpreted his praise. She would be grateful, she said, if he would write a brief introduction for her projected volume. Frost, already under double obligation to his attractive hostess, agreed to do so as soon as he could find time, but apparently he never could.[16]

2

FROM NOWHERE UP TO SOMEWHERE

If you should rise from Nowhere up to Somewhere,
From being No one up to being Someone,
Be sure to keep repeating to yourself
You owe it to an arbitrary god
Whose mercy to you rather than to others
Won't bear too critical examination.[1]

AS SOON as Robert Frost completed his first round of campaigning in New York City, he was caught up in an unexpected series of adventures. Instead of starting for New England he made an impulsively compassionate journey southward for a distance of one hundred and fifty miles to visit his sister, Jeanie. She was teaching in Wildwood, New Jersey, down near the tip of Cape May, when last she had written him, and he went there by train from New York without trying to give her any hint of his coming. He knew that the nervous instability which had troubled her since childhood had been reflected recently in her failure to keep any teaching position for more than a year, but she had told him in her letter that this her first year at Wildwood had started well. When he got there, he was upset by his discovery that she had already been discharged and that she was now teaching in South Fork, Pennsylvania—a coal-mining town in the narrow valley of the Conemaugh River, not far from Pittsburgh and more than three hundred miles westward.

He could easily have made excuses to himself for avoiding the long trip to South Fork. His wife and children were waiting for him in New Hampshire and he had little cash. Nevertheless, to South Fork he went, and when he found Jeanie there she was already distraught by what she described as the rudeness, even brutality, in her new school. "My pupils are nearly all of German extraction and have peculiar temperaments," she had written to a friend. "One of the teachers in attempting to use corporal punishment, was attacked by several of the pupils and hurt quite badly."[2]

Jeanie's brother listened to her wild account of all she said she had suffered since he last heard from her. She regretted that she had not made better uses of the annuities received from her grandfather's estate, and that she had not continued her education to a point where she could obtain a first-rate teaching position. Her brother, trying to comfort and encourage her, insisted that it was not too late for her to earn a college degree. She was so bright, he told her, that she could do the necessary work in three years. He also assured her that most of her expenses could be paid from the funds continuously provided by the annuity, and he offered to give her additional financial aid as soon as he was established. Deriving fresh hope from her brother's practical suggestions, Jeanie at once began making college plans which she later carried out. She was so grateful for his visit that he was glad he had made the effort to find her. At the same time, he was equally glad to take leave of her and set out for New England.[3]

The unexpected expense of his journey to Wildwood, and then to South Fork, Pennsylvania, caused him to rearrange his route northward. He went first to Lawrence, Massachusetts, immediately important to him as the home of his friend and lawyer Wilbur E. Rowell, who had already served for fourteen years as the executor and trustee of the William Prescott Frost estate. The poet had repeatedly written from England to Rowell, counting much on his friendship and asking for advance payments on the $800 annuity customarily paid in July. To Rowell he had also sent inscribed copies of *A Boy's Will* and *North of Boston,* as soon as each book had been published in London, and had received enthusiastic acknowlegments. When he reached Lawrence early in March of 1915, he was given such a cordial reception by Mr. and Mrs. Rowell—and was so quickly granted an advance of $200 —that he could not refuse their invitation to stay with them for an extra day or two.[4] Nor could he deny himself the pleasure of walking along the familiar streets of Lawrence and of calling briefly on a few of his old friends.

Some of these visits were more embarrassing than he had anticipated. Ernest Jewell, with whom he had been closely associated during and after their high-school days, received him coldly. Neither one of them mentioned the considerable debt which Frost had owed Jewell since the Derry period when Frost had speculated too optimistically in poultry futures, with the aid of a loan from Jewell; but it was obvious from Jewell's manner that he had neither forgotten nor forgiven the twelve-year lapse in the promised payments.[5] A far more affable reception was given him by several of his former high-school teachers, into whose classrooms he cautiously intruded. One of them persuaded him to set a precedent by reading aloud—or rather by saying from memory—to the students in her literature class, a few of his own poems.

Before leaving Lawrence, Frost decided he had reason enough for delaying still longer his departure for New Hampshire so that he might call on at least one literary figure in Boston: Ellery Sedgwick, editor of the *Atlantic Monthly*. For years, Frost had been unsuccessful in his attempts to place any of his poems in the *Atlantic*. From Derry, shortly after the turn of the century, he had submitted to the *Atlantic* poem after poem. Later, from Gloucestershire in England, he had sent several of his longer narrative poems, with a letter in which he explained that the Boston mentioned in the title of his forthcoming book was in Massachusetts and not in Lincolnshire; he would therefore be pleased if a few of these poems might be published at home, in the *Atlantic*, before they appeared in England. Back they had come, with a one-sentence letter from "The Editors," saying, "We are sorry we have no place in the *Atlantic Monthly* for your vigorous verse."[6] At the time, Frost had scornfully wondered whether such a comment implied that his poems were too vigorous, or whether the *Atlantic* was currently publishing far more vigorous poems. If the latter were true, he had decided, times had really changed. Now, partly for reasons of spite, he wanted to visit Sedgwick just to see if recent developments might have softened his attitude. Impulsively, Frost started for Boston on Friday, the fifth of March, choosing to leave his suitcase with the Rowells in Lawrence, and assuring them he would return before dark.

The visit to the editor of the *Atlantic* turned out to be far more of an adventure than Frost had expected. Sedgwick, informed that the caller was Mr. Robert Frost, came forward from his inner office with a seemingly hypocritical display of warmth: he stretched out both hands in greeting, as though he were welcoming a long-absent friend. Even worse, he said he was glad to see that Frost had returned to the United States, and added that the *Atlantic* was "going to hold you up to your best." When the two men retired to the inner office and were seated, neither one of them spoke of all those poems which had been rejected. Instead, Sedgwick said he had first heard about *North of Boston* from Amy Lowell, and now he wanted the whole story. Frost began talking, and in a short time he succeeded in charming the editor of the *Atlantic* to such a degree that Sedgwick made a surprising gesture. He hoped Frost was free to be a guest in the Sedgwick home that evening at a little dinner party already planned: it would be a pleasure to introduce the newly discovered poet to two of the Sedgwicks' close friends in Cambridge. Frost hesitated only a moment before accepting.[7]

The two other guests at the Sedgwicks' that evening were Mr. and Mrs. William Ernest Hocking. Only one year older than Frost, and newly appointed as a professor of philosophy at Harvard, Hocking had gained wide attention three years earlier with his first book entitled *The Meaning of God in Human Experience*. In it, he had pointedly emphasized the religious aspects of his philosophical idealism. Although Frost was often shy about acknowledging his own religious beliefs, he always responded with eagerness to any practical idealist like Hocking. Under the circumstances, it was appropriate for Frost to display—as he did—his knowing admiration for the writings of Harvard's celebrated pragmatist, the late William James.

Hocking's attractive Irish wife surprised Frost by saying she was the daughter of the poet John Boyle O'Reilly, who had come to Boston from an Australian prison where he had been confined as a result of his revolutionary activities in Dublin. Frost, priding himself on his own Scottish-Celtic heritage and genuinely fond of the Irish, impressed Mrs. Hocking by demonstrating his knowledge of her father's poetry. Back in Frost's romantic days as a high school student, he and many other young rebels had memorized a poem of O'Reilly's, beginning,

I'd rather live in Bohemia than in any other land;
For only there are the values true,
And the laurels gathered in all men's view. . . .

and ending,

Oh, I long for the glow of a kindly heart and the grasp
of a friendly hand,
And I'd rather live in Bohemia than in any other land.[8]

The Hockings regretfully left the dinner party early because they had previously committed themselves to attend
a lecture, and Frost did not stay late with the Sedgwicks. Before
his departure, he apparently asked for more details connected with one story which Sedgwick had told to the Hockings
at the dinner table. That morning, soon after Frost had made
his visit to the office of the *Atlantic*, Sedgwick had learned
that two of Boston's literary notables—Nathan Haskell Dole
and Sylvester Baxter—were already admirers of Robert Frost's
poetry: they were going to read some poems from *North of
Boston*, and talk about these poems, that very day, at the
weekly luncheon of the Boston Authors' Club. Sedgwick, unable to attend the luncheon, could not resist boasting that he
was to be the host of Robert Frost that evening. This boast
was circulated as news, at the Boston Authors' Club, for it
was the first available announcement that the newly discovered poet was in Boston. That afternoon, Dole and then
Baxter telephoned Sedgwick to protest that Frost should not
leave Boston until they could meet him.

Although Frost had never met either of these admirers,
he had heard and seen their names for years. Dole, the older
of the two, had been graduated from Harvard the year Frost
was born: 1874. Not only a poet but also a teacher, newspaperman, editor, and translator, Dole had specialized in
translating poetry and prose from the works of Russian
authors. Sylvester Baxter, sixty-five years old and extremely
proud of his descent from Pilgrim ancestors, was also a poet
and newspaperman. Educated in Germany and fond of traveling, he had served as a foreign correspondent for two Boston
newspapers and had lived for years in Mexico, Panama, and
Brazil.

Frost, apparently urged by Sedgwick to accept the friendly

gestures of Dole and Baxter, made a telephone call to Dole in the Boston suburb of Jamaica Plain that evening, soon after he left the Sedgwick home. Showing an unusually Bohemian disregard for the amenities, he introduced himself over the telephone and asked if it was too late in the evening for Dole to receive a visitor. Dole expressed his delight by insisting that Frost should come right along, and should plan to spend the night.

The friendship which began in this odd way was quickened by Dole's eagerness to campaign on Frost's behalf. The next morning, Dole insisted on bringing to his home, to meet Frost, the half-Negro and half-white poetry editor of the Boston *Evening Transcript,* William Stanley Braithwaite, whose considerable success with his weekly articles on the new poetry had led to the annual appearances of his *Anthology of Magazine Verse.*[9] Dole was correct in his prediction that Braithwaite would jump at the chance to obtain an interview with the author of *North of Boston,* and Frost's conversation with the poetry editor began pleasantly. He had read and liked "The Death of the Hired Man," when it appeared in the *New Republic*; he had also read Amy Lowell's review. Although he had not previously seen the book, *North of Boston,* he insisted on buying an extra copy which Dole possessed. Frost, touched by these indications of sympathy, promised to send Braithwaite a copy of *A Boy's Will,* together with some jottings of biographical facts that might be useful in preparing the article which Braithwaite did indeed want to write.[10]

At noon, Dole took Frost into Boston to meet Sylvester Baxter, and the three men discussed literary matters during their luncheon at the Boston City Club. Although Frost insisted that he must catch an early afternoon train for Lawrence so that he might start for New Hampshire that night, circumstances again caused him to change his plans. Escorted by his two new friends, he progressed only as far as the North Station when the trio happened to meet Mrs. Hocking. She exclaimed with delightful Irish ardor that she and her husband had been so sorry to leave Ellery Sedgwick's dinner party so early the night before: they both had belatedly wished they had thought to invite Mr. Frost to have tea with them in their Cambridge home before he started northward. Frost, with all the impulsiveness of a Bohemian, met the occasion:

"When do you want me?"

"At four-thirty this afternoon."

"I'll be there."[11]

Professor Hocking later gave his own account of what happened as a result of that accidental meeting in the North Station: "He came, and we began talking; he stayed the night, he stayed the next day and the next night. When I had to go to class [on Monday morning], Agnes Hocking took him on; and when she had to get a meal, I took him on. We had a great time. In three days, we had done a fair two-years' job of ripening friendship."[12]

Something other than this friendship caused Frost to linger with the Hockings in Cambridge from Saturday afternoon to Monday afternoon. He must have told them that, soon after he had made his promise to Mrs. Hocking in the North Station, he telephoned Amy Lowell in Brookline, simply to express his thanks for her review of *North of Boston*. She responded with typical imperiousness. She was having a small dinner party three nights hence, she said, and he must be her guest on that occasion. He would take the blue-painted streetcar from Boston to Brookline, and would get off just past the reservoir, at Heath Street. Then he would walk uphill to a gate where he would find a sign warning guests in motorcars not to run over her precious dogs. Her gate-keeping gardener would be waiting to escort him through the park of her estate—and past the dogs—to the front door of her home, Sevenels. Frost must have told the Hockings—as well as Dole and Baxter—that he had promptly accepted the invitation.

On the afternoon of his departure from the Hockings' home, he had no difficulty in following Miss Lowell's directions. When he left the trolley at Heath Street, he asked a delivery boy (carrying a handsomely wrapped gift-package) how to reach Miss Lowell's house. The boy said he was going there and would serve as guide, but he warned that Miss Lowell's big dogs roamed the park near the gate and if the gardener was not handy to protect callers the dogs could be a nuisance. They were waiting at the gate: huge overfed Old English sheepdogs, their eyes almost hidden under long hair. No gardener was in sight, and as the boy rattled the gate the dogs began barking. The boy explained the next procedure. All you had to do, he said, was to pick up throwing-stones from the crushed rock of the driveway entrance and threaten whichever dog came nearest. Amused, yet nervous, Frost selected a handful of stones and followed the boy through the gate. The instructions were correct. Each threatening dog showed respect whenever Frost cocked his arm. But as he walked through the park with his companion toward the front door of Sevenels, he worried for fear his distinguished hostess might be watching this undignified approach.

The maid at the door informed him that Miss Lowell was waiting for him in the library, and as he followed he could hear a man reading English verse with a Spanish accent. The voice stopped when Miss Lowell rose from the sofa to greet her new guest. He had been warned that she was a huge woman whose corpulence was caused by a glandular ailment, but he was quickly put at ease by the liveliness of her manner and the genuine cordiality of her welcome. The man who had been reading aloud was introduced as the Nicaraguan poet Salamon de la Selva, and he seemed to resent the interruption. Somewhat petulantly he asked if he might at least finish, before he left, the long poem he had been reading. Frost, temporarily relegated to the role of listener, and quickly bored by what he heard, surveyed the elegance of Miss Lowell's library. The spacious room was paneled with oak and each of the two fireplaces was framed within elaborate wood-carved arrangements of fruit and flowers, and the two high doors leading into the hallway were crowned with wood-carved festoons. Three glass chandeliers hung from the white plaster ceiling which was ornamentally decorated with mouldings done after the manner of Robert Adam. Along the entire length of the inner wall, the recessed bookcases were crowded with new and old books. (Frost was later shown that the book-case at the far end of the library was merely a façade which concealed the entrance to Miss Lowell's room-sized and fire-proof vault, in which she kept her treasures of Keats books and manuscripts.) Never before had he seen such a library; never before had he been entertained in such a mansion. Although he was inclined to scorn any such display of wealth, he was impressed.[13]

When the Nicaraguan poet finished his tedious reading he said brightly to Miss Lowell, "Shall I read another, or have you got my number?" Miss Lowell assured him, with a thinly concealed sarcasm, that she thought she had his number, and then she said the maid would show him out. Miss Lowell did not even wait until his back had disappeared through the library door before she gave him a derisive thumb-to-nose dismissal. Frost, delighted with the unexpected crudeness of the gesture, immediately decided that he and Miss Lowell would get along well, no matter how much they might disagree over the present state of New England or of poetry.

The only other guests at Miss Lowell's "small dinner" that evening were the poet, John Gould Fletcher, and the retired actress Ada Dwyer Russell—the latter a permanent member of Miss Lowell's household. The conversation began with literary gossip, and Frost was thoroughly entertained by the raucous prejudices of his hostess. She had gaily participated in every important literary battle since the beginning of the New Poetry movement, three years earlier. A mention of Harriet Monroe's magazine, *Poetry*, was enough to make Amy —even Frost was calling her Amy before the evening ended— explode into a wittily wrathful remembrance of all the stupidities and injustices Harriet had heaped on her. They had been friends at the start, and Amy had helped finance *Poetry* for a while. It was through the pages of *Poetry* that she had been attracted to Ezra Pound. When he had begun explaining the mystique of the "Imagistes" to the readers of *Poetry* and had sent Harriet a poem signed by "H. D., Imagiste," published in the issue for January 1913, Amy had exclaimed to herself, "Why, I, too, am an Imagiste!" She had sailed for England that summer carrying with her Harriet's letter of introduction to Ezra, but of course she wasn't prepared to have Ezra rewrite some of her poems to demonstrate that she hadn't yet mastered the principles of "Imagisme." He had at least enabled her to make the acquaintance of her present guest John Gould Fletcher—Arkansas born, Harvard educated, and wealthy.

(Listening, and given very few chances to talk, Frost had no intention of adding his own account of how Ezra had offered him a chance to meet Amy during the summer of 1913; of how Frost had refused, saying he knew the president of Harvard College, and therefore had no desire to meet the president's sister.)

Continuing her monologue, Amy admitted that there had been no declared warfare against Ezra during these meetings. In retrospect, she did feel that he had insulted her deliberately when he had included only one of her poems in his volume, *Des Imagistes: An Anthology.* She also suspected he had poisoned Harriet's attitude toward her, that the first sign occurred when Harriet either perpetrated or permitted an egregious typographical error in Amy's poem entitled "The Forsaken," which had appeared in the issue of *Poetry* for April 1914. The central character in the poem was a girl whose lover had been killed and whose child was soon to be born. Harriet, dropping one line, where delicacy was imperative, Amy said, had made a disagreeable kind of sense which was far worse than nonsense. In her fiery protest, Amy had overheated the telephone wire to Chicago.

According to Amy, Ezra had gone back on the Imagists by the time she returned to England in the summer of 1914: he was all wrapped up in Vorticism, and he further offended her by giving a big dinner party to which he invited all the literati in London, except Amy. She was more polite. Ezra was invited to her far more sumptuous dinner party, given two weeks later, in the same London restaurant. That evening she had announced to the Imagist poets H. D. and Richard Aldington that she liked the way the editors of *Georgian Poetry* brought out a volume annually, and she was going to edit the next annual volume of poems written by Imagists. Ezra had been furious with her for butting in. "He accused me of trying to make myself editor instead of him, and finally tried a little blackmail," Amy had written to Harriet. "Ezra has always thought of life as a grand game of bluff. He never has learned the wisdom of Lincoln's famous adage about 'not being able to fool all the people all the time.' "[14]

Before she left England that summer, Amy said, she had enlisted the support of her present guest, John Gould Fletcher, also of H. D., Aldington, and D. H. Lawrence. Recently, they had sent her poems for the next annual volume, which she was going to call *Some Imagist Poets.* It was due to be published within a month. Before its appearance, she hoped to give the book a good push by presenting the cause of Imagism at the March meeting of the Poetry Society in New York.

Very few people were able to outtalk Robert Frost on occasions like this, but Amy Lowell did. Fletcher later said that during the entire evening the newcomer "sat on her sofa and said little."[15] Frost was able to say that his one visit to the Poetry Society, with Robert Haven Schauffler, made him realize that the majority of those present were hostile to the Imagists. Miss Lowell had a low regard for that crowd, particularly for Schauffler. Less than two months earlier, she and Schauffler had discussed "The Failure of American Poetry and Its Remedy," at a Twentieth-Century Club luncheon in Boston. Schauffler had first annoyed her by claiming, in his notorious "Scum o' the Earth," that the foreign blood of immigrants would revitalize the degenerate American stock. He had further infuriated her by saying poetry in America was being ruined by the drudgery of moneymaking, and American poets should be subsidized. Such nonsense, said Miss Lowell, was "simply abominable."[16]

Before Robert Frost left Amy Lowell's home, he had acquired a new understanding of how and where the battle lines were drawn between the liberal and the conservative poets in America. He was convinced that, although he did admire the gusto with which Amy conveyed her prejudices, his old-fashioned ways of making new poetry placed him apart from the immediate lines of battle.

Just how successful he had been in making an impression on the literati of Boston, during his unexpected tarryings, he did not know until he reached Bethlehem. His new friend, Sylvester Baxter, wrote enthusiastically of his homecoming from England and published his article in the Boston *Herald*:

"Boston's literary sensation of the day has been the homecoming of Robert Frost. Three years ago a young New Hampshire schoolmaster went over to England, lived in retirement for a while, and published a volume of poems which won him many friends in a quiet way. Some time ago another volume of verse went to the same publisher and one morning Robert Frost found himself famous. His work was hailed as striking a new note in modern poetry. He was sought on every hand in the circles where literary values count and was acclaimed one of the elect—ranking with Masefield, Gibson, Abercrombie and others of that high grade in the younger generation of British poets. The book was called 'North of Boston,' and its contents bore out the title, being a series of vivid pictures of New England life and character. . . .

"In due time copies crossed the water and appeared in the bookstores and the libraries. Readers began to discuss the remarkable work and ask, 'Who is Robert Frost?' Nobody could say, in spite of diligent inquiry, and 'Who's Who?' was silent.

" 'You'd better get hold of him,' said a friend to the editor of the *Atlantic*—'he's another Masefield.'

"Then came the news that Frost had just landed in New York with his family, on his way back to New Hampshire, to take up farming again—he had been a farmer as well as a school teacher.

"Last Friday they were discussing Frost at the monthly 'shop talk' of the Boston Authors' Club; one of the members, reading from his work, said that Frost was doing for New England in verse what Alice Brown, Mary Wilkins and Sarah Orne Jewett had been doing in prose. Another member announced that Mr. Frost was in Boston that day, and was dining that evening with Mr. Ellery Sedgwick and some literary friends. It seems that he had come to Boston from friends in Lawrence, the home of his youth, and had expected to spend only a few hours in the city, for he had with him only the clothes he had on. But his new friends insisted upon his staying over, and meeting various people he ought to know and who wanted to see him. So he did not get away until last evening.

"He has been the guest of Mr. Nathan Haskell Dole at his home in Jamaica Plain. Last evening he dined with Miss Amy Lowell and friends in Brookline and yesterday he was entertained at luncheon by Prof. Hocking of Harvard and Mrs. Hocking at their home in Quincy Street, Cambridge. . . . Mr. Frost is expected to return to Boston in the near future. He is a most agreeable personality—'one of the most loveable men in the world'—declared one of his new literary friends, prominent in New England letters. He is still in his thirties, but remains youthful in face and figure; dark brown hair, handsome gray-blue eyes, a well-modelled head and mobile features. . . ."[17]

Frost was not embarrassed by such advertising. It was proof enough to him that the initial phase of his campaigning had not been a waste of time. As soon as he reached the Lynch farm in Bethlehem and could look back at all he had done since his arrival in New York, he could even risk boasting, to one of his old friends: "I didn't get through New York and Boston without more attention than you may think I deserve from my fellow countrymen. The Holts are splendid. If you want to see what happened in Boston, look me up in the Boston Herald for Tuesday March 9 under the heading Talk of the Town. . . . If the fellow who wrote it seems to know more of my goings and comings than he could without complicity of mine, the reason is because he is a lovely old boy and quite took possession of me while I was in Boston. When he wasn't actually with me like Mary's lamb he was keeping track of me by telephone. I believe he is doing for me on principle. He's got me on his conscience. The Ellery Sedgwick of the piece is mine ancient enemy the editor of The Atlantic."[18]

3

MY OWN STRATEGIC RETREAT

My own strategic retreat
Is where two rocks almost meet,
And still more secure and snug,
A two-door burrow I dug.[1]

AFTER his adventures in New York and Boston, Robert
Frost was in a mood to relish the solitude of winter life on
John Lynch's farm in the White Mountains. Never before had
he seen the place with icicles on the eaves, with rounded
and wind-carved caps of snow on the roofs of house and shed
and barn, with deep paths shoveled about the yard, and with
snow piled high along both sides of the driveway. In England,
where winter brought so much rain that back roads and paths
too much resembled mud-time in New England, he had
missed the sparkle of landscapes and dooryards buried under
snow. Still remembering how his muscles were lamed by
shoveling the stuff, either wet or dry, on his Derry farm, he
could now enjoy all this whiteness stretching miles beyond
the Lynch farm to the peaks of mountain ranges which would
hold the snow for another month or more. Years earlier, sharing
with Susan Hayes Ward his memories of summer days on
the Lynch farm, he had mentioned the "snug downhill churn-
ing room" there, "with the view over five ranges of mountains . . . and the blue-black Lafayette [Mountain]." He had
concluded, "There is a pang there that makes poetry. I rather
like to gloat over it."[2]

He had new reasons to gloat, as he returned now to these
cherished scenes after so long an absence. Homecoming, for
him, had little to do with getting back to New York or Boston;
he had been homesick for the rural scenes and people in
New Hampshire, for such warmth of greeting as was given
him by these affectionate friends, the Lynches. His many

[23]

delays in reaching Bethlehem had been explained to his family, apologetically, by postal cards and letters. Now he was required to tell the whole story in more detail, starting with the complete account of what had happened to Mervyn Thomas at Ellis Island. His children, giving him only time enough to get one good night of sleep, insisted that he must accompany them on various rounds of snow-adventures and explorations—on well-used snowshoes and skis found for them by John Lynch in his attic. Frost was in the mood for letting his children show him how to celebrate their return to the region they loved as much as he did. Yet it was only after he had begun to relax at the Lynch farm that he discovered how tired he was. As soon as he could muster enough courage to write letters of thanks to his newly made friends, he confided his predicament to Nathan Haskell Dole:

"I am slow to recover from the awful dazing you gave me in Boston. I was afraid my special pertness was never coming back. I sat on the edge of the bed for days together rubbing my eyes . . . 'The cuss is all gone out of me!' Possibly it is. I shall know better when I have made up the rest of my lost sleep."[3]

He did not deny to himself or to his friends that there was a continuing excitement in his beginning to realize some of the hopes he had nurtured secretly and persistently through more than twenty years of discouragement. To the closest of his old friends, John Bartlett—who had by now returned from Vancouver with his wife and child to Derry, New Hampshire—he gave some hints of how he responded to "the winning subject of the fortunes of my book," *North of Boston:*

"You can't wonder that it is a good deal on my mind with a review appearing every few days and letters coming in from all quarters. I wish I could describe the state I have been thrown into. I suppose you could call it one of pleasurable scorn when it is not one of scornful scorn. The thought that gets me is that at magazine rates there is about a thousand dollars worth of poetry in N. O. B. that I might have had last winter if people who love me now had loved me then. Never you doubt that I gave them the chance to love me.[4] What, you ask, has come over them to change their opinion of me? And the answer is What?—Doubtless you saw my countenance displayed in The [Boston] Herald one day.[5] The Transcript will [do] me next.[6] The literary editor of The Chicago

Post writes to say that I may look for two columns of loving kindness in The Post in a day or two.[7] It is not just naught— say what you will. One likes best to write poetry and one knew that he did that before one got even one reputation. Still one can't pretend not to like to win the game. One can't help thinking a little of Number One."[8]

He might have confided to Bartlett that after all these years of neglect in which it was easy to imagine that he had fewer friends than enemies, and even some enemies among his friends, his delayed victory aroused a retaliatory sense of vindictiveness which he did not try to restrain. Hints had been given to Bartlett from England, immediately after the publication of A Boy's Will: "What do you say if we cook up something to bother the enemies we left behind in Derry?"[9] When Bartlett had failed to respond, Frost had written apologetically, "I ought not to give way to thoughts of revenge in the first place. Still there were a few people in Derry who vexed me and one or two who did more than that and I am human enough to want to make them squirm a little before I forgive them."[10]

Among the unforgiven was Carl Burell who was treated harshly even after he had helped to save Frost's life during the worst period on the Derry farm. Not unrelated to the vexation was Burell's desire to make a name for himself as a poet, a desire just as intense as Frost's. They had shared the pleasures of seeing their early poems in the Lawrence High School Bulletin while they had been students there.[11] From the Derry farm they had sent out their poems to magazines and had compared rejection slips. After commiserating as failed poets during those early days on the farm, they had built up so many other common interests that they had reasons for keeping in touch with each other. Carl had tried, but Frost had discouraged him. From England, Frost had sent a copy of A Boy's Will to Carl, partly to boast and partly to make amends. After the return to America, he sent Carl a copy of North of Boston. If these two gifts were actually motivated by a vindictiveness which reflected an unforgiving nature and a desire to even the score with Carl for wrongs and injuries which existed only in Frost's imagination, Carl's response typified his refusal to recognize hurts even when deliberately aimed. He was forced to send his letter of thanks by way of the publisher:

[25]

"Dear Rob

Your 'North of Boston' came some time ago—but no post mark—so did not know where you were—and expected a letter but none rec'd as yet—

I read & re-read (with friends) North of Boston and am still alive and at times hungry & thirsty. But when I read the review of your books in . . . Literary Digest, I just had to let out my waist band—*That is great!* and you can't know how glad I am to have you get American recognition—It *is* great.

Hope others may follow the good example set by the Literary Digest. . . .

Really I think I like 'The Wood-Pile' the best of any—but I do not notice any one in the two vols that could well be left out.

I am glad all through that you have won out.

Yours sincerely

Carl"[12]

Such a letter might have succeeded in making Frost regret and even relinquish his unforgiving attitude toward Carl, but it did not. Burell received no answer.[13] Matters which seemed more practical required attention, including the urgent need to find and buy a home which would suit the tastes of his wife, their children, and himself. The Lynches were intimately acquainted with the insides and outsides of such farms as were or might be for sale along their hillside, but their location was too far from any school.

No attempt had been made to hurry Lesley, Carol, Irma, and Marjorie into classrooms after they reached the Lynch farm in February. Frost insisted that they had been out of school so long in England that there could be no harm in letting them stay out for the remainder of the year. If their father had had his way, he might also have insisted that the desultory education given them by their parents was far better suited to their needs than the humdrum boredom of usual classroom teaching. Each of them had progressed well enough, in learning, since the formal school year at Plymouth in 1911–1912. Mrs. Frost had other views, for she had carried the heavier burden of trying to work with them, as teacher, in spite of their very strong resistance to studying.

Now she wanted them out of the house and in a school near enough for walking. Down in the valley of the Gale River, at the western foot of the Lynch mountainside, the village of Franconia could provide a grammar school and, in Dow Academy, a complete high-school program. If the Frosts could find a place to live down there in that valley, their mother would like it.

As soon as April sunlight began to dry up the puddles of melted snow on the dirt roads, Frost extended his daily walks down into Franconia, searching for a small farm that would be suitable. Always idealizing possibilities in matters of real estate, he felt that anyone who admired mountain scenery as much as he did should carry exploration just far enough beyond the village to search for a house and barn perched on a foothill or a shoulder of mountain, just for the sake of the view. He soon found what he was looking for. On the seventeenth of April 1915 he wrote to Edward Thomas, "We are still unsettled. Hopes grow. . . . Looked at a little farm yesterday right forninst Lafayette."[14] Although the mountains flanked all sides of the Franconia village with varying degrees of abruptness, the panorama which appealed strongly to Frost was the one seen best from the southern outskirts of the village: the entire Franconia Range—Garfield, Lincoln, Haystack, and Liberty—dominated by the rocky peak of Lafayette. Using that peak for his orientation, in his calculated wanderings, he had been attracted to the little farm mentioned in his letter to Thomas. It was only a mile or so from the center of town, and the man who chose to build a small house and barn on that shoulder of what was locally known as Ore Hill plainly had an eye for mountain splendors. The road which climbed past that farm soon curved and ascended more steeply in the direction of Sugar Hill, another village famous for hotels which attracted wealthy summer visitors.

Frost was not immediately concerned with possible intrusions from Sugar Hill. The serious hitch was that there seemed to be little chance of displacing the present owner, whom he found raking dead leaves away from the front of the house. Entering the dooryard and striking up a conversation, the intruder explained that he was just out tramping, but wasn't a tramp; he wanted to buy a farm, and this was the one he liked best. The owner, Willis E. Herbert, amused by the bluntness of the visitor's approach, said maybe they could help each other. Herbert, needing more pasturage than he had here for his livestock, had taken a fancy to a larger farm, half a mile farther up the road. The larger farm was being rented at present by Herbert's brother, who wanted to give it up and find work in the village. So if the blunt-spoken visitor wanted this little farm and was willing to pay a thousand dollars for it, Herbert would move in a hurry.[15]

A few days later, Frost brought his wife and children over for a tour of inspection. Although the house was extremely small, and had neither bathroom nor furnace, the entire family liked it. The water supply came from an uphill spring, and was fed into the house by gravity, leaving enough surplus to fill a brook which flowed down into the Ham Branch of the Gale River. The barn was not so large as the one the Frost children remembered from their Derry days, but Frost was looking only for space enough to winter a few hens and a cow or two. Uphill, beyond the barn, was a hayfield and a pasture; above them were woodlots with good stands of white birch, maple, poplar, tamarack, and (most attractive of all) a grove of spruces pretty enough to be marketable for Christmas trees. One of those uphill woodlots was a sugar orchard, with a sugar house.

As soon as Frost had gained the approval of his family, he began to talk finances with Herbert. Apologetically, he said that he couldn't find a thousand dollars very fast, although he might be able to draw on the trust fund from which he received an annuity of $8oo, and he knew that John Lynch in Bethlehem would serve as reference for his credit. Herbert may never before have met a New Hampshire farmer with so large an annuity, and he closed the deal with a handshake, "nothing down." When Frost explained that the furniture from his Derry farm was in storage, down in Plymouth, Herbert very generously said there would be no need for the Frosts to wait. It would be easy for the Herberts to move in with Will's brother's family and leave their own furniture— beds and all—for the Frosts to use. Grateful for the friendliness of the gesture, Frost explained that he and his family would prefer to stay with the Lynches in Bethlehem until a carpenter could be found to make a few alterations and additions.

The carpenter, when found, went about his task with such

deliberation that the Frosts continued renting rooms at the Lynch farm throughout the spring of 1915. Before the actual move could be made, all of these pastoral arrangements were interrupted by two invitations which frightened the poet almost as much as they pleased him.

4

RETURN TO BOSTON

May no fate willfully misunderstand me
And half grant what I wish and snatch me away
Not to return. Earth's the right place for love:
I don't know where it's likely to go better.[1]

THE Delta Chapter of the Phi Beta Kappa Society, at Tufts College in a suburb of Boston, wrote to Robert Frost in Bethlehem, New Hampshire, requesting him to read at least one unpublished poem at its annual meeting on the fifth of May 1915. Back of this invitation was the poet Nathan Haskell Dole, who simultaneously prompted Sylvester Baxter and the Boston Authors' Club to urge that Frost talk before its members after a luncheon on the fifth of May. These attractive invitations added fuel to a disagreement which had smoldered between Robert and Elinor Frost since the publication of *A Boy's Will* in England.

There were times when it seemed to Frost that the sharp differences of opinion between his wife and himself had seriously injured their marriage, from the day of their wedding. At first he had thought that two people who disagreed so violently with each other should obtain a divorce. It also seemed that, even prior to their marriage, she had misunderstood him to such an extent that she had mistakenly hoped to make him over into an ordinary and responsible citizen; when this hope had failed she had decided to throw her life away with his, self-sacrificially, and to honor him as a good poet who had failed to win attention. As long as he had remained a complete failure on the farm in Derry, she seemed to luxuriate in the sadness and loneliness of their predicament. But as soon as he began to be noticed in England with his first book, she seemed to become jealous of the success which threatened to destroy what she had accepted as her ideal. Now the double invitation from

Tufts College and the Boston Authors' Club caused her to reproach him with charges that he was too eager to win the wrong kinds of attention—that he was willing to buy attention and flattery at the expense of the time and energy he should conserve for writing more poems.[2]

In his own defense, Frost tried to explain that he never had been, and never could be, content to write poetry merely for his or her enjoyment. Since the time when he first began writing, he had hoped his poems would some day win acclaim. He was willing to admit that it would be easier for him to refuse all invitations from those who wanted to see him and hear him. Never before had he stood facing a large public audience for the purpose of reading or talking about his poems. He knew it would be as painful for him to do that now as it had been when the mere thought of it had caused him to refuse the Rev. Merriam's invitation to read "The Tuft of Flowers" before the Men's Club in Derry, back in 1906. Nevertheless, he was determined to suffer through whatever torture of nervousness and pain such an experience would inflict, and he would do it not only to advance his own standing as a poet but also to earn money for the support of his wife and family.

While he was accepting these two invitations, he further calculated that this return to Boston would give him a chance to improve relations with influential editors and critics, such as his "ancient enemy" Ellery Sedgwick and his new friend William Stanley Braithwaite. In addition, he looked forward to meeting other literary figures who were still strangers to him. One such was the poet and critic Louis Untermeyer, whose correspondence with Lascelles Abercrombie, while the Frosts were living in Gloucestershire, had brought the name into frequent conversations. Not long after Frost reached New Hampshire from England, Untermeyer had written a friendly letter to convey his admiration for *North of Boston* and to say he would soon be giving the book strong praise in the Chicago *Evening Post*. There were obvious advantages in cultivating the friendships of such men as Untermeyer and Braithwaite, and these possibilities aroused all of Frost's calculating shrewdness. Soon after his arrival in Bethlehem he had kept his promise to Braithwaite by sending him a copy of *A Boy's Will* and a long letter containing biographical information for use in the article which Braithwaite was going to write.[3] On the same day, he had answered Untermeyer's letter with a cordiality which was calculated to flatter. ("There's not a person in New York I should have had more pleasure in meeting than Louis Untermeyer."[4]) The strategy proved to be rewarding. Untermeyer's response had clearly indicated that, with proper cultivation, he could be counted on to give continuing and vigorous support. Frost had also liked the way in which Untermeyer defended him against other poets and critics who found fault with him for being "too daringly bold" in dropping to a level of poetic diction that (as Frost had once boasted to Mosher) "even Wordsworth kept above."[5] The best part of Untermeyer's defense, in the Chicago *Evening Post*, was the polemical:

"I have little respect—literary respect—for anyone who can read the shortest of these poems without feeling the skill and power in them. But I have far more respect for the man who can see nothing at all in this volume than for him who, discovering many other things in it, cannot see the poetry in it. For that attitude represents a theory of poetry as false as it is doctrinaire. And also as common. Even some of Mr. Frost's most ardent adherents begin and end their praise by saying with a more or less deprecatory gesture, 'Whether this is poetry or not . . .' or even, more frequently, 'While this may not be poetry in the strict sense. . . .' And so on, to less cautious stammerings."[6]

For Robert Frost, still nursing the wounds caused by years of neglect, there was a thoroughly vengeful pleasure in standing apart, scornfully, in his White Mountain hideaway, and witnessing the numerous printed evidences that his admirers and detractors were fighting over him. Even as he had flattered Braithwaite by saying that when next Frost got down to Boston he hoped they could "have a talk about poetry by ourselves alone," so now he flattered Untermeyer. After acknowledging his review and adding that there were "a dozen things in the article that I should like to thank you for in detail," he chose just one: "You make the point that there must be many poetical moods that haven't been reduced to poetry. Thanks most of all for seeing that, and saying it in a review of [a] book by me." In the same letter, Frost acknowledged receipt of Untermeyer's second volume of poetry, *Challenge*. Although Untermeyer's lyrics sang too passionately of sex, of beauty, and of social values to win the genuine admiration of this puritanical New England poet, he side-stepped these matters gracefully by saying he was just now reading *Challenge* and was "full of the

large spirit of it." Continuing, he expressed the wish that Untermeyer might indeed be in Boston, as planned, near the time
when Frost would be performing there; he hoped they might
meet at Sylvester Baxter's house and then "steal away somewhere by ourselves" to talk about their mutual literary interest.[7]

The Boston visit began unpleasantly.[8] As soon as Frost
reached the Authors' Club he learned from his immediate host,
Nathan Haskell Dole, that he was sharing honors with another poet. The first after-luncheon speaker was to be Josephine
Preston Peabody, whose lyrics and plays were far too conventional and old-fashioned to please Frost, even though she was
exactly his age. He had not previously met her, but since the
nineties he had been reading her sweet lyrics in magazines, and
he had come to think of her as an outmoded sentimentalist
who wrote too many poems about the moon. Now he was even
more disgusted—and jealous—because he had let himself in
for the ordeal of sharing attentions with her. He also resented
the prospect of having her read poems just before he spoke on
the topic of his choice: his theory of sound-posturing, or of the
sound of sense.

He might have taken consolation in his knowledge that the
poetry of Josephine Preston Peabody would serve to illustrate,
implicitly, his complaint against the persistent use of an out-
worn musical vocabulary. Instead, he worried over the fact that
she was bound to cast him in the role of an outsider; everyone
admired her and bowed down before her as Boston's best. As
soon as he met her, all his suspicions seemed to be confirmed.
Although she carried herself as a high priestess of poetry, she
seemed to Frost coy and insincere. He sulked through the
luncheon, played with the food he could scarcely touch, became increasingly nervous as Nathan Haskell Dole introduced
the first speaker, listened scornfully as the fine lady read several of her latest poems, and then he began to shake.[9]

When he was introduced, Frost was in such a dour and
frightened mood that even his voice trembled and his words
came awkwardly. As he listened to himself, fumbling along
through this first public performance before such an audience,
he was inclined to think that perhaps his wife was correct in
saying he should not be here. He felt that he did not even say
his own poems well, and when he finished he was miserable. In spite of the assurances given him by Dole and Baxter,
in spite of the praise expressed by strangers who shook his

hand, he was disgusted with himself for having botched the assignment.

There was one way to make amends, and Frost took it. Having promised to have a session with Braithwaite in order to help him shape materials for a second *Transcript* article, Frost arranged to explain his theory of poetry to Braithwaite, at great length, during two interviews while he was in and near Boston, and he carefully dictated statements which he apparently requested Braithwaite to quote. The article appeared in the *Transcript* while Frost was still in Boston, and it conveyed all of the essential points the poet feared he had spoiled in his talk before the Authors' Club. Braithwaite began: "The success which has immediately come to the poetry of Robert Frost is unique. It has no exact parallel in the experience of the art in this country during the present generation." After these preliminaries, the article quickly settled into direct quotations from Frost:

" 'First,' he said, 'let me find a name for this principle which will convey to the mind what I mean by this effect which I try to put into poetry. And secondly, do not let your readers be deceived that this is anything new. Before I give you the details in proof of its importance, in fact of its essential place in the writing of the highest poetry, let me quote these lines from Emerson's "Monadnoc," where, in almost a particular manner, he sets forth unmistakably what I mean:

> *Now in sordid weeds they sleep,*
> *In dulness now their secret keep;*
> *Yet, will you learn our ancient speech,*
> *These the masters who can teach.*
> *Four-score or a hundred words*
> *All their vocal muse affords;*
> *But they turn them in a fashion*
> *Past clerks' or statesmen's art or passion.*
> *I can spare the college bell,*
> *And the learned lecture well;*
> *Spare the clergy and libraries,*
> *Institutes and dictionaries,*
> *For that hearty English root*
> *Thrives here, unvalued, underfoot.*
> *Rude poets of the tavern hearth,*
> *Squandering your unquoted mirth,*

Which keeps the ground and never soars,
While Dick retorts and Reuben roars;
Scoff of yeoman strong and stark,
Goes like bullet to its mark;
While the solid curse and jeer
Never balk the waiting ear.' "

(Braithwaite did not know Frost well enough to realize that several of his prejudices—which had nothing to do with his theory of poetry—could be found reflected in this passage from Emerson. Frost would have substituted the word "scorn" for the word "spare" in passing judgment on the "college bell," the "learned lecture," the "clergy and libraries, institutes and dictionaries.") Braithwaite continued his direct quotation:

" 'Understand these lines perfectly and you will understand what I mean when I call this principle "sound-posturing," more literally, getting the sound of sense. What we do get in life and miss so often in literature is the sentence sounds that underlie the words. Words in themselves do not convey meaning, and to prove this, which may seem entirely unreasonable to anyone who does not understand the psychology of sound, let us take the example of two people who are talking on the other side of a closed door, whose voices can be heard but whose words cannot be distinguished. Even though the words do not carry, the sound of them does, and the listener can catch the meaning of the conversation. This is because every meaning has a particular sound-posture, or to put it in another way, the sense of every meaning has a particular sound which each individual is instinctively familiar with, and without at all being conscious of the exact words that are being used is able to understand the thought, idea or emotion that is being conveyed. What I am most interested in emphasizing in the application of this belief to art, is the sentence of sound, because to me a sentence is not interesting merely in conveying a meaning of words; it must do something more; it must convey a meaning by sound.'

" 'But,' I queried, 'do you not come into conflict with metrical sounds to which the laws of poetry conform in creating rhythm?'

" 'No,' the poet replied, 'because you must understand this sound of which I speak has principally to do with tone. It is what Mr. Bridges, the poet laureate, characterized as speech-rhythm. Metre has to do with beat, and sound-posture has a

[35]

definite relation as an alternate tone between the beats. The two are one in creation, but separate in analysis. If we go back far enough we will discover that the sound of sense existed before words, that something in the voice or vocal gesture made primitive man convey a meaning to his fellow before the race developed a more elaborate and concrete symbol of communication in language. I have even read that our American Indians possessed besides a picture-language, a means of communication, though it was not said how far it was developed, by the sound of sense. And what is this but calling up with the imagination, and recognizing, the images of sound? When Wordsworth said, "Write with your eye on the object," or in another sense, it was important to visualize, he really meant something more. That something carries out what I mean by writing with your ear to the voice.

" 'This is what Wordsworth did himself in all his best poetry, proving that there can be no creative imagination unless there is a summoning up of experience, fresh from life, which has not hitherto been evoked. The power, however, to do this does not last very long in the life of a poet. After ten years Wordsworth had very nearly exhausted his, giving us only flashes of it now and then. As language only really exists in the mouths of men, here again Wordsworth was right in trying to reproduce in his poetry not only the words—and in their limited range, too, actually used in common speech—but their sound.' "[10]

Frost had reason to be satisfied with Braithwaite's assistance in conveying to the public these extremely important principles concerning the sound of sense. In addition, the *Transcript* article enabled the proponent of these principles to reach a larger audience than the Authors' Club.

The visit to Tufts College in Medford was far more pleasant than he had expected. He was escorted there not only by his sponsor, Nathan Haskell Dole, but also by Dole's attractive teen-age poetry-writing daughter Margaret, and the three of them were guests for the night at the home of Charles Ernest Fay. Well known as a professor of modern languages at Tufts, Fay was more widely hailed as the "dean of American mountaineering." He had climbed all of the best mountain trails on those peaks visible from the porch of Frost's new home, and he talked enthusiastically about the Franconia region. But he was equally enthusiastic in his conversation about the new poetry, and he proudly said he had first heard the name of Robert Frost during a recent visit to England.

During dinner at Fay's home, the main subject for conversation was the news that the young English poet Rupert Brooke had just died in the war and had been buried on the isle of Lemnos in Greece. Asked to tell of his friendship with Brooke, who had helped to edit the Georgian publication *New Numbers* from Abercrombie's thatched cottage in Gloucestershire, Frost easily participated in the grief over the young soldier's death and as easily managed to keep silent about his jealousy of Brooke.[11] Throughout the dinner he found it easier to talk than to eat; the prospect of reading before the Delta Chapter of Phi Beta Kappa brought on an attack of nervous indigestion. But the reading went well, and the campus reporter spoke of "the pleasing impression made by the poet, of the simplicity of his manner, the sincerity of his voice and the beauty of his three poems."[12] He first read "Birches," written in Buckinghamshire during a phase of homesickness; then "The Road Not Taken," inspired by Edward Thomas and only recently completed; and finally "The Sound of Trees," written at Abercrombie's cottage in Ryton.

Among those whom Frost met at the reception which followed was a stranger named George H. Browne who made an attractive offer: If the Phi Beta Kappa poet would be willing to give a reading of some poems, without renumeration, before the boys at the Browne and Nichols School in Cambridge, on the following Monday morning, Browne would arrange for Frost to receive $50 for each of four other readings at private schools in the Boston area. Although he had not intended to linger in Boston this time, Frost could not resist the opportunity to advertise his poetry while picking up $200 so easily. In the meantime, he counted on the hospitality of Sylvester Baxter.

As he returned to Boston from Tufts College the next morning, he had in mind another financial scheme. He wanted to see whether he could sell to his enemy, Sedgwick, the three unpublished poems in his pocket. Sedgwick's previous show of friendliness had not caused Frost to forgive the fact that the *Atlantic* had never yet accepted any of his poems, and so the planned visit was motivated in part by a desire for revenge. Again Sedgwick surprised Frost, not by holding out both hands but rather by greeting him in the *Atlantic* office with the announcement that the poet had arrived just in time to share some news about himself. The news could wait, Sedgwick said, until he found out if Frost had brought some poems for the *Atlantic*. Pretending to be surprised and hurt, Frost reproachfully asked if he looked like the sort of beggar who went around to editors pleading with them to take a poem. Of course not, Sedgwick said. He just wanted Frost to remember that whenever he had some poems available, the *Atlantic* would be glad to publish them—and would pay well for them. Did he mean he'd take a Frost poem sight unseen? To Sedgwick, it must have seemed safe to reply as he did, "Yes, sight unseen." Maliciously, Frost reached toward his coat pocket as he went on to explain that he was just returning from Tufts, where he had read three poems at the annual Phi Beta Kappa meeting, and that as a consequence he did have with him the manuscripts of these three poems. He took them out of his pocket, held them high, as though he were an auctioneer, and carried on his teasing: "Are you sure—that you want to buy—these poems?" Sedgwick had no choice but to say that of course he was sure. Slowly, Frost lowered the manuscripts into Sedgwick's hand and said with finality, "They—are—yours."[13]

It was Sedgwick's turn for teasing, and he had his own gift for it. The news, he said, was that the *Atlantic* had just received a letter from one of England's most distinguished critics, Edward Garnett. With the letter, Garnett had sent an article which Sedgwick might or might not be able to use in the *Atlantic*. It was entitled "A New American Poet" and it was devoted entirely to Robert Frost. After Sedgwick settled his visitor in a chair, he read aloud a portion of Garnett's letter:

"Of Mr. Frost I know nothing personally, but a few particulars given me by Mr. Edward Thomas who sent me 'North of Boston.' Possibly you know more than I do—which is simply that he hails from a New England farm, has paid a long visit to England, & has returned only a few weeks ago to the States. Mr. Frost as a poet, however, *is a very considerable figure indeed*, not to be classed in any way with Mr. Untermeyer & his associates, who I see are vociferously advertising the claims of 'The New Poetry,' or with the class of poetic dilettanti who contribute to Miss Harriet Monroe's magazine 'Poetry.'

"From what Mr. Thomas told me I fancy these fellow poets, or poetlings, are not particularly anxious to herald Mr. Frost's achievement; the former, if I may judge from my examina-

tion of 'their' work in 'Poetry,' are *negli[gi]ble,* whereas **Mr.**
Frost is really *representative,* carrying on those literary traditions of New England, which are associated with talents as
diverse as Hawthorne, Thoreau & Sarah Orne Jewett. If anything I have erred in *understating* Mr. Frost's claims to the attention of American readers; but I prefer that my verdict should
be cool & unbiassed. Although I rely entirely on my own judgment in this matter, I understand from Mr. Thomas that the
few notices of 'North of Boston' received on this side, though
short, owing to the War, practically confirm my belief that
since Whitman's death, no American poet has appeared, of so
unique a quality, as Mr. Frost.

"It is possible that by the time my article reaches you that
your own critic of poetry may have written something for 'The
Atlantic Monthly' on Mr. Frost's claims. . . ."[14]

Frost was elated, until Sedgwick explained with a straight
face that Garnett was correct in supposing the arrangements
had already been made for an American reviewer to include
North of Boston in a general survey of poetry; it might not be
possible, therefore, to use Garnett's article. But, Frost protested,
how could the *Atlantic* refuse to print an article by Garnett?
Ah, but the article hadn't been requested. Still teasing, Sedgwick went on to explain that the situation was awkward, and
that nothing could be decided on the matter for the present.

Frost left the *Atlantic* office in a rage. Two evenings later,
while staying as guest in Sylvester Baxter's home in Medford,
he was in no mood for recognizing or enjoying the next move
in Sedgwick's game of counterteasing. He telephoned Frost at
Baxter's to say with mock seriousness that although he had
read and liked the poems, he would have to consult his poetry
editor before he could say for certain whether the *Atlantic*
would publish any of them. If Frost had been on the giving end
of such a tantalization, he would have enjoyed it. He had not
yet recovered from his rage, and now he bellowed over the
phone, "Oh no you don't! You accepted those poems for publication, sight unseen, and I'm going to hold you to it." Sedgwick, pretending reproach, ironically urged Frost not to get too
excited. "I'm not excited," Frost said, again bellowing. "I'm—
inexorable!" With this pronouncement, he ended the conversation by slamming the receiver into place.[15]

One of the guests who heard the entire story at Sylvester
Baxter's home that night was Louis Untermeyer, who had ac-

cepted Frost's invitation to meet him there. Frost liked the breezy manner in which this New Yorker handled gossip about literary matters, including Frost's malicious account of his difficulties with Sedgwick. Sufficiently familiar with the oddities of many New England editors and authors, Untermeyer also knew the latest gossip about poets and novelists in other parts of the country. Only twenty-nine years old, he seemed to Frost to be a witty jester. He had a hawklike nose, a fondness for outrageous puns, and a surprising ease in joking casually about his Jewish heritage.[16] Frost, using his knack for getting strangers to talk about their past, very quickly obtained the most picturesque details of Untermeyer's story. His paternal grandfather, having come to America from Bavaria, had established himself as an ordinary butcher in Waldoboro, Maine, had gone from there to Boston, and had developed a prosperous meat market. The butcher's son, transferring his own skills and interests to the making of inexpensive jewelry, had established a wholesale firm in New York City. He had married a southern woman who "played Chopin desperately," and under her influence their son Louis had been well educated in music. As a boy, he had become impatient with formal education and had escaped from it before he finished high school. He had written his first poem when he was thirteen, had entered his father's jewelry business when sixteen, had married a poet named Jean Starr when he was twenty-two, and had published a book of lyrics, *First Love*, when twenty-six. Early in his career as an author, he had begun writing reviews for various newspapers, and he was now an editor of a leftist periodical, the *Masses*, which had published a typically youthful manifesto containing the boast that the editors would offer their readers a "revolutionary and not a reform magazine—a magazine with a sense of humor and no respect for the respectable."[17]

Among the editors and contributors to the *Masses* were other youthful leftists about whom Frost knew next to nothing: John Reed (Harvard, Class of 1910), Max Eastman (an assistant professor in philosophy at Columbia), and Floyd Dell (formerly editor of the literary supplement of the Chicago *Evening Post*). Frost, in his eagerness to make an ally and defender of Untermeyer, concealed his own political conservatism by assuring Untermeyer that this group of young men seemed very attractively romantic.

Sylvester Baxter, when given a chance to add some literary

news, informed his guests that all the recent stirrings among the New England poets had caused him to join Braithwaite, Edward J. O'Brien, and others in planning to organize a Poetry Club of New England. The first meeting was to be held at the Authors' Club a few nights hence, on Tuesday, the eleventh of May 1915. It would be an advantage for Frost, and an entertainment for Untermeyer, if each of them could attend that meeting. Frost, having committed himself to remain in the Boston area for the readings arranged by George H. Browne, accepted the invitation.

The pleasant literary gossip in Sylvester Baxter's home was darkened by the arrival of the news that a German submarine had torpedoed the British luxury liner *Lusitania* without warning, earlier that day, off the Irish coast. According to the first estimates, the ship had gone down so fast that over a thousand passengers (including at least a hundred American citizens) had lost their lives. Up until this time there had been considerable American sympathy for Germany, but it was clear that there would soon be strong demands for an immediate declaration of war by the United States. Untermeyer made it clear that he and the editors of the *Masses* would oppose such a declaration; Frost was equally certain that he would be in favor of it. He later conveyed his views to Untermeyer quite strongly: "Nothing is true except as a man or men adhere to it—to live for it, to spend themselves on it, to die for it. Not to argue for it! There's no greater mistake than to look on fighting as a form of argument. To *fight* is to leave words and act as if you believed—to *act* as if you believed. . . ."[18] From Sylvester Baxter's, the next morning, Frost wrote briefly to his friend John Bartlett, on whom he planned to call as he returned home from Boston:

"I got through my Phi Beta Kappa and my speech before the Authors' Club but what does it matter about me. I'm sick this morning with hate of England and America because they have let this [sinking of the *Lusitania*] happen and will do nothing to punish the Germans. They can do nothing. I have no faith in any of them. Germany will somehow come out of this war if not completely victorious at least still formidable and needing only time to get wind for another round. Dammit. . . ."[19]

During the next few days, which Frost spent in Boston, the shock of the *Lusitania* sinking was almost eclipsed for him by the excitement of literary warfare. When the incipient members of the New England Poetry Club met on the evening of May eleventh to create the organization and to elect officers, it became apparent that the primary instigators of this gathering were Amy Lowell, Braithwaite, Edward J. O'Brien, and Baxter, but it seemed that the influence of the older poets might be stronger than that of the new. The most ancient supporter of the plan for the Society was the eighty-eight-year-old John Townsend Trowbridge, who had delighted Boston years earlier with his light-verse account of Darius Green and his flying machine. Next in age, as a prominent supporter, was the eighty-year-old Harriet Prescott Spofford, not so well known for her poetry as for the prose-tales she had been publishing in the *Atlantic* since 1859. More important to Frost, in the light of later developments, were two inseparable spinster ladies, Helen Archibald Clark and Charlotte Endymion Porter, who had founded the magazine *Poetry Lore* some twenty-six years earlier. These two busy ladies had also directed the Boston branch of the Browning Society from its beginning and were currently making arrangements to produce little verse-plays (including two of Frost's dramatic narratives) for the American Drama Society in Boston. Also present at this first meeting was Denis Aloysius McCarthy, a local singer cherished by the Boston Irish because of his lyric which began, "Ah, sweet is Tipperary in the springtime of the year." Absent, because of illness, was the uncrowned queen of the Boston poets, Josephine Preston Peabody.

The warfare broke into the open as soon as the business session began, with Sylvester Baxter presiding. Only two nominations were made for the presidency: the absent Miss Peabody and the obviously present Miss Lowell. In the discussion, those who spoke in favor of Miss Peabody pointed out that she was the first woman poet who had achieved important recognition in New England, even in the United States, and even prior to the discovery of Emily Dickinson. It was further pointed out that she had obtained international eminence in 1910 when her five-act drama, *The Piper*, symbolizing the struggle between the devil and Christianity, had won first place in the Stratford-on-Avon competition. As the discussion continued, with increasing evidence that the supporters of Miss Lowell were far less articulate and might be in the minority, the impetuous Amy chose not to remain. With a flourish, she rose to her feet, as if to speak, then strode out of the room, alone. The self-appointed peacemakers who scurried after her included Braithwaite and O'Brien. They were told by Miss Lowell, flatly, that there was only one way for them to make peace. If she couldn't be president, she didn't want to have anything to do with the New England Poetry Club. Her two supporters insisted that she could be president if only she would be willing to let them nominate the ailing (and actually dying) Josephine Preston Peabody as honorary president. It was too late, that night, for peace to be made, but their plan was carried through at a meeting which was held one week later.[20]

Frost was amused by all these frictions between celebrated literary personalities, partly because it provided such a wealth of material for gossip. "I like the actuality of gossip, the intimacy of it," he had told Braithwaite.[21] He certainly did, but he also liked the chance to become intimately acquainted with some of these friendly enemies who would remain competitors, at least from his viewpoint, in his unflagging struggle for honors and glories. One of them, present at this meeting of New England poets, was Edwin Arlington Robinson, whom Frost had already met under awkward circumstances.

It was easy enough for Frost to trace his jealousy of Robinson back to the days in 1905 when newspapers and magazines had carried the story of how President Theodore Roosevelt had singled out the Tilbury Town poet for special attention. Thereafter, Robinson's reputation increased while Frost continued to gather rejection slips. In 1913, shortly after Frost published his first book in England, the British poet Alfred Noyes visited Boston and startled complacencies by announcing that the greatest living American poet was Robinson. When Frost landed in New York City from England the issue of the *Literary Digest* on the newsstands carried an article describing Robinson as the one "who had received higher praise from discriminating critics than any other living American poet." Among these critics was Braithwaite, who sharpened Frost's awareness of being in competition with Robinson. Braithwaite in his first *Transcript* article on Frost had begun clumsily with a survey of those New England poets who had attracted special attention during the nineteenth century, and he had named Longfellow as the most popular of them all. He continued: "One came after him, much later, who is today our foremost poet in whom the very fundamental substance of New England life

burns with extraordinary intensity. This poet is Edwin Arlington Robinson . . . There comes now another poet to help Robinson uphold the poetic supremacy of New England . . . Robert
Frost."[22]

Braithwaite's well-intended manner of putting Frost in second place as the helper of another poet was at least indelicate,
and soon thereafter Braithwaite made another mistake. When
Frost said that he also considered Robinson one of the best of
the living American poets,[23] and would like to meet him, Braithwaite volunteered to introduce them. Plans were made and
carried out while Frost was visiting Baxter during this second
visit to Boston, and Baxter went with Frost and Braithwaite to
Robinson's tiny apartment in Cambridge. Unfortunately, the
introduction was handled with a crudeness which must have
been as embarrassing to Robinson as to Frost. When the two
men stood face to face, Braithwaite began the ceremony by
saying, "Frost, when anybody thinks of poetry in America, he
always thinks of Robinson as our greatest poet. . . ." In his
reminiscences, Braithwaite said of this awkward moment, "So
I introduced them, and I don't think Frost ever forgave me the
fact that I, before Baxter, made the statement that Robinson
was the greatest of our poets."[24] Frost never did forgive him,
and much of the vindictiveness he later aimed at Braithwaite
stemmed from this moment.

Robinson tried to make amends. After the organization meeting of the New England Poetry Society, he waited for a chance
to speak again with Frost. With his typically owlish humor, he
said he detected a slight hoarseness in Frost's throat and gathered that bitters would be a good lubricant. There was a bar
nearby, he said, where they could go alone to have a drink.[25]
Frost accepted the invitation, although he was not accustomed
to frequenting bars, and the two men found plenty of subject
matter, fresh at hand, for conversation. The immediate conflict
between Miss Peabody and Miss Lowell was viewed with
amused detachment by each of these men who had earned his
own separate place. Before they left "The Place of Bitters," as
they later called it, they agreed that it didn't matter how arrant
an experimentalist or how arrant a reformer any poet might be,
so long as he or she created real poems. They further agreed
that no poem was likely to succeed merely because of the theory
on which it might be written.[26]

When Frost and Robinson parted that evening each promised to send the other a book. Robinson was the first to keep his promise. He had just published his second prose play, *The Porcupine*, and he quickly mailed a copy of it to Frost in Bethlehem. Handled in the familiar Robinsonian manner, the play is a study in mismating. The irresponsible protagonist stands outside the conflicts of the estranged pair and tries to provide them with "a way out" of their predicament, but the protagonist is dramatically represented as failing to realize that he himself has previously caused the crucial difficulty. Just before the final curtain, the heroine—who has fallen in love with the protagonist without his knowing it, and who is called a porcupine by her husband because she wears "an armor of invisible knives"—desperately finds her way out, through suicide. Robinson's sympathies, clearly given to the heroine, might have been shared by Frost, if only on the ground that he himself had once tried a similar means of resolving a love-triangle which threatened to deprive him of the girl he wanted to marry.[27] Instead, in his belated letter of acknowledgment, he used the play as a springboard for discussing his own theories about the sound of sense:

"Don't think I have been all this time trying to decide what your play is if it isnt comedy. I have read it twice over but in no perplexity. It is good writing, or better than that, good speaking caught alive—every sentence of it. The speaking tones are all there on the printed page, nothing is left for the actor but to recognize and give them. And the action is in the speech where it should be, and not along beside it in antics for the body to perform. I wonder if you agree with me that the best sentences are those that convey their own tone—that haven't to be described in italics. 'With feline demureness' for instance is well imagined as it is, but do you suppose it wouldn't have been possible to make the sentence to follow indicate in itself the vocal posture you had in mind. I don't say. I see a danger, of course, not unlike the danger of trying to make the dialogue describe the dress and personal appearance and give the past history of the characters. This is no spirit of fault-finding. I merely propose a question that interests me a good deal of late.

"I have had to tell a number of people in my day what I thought of their writing. You are one of the few I have wanted to tell—one of the very few. Now I have my chance to tell you. I have had some sort of real satisfaction in everything of yours I have read. I hope I make that sweeping enough.

"I owe Braithwaite a great deal for our meeting that day."[28]

Even when he tried to conceal his jealousy of Robinson, Frost was unable to do any better than make these awkward motions. The possible friendship between these two major New England poets of the twentieth century never developed. After these preliminaries, they rarely saw each other and, during the next twenty years, their correspondence with each other was limited to only a few brief letters.[29]

5

MAKING FRIENDS—AND ENEMIES

"I can see that I am going to make enemies if I keep on."[1]

"I am . . . that discouraged it would do my enemies (see roster of the Poetry Society of America) good to see me. . . . You needn't tell anyone I am so down or I shall have everybody on top of me. You know what a wolf-pack we are."[2]

ROBERT FROST did not go straight home after his second round of campaigning in Boston. On the way, he stopped overnight in Derry, New Hampshire, to visit with the married couple who had been his favorite students when he taught at Pinkerton Academy: John and Margaret Abbott Bartlett. Until the start of the war, John had done well enough as a newspaper reporter in Vancouver. Forced out by wartime curtailments, he and his wife had made a discouraged retreat, with their year-old son, to the Derry farm owned by Margaret's parents. If John should give up his plan to make a career of writing, he could become a farmer, but he disliked farming. Frost, full of his latest triumphs, sympathetically gave the young people genuine reassurance that he would stand by them and help in any way he could. His response to their problems was deepened by the analogies he saw between John's predicament and those through which Frost himself had suffered during the days when he had first come to Derry, ill with asthma or perhaps tuberculosis, and convinced that his grandfather had wanted him to "go on out and die." Writing to John from the Lynch farm in Bethlehem soon after this visit, he continued his encouragements:

"Just you hold on a bit till I know where I stand with my Boston friends and I will do so for you (and more also) as I needed someone to do for me, when I was your age. At least I will try. There are a dozen sorts of things you could do and make more money in a week than I ever could in a year. . . ."[3]

His own immediate problem was to learn from the Franconia farmer, Willis E. Herbert, where they both stood concerning the Franconia property Frost hoped to buy with funds from his grandfather's estate. While Frost had been in Boston, Herbert had called on John Lynch to say he'd seen Frost's picture in a Boston paper and had decided that this newcomer was famous enough to pay a little more than a farmer would ordinarily pay. Frost explained this awkwardness to Untermeyer: "I ought to say dammit that the farm I was to have had for a thousand dollars has gone up a hundred or two owing to the owner's having seen my picture in the paper."[4] Nevertheless, Herbert continued his neighborly offer to let the Frosts move into his house, "nothing down," and to use the furnishings left there by the Herberts. The Frost family eventually accepted the arrangement and moved from the Lynch farm to the Herbert Farm early in June 1915.

For a time the poet devoted all his energies to farming. Each day began with his milking the two cows and staking out the two calves he had purchased from Will Herbert. The children helped him plant a good-sized vegetable garden of corn, peas, beets, squash, cucumbers, and cauliflower. From England, Edward Thomas teased him gently: "I hope people aren't going to crowd to see you milking & find out whether your private life is also like a page from Theocritus. It will spoil the milk."[5] If his admirers had crowded around, they might have noticed the clumsiness of hands never skillful at milking, and the consequent nervousness of the cows. The trouble did not last long, and Frost very soon boasted, "You will be glad to hear that my cows and I have composed our differences and I now milk them anchored at one end only. They have accepted me as their milker in place of the calves. The trouble was that I wasn't enough like the calves, which are black and ring-streaked, to impersonate them. And I lacked the calves' little ways. I was easily known for a changeling. Isn't it the usual thing to wind up a bucolic like this with an Ah here we touch the realities of life?"[6]

As soon as he had re-established himself as a gentleman farmer who, playing his favorite game, enjoyed the work because so much of it could be neglected, Frost began to recover his old concern for weather. Each morning when he got up—

never early—he started the day by studying clouds and mountains to the north of Lafayette, hoping for signs of an easterly rain. While he was brooding over prospects for his garden, with newly planted seeds, he complained if the skies were too clear for too many days. "A little rain today," he wrote John Bartlett, "—not enough to pay for prayers at the regular pulpit price."[7] A month later he was protesting over too much rain: "I'll bet there is nearly as much water here today as there is where you are. And we care personally. We have to care. We have a garden we don't want drowned. We easily fall into bitter apostrophe when the weather goes wrong—and we don't stop to ask whom to."[8] Early in the summer, the downward flow of cold air off the mountains added the new fear that garden crops might be frozen before they could ripen. The first nip came in August; the first real freeze in September, leaving nothing more to harvest than beets and turnips. "So it goes," Frost wrote to Bartlett. "I doubt if what we have had from our summer's planting has cost us any more than it would have in the market."[9]

For the Frost children, the first summer in Franconia was idyllic. They soon made friends in the village and were delighted to find that their home was near excellent swimming holes in the Ham branch of the Gale River. Within a few weeks Carol and Lesley and Irma had learned to swim, but the ten-year-old Marjorie could not keep up with them because she feared deep water. In a field near the river, all of the children played baseball with their father, making enough of a crowd for scrub, the "moving up" version of the game. Carol became so proficient that he sometimes played with village boys in pick-up games on the diamond near the Dow Academy.

Berrying was another favorite entertainment for all. Will Herbert told them where they could find high- and low-bush blueberries on their own land. Always entertaining them with his tall tales, he claimed he knew one place on Ore Hill where there were blueberries so big you could get just one in a bushel basket, but of course he wasn't going to tell where these berries grew. At any rate, the children were well satisfied with what they found. Berrying expeditions were organized with the excitement of preparations for a picnic: milk and sandwiches were taken for those who might grow thirsty or hungry before the party returned home with heaped pails of berries.

All the children had been taught to share their father's keen pleasure in botanizing. As soon as they had settled on their farm, they helped him transplant wildflowers, trees, and shrubs from the woods and meadows to their own backyard or to the side of the brook which flowed from their spring. The brook itself became a favorite place for the children to play. It even inspired their father to a trial-flight of a poem which never shaped up well enough, he thought, to merit more attention than might be given it by lenient friends:

FISH-LEAP FALL

From further in the hills there came
A river to our kitchen door
To be the water of the house
And keep a snow-white kitchen floor.

The fall we made the river take
To catch the water in a dish
(It wasn't deep enough to dip)
Was good for us, but not for fish.

For when the trout came up in spring
And found a plunging wall to pass,
It meant, unless they met it right,
They glanced and landed in the grass.

I recollect one fingerling
That came ashore to dance it out;
And if he didn't like the death,
He'd better not have been a trout.

I found him faded in the heat.
But there was one I found in time
And put back in the water where
He wouldn't have the fall to climb.[10]

Into this idyllic atmosphere on the Frost farm came too many reminders, by mail, that such an enjoyable retreat could be only part of the poet's life henceforth. Early in June of 1915, Ellery Sedgwick made his peace by writing to say he was going to publish, in the August issue of the *Atlantic*, not only Edward Garnett's article in praise of Frost but also the group of new poems, "Birches," "The Road Not Taken," and "The Sound of Trees." He said he had been planning to do this from the start, and that Frost should have seen through his teasing. Greatly relieved, the farmer-poet passed the news along to Untermeyer:

"The three poems you have interested yourself in are with Ellery to stay. Ellery has said it: he is going to be good to me. He is even going to print the article by my new-found friend Garnett. He says it overpraises me, but never mind, it may not hurt me: he has never known a man's head turned when his hair was turned already."[11]

Wanting to thank Garnett, well in advance of publication, Frost had difficulty in doing so without showing too much bitterness against American editors and critics who had either ignored or misinterpreted him. The letter to Garnett, when finally written, still retained some traces of impatience:

"What you say for me is bound to have a tremendous effect. I can see the impression you made by the way you came to judgment last winter on the novelists.[12] We are all prepared to envy anyone you think well of.

"Most of the reviewers have made hard work of me over here. That is partly because they use up their space groping for the reason of my success in England. (I was rather successful though not with the editor of The English Review—as you observe.)[13] What you are good enough to call my method they haven't noticed. I am not supposed to have a method. I am a naive person. They get some fun out of calling me a realist, and a realist I may be if by that they mean one who before all else wants the story to sound as if it were told the way it is because it happened that way. Of course the story must release an idea, but that is a matter of touch and emphasis, the almost incredible freedom of the soul enslaved to the hard facts of experience. I hate the story that takes its rise idea-end foremost, as it were in a formula such as It's little we know what the poor think and feel—if they think and feel at all. I could name you an English poet the editor of the English Review admires, all of whose stories are made on just that formula.[14] The more or less fishy incidents and characters are gathered to the idea in some sort of logical arrangement, made up and patched up and clothed on. . . ."[15]

The polemical undertone in his letter to Garnett was inspired partly by the way Garnett's article upbraided American readers and editors for their failure to be first in recognizing this "new American Poet" who was "destined to take a permanent place in American literature." No American reviewer had dared make a statement so sweeping as that. Garnett admitted, with ironic condescension toward American readers, that "originality of tone and vision is always the stumbling-block to the common taste when the latter is invited to readjust its accepted standards." After praising "The Death of the Hired Man" for its "exquisite precision of psychological insight," the English critic again bore down on the common taste: "Yes, this is poetry, but of what order? the people may question, to whom for some reason poetry connotes the fervor of lyrical passion, the glow of romantic color, or the play of picturesque fancy. But it is precisely its quiet passion and spiritual tenderness that betray this to be poetry of a rare order, 'the poetry of a true real natural vision of life,' which, as Goethe declared, 'demands descriptive power of the highest degree, rendering a poet's pictures so lifelike that they become actualities to every reader.' " In further defense of Frost, against the common taste, Garnett again quoted Goethe:

" 'At bottom no subject is unpoetical, if only the poet knows how to treat it aright.' The dictum is explicit: 'A true, real, natural vision of life . . . high descriptive power . . . pictures of life-like actuality . . . a lively feeling of situations'—if a poet possesses these qualifications he may treat any theme or situation he pleases. Indeed, the more prosaic appears the vesture of everyday life, the greater is the poet's triumph in seizing and representing the enduring human interest of its familiar features. In the characteristic fact, form, or feature the poet no less than the artist will discover essential lines and aspects of beauty. Nothing is barred to him if he only have vision. But is Mr. Frost then a humorist? the reader may inquire, seeing a gleam of light. Humor has its place in his work . . . But . . . his humorous perception is interwoven with many other strands of apprehension, and in his *genre* pictures, sympathy blends with ironical apprehension of grave issues, to endow them with unique temperamental flavor. . . ."[16]

Pleased as Frost was by the prospect of having this article in print, he worried over Garnett's characteristically British tone of condescension and over its effect on American critics and reviewers who had already devoted too much space to "groping for the reason of my success in England." Frost himself had helped to precipitate a concern for this question when he had provided information for use in Braithwaite's first article. It contained this: "It must be remembered that Mr. Frost had no influence to attract this critical attention except what the work itself commanded. He has accomplished what no other American poet of this generation has accomplished, and that is, unheralded, unintroduced, untrumpeted, he has won the acceptance of an English publisher on his own terms, and the unqualified approbation of a voluntary English criticism."[17] Other American critics had gone out of their way to stress the same point, until Frost had begun to worry for fear that such praise might backfire. An editorial by Llewellyn Jones in the Chicago *Evening Post* had brought Pound back into the controversy: "Whether it is the American public's own fault that Mr. Frost's work was not accessible to it sooner, we cannot say, but if we remember correctly, Ezra Pound wrote in *Poetry* a year or so ago to the effect that Mr. Frost had been refused a hearing by American publishers before David Nutt of London issued his works. . . ."[18] When the backfire came, it was directed by Miss Jessie B. Rittenhouse, recording secretary of the Poetry Society of America:

"When an American poet comes to us with an English reputation and prints upon his volume the English dictum that 'his achievement is much finer, much more near the ground, and much more national than anything that Whitman gave to the world,' one is likely to be prejudiced, not to say antagonized, at the outset. Just why a made-in-England reputation is so coveted by the poets of this country, is difficult to fathom, particularly as English poets look so anxiously to America for acceptance of their own work. . . ."[19]

Miss Rittenhouse also called the British praise of his works "fulsome and unconsidered," and Frost made his first complaint against her to his friend Sidney Cox: "The only nastiness in Jessie B's article is the first part where she speaks of the English reviews as fulsome. There she speaks dishonestly out of complete ignorance—out of some sort of malice or envy I should infer. . . . She has no right to imply of course that I desired or sought a British-made reputation. You know that it simply came to me after I had nearly given up any reputation at all."[20] It would be necessary, Frost decided, to find some way of publishing his own answer to these charges.

Before he could decide how to cope with the danger, Ezra Pound heightened it by reacting against a well-meaning review written by Edmund J. Wheeler, president of the Poetry Society of America and editor in chief of *Current Opinion*. Speaking on behalf of all American poets, Wheeler began, "No less than a year ago, the pugnacious Mr. Pound made the accusation in *Poetry* that Robert Frost had been refused a hearing by American publishers before his work was published by David Nutt of London." Continuing, Wheeler quoted Braithwaite's *Transcript* statement that Frost had accomplished in England what no other American poet of this generation had accomplished. The photograph which accompanied the article bore the caption, "ENGLAND ACCLAIMED HIM FIRST," and the subcaption, "Tho his wonderful poetry of New England life is said to be even more American than the work of Walt Whitman . . ."[21] Pound, reacting with his usual violence, sent a pugnacious riposte to the editor of the *Transcript*:

"I don't know that it is worth my while to call any one of your reviewers a liar, but the case has its technical aspects and the twistings of malice are, to me at least, entertaining.

"I note in *Current Opinion* for June a quotation from your paper to the effect that my friend Robert Frost has done what no other American poet has done in this generation 'and that is, unheralded, unintroduced, untrumpeted, he won the acceptance of an English publisher on his own terms' etc.

"Now seriously, what about me? Your (?negro) reviewer might acquaint himself with that touching little scene in Elkin Mathews' shop some years since. . . .

"No, sir, Frost was a bloated capitalist when he struck this island, in comparison to yours truly, and you can put that in your editorial pipe though I don't give a damn whether you print the fact.

"You might note *en passant* that I've done as much to boom Frost as the next man. He came to my room before his first book *A Boy's Will* was published. I reviewed that book in two places and drew it other reviewers' attention by personal letters. I hammered his stuff into *Poetry*, where I have recently reviewed his second book, with perhaps a discretion that will do him more good than pretending that he is greater than Whitman. . . ."[22]

It was true that Frost, living on his annuity while in England, and therefore not required to earn a living, had been much better off than Pound. It was also true that Pound had given him considerable assistance in England, as a friend, and that the hostility between them had been one-sided: Frost had broken away from Pound for reasons more imagined than real, and Pound had remained friendly even after the break-away.[23] Nevertheless, the hostility still remained, on Frost's side, and found expression in his answer to Braithwaite's question whether he had seen Pound's letter to the *Transcript:* "No I haven't seen Pound's letter. What new terms of abuse has he found for your review? Why would you review him? He needs letting alone. The English have ceased to give him space in their papers."[24] Frost was willing to leave Pound alone, even if the English weren't; but he could not leave alone the far more dangerous possibility that his cause would be hurt if he failed to quiet the claim first made by Pound (who was actually quoting Frost) to the effect that Frost had gone to England only after he had been snubbed by American editors and publishers. Appealing to Alfred Harcourt, Frost used the same methods he had already used in manipulating Braithwaite and Untermeyer as voices for his views. If Harcourt could exert his influence to get something published in denial of the current thrusts at American publishers, Frost would be grateful. Harcourt knew the ropes, and within a few days after the request was received, he planted an editorial in the New York *Times:*

"That Mr. Robert Frost's volume of poems, 'North of Boston,' made its first appearance under the imprint of an English instead of an American publisher has disturbed some of our reviewers and revived the old complaint that we are unappreci-ative of true excellence when it knocks at the door of our native literature. Mr. Frost's poems are pre-eminently worth while, they are thoroughly original in theme and treatment, they are genuinely interpretive of certain phases of American life— why, then, were they published first in England? The query has suggested dire possibilities by way of answer. But now Mr. Frost himself comes to the rescue with an explanation the simplicity of which should allay at once any international jealousies or suspicions. Writing to his present American pub-lishers he tells them that he happened to be in England when the idea came to him of collecting his poetry manuscripts into a volume. He did this, and, with the manuscript in his pocket, went up to London and left it with a publisher, who promptly accepted it. He declares, moreover, that he 'never offered a book to an American publisher, and didn't cross the water seeking a British publisher.' The thing 'just happened.' And so, there is not 'another case of American inappreciation' to record."[25]

That this editorial did not contain the whole truth, and that Frost was willing to differentiate between what he would say in private and wouldn't say in public, he very quickly demonstrated in his letter of thanks to Harcourt for assistance: "If I ran away from anything when I went to England it was the American editor. Very privately in the inmost recesses of me I suppose my Hegira was partly protest against magazine poets and poetry. We won't insist on that now, but please remember it when I am dead and gone."[26]

In spite of his nervousness, worries, and fears over the public responses, Frost enjoyed the private game of jockeying for position and of demonstrating his power to manipulate those he could use. He further enjoyed noticing that, as the controversy continued, the sale of his books increased. Long before the summer of 1915 was over, Harcourt proudly informed him that *North of Boston* was on the best-seller list and that a fourth printing had been ordered. This was enough to start the poet on a new campaign calculated to make the most of his advantages. In a letter to Amy Lowell he managed to mention the news in his first sentence: "There is an ominous note in your letter that seems to tell me you are getting ready to throw me over as a poet of the elect ostensibly on the ground that I am become a best-seller . . ."[27] The next day, in a flattering letter to Braithwaite, he built up to his point by urging that the poet-critic should come and visit him in Franconia, where they could fill a week of days walking and talking. He concluded, "If you don't come I shall be sure it is because you are too nice to have anything to do with the author of a Best-seller (non-fiction) which is what I am told I have become. Isn't it —well hard to know how to take?"[28]

He plied his advantage in other ways. Thoroughly disgusted with the pretentiousness of the Imagists, in their theories and practices, he nevertheless found excuse now for identifying himself with Amy Lowell's fight to advance the cause of the "new poetry" movement. In writing to thank her for her gift of *Sword Blades and Poppy Seeds,* he praised her, taking exception only to her following Browning in "some of the broader intonations he preempted." He continued, "But that's a small matter (or not so large as it might be); the great thing is that you and some of the rest of us have landed with both feet on all the little chipping poetry of awhile ago. We have busted 'em up as with cavalry. We have, we have we have. Yes I like your book. . . ."[29]

There were reasons enough for cultivating Amy Lowell, and at least one immediate reason for strengthening his ties with Braithwaite. Having published no new poems since his return from England, except the three in the *Atlantic*, he wanted Braithwaite to pick up at least one of these poems for his *Anthology of Magazine Verse for 1915*. His inviting Braithwaite to visit the Frosts in New Hampshire was thoroughly successful as campaign strategy. Braithwaite sent his regrets, saying he was so busy compiling his *Anthology* that he could not get away just now. But he did hope that Frost would be willing to let him use in the *Anthology* "Birches," "The Road Not Taken," and (because it had appeared in the *New Republic*) "The Death of the Hired Man." Frost replied expansively, "I shall be honored if you will use the poems in your book, honored enough if you will use two, honored beyond dreams if you will use three."[30]

A more important honor came from the Dean of American Letters, William Dean Howells, in his "Editor's Easy Chair" column in *Harpers* magazine for September. After condemning *vers libre* as having newness only in the sense of being "what we may call the shredded prose," and after treating harshly not only Amy Lowell's *Sword Blades and Poppy Seeds* but also Edgar Lee Masters' extremely popular *Spoon River Anthology*, Howells gave almost unreserved praise to *A Boy's Will* and *North of Boston*: "Here is no *vers libre*, no shredded prose, but very sweet rhyme and pleasant rhythm, though it does not always keep step (wilfully breaks step at times, we should say), but always remains faithful to the lineage of poetry that danced before it walked." Continuing at some length, Howells singled out for praise one aspect which no other critic had mentioned:

"His manly power is manliest in penetrating to the heart of womanhood in that womanliest phase of it, the New England phase. Dirge, or idyl, or tragedy, or comedy, or burlesque, it is always the skill of the artist born and artist trained which is at play, or call it work, for our delight. Amidst the often striving and straining of the new poetry, here is the old poetry as young as ever; and new only in extending the bounds of sympathy through the recorded to the unrecorded knowledge of humanity. One might have thought there was not much left to say of New England humanity, but here it is as freshly and keenly sensed as if it had not been felt before, and imparted in study and story with a touch as sure and a courage as loyal as if the poet dealt with it merely for the joy of it. But of course he does not do that. He deals with it because he must master it, must impart it just as he must possess it."[31]

Howells gave Frost more than public praise. He wrote a personal letter, in advance of his article, and asked Frost to call on him whenever the poet was next in New York. He did, and the visit with Howells was far more intimate than Frost had expected. Howells had a secret to confide: the triumph of *North of Boston* amounted to a fulfillment of a hope Howells had entertained forlornly in 1909, when he had published what he now considered to be a similar volume of blank-verse poems, *The Mother and the Father: Dramatic Passages.* Apparently, Howells said, the reading public had not been ready for the poetic realism he had offered at that time. Glad that Frost had succeeded where he himself had failed, the poet-novelist inscribed a copy of *The Mother and the Father* as a gift which Frost proudly accepted.[32]

Neither in his conversation nor in his article did Howells raise one question which bothered so many conservative reviewers: whether the dramatic narratives in *North of Boston* might have been handled just as well as short stories or sketches, in prose. Frost was still chafing under Amy Lowell's having compared his poetic tales with the prose stories of Alice Brown, and under the additional claim that while Alice Brown had "a rare sense of humor," Frost seemed to have none.[33] Commenting sarcastically on this latter point, in one of his letters to Edward Thomas, after giving a comical illustration of Gibson's innocence, Frost wrote, "Amy Lowell says I have no sense of humor, but sometimes I manage to be funny without that gift of the few. Not often, you know."[34] Often enough, he thought, to have woven comic touches into more than half the poems in *North of Boston.* He felt that if anyone should read "Mending Wall" properly there should be no difficulty in finding a variety of humorous elements there. "The Mountain" specifically contained his view of the basic New England knack for conveying humor: ". . . all the fun's in how you say a thing." Could anyone read through "A Hundred Collars" without seeing the central situation as comical? And wasn't "Blue-berries" built around a humorous portrayal of the central character, even as a grim joke provided the crucial moment in "The Code." He wondered if Amy Lowell found no humorous overtones on either side of the conversation between the two young people in "The Generations of Men," and whether she missed entirely the clergyman's quiet humor in "The Black Cottage." As for his earlier book, he had supposed his best readers would notice how the entire structural arrangement of poems in *A Boy's Will* conveyed his own retrospective detach-ment and humorous objectivity concerning poems which re-flected his immature moods: his "program notes" had been calculated to heighten an awareness of the humor there. As for his humorous employment of irony and sarcasm, even Ezra Pound had laughed sympathetically over the five lines of "In Neglect."[35]

Tones, tones, tones. He was certain that he had succeeded in building enough humorous tones of voice into his poems to spare him too much concern over Amy's apparent tone deafness. But he was seriously annoyed when others repeated her insinuation that he was a writer of short stories in verse. Mark Sullivan said it bluntly, in *Collier's:* "Poets like Masefield and Gibson, and, among Americans, Robert Frost and Edgar Masters are really short-story writers who use verse to tell their stories."[36] Franklin P. Adams, the so-called licensed jester of the New York *Tribune,* carried the insult one step further when he demonstrated that Frost's verse-tales, printed as prose, revealed their prosiness.[37] An editorial in the New York *Eve-ning Post* carried the insult further by insisting that "it was hardly necessary to run Robert Frost's lines solid in order to show that they are essentially prose. . . . Disguised as poetry, the . . . short story is finding a market."[38] It seemed to Frost that Edward Garnett had answered these insults best when he had come to Frost's defense by declaring him to be "a mas-ter of his exacting medium, blank verse." Going even further, Garnett had restated the question raised by readers who were deaf, and then had answered well:

"But why put it in poetry and not in prose? the reader may hazard. Well, it comes with greater intensity in rhythm and is more heightened and concentrated in effect thereby. If the reader will examine 'A Servant to Servants,' he will recognize that this narrative of a woman's haunting fear that she has inherited the streak of madness in her family, would lose in distinction and clarity were it told in prose. Yet so extraordinarily close to normal everyday speech is it that I anticipate some person may test its metre with a metronome, and declare that the verse is often awkward in its scansion. But so also is the blank verse of many a master hard to scan, if the academic footrule be not applied with a nice comprehension of where to give and when to take."[39]

A particular failure in "nice comprehension" of his implied meanings aroused Frost to impatience and anger when he went down to Boston in the fall of 1915 to attend dramatic productions of two of his blank-verse dialogues. He was infuriated by those who played the parts of Warren and Mary in "The Death of the Hired Man." These two actors, obviously well-educated city people, seemed to feel that they could best convey the rural qualities of these characters by talking crudely and by taking clumsy steps across the stage. After the performance, when Frost was taken behind the curtain, he scolded the man who had played Warren. Wasn't it clear from the lines, Frost asked, that Warren was no fool, no clodhopper? Wasn't it clear that Warren and Mary were dramatically represented as intelligent people? No? "Well," said Frost, sarcastically, as though he were giving acceptable proof, "both of those characters are college graduates."[40]

Frost was always conscious of the need for conveying his criticisms subtly—even the need for concealing them entirely —whenever his opponent was being useful to him. His newly made friend Untermeyer, for example, had already established himself as a defender of Frost against those who belittled his poetic abilities, and Frost was as flattering to Untermeyer as to Braithwaite. For a time, he continued to conceal his annoyance with Untermeyer for his work as editor of the liberal socialistic-communistic sheet entitled the *Masses* and for his contributions (under the pseudonym, Owen Hatteras) to the magazine the *Smart Set*, which Frost disliked because of its title alone. During their first meeting at Sylvester Baxter's, Untermeyer had apparently given Frost a few current issues of the *Masses* and of the *Smart Set*. Commenting on them, after his return to Bethlehem, Frost had written, "You needn't be afraid of being too romantic for me—you or your friends. I liked you all as I found you sprinkled through the Masses. It's all sorts of a world. . . . You are a lot of fun as Owen Hatteras and something of a terror. I'm glad you didn't bite me."[41] Such compliments obliquely reflected Frost's desire to hold Untermeyer's hands so that the polemical critic couldn't strike Frost. "You have a scourging pen," Frost wrote to him. "Scourge away."[42] Again, "Down with our enemies . . ."[43] Again, "Iron cross for you if you kill more than so many of my enemies at once."[44] There were many times when Frost poured out his resentments against enemies real or imagined, knowing that some of his prejudices thus expressed would help to color Untermeyer's critical writings. Even so, there were times when his bitterness shocked Untermeyer enough to evoke comments which Frost had to answer with playful countercomments:

"You do just right to humor me when I am like that: one of my wife's relatives married into a family in which there was a taint of insanity.

"That was a bad letter I wrote you the other day and what was worse I sent it. . . .

"I wrote of everything, I believe, but what was really bothering me, which was no more important a person than [the poet] Richard Burton—poor dear—author of the mortal line (I don't lie) 'The Sough of winds in Immemorial trees' (caps not his), which brings together in some sort of relation the two worst poeticisms of our poetical bankruptcy. Why should I mind Richard, you say. I don't mind him today. But I did two or three days ago while his offense was still fresh on the floor. He was writing to a common friend a pious wish that, for my own sake, I weren't quite so 'daringly radical.' It's the damned hypocrisy of his 'daringly' that seems like the whole nation against me. You see the force of it and you smell the device. It makes him seem to speak as a well-wisher. Torment his picture."[45]

Oversensitive, and suffering too often under the delusion that he was being persecuted by those who might set the "whole nation" against him, Frost needed the playful and witty support given him by many of his understanding friends, including Untermeyer. But Edgar Lee Masters was one competitor who was praised too highly and too often by Untermeyer. Even worse, Frost noticed, Untermeyer and Braithwaite coupled Frost with Masters as the two best finds of the year 1915. Resenting even the qualified praise which Untermeyer gave Masters, Frost tried to correct him: "It grieves me a little that you shouldn't have felt that what I wanted to say about

Masters but couldn't say because it would sound strange coming from me—couldn't say in so many words at least—was that he was too romantic for my taste, and by romantic I'm afraid I mean among other things false-realistic."[46] Masters' next book, *Songs and Satires*, disappointed all the critics, including Untermeyer. Delighted by this development, Frost privately gloated over his belief that Masters was dead as a competitor. A blurb, written by Masters for Sandburg's *Chicago Poems*, gave a chance for extra gloating to Untermeyer:

"Meanwhile and till I can go to join him here's a sigh and a tear for poor old Masters. That stuff on the outside of Sandburg's book is enough to prove my original suspicion, not that Masters is just dead but that he was never very much alive. A fellow that's that way can't ever have been any other way. But we won't labor that. We won't labor or belabor anything and so we shall save ourselves from all things dire. Nothing but what I am 'forced to think,' forced to feel, forced to say, so help me, my contempt for everything and everybody but a few real friends.

"You are the realest of these. Who else has struck for me so often in swift succession. I had seen what you wrote in Masses. The devil of it is I am getting so I rather expect it of you. Don't fail me!"[47]

Untermeyer was not the only poet-critic who annoyed Frost by refusing to accept the notion that Masters should be ignored. Braithwaite, in his *Anthology* for 1915, did something worse than repeat that Masters and Frost were the two poets who had made the biggest splash in 1915. He placed Frost in unpleasant company by choosing as the five best poems published in 1915 Amy Lowell's "Patterns," Odell Shepard's "The Adventurer," Margaret French Patten's "Needle-Travel," Frost's "The Road Not Taken," and Wallace Stevens' first important poem, "Peter Quince at the Clavier." Untermeyer again came to Frost's rescue by publicly criticizing Braithwaite and then by sending his criticism to Frost. Consoled, and eager to encourage such faultfinding, Frost warmed to the subject, again flatteringly, in a letter acknowledging the review:

"You and I are not clever, Louis: we are cunning, one with the cunning of race the other with the cunning of insanity. (All women are cunning with the cunning of sex.)

"Anybody can tell you are cunning by the way you phrase yourself on the subject of Braithwaite's five best poems. The selection 'staggers you.' That is to say you don't say it is not good and you won't say you don't know what good is. You seem to allow that the poems have merit, though you don't see it. They have none. Amy's is just nothing to the eye, ear, or peritoneum. How completely outside of herself she gets and how completely outside of everybody else she keeps. She executes a frightfulness. Somewhere else she brings in the Peeping-Tom idea. The Adventurer is a Blissful Carman—a voice from the nineties. Mosher would like it. But to be novel you have to revive something older than the nineties. Susanner [in "Peter Quince at the Clavier"] simply bothers me. A priori I ought to like any latter-day poem that uses the word 'bawdy.' I don't know why I don't like this one unless it is because it purports to make me think. A bawdy poem should go as easy as a song: 'In Amsterdam there lived a maid,' frinstance.

"But why try to discriminate in this world? It ill becomes the author of poems not to like the other fellows' poems, because the more he doesn't like the other people's poems the more he seems to his suspectors to like his own. Me for Hudson Bay!

". . . As you say, few of these poets are much bothered by anything that is in them. I wish you would give them all Hell and relieve my feelings without involving me in the odium of seeming jealous of anybody. . . ."[48]

Similar moods of scorn and condemnation were indulged by Frost whenever his lack of confidence in his own abilities to sustain his own powers was intensified by other fears which also drained his energies. Throughout the fall of 1915, he was frightened by a serious illness which overtook Mrs. Frost and which seemed related to her being pregnant. From the time her first child had been born, she had been warned repeatedly by various physicians that she had a heart ailment which made childbearing dangerous. Now that she was carrying her seventh child, she was told by her new doctor in Franconia that her heart was not in good condition and that she must be very careful. Frost, writing to his British friend Lascelles Abercrombie, confided, "You will be sorry to hear that Elinor is altogether out of health and we are in for our share of trouble. . . . It is the old story: what she has been through so many times. . . . The doctor frightens me about her heart. But this is something you mustnt mention in your letters."[49] Late in November, Mrs. Frost suffered a miscarriage, and Frost quickly conveyed the news to Abercrombie in a brief note: "Just a word to you and Catherine to let you know that we are out of those woods—though perhaps not yet far enough to feel safe in crowing. We are still six in the family, no more and, thank God, no less."[50] After telling Untermeyer that the crisis had passed, he added, "We are lucky in all being still alive. I am nurse, cook, and chambermaid to the crowd, and that discouraged it would do my enemies (see roster of the Poetry Society of America) good to see me. . . . You needn't tell anyone I am so down or I shall have everybody on top of me. You know what a wolf-pack we are."[51]

While this bitter mood lasted, he gave way to new outbursts aimed at those he now viewed as enemies. A copy of Braithwaite's *Anthology of Magazine Verse for 1915* received from Untermeyer annoyed Frost so much that he had to find a special way to vent hostility. While he had been on friendly terms with Braithwaite, and indebted to him for the two long *Transcript* articles which they had collaboratively written, Frost had completely ignored the fact that Braithwaite, who appeared to be a white man, was in part a Negro.[52] Largely because of Braithwaite's preference for Robinson, however, Frost turned against Braithwaite, and began to make remarks which revealed some of his deep-seated prejudices. Near Christmas of 1915 he sent to Untermeyer a one-sentence foreshadowing: "Sometime at a worse season I will tell you what I think of niggers and having said so much to pollute this letter I will break off here and begin over on a fresh sheet which I will mail under separate cover." The continuation was a tirade against Braithwaite and others whom he now considered to be his enemies:

"And again: to be niggerly is not necessarily to be niggardly. It is niggerly for instance to single out Fannie Stearns Davis for dispraise, but it can't be called niggardly to name nobody else in the world but to praise them. In the case of Fannie you can't help suspecting something in the woodpile, a nigger scorned or slighted or not properly played up to.

"Mind you I haven't read Fannie and I haven't read Braithwaite's g. d. book—I got one of the children to read it for me and tell me about it. All that saved the fat obstacle from the worse fate that overtakes paper was your name and mine on the flyleaf."[53]

After this beginning, he digressed to tell a story which provided him with the profane expletive he wanted, to express his disgust: "Holy jumping *Jesus Christ!*" He continued:

"Maybe you don't like me to talk this way. I can see that I am going to make enemies if I keep on. Still that won't be anything new or strange. I had nothing but enemies three years ago this Christmas.

"Why go into details? Granted that there are a few good poems in the book—I read yours and liked it because it *says* something, first felt and then unfolded in thought as the poem wrote itself. That's what makes a poem. A poem is never a put-up job so to speak. It begins as a lump in the throat, a sense of wrong, a homesickness, a lovesickness. It is never a thought to begin with. It is at its best when it is a tantalizing vagueness. It finds its thought and succeeds, or doesn't find it and comes to nothing. It finds its thought or makes its thought. I suppose it finds it lying around with others not so much to its purpose in a more or less full find. That's why it oftener comes to nothing in youth before experience has filled the mind with thoughts. It may be a big big emotion then and yet finds nothing it can embody in. It finds the thought and the thought finds the words. Let's say again: A poem particularly must not begin thought first. . . .

"You mustn't mind me. Some day you would think I knew it all, to see me on paper. In reality I am only a poor man on ration. Its a hard winter and I'm hard up and sometimes I harden my heart against nearly everything."[54]

Untermeyer didn't mind. It frequently happened that when Frost was roiled by his uncontrolled hatreds he could depart from them and (either because of them or in spite of them) could give expression to some of his best insights concerning the constructive relation of art to life.

6

MY VOICE AND MANNER

I felt rather lost with my brief poem in all the smoke and noise. I would do better another time . . . and should know from experience how to make more of my voice and manner. . . . all new to me.[1]

IN THE MIDDLE of winter—on the morning of Friday, the eleventh of February 1916—a Boston newspaper reporter arrived in Franconia, unannounced. He had hired a driver to take him by sleigh from the railroad station in Littleton, and he stopped at the village store to ask where the poet Robert Frost lived. The woman in charge told him: Follow this road to the first bridge, keep to the right, take the second bridge, and about a mile up his house is on the right. The morning was a cold one, even for Franconia: twelve degrees below zero. The villagers seemed to be staying indoors, sensibly. When found, the house seemed too small to be the home of a man who was known to have a wife and four children. Nothing stirred, except smoke from the chimney. The reporter climbed out of the sleigh, knocked at the kitchen door, and waited. The door opened, scarcely more than a crack, and a woman peered out. She was tall, with a serious face, and with her hair drawn back in a knot. A college woman, a teacher, the reporter told himself. She answered his question by saying that Mr. Frost did live here, but he wasn't up yet. When told the purpose of the visit, she said she'd wake her husband and tell him. Then she shut the door, leaving the two men out in the cold. Walking back to the sleigh, they tried to keep warm by swinging their arms and slapping their shoulders. Hens and roosters in the barn behind the house were apparently disturbed by what the reporter described as this "commotion in the midst of this deathly morning mountain mid-winter silence." Their crowing and cackling was still going on when the door opened again and a tall man in a brown suit, fully dressed even to collar and necktie, said to both men, apologetically, "Come in, come in—and try to be warm."

The parlor contained a tall wood-burning cast-iron stove which reached almost to the ceiling and threw out enough heat to thaw the shivering intruders. The poet began talking before they were seated: "I don't usually wear a collar as early as this, but I wore these things last night to a meeting of a Parent-Teachers' Association, so I just put them on again this morning." He admitted that the villagers had paid no attention to him when he first settled in Franconia, but that enough summer visitors had called at the Frost home to suggest that he must be somebody. So the villagers had elected him president of the Parent-Teachers' Association. As the poet talked, the reporter glanced around the parlor, which seemed to serve as a study for the poet. There were books enough in evidence and a desk covered with a scattering of apparently unanswered letters. The poet said that he liked to play at farming, that he had lived on a farm in Derry, New Hampshire, for several years with his wife and four children before going to England. But how could a house with four children be so quiet? Oh they had gone to school shortly before the reporter arrived: "Lesley, my oldest girl, is sixteen; then comes my boy, Carol; then Irma; and then Marjorie . . . Carol does most of the work around the farm."

"Who chopped the woodpile that we saw buried in the snow?"

"Oh, I didn't. You know, I like farming, but I'm not much of a success at it. Some day I'll have a big farm where I can do what I please."

The smile suggested that the poet enjoyed the luxury of laziness; he admitted as much as he continued talking.

"I always go to farming when I can. I always make a failure of it, and then I have to go to teaching. I'm a good teacher, but it doesn't allow me time to write. I must either teach or write: can't do both together. But I have to live. . . . I've had a lazy, scrape-along life, and enjoyed it. I used to hate to write themes in school. I hate academic ways. I fight everything academic. The time we waste in trying to learn academically —the talent we starve with academic teaching!"

Where did he do his writing? The poet pointed to a home-made contraption, standing in a corner of the parlor. Two short boards, held together by two wedge-shaped cleats which could be rested on the arms of a nearby Morris chair. For writing, the poet said, this gadget was better than a lapboard, especially if one liked to slouch in a comfortable position. And when did he write?

"Oh, I haven't any set times. I write when I feel like it. Sometimes I write nothing for months. Then I'll work a blue streak, and rave around all day till it's off my mind. I can't do as many writers do, write to keep my hand in. . . . I hear everything I write. All poetry is to me first a matter of sound. I hear my things spoken. I write verse that might be called 'free'—the free-versers have accepted me!—but I believe, after all, that there must be a cadence, a rhythm, to all that is to be poetry at all. I don't mean jingle. I hate jingle. I want drama, too. Some day I may write a play. But I avoid the sublime, the ecstatic, the flights that three hundred—or is it three thousand?—minor poets of America slop into the magazines month after month. Meaningless twaddle, with a few worn-out tones. You know what I mean by tones? I'll explain. . . . Take, for instance, the expression 'oh.' The American poets use it in practically one tone, that of grandeur: 'Oh, Soul!' 'Oh Hills!'—'Oh Anything!' That's the way they go. But think of what 'oh' is really capable: the 'oh' of scorn, the 'oh' of amusement, the 'oh' of surprise, the 'oh' of doubt—and there are many more. But these are disdained by the academic poets. America must get away from the schools."

The reporter asked what the poet was writing now.

"Well, my publishers say I'm getting out a new book next fall, but—I don't know."

"Will your new poems be also about the country?"

"I shall always write about the country. I suppose I show a sad side to it too often. It only seems sad to those who love the city. I used to think the mill people, scooting home in the dusk, were sad, till I worked in the mill and heard them singing and laughing and throwing bobbins up at me as I stood on the ladder fixing the lights. . . . To get back. If American poets will only try to use all the tones of life and will drop the eternal sublime and see that all life is a fit subject for poetic treatment, they will do better. We must have new subject matter, new treatment of it, and we must employ the neglected tones and forget the overworked ones."

After much more conversation, the reporter finally said he

had to be getting back to the station. The poet had one thing more to add, at the door.

"I'll come to see you when I'm in Boston. . . . I want to spread my gospel of getting away from those deadly professors!"

Three days later, when the interview appeared in the Boston *Post* under the caption, "Finds Famous American Poet in White Mountain Village,"[2] the reporter placed his story in a context which did not please the Franconia villagers. He began by describing Franconia as a place "forgotten by the whole world." He went on: "Buried in the snow, with more snow and more snow, nobody comes here. Once a day an old man in a pung drives over with a few bundles, and leaves them, and drives off again in his old pung." He mentioned "the old woman in the deserted general store." That was enough. The "old woman" was relatively young. She was also articulate, and she wrote a sarcastic retort which was published:

"To the Editor of the *Post:*

SIR—Will you kindly inform your staff correspondent Mr. Carl Wilmore that . . . [if] he for a moment thinks . . . [he] can come to our beautiful little village of Franconia and then give us and our abode such a slam as came out in *The Boston Post* on Monday last, without causing some little stir, he is very much mistaken.

" 'Forgotten by the whole world.' What a statement! Had there been 'anybody home' your reporter would have known better than to have undertaken a five- or six-mile ride in northern New Hampshire on February eleventh with nothing on but a summer overcoat. No wonder his appearance caused Mr. Frost's hens and roosters to cackle and crow. . . .

"Again, had there been 'anybody home' . . . [your reporter] would have known by the way their sleigh-runners grated . . . that Franconia could not boast of snow enough for even decent sleighing. Here we have been praying for snow for the past four weeks so we could enjoy a good sleigh ride, to say nothing of business lying idle for the want of it, and your reporter reports to the world that we are literally buried in snow and then more snow. . . .

"Does he expect to find a crowd in a country store at nine o'clock in the morning? If he had only sent his card ahead, what a scramble there would have been to have gotten to that

deserted place so the poor snow-bound country folks could
have seen a real smarty chap from the city.

". . . if that reporter ever happens this way again he had
better provide himself with an armour plate or he may never
live to send in another report, and he will realize more fully,
to quote his own words, what this 'deathly mountain mid-winter
silence' means.

'The Old Woman in the Deserted Store' "[3]

Other letters of protest were sent from Franconia to the *Post*,
apparently, and the reporter became sufficiently embarrassed
to write a note of apology to Frost: "My little yarn has stirred
up such a lot of village ire (I don't say this contemptuously)
that I have begun to worry lest you too have felt resentment,
not so much because of my pictorial isolation of Franconia,
as because of my describing you as (I hesitate)—lazy."[4] Part
of the resentment which Frost did indeed feel may have been
directed against his own carelessness in making remarks about
the villagers—remarks which could have seemed harmless
until he saw them in print. This was not the first time he had
been embarrassed by printed quotations of his own words.
In England, shortly before the appearance of *A Boy's Will*, he
had given Ezra Pound, during their first meeting, a romantic
and partly fictitious account of the years of poverty on the
Derry farm, and then had been reproached by Mrs. Frost
when Pound summarized the account quite accurately in his
review of *A Boy's Will*.[5] Mrs. Frost may have scolded him anew
for these latest indiscretions, hinted at in Frost's next letter
to Untermeyer: "We are all well of some things but we are
sick of some others. Something that appeared in The Post a
week or so ago nearly ruined us."[6] The reporter, learning that
Frost feared criticism from the townspeople, because of the
newspaper article, urged that the easiest way out was to blame
the reporter: "Say I misquoted, and all that: I've heard it for
ten years, and won't mind a bit." He added, ". . . perhaps I *did*
put it into your mouth that you were lazy. But nobody takes
such things seriously. Anyway, down deep in your heart you
know it's true."[7]

Such a challenge came close to another problem which
continued to worry Frost during these early days of success:
how to prepare a face for the faces that he met. The problem
called for some acting, some pretending, and some masking

of what seemed to him to be his essential weaknesses. During the years on the Derry farm, when he was trying to discover who he was and what he might become, he had explored such a gamut of hopes and fears that he had confronted others with a variety of faces. At times his best protection had been to treat the whole world with scorn. At other times, when he needed help, he had not hesitated to wear a mask of ingratiating obsequiousness, although he hated that posture. On the farm, if neighbors appeared in the yard so that he could see them before they saw him, there had been times when he hadn't even bothered to prepare a face: he had often stayed behind a closed door or he had hit for the woods. Irritating thoughts of confrontations frequently drove him into furtive acts of self-defense. When he began teaching at Pinkerton Academy he had hoped that nobody could guess the pain and anguish required by the act of walking into the classroom to face those boys and girls who knew him only as a local hen-man, now teaching because he had failed at farming. His dour Scottish manner during those early days at Pinkerton had completely masked his pleasure in being playful, witty, amusing, entertaining. As soon as he had won the confidence and admiration of the students, however, he had come out from behind that mask. By the time he had moved from Derry to Plymouth he had developed so much confidence that he had actually swaggered before the Normal School girls.

In England, all the old cringing and furtiveness had overwhelmed him anew. He had been almost overcome by his inner fears and outer tremblings when he had carried the manuscript of *A Boy's Will* into Mrs. Nutt's London office. Of course the success of that visit had given him courage enough to seek out literary friendships by invading Harold Monro's Poetry Bookshop, and by knocking on the door of the stranger named Ezra Pound. His growing confidence had been strengthened by the success of *North of Boston*, and even before he had returned to America from England he had been provided with a public image by the British reviewers: He was a Yankee farmer who had made admirable poetry out of his farming experiences, and all he needed to do after that, to play the self-assigned part, was to "become Yankier and Yankier." After he landed in New York he had performed so well in his confrontations with strangers that his apparently pleasant ease of manner had given him new assurance. Sylvester Baxter had even said in print that Frost had "a most agreeable personality." Baxter had quoted someone else as claiming that Frost was "one of the most loveable men in the world."[8] Frost knew that wasn't true, but he didn't mind taking credit for the success of his performance.

If he had resisted invitations to give talks and readings in public he might easily have protected the easygoing and agreeable image. He would never forget how those first invitations —from Tufts College and the Boston Authors' Club—had made him turn over inside. He had been almost ill at the very thought of standing before a large audience either to read his own poems or to explain his own theories. Having determined to suffer whatever the cost to his nerves, so that he might improve his own poetic stature through making such public appearances, he had done his best to assert courage, boldness, daring. Yet when he had stood up to speak before the audience at the Authors' Club his hands had trembled so much that he had feared he would drop the book he held. Before he had uttered a single word he could feel his lips trembling, and his voice had actually quavered, noticeably. He had seen that some of his listeners were suffering with him. One of them, Katharine Lee Bates, in making plans for him to give a later Boston reading, had asked their mutual friend Nathan H. Dole to introduce Frost and then to sit on the platform just to give him support. Trying to explain, Miss Bates had written to Dole:

"The fact is, I was a good deal concerned when I heard Mr. Frost read his poems, for the reading was evidently so difficult for him that I wondered how he would be able to keep it up for a continuous hour. . . . I see that he talks more easily than he reads. I only wonder that so sensitive a poet can bring himself to face an audience at all."[9]

Frost could have told her all the reasons why he was determined to "face an audience." Nevertheless, during this trial period he was the one who found most fault with the ways in which he performed. Shortly before the *Post* reporter made the Franconia visit, he had put himself through a variety of paces in a tour which had forced him to behave like a grasshopper jumping in contrary directions: from Franconia to the Boston area for several appearances, then up to Hanover, New Hampshire, then all the way down to New York City, then back to Boston, and to Exeter, New Hampshire. The geographical changes had not bothered him so much as the necessary changes in manner.

At the start of these gyrations, the afternoon performance for Miss Bates, before a group of elderly Bostonians in the Hotel Vendome, went well enough to satisfy him. His next appearance, before the girls of Abbot Academy in Andover, Massachusetts, was much more difficult.[10] Then there was a sort of homecoming ritual in Lawrence, where so many of the faces in his audience were so familiar to him that he was able to relax more than usual.[11] At Dartmouth, he had the advantage of being introduced as one who had suffered through part of a semester there, back in 1892, and this helped to establish a rapport with the students.[12] The townspeople in Exeter made him feel relatively comfortable.[13] A few nights later, when he attended a huge banquet at the Copley-Plaza Hotel in Boston to read one poem at the end of the annual meeting of the Dartmouth Alumni Association, he felt miserably out of place. The cigar smoke became so thick before he stood to read his poem that he felt suffocated.[14] The worst misery in this extended schedule of performances occurred in New York City, where he made the mistake of trying to give the hostile Poetry Society of America a serious defense of his poetic theory. As the third of four speakers, there, he was followed by Untermeyer, who read with a straight face some uproariously successful parodies of peculiarities in the works of Robinson, Masters, Frost, Amy Lowell, and Vachel Lindsay. Frost tried to conceal his annoyance. But there was no pleasure in sitting there, after the failure of his own performance, and listening to the mossbacks laughing over a parody of the poetry he had just been trying to defend.[15] Home he went to Franconia, sick in spirit, heart, head, stomach, and his illness was serious enough to keep him in bed for a week. Brooding over the pleasure his enemies in the Poetry Society would derive from the news of his collapse, if they should hear it, he tried to cheer himself up by dictating to his daughter Lesley a declaration calculated to amuse the loyal Untermeyer:

"Just to protest that though in bed with the temperature of a setting hen I ain't a'goin' to die to please

Ella Wheeler Wilcox
Richard Underwood Johnson
Richard LeGallienne

[73]

> Abbie Farwell Browne
> Benjamin R. C. Low
> Brian Hooker
> Joyce Kilmer
> Cale Young Rice
> Florence Earle Coates
> Richard Burton
> Arthur Guiterman
> Olive Tilford Dargan
>   or any other
> Old-believer,
>   Whatsoever."[16]

He had to say something about the success of Untermeyer's parodies at the dinner, and in a later letter he added,

"I'm glad you found it in you to give Robinson his due because he gave you yours, you devil, the night of the Poetry Meal. The way he snickered over you was the next best thing to you there, confirming me in what I had about made up my mind was the best quality in his books. You are only more witty than he.

"Sometimes I think you are a blinding flash—as in that preface to '—and Other Poets.' And don't think that because I don't think you as successful with me as with Masefield, Yeats, Lindsay, Masters, Pound, and some others I don't like the whole book as well as any part of it. There ain't been no such book for brilliance."[17]

Such praise, written under difficult circumstances, was proof enough of skill in masking his inner feelings. At the same time, he was convinced that he had not yet learned to cope with his new task of performing adequately under so many different public circumstances. He was working on precisely this problem when he wrote to Bartlett, as soon as the setting-hen temperature subsided:

"The Exeter evening was better than the Dartmouth dinner. I never can tell where I am going to like my job. Lawrence was rather a success: most of the schools and colleges have been. The Dartmouth Dinner was for the politicians. I felt rather lost with my brief poem in all the smoke and noise. I would do better another time; for I would bargain for an early place on the program and should know from experience how to make more of my voice and manner. I wasnt particularly good at the New York Dinner either. There I struck too serious a note. Dinners are all new to me."[18]

He ran into more that was new when the next round of readings took him to Mt. Holyoke College in the winter of 1916. In that performance he followed his usual custom of reading some of his poems before he talked on his theories of poetry, and both parts of the program were well received. But his hostess, Miss Jeannette Marks, a professor of English at Mt. Holyoke, caught him off guard when she asked him to serve as a judge in a poetry contest which she was conducting for undergraduate students in the New England area. Dreading the amount of work he might be letting himself in for, he saw no way of backing out. He stayed overnight at Mt. Holyoke, and the next morning Miss Marks again took advantage of his generosity by persuading him to talk informally about some of his favorite nineteenth-century poets, before one of her classes.[19] Although the assignment was not difficult, it increased the drain on his nervous energies.

An entirely different exercise awaited him when he went from Mount Holyoke to Boston for his next engagement. His newly made friend and admirer George H. Browne had made him promise, months ahead of time, that he would talk before the New England Association of Teachers of English, in the Boston Public Library, on the eighteenth of March 1916. His announced subject was "Having a Literary Moment," and he had decided that he would attack the customary way of teaching literary composition in secondary schools: the approach of the rhetoricians who harped on figures of speech, grammar, syntax, and even spelling. Speaking from his own experience as a teacher at Pinkerton Academy, from 1906 to 1911, he told of how he had encouraged his pupils to write from their own experience, and of how he had picked out words or phrases or sentences or paragraphs which he could praise simply by saying, "There you did it." Such encouragement, he said, provided the best stimulus to greater effort. Of course the teacher who had never had literary moments of his own would have difficulty in detecting one in the uneven writing of a pupil. Paraphrasing what Emerson had said in "Monadnoc" about rude poets of the tavern hearth, Frost described what he meant by figures of speech. Students could be shown how to use their ears in gathering materials for their literary compositions. They could be shown various ways in which contexts would serve to fasten tones of voice to a page so that readers could hear them. At the conclusion of his talk to the Teachers of English, he was questioned in ways which made him know he had offended and puzzled some of his listeners. He was glad for the chance to rumple the prejudices of the rhetoricians, but again he did regret the amount of energy he had spent on what seemed to him a nearly hopeless cause.[20] As soon as he got back to Franconia he began his next letter to Untermeyer, "I wish I could remember where-all I've been in the past week or so and who-all I've baptized into my heresies. Here I am home again in disgrace with those who see through me and ready with pen and the same kind of note paper to resume inkling."[21] In disgrace he was, with his wife, who saw through him to the extent of knowing he was too exhausted to do anything more with pen and paper than waste his time writing letters.

In less than two weeks after this return, he was packing his bag in readiness for another strenuous peddling of heresies, this time in Philadelphia. The invitation which took him there had been made especially attractive by the circumstances which had built up to it. One of the earliest letters of praise for *North of Boston* received shortly after the return from England had come from Cornelius Weygandt, a professor of English literature at the University of Pennsylvania. Weygandt and his family spent their summer vacations in the White Mountain village of Wonalancet, not many miles to the north of the Ossipee Mountain neighborhood where Frost had courted Elinor White during the summer of 1895.[22] From Wonalancet, in August of 1915, Weygandt had brought his family by car to spend an afternoon visiting with the Frosts in Franconia, and the friendliness quickly established between the two families had been exceptionally warm. After this visit, Weygandt had offered Frost the chance to earn money by extending his bardings farther south than he had previously done. The acceptance of this invitation took him to Philadelphia on the first of April 1916. He stayed with the Weygandt family in Germantown, gave a reading of his poems to a group of friends in Weygandt's home, as a sort of warm-up, and then performed before an audience of five hundred students in the College Hall Chapel at the University of Pennsylvania the next day. A luncheon was given in his honor at the Philadelphia Art

Club, where he was also interviewed by a reporter from the Philadelphia *Public Ledger.*

During this interview he was given another chance to practice discretion while conveying his literary and educational prejudices. He surprised the reporter by saying that New England puritanism could provide some hints useful to literary theory if only one could get back to the root-meanings: purification from unscriptural and corrupt forms of ceremonies, renewal of original meanings in words, disciplined simplification of human responses. For the benefit of the reporter, he offered an example of what needed to be purified in the gushing and undisciplined verse of so many modern lady-poets, and added,

"Never larrup an emotion. Set yourself against the moon. Resist the moon. If the moon's going to do anything to you, it's up to the moon. . . . Love, the moon, and murder have poetry in them by common consent. But it's in other places. It's in the axe-handle of a French Canadian woodchopper. . . . You know the Canadian woodchoppers . . . [make their own] axe-handles, following the curve of the grain, and they're strong and beautiful. Art should follow lines in nature, like the grain of an axe-handle. False art puts curves on things that haven't any curves. . . . [puritanism] hasn't had its day, and it might be fun to set it up as an artistic doctrine."

The *Ledger* reporter gave the visiting poet a chance to offer another example of how the uses of imagination should be purified. Frost quoted from a White Mountain guidebook a passage which could be set in free verse—as the reporter set it:

"One of the most deplorable facts about the White Mountains
Is the lack of legends.
Imagination, therefore, must be requisitioned
To supply the story
That gave a name to this beautiful spot."

Frost continued: "The point I'm making lies in that line, 'Imagination . . . must be requisitioned.' The curse of our poetry is that we lay it on things. Pocketsful of poetic adjectives like pocketsful of peanuts carried into a park for the gray squirrels! You can take it as gospel, that's not what we want.

"But people say to me: 'The facts themselves aren't enough.

You've got to do something to them, haven't you? They can't be poetical unless a poet handles them.'

"To that I have a very simple answer. It's this: Anything you do to the facts falsifies them, but anything the facts do to you—yes, even against your will; yes, resist them with all your strength—transforms them into poetry."

The reporter understood Frost well enough to conclude that the poet's observations threw light on essentials in his recent success: "He is a Puritan who has fought the soil for sustenance and has fought the world for recognition as a poet. He has won success because he has fought his own emotions, digging into them and behind them, the better to strike the universal note that makes poetry out of axe-handles."[23]

Frost had reason to feel content with the quality of his performances in Philadelphia, and he foresaw no difficulty in handling his next important commitment. A group of undergraduates at Amherst College had invited him to give a reading of his poems, on their campus, and they had offered a satisfactory honorarium. Their invitation had been supported by Stark Young, a member of the Department of English at Amherst, and Frost had accepted.[24] When he reached Amherst on his way home from Philadelphia he found that his immediate host and guide was the attractive and witty Stark Young, a thirty-five-year-old Missourian. During the previous ten years, Young had published two novels, several short stories, and some poems. He had recently been brought to Amherst from the University of Texas by the provocative and controversial new president of Amherst, Alexander Meiklejohn. Although Young proved to be a genuine admirer of Frost's poetry, and a gracious host, he embarrassed Frost by asking favors. In the quiet of Young's prettily decorated apartment, he asked for permission to read aloud some of his own poems. Frost listened politely, was not impressed, and had some difficulty in finding enough kind words. Then Young further embarrassed him by asking for help in securing a publisher for a book which would contain these poems. Still trying to be polite, Frost suggested that Young send his manuscript to Alfred Harcourt at the office of Henry Holt and Company; Frost would do what he could. Not long after he returned to Franconia from Amherst he received a letter from Harcourt: "Stark Young of Amherst writes that he has had two fine days with you and that you went over his verses and liked them, and wanted him to bring them to me. . . ."[25] Frost answered by telegram in two words: "THUMBS DOWN."[26]

The accumulation of all these distracting experiences annoyed Frost because he had half-promised Harcourt another volume of poetry, which might be published in the fall of 1916, even though it seemed impossible that he could have the manuscript ready by then. The Phi Beta Kappa Society at Harvard had invited him to be the poet for its annual public meeting in June of 1916, and he had already set aside for that occasion two almost-completed poems: "The Ax-helve" and "The Bonfire." Both of them needed further revision, and he seemed unable to find the right mood for making revisions.

His wife, understanding the ways in which his intermittent moods of grouchiness and sulking were heightened by the strain of his barding ventures, continued to say that his first loyalty should be to his writing. Each time he returned from another tour, boastful of the successes he had achieved, her silences were sufficient reminders of her belief that the gains from these trips did not offset the losses. She understood all his needs for public attention and recognition. She also knew how important it was to him to flaunt his heresies before assemblies of old-fashioned poets and academicians, but she kept urging him to put the poetry first. After he came back from Amherst he was apparently overcome by a new wave of depression and discouragement. Repeatedly he told himself and others that the best work of any poet is completed before he reaches thirty. Now it seemed that if he had outlived his poetic powers he might as well be dead. At best, he could merely cull from yellowed manuscripts, written on the Derry farm years ago, offerings which might be stopgaps. In a particularly low mood, he poured these fears into a letter calculated to bring consolation and reassurance from Untermeyer:

"When I have borne in memory what has tamed Great Poets, hey? Am I to be blamed etc? No you ain't. Or as Browning (masc.) has it

> *That was I that died last night*
> *When there shone no moon at all*
> *Nor to pierce the strained and tight*
> *Tent of heaven one planet small.*
> *Might was dead and so was Right.*[27]

"Not to be any more obvious than I have to be to set at rest your brotherly fears for my future which I have no doubt you assume to be somehow or other wrapped up in me, I am going to tell you something I never but once let out of the bag before and that was just after I reached London and before I had begun to value myself for what I was worth. (Toop.) It is a very damaging secret and you may not thank me for taking you into it when I tell you that I have often wished I could be sure that the other sharer of it had perished in the war. It is this: The poet in me died nearly ten years ago. Fortunately he had run through several phases, four to be exact, all well-defined, before he went. The calf I was in the nineties I merely take to market. I am become my own salesman. Two of my phases you have been so—what shall I say—[kind?] as to like. Take care that you don't get your mouth set to declare the other two (as I release them) a falling off of power, for that is what they can't be whatever else they may be, since they were almost inextricably mixed with the first two in the writing and only my sagacity has separated or sorted them in the after-thought for putting on the market. Did you ever hear of quite such a case of Scotch-Yankee calculation?"

Apparently purging himself of discouragement and self-disgust through the mere process of writing this much, he added to the letter a poem on "Old Age" and led up to it with these introductory remarks: "I must give you a sample from the fourth book, 'Pitchblende.' As a matter of fact and to be perfectly honest with you there is a fifth unnamed as yet, the only one unnamed (the third has been long known as 'Mountain Interval')[28] and I think the most surprising of the lot (circa 1903). But none of that now."[29]

The dark mood had passed before Untermeyer could send reassurances, and although it was followed intermittently by other moods just as dark, he was soon lifted by a sequence of events which honored and cheered him. One of these events was an invitation from Untermeyer to serve as a contributing editor on the staff of a projected monthly periodical to be called *The Seven Arts*. Another was his extremely triumphant visit to Harvard, as Phi Beta Kappa poet, at commencement time in June of 1916.

Even before the Harvard visit occurred, preparations for it included pleasant surprises. A retired professor of philosophy there, George Herbert Palmer, wrote to say that when the poet appeared in Cambridge he should bring Mrs. Frost with him and that they both would be welcomed as guests in the Palmer home over the commencement weekend. A year earlier, Palmer had written to congratulate Frost on the success of *North of Boston*, and in replying Frost was able to boast that he had once attended an "open house" poetry session arranged by Palmer for Harvard undergraduates, back in the 1890s. He could have added that he greatly admired, and had frequently read aloud to his children from Palmer's felicitous translation of the *Odyssey*. The immediate problem of accepting Palmer's invitation was complicated, however, by the question of whether the Frost children were old enough to keep house for themselves while the Frosts were away.

Franconia neighbors solved the problem. Not too far beyond the Frost farm, and on the same side of Iron Mine Hill, was a farm (more nearly an estate) occupied in summer by a wealthy retired minister—the Reverend J. Warner Fobes of Peace Dale, Rhode Island. Mr. and Mrs. Fobes had been among the first to call on the Frosts after the move to Franconia, and the friendship begun between the two families was exceptionally cordial. Mrs. Fobes, learning of the Palmer invitation, insisted that the four Frost children could easily be cared for in the spacious Fobes summer home, and Mrs. Frost was thus able to accompany her husband to Cambridge.

The attentions given the Frosts by the Palmers in Cambridge were flattering, and the poetry readings went well. At the public meeting of the Phi Beta Kappa Society, Frost said his war poem entitled "The Bonfire," and at the Phi Beta Kappa dinner that evening he said his education poem, "The Ax-helve." The responses to both poems were thoroughly satisfying to him, and the entire weekend was a memorable one for the Frosts.

The poet's confidence was further strengthened by another invitation which was accepted that summer. His friend and former boss, Ernest Silver, asked him to give five lectures in one week at the Plymouth Normal School, and to bring the entire Frost family with him, to stay as Silver's guests in the home where they had lived while Frost was teaching there. The week at Plymouth went happily, and the six Frosts were next escorted to the nearby White Mountain town of Wonalancet to stay as guests of the Weygandts for a few days.[30] By the time this flurry of events ended, Frost was in the proper mood for settling down in Franconia to complete the manuscript of *Mountain Interval.*[31]

The mood was broken when a visitor came unexpectedly to Franconia. He was Stark Young, and he brought from President Meiklejohn at Amherst the request that the poet serve as a member of the Amherst faculty for at least one semester, with the rank of full professor, for a salary of $2,000, starting in January of 1917. The sudden move was caused by the resignation of Professor George Bosworth Churchill, who had been elected to office in the Massachusetts State Legislature.

Frost was at once attracted and repelled by the prospect. "I'm a good teacher," he had told the *Post* reporter, "but it doesn't allow me time to write. I must either teach or write— can't do both together. But I have to live." Recently he had almost convinced himself that he had risen above the need to teach, now that he could supplement his income from royalties by going about the country as a bard. If he should crawl back into teaching now, under the excuse that he needed more money to support his family, could he tolerate the academic? In spite of his occasional doubts concerning the wellsprings of his creative abilities, he wanted to keep trying to write more poems. If he assumed the voice and manner of a professor, might it cause him to lose the voice and manner of the poet, completely?

Again Frost needed a wailing wall, and this time he turned to Alfred Harcourt. Working toward his new problem, he complained first about an article in a poetry magazine newly established in Boston by Braithwaite and O'Brien. The article implied that Frost's reputation as a poet had been achieved primarily through the skillful advertising of his publisher:

"Here's that damned Hell-I-Can turned up again with the base insinuation that people like what I write because of the reputation you have made for me. I don't like the business but I don't want to antagonize anyone whose friendship won't hurt us.[32] Am I too hard on O'Brien? Do you approve of that pair (him and Braithwaite)? I get to railing and I can rail myself into damning my best friends to Hell. Sometimes I think I need holding in.

"A case in point. You remember how I flew off the handle because I suspected a certain poet got me to read my poetry at his college in order to get me to find him a publisher for his poetry. Well I didn't find him a publisher did I? And here he comes with an invitation to me to give two half courses at his college from January on for $2,000. I'm humiliated. And it ain't the first time in forty years. I seem to go plum crazy.

"This about the college must be a secret. I haven't decided yet."[33]

In spite of all he had said about the academicians, Frost continued to idealize one possibility. From England he had written to Sidney Cox, "I should awfully like a quiet job in a small college where I should be allowed to teach something a little new on the technique of writing and where I should have some honor for what I suppose myself to have done in poetry. Well, but I mustnt dream."[34] He hadn't entirely relinquished that dream, and his recent visit to Amherst had made him realize that it was an exceptional college, newly dedicated to certain goals which Frost admired. "The Amherst Idea," proposed by alumni from the Class of 1885, and accepted by the trustees in 1911, had been a plan to abolish the degree of Bachelor of Science there and to concentrate on a liberal arts program which would shift the emphasis from the sciences to the humanities. At a time when the trend of education was so markedly toward the scientific and the vocational, Amherst had advanced the notion that young men were better trained for later specialization if they spent four years building a broad base through disciplines provided by studying the classics, languages, history, philosophy, with programs of outside activities which would include dramatics, music, literary publications, intercollegiate debates and oratical contests.[35] Such a retrenchment seemed old-fashioned and reactionary to some educators, but President Meiklejohn had grafted to this program some ideas of his own which were highly flexible and experimental. Only two years older than Frost, Meiklejohn had taught courses in logic and philosophy at his Alma Mater, Brown University, before and after he had begun serving as dean there. When he accepted the presidency of Amherst in 1912, he had given strong support and implementation to "The Amherst Idea" and had very quickly become popular with the students, the faculty, and the trustees. He had even been bold enough to oppose the indiscriminate application of the elective system made popular by Eliot at Harvard. Meiklejohn insisted that any undergraduate, permitted to choose whatever courses he liked, was too often motivated immaturely by "the love of vocation, the line of 'snaps,' the line of a certain profession, or the days that will let the student get out of town."[36]

It was easy for Frost to assume that Meiklejohn was a boldly independent rebel whose procedures in handling a small college like Amherst could make room comfortably for Frost's own brand of individuality. Now that the poet had gained some literary recognition he was able to look back over his first forty years of life and interpret them as containing proofs that he had successfully declared his independence from all the conventional responses to educational, economic, social, and political programs. The years of isolation on the Derry farm had heightened his awareness of his being separate. He had even run away from America long enough to complete his first two volumes of poetry. Instead of aligning himself with any literary schools or movements when he returned to America, he had again deliberately isolated himself on a small farm in the White Mountains. The friends who meant the most to him were those who showed their own individuality. He had even tried to convince Untermeyer that the two of them could join forces as rebels if only Untermeyer would break away from that socialistic-communistic radicalism represented by the so-called liberals who wrote for the *Masses*. Frost had tried to spell out his own sense of the difference between radicalism and rebelliousness:

"I thought you and we was going to be rebels together. And being rebels doesn't mean being radical; it means being reckless like Eva Tanguay.[37] It means busting something just when everybody begins to think it so safe it's safe. (See Rheims Cathedral—next time you're in France.)[38]

"These folks that get on by logical steps like a fly that's climbed out of the molasses a little way up the side of the cup—them I have no use for. I'm all for abruption. There is no gift like that of suddenly turning up somewhere else. I like a young fellow as says 'My father's generation thought that, did they? Well that was the Hell of a way to think, wasn't it? Let's think something else for a change.' A disconnective young fellow with a plenty of extrication in his make-up. You bet your sweet life. What would the editors of the Masses say to such onprincipled[39]—what shall I call it.

"The only sorrow is that I ain't as reckless as I used to be. That is to say not in as many departments."[40]

Even in assuming that his own brand of rebelliousness would

mix well enough with Meiklejohn's, Frost hesitated for fear that the President's leanings toward logic and philosophy might indicate a lack of appreciation for literary art. The poet's views were more closely akin to those of George Edward Woodberry, another poet-teacher, who had taught for one year at Amherst after retiring from Columbia. Woodberry had been attacking Columbia rather than any small college such as Amherst when he had criticized the failure of American universities to encourage the writing of American literature: "The universities have not, on the whole, been its sources or fosterers, and they are now filled with research, useful for learning but impotent for literature."[41] Frost went further than Woodberry and insisted that the university approach was "the worst system of teaching that ever endangered a nation's literature."[42] In mentioning Woodberry's complaint he had offered his own belief concerning where the emphasis ought to be placed, in the study of literature: "No one is taught to value himself for nice perception and cultivated taste. Knowledge knowledge. Why literature is the next thing to religion in which as you know or believe an ounce of faith is worth all the theology ever written. Sight and insight, give us those."[43] But in a college as small as Amherst there should be a chance to show the students the way in which literature should be approached, provided the academicians would not be too much of a hindrance. "There are a lot of completely educated people in the world," he sarcastically observed, "and of course they will resent being asked to learn anything new."[44]

The Amherst offer was made attractive by other factors which Frost was just then considering. Although mountain air helped him and other hay-fever victims, during the pollen season, he and his family had discovered that so much below-zero weather during the winter months was harsh on sensitive lungs. ("Fifteen below here this morning. Twenty-five below the morning I left for my last tour.")[45] He had been confined to his bed, repeatedly, with feverish colds which plagued him too often. His son Carol had developed a sore throat and cough which was so persistent that his Franconia doctor feared he might have tuberculosis. After the boy had been taken to Boston for medical examinations by a specialist, his father had written, "Carol is going to be an anxiety—that much is settled by our conference with the doctors. . . . The one certainty is that I shall have to be making money somehow to provide for the family in new quarters next winter."[46] Carol wanted to become a full-time farmer as soon as he finished high school, and his interests helped to persuade his father that there was no sense in trying to raise crops of fruit and vegetables at a mountain level where freezing temperatures occurred even in summer months. After the first gardening disappointments in Franconia he had confided to his farmer-friend Bartlett,

"I see a possibility of my getting south to farm sooner or later. I am not going to be satisfied with just grass-farming. But this place will have to serve for a year or two or until I am rich enough to let it lie idle all but two or three months in the year. I should always want to keep it as a summer resort. I wish it were so we could have it together. We could be neighbors in some good fruit region down your way and up here we could all live together for the hay fever season. Wouldn't that be about right."[47]

If the Amherst offer were accepted Frost and his family would be in a good position to search for a more practical farm in the region of the Connecticut River Valley. After more soul-searching, he decided that he would make no choice until he had gone to Amherst once more, to lay all his doubts and fears before President Meiklejohn. The President's considerateness and warmth of personality made the opportunities very attractive, and he accepted the offer. Soon after he returned to Franconia, following the second visit, he heard from the President:

"This morning at the chapel service I read 'The Road Not Taken' and then told the boys about your coming. They applauded vigorously and were evidently much delighted at the prospect. I can assure you of an eager and hearty welcome by the community. I hope you did not get too tired when you were with us and that the cold is altogether gone. I beg of you to let us know if there is anything that anyone here can do to help in the plans which Mrs. Frost and you are making for coming and getting settled. . . ."[48]

7

DEATH OF A SOLDIER-POET

You went to meet the shell's embrace of fire
On Vimy Ridge; and when you fell that day
The war seemed over more for you than me,
But now for me than you—the other way.[1]

SHORTLY before Robert Frost started for Amherst College
with his family, from Franconia, in January of 1917, he began
a successful effort to find an American publisher for the poems
of his Welsh friend Edward Thomas. Unable to proceed earlier
in this effort because Thomas felt he had not yet achieved
maturity as a poet, Frost had tried to overcome the reluctance
by repeating his claim: The genuine poetry in so many of the
prose essays published by Thomas during the past ten years
stood as convincing evidence that Thomas had curiously denied
himself the right to be the one thing he couldn't help but
be. Once, when Thomas expressed his fear that he was a fool
to hope he could ever establish himself in this field which was
new to him, Frost replied impatiently, "You are a poet or you
are nothing. . . . I told you and I keep telling you. But as long
as your courage holds out you may as well go right ahead making a fool of yourself. All brave men are fools."[2] The help
and friendship meant so much that Thomas repeatedly hoped
he might move with his family to New Hampshire and live next
door to Frost. Early in 1915 he said it again: "Of course I keep
thinking about the chance of coming over this year."[3] At the
same time he was frank in admitting that, much as he dreaded
the thought of physical combat, he felt he should fulfill his
responsibilities as a British subject by enlisting in one of the
armed services.

Frost was familiar with all of the unavoidable excruciations
through which this dour Welshman went each time he was
required to make a choice. Repeatedly, while these two men had

botanized in England together—Thomas leading the way through his favorite countryside in the hope of showing his American friend an extraordinary station of rare plants— these ventures had ended with self-reproachful sighs and regrets. Even the most successful of these walks failed to satisfy Thomas's fastidiousness. He blamed himself for having made the wrong choice of location, and would sigh wistfully over the lovely specimens he might have shown if only he had taken Frost to a different place. Frost, disciplined by his mother's puritanical and stoic insistence on quoting the biblical adage that the worthy plowman never looks back, was amused by these laments. Teasing gently, he accused Thomas of being such a romantic that he enjoyed crying over what might have been. After one of their best flower-gathering walks, he had said to Thomas, "No matter which road you take, you'll always sigh, and wish you'd taken another."[4] It seemed to Frost that such an amusing attitude should provide the makings of a poem which could represent, with dramatic and ironic subtlety, the very human and familiar posture of his romantic friend. Near the end of his stay in Gloucestershire, he had written at least one stanza:

> *I shall be telling this with a sigh*
> *Somewhere ages and ages hence:*
> *Two roads diverged in a wood, and I,*
> *I took the one less traveled by,*
> *And that has made all the difference.*[5]

Not until he reached New Hampshire and began to find in the many letters from Thomas further reflections of the same wistful brooding over alternatives, did Frost complete this poem which he first called "Two Roads." As soon as it was done to his satisfaction he sent a fair copy of it to Thomas, as a letter, with nothing else in the envelope. The hope was that Thomas would take the poem as a gentle joke and would protest, "Stop teasing me." Instead, Thomas praised the poem in ways which indicated that he viewed the speaker of this dramatic lyric as Frost, not as Thomas. Although he liked the poem and even said he found it "staggering," he stopped there. Frost in his next letter asked why Thomas called the poem "staggering." The answer, when it came, clearly revealed that Thomas had not yet suspected that his own viewpoint—or any viewpoint like his—had been parodied and quietly mocked.[6] It was embarrassing to Frost to explain this joke which had failed, but he did explain. Thomas replied, "You have got me again over the Path not taken & no mistake. . . . I doubt if you can get anyone to see the fun of the thing without showing them and advising them what kind of laugh they are to turn on."[7]

If the failure of insight rested with Thomas, part of his blindness was caused by his being in no mood for laughter of any kind at this particular time. In the same letter, dated 11 July 1915, he said quite simply, "I am going to enlist on Wednesday if the doctor will pass me." Thus ended the days, weeks, months of his agonizing over this particular choice— an agonizing which had been sufficiently apparent between the lines of a previous letter:

"I have been talking to my Mother about going to America. She does not really resist much, but pretends to assume I mean after the war. . . . There is a weak effeminate me too—if some branch of the army will take me in spite of my weak foot: I believe the Royal Garrison Artillery might. Frankly, I do not want to go, but hardly a day passes without my thinking I should. With no call the problem is endless. It would mean Bronwen going to some very cheap school & my letting Mervyn slide rather, unless I had the boldness to have all my savings used up in one year & leave the rest to chance. It all comes of not believing. I will leave nothing to chance knowingly. But, then, I suppose the believers calculate to the best of their ability. It means stepping out alone into company when I should expect to remain alone, with neither faith nor forgetfulness but just a reluctant admission of necessity. How much of it comes from unwillingness to confess I am unfit."[8]

As soon as Thomas announced that he was in uniform, Frost responded sympathetically:

"I am within a hair of being precisely as sorry and as glad as you are.

"You are doing it for the self-same reason I shall hope to do it for if my time ever comes and I am brave enough, namely, because there seems nothing else for a man to do.

"You have let me follow your thought in almost every twist and turn toward this conclusion. I know pretty well how far down you have gone and how far off sideways. And I think the better of you for it all. Only the very bravest could come to the sacrifice in this way. . . .

"I have never seen anything more exquisite than the pain you have made of it. You are a terror and I admire you. For what has a man locomotion if it isnt to take him into things he is between barely and not quite standing.

"I should have liked you anyway—no friend ever has to strive for my approval—but you may be sure I am not going to like you less for this.

"All belief is one. And this proves you are a believer.

"I can't think what you would ask my forgiveness for unless it were saying my poetry is better than it is. You are forgiven as I hope to be forgiven for the same fault. I have had to over sate myself in the fight to get up. Some day I hope I can afford to lean back and deprecate as excessive the somewhat general praise I may have won for what I may have done.

"Your last poem Aspens seems the loveliest of all. You must have a volume of poetry ready for when you come marching home. . . ."⁹

As Thomas moved from one training camp to another, he still found time to keep writing poetry, and he relished this creative experience as an exciting, fearful, breath-taking adventure: "I can hardly wait to light my pipe."¹⁰ By the time he was transferred to the Royal Artillery Barracks, where he was trained as a gunner-cadet, some of his poems had already appeared in print under the pseudonym, Edward Eastaway. In December of 1916, he volunteered to go out to France with the next draft, and before he went he had seen eight of his poems in print. He also arranged for the publication, in London, of a sixty-four-page book to be entitled *Poems,* by Edward Eastaway, and asked that it be dedicated to Robert Frost. He was at home with his wife and children, on leave, for Christmas of 1916, just prior to his departure for France, and his letters were in part the inspiration for Frost's imaginative war poem entitled "Not to Keep":

> They sent him back to her. The letter came
> Saying . . . And she could have him. And before
> She could be sure there was no hidden ill
> Under the formal writing, he was there,
> Living. They gave him back to her alive—
> How else? They are not known to send the dead.—
> And not disfigured visibly. His face?
> His hands? She had to look, to look and ask,

"What is it, dear?" And she had given all
And still she had all—they had—they the lucky!
Wasn't she glad now? Everything seemed won,
And all the rest for them permissible ease.
She had to ask, "What was it, dear?"
                                        "Enough,
Yet not enough. A bullet through and through,
High in the breast. Nothing but what good care
And medicine and rest, and you a week,
Can cure me of to go again." The same
Grim giving to do over for them both.
She dared no more than ask him with her eyes
How was it with him for a second trial.
And with his eyes he asked her not to ask.
They had given him back to her, but not to keep.[11]

Early in 1916, Frost began to receive letters from France, in which Thomas described casually and in a typically matter-of-fact way his experiences at the front, his work in an observation post near the big guns of his siege battery, the villages in view, either damaged or completely destroyed by artillery fire from both sides. One letter mentioned "the moan of the approaching & hovering shell & the black grisly flap that it seems to make as it bursts."

By the time Frost had gained permission from Thomas to seek American publishers for the poems of Edward Eastaway, it was necessary to handle the business through Mrs. Thomas, because of the difficulty in getting letters to and from France. Sending a group of these poems to Harriet Monroe, Frost wrote in January of 1917:

"Here I sit admiring these beautiful poems but not daring to urge them on anyone else for fear I shall be suspected of admiring them for love of the author. If Edward Eastaway gets killed before the war is over (he is with the artillery) there will be plenty found to like them and then where will my credit be for having liked them first. After all is it any worse for me to like them because I know their author (but I *don't* like them for that reason) than for others to like them because they know he is dead. . . ."[12]

Fortunately, Harriet Monroe did like them and promised to publish them in *Poetry* as soon as possible. At Frost's suggestion, Alfred Harcourt arranged with Thomas's London publisher to bring out an American edition of the book. The good news was sent to Helen Thomas by Frost in a letter which began, "I am writing this to you because I think it may be the quickest way to reach Edward with questions I must have an answer to as soon as possible. I have found a publisher for his poems in America. But there are several things to be cleared up before we can go ahead." One of the questions was whether, for the American edition, Thomas might be willing to use his own name and to give up the pseudonym. She answered, in March:

"What a bit of luck to get your letter at all. I thought all the mails had gone down in the Laconia, but evidently not. I'm *so* excited & happy about your splendid news, & I've already written to the dear man & told him. . . . I'm not at all sure that Edward Eastaway will consent to be Edward Thomas. . . . It's all very good news & you sound as pleased as you knew we would be.

"By now you will have heard from him. He's at Arras & expecting a hot time presently. I don't suppose I can tell you much about it may I. He's at present at headquarters as adjutant to a ruddy Colonel whose one subject is horse racing and tracking & such . . . tho he's longing to be back at his battery, he's afraid the Colonel has taken a fancy to him and will keep him. It will probably mean promotion, but Edward wants the real thing & won't be happy till he gets it. What is one to do with such a poet. In a pause in the shooting he turns his wonderful field glasses on to a hovering kestrel & sees him descend & pounce & bring up a mouse. Twice he saw that & says 'I suppose the mice are travelling now.' What a soldier. Oh he's just fine, full of satisfaction in his work, & his letters free from care & responsibility—but keen to have a share in the great stage when it begins where he is.

"At first after we'd said 'Goodbye' . . . I did not live really, but just somehow or other did my work. . . . I must tell you that [on the] last evening we were talking of people—of ourselves, of friends, & of his work & all he'd like done. And he said, 'Outside us & the children & my mother, Robert Frost comes next.' . . . I send you this photograph [of Edward Thomas]. Merfyn took it. . . .

"I'll leave this letter open so details can be added about the book. Edward will be 39 tomorrow, March 3rd & we are hoping our parcels of apples and cake and sweets & such like luxuries will get to him on the day. . . ."

Two weeks later, Helen Thomas continued the letter:

". . . Eastaway will not be Thomas & that's that he says. . . . Edward's letters are still full of interest & life & satisfaction in his work. He's back on his battery now in the thick of it as he wanted to be, firing 400 rounds a day from his gun, listening to the men talking, & getting on well with his fellow officers. He's had little time for depression and homesickness. He says 'I cannot think of ever being home again, & dare not think of never being there again' & in a letter to Merfyn he says 'I want to have six months of it, & then I want to be at home. I wish I *knew* I was coming back. . . .'"

There was a postscript, added by Helen Thomas:

"This letter was returned by the Censor ages after I posted it. I have had to take out the photographs. But lately I have just received the news of Edward's death. He was killed on Easter Monday by a shell. . . ."[13]

Jack Haines and Lascelles Abercrombie had already sent other details. The big British attack had opened to the east of Arras on a forty-five mile front which stretched to the north and south, at seven o'clock on the morning of the ninth of April 1917. Thomas had been among those who watched from his artillery post the first waves of British troops crossing no man's land. A few minutes later, he was killed by the concussion from an exploding shell.

Until Frost received word of the death of Edward Thomas, he had managed to keep himself from being too deeply involved with even his own secret hopes and fears. No other war loss could have affected him more profoundly. The bond between these two men had been forged not so much by their common tastes in literature as by far deeper similarities in temperament. At the time of their first meeting, Thomas had been in a psychological depression from which he might not have recovered if Frost had not been there to help him. Now, just after the soldier had found himself as a poet and had begun what amounted to a new and more valid way of life, all the mutual hopes of these two men had been obliterated by that shell. The immediate task was to say something to the bereaved widow:

"People have been praised for self-possession in danger. I

have heard Edward doubt if he was as brave as the bravest. But who was ever so completely himself right up to the verge of destruction, so sure of his thought, so sure of his word? He was the bravest and best and dearest man you and I have ever known. I knew from the moment when I first met him at his unhappiest that he would some day clear his mind and save his life. I have had four wonderful years with him. I know he has done this all for you: he is all yours. But you must let me cry my cry for him as if he were *almost* all mine too.

"Of the three ways out of here, by death where there is no choice, by death where there is a noble choice, and by death where there is a choice not so noble, he found the greatest way. There is no regret—nothing that I will call regret. Only I can't help wishing he could have saved his life without so wholly losing it and come back from France not too much hurt to enjoy our pride in him. I want to see him to tell him something. I want to tell him, what I think he liked to hear from me, that he was a poet. I want to tell him that I love those he loved and hate those he hated. (But the hating will wait: there will be a time for hate.) I had meant to talk endlessly with him still, either here in our mountains as we had said or, as I found my longing was more and more, there at Leddington where we first talked of war.

"It was beautiful as he did it. And I don't suppose there is anything for us to do to show our admiration but to love him forever."[14]

There was one thing left to do for Edward Thomas, and Frost threw himself genuinely into the task of making other people realize that the dead man deserved the recognition he had not yet been given as a poet. Two days after writing to Helen Thomas, he wrote to Garnett, who had learned from Thomas about *North of Boston*:

". . . Edward Thomas was the only brother I ever had. I fail to see how we can have been so much to each other, he an Englishman and I an American and our first meeting put off till we were both in middle life. I hadn't a plan for the future that didn't include him.

"You must like his poetry as well as I do and do everything you can for it. His last word to me, his 'pen ultimate word,' as he called it, was that what he cared most for was the name of poet. His poetry is so very brave—so unconsciously brave. He didn't think of it for a moment as war poetry, though that is what it is. It ought to be called Roads to France. 'Now all roads lead to France, and heavy is the tread of the living, but the dead, returning, lightly dance,' he says. He was so imperturbably the poet through everything to the end. If there is any merit in self possession, I can say I never saw anyone less put off himself by unaccustomed danger, less put off his game. His concern to the last was what it had always been, to touch earthly things and come as near them in words as words would come.

"Do what you can for him and never mind me for the present. . . ."[15]

With the same intensity of anguish, Frost sought assistance from his friends in America. As soon as the American edition of Thomas's *Poems* was published, he helped his newly made friend George Whicher at Amherst write an essay for publication in the *Yale Review*.[16] He collaborated with Louis Untermeyer in another carefully written and comprehensive essay on Edward Thomas.[17] Wanting to write his own tribute, he could not trust himself immediately to keep his grief under the severe artistic controls required by his temperament. The poem he finally wrote was simply entitled "To E. T."

> *I slumbered with your poems on my breast,*
> *Spread open as I dropped them half-read through*
> *Like dove wings on a figure on a tomb,*
> *To see if in a dream they brought of you*
>
> *I might not have the chance I missed in life*
> *Through some delay, and call you to your face*
> *First soldier, and then poet, and then both,*
> *Who died a soldier-poet of your race.*
>
> *I meant, you meant, that nothing should remain*
> *Unsaid between us, brother, and this remained—*
> *And one thing more that was not then to say:*
> *The Victory for what it lost and gained.*
>
> *You went to meet the shell's embrace of fire*
> *On Vimy Ridge; and when you fell that day*
> *The war seemed over more for you than me,*
> *But now for me than you—the other way.*

How over, though, for even me who knew
The foe thrust back unsafe beyond the Rhine,
If I was not to speak of it to you
And see you pleased once more with words of mine?[18]

8

THE AMHERST IDEA

The latest thing in the schools is to know that you have nothing to say in the days of thy youth, but that those days may well be put in learning how to say something 'gainst the evil days draw near when thou shalt have something to say. Damn these separations of the form from the substance. I don't know how long I could stand them.[1]

ONE OF President Meiklejohn's young professors, newly acquired to help revitalize the department of English at Amherst, said that when Robert Frost gave his first public talk and reading at Amherst the poet seemed to be "dead set not to appear either academic or literary." It was apparent that he was "all farmer." The listening students and townspeople were charmed by this man who was "sturdily built . . . in his early forties, wearing rumpled clothes and a celluloid collar, with unruly brown hair, blunt features, and eyes of seafarer's blue that had a way of magically lighting up." The poet spoke hesitatingly, almost as though he were inviting his audience to help him find just the right words. Often he rolled up a sentence "with many heaves as though it were a stone to be placed in a wall that needed mending." The audience felt that they were "watching an arduous creative triumph, the shaping into form of ideas drawn from the dark abyss of the unconscious mind."[2]

Frost and his family, in turn, enjoyed the process of getting acquainted with the village of Amherst, which had grown up around a broad and parklike common, shaded by elm trees. The southern reach of the common started uphill toward a cluster of brick and granite college buildings placed casually along the hill crest. From that crest the panoramic view to the south extended impressively across miles of fertile countryside and farmlands in the Connecticut River Valley to the range of hills which rose in size to the peak of Mt. Tom, down below Northampton. In the center of town and well beyond the little shopping district, the Dana Street house rented by the Frosts stood within easy walking distance of the campus. Friendly neighbors helped the poet and his family settle into the village routine, which included public school schedules for the four Frost children.

Of the courses which the poet had agreed to teach, the most attractive to him was the special seminar devoted to the appreciation and writing of poetry. A group of students who had elected the seminar explained to their new professor that there was no classroom on campus which could provide the atmosphere suitable for such a course. They asked him to consider holding class one night each week in a large room shared by four of them on the second floor of the Beta Theta Pi fraternity house, facing the common. The offer was accepted, although the atmosphere of the room was rather precious for the tastes of Robert Frost. On winter nights in January of 1917, when the seminar met, the lights were subdued and the open fire gave a friendly glow to the room. Above the fireplace a small Bellini Madonna was flanked on the mantel by two guilded pottery candlesticks, with candles burning. A long cushion before the hearth was covered with a predominantly blue Baluch rug. Against the wall to the right was a long divan, heaped with pillows, the wall behind it draped with a huge tapestry, dull green and gold. To the left of the hearth was a Morris chair, always reserved for the poet. The rest of the room was lost in shadows, out of which stood the softened white of a plaster cast of the Psyche of Capua.[3]

Each of the seminar sessions held in this room was unpredictably different, and the students quickly discovered that their new teacher was indeed set against the customary academic approach to literature. He liked to slouch or recline in the Morris chair, and he seemed to begin each evening casually, with whatever thought might cross his mind. He was blunt in his attacks on what he viewed as the inexcusable procedure of trying to separate form from content in the study of how to write poetry—or how to appreciate it. As a corrective he preached the Emersonian doctrine of the instant dependence of form on soul; the Emersonian insistence that a poem grows out of heartfelt thoughts, finds its expression in sentence tones, and in this way creates its own architecture. The students, invited to read their own poems aloud, were relieved to find that Frost was gentle with any offering which was not pretentious. He had his own quiet ways of teasing and mocking anyone who tried to lean on the musicality of words for purposes of creating sublime poetic effects.

There was a regular time during each of these seminars when the class—as class—was dismissed: those who could not linger for informal conversation were given the chance to leave. The students who stayed were usually entertained with a brilliant flow of monologue in which Frost revealed to them not only his prejudices concerning many subjects but also his fondness for gossip. One evening he surprised a small number of them with his denunciation of Greenwich Village life in New York City. It was talk which, as one of them later said, "would have delighted the ears of any fundamentalist preacher in that wicked town."[4] At the end of each evening—usually well after midnight—one or two of the students escorted the poet-professor to his front door on Dana Street.

Other surprises awaited those who were taking the course in pre-Shakespearean drama. Frost had been given permission to handle the subject in any way he chose, although he had been shown how far Professor Churchill had progressed through the class text: J. M. Manly's *Specimens of the Pre-Shakespearean Drama*. One student, making notes from Churchill's final lecture, had ended with these facts: "In 1264 the Feast of Corpus Christi was instituted by Pope Urban IV, and its restoration was ordered by Clement in 1311." Frost made it clear, when first he met the class, that he would be giving no lectures on historical backgrounds. He implied that because the convenience of printing had been invented some time ago he thought it should be easier for the students to get their facts and dates from books in the library, rather than from him. He preferred to talk about the plays as plays. Before long, he was acquainting them with his favorite notions, and the same note-taking student continued: "The first dramatic principle is to think in terms of situation; the second, to imagine tones of voice. Deeds or actions are important in drama, rather than conversation. Tones of emotion and voice are essential."[5]

One of the first assignments was *The Four P's*, by John Heywood, that "new and very mery enterlude of a Palmer, a Pardoner, a 'Pothecary and a Pedler." Volunteer students, to whom parts were assigned, followed instructions to modernize their lines by removing didactic passages and by rewriting archaic constructions. When ready to demonstrate, these four students stood before the class and read their parts with so much feeling for the dramatic tones of voice that the old interlude became "surprisingly lively and entertaining." Within three months, the class had made similar adaptations of parts selected from *Gammer Gurton's Needle*, Kyd's *Spanish Tragedy*, Marlowe's *Doctor Faustus*, and Shakespeare's *Othello*. The results pleased the students so much that they gave public presentations of the five abridgements.[6]

From the start, Frost conducted these experiments with the hope that he could heighten literary tastes and insights, but he was soon disappointed. In spite of the warm enthusiasm shown by some students in this good-sized class, he was hurt to find that the good work was done by only a few and that too many seemed indifferent. One of his best students, a Colorado boy named Gardner Jackson, felt that part of the difficulty grew out of the casual way in which Frost handled requirements. Retrospectively Jackson gave this account:

". . . he required no papers. He hardly gave any test or examinations. His class was the most loosely run and undisciplined class of any of the classes I attended in college. I used to talk with him about that because the boys in the back row would actually be playing cards together while he was holding forth. It wouldn't disturb him at all. He said, 'If they want what I have to give, they can take. If they don't, that's all right.' It was a 'gut' course. I don't believe he flunked [anyone] in that course."[7]

Frost was disturbed by the failure of his attempts to carry out provocative experiments not only in this course but also in his section of the freshman composition course. Part of the trouble, as he saw it, was that the elderly professor in charge of composition was content to demand that his instructors drill the students in differentiating between the literary forms of exposition, description, narration, while giving proper attention to grammar, spelling, and punctuation. Frost was indignant. Here again he was eager to convey his belief in the Emersonian concept that good writing in either prose or poetry grows out of having something to say. He urged the freshmen to write brief compositions based on their own observations and insights, and he expected that the students would relish this freedom to fashion their descriptions or narrations out of their own experiences. When the boys seemed at a loss to know how to follow these general instructions, he blamed their previous instructors. Sarcastically, he summarized his findings in a letter to Untermeyer:

"The latest thing in the schools is to know that you have nothing to say in the days of thy youth, but that those days may well be put in learning how to say something 'gainst the evil days draw near when thou shalt have something to say. Damn these separations of the form from the substance. I don't know how long I could stand them."[8]

Frost was also annoyed to discover that so many of these young men who had nothing to say seemed to have no capacity for thinking with any originality, and were therefore willing to have their professors do their thinking for them. Again he complained: "A well-educated college boy said to something I said the other day 'Do they say that?' and I answered 'I may say unto you for the twentieth well educated college boy I have said it unto, 'No! *they* don't say that. I say it. But they will after me presently.' What's the matter with these fellows? Do they want ideas merely authorized or do they want them authorized from abroad? Have they had to stay in the receptive attitude so long that they have stiffened in it and what's worse never expect to meet in the flesh anyone who hasn't stiffened in it?"[9]

Given repeated opportunities to share his teaching problems with President Meiklejohn, Frost received sympathetic encouragement to continue whatever provocative forms of experimentation he chose. Meiklejohn was quite frank in admitting that the most serious hurdle he himself faced, in trying to develop new methods of approach for the undergraduate program of study at Amherst, was the deadwood on the faculty— deadwood he had inherited from his predecessor, and could not get rid of. He took pride in saying that progress was being made by adding steadily to his teaching staff men with bold and original ideas.

One of Meiklejohn's first ways of applying leverage against the lethargic intellectual atmosphere created by faculty and students had been to require that each freshman take a course in logic, a course taught by Meiklejohn himself. Another stimulus calculated to awaken new concern for living issues of the day was a newly instituted course entitled "Social and Economic Institutions," taught by a brilliant young professor, Raymond G. Gettell. With Meiklejohn's encouragement, Gettell was soon taking his students on field trips to the nearby cities of Northampton and Holyoke to study living and working conditions of the laboring classes. Meiklejohn was also trying to provoke thought and debate among students and faculty by bringing as lecturers to the Amherst campus a few dedicated radicals, including the American anarchist Emma Goldman. All these stratagems were designed to shock the boys into having something to think about, talk about, write about.

To Frost, such an unusual array of experiments seemed dangerous because it ran counter to his own fondness for preaching the gospel of self-reliance and rugged individualism. He made one of these preachments off campus soon after he began teaching at Amherst. Given permission to be absent for a few days in order to fill commitments previously arranged, he went to Baltimore for two speaking-and-reading engagements. The summer before, he had been visited in Franconia by a wealthy Baltimore lady, Miss Mary Goodwillie, who had walked down to his home from her hotel on Sugar Hill to say she was an admirer of his *North of Boston*. Out of that first meeting had come her later request that he talk and read, for pay, to a group of young ladies who did volunteer social work in Baltimore under her guidance.[10] Frost accepted the invitation, correctly anticipating that he would face an audience who might as well be Junior Leaguers, and as a consequence he planned his talk with malicious care. His own version of the event, given retrospectively, showed his impatience with such an assignment:

"When I meet very wealthy people, I have to face them. I remember facing once a small group. . . . I did it for a charity-working friend of mine. She told me that the girls I must speak to must be gone for: they were worth at least a million apiece, and I could be rough on them. I knew they were all helping her in her charity work, so you can see my state of mind. I felt cross to be there. I took for my text, 'Let not man bring together what God hath set asunder.' Let the rich keep away from the poor for all of me, as the slang is. Well, that's just the way I feel. I suppose I take that position as an artist. 'You wrote about the poor,' they said. I never measured that. I wouldn't have done it if I knew anything was going to be made of it. I didn't do it to get rid of the poor. . . . I need them in my business."[11]

At Amherst, during the winter and spring of 1917, Frost expressed similar views as he increased his criticism of President Meiklejohn and of Professor Gettell for what seemed to him their socialistic and even communistic leanings. One of his students, later admitting to "being shocked at the moral intolerance, the scorching anger behind his words," added, "I was under the assumption that he was liberal in thought, broad-minded, humanistic. I found none of this kind of thing. He had violent prejudices and hatreds; he descended to gossip with a genuine relish and abused even teachers close to him on the campus. . . . As one came to know him further and the 'asides' of talk became more frequent this aspect of his character impressed me. It did not fit at all with the author of those poems in *North of Boston* which carried such a singular attitude of acceptance of the variety of personality and human types, of realistic detachment from causes and the principles of ethics and religion. This discrepancy bothered me at the time; my loyalty to the Socratic atmosphere in the college under Meiklejohn was aroused and was inclined to be shocked and troubled . . . [by the] strong irritable anti-intellectualism in Frost's talk. . . ."[12]

All the students at Amherst were aware that Meiklejohn consciously and deliberately endowed the words "intellectual" and "anti-intellectual" with special meanings. To assist him, he carefully selected not only the newcomers to his faculty but also the steadily increased parade of visiting lecturers. One of these was a young Columbia professor, John Erskine, who had previously taught at Amherst and who attracted special attention in 1915 when he published a volume of essays entitled *The Moral Obligation to Be Intelligent*. Previously, his title essay had been delivered as a paper before the annual public meeting of the Amherst chapter of Phi Beta Kappa, and Meiklejohn had said that Erskine's ideas fitted nicely into those of the educational program at Amherst.[13] In his paper, Erskine claimed that while the Greeks considered intelligence a virtue, Anglo-Saxon ethics gave it a more humble place. Character, strong character, seemed to be the predominant virtue in English poetry, drama, fiction, where intelligence was disparaged by associating it with the actions of evil individuals. Milton, in *Paradise Lost*, had given the intellectual honors to Satan. Shakespeare, in *Othello*, endowed his Machiavellian Iago with far more intelligence than was displayed by the gullible hero. Erskine's point was that in the American as well as English tradition no moral obligation was usually attached to the act of being intelligent, of being aware of the essenial facts of human nature and the universe, or even of the act of training the mind for the making of wise decisions. Instead, men were more often praised for their pluck and heroism or for their being good, even if they were otherwise stupid. He gave as another example Tennyson's "Charge of the Light Brigade," wherein the heroes praised were those who had obediently ridden to death knowing that someone had blundered and that their sacrifice was unnecessary. Urging a return to classical notions, Erskine stressed the need to re-establish intelligence as a modern virtue. He further hinted that authors like Milton and Tennyson were disposed to use the term "right reason" as an unsatisfactory substitute for the word "intelligence."[14]

Frost, who later met Erskine, and became well acquainted with him, had no more sympathy for this notion of moral obligation to be intelligent than he had for Meiklejohn's notions of the need for social amelioration. Whenever his intolerance was stirred by such currents of thought, he tried to counteract them by preaching another aspect of his doctrine. In classroom and out, he told the Amherst students that there was no valid connection between real life and the artificiality provided through academic programs which pretended to fit young men for what lay ahead. The poet liked to offer the story of his own experience as an exemplum: he had fashioned his life successfully because he had been enough of an individualist to foresee the value in running away from college—first from Dartmouth and next from Harvard. It seemed to him that the brightest and most independent of the Amherst students ought to find reasons enough for escaping from all the poisonous nonsense peddled as "the Amherst idea." One sympathetic listener to this advice was the junior from Colorado, Gardner Jackson, who disliked seeing lazy students playing cards in the back row of the drama class. His almost worshipful admiration of Frost was rewarded by special attentions, and Frost became better acquainted with him than with any other student during that spring term of 1917. Reviewing the circumstances, Jackson said:

"I really can't explain why Robert Frost singled me out of the class to become his friend. My recollection is that he started by asking me to go on a walk with him one Saturday out across the Connecticut Valley. It had snowed and was very beautiful. We walked, I imagine, ten or twelve miles on that first walk. Right away, Frost began questioning me as to why I thought

I was in college, and what I was getting out of it and whether I thought I ought to stay. Upon my trying to answer his questions, he quite quickly, in his turn, began to argue with me about going on in college. He thought that I oughtn't to, that it was a waste of my time, and that I ought to do what he said he had done, which was to interrupt his college course by going on the bum for a couple of years. I think he had a notion that I, in his judgment, had potentials as a writer. He thought that I would encourage those potentials much more by not doing the academic work. He felt that the contact with reality in the workaday world would be more likely to stimulate me into a creative use of what he thought, apparently, I had as potential talents."[15]

Like several other students, Jackson was surprised to discover that Frost took an extraordinary pleasure in gossiping about teachers close to him, particularly his colleagues in the English department. The very popular Stark Young remained a special target for Frost's animosity, and Jackson was cross-examined concerning Young's ways of dealing with the students. Part of the difficulty, here, was that Young was the most witty and skillful teacher in the English department at that time, and Frost was jealous of the ways in which he was succeeding while Frost was losing control of his classes.

Unintentionally, Jackson gave to Frost the weapons needed for acts which went beyond gossip. During Jackson's freshman year he and another boy had been amused rather than annoyed by the unsuccessful attempts of Stark Young to educate them in forms of eroticism which did not appeal to them. As their instructor in freshman composition, he had invited them several times to his apartment on Amity Street. With lights dimmed and incense burning, Jackson said, he read them homosexual passages while "trying to induce us into the joys of the abnormal business."[16] It was difficult for Jackson to understand why Frost seemed so eager to collect more and more details about the seductive habits of Stark Young, and it never seemed to occur to him that Frost might use the information for the purpose of urging President Meiklejohn to dismiss Young from his position.[17] Even in retrospect, Jackson expressed his puzzlement:

"Of course our relationship became one involving rather intimate discussion about other members of the faculty and particularly about Stark Young, because he seemed to find in

Stark Young the exact oposite of himself and an opposite that he, in his expression, certainly seemed to loathe. He loathed him even too much. It was so much that it seemed to me to indicate an envy or a wishing that he might have some of the qualities or interests that Stark Young had. He seemed to me almost obsessed with a preoccupation to paw over Stark Young's eroticism and interest in erotic literature. . . . I found in Frost something of my own Puritan background, Puritan upbringing, and an interest in, and maybe an over-emphasized interest in, the stuff that was anti-Puritan."[18]

There were some students at Amherst who were attracted to Frost because he kept protesting that atheism was one of the evils encouraged by Meiklejohn's liberalism. A few of them, after hearing him make remarks which might indeed have "delighted the ears of any fundamentalist preacher," invited him to talk before the members of the Amherst Christian Association. Accepting, he built his talk around a selection of poems largely available to him in *The Oxford Book of English Verse*, seeming to take as his topic the romantic belief that "the world is a place to get away from"—through love or art or nature or science or religion. To illustrate the first belief he read Browning's "Love among the Ruins," in which a contrast is made between the rewards of love and the losses of civilizations which have come to nothing. The final stanza:

> *Oh heart! oh, blood that freezes, blood that burns!*
> *Earth's returns*
> *For whole centuries of folly, noise and sin!*
> *Shut them in,*
> *With their triumphs and their glories and the rest.*
> *Love is best.*

To illustrate the different claim that art is best, as a means for getting away from the world, he read Yeats's early lyric, "The Song of the Happy Shepherd." Continuing, he amused his audience with poems which represented romantic notions of escape from this world by means of scientific inventions and discoveries such as the flying machine of Darius Green. But he became more serious as he pointed out that, whether we like it or not, death eventually provides the unavoidable means of getting away. He read to them Christina Rossetti's little dialogue entitled "Uphill," which ends,

Shall I find comfort, travel-sore and weak?
  Of labour you shall find the sum.
Will there be beds for me and all who seek?
  Yea, beds for all who come.

Finally, and with a seriousness which the students of the Christian Association understood, he read Richard Blackmore's "Dominus Illuminatio Mea":

In the hour of death, after this life's whim,
When heart beats low, and the eyes grow dim,
And pain has exhausted every limb—
  The lover of the Lord shall trust in Him.

When the will has forgotten the lifelong aim,
And the mind can only disgrace its fame,
And a man is uncertain of his own name—
  The power of the Lord shall fill this frame.

When the last sigh is heaved, and the last tear shed,
And the coffin is waiting beside the bed,
And the widow and child forsake the dead—
  The angel of the Lord shall lift this head.

For even the purest delight may pall,
And power must fail, and the pride must fall,
And the love of the dearest friends grow small—
  But the glory of the Lord is all in all.

Frost had apparently designed this talk to pivot ambiguously and provocatively on the word "romantic," but he gave the best students in the Amherst Christian Association enough hints of his deep religious convictions to permit their reporter to end his detailed article, "Professor Frost's entire talk was given in an interesting manner and explained the attitude of the poet to his listeners. He concluded his readings with a serious poem ending in 'The glory of God is all in all.' "[19]

Before the first term of the poet's stay at Amherst was completed, the United States declared war against Germany and her allies. Immediately, the entire teaching program underwent a rapid series of changes, and one of the first students to enlist was Gardner Jackson, encouraged by Frost's talks about the heroism of offering one's services to country at such a time.[20] Those who upheld any form of pacifism aroused his outspoken and scornful disgust. "Glorious war, isn't it?"[21] he wrote to one of his friends. To another he said, "Write a lot. Enjoy the war. I've made up my mind to do the second anyway. I don't see why the fact that I can't be in a fight should keep me from liking the fight."[22]

Not even the war could help him ignore the accumulation of campus annoyances which got on his nerves so much that he was sorry he had accepted the Amherst offer. "I'm sick as hell of this Stark Young imbroglio," he wrote to Untermeyer, "and I'm thinking of going out and getting shot where it will do some good."[23] When he told his wife much the same thing, she infuriated him by saying he wouldn't dare to become a soldier. Deciding to punish her for saying that, he made one move toward enlistment. A retired Army officer in Amherst had begun giving civilian volunteers a chance to learn rifle practice and marching drill, on the village common. The day his wife taunted him, Frost appeared at the common, with other civilians, for the afternoon drill. Shown how to carry a Springfield rifle, how to present arms, and how to march in step with the rifle on his shoulder, he completed the afternoon session. That was enough—particularly after he found that Mrs. Frost seemed completely indifferent to the news of what he had done; equally indifferent to his boast that he was now going to enlist.[24] Under the circumstances, he found more satisfaction in turning once again to vent his fury on Stark Young, in another letter to the pun-loving Untermeyer:

"I was melancholy when I wrote [last] and disposed to play with sad things. I'm still melancholy. He may be stark young but I'll say this[:] if he was much stark younger I should go stark crazy before I got back to my side hill. He has spoiled everything here that the coming of the war hasn't spoiled. And he's so foxy about it. He walks up close to me on the street and passes candy from his pockets to mine like a collier passing coal to a warship at sea. It makes everybody think that he must say with sorrow everything he says against me when he loves me so much in spite of all. But it will make a melodrama."[25]

He might have added, "Another melodrama," for he had published a little one entitled "A Way Out" in *The Seven Arts* for February 1917, and it was later produced in Northampton by some of his Amherst students. The writing of "A Way Out" could have drained off, temporarily, some of his murderous bitterness. The setting of the piece is "a bachelor's kitchen bedroom in a farmhouse with a table spread for supper." The owner and sole occupant, Asa Gorrill, shuffles across the stage to answer a knock and is confronted by a stranger who pushes into the room. "Huh," says the stranger, "so this is what it's like. Seems to me you lock up early. What you afraid of?" Asa insists that he is " 'Fraid of nothing, because I ain't got nothing —nothing't anybody wants." The stranger hastily cross-examines Asa, as though he has reason for wanting to learn much, fast, about this hermit. The two men are the same height and have features so much alike that they might pass for twins, but Asa has never before seen the stranger and can't imagine what he wants. Gradually Asa learns that the intruder has killed someone and is trying to escape from those in pursuit. Having been told that he looks like Asa, the stranger has decided that his best means of escape—his best "way out"—is to cast himself in the role of Asa Gorrill. Practicing, he puts on some clothes which belong to the hermit, and he imitates the way the hermit talks. By the time the posse begins hammering at the door, the intruder has killed Asa and hidden the body offstage. Shuffling to the door, and opening it cautiously, he successfully deceives the posse by playing the role of Asa Gorrill very well.[26]

Many times, when Frost indulged his passionate hatred, he couldn't resist imagining that he himself had used murder as a means of liberating himself from a torturing enemy. Escape of some kind—real or imaginary—was his favorite solution for many of his problems. Early in 1917, when he had heard from John and Margaret Bartlett that she was on the verge of a nervous breakdown, because of tensions involving her in-laws and her two small children, Frost made a characteristic pronouncement concerning the psychological virtue of escape:

"And speaking of war, what kind of a trouble have you children got yourselves into? Didn't I tell you you would have to stick at nothing to get over these hard times? You have still your reserves—things you wont give up. But you'll have to give up everything for a little while. Those boys ought to go on a visit to one of their grandmothers. You can do a lot for them. But if you're the least like me, not enough to take them entirely off Margaret's mind. She's got to be relieved of them to get well. That's sure. I have seen right in my own family one person lost by not taking instant and out-and-out measures and another person saved by taking them. The business can go either way you want it to, but I'm afraid generally as most of us are entangled in life and obligations, it inclines to go the wrong way. Cut and run away from every care: that is the rule. Nothing else will do. No faltering. I saw the way my father fed his hopes on one concession after another. It was my first tragedy."[27]

For Frost, one of the strongest temptations was to cut and run away from every care at Amherst by escaping to Franconia and by refusing to go back. "Oh I don't know about teaching after all," he wrote to Amy Lowell in the spring of 1917. "When I am fifty, say—ten years from now—when the war is over. I want to write a few things first if I can only happen to."[28] A month earlier, he had written to Harcourt, "Franconia beckons to us. We have had enough of Stark Young's stark disingenuousness. Welcome the wilderness where no one comes or has come except in an expensive touring car. . . .The best of misunderstanding any one is that it sort of disposes of him and clears your mind of him and so leaves you with the one less detail in life to be bothered with. Of course it is the same with understanding. Of what use is either understanding or misunderstanding unless it simplifies by taking away from the sum and burden of what you have to consider. There are a hundred poets in a new anthology for example; I get rid of one half of them by understanding, of the other half by misunderstanding, and the danger of my mind's being overcrowded with poets or my brain's being congested with 'em is passed. What a thing misunderstanding is. I sing misunderstanding."[29]

To Franconia he did go, with his family, just as soon as the school year was over for him and for his children. He had not made up his mind whether he would return to Amherst in the fall, but he carried with him an attractive offer. President Meiklejohn knew how to deal with this poet who was a stimulating presence at Amherst, even when he did sing misunderstanding. The Amherst offer, based on a wartime reorganization of the course program, gave the poet a chance to teach only two (instead of three) courses; the chance to choose these courses; the chance to continue in the rank and in the salary-scale of a full professor; even the chance to be absent from the campus, whenever convenient, to give readings of his poems. The decision to reject such an attractive offer might have been possible if he could support himself and his family from the proceeds of his writings, but royalties from his third book, *Mountain Interval,* were disappointingly small. Payments for poems sold to magazines might have amounted to more if he had found more time or inclination, at Amherst, to write. During the semester just completed, he had not offered a single poem to any magazine. How, then, to earn a living? The last thing he wanted to do was to try to make a go of it by earning a living as a farmer. Under the circumstances, Meiklejohn's generosity would provide a comfortable subsistence—more than he had ever made before—even if it did require rubbing shoulders unpleasantly with Stark Young. In August of 1917, Frost wrote to his farmer-friend John Bartlett, "We are all going back to Amherst next month."[30]

Where the Frosts would live, during their first full academic year at Amherst, was a problem nicely solved by one of the most pleasant real-estate dealers Frost had ever met. His name was Warren R. Brown, and he had been present at Frost's first reading of his poems in Williston Hall at Amherst in March of 1916. Brown had sat in the front row, that afternoon, with his right hand cupped behind his ear. The twinkle in his eye and the way he smiled at just the right time, during the reading of certain poems in *North of Boston,* had won Frost's heart. After the reading, Brown had waited until he could introduce himself and ask a question. He said he'd never gone very far with schooling but that one of his favorite books was Thoreau's *Walden.* He felt there was something in Frost's poems that suggested a kinship of interest between Thoreau and Frost. Was he right? That question alone provided a sufficient basis for friendship. The two men quickly became well acquainted, and so fond of each other that it was a pleasure for Frost to seek Brown's help, during the summer of 1917, in searching for a suitable house which might be rented. The place had to be just far enough out of town to give the Frost family a chance to escape from the villagers, the students, the faculty; a true sense of living in the country.

Brown knew what Frost wanted, and he showed him an attractive property on the Pelham Road not too far out in the country—just across the Amherst town-line, in West Pelham. It was a two-story shingled cottage which nestled in against a grove of tall pines. Large enough for a family of six, the cottage had a picturesque setting which immediately appealed to

Frost. Through the pine grove, a deep gorge had been made by the innumerable spring freshets of a small stream known as Orient Brook. To the east of the gorge rose a tree-covered hill, locally known as Orient Mountain. The whole region offered a fine variety of places for botanical explorations, or just for casual walking. Frost was well satisfied and he looked no further.

When the two men returned to Brown's real-estate office in Amherst to draw up a rental contract, Frost started to write out the necessary check to the order of Warren R. Brown, and hesitated. He had just realized, he said, that he didn't know what "R." stood for. Brown evaded the question at the time, and later confessed that he had been christened with only one given name: he had added the initial to commemorate his failure to win the schoolgirl he had loved and courted. Her name was Rebecca, and when she refused to take his name he had told her she couldn't help giving him hers. From that time on, he had signed himself Warren R. Brown.

Among all the Amherst townspeople whom Frost knew as friends, nobody charmed and entertained him as much as Brown. This easygoing and Thoreau-admiring real-estate man who seemed better cut out to be a farmer was usually ready for a walk in the country whenever Frost wanted companionship. At the same time, Brown was demonstrating modest literary gifts. For years he had been the local newspaper correspondent for the Springfield *Republican,* and he was well stocked with stories of odd characters in the region. Frost liked best the one about a local farmer whose cow was just ornery enough at milking time to wait until the pail was almost full before lifting a hind leg and lowering the dung-covered hoof through the foam. Just once the farmer lost his temper. He jumped up, placed both hands on the cow's back, closed his fingers until a ridge of hide appeared between his hands, leaned forward, and sank his teeth into the ridge of hide as hard as he could. The cow, bellowing surprise and pain, leaned sideways against the man until she pinned him against the side of the stall. Then she kept leaning, harder and harder, until the man shouted, "Wait a minute, wait a minute! Who begun it, goldern ya, who begun it?"[31]

That farmer's question was the one which Frost asked himself, reproachfully, as soon as he began to feel pressed against the academic stall, after his return to Amherst in the autumn of 1917. Many of the students had enlisted, classrooms were half empty, and those in attendance showed little concern for studies. The poet, made irritable by campus duties and regulations, was in no mood for devoting his newly acquired budget of spare time to writing poetry. It seemed that all he could do to relieve his irritabilities was write letters attacking anything in sight. Untermeyer had offended him by helping to transform *The Seven Arts* into a propagandistic weapon for attacking the government and for espousing peace. The leftist radical John Reed, who later died in Moscow and was buried at the Kremlin, was nearly jailed in New York City for contributing to *The Seven Arts* a blistering article entitled "This Unpopular War." The crippled hunchback Randolph Bourne carried his plea for pacifism too far, in a series of six antiwar articles, and soon thereafter the wealthy backer of *The Seven Arts*, withdrawing support, brought the magazine to its end with the issue for October 1917. Frost started mocking Untermeyer's share in this fiasco by sending him a limerick:

THE SEVEN ARTS

In the Dawn of Creation that morning
I remember I gave you fair warning:
The Arts are but Six!
You add Politics
And the Seven will all die a-Bourneing.

He continued his attack, in prose, then shifted to a self-revealing discussion of his own recurrent moods of gloom and melancholy:

"Under separate cover I have told you why I ain't got no sympathy for your total loss of all the arts. You tried to have too many at the present price of certified milk. Why would you be a pig instead of something like a horse or a cow that only has one in a litter, albeit with six legs sometimes, for I have seen such in my old mad glad circus-going days. But that's all put behind me since I discovered that do or say my damndest I can't be other than orthodox in politics love and religion: I can't escape salvation: I can't burn if I was born into this world to shine without heat. And I try not to think of it as often as I can lest in the general deliquescence I should find myself a party to the literature of irresponsible, boy-again freedom. No, I can promise you that whatever else I write or may have been writing for the last twenty-five years to disprove Amy's theory that I never got anything except out of the soil of New England, there's one thing I shan't write in the past, present, or future, and that is glad mad stuff or mad glad stuff. The conviction closes in on me that I was cast for gloom as the sparks fly upward, I was about to say: I am of deep shadow all compact like onion within onion and the savor of me is oil of tears. I have heard laughter by daylight when I thought it was my own because at that moment when it broke I had parted my lips to take food. Just so I have been afraid of myself and caught at my throat when I thought I was making some terrible din of a mill whistle that happened to come on the same instant with the opening of my youth to yawn. But I have not laughed. No man can tell you the sound or the way of my laughter. I have neighed at night in the woods behind a house like vampires.[32] But there are no vampires, there are no ghouls, there [are] no demons, there is nothing but me. And I have all the dead New England things held back by one hand as by a dam in the long deep wooded valley of Whippoorwill, where, many as they are, though, they do not flow together by their own weight. . . . I hold them easily—too easily for assurance that they will go with a rush when I let them go. . . ."[33]

In these lacerating and self-lacerating moods, Frost constantly used letter-writing to release the pent-up energies caused by his hatreds of self and others. An extraordinary sequence of rages, which he piled up like dark thunderclouds during the fall of 1917, took so much out of him that he may not have avoided mental illness, entirely. One serious upset, during the sequence, was caused by Amy Lowell. After she had given a course of lectures on modern poets, she published them in the fall of 1917 under the title, *Tendencies in Modern Poetry*. Frost was infuriated because the chapter devoted to him came second, and Robinson came first. Nevertheless, Amy Lowell's essay on Frost stood out as the most extended and most favorable critical treatment given him by an American. He was aware of its value in this regard, and he wrote a restrained letter of thanks.[34] Without restraint, a few days later, he cut loose to Untermeyer, complaining that Amy's fumbling approach was a dreadful misrepresentation. Halfway through the letter, he once again took issue with her claim that his grimness showed that he lacked a sense of humor, and he continued:

"I doubt if she is right in making me so grim, not to say

morbid. I may not be funny enough for Life or Punch, but I have a sense of humor enough, I must believe, to laugh when the joke is on me as it is in some of this book . . .

"I really like least her mistake about Elinor. That's an unpardonable attempt to do her as the conventional helpmeet of genius. Elinor has never been of any earthly use to me. She hasn't cared whether I went to school or worked or earned anything. She has resisted every inch of the way my efforts to get money. She is not too sure that she cares about my reputation. She wouldn't lift a hand or have me lift a hand to increase my reputation or even save it. And this isn't all from devotion to my art at its highest. She seems to have the same weakness I have for a life that goes rather poetically; only I should say she is worse than I. It isn't what might be expected to come from such a life—poetry [—] that she is after. And it isn't that she doesn't think I am a good poet either. She always knew I was a good poet, but that was between her and me, and there I think she would have liked it if it had remained at least until we were dead. I don't know that I can make you understand the kind of person [she is]. Catch her getting any satisfaction out of what her housekeeping may have done to feed a poet! Rats! She hates housekeeping. She has worked because the work has piled on top of her. But she hasn't pretended to like house-work even for my sake. If she has liked anything it has been what I may call living it on the high. She's especially wary of honors that derogate from the poetic life she fancies us living. What a cheap common unindividualized picture Amy makes of her. . . ."[35]

While Frost was growling over the faults of Amy Lowell, he was building up an enormous rage over what he viewed as the stupid mistreatments of his eldest daughter, Lesley, during the first term of her freshman year at Wellesley College. Lesley, having studied for most of her life with her father and mother, had become conditioned to share her father's impatience with any rigorous academic discipline. She had been exposed to only a smattering of formal education at Derry, Plymouth, Beaconsfield, Franconia, Amherst. Her choice of Wellesley had been stimulated by her making the acquaintance of Professor Charles Lowell Young, who taught a course in American literature there, and whom her father had accidentally met during a climb up Lafayette Mountain in the summer of 1917.[36]

Young had assisted Lesley in making a successful, although

tardy, application for admission to Wellesley. After she arrived there, he had also given her counsel in choosing courses. But because she had acquired her father's knack for expressing furious indignation against anyone who found fault with her independent ways, she very soon began to complain that she was being mistreated by two of her professors—Miss Fletcher in Latin and Mr. Coe in French—both of whom gave her midterm marks which she considered disgracefully low and unfair. Her father, responding with sympathy, wrote a diatribe to Miss Fletcher.[37] Professor Young did what he could to soothe all of the contestants, but Frost was still angry at the so-called linguists when he sent his thanks to Young:

"You are a great friend and we are fortunate in our misfortunes to have one so great. You may not know all you have done to be called great. Among a lot of other things you have given us support, and what is better and harder to give, self-support.

"As for that precisian in syntax [Miss Fletcher] I can't quite get over her. She is nothing new mind you. If I showed surprise in running into her it is not because I had never seen her before, it is because I hadn't seen her for so long I had begun to fool myself into the notion that I had talked her off the face of the earth—laughed her off the face of the earth. I had fallen into a mellow reminiscent way about her in my public utterances that was almost good-natured and forgiving. Now I get my punishment (and not alone) for letting myself believe even for the least division of an hour that there is any such thing as progress. Mea culpa. The fault is mine and the punishment is half Lesley's. I gave a lecture somewhere once upon a time[38] on 'The Waiting Spirit: How Long Will It Wait,' in which I showed how I thought we had revised our teaching in English and ought to revise it in other subjects to give the spirit its chance from the very first day in school and every step along the way, not counting on it to wait at all. I asserted that there wasnt an English teach[er] left who would be for putting off the day of the spirit in reading and writing till the hard mechanics of the subject could be learned. It has been found that the spirit won't be put off. Either it will be engaged at once and kept engaged or it will take sanctuary in the sun returning unto the God who gave it. So I said in folly and so I made Lesley believe we all believed. And then on top of all the pains your Latin department takes to make Latin painful, comes your

French department to exclaim against a child for so far forgetting herself as to write a poem in French before she has studied French prosody. 'Let the spirit wait,' says your Whitechapel Frenchman: and the spirit can wait or go—it is all one to him. I remember four lines to the tune of Tararaboomdeay I once addressed to Sheffy[39] at Harvard:

> *Perhaps you think I am going to wait*
> *Till I can write like a graduate*
> *Before I write to my friends any more*
> *You prig stick, what do you take me for.*

"How it all comes back to me! You see I was angry at the general disposition to take everything written by an undergraduate as an exercise. I never wrote exercises in my life. I was the same sixpence then as now and so is Lesley's Latin teacher the same old scourge blight and destitution that held marks over me for seven years of Latin and then left me nowhere in the end. It's sure she's an argument against taking Latin as literature but isnt she just as much an argument against taking it as a discipline in the hope that the close thinking it calls for in accurate translation will serve in any other walk of life than Latin. Precise in syntax, you would say, precise in business, precise in justice. But not so. I say I have seen Miss Fletcher before. And never in all the years have I found her able to think closely of anything but Latin. I have always found her miserably minded. Was Miss Fletchers handling of the crime she thought she had caught Lesley at[,] precise? It was slovenly. I hope I made her look ridiculous to herself. And it didnt take me five questions. Yet I hardly feel as if I had had satisfaction. She may have to hear further from me. She is a bad woman. To Hell with her piddling accuracy in Latin. I should know it could come to nothing lovely and to nothing lovely it came.

"But you have thought of all this in a lifetime of teaching and dismissed it for something the matter with it that I dont see. You don't listen with much patience, I notice.

"Lesley says you had a talk with the Whitechapel Frenchman. I wonder if you found him implacable in his magisterial self-importance. Has Lesley the least hope of success with him? Prosody! I was hoping the mere word might be kept from Lesley as long as possible. I've been telling Lesley how little embarrassed Wilfrid Gibson was when he had to confess before all the assembled professors at Chicago last winter that he didn't know one form of verse from another. I believe I don't know a single poet who knows any prosody, except always Robert Bridges. I once asked De la Mare if he had noticed anything queer about the verse in his own The Listeners and he answered that he hadnt noticed anything at all about the verse in it queer or unqueer.

"But blast all this. What a father I am! I promise never to talk to you about my children again—any of them. That is if you will forgive my having talked this time and the last time and the time before that and so on back to the day on top of Lafayette. . . ."[40]

Lesley pleased her father by withdrawing from Wellesley at the end of her freshman year and by doing wartime work with other girls in an airplane factory. As soon as classes ended at Amherst, and the summer vacation of 1918 began, Frost made a quick retreat to Franconia. "Two weeks' farming has made me think better of teaching than I did when I left it at Commencement," he wrote to Whicher.[41] "This is a lovely region," he told Untermeyer. "It is away off."[42]

President Meiklejohn had found several ways to make the restless poet think better of teaching, even prior to commencement: the undergraduate newspaper for the sixth of May 1918 carried the announcement that an honorary degree had been given Professor Frost, by Amherst; that he had been "reappointed professor of English Literature with the understanding that he is to teach in the first semester only, giving two courses."[43] The seniors had given him a further honor by inviting him to be their speaker at the traditional Senior Chapel exercises. Perhaps in no mood for addressing them, he begged off at the last moment on grounds of illness. The students, well accustomed to the poet's knack for getting out of his academic obligations, were given to making jokes about it, and the satirical speaker in the Class-day Address, at commencement time, delighted his audience by paying special attention to his performance during the year:

"Frost has been trying his hardest to make his own course gutty enough to take the place of all the guts which have recently evaporated. Under the strain of doing as little as possible . . . he fell sick just in time to get out of making the Senior chapel address—the one piece of work he was in danger of doing. It is true Stark Young was a noble eleventh-hour hero and came across nicely; and nobody but Stark Young could say so much so well on such short or no notice. . . . It is hard to imagine what the college would do without Stark Young. We nominate and elect him to the Hall of Fame."[44]

Any praise of Stark Young had for Frost the bitter taste of wormwood, but by the time the Frost family returned to Amherst in the fall of 1918 there was one important diversion. President Meiklejohn had asked Frost to give a new course which was to be merely a series of discussions, designed to appeal to those Amherst students who were thinking primarily of when they might be called into one of the armed services. The course was to be called "War Issues," and the president was confident that such a seminar, devoted to the exploration of conflicting attitudes toward the war, toward pacifism, toward the draft, toward freedom of speech, could be made stimulating by Frost's reactionary prejudices. Frost explained his attitude toward it, in a letter to Untermeyer:

"This is a war college and I am teaching war issues: so it's a lucky thing I have always taken a sensible view of the universe and everything in it. Otherwise I might have to knuckle to the war department were it ever so little or else go to jail like old Gene Debs. I am out to see a world full of small-fry democracies even if we have to fill them two deep or even three deep in some places.

"Lesley is worse than I am. She is manufacturing hydroplanes with the Curtiss company and I'm afraid if she wasn't so fond of seeing people licked, anybody licked, she might want to see the war go on forever. In other words she is one of the interests.

"Too much war; I swear if there's another war on top of this one I shall refuse to know anything about it. I have ordered all my papers and magazines discontinued after July 4, 1919. No more politics for me in this world, once I am sure all throwns are throne down."[45]

As it happened, the war was blamed for causing one epidemic from which Frost did not escape. During the fall of 1918, the spread of influenza became so acute and serious that during one day—the first of October—209 people died in the city of Boston. Frost, confined to his bed with a severe case of the disease, was too ill to celebrate Armistice Day. He remained seriously ill during the next two months, but by the fourth of January he had recovered sufficiently to joke about his ordeal:

"Here it is as late as this (1919 A. D.), and I don't know whether or not I'm strong enough to write a letter yet. The only way I can tell that I haven't died and gone to heaven is by the fact that everything is just the same as it was on earth (all my family round me and all that) only worse, whereas, as I had been brought up in Swedenborgianism to believe, everything should be the same only better. Two possibilities remain: either I have died and gone to Hell or I haven't died. Therefore I haven't died. And that's the only reason I haven't. I was sick enough to die and no doubt I deserved to die. The only question in my mind is could the world have got along without me?"[46]

A serious question kept troubling him throughout the spring of 1919, and again when he returned to Amherst College that fall. He kept asking himself how and why he had made the mistake of nearly giving up being a poet, and of becoming a mere teacher. As soon as he decided that he had indeed made a mistake, and that he should fight his way out of Amherst, he began to seek excuses for resigning. His capacity for rage was always helpful to him under such circumstances, and he liked to say, repeatedly, "I always hold that we get forward as much by hating as by loving."[47] Late in January of 1920, he brought to the boiling point his indignation against Stark Young and President Meiklejohn, particularly because their talk about "freedom" seemed to him far too academic, far too liberal, to be tolerated. It also seemed to Frost that Meiklejohn was so obsessed with the pleasures of debate and argument that he encouraged the Amherst students to express, freely, attitudes which were treasonable. In addition, he became convinced that Meiklejohn's leanings were immoral, undemocratic, and atheistic. As soon as the poet's rage was hot enough to satisfy him, he demanded a private session with Meiklejohn, and delivered an ultimatum: Stark Young must be fired because he was a bad moral influence on the students. If he stayed, Frost would quit. Meiklejohn tried to reason with Frost by asking where the boys were likely to go, in later life, without coming into contact with individuals who had moral imperfections. The president was willing to let the boys build their own defenses against such imperfections, in this Amherst atmosphere where men like Frost would counteract whatever might be immoral in the influence of men like Young. Frost took the opening thus offered. "I did not come here to counteract," he said. Then he resigned.[48]

No public announcement was made of Frost's resignation, but the poet himself spread the word privately. Having been asked to serve as an after-dinner speaker before a group of Amherst alumni, and having made a provisional acceptance, he wrote that there were circumstances which made it impossible for him to accept:

"I am forced after all to give up the idea of speaking at the Amherst dinner, and I owe you something more than a telegram of explanation. I have decided to leave teaching and go back to farming and writing. Strange enough, I was helped to this decision by your invitation. It was in turning over in my mind my subject chosen for the dinner that I came to the conclusion that I was too much out of sympathy with what the present administration seems bent on doing with this old New England college. I suppose I might say that I am too much outraged in the historical sense for loyalty. I can't complain that I haven't enjoyed the 'academic freedom' to be entirely myself under Mr. Meiklejohn. While he detests my dangerous rationalistic and anti-intellectualistic philosophy, he thinks he is willing to have it represented here. But probably it will be better represented by someone else who can take it less seriously than I. . . ."[49]

After making his decision, Frost gathered his family and retreated with them to Franconia, in February of 1920. Words of solicitude sent to him by Wilbur Cross at Yale gave him another chance to clear his own mind concerning what he had learned at Amherst, and why he had decided to break away:

"I should have answered your letter sooner, but I have been busy retiring from education. I discovered what the Amherst Idea was that is so much talked of, and I got amicably out. The Amherst Idea as I had it in so many words from the high custodian is this: 'Freedom for taste and intellect.' Freedom from what? Freedom from every prejudice in favor of state home church morality, etc.[50] I am too much a creature of prejudice to stay and listen to such stuff. Not only in favor of morality am I prejudiced, but in favor of an immorality I could name as against other immoralities.[51] I'd no more set out in pursuit of the truth than I would in pursuit of a living unless mounted on my prejudices. There was all the excuse I needed to get back to my farming. [William Ernest] Hocking says if I probed any college to its inmost idea I couldn't teach in it. But by any college Hocking means simply Harvard. The trouble with Hocking is he belongs at Yale where he formed himself in the plastic age. He will never be happy anywhere else. Neither will Mrs. Hocking.

"But why these confidences in a letter to one who has never shown the least curiosity in my hearing about Amherst? What I set out to tell you was that, having kicked myself free from care and intellectuality, I ought to find time to polish you off the group of poems I had in mind to offer you . . ."[52]

9

JEANIE

And I suppose I am a brute in that my nature refuses to carry sympathy to the point of going crazy just because someone else goes crazy, or of dying just because someone else dies.[1]

SOON AFTER Robert Frost withdrew from Amherst College and took refuge in Franconia, with his family, he received word that his sister Jeanie was in jail. He had heard nothing from her, and very little about her, for more than a year, and when last they had met they had exchanged harsh words and had quarreled bitterly. Their friend Wilbur Rowell, who regularly sent each of them annuity payments from their grandfather's estate, kept in far closer touch with Jeanie than her brother did.

The immediate trouble seemed to begin when Jeanie disturbed the peace in Portland, Maine. Using a public telephone in a drugstore, she tried to place a call to Rowell in Lawrence, Massachusetts, to ask for money. Failing to reach him, she became hysterical, and the druggist had summoned the police. Jeanie, obsessed for years by the notion that she was in constant danger of being captured by underworld characters who wanted her for their white-slave trade, fought the policemen and protested that she was being kidnapped by criminals who were only pretending to be officers of the law. She was subdued by force, taken to the police station, and locked in a cell. A physician, brought in, gave her sedatives, pronounced her demented, and said she should be placed in an asylum for the insane. Whatever her condition may have been, she did have enough presence of mind to ask that word of her plight be sent to her friend, Miss Louie Merriam, with whom she had been living—and wandering from one teaching position to another. Miss Merriam came quickly, explained that she understood Jeanie's case, and offered to assume complete responsibility for her care if the police would let her go. The police, unwilling to accede until they had instructions from the nearest of kin, asked about relatives. Both of these women had their reasons for avoiding any mention of Jeanie's brother. Instead, they named Rowell as Jeanie's lawyer and guardian. Frost learned of Jeanie's predicament only when he received Rowell's letter written on the thirty-first of March 1920:

"Last Thursday morning the Police Department of Portland, Maine, telephoned to me saying that they had Jeanie Frost in confinement and that she was demented. They wanted me to come there and take her off their hands. This I declined to do. I have neither the authority nor the means to take care of her.

"She has been in various places during the fall and winter. When I last heard from her she was in North Yarmouth, Maine. She, with her friend, Miss Merriam, were in Lowell and Haverhill during the winter. They were both ill in Haverhill with influenza but apparently they were not so badly off, so they managed to take care of themselves. I have paid her during the year $300 [advance on her annuity] so that there is little less than nothing available for her now.

"I wonder what we ought to do and what we can do for her welfare. If she is really insane and it is necessary for her to be confined in some institution it might be important to know whether she has, anywere, a legal settlement. . . ."[2]

Answering Rowell's letter as soon as he received it, Frost wrote,

"This is no worse than I have been expecting. . . . If no state will have her and I haven't the means to have her taken care of in a private institution, what happens then? I am too shaken at the moment to know what to propose. It may not be an incurable case. My hope is that what has been pronounced insanity may turn out no more than the strange mixture of hysteria and eccentricity she has shown us so much of. If so, she might be perfectly manageable at large in the company of somebody like Louie Merriam. But I should want them to come to rest somewhere and should feel obliged to contribute a little to make it possible. . . .

"We are just back from Amherst and in here where letters seem forever in reaching us. Will you wire at my expense if you wish to see me to instruct me as to how I shall approach the Portland police without assuming more responsibility than I am equal to? I may say that there isn't the haste that there would be if my personal attendance could do anything to soothe or comfort Jean. It's a sad business."[3]

On the same day that Rowell informed Frost of Jeanie's predicament, her friend Miss Merriam wrote to Rowell, "This in confidence: I do not have confidence that her *brother* would not be cold and heartless; *but,* will *you* try to see if he will help bear expense at sanitareum, if she has not enough [from her annuity]. A few weeks or months. I would go with doctor and her to Boston, when she goes—I must! If only I might remain with her. She will be frantic *when I leave her.*"[4]

Frost gained additional instructions from Rowell before starting alone by train through the White Mountains to Bethel, Maine, and down to Portland. The long and tedious journey gave him time enough to weigh his own responsibilities to his sister, and to mull over the insinuation that he had been "cold and heartless" to her. From childhood days, he and Jeanie had been so much alike in so many ways that they had found special methods of taunting and tormenting each other. While their mother was alive she had managed to serve as a buffer between them. She had educated them at home, in San Francisco, because their sensitivities made it painful for them to tolerate the atmosphere of public schools, and their nervous problems had caused their mother to indulge them, always with the best of intentions.

During those childhood days in San Francisco, Jeanie had naturally matured faster than her brother. By the time he was ten and she was eight, she could read and write better than he. Prior to this triumph, she frequently gave way to long spells of crying which puzzled her mother. But Jeanie's rapid advances in learning to read and write seemed to give her a new confidence which expressed itself in boasts of superiority over her brother. After they moved to New England and completed their grammar school education in their mother's Salem classroom, Jeanie did so much better than Rob in taking entrance examinations for high school that he was made miserable by his own lack of self-confidence. They entered the freshman class in Lawrence at the same time, but at the end of the year their report cards showed Jeanie could no longer be scornful of her brother's stupidity: he led the class. As though in self-defense against all of her difficulties,

Jeanie began to withdraw into a realm of make-believe. As a high-school sophomore, she slipped back into much the same moods of tears and depression through which she had so often suffered, years earlier, in San Francisco. Her mother became increasingly perplexed by Jeanie's frequent spells of hysterical raving. Once, when her brother tried to bring her out of a particularly noisy crying-spell, he slapped her across the face and stopped her long enough to prompt her to say, with reproachful scorn, "You cad, you coward."

After their mother died in 1900, Jeanie and Rob became increasingly hostile toward each other. He would never forget the dreadful scenes she had created, in the presence of his baffled children, at the Derry farm while occasionally visiting there. Her most embarrassing performance, there, occurred in June of 1907, when Elinor was away at a lying-in home, awaiting the birth of her sixth child. That time, altercations between sister and brother built to the crisis which occurred when Jeanie ran out of the house and up the road, spilling coffee from the cup in her hand, and screaming hysterically. Her brother, upset by what the neighbors might say or do, took from its hiding-place the revolver he always kept loaded, ran after her, and threatened to kill her if she didn't get back in the house. Jeanie was fascinated by the discovery that her brother had a revolver, and she returned with him, promising to leave town immediately if he would give it to her. The offer seemed a bargain, and he gladly gave her the weapon, unloaded, not caring what she might do with it.

There had been no further visits from Jeanie while the Frosts lived in Derry, and no further contacts prior to the departure of the Frost family for England in 1912. Elinor tried to keep up some contact by writing to her occasionally, and Jeanie's answers usually contained requests for money. For a time, her annuity and the salary she earned from school-teaching provided adequate support, although she was constantly imploring Rowell to send her advances.[5] Frost had written her from England, at least once, to tell of his triumph in getting two books published. He had also sent her, from England, some of the most favorable reviews.

When he returned to the United States and tried to create a new basis of rapport between them by going out of his way to visit her, she seemed particularly grateful to him for his urging that she should stop teaching, long enough to acquire a college degree. In the fall of 1915, she tried to enter the University of Michigan. as a special student, and encountered difficulties because she had never completed the fourth year of her high-school program. After generous concessions were made by the authorities, she was admitted to the University of Michigan in February of 1916, and her brother did give her some financial support.

During the summer of 1916, Frost had met in Franconia a professor of English who was on vacation from the University of Michigan, Morris P. Tilley. The two men spoke of the extraordinary fact that Frost's sister, forty years old, was a special student at Michigan, and Tilley offered to do what he could for her when he returned. That fall, he wrote to say he was in touch with Jeanie, who seemed to be getting along remarkably well, considering her odd academic status. She had slowly been passing entrance examinations and was bold enough to believe she could complete her four-year course in two and a half years, if she worked through each summer session. Tilley, having talked with several people who knew Jeanie, was forced to admit that she had "made last year upon two of her instructors and two of the college officers . . . the impression of extreme eccentricity." He concluded, "Since a good position after graduation will in good part depend upon recommendations of her professors, I shall impress upon her the necessity of winning their good opinion."[6]

While Jeanie was trying to complete the entrance examinations that would enable her to be graduated at the end of two and a half years, her brother and Wilbur Rowell frequently shared their acquired evidences that she did indeed give the impression of "extreme eccentricity" at Ann Arbor. Her place of abode changed frequently, and the problems she encountered with her various landlords were pathetic. She was consistent only in her habit of making last-minute appeals for gifts, loans, or advances on her annuity, in order to pay pressing bills, and both men continued to help her financially. Her brother became increasingly disturbed, however, by her radical opinions concerning social and political questions. Her idealistic liking for extreme forms of socialism and communism was oddly counterbalanced by her love for Kaiser Wilhelm and the German people. She bitterly opposed the entry of the United States into the war and participated in protest marches. Nevertheless, she did complete her planned course of study at Michigan, and was graduated with a Bachelor of Arts degree in August of 1918.

Adequately prepared to teach German, Latin, and French, at the high-school level, Jeanie was not able to secure a good position. With the aid of her friend Louie Merriam, who had taken some courses with her at Michigan, she returned to New England and started teaching again. The high-school position she obtained was in the town of Mill River, Massachusetts, about fifteen miles north of Amherst, and so close to her brother that he was displeased. Students and townspeople in Mill River soon became annoyed by her indiscreet ways of expressing her pacifist views and her sympathies for Germany. One day when she accidentally walked into a Red Cross gathering, where the ladies were knitting, she was asked to help them complete their quota of sweaters for the boys overseas. With typical scorn, she replied, "Send the boys home, and their mothers will knit for them."[7] That single remark precipitated a series of persecutions calculated to drive her out of town. The worst moment occurred on the morning of Armistice Day, 1918, when one of the teachers "demanded in an altogether insufferable manner" that Miss Frost celebrate with them by saluting the flag.[8] She refused, and was nearly mobbed by students and teachers alike. Fearing violence, she fled from the high school, called a taxi, and gave directions to the home of her brother in Amherst.

Frost, sick in bed with influenza, had been in no mood to learn that his sister had arrived, unexpectedly, with a request that he pay the bill for the taxi fare from Mill River to Amherst. Jeanie, storming into his bedroom, infuriated him with her account of how she had barely escaped being murdered by the brutes in Mill River. She had no money, and her brother gave her a few dollars. But when she asked if he would help her find another teaching position, he refused. Taunting her with sarcasms, he said he had friends who wrote for the socialistic-communistic sheet called the *Masses* in New York City, and maybe he could get her a job with those who thought as she did. Enraged by his mockery, she fled again. That evening she telephoned her sister-in-law to say there was no need to worry about Rob's influenza: people as bad as he never died of illness.[9] That was the last word from Jeanie until Frost learned that she had been locked up in Portland as a "demented" case. To Rowell, he then commented on her Amherst visit:

"The last time we saw Jean she came to us at Amherst a fugitive from a mob that was going to throw her into a mill-pond for refusing to kiss the flag. The war was just ending and she was actually in tears for the abdicated Emperor. Nothing she said or did was natural. I should have had her examined by an alienist then if I had known how to manage it without disturbing her. Looking back I can see that she hasn't been right for years. She has always simply dismayed the children with her wild talk. . . ."[10]

If Frost, during his winding ride through the mountains by train from Littleton, New Hampshire, to Portland, Maine, did use his leisure to review these past relations with his sister, he may have been in no mood to sympathize with her for what subsequently happened. He expected to find her still held in custody by the police. Instead, he learned that Miss Merriam had rescued her by finding a doctor in West Pownal, Maine, who had taken Jeanie into his own home for observation and treatment. The police told Frost about the decision of the other doctor, who had insisted that Miss Frost should be placed in a mental institution.[11] On the strength of this information, Frost began to suspect the motives of Miss Merriam, who might want control of Jean's annuity. Having decided that his sister should be taken to the State Hospital in Augusta, he obtained the necessary papers for commitment, and was accompanied to West Pownal by a woman authorized to serve as a sheriff. He was not well received: Miss Merriam clung to Jeanie and insisted that Frost's decision was further proof that he was "cold and cruel." After an unpleasant fracas, in which Miss Merriam used her fingernails enough to draw blood on Frost's face, he and the sheriff managed to force the hysterical Jeanie into a taxi. They took her to the State Hospital, and the understanding there reached with the doctors was that Frost would be notified if or when his sister was able to leave.[12] Not long after he returned to Franconia from Maine, he confided to his friend Untermeyer his thoughts concerning what had happened:

"I must have told you I have a sister Jeanie two or three years younger than myself. . . .

"The police picked her up in Portland Maine the other day insane as nearly as we can make out on the subject of the war. She took the police for German officers carrying her off for immoral use. She took me for someone else when she saw me.

She shouted to me by name to save her from whoever she thought I was in person.[13]

"I was prepared for this by what I saw of her a year ago (a year and a half ago) when she came to us at Amherst, a fugitive from a mob in a small town fifty [fifteen] miles away who were going to throw her into a mill pond for refusing to kiss the flag. She got Hell out of the war. She turned everything she could think of to express her abhorrence of it: pro-German, pacifist, internationalist, draft-obstructor, and seditionist.

"She has always been antiphysical and a sensibilitist. I must say she was pretty well broken by the coarseness and brutality of the world before the war was thought of. This was partly because she thought she ought to be on principle. She has had very little use for me. I am coarse for having had children and coarse for having wanted to succeed a little. She made a birth in the family the occasion for writing us once of the indelicacy of having children. Indelicacy was the word. Long ago I disqualified myself from helping her through a rough world by my obvious liking for the world's roughness.

"But it took the war to put her beside herself, poor girl. Before that came to show her what coarseness and brutality really were, she had been satisfied to take it out in hysterics, though hysterics as time went on of a more and more violent kind. I really think she thought in her heart that nothing would do justice to the war but going insane over it. She was willing to go almost too far to show her feeling about it, the more so that she couldn't find anyone who would go far enough. One half the world seemed unendurably bad and the other half unendurably indifferent. She included me in the unendurably indifferent. A mistake. I belong to the unendurably bad.

"And I suppose I am a brute in that my nature refuses to carry sympathy to the point of going crazy just because someone else goes crazy, or of dying just because someone else dies. As I get older I find it easier to lie awake nights over other people's troubles. But that's as far as I go to date. In good time I will join them in death to show our common humanity."[14]

The first trip which Frost made to Augusta, to call on Jeanie after she had been committed, was in May of 1920, and he found her sane enough to express her bitterness against him for his decision to have her put away. Answering his questions as briefly as possible, she sat rigidly on a straight-back chair, facing him, her eyes closed.[15] After his next visit, about two months later, he wrote to Rowell:

"I have been over twice to see Jean, and should have been oftener if the journey weren't so long and expensive. When I was with her she was nearly rational—not quite. But she is in a semi-violent ward and the doctors tell me she is noisy and destructive at times. Her general health is bad. I should think she might not live long. Whether she is happy as may be where she is I don't quite make out. She expressed to me a wish to stay and 'take the treatment.' She shows a disposition to run away, though, that deprives her of the freedom that milder cases have of walking in the yard. The doctors say she must have been years in reaching her present state. . . ."[16]

Some time earlier, he had written to Rowell in regard to the suggestion that Frost be made guardian of his sister so that the annuity to which she was entitled (insufficient to pay her expenses) might be turned over to the hospital through his hands: "I'm sure Jean wants me made her guardian now. . . . Jean hoped for a long time that she was going to be able to try the world again. She has about given that up now. The most she can expect is to be made to feel at home where she is. She will be easier in her mind, I'm sure, when she is using her own money to pay her expenses."[17]

Mrs. Frost went once with her husband to visit Jeanie, and their separate impressions were quite different. Frost wrote to Rowell, "It's good Jean wants me appointed her guardian. She can be very sane in a letter—and in conversation too at times. Elinor and I went to see her a few weeks ago and found her fairly well. I was surprised at the personal interest Dr. [Forrest C.] Tyson, the Superintendent, showed in her and the special account he was able to give of her case. I am sure she has the best care and is at least as happy as I have seen her for years. That's not happy enough to smile much. I just mean she has her satisfactions from day to day almost like a normal person."[18]

Mrs. Frost wrote, "We were in Augusta the first week in May, and she was not able to talk sensibly or coherently for five minutes. Dr. Tyson is a man of ability, culture, and great sympathy. He takes a special interest in Jean, and I think they have tried very hard to cure her, but he does not now expect that she will ever be able to live outside an institution." Mrs. Frost's main purpose in writing was something else:

"I am enclosing a letter which Robert received from Jeanie a few days ago. Some of her letters sound very sane, but many of them reveal clearly the condition of her mind, and I think this one does that, and is also very pathetic."[19] Jeanie's letter contained, among other things, her attempt to explain her condition and the causes of it:

"Dear Rob,-

"I was sorry Elinor could not come to see me. A week with her might do me a very great deal of good.

"I am not well, not able and never have been since being here able to be on parole to go out walking on the grounds. I am depressed nearly all the time and when I get a slight relief from that I have spells of excitement when they dont know what I would do.

"I am very peculiar and did not start right. If I ever was well and natural it was before I can remember. I hate to have anyone understand how I feel in a way. To the mind of anyone who could understand the condition of my mind, there could not be any worse horror. That is the way I have been for the past twenty years and before that, only I did not use to understand—I used to lay it to causes that had nothing to do with it. I used to think if I could only get out of Lawrence I would be all right, etc.

"People always slight me. That's what I used to mind. It isnt that really now I think. It's just entire boredom, lack of interest in books, everything. My heart is steel, I cannot see, I cannot feel.

> *This heart of stone*
> *Ice-cold, whatever I do*
> *Small and cold and hard*
> *Of all hearts the worst of all*

"When I have been sick here as I have been twice, delirious, so that I couldn't recognize anyone, I imagine myself forever unable to move and without any feeling or interest, or else I pace back and forth feeling forever glum, caring for nothing. It isn't what I see interests me. I wouldn't care if I was blind and couldn't see a thing. It's only what I am that I care about. On the other hand I resist that I *won't* be *ambitious*. . . .

"Then of course there's that contradiction in one that makes me say to 'H--- with praise or success' and think I'd as soon crack a safe as to be proud of anything I'd done or knew. The summer I was eight when you and I were with 'Aunt' Blanche at Mrs. Braggs in Napa[20] my head got into a rather bad condition owing to being separated from mama for such a long time, six weeks. I was not homesick, nor would have been especially glad if mama had come. . . .

"The doctor says I put up a defense around myself. Of course I don't consciously. As the doctors say I must fight this off. I think I will make up my mind to have a good time. That's the whole trouble. Want to and can't.

"The other night we had a little birthday party on the violent ward. I enjoyed that and they did. The best patients are on the worst wards, but I suppose they would break glass out here.

"Wouldn't you buy me a small graphaphone, the smallest size you can find? It wouldn't cost more than ten or twenty dollars, would it? The patients would like it and could dance by it and we might have some pleasant times. When there's a party now sometimes there's nothing to do for the very insane ones can't play cards.

"They have enjoyed the candy you and Elinor have given me for them but now I'd rather give them the music. . . .

"When I get these excited spells I feel quite a little better, my nose bleeds slightly. When I put my handerkerchief in just once there's blood on it and my hands won't stop bleeding. But when I'm quiet and rational my blood doesn't flow in such a way as to cause me pleasure. It's my mind, as they say is controlling the circulation of my blood. . . .

"That was a fine lot of magazines you and Elinor sent me. Have you got any more? And if not too much trouble I would like Theatre Classic and Photoplay but I won't ask for these motion picture magazines again as I suppose you have to buy them on purpose. The patients need the magazines. . . .

"When one is almost absolutely without resources, doesn't care for travel, books or music, he or she is badly off. Jean."[21]

Jeanie lived for nine years in the State Hospital in Augusta, Maine, and died there from natural causes, at the age of fifty-three, on the seventh of September 1929.[22] Her brother, three years after her death, talked to his close friend John Bartlett concerning her, and Bartlett made the following notes:

"The talk had turned to the subject of adjustment and maladjusted. Frost . . . observed how he could look back, probably Bartlett could look back, and see times when it seemed a miracle they had 'come through.' Will had something to do with it. He could contemplate his sister's life . . . and see half a dozen times when by making the right decision she could have saved herself. To an extent, it was a matter of choice. One could run away from things in cowardice . . . one could run away from them and retreat into the ego, in the direction of paranoia. . . . We all have our souls—and minds—to save. And it seems a miracle that we do; not once but several times. He could look back and see his hanging by a thread. His sister wasn't able to save hers. She built the protecting illusion around herself and went the road of dementia praecox."[23]

10

TROUBLE IN FRANCONIA

"One of the books I am writing at the moment is to be called On Looking into the Rich. Won't I consider them, though! I count myself peculiarly qualified for looking into them by my freedom from prejudice against them. Neither they nor their trappings make me the least bit embarrassed self-conscious or unhappy with the bitches and sons of bitches."[1]

DURING the summer of 1920, Robert Frost felt himself surrounded by too many troubles in Franconia, and he began to look for avenues of escape. He and his sister had acquired from their mother a romantic habit of idealizing distant scenes, particularly when immediate irritations became annoying. His impulsive acts of running away, in the past, had often surprised his neighbors. While he lived on the Derry farm he once arranged with a nearby farmer to care for Frost's cow, chickens, and horse long enough to let him escape completely from the dreariness of early spring mudtime. On that occasion, he had taken his family to New York City, had rented a furnished apartment alongside the Sixth Avenue elevated railway, and had stayed there for a full month.[2] Shortly after his return from that trip he had confided to a friend, "Sometime we intend to be [living] nearer New York than we are, if it can come about in the right way. But that is one of the dreams."[3]

Summer after summer, during those Derry years, he had further surprised neighboring farmers by letting his garden go to weeds while he and his family took month-long vacations in either the White or the Green Mountains.[4] Later, the runaway venture to England had been motivated in part by the dream of living under thatch, but soon after the Frosts reached England all of them grew homesick. From that distance they wistfully remembered as idyllic the life on their Derry farm: "We can't hope to be happy long out of New England. I never knew how much of a Yankee I was till I had been out of New Hampshire a few months. I suppose the life in such towns as Plymouth and Derry . . . is the best on earth."[5] But he did not choose to live in either Plymouth or Derry after his return from England, and he had barely settled on the farm in Franconia when he began to regret it: "I see a possibility of my getting south to farm sooner or later," he wrote to Bartlett. "But this place will have to serve for a year or two . . ."[6] Mrs. Frost, worrying about school arrangements for the children in Franconia, and dreading "the possibility of their disliking the whole place," had suspected that it might be "still harder to sell the farm than it had been to buy it."[7]

For a time, however, all of the Frosts had been delighted with their Franconia hideaway and had been charmed by the picturesque games they played on that hillside farm. Among those games was the chance to participate, each spring, in the elaborate ritual of tapping their own maple trees, collecting the sap, carrying tin pails of it to the sugar house, and boiling it down into either maple syrup or sugar. Willis Herbert, former owner of their farm, easily convinced them that any successful handling of the entire syrup-making operation required expert supervision; he and his family would be glad to take charge of the enterprise, accepting as remuneration for their work nothing more than a fair amount of syrup. The arrangement was worked out satisfactorily, for it did permit all of the Frosts to do as much or as little work as they liked in the sugar orchard.

Just once Frost and a friend volunteered to keep the fire stoked under the steaming pans of sap, throughout a night, so that Will Herbert and his relatives could go home and sleep. The friend was a young man from New York City, Raymond Holden, whom Frost had first met under odd circumstances, in Franconia during the summer of 1915. Invited to read his poems and talk before a group of wealthy summer visitors at a nearby hotel called the Forest Hills House, Frost had felt that most of his listeners on that occasion had treated him as a mere curiosity. By contrast, young Holden's attention had been so rapt and sympathetic that Frost had instinctively made him the focal point of that audience. At the conclusion of the reading, Holden was introduced as one

[136]

who wrote poetry and aspired to become a poet. Born in New York, and educated in a private school there, he had gone to Princeton, where he would have been graduated with the Class of 1915 if he had not withdrawn, during his senior year, after growing disgusted with courses he was required to take. Liking Holden as poet and rebel against the academic, Frost deliberately cultivated a friendship with him. The Frost farm was only a mile or so from Sugar Hill, where Holden was staying, and he was encouraged to become a regular visitor at the farm. During the remainder of that summer, he became well acquainted with all of the Frosts, joining them in their swimming expeditions, their baseball games, their berry-picking, and their mountain-climbing. With the famous poet, he helped clear the brush from paths through the woods on the farm, walked the country roads, made shopping trips to the village, and shared views on versification.

The friendship thus begun was tested by circumstances which began when "Pancho" Villa's depredations along the Mexican border caused President Wilson to send troops to Texas under the command of General Pershing. Holden, having enlisted in a cavalry squadron of the New York State National Guard, was among the forces used to patrol the Mexican border. As a result, he was absent from Franconia during the summers of 1916, 1917, and 1918. Throughout his stay in the service, however, he and Frost corresponded with each other, and Holden confessed in his letters that as soon as he could return to civilian life he hoped to take up residence in Franconia. By the time he did return there, in the summer of 1919, he had married and had acquired a substantial inheritance from his grandfather. After gaining his wife's consent, he announced that they would live in Franconia year-round, so that he might be near Frost while continuing his effort to establish himself as a poet.

While Holden was exploring Franconia real estate in the hope of finding a vantage point on which to build his home, Frost offered to sell him the uphill half of Frost's own fifty-acre farm. Delighted with the possibilities thus made available to him, and considering himself richer than he was, the young man did not even realize that Frost was driving a hard bargain. Having paid $1,000 to Willis Herbert when he had bought the farm, Frost offered to sell Holden the twenty-five upland acres for $2,500 on the condition that if the time should come when Frost should be forced by circumstances to sell the other half of the farm—containing house and barn—Holden would buy it from him for an additional $2,500. These terms were immediately accepted.

Although Frost might have hesitated over being so ruthless in gouging a worshiper, there was an element of vindictiveness in arranging these terms. Frost's attitude toward the wealthy was controlled in part by his pleasure in bolstering his own ego through outsmarting any one of them. In this case, his liking for Holden and for the young man's poetry was apparently counterbalanced by his eagerness to get back at him for being rich, at a time when Frost needed money. Holden quickly paid the first $2,500 and began building his house before the summer of 1919 ended. Immediately, the friendship between the two men seemed much closer than it had been, and Holden was glad for the excuse to spend more time with the Frost family.

The better acquainted he became with the Frost children, the more deeply Holden recognized the tensions in the relationships of all four to their father. The spirited and attractive Lesley, twenty years old, seemed to become increasingly capable of standing up to him in asserting her own wishes and prejudices. The dour and frequently sullen Carol, seventeen, was inclined to use silence and withdrawal as his best defenses against his father's persistently harsh faultfinding. The attractive Irma, sixteen, had odd mannerisms which seemed to reflect the prudishness of both her parents concerning sexual matters. The fourteen-year-old Marjorie, fragile and shy, seemed to be her father's favorite. Each of these young people showed artistic gifts, and all of them spent considerable time in writing, although their father did not seem enthusiastic over their attempts to write poetry.[8] He implied, half humorously and half seriously, that one poet in the family was enough.[9]

Holden noticed other tensions in the Frost household. It frequently happened that when he came down through the woods to Frost's back door, from the Sugar Hill place where he and his wife and son were living while their house was being built, he would hear sharp words being exchanged in unpleasant arguments between Mr. and Mrs. Frost. His knock on the door always brought these arguments to an abrupt end, and even when he and Frost left the house for walks in the woods, or down to the village, no word was ever spoken of whatever trouble they had left behind. Once, after there seemed to be much heat in what Holden overheard before he knocked, Frost was not immediately ready to go, as planned. He disappeared for a few moments, and came back with a gift for Holden: a manuscript copy of a poem Frost said he had finished writing the night before. Whether Holden was supposed to find any metaphorical hints of the silenced argument, here, he was not sure. The poem was "Good-by and Keep Cold":

This saying good-by on the edge of the dark
And the cold to an orchard so young in the bark
Reminds me of all that can happen to harm
An orchard away at the end of the farm
All winter, cut off by a hill from the house.
I don't want it girdled by rabbit and mouse,
I don't want it dreamily nibbled for browse
By deer, and I don't want it budded by grouse.
(If certain it wouldn't be idle to call
I'd summon grouse, rabbit, and deer to the wall
And warn them away with a stick for a gun.)
I don't want it stirred by the heat of the sun.
(We made it secure against being, I hope,
By setting it out on a northerly slope.)
No orchard's the worse for the wintriest storm;
But one thing about it, it mustn't get warm.
"How often already you've had to be told,
Keep cold, young orchard. Good-by and keep cold.
Dread fifty above more than fifty below."
I have to be gone for a season or so.
My business awhile is with different trees,
Less carefully nurtured, less fruitful than these,
And such as is done to their wood with an ax—
Maples and birches and tamaracks.
I wish I could promise to lie in the night
And think of an orchard's arboreal plight
When slowly (and nobody comes with a light)
Its heart sinks lower under the sod.
But something has to be left to God.[10]

Raymond Holden did not know that the last line in "Good-by and Keep Cold"[11] touched on a notion which provided a subject for continuing argument between Frost and his wife. According to Mrs. Frost, it was safer to leave nothing to God, even to view God as nothing. Her atheistical views, often expressed with bitterness, had found reflection in two of her husband's early poems.[12] While in Franconia, he gave one brief account of an almost pleasant argument with his wife over religious matters:

"Elinor has just come out flat-footed against God conceived either as the fourth person seen with Shadrack, Meshack and Tobedwego in the fiery furnace or without help by the Virgin Mary. How about as a Shelleyan principal or spirit coeternal with the rock part of creation, I ask. Nonsense and you know it's nonsense Rob Frost, only you're afraid you'll have bad luck or lose your standing in the community if you speak your mind. Spring, I say, returneth and the maple sap is heard dripping in the buckets—allow me to sell you a couple. (We can quote you the best white first-run sugar at a dollar a pound unsight and unseen—futures.) Like a woman she says Pshaw."[13]

Frost never mentioned to Holden, during their many conversations, anything specific about his own religious belief or his wife's unbelief. Much of the talk, during their periods of working, playing, walking, was devoted to local gossip, and Frost's prudishness revealing itself at times in his comments on sexual irregularities among the villagers. Once when the two men spent an afternoon clearing out brush and weed-trees in an area which extended uphill between Frost's house and the site where Holden was building, Frost began talking about an attractive local girl. She was only sixteen or seventeen, but according to village gossip she didn't spend many summer evenings at home. It seemed to Holden that Frost took pleasure in recounting one story about this girl's amorous exploits with a local man, of how someone had recently come on them at an awkward moment in the woods. Frost concluded his account by saying, after the colloquial manner of the region, "Ain't that sumpin?" Before the afternoon of wood-cutting was over, the girl herself appeared at the edge of their clearing. Holden later described the incident:

"It happened that while we were working . . . this young woman, wearing a thin cotton dress without sleeves, her hair tied behind her neck, and falling from the knot loosely down her back, came walking barefoot down the woods path along the edge of the clearing. She held a long piece of Timothy grass between her teeth. As she passed us, she looked at us with wide eyes, as if they had stopped moving while the rest of her moved on. Robert looked at me. He knew that I knew who she was. He nudged me with his elbow, picking up his axe with the other hand. The girl's face changed a little, but she didn't smile. If Robert greeted her, I didn't see him do it. When the girl had gone, her haunches moving pleasantly as she steadied herself on the uneven path, Robert sat down and looked at me. He said nothing as he rose to his feet. We both began chopping vigorously. Neither of us mentioned the girl again that day."[14]

There was another topic of sexual love which the two men almost discussed, that same day. In spite of Holden's reticence, Frost had correctly guessed that Holden's wife, accustomed to the city, had grown unhappy over the prospect of living in the woods, year round, and had begun to look for ways to escape. What worried Frost was that Raymond's marital estrangement seemed to be reflected in his becoming too intimate with Lesley. These fears and suspicions were heightened, during the summer of 1919, when Lesley announced to her parents that she and Carol were going to climb Mount Washington with Raymond and with a male guest[15] then visiting with the Holdens. The four of them carried blankets, together with enough food for the two-day trip, and slept under the stars near the top of the mountain. Not long after their return to Franconia, Holden wrote a poem inspired by this experience. It was entitled "Night Above the Tree-Line," and when he sold it to *Poetry* magazine that winter, he dedicated it to Lesley. Pleased, Lesley told her father about it, and Frost sternly demanded that Holden must wire Harriet Monroe instructions to cancel the dedication. The demand was carried out, but Holden was hurt.

Although the underlying awkwardness gradually increased between Frost and Holden, there were many days when their friendship seemed to remain at a high level of mutual cordiality. During one of their longest hikes—over Moosilauke Mountain and down into the township of Warren—Holden told Frost a story he had recently found in a local history of Warren: a story about a woman who had become a pauper there and who had been accused of being a witch, with evil powers over her husband and other men. Frost was fascinated by the possibilities of poetic extensions, in the story, and asked if he might borrow the local history. The book was lent as requested, and Frost used the story as the basis for his dramatic monologue entitled "The Pauper Witch of Grafton."[16]

The last important sharing of experiences between Frost and Holden in Franconia occurred in late March of 1920, during the night they spent keeping the fire blazing under the pans in the sugar house. Some details of that night remained vivid for Holden years after: "The sense of Robert's talk, uninhibited and genial, probing and revealing, the firelight flickering through the stove doors on his face as he sat crouched, fingering a piece of wood, the smell of the thickening sap and its wavering steam, have never left me. Most of all, I have never forgotten Robert's extraordinary face which, with its full lips, always gave the impression that it was trying to decide whether to speak or to whistle. He was happy in a task like that in which we were engaged, and his remarkable countenance showed the happiness coming from the kind of work which blended effort and will without too much pressure upon either and which resulted in the making of something, the importance of which did not have to be considered."[17] As the night vigil continued, both men took turns making the slippery journey out around the sugar house to the shed in the rear, where the wood was stored. Sometimes they both stepped out into the cold night and stood in the moonlight watching the "glitter of the frozen rivulets which, in the warm sun of the afternoon before, had been runnels of thaw-water, running down the sloping floor of the sugar orchard."[18] Frost later caught those "silver lizards" in his poem entitled "A Hillside Thaw." He caught something else in another poem, "Evening in a Sugar Orchard," based on the adventure of that night:

> From where I lingered in a lull in March
> Outside the sugarhouse one night for choice,
> I called the fireman with a careful voice
> And bade him leave the pan and stoke the arch:
> "O fireman, give the fire another stoke,
> And send more sparks up chimney with the smoke."
> I thought a few might tangle, as they did,
> Among bare maple boughs, and in the rare
> Hill atmosphere not cease to glow,
> And so be added to the moon up there.

The moon, thought slight, was moon enough to show
On every tree a bucket with a lid,
And on black ground a bear-skin rug of snow.
The sparks made no attempt to be the moon.
They were content to figure in the trees
As Leo, Orion, and the Pleiades.
And that was what the boughs were full of soon.[19]

During all of these pleasantly shared experiences, Frost said nothing to Raymond Holden about the development of a plan to look farther south in New England for another farm. Still remembering his former dream of living closer to New York City, he did gather suggestions from friends, and actually began looking at property in Connecticut and southern Massachusetts early in May of 1920. After two exploratory trips he came so near to reaching a final decision that he was ready to accept the offer of a loan. "All right then," he wrote to Untermeyer early in June of 1920, "if you have a thousand dollars you can lend me please send it with your blessing to my brand new address Monson, Mass. some day this week."[20] A short time later, he returned the check for $1,000, implying that he didn't need it. His interests had actually shifted from Massachusetts to the region around Arlington, Vermont, where Alfred Harcourt spent his summers.

Frost had another way of getting money easily for the purchase of a new farm. All he needed to do was to inform Holden that the Frosts were leaving Franconia, and that under the terms of their agreement it was now necessary to ask that Holden buy the other half of the Frost farm for $2,500. So far, however, Frost had not given Holden even so much as a hint of the plan to move, and perhaps the delay in bringing up the subject was caused in part by Frost's troubled conscience. What he seemed to need was a preliminary way to rationalize and justify the fact that he must hurt and disappoint Holden. Untermeyer helped, innocently, by writing to ask Frost's opinion of another young poet, Merrill Root, who had formerly been one of Frost's students at Amherst. In his answer, Frost found excuse for mentioning Holden, praising him as a poet, and condemning him as one of the rich. The answer began with considerations of Merrill Root:

"I count him a friend, and just for that reason I have left him to break in among you poets without my doubtful help.

Now that two or three of you have noticed him of your own motion I should think I could speak without prejudice to his chances. He's not in the same classification with Raymond Holden whom I throw out the window onto your spear-points. I'm pretty sure he's a poet. It would please me a lot if you should see it as I see it. Max Eastman's good opinion ought to weigh with you if Harriet Monroe's doesn't. I say no more. But I think you ought to make your half-inclination whole and go in for Root, or rooting for Root, a little. He's some sort of a homely devil of perversity that should commend itself more to you than to me. His father is a poor preacher and Merrill is himself a Quaker preaching, though not ordained, in orthodox pulpits. I don't know how he gets by in any pulpit with the radical stuff that froths out of him. He had his troubles as a conscientious objector before the fact, if you are not too tired of the breed.

"But Raymond Holden. They say we poor expect the rich to consider the poor but when we are asked to consider the rich, we start talking a priori. One of the books I am writing at this moment is to be called On Looking into the Rich. Won't I consider them, though! I count myself peculiarly qualified for looking into them by my freedom from prejudice against them. Neither they nor their trappings make me the least bit embarrassed self-conscious or unhappy with the bitches and sons of bitches. I have come right up to them and looked in without fear and without even dislike. I believe I honestly liked them not only for themselves but for their money before I looked into them. I was just the one for doing them justice, I should say. But what have I seen in them? Well, the book tells that. Buy the book."[21]

It was apparently necessary to make some kind of case against Raymond Holden, defensively. Holden later said, "I did not in 1919, and I do not now know how much planning to take himself away from Franconia he had done before we reached our agreement. I do know that if I had believed that he would be gone from Franconia almost before the home I built on the land I bought from him was completed, I should have thought twice about making such a deal. I didn't know, either, that while he was negotiating with me, he was also dealing with Louis Untermeyer, to borrow money to buy a farm elsewhere. In the spring of 1920, he did borrow $1,000 from Louis which he returned almost immediately. It may well be that the second part of his agreement with me had occurred to him as a better way of solving his problem. . . . This turn of affairs affected me deeply. I reluctantly felt that he had used me as a convenience. I even, for a time, believed that his friendship for me was insincere and motivated by what he thought he could get out of me. This feeling did not persist."[22]

At the time, Holden's feeling did not develop fast enough to keep up with events. Early in the fall of 1920, his Franconia home was so nearly completed that he was able to move into it with his estranged wife and, by then, their two children. At about the same time, Frost was stripping his Franconia house and shipping his furniture to South Shaftsbury, Vermont, by freight. Lesley was sent away for her own safety, according to Frost; she spent the summer of 1920 working as a bookseller in New York City. Carol and Irma departed for South Shaftsbury first, in the Frosts' newly acquired secondhand Overland car, loaded with belongings. A few days later, near the end of September 1920, Raymond Holden used his own car to carry the Frosts and their daughter Marjorie from their emptied Franconia home to the Littleton railway station. It was an awkward leave-taking, for reasons which Holden regretfully stated years later: "It turned out . . . that I had not only contributed to his desire to leave the place he really loved but had also given him the means of doing it."[23]

11

TRANSPLANTED: A NEW START

*I've been sick. . . . The trouble seems to be that I wasn't
taken up carefully enough in Franconia nor replanted
soon enough in South Shaftsbury. It has been a bad job
of transplanting. . . ."*[1]

NEITHER Raymond Holden nor Louis Untermeyer knew that
during the twelve months prior to the actual move from Franconia various members of the Frost family had made exploratory visits to the southern part of Vermont. The first nudge in
that direction had been given by Mrs. Dorothy Canfield Fisher,
the attractive and successful poet-novelist whom Frost had met
in Boston in December of 1915 when she attended the dramatization of his narrative dialogues. Soon after that meeting
she had written him from her home in Arlington, Vermont,
"That was by far the best part of my Boston trip—meeting you
and hearing you voice my secret and up-to-the-present-time
humble views about poetry. I'm writing to tell you how much
good it did me. . . ."[2] Later, Frost learned from Alfred Harcourt
that Dorothy Canfield and her neighbor Sarah Cleghorn had
recently helped to organize the Poetry Society of Southern
Vermont; around them had grown a literary group held together by nonliterary friendships. In the summer of 1919,
Frost had received from Mrs. Halley Phillips Gilchrist, secretary of that Society, a gracious letter inviting him and Mrs.
Frost to visit friends and admirers in Arlington, to stay as
guests with the Gilchrists there, and to give a reading of his
poems at a meeting of the Society, in the Gilchrist home. He
had answered,

"I had some idea I would be in friendly country in Arlington. I knew Mrs Fisher and Miss Cleghorn were there and I
hoped I might find the Harcourts still there if I came soon
enough . . ."

He went on to say that if the Society would be willing to wait until the hay-fever season had passed, he and Mrs. Frost would gladly accept the invitation: they would plan to stop at Arlington en route to Amherst. He added, "We shall look forward to the ride across states and to seeing you all at Arlington— even a little to reading to you, though I'm not the minstrel I sometimes wish I were and don't pretend to give or experience the pleasure Vachel Lindsay does in public performance."[3]

The plan had been carried out, and the genuinely affectionate reception given the Frosts during their visit in Mrs. Gilchrist's home was pleasurably different from the response provided by the curious and quickly bored summer-people to whom Frost had first read in Franconia. He was flatteringly told that his Arlington reading was an historic event, the likes of which had not occurred in southern Vermont since the celebrated day when Daniel Webster had come over from New Hamphire to deliver a political address on the southern side of nearby Stratton Mountain. The same comparison was pleasantly invoked when the occasion was reported (probably by Mrs. Gilchrist) as news for the Bennington *Banner:*

"Arlington has something at last to match with Stratton's memories of the Daniel Webster visit and address, for Robert Frost, the poet, has visited Arlington and spoken there. There is, however, something quaint in comparing the traditional bombastic presence of the oratorical Webster with the utter quiet sincerity and spontaneity of Mr. Frost. To the large and breathlessly attentive audience which gathered at Mrs. Gilchrist's house to hear him, he read poem after poem as though he were that moment composing them; as though they were as new to him as to anyone. And the people before him, never taking their eyes from his face, listened as though their lives depended on their catching every syllable uttered by this quiet, humorous, sincere voice, for it is to the word sincere that one comes back always in speaking of Mr. Frost."[4]

Still unappeasably hungry for such adoring response, after having been deprived of any public literary attention until the thirty-ninth year of his life, Robert Frost could not help but be attracted by these Vermonters. The same rapt adulation had pervaded the special dinner given by Mrs. Gilchrist in honor of the Frosts, after the reading. Other guests at that dinner included the Fishers, Sarah Cleghorn, and Madison C. Bates, the latter being not only the president of the Poetry

Society but also the principal of Burr and Burton Seminary in nearby Manchester. In this cordial atmosphere, the Frosts confided that they were planning to move down out of the White Mountains to a region where their son might be more successful as farmer and apple-raiser. This beautiful Green Mountain valley, flanked by relatively low and tree-covered or even pasture-crowned mountains, made the Frosts wonder if any suitable farms might be available in or near Arlington. The very next day, they were escorted through the region to consider possibilities.[5] Although they reached no decision before they drove on to Amherst, they returned to Arlington at the start of the Christmas vacation—and they returned again, during the early summer of 1920.[6]

Dorothy Canfield Fisher was the one who finally showed the Frosts the farm they chose to buy: the Peleg Cole place, at the brow of a hill not far below the village of South Shaftsbury —halfway between the towns of Arlington and Bennington —with impressive views of the Green Mountains, to the eastward, and of the Taconic Mountains, to the westward. The farmhouse itself was a colonial oddity, built in 1779: a half-stone cottage, the thick and rough-hewn blocks of stone reaching up to the eaves of the steeply pitched gable roof, front and back; the same stone structure rising to the same height on the sides, with wooden clapboards and trim, painted dark red, ascending above the stone to the gable peaks; a large wooden gable and window thrusting out through the front roof directly over the front door; all the windows and doorways deeply recessed.

The immediate setting heightened the charm of the cottage, shaded by ancient maple, horse chestnut, and elm. Behind the house was a small apple orchard, almost too old to be worth much. To the south of the orchard stood an unpainted weather-beaten barn, and across the road in front of the house stood another barn which belonged with this ninety-acre farm. Downhill to the west of the farmhouse, there was a good-sized pasture with a brook running through the entire length of it.

Several factors made the Frosts hesitate, even after they agreed with each other that they were strongly attracted to the Peleg Cole place. This old farmhouse had no furnace, no running water, no bathroom—and the roof leaked. If they bought it, they could not make the necessary repairs and improvements before it would be time for their fifteen-year-old Marjorie to start her sophomore year in the high school at nearby North Bennington. Mrs. Fisher, serving as cheerful assistant to the Frosts during every step of their deliberations, overcame their doubts by offering them free rooms in what had been her family home before her marriage. It was called The Manse or Brick House, and it was conveniently located on the main street in Arlington, not far away from South Shaftsbury. Her offer was accepted, the bargaining for the Peleg Cole place was completed, and friends were notified long before the actual move was made from New Hampshire to Vermont. As early as June of 1920, when Frost returned to Untermeyer the $1,000 check, he had given fair warning that he would no longer seek a home within commuting distance of New York City:

"I will probably go further off for my farm and fare cheaper. This came to me a trifle suddenly the day I got to Monson. The object in life is hard to keep in mind. I let it slip sometimes, but never for long—never for good and all anyway. In this instance it is apples bees fishing poetry high school and nine or ten rooms. Nothing else matters. Nearness to no particular city matters. . . . Fishing bees poetry apples nine rooms and a high school! All of which we now think are within our unaided means. . . ."[7]

The actual move was made in a piecemeal manner, and on the eighteenth of September 1920 Frost again wrote to Untermeyer from Franconia, "Still here more than anywhere else, though I now practically own a farm (all but paying for it) in South Shaftsbury Vermont and one half of my family remains with me, one third of it [Carol and Irma] being at Arlington Vermont in the manse and one sixth [Lesley] in New York campaigning, not for Cox, not for Harding (whom I should like to see elected if only I was surer he was anti-international), but for [Frederic G.] Melcher of the National Association of Book Publishers."[8]

Even after all the Frosts except Lesley were gathered in Arlington, the repairs and renovations at the Peleg Cole house took longer than had been expected. There was a well with a hand-pump in the front yard, but a better supply of water was found: a hillside spring, some distance across the road from the house. A storage tank had to be built below the spring, and pipes to the house had to be sunk deep enough to keep from freezing in winter. Not until near the middle of November 1920 was Frost able to write, "We're at South Shaftsbury at last. Part of the roof is off for repairs, the furnace is not yet under us and winter is closing in. But we're here."⁹

Exhausted by all these tedious preliminaries, Frost was scarcely in his new home before he began to have reservations about the farm he and his family had chosen to buy. He made the announcement of his decision to one of his friends who had been urging him to look for a farm in the Berkshires. Frost added, "To you alone I will confess I am still looking for a home. I may settle down and like this place. My present agony may be home-sickness for the home I've left behind me rather than for the home that never was on land or sea. . . ."¹⁰

Another cause for hesitation at this time was the poet's financial status and the consequent question of how he could earn money enough to cover living expenses for his family while paying for this farm an amount greater than he had saved from the sale of the Franconia farm. Any ordinary farmer in this fertile valley of the Green Mountains would have considered himself comfortably fixed if he could have counted on the $800 annuity which Robert Frost received without fail from the estate of his long-dead grandfather. But this was going to be no ordinary farm and Frost was no ordinary farmer. As he had hinted, his dream was to work for just one main crop, apples, and to let Carol do most of that work. Still dreaming in that pleasant way, after his arrival at The Manse in Arlington, he had playfully written to another friend who had not yet heard where he was:

"I depose that I have moved a good part of the way to a stone cottage on a hill at South Shaftsbury in southern Vermont on the New York side near the historic town of Bennington where if I have any money left after repairing the roof . . . I mean to plant a new Garden of Eden with a thousand apple trees of some unforbidden variety."¹¹

. . . If he had any money left. The regular salary from Amherst had supplemented royalities, annuities, and profits made at the expense of Raymond Holden. Having walked out of Amherst, because of his rage against Meiklejohn's liberalism, he was now forced to calculate how he could earn the equivalent of that Amherst salary—$4,000 a year. Returns from public readings would help. He was receiving either $50 or $100 for each reading, but at that rate of pay he would be required to give forty to eighty performances in order to gross $4,000 a year from them. Royalties from his three books had never brought him more than a few hundred dollars each year, even when *North of Boston* had been a best seller. The individual poems he sold to magazines (when asked) brought prices ranging from $15 to $30 apiece, but after the publication of *Mountain Interval* his reputation had declined so sharply that few editors seemed eager to ask. Only three new poems of his had appeared in magazines during 1917, only one in 1918, none in 1919, and none in 1920—up to the time of his decision to buy the Peleg Cole place in South Shaftsbury.[12]

All of these discouraging factors had been accumulating since the day he had resigned, in a rage, from Amherst College. Easily victimized by his fears, he worried so much about his future, even before he moved from Franconia, that he seemed to make himself ill. The Franconia doctor informed him that the symptoms—irritability, peevishness, grouchiness, nervous depression, and lack of appetite—suggested jaundice, except that the ailment had failed to turn him yellow: "The doctor was flattering enough to say it would have turned me yellow if there had been any yellow in me to bring to the surface. Little the doctors really know us in our true moral inwardness. If they did they would not make such wild misses in prescribing for us."[13]

One fact afforded cautious encouragement. During the past years, while fewer and fewer poems of his were appearing in print, he had written enough of them to increase his confidence in his having improved his capacities. He needed this confidence, for there continued to be moments when he was nearly paralyzed by the fear that the period of his best writing had ended. One by-product of such moments had been the letter to Untermeyer in which he had said the poet in him died nearly ten years ago, and the most he could do henceforth was to market what he had written back in the nineties. But he was now accumulating so many new poems that he thought he might be ready to start planning for another book. What he liked best was his recently developed knack for making some of his lyrics almost as tight as the classical epigrams he so greatly admired. One of them he called "Fire and Ice":

> *Some say the world will end in fire,*
> *Some say in ice.*
> *From what I've tasted of desire*
> *I hold with those who favor fire.*

> *But if it had to perish twice,*
> *I think I know enough of hate*
> *To say that for destruction ice*
> *Is also great*
> *And would suffice.*[14]

Here was a new style, tone, manner, form, for him, and he had never before managed to achieve such powerful compression. The nearest he could remember was his five-line sarcasm entitled "In Neglect," where the tone and posture differed sharply from "Fire and Ice." Another new poem, "Dust of Snow," recently written, and satisfactory to him in its terse manipulation of opposites, was a quietly symbolic study in blacks-and-whites, all in a single sentence:

> *The way a crow*
> *Shook down on me*
> *The dust of snow*
> *From a hemlock tree*
>
> *Has given my heart*
> *A change of mood*
> *And saved some part*
> *Of a day I had rued.*

While these and other new poems had just begun to accumulate, and while he had still been teaching at Amherst in December of 1919, two other cheering events had occurred. The first of these was a perceptive article entitled "The Neighborliness of Robert Frost," in the *Nation* for the sixth of December 1919. The author, a complete stranger to him, was George Roy Elliott, a Canadian, teaching at Bowdoin College. The article began:

"That very readiness with which critics have responded, during the past five years, to Robert Frost's singular charm has withheld attention from his representative meaning. The local and individual qualities of his art have been praised at the expense of its wider significance. Considered broadly, his work appears as the poetry of true neighborliness emerging from the romance of human brotherhood. The aspiring poetry of human love and fellowship, which has been flowering and reflowering for more than a century, has no doubt had at its root an actual social desire for such brotherhood of man as the world has never yet attained. But the expression of that desire in verse has persistently remained over-idealistic. This is most strikingly the case in such recent 'realistic' poetry as, while determinedly reacting from romance in several other respects, has still clung to certain thinly idealistic notions of human brotherhood. Mr. Frost is distinguished among our realists by his degree of freedom from such notions. He has attained this freedom, not by reacting from romance still more urgently than his fellow-craftsmen, but by keeping his eye more faithfully than they on the facts of human nature in the immediate neighborhood. . . .

"In failing to follow out the implications of this spirit, interpreters have failed to trace the distinctive pattern of Mr. Frost's work as a whole. Miss Amy Lowell has exaggerated its dramatic sadness, and Mr. Louis Untermeyer by way of reaction has exaggerated its lyric gladness. Centrally, however, it is neither sad nor glad. The burdens and limitations of the neighborhood keep the poet from being very glad; but his faith in the latent value of the neighborly spirit prevents him from being very sad. He is more dispassionate and more veracious than his fellow-craftsmen when contemplating the limitations of common life. . . . Keeping his eye on 'Truth with all her matter-of-fact,' and with a smile at once sympathetic and quietly corrective, the poet moves temperamental longings from the center of life to its fringe, where they belong. He uses them to relieve, and prevents them from disrupting, the everyday neighborhood. . . ."[15]

Robert Frost, liking the article and describing it as "one of the most understanding things ever written about me,"[16] believed it to be responsible for the second event which also occurred in December of 1919. To visit him in Amherst came another stranger, Mr. Joseph Anthony, requesting that *Harper's* magazine be allowed to publish in one issue several new Frost poems. Given considerable time to decide how he would meet the request, he had sent to *Harper's* from Franconia, soon after the retreat from Amherst, two long poems and two short ones—a total of 134 lines: "Place for a Third," "Good-by and Keep Cold," "Fragmentary Blue," and "For Once, Then, Something." In response, *Harper's* had done more than pay well for the poems received. The editor-in-chief had requested another cluster of poems at Frost's convenience. Delighted, he had sent four more, totaling 156 lines: "Fire and Ice," "Wild Grapes," "The Valley's Singing Day," and "The Need of Being Versed in Country Things."[17] When Wibur L. Cross sought one poem for the Yale *Review*, Frost replied, "Do you think you could stand an unrelated group such as Harpers is about to publish? My plan would be to return to print hurling fistfulls right and left. You may not be willing to fall in with anything so theatrical. I wonder if I know you well enough to ask you to let me wait till some number when the poverty of your material would thrust me automatically into the place of prominence in your make-up."[18] A few months later, the Yale *Review* printed in one issue "Dust of Snow," "The Onset," "Misgiving," and "A Star in a Stoneboat."[19]

Deeply superstitious, and slightly embarrassed to confess as much, Frost had taken these bunched events as omens. He told himself they marked a turning point in his career, and he began to say so, to his friends, even before the first of these poems appeared in print. In his letter of thanks to Professor Elliott, Frost had written, "I had begun to be afraid certain things that had been said about me in the first place (and in praise, mind you) by people who had hardly taken the trouble to read me would have to go on being said forever. You broke the spell. You took a fresh look. . . . I have asked my daughter at Barnard to send you a copy of one of my less amiable poems in character called Place for a Third. I'm sending herewith several shorter ones I like better myself. The time draws near publishing again. I shall let a few out into the magazines this year and next year book a good many."[20] His next letter to Elliott, written in April of 1920, had been more specific: "I return to the magazines with a group in Harpers in July . . . It is so long since I printed anything I feel as if I were about to begin all over again."[21]

At the same time, he was about to begin all over again as lecturer and bard, with an eye to the necessity for crowding several public appearances into each month of the year. Before the workmen had completed repairing and improving the Stone Cottage in South Shaftsbury, he was off for Philadelphia to give a reading at Bryn Mawr College. The girls were charmed by his performance; indeed, a group of them (borrowing from Lewis Carroll their name, "The Reeling and Writhing Club") made a special plea to him that he return under the sponsorship of their club to give a brief three-session course in reading and writing, just for the members of the club.[22] Flattered, and needing the money, he accepted.

On his way back to South Shaftsbury from Bryn Mawr he stopped in New York City long enough to discuss his financial problems with a new member of his publishing firm. Henry Holt and Company had been suffering through a crisis during the past few years, and the trouble had begun when the elderly Mr. Holt, past eighty, placed more and more power in the hands of those he thought he could trust. A thoroughly reliable senior member of the firm, Edward N. Bristol, had been elevated to the position of chief director for all departments. The younger men, Alfred Harcourt and Donald Brace, who began to work for Holt immediately after their graduation from Columbia in 1904, were advanced in rank until Harcourt became head of the trade department and Brace head of production. They had resigned in May of 1919 to establish their own publishing house, hoping to take with them some of Holt's most valuable authors, including Robert Frost, When formally invited to go with Harcourt, Frost had replied. "There is only one answer possible to your question. I am under obligation to Henry Holt & Co for endless favors. But as far as I am concerned you are Henry Holt & Co. You are all the Henry Holt & Co I have known and dealt with. I promise to do all I can to make you a great publisher even as I expect you to do all you can to make me a great author."[23] Given further information about plans for the new firm, Frost confided to Harcourt, "I suppose I should be more excited if I hadn't been looking for it to happen ever since something you said to me somewhere in a narrow side street as we walked across town to lunch two or three years ago."[24]

Bristol's resentment over Harcourt's attempt to steal Holt authors was softened somewhat by Bristol's belief that textbooks were more profitable than novels and poetry. He implied something else when he informed the elderly Mr. Holt that no great loss would be suffered if Harcourt took almost all the trade department authors, including Carl Sandburg and Walter Lippmann; then he added: "Mrs. [Dorothy Canfield] Fisher and Frost (if Frost) and possibly Untermeyer are all that count."[25] Untermeyer and Mrs. Fisher went with Harcourt, but a legal point was ingeniously invoked to keep Frost from going. Bristol informed him that Holt had worked hard to obtain the copyright for *A Boy's Will* and *North of Boston;* Holt also had *Moun-*

tain Interval under copyright. If Frost chose to go with Harcourt and planned someday to have a volume of collected poems, it would be impossible to include under a Harcourt imprint the contents of the three books on which Holt held the copyright. Sullenly, Frost chose to stay with Holt.

Bristol was quick to make amends. He sent to Franconia for a visit with Frost, the newly appointed head of Holt's trade department, an attractive young Harvard graduate, Lincoln MacVeagh. Having worked for two years in the Holt office shortly after his graduation from Harvard, MacVeagh had joined the Army in 1917 and had served overseas until the end of the war. Soon after his return, he was given the position left vacant by Harcourt. During his visit with the Frosts in Franconia, he had greatly impressed Frost by displaying a genuine delight in and knowledge of Greek and Latin literature—and an equally genuine admiration for the classical and nonclassical elements in the poetry of Robert Frost.

To MacVeagh's office Frost went, on the ninth of November 1920, as he was returning home from Bryn Mawr, and to MacVeagh he described the financial worries which had been bothering him since his resignation from Amherst. Hoping simply for an agreement on higher royalties from Holt, the poet was not prepared for MacVeagh's sympathetic proposal that Frost should be helped immediately with a sinecure, as consulting editor on the Holt staff, at a regular salary of $100 a month. The day after their pleasant discussion of these plans, MacVeagh wrote to Frost, "I am glad to enclose our check for $100 for the month of November, as I promised yesterday."[26] Frost's reply from South Shaftsbury amounted to an act of tossing his friendship with Harcourt into the discard:

"Not so much what you did as the way you did it convinces me that I have been right all along in looking for a business relationship into which friendship could enter. I like to see the opposite of cynicism in me rewarded. Of course thanks no end. And thanks to Bristol, too, if you'll convey them. Now we're away for a fresh start and nobody's on our conscience. What's to prevent our achieving something? . . . I shall see you somewhere around December 9th when I'm down for my next at Bryn Mawr."[27]

Relieved and encouraged by this unexpected development, Frost could not resist sharing it with his other new friend, Professor Elliott at Bowdoin College:

"I'm just going to tell you a matter that may amuse you. You know I left Amherst all so irresponsible. You must have wondered how I could go and come as I pleased on nothing but poetry and yet seem to be taken care of as if I hadn't defied fate.[28] I've wondered myself. The latest interposition in my favor when I had ceased to deserve further clemency is an appointment as *Consulting Editor of Henry Holt and Co.* I owe this under Heaven to Lincoln MacVeagh a younger member of the firm. The pay will be small but large for a poet and the work between you and me will be nothing but seeing MacVeagh once in a while in friendship. . . ."[29]

EXPLORATIONS

*. . . we aren't getting enough American literature out of
our colleges to pay for the hard teaching that goes into
them. After getting a little American literature out of myself the one thing I have cared about in life is getting a
lot out of our school system.*[1]

BEFORE the first heavy snow began to fall on the Green
Mountains in the winter of 1920, the Stone Cottage on the
farm in South Shaftsbury became for Robert Frost more like
a hostelry, intermittently visited, than a permanent home. He
rested briefly there between trips to far-scattered colleges which
invited him to read his poems before large audiences, and to
talk with small groups of undergraduates concerning his poetic
theories. The club of girls at Bryn Mawr, having arranged to
pay him for three extra visits, had caused him to reconsider his
notions about the ways in which established authors might
help educational institutions. After the first of these extra
sessions at Bryn Mawr, early in December of 1920, he stopped
in New York City just long enough to learn, quite by accident,
that at least one Midwestern university had gone so far as to
establish a poet in residence on its campus.

At this time, Frost knew little about the Midwest, other than
that some outrageous claims for American literature had been
made there by such poets as Carl Sandburg, Vachel Lindsay,
Harriet Monroe, and his first serious rival, Edgar Lee Masters.
Back in 1917, when he had given several readings in Chicago,
his hostess had been the widow of the poet William Vaughn
Moody. Immediately following her husband's death, she had
gone to the aid of visiting poets by making her luxurious Chicago home a rendezvous for them. After helping Frost save
money by offering him lodging whenever he might be in Chicago, she had extended her hospitalities by telling him that she

maintained an apartment which other poets used in New York City—at 107 Waverly Place in Greenwich Village—and that she hoped he would stay there whenever convenient. Accepting, he had found at 107 Waverly Place the Midwestern poet, Ridgely Torrence, who had been a close friend of Moody's. Torrence and his wife seemed to commute between New York City and Xenia, Ohio, where Torrence had grown up, and so for a time Frost gained little more than glimpses of the Torrences. His first lengthy visit with them had been reported to Mrs. Moody by Torrence, writing from 107 Waverly Place on the fourth of March 1919:

"Robert Frost came here to dinner last night. He called us up on Sunday and asked whether you were here and he was so disappointed to hear how narrowly he had missed you. He is certainly one of your most loyal appreciators. He agreed to come to dinner yesterday evening and we had a grand evening. We invited the Colums but Molly had just been discharged from the hospital and they couldn't come to dinner. Padraic came later in the evening and added to the general liveliness. We had never had a real heart to heart with Frost before and we were quite carried away by him. He is a man, a noble character in addition to being a noble poet."[2]

Frost had also written to Mrs. Moody soon after that visit and had mentioned "the good evening at your house in New York with the great-faced Ridgely."[3] More than a year later, when Torrence had been given the position of poetry editor on the staff of the *New Republic*, Frost wrote to him with typically serious playfulness, "You'll begin to think I don't see the beauty of having a friend on the editorial staff of The New Republic. But I do and I mean to show it by sending you some poems I have on hand just as soon as I can. . . . You're not going to be where I can run across you in my first descent on the settlements this week. I must see you, though, when I am down in December if we are going to continue to be anything more to each other than respecters of each other's poetry."[4] They did see each other at 107 Waverly Place in December of 1920, and on this occasion Frost learned that the latest Midwestern doings on behalf of American literature might eventually involve him.

His informant was the poet and dramatist, Percy MacKaye, another friend in the Torrence-Moody circle, briefly staying with the Torrences in Mrs. Moody's apartment. MacKaye was in a talkative and even boastful mood because a recent event had changed his way of life: Miami University in Oxford, Ohio, had honored him in the fall of 1920 by appointing him poet in residence. A studio had been built for him on the campus, and he had been promised freedom from too much academic intrusion. The plan had been developed through the initiative of President Hughes of Miami, and shortly after MacKaye was settled on the campus President Hughes had proposed to the annual meeting of the National Association of State Universities that other institutions of learning should follow this example. "There is no one that is in the main more poorly paid than the creative artist," Hughes had said in his address. He had added that "nothing would do more to leaven the increasing materialism of the American university than to have a creative artist working on the campus." This should not be a professorship and it should not involve classroom assignments. The primary obligation of the artist should be to work in his own way in his chosen field. It seemed to President Hughes that fifty or perhaps even one hundred colleges in America could afford to support at least one working artist in this way.[5]

MacKaye's story was a revelation to Frost, who said he would certainly like to find an institution which would ask him to do nothing except serve as poet in residence. If he was seriously interested, MacKaye said, President Hughes should be informed because he knew the colleges and universities which had responded favorably to his proposals. MacKaye promised to talk with President Hughes about Frost, and soon thereafter the University of Michigan made preliminary overtures. Gratefully, Frost wrote to MacKaye:

"The arts seem to have to depend on favor more or less. In the old days it was the favor of kings and courts. In our day far better your solution, that it should be on the colleges, if the colleges could be brought to see their responsibility in the matter. We are sure to be great in the world for power and wealth. . . . But someone who has time will have to take thought that we shall be remembered five thousand years from now for more than success in war and trade. Someone will have to feel that it would be the ultimate shame if we were to pass like Carthage (great in war and trade) and leave no trace in the spirit."[6]

Not long after his return to South Shaftsbury from his December meeting with Percy MacKaye, and before he felt any confidence that anything would eventuate from the Michigan preliminaries, Frost began making other exploratory gestures. In Vermont, the most recent educational innovation which had attracted him was a summer school newly started by Middlebury College during the previous summer. Middlebury, having pioneered separate programs in the languages and literatures of France, Russia, and Spain, had recently inherited some real estate which offered an ideal setting for an unusual School of English, not far from Bread Loaf Mountain, in Ripton, Vermont. A hotel known as Bread Loaf Inn, together with several outlying cottages and barns, had been given Middlebury College in the will of the late Joseph Battell, who had been (among other things) a proprietor of a local newspaper, a breeder of Morgan horses, and a spirited lover of mountain splendors. Frost was so much taken by the possibilities for conducting an extraordinary English program in such a mountain retreat that he apparently asserted his own initiative in trying to make a rapprochement. To Professor Wilfred E. Davison, newly appointed head of the Bread Loaf School of English, Frost wrote from South Shaftsbury on the nineteenth of December 1920:

"I have been a good deal interested in your new Summer School from afar off. I have been wondering if what is behind it may not be what has been troubling me lately, namely, the suspicion that we aren't getting enough American literature out of our colleges to pay for the hard teaching that goes into them. After getting a little American literature out of myself the one thing I have cared about in life is getting a lot out of our school system. I did what in me lay to incite to literature at Amherst. This school year I shall spend two weeks at each of two colleges talking in seminars on the same principles I talked on there. School days are the creative days and college and even high school undergraduates must be about making something before the evil days come when they will have to admit to themselves their minds are more critical than creative. I might fit into your summer plan with a course on the Responsibilities of Teachers of Composition—to their country to help make what is sure to be the greatest nation in wealth the greatest in art also. I should particularly like to encounter the teachers who refuse to expect of human nature more than a correct business letter. I should have to cram what I did into two or at most three weeks."[7]

Professor Davison answered promptly from Middlebury, accepting the plan and apparently offering to pay $150 for the proposed course on the Responsibilities of Teachers of Composition. Frost replied, "We are agreed on everything but the money. I suppose you offer what you can. But I really couldn't give of my time and strength at that rate—particularly of my strength, which I find I have more and more to consider. It would be stretching a point to offer to come for a week and give five lectures for $150 and my expenses. I am sorry if that seems too much, for I wanted the chance to show my belief in what you have undertaken in literature and teaching."[8] Shrewdly, Davison answered by saying that he would like to visit Robert Frost at South Shaftsbury, at such time as might be convenient, to discuss the Bread Loaf idea and any mutually satisfactory ways of bringing Robert Frost to Bread Loaf. The proposal was accepted, and the visit occurred late in January 1921.[9]

There were conflicting motives behind Robert Frost's aggressive concern for what might be going on at the Bread Loaf School of English. They included his desperate fear that his purchase of the new farm, while he was trying to get along without the benefit of a regular salary, might place on him financial burdens heavier than he could meet. Shortly before Davison's visit to the Stone Cottage, Frost had been forced to borrow money, even though it hurt his pride to do so.[10] New complications were caused when the University of Michigan made a formal proposal as a result of MacKaye's hints. Although Frost was reluctant to leave New England, even temporarily, the $5,000 offered him for a one-year stay at Michigan was very attractive. A few days prior to Davison's visit, Frost wrote to Harriet Moody, "We want to see you . . . before we do or don't decide to take this step into Michigan."[11] The visit from Davison made the poet consider the possibility of aligning himself on a full-time basis with Middlebury College, but he feared that if he did that he might go into another writing slump as bad as the one caused by his going to Amherst in 1917.

Just when he was feeling nervously upset by all these considerations, he was hurt by a trivial criticism made by Henry Seidel Canby in the literary supplement to the New York *Evening Post*. At the same time, Untermeyer's report that Braithwaite had been unkind to Untermeyer in a *Transcript* article caused Frost to anticipate the opportunity to share sympathies with Untermeyer on the twenty-third of February. On that day, Frost was to give a reading at the Cosmopolitan Club in New York City—if he felt well enough to go. On the twenty-seventh of January 1921, he wrote to Untermeyer:

"Robert Frost is coming he *says*, with the accent on the says: but he says it by telegram which isn't very binding, especially on a sick person, if he should manage to be sick. He has started to be sick now. The only question is, shall he continue to be sick till Feb. 23rd, or shall he get well, enjoy a period of good health, then get sick again in time to make his excuses. Let us pray for light on this subject. I write this by the hand of an-other, or rather I dictate it from a bed of pain. . . .

"You can't honestly say that the Transcript Nigger treated you any worse than the Post Canby treated me and some other Americans in an article called 'Ham and Eggs' Saturday. What are we going to do about such things? More when I'm better."[12]

He did not recover as quickly as he wished. The local phy-sician said his aches seemed caused by a combination of grippe and neuralgia, but Frost imagined that the ailment must be caused by something worse than that. Shortly after Groundhog Day he wrote again to Untermeyer: "I crawled out (I was go-ing to say out of going to The Cosmopolitan)—I crawled out in the sun today and failing to cast any shadow, asked to be carried back to bed again. I guess it is the carving knife for mine: and I wouldn't care nearly so much if there was any advertisement in it. There is a Masters Mountain and right be-side it a Frost Hollow hereabouts. What can be done to bring low the mountain and cast up the hollow? You say."[13]

While still recovering slowly from the illness, he received a special invitation to praise American literature in a way which appealed to him. The novelist Hamlin Garland (whose acquaintance Frost had made at a meeting of the National Institute of Arts and Letters) wrote saying he hoped Frost would take part in a memorial service to be held in the New York Public Library on the first of March 1921, to honor the late William Dean Howells. Frost answered,

"Sick man as I am (I am just up from a week in bed) I am tempted to accept your invitation for the chance it would give me, the only one I may ever have, to discharge in downright prose the great debt I owe Howells.

"Howells himself sent me The Mother and the Father after he saw my North of Boston. It is beautiful blank verse, just what I should have known from his prose he would write. My obligation to him however is not for the particular things he did in verse form, but for the perennial poetry of all his writing in all forms. I learned from him a long time ago that the loveliest theme of poetry was the voices of people. No one ever had a more observing ear or clearer imagination for the tones of those voices. No one ever brought them more freshly to book. He recorded them equally with actions, indeed as if they were actions (and I think they are).

"I wonder if you think as I do it is a time for consolidating our resources a little against outside influences on our literature and particularly against those among us who would like nothing better than to help us lose our identity. I dont mean the consolidation so much in society as in thought. It should be more of a question with us than it is what as Americans we have to go on with and go on from. There can be nothing invidious to new comers, emigrant Russians Italians and the like, in singling out for notice or even praise any trait or quality as specially American. . . . Our best way to define to ourselves what we are is in terms of men. We are eight or ten men already and one of them is Howells. . . ."[14]

Frost's concern for giving support to a truly American literature always found best expression when he saw the chance to oppose "those among us who would like nothing better than to help us lose our identity." That concern had been heightened while he was living in England from 1912 to 1915. He had gone there, not to settle permanently, not to imitate British mannerisms, and not even to acquire a merely British literary reputation. From there he had confided his hope that he might get started in London and then return home to "get Yankier and Yankier."[16] Just before leaving England, he had read and praised the plea of another American poet-teacher, George Edward Woodberry, that new efforts should be made to advance the cause of American literature.[16]

Repeatedly, after he returned to the United States, Frost made outspoken protests against the various ways in which some of his countrymen seemed to pay too much attention to British poets. In 1917, when he stayed as guest in the Chicago home of Mrs. William Vaughn Moody, he had been furious because she welcomed to her home, just before Frost left, an English poet newly arrived in America to give lectures and readings: Frost's friend-and-enemy, W. W. Gibson. In his next letter to her, Frost scolded Mrs. Moody for being an Anglophile:

"Enter distinguished Englishman, exit extinguished American. Padraic [Colum] may think my sympathy with his Ireland is just Blarney I give him. It's not that I love Ireland more for loving England less and less. But I do love a country that loves itself. I love a country that insists on its own nationality which is the same thing as a person's insisting on his own personality. Isn't an idea any better for its being my own out of my own life and experience? Isn't it? Isn't a literature any more to us for being our own? It is, whether you think so or not. No danger about our not insisting on our own nationality in business and diplomacy. But that is only on the material plane. My concern is that some day we shall go in to back ourselves on the intellectual and spiritual plane. Don't we seem poor stuff the way we whoop it up for anything imported in the arts? Other things being unequal, the visitor having all the advantage in other things, I should still make him feel if I were an American that, just because he was imported, he couldn't expect any more adulation than our own home-grown poet. But of course I'm not an American. Let's go back on America together."[17]

The same playfully serious approach to the identical problem was used in another letter he wrote Mrs. Moody in January 1921:

"I should be more pleased with your good opinion if you hadn't told me that time [in Chicago, March 1917] that I might be the best poet in America, but the best in America couldn't hope to come up to the worst in England. Have a little national pride. Don't you know it's provincial to look up to England? So is it to brag about America. What isn't provincial then will be the question before the house at our next meeting."[18]

Having decided what he would say in praise of American literature in general and of the late William Dean Howells in particular, if he could attend the memorial service on the first of March 1921,[19] Frost recovered from his illness soon enough to give three performances in New York and Philadelphia even before the end of February.[20] Early in March he was able to return to New York and Philadelphia for two more performances.[21] Then he spent a week as poet in residence at Queens University in Kingston, Ontario, before the end of March.[22]

Out of all these winter jauntings, one which simultaneously pleased and troubled him was a brief visit to Princeton University, where he met and seemed to start a friendship with Paul

Elmer More, distinguished author of the *Shelburne Essays.* When Frost gave his reading at Princeton, on the ninth of March 1921, under the auspices of the Freneau Club, More was in the audience. After the reading and the discussion period with the students, More took Frost home to spend the night. In their conversation they quickly discovered various ways in which their experiences had overlapped. Ten years older than Frost, More had served as a contributing editor for the *Independent,* to which Frost had first sold a poem, back in 1894. Both Frost and More had become well acquainted with the editor-in-chief, William Hayes Ward, and with Ward's sister Susan, poetry editor for the *Independent.* Before the evening was over, More confessed that he himself had begun his literary career with the writing of poetry, and his first two books had been collections of his early lyrics. Then he had turned to scholarship, and while doing graduate work at Harvard he had studied Greek, Latin, and Sanskrit. In 1898, the year Frost entered Harvard as a special student, More published a volume entitled *A Century of Indian Epigrams, Chiefly from the Sanskrit of Bhartrihari.* The poet-translator still owned an extra copy of this work, and he inscribed it as a gift for Frost, before the two men parted. That same day, More wrote to his sister,

"Robert Frost was in Princeton yesterday reading and talking to the Freneau Club, and I had him here over night.

"I have always rather admired his poetry, which is modern in some respects, but has balance and measure and deals with the real things of life. It was a pleasure to talk with him—we sat up until about one—and hear how sound his views on art and human nature are. He knows all the wild men now snorting up the sides of Parnassus, has heard the infinite scandals of their life, and can prick them out in epigrams to the king's taste. It was rather exhilarating to listen to him, and I think too he went away somewhat encouraged from his contact with a kindred soul. . . .

"I was interested in seeing how Frost managed some of our ultra esthetes who gathered about him after his lecture and asked him the old foolish questions: does not thinking dull poetic genius, and must not a poet welcome all (particularly the base) experiences of life? He handled the boys with a good deal of tact, but made them feel rather silly."[23]

Paul Elmer More was correct in believing that Frost "went away somewhat encouraged from his contact with a kindred soul," and there was indeed a potentially firm basis for the development of a strong friendship. But Frost was annoyed by More's confession that he had started as a poet and then had deserted poetry for scholarship; had gradually strayed from American literature to the study of Sanskrit. On the train, starting back toward South Shaftsbury, Frost suspiciously began reading More's "Introduction" to *A Century of Indian Epigrams,* and strongly disliked one particular passage:

"Now the Vedanta teaches the same doctrine of knowledge and ignorance; but it goes a step further, and herein lies its clearness and originality. Regarding the world without, we have only ignorance or false opinion. It therefore exists for us only in these, and for us ignorance is the cause of the world. With the acquisition of knowledge ignorance is destroyed, and the world of which it is the cause ceases for us to exist. We win deliverance by knowledge—and knowledge of what? By apprehension of this definite truth, that the soul has real existence, and that the world has only a phantom existence in illusion."24

In his conversation with More during the previous evening, Frost had learned that while he and More shared a deep admiration for Emerson, they read him differently. Frost liked the fact that the Concord sage had firmly rejected the notion that "the world has only a phantom existence in illusion." In his first published essay, *Nature,* Emerson had made the following statement in taking exception to the view of nature as illusion: "Idealism is a hypothesis to account for nature by other principles than those of carpentry and chemistry. Yet, if it only deny the existence of matter, it does not satisfy the demands of the spirit. It leaves God out of me." By contrast, More's "Introduction" was far too Platonic or Neoplatonic for the tastes of the man who had written, "Earth's the right place for love: I don't know where it's likely to go better." Frost, viewing himself as a discriminating dualist in his beliefs, was impatient with that form of monism to which More seemed to subscribe.25 By the time he reached South Shaftsbury, he was still trying to decide how he could tactfully write a letter of thanks to More for his hospitalities and for the gift of the unsettling book. He never did decide; at least, he did not write even a note to More. This silence ended the possibilities of friendship between these two men who, as it happened, never saw each other again.26

After having been away from home so much during the fall and winter, Robert Frost was glad to forget literature long

enough to spend most of the springtime improving his acquaintance with his farm. Previously, he had not found spare
time or energy to walk all the boundaries of his ninety acres,
or even to explore some of his own woodlots, hillsides, and
meadows which he could see from the windows of the Stone
Cottage. Carol was happy to have his father's help in arranging
for the purchase of apple seedlings grafted with Astrachan or
McIntosh scions. Together they set out enough of them to
start the first of several projected orchards, knowing that years
must pass before anyone would find the first fruit—or even the
first blossom.

Dorothy and John Fisher had convinced the Frosts that pine
lumber was a crop which could be grown at a profit without
tending. Eight years earlier, in 1913, the Fishers had enjoyed
planting hundreds of six-inch white pine seedlings. They had
done this, partly to protect from erosion a sloping hillside on
their own farm in Arlington, and the incipient grove was
already a beautifully decorative addition to their real-estate
holdings. Liking the Fishers' suggestion, Carol and his father
bought a thousand red pine seedlings, cleared brush from a
hillside area not far to the northwest of the Stone Cottage, and
planted the little trees very quickly.

They proceeded slowly in acquiring livestock. A good Jersey
cow was found and bought just before she was due to come in.
The lively stepping mare, called Beauty or Beaut, purchased
from Willis Herbert in Franconia, had become such a family
pet that she had not been left behind. Sent by rail from Franconia to White River Junction, she was brought the rest of the
way by Carol, who rode her a distance of eighty-two miles to
South Shaftsbury, camping each night near the tethered Beaut.
Frost quickly acquired a buggy so that he could ride about the
countryside at leisurely pace, as he had enjoyed doing when he
was a New Hampshire farm-poultryman in Derry. Carol might
prefer to use their secondhand Overland automobile for errands,
but his father easily found excuses for hitching Beaut into
the shafts of the buggy—if only to go down the hill to the
local store-and-post-office in the nearby village of South Shaftsbury.

Mr. Clifford Hawkins, postmaster and part-owner of the
store, was the first person in South Shaftsbury whom the Frosts
knew by name. Gradually, through him, they became well

[168]

acquainted with several other members of the Hawkins family. One of the most appealing was young Wales Monroe Hawkins, twenty-four years old, who had completed a college course in engineering at the University of Vermont, had established himself over in New York State, had developed tuberculosis, and was now home as an invalid. Frost enjoyed talking with this alert and well-informed young man, who lived not far from the Hawkins store. Even more picturesque and entertaining was Charles A. Monroe, uncle to Wales, and only two years younger than Frost. Monroe, born in South Shaftsbury and educated at the nearby North Bennington High School, had taught for a time in rural schools around the Shaftsbury region. In 1899, he had acquired a position more to his liking, as clerk in the Railway Postal Service.[27] Monroe was a highly respected and active member of the community. His neatly trimmed Van Dyke beard and his shrewd eyes, always twinkling behind his steel-rimmed glasses, distinguished him from the other townsfolk. He was an authority on local history, apples, and bees. His little farm at the edge of the village—not much more than a mile away from the Frost Stone Cottage—gradually became a favorite visiting-place for the poet whenever he knew the Railway Postal clerk was at home. Monroe did more than arrange to provide the Frosts with a hive of bees: he suggested that if Frost was so much taken with the activities of bees he should let Monroe build him a little hive, with one side made of glass, and place it on the ledge of a living-room window. The plan was carried out, and the Frosts enjoyed watching the bees make the combs in which they stored honey.[28] Monroe was one of the neighbors whom Louis Untermeyer met during his first visit with the Frosts in South Shaftsbury, and soon after that visit Frost wrote to Untermeyer, making a little parable out of Monroe's latest bee-adventures:

"Monroe says the buckwheat has been behaving very badly with the bees. It will be sweet for a few hours in the morning and then for the rest of the day unyielding. It has put the hives all out of temper. Ordinarily Monroe does what he likes with the bees, shakes them off the combs, sweeps them into heaps, and carries them in his bare hands without being stung. They stung him twenty-five times when he walked between the hives where he had a perfect right to be. They came looking for him away on the porch of his house to sting him right before me.

The buckwheat had just the same effect on them that that kind of woman has on a man. And that's no tale from Maeterlinck."[29]

These casual and idyllic ways of observing and participating in rural pleasures, during the spring and summer of 1921, gave Robert Frost the relaxation he so much needed. In this mood, he could even adjust himself to whatever intrusions outsiders might make. A reporter sent by the Boston *Traveler* appeared unannounced in April of 1921, and stayed long enough to gather some good impressions:

". . . that quaint old house; gray block stone two-thirds of the way up, with dark-red clapboards continuing on above to the long, sweeping roof. Dutch curtains, patterned in dark brown, swished and rippled just within the open windows. On the wide doorsill of the massive colonial doorway, comfortably resting against one side, sat a silver-haired gentlewoman in buff and white, her fingers and needle dancing in and around a strip of crochet work which overlapped her wrist and fell into her lap. A tall, thin young man in blue overalls, whom I shortly learned was the son of the family, thumped a big, flat rock down into the brown earth path he was making new. . . . There was a green iron pump immediately to his left, with a shining dipper upside down on the snout. A few weeks more and the pump will be in the shade of maple leaves. . . .

"What a world of contentment and peace! And the eyes of the doorstep figure—full, rich, brown eyes—reflected it all. So did the eyes of Lesley Frost, who had appeared . . . in the doorway behind her mother. She was twenty-one and wore a brand new pair of oxblood oxfords with sensible heels.

" 'He' would be back presently. He had just walked down the road . . . with a young student poet from Amherst who had been spending a few days with them.

"In that first moment of meeting Mrs. Frost, in which she had invited me into the 'cool of the house,' I well knew that her talk would not be of the local church social or about the man on the farm below who had been kicked by his horse last Thursday afternoon. She had been a bit disappointed in Sinclair Lewis's *Main Street*. . . .[30] Oh, it was a charming chat we had in that simple, spacious living room waiting for 'him' to return. . . .

"I arose and went to meet him, and I noticed his suspenders first as the sunlight brought the straps into high relief against his dark gray flannel shirt. He wore no hat. I do not quite remember how it all occurred, but from the moment I joined him I seemed to be walking along the road by the side of an old friend and just talking naturally of many things.

"One of his literary friends prominent in New England letters had told me some time ago that Frost was 'one of the most lovable men in the world.' I could not help thinking of this remark as I gazed into the remarkable face of the man by my side and listened to his talk. It is a large face with mobile features—strong features that radiate peace, contentment, and the perfectly balanced solidarity of the inner man. . . .

"His movements were most deliberate and his grayish hair was plain 'mussed up.' He wore a very old pair of bluish-gray, striped trousers, mended a bit on the inner side of the bottoms. A wisp of worn leather flipped and flapped from the bottom of one shoe, near the toe, as he walked along. . . . We paused under the maple tree by the pump, he taking the straight-backed chair which leaned against the bark and I the more comfortable armchair which faced him. He had insisted that such should be the order. . . ."[31]

Robert Frost's pleasure in playing at farming, and even in playing host to visitors, was spoiled when the pollen began to float. As early as the seventeenth of July he wrote to Raymond Holden in Franconia, "I am beginning to sniff the air suspiciously, on the point of taking flight from these weedy regions. It can't be long before you hear me come crashing through the woods in your direction. Don't shoot till you're sure who it is anyway."[32] Back of the humor was a guilty awareness that Holden might feel he had new reasons for shooting: Frost had arranged to borrow from Holden, during the approaching hay-fever season, the same farmhouse Holden had bought from Frost at a fancy price and under disappointing circumstances less than a year earlier.[33]

In anticipation of the drive to Franconia, in the family Overland, from South Shaftsbury, Frost had already completed plans to give one reading en route. Having initially offered his services to Davison at the Bread Loaf School of English, for two or three weeks, then having trimmed the offer down to a few days, he had ultimately settled for just one evening's performance. But he had decided to give the school something more than had been bargained for. When he appeared there as scheduled, with Mrs. Frost, he began his evening program as usual, reading generously from his poems. Then he launched into a thoroughly serious talk, in which he foreshadowed what later became the basic idea for the Bread Loaf Writers' Conference.

He began his talk by saying that what Bread Loaf wanted for a teacher was an author with writing of his own on hand; one who would be willing to live for a while on terms of equality—almost—with a few younger writers. He said he was not suggesting that such an author-teacher need go so far as to carry his own manuscripts to the students, but rather that they would be free to bring theirs to him. In such a course, the teacher would no more think of assigning work to the students than they would think of asking him to write something for them. In discussions, such a teacher would expect to take as well as give, insofar as an exchange of ideas was possible—if not ideas of form at least observations of life. Such a teacher should address himself mainly to the subject-matter of the younger writer, but conversations would take the place of lectures. Instead of correcting grammar, in red ink, he would try to match experiences of life and experiences of art with his students. Individual conferences could best be conducted during long walks into the country or, on rainy days, long talks before a fireplace. If he had to find fault, he might say nothing more pointed than, "The trouble with it is that it hasn't enough to it. Let the next piece have more to it—of Heaven Earth Hell and the young author." But the manuscripts offered to the author-teacher would not be "exercises," because the young writer's whole nature should be in every piece he set his hand to; his whole nature should include his belief in the real value that the piece would have when finished.[34]

Four years passed before Robert Frost's ideas concerning the possibility of conducting a writers' conference along these lines became an actuality at Bread Loaf, quite apart from the Bread Loaf School of English. For the present, Davison's program was moving in another direction. Although the poet was greatly taken with the Bread Loaf setting, on a meadowy shelf of the Green Mountains, he was infuriated by what seemed to him the discourteous way in which Davison and his staff ignored and neglected Mrs. Frost. When asked to return for another talk and reading, a year hence, he avoided making any commitment. But even before he drove away from Bread Loaf toward Franconia, he had firmly decided that he would not go back there in 1922; his absence would be his way of punishing Davison and the staff for their neglect of Mrs. Frost.[35]

The return to Franconia was pleasant, even though Frost had to make awkward amends to Raymond Holden. It was easy enough to give the impression that the Frosts were sorry they had been required to leave Franconia, because of Carol's farming plans; it was also easy to let an ignorant newspaper reporter assume that Frost still lived in Franconia, year-round:

"With the opening of the college year, Robert Frost the New Hampshire poet is leaving his white farmhouse in the interval below the Franconia Mountains for the campus of the University of Michigan. . . ."[36]

The reporter would have been more accurate if he had said that Robert Frost the Vermont poet, leaving Raymond Holden's white farmhouse in Franconia, at the end of the hay-fever season, was returning to South Shaftsbury to close up his farm there before going to Michigan.

THE MICHIGAN FELLOWSHIP

*. . . It will be a year-long picnic and we are free minded
enough as a family to break off our several affairs and
take them up as seriously as ever again after the picnic
is over. . . . There'll be music and dancing and college
yelling. We all like such things.*[1]

MARJORIE FROST had already started her junior year at
North Bennington High School, sharing a rented room in the
village there with her closest friend, Lillian LaBatt, when the
rest of the Frost family set off for Ann Arbor early in October
of 1921. The adventurous uncertainty of it was appealing.
They knew nothing about what it would be like to live on the
edge of a large state-supported Midwestern campus, with more
than ten thousand students enrolled. Carol, who liked to follow
newspaper accounts of professional baseball and college football, knew that Coach "Hurry-up" Yost had made a famous
record at Michigan with championship elevens, and that he
was expected to have another good team this fall. Lesley, temporarily giving up her work in the New York City book trade,
wanted to take a few courses as a special student at the University. Irma, hoping to become an artist, planned to audit
courses in the history of art while continuing her painting,
drawing, and sculpture at home. Mrs. Frost was worried about
the size of the house awaiting them at the Ann Arbor address
they already knew: 1523 Washtenaw Avenue. The authorities
had rented for the Frosts an elegantly furnished home owned
by the widow of Dr. Martin L. D'Ooge, who had distinguished
himself as a classicist, but the house was said to be so big that
a maid would be needed. The assistance of a maid would be,
for Mrs. Frost, a strange experience. Her husband, writing to
Percy MacKaye from South Shaftsbury, had given his own
reaction to the style in which they were expected to live: "The

house is very large, there'll be no hope of running it without one servant. So the money goes. But never mind, it's their money in a sense and they want me to live in a style worthy of their high idea of me. We've made up our minds to be in their hands for a good time and damn the economies."[2]

When they reached Ann Arbor they were all delighted to discover that this hilly town on the Huron River seemed to be built in a forest of trees, and that the surrounding countryside was a fruit growing area.The entire setting reminded them so much of New England that they felt very much at home. The beautiful campus, stretching outward for hundreds of acres under its own canopy of trees, and comprising such a variety of classroom buildings, laboratories, schools and graduate colleges, fraternities and sororities, seemed bewilderingly vast. As for the house to which they were taken at 1523 Washtenaw Avenue, it had an old-fashioned Victorian architectural quality unlike anything they had lived in before. There was certainly more elegance in the furnishings than they were used to, but they quickly decided they would rather do the housework themselves than put up with the inconvenience of having a servant under foot.

As soon as they had settled in, they were all curious to know how Robert Frost, the poet in residence, would be asked to carry himself for the purpose of living up to whatever was expected of him. The President, Dr. Marion LeRoy Burton, had said that the poet would be paid $5,000 for the year of this "Fellowship," but had not said how much time he should make available to the students, faculty, and community. Frost was prepared to grope his way into whatever service seemed consistent with these generous terms; in fact he had begun his groping when he had written to President Burton from South Shaftsbury:

"You had my telegram accepting your offer. It remains for me to thank you for having chosen me to be a representative of creative literature in this way at Michigan University. We'll waive the question of whether you might not better have chosen someone else for the honor. I should have thanked you almost as much if you had. The important thing is that you should have chosen anyone. I don't know why I am so gratified unless it is because I am somewhat surprised when men of your executive authority (yours and Mr. Osborn's)[3] see it as a part of their duty to the state to encourage the arts . . .

"I can see that the appointment may contemplate the bene-fit of education a little as well as of poetry and one poet. You would like it to say something to the world for keeping the crea-tive and erudite together in education where they belong. And you would like it to make its demands on the young student. He must be about some achievement in the arts or sciences while yet he is at his most creative period and the college in-terposes to keep the world off his shoulders. . . ."[4]

Apparently President Burton was also groping, for he had replied, "You have sensed and expressed so much more ade-quately than I can just the purposes which we have in mind, that it increases my anticipation of your residence among us . . ."[5] The President's interest was, nevertheless, warm-hearted and genuine, as he demonstrated when the Frosts arrived in Ann Arbor. The poet was impressed with Burton's dynamic personality and his obvious abilities as the adminis-trator of a rapidly expanding educational program. The man placed in charge of this new venture in the creative arts was another warm-hearted and cordial human being, Joseph A. Bursley, Dean of Students. But everyone seemed so eager to let Frost make his own way, at his own pace, that he feared he might spend the entire year in this large institution without having any effect on either the students or the faculty.[6]

He did have one old friend to whom he turned for counsel at Michigan: Morris P. Tilley, the English department professor who had spent many summers with his family in Franconia while the Frosts were living there.[7] Through him the poet gradually became acquainted with the senior members of that department, but introductions had not progressed far before Frost heard of resentments on the part of certain drones who disapproved of paying a mere poet $5,000 to sit around and do nothing all year while they slaved in classrooms. One exception was Professor Roy Cowden, who enjoyed supervising the pub-lication of the undergraduate literary magazine. The editors traditionally held their staff meetings in Cowden's home, and Frost was invited to meet them there. Cowden apologetically explained that the students called their literary magazine *Whimsies*, but that it wasn't as bad as it sounded.

Glad to find this pleasant way of establishing contact with these hopeful young writers, Frost met first with the *Whimsies* staff at Cowden's home on the tenth of October 1921, and seemed particularly charmed by the bobbed-hair styles of the attractive girls.⁸ They, in turn, were relieved to find they could talk easily with their distinguished visitor, who was as informal as their beloved Professor Cowden. When the meeting settled down to formalities, the procedure was simple. Manuscripts were read aloud, for consideration, Cowden gladly deferred to his guest for comments, and Frost made his criticisms gentle.

Officially, the poet was introduced to the undergraduates at a reception in the assembly hall of the Union Building only a few nights after he had met the *Whimsies* staff. The reception line, which started forming at eight o'clock, extended around the entire periphery of the hall before Frost arrived. Introduced by the Assistant Dean, Professor W. R. Humphries, the poet again impressed his listeners: "With a complete informality that brought an immediate response from the hundreds of students and faculty men that filled the room he talked to his audience about his poetry, his artistic ideals, and his aims in visiting the Michigan student body, ending with . . . [several poems which were] transformed by his colloquial charm and interpolated explanations, given with complete informality."⁹

These first two events encouraged him to feel that he might gradually establish enough rapport on the campus to justify the program which Percy MacKaye had helped start. Reporters who called at his elegant house on Washtenaw Avenue gave him further chances to make it plain that he did not want to play the role of poet-in-retirement. Not all of the reporters were impressed, nor was all of the publicity flattering. One interviewer began his article by wondering whether it was worthwhile to pay a poet $5,000 and then not ask him "to do anything, not even to twirl his thumbs, if he does not so desire." The same interviewer expressed surprise over some theological implications of certain things the poet had said:

"The attention of Mr. Frost was drawn to the fact that some of the squirrels in Ann Arbor were dying; that a mysterious disease was carrying them to 'timely' graves, 'timely,' because they were getting too numerous. So, speaking of the lessening number of squirrels, he remarked,

" 'That is nature's way. Animals breeding rapidly after a time become a menace for one reason or another. Then comes a scourge and they die off. It is true of humans. When the world becomes so over-populated that its organizations can no longer protect its people there will come a pestilence, a famine, a scourge of disease—possibly a war—and men die by the thousands or are killed by the hundreds of thousands and then once more organization is able to care for the people of a great world.' "

The reporter, amazed, completed the article sarcastically:

"How simple. The great world war was nothing to be regretted but simply God's way of thinning us out. Poor ignorant man may think he blundered, but Mr. Frost doesn't think so. The black plague, tuberculosis, grippe, smallpox, scarlet fever—these must be looked upon as God's blessings in disguise to prevent over-population.

"God first creates too many stomachs and backs to get along comfortably and then He sends His servants in the shape of war and pestilence to thin us out.

"One might well argue that man has no right to try to interfere with God by endeavoring to cure disease or to prevent wars. Doesn't God know best?

"The University of Michigan is welcome to Mr. Frost and his theory of God's ways . . ."[10]

It was true that the Christian doctrine of acceptance, taught so early to Frost by his mother, continuously enabled him to rationalize oddities in his view of God's ways, but such a view did not hinder Frost from playing his own God-like role in designing and then helping the editors of *Whimsies* to accomplish a near-miracle at Ann Arbor. It all began with the suggestion that it might be possible to arrange a series of readings by several celebrated proponents of "the new poetry"—including Amy Lowell, Vachel Lindsay, and Carl Sandburg. Frost, with characteristic furtiveness, chose to stay behind the scenes in making the arrangements for the series, and to do any necessary wirepulling through private correspondence. The reluctant Amy Lowell received a special plea from him soon after she had refused the invitation sent by one of the students:

"Miss Uki Osawa asks me to intercede with you for the young people who have been trying to bring you here to talk and read. They are children. They tell me they began by not offering you enough money. They had nothing to reason from except the hundred dollars they gave Jack Squire, their only poet English or American so far this year and I guess for several years. If a hundred isn't enough ask a little more, but come and read to them. . . . They are taking a great deal on themselves in bringing so many poets at once where so few have ever been before. I suppose they told you they are having Louis, Carl, Vachel, and Witter Bynner too. It will be a great stirring up of poetry here. . . ."[11]

Amy Lowell was persuaded, but she let it be known that she would stay in Detroit, at a hotel where she could take enough rooms for her usual retinue of servants.

Padraic Colum, fresh from Ireland, was the lead-off poet, calculated to attract interest because of the American sympathy with new developments in Ireland. After so many years of struggle, the Irish Free State which had been officially established in January of 1921 had plunged the country into a new civil war precipitated by those who refused to accept even a dominion status and the separation of Northern Ireland. Colum drew a good crowd. Before he read some of his own poems in his colorful brogue he talked on "The Development of Irish Literature" with special emphasis on the rise of the Abbey Theatre and the presentation of plays written in the peasant vernacular.[12] Immediately after his talk and reading, a reception was given him by the editors of *Whimsies* in the parlor of Frost's home. The students, delighted by the informal give-and-take of witty nonsense, asked Colum if he had ever been associated with the Sinn Fein movement. Of course. Would he stay in the United States? "No, no. I'm leaving for Ireland in July, though I'll always be connected with this country. It's my market, you know, and I have some plays going the rounds now."[13]

Next in the series came Carl Sandburg, whom Frost had met in Chicago in 1917—and had immediately disliked. The New England poet correctly assumed that the Chicagoan would appear in Ann Arbor affecting his Whitmanesque mannerisms and garb in order to show his deep sympathy with the working classes: the blue shirt with the collar open at the throat and the prematurely gray hair tumbling over his forehead. His announced topic was, "Is There a New Poetry?" By way of answer, he praised free verse as the surest indication of what was new. Then, accompanying himself on his guitar, he sang several American folk songs including the ballad containing "Oh my name it is Sam Hall, and I hate you one and all, damn your eyes."[14] Most of the hating was done by Robert Frost that afternoon in Hill Auditorium, and Sandburg had scarcely left town when Frost reacted bitterly in a letter to MacVeagh:

"We've been having a dose of Carl Sandburg. He's another

person I find it hard to do justice to. He was possibly [three] hours in town and he spent one of those washing his white hair and toughening his expression for his public performance. His mandolin [guitar] pleased some people, his poetry a very few and his infantile talk none. His affectations have almost buried him out of sight. He is probably the most artificial and studied ruffian the world has had. Lesley says his two long poems in The New Republic and The Dial are as ridiculous as his carriage and articulation. He has developed rapidly since I saw him two years ago. I heard someone say he was the kind of writer who had everything to gain and nothing to lose by being translated into another language."[15]

Following Carl Sandburg, in the series, came Louis Untermeyer, who chose for the subject of his talk, "Certain American Poets." If the talk had been written by Frost as a deliberate parody of self-advertising, it could scarcely have been improved. It was summarized at length in the Michigan Daily:

"Untermeyer placed Robert Frost as the greatest of American contemporary poets. He read several of Frost's poems that are not included in his books . . . and stressed the fact that these poems . . . are full of a warm undertone that goes beyond superficial realism. Frost, he said, embodies a whimsical and at times fanciful note in his poetry. In speaking of Robinson, Untermeyer said he possessed some of the same austerity and realism that Frost does. Summing up the differences . . . Untermeyer said, 'Frost writes in a manner that gives the impression of continuing life, while Robinson portrays episodes that are closed and causes the reader to picture life concluded. Sandburg represents one extreme swing of the pendulum, while Frost represents the other. Frost may be called the intellectual aristocrat, while Sandburg may be called the emotional democrat. . . .' "[16]

At the reception for Untermeyer, and for his poet-wife Jean Starr Untermeyer, it was Frost's turn to be generous with praise. He described Untermeyer as a radical, an aristocrat of radicals, and added, "He's this kind of radical: he'll let other people walk all over his property but he won't take anybody else's."[17] The reporter gathered that Untermeyer's fourteen-year-old son Richard was far more of a radical that his father: "For one thing, Dick, cherished as a promising young Bolshevik, recently gave his parents a shock of surprise by writing a play in blank verse, with Napoleon for hero!" During the reception, both Untermeyer and Frost confided to their listeners some disparaging comments on other poets: "Speaking of [Edgar Lee] Masters, Untermeyer said he had the mind of a country doctor who had read analytical psychology too late in life to do him any good. He is a diagnostician rather than an artist." As for Jean Starr Untermeyer's poetry, Untermeyer was more generous—and witty: "He said that he could speak of her with a cool detachment since she was related to him only by marriage."[18]

One of Untermeyer's remarks was saved, by the undergraduate reporter, for use in announcing the arrival of the next poet in the series, Miss Amy Lowell. He was then quoted as saying, ". . . no individual has been more fought for, fought against, and generally fought about than Amy Lowell. She has been hailed and hooted in the triple capacity of person, propagandist [for free verse] and poet. Nothing is so characteristic of Miss Lowell as her power to arouse."[19] Frost had especially wanted her to appear in the series partly because she could be counted on to give a show which might ascend to genuine histrionics or descend to vaudeville. On stage, she was always a spectacle—stout, pompous, officious. When she appeared at Ann Arbor on the night of the fourth of May 1921, before an overflow audience of 2,500 people, in the Hill Auditorium, she was in fine spirits. Everyone was amused by her gesture of sweeping her pince-nez off her capacious bosom, her way of plucking a large pocket-handkerchief out of a hiding place in the rear of her skirt, and her bumbling about with the special reader's lamp she always carried with her. Those of the audience who were sitting in the front rows were delighted by her stage-whisper asides to Frost about where the lamp should be placed. Then Frost, toying with it and explaining its importance, as he began his introduction, increased the hilarity by pulling too hard on a wire and causing the lamp to blow a fuse which threw the whole audience into darkness. While the authorities scurried for the janitor, Frost and Miss Lowell "kept the invisible audience in howls of laughter by their impromptu jests."[20] After some time, the lights went on again, and the audience settled down for the remainder of the introduction. As Frost finished and turned away from the podium, bowing toward Miss Lowell while she was making her huge way from her platform chair, he accidentally tripped over the cord of the reading lamp, and in the excitement that followed he upset a pitcher of ice water especially set on the speaker's table for Miss Lowell.[21]

Finally, when she could begin her talk, Miss Lowell announced with customary arrogance that she would spend what remained of the hour talking about herself, her theory of poetry, and her practice of it. There were only two kinds of poetry, she said: good and bad. The form of the verse didn't matter; she happened to choose free verse as the form which most interested her. The crowd took all these remarks in good-humored fashion. When she began to read her poems, however, and to explain her meanings as she went, she gave the effect of talking down to her listeners as though they were grammar-school children—and many of them were indignant. Her defense, afterward, was that she didn't see how she could be expected to anticipate a sophisticated audience in "Edgar Guest's State."[22]

Although it would have been difficult for any poet to follow Amy Lowell, in this series of talks and readings at Ann Arbor, the next one scheduled was the best showman in this higher vaudeville business: Vachel Lindsay, who had his own ways of transforming an ordinary session of poetry-reading into a special performance. Naïve and childlike in his ability to lose himself in the spirit and mood of such poems as his "General Booth Enters Heaven" or "The Congo," he acted out and chanted them. Awkward in his long-armed and long-legged struttings about the stage, he never seemed to guess that anyone might find an element of clowning in his performance. For those who were sympathetic admirers, he was more nearly an inspired mystic than a clown. A few months earlier, however, when he had achieved spectacular triumphs in England, reading in Oxford and Cambridge, one of his listeners had been T. S. Eliot, whose fastidiousness was so deeply offended by Lindsay's gymnastics that Eliot had exclaimed, "I am appalled . . ."[23]

Long before Lindsay made his brief visit in Ann Arbor, Frost had become well acquainted with him. Prior to their meeting, Lindsay had sent Frost a copy of *The Congo and Other Poems,* with an elaborate inscription dated "Sept. 22, 1915" and containing the statement, "It gives me joy to know the good Louis Untermeyer has interceded with you on my behalf."[24] They had first met in Chicago, through the mutual friendship of Harriet Monroe; they had met again at Untermeyer's apartment in New York City in February of 1918 when Lindsay had urged the assembled poets (including Sara Teasdale) to write verse in memory of the recently deceased world heavyweight boxing champion John L. Sullivan. Frost had responded with a good forty-two-line parody entitled "John L. Sullivan Enters Heaven."[25] They had seen each other again when Lindsay, newly returned from his triumph in England, appeared in Bennington to read under the auspices of the Poetry Society of Southern Vermont.[26] Frost had urged the *Whimsies* staff at Michigan to seek Lindsay for their series because the students would surely get their money's worth. They did, and they responded to his vaudeville act with uncritical enthusiasm. Afterward, Lindsay delighted the girls in particular as he moved around to talk with each one of them, asked the name of each, and then made for each an individualized pen-and-ink drawing, developed around the "suggestions" he found in the girl's name. He boasted that he had begun as an artist and that most of his poetry had been written initially to illustrate his drawings.[27]

The "Poet Series" ended with Lindsay, even though many on the campus did their best to persuade Robert Frost that he should provide the climax with an evening of readings from his own poems. He was content to stay on the edge of things, participating in no apparent way except to introduce some of the poets, to entertain them, and when possible to make them linger for a meeting of the *Whimsies* staff. The strategy worked so well that President Burton, addressing an alumni dinner in Louisville, Kentucky, said (before the "Poet Series" was over) that he was uncertain whether the most popular man on the Michigan campus was Coach Yost or Robert Frost. When asked to comment, Frost said he was willing to demonstrate which man had the stronger drawing power. He would wait until the next football game, and would schedule for that same Saturday afternoon a Robert Frost reading in the Hill Auditorium. On that afternoon, he declared, the stadium would be filled and nobody would be in the Hill Auditorium, "not even myself, because I'll be at the football game."[28] President Burton's remark was taken more seriously by an undergraduate who wrote an editorial on it for the Michigan *Daily*:

"Of course, the President made this remark more or less in a spirit of fun, but nevertheless it did drive home with particular effectiveness the realization of the University's progress during the present year towards the general appreciation of things cultural. The interest in literature and in any pursuit which deals with the arts has become widespread, and perhaps the best example of this is the enthusiastic attendance at the Poets' Lecture Series, an attendance of such size that Sarah Caswell Angell Hall had to be replaced by Hill Auditorium in order to accommodate the crowds. President Burton attributes the cultural spurt largely if not entirely to the stimulating influence of Robert Frost in our midst, and few can deny that the fellowship made possible through the generosity of Chase S. Osborn has produced excellent results. . . ."[29]

Frost was able to measure the popular success of his performance at Michigan in another way. As the end of the spring term approached, he confided to one of his friends, "Terrible pressure being put on me to bring me back to Ann Arbor."[30] Although he kept speaking of himself as being merely a part of "President Burton's window-dressing," he had enjoyed all the attentions showered on him during the year. He also liked sitting on the platform during the commencement exercises and sharing honors with Secretary of State Charles Evans Hughes and others in receiving from President Burton an honorary degree. Although he grumbled pleasantly over the fact that Hughes was given an LL.D. while the poet was asked to settle for a mere M.A., he found no fault with the citation:

"Robert Frost, M.A., poet and teacher, trained at Dartmouth and Harvard; yet more truly a fashioner of his own education through sympathetic and penetrating studies of man and nature. As a Fellow in Creative Arts, Mr. Frost has been a welcome sojourner in our academic community—wise, gracious, and stimulating."[31]

Very few people outside the immediate family of Robert Frost could imagine the expenditure of nervous energy which had gone into such an extraordinary performance. He had found little time for the one thing the "Fellowship" had been calculated to advance: work on his own poetry; indeed, not enough time to participate in the lonely and frustrating activities of his own children. Lesley, having dabbled once again in academic life and having joined a sorority, quickly became hostile toward the professors in her classes and toward the girls in Alpha Phi. Her father, trying to find something to serve as a diversion for her, had written to Harriet Moody in Chicago:

"I'm bringing Lesley. . . . If it could be arranged I should like to leave her a little while with you in Chicago for the good you would do her. The poor kid is rather sick of this institution and that through no fault of hers. She's had splendid marks and liked seventy five percent of her teachers. But my line of talk isn't calculated to make her like any institution. You know how I'm always at it against colleges, in a vain attempt to reconcile myself with them. The part of them which the youngsters are most free in or where they could be most free, their own so-called activities, they are the most slavish and conventional in. Self sacrifice there must always be in religion and out of religion and with small people it seems to take the form of sacrificing their initiative and independence. . . . it's Alpha Phi that has done for Lesley's love of Ann Arbor."[32]

Lesley's father could have explained her predicament by confessing that his habit of caustic disparagement, reflexively employed as a form of self-defense and aimed at human beings more often than at institutions, had proved to be so contagious that all his children had acquired that habit from him. Lesley was not the only member of the family who wanted to escape from Ann Arbor at exactly the time when the poet was reveling in attentions there. Irma had been miserable from the start and had spent much of her time sulking. Marjorie, lonesome in Vermont and discouraged by her high-school assignments, had written letters which had so upset her mother that Mrs. Frost had twice gone back to North Bennington to visit with her. Carol, inclined to be suspicious of strangers, had grown restless as soon as Yost's very successful football season ended. One spring night, after his father had harshly criticized Carol, the boy simply walked out of 1523 Washtenaw Avenue and did not come back. His parents and sisters could only guess where he had gone, but as the hours of his absence turned into days there was general agreement that he was probably hitchhiking eastward toward the Stone Cottage in South Shaftsbury.

The harsh words directed at Carol had occurred during a family discussion in which Carol said he would like to raise chickens on the South Shaftsbury farm so he could sell eggs as a sideline to apple-raising. He had been studying poultry catalogues, he announced, and he had decided to buy a $35 rooster for his projected brood of hens. His father had explosively protested against such a waste of money, and had ridiculed the boy's proposal. All the children were familiar with the occasional tone of vindictiveness which occurred at certain times when their father went into a rage against anyone who tried to defend opinions which differed from his. During such arguments, Carol seemed to bring down on himself some of his father's most savage attacks, in spite of (or perhaps because of) the way in which the boy's mother frequently tried to defend him. This time, as soon as it became apparent that Carol's disappearance from Ann Arbor was not a temporary affair, his parents phoned Marjorie in North Bennington. They explained what had happened and suggested that she might be on the lookout for her brother; might find him at the Stone Cottage in South Shaftsbury when next she passed it on her way to the home of her roommate, Lillian LaBatt, in nearby Sunderland. A few days later, they received word from Marjorie that Carol was keeping house alone in the Stone Cottage, and seemed to be having a fine time building a henhouse.[33]

Carol's independent return to South Shaftsbury was enough to precipitate a further exodus from Ann Arbor. Irma and Lesley, pleading for permission to go home and keep house for their brother, were allowed to leave. Their father, trying to conceal all the tensions caused by these family events, later wrote to John Bartlett, who had moved from New Hampshire to Colorado for reasons of health:

"I'm still at Ann Arbor, Mich but the climax of annual improvements is about reached and it wont be many days before we book for home. We are Elinor and I. The children long since went ahead of us to set the hens and watch the apples and pears set themselves. . . . Lesley Carol Irma and Margery write that there's all that heart could wish going on on the farm we have. We have a small horse (Morgan) we bought for a saddle horse when very young. We brought it with us at too much expense from Franconia. It has eaten its head off several times over when we have had to board it out in our absence on various errands of mercy and education in the winters. We were just beginning to resent what it had cost us when lo and behold on converting it into a driving horse we find we have a trotter. You may hear of Carol or me on the turf next."[34]

Although Frost kept trying to keep his mind off unpleasantness as he prepared to leave Ann Arbor, he was driven into another fit of rage by the widow from whom he had rented the elegant home on Washtenaw Avenue. In the final settling of accounts, she implied that all was not in proper order and that the Frosts had been inconsiderate tenants. This time, Frost gained some relief from his anger by raging to Untermeyer:

"I wrote you a letter a week ago which you paid no attention to because I never sent it. It was all about the way the distinguished Greek and Latin Professor's Widow (pronounced Dogie as in The Chisholm Trail) accused me out of a clear sky of having stolen or otherwise nefariously made away with one of the five iron pisspots she would swear she had distributed to the five bedrooms of the house she rented to us in Ann Arbor. She wouldn't claim it was an Etruscan vase. Neither was it Mycenaean or Knossian ware. Nevertheless it represented a loss of fifty cents and she proposed to make a stink about it if not in it. I haven't admitted that I could have stolen a thing I no longer have any use for since I stopped drinking. If I did anything with it, I probably took it out into society to make conversation and lost it. I remember trying hard to break it over Carl Sandburg's head for his new mysticism and madness prepense—but in vain. I may have dented it ten cents worth. I have asked her to let the ton of coal we left her in the cellar go toward that.

"I got too bitterly funny about the episode in my other letter. I decided that I didn't mind the bitch as much as I made myself appear. I'm served exactly right for having spent so much of my life tolerating the lower and middle classes. I've been punished often enough in the past for pretending not to see what was wrong with the poor. This is the worst I ever got it for affecting to stand in with the comfortably off. Men[c]ken wins. My democracy has been 99 per cent unrealization. I left the world when I was young for reasons I gradually came to forget. I returned to the world at thirty three (sharp) to see if I couldn't recover my reasons. I have recovered them all right, 'and I am ready to depart' again. I believe I will take example of [Emerson's] Uriel and withdraw into a cloud—of whiskers. . . ."[35]

14

THE LONG TRAIL

I came back from Michigan University all puffed out with self-hate that would have curdled the ink in my pen if I had tried to write to you at that time. There was nothing for it but to get away from myself. You know they say there is no such thing as leaving ourselves behind. . . . But if we will do it on foot . . . the escape from self is complete. It has been so complete in my case that no one would know me . . .[1]

WHEN Robert Frost returned to South Shaftsbury from Ann Arbor in June of 1922, he felt thoroughly exhausted. The whirl of activities during the spring term had shaken him physically and had made him regretful enough to complain that he should never have let himself in for such an ordeal. Unfortunately, he now complained, his various performances had been so highly successful that the students, the faculty, and the townspeople hoped the one-year appointment was but a beginning. President Burton, in their final conversation before Frost's departure, had said that if money could be found for carrying on the experiment, Frost would certainly be invited back for at least one more year of residence at the University of Michigan. In his immediate state of weariness, the poet had not been elated by the prospect. He had told the president, bluntly, that if he came back he would expect the arrangement would contain reliable provisions for protecting him from being overwhelmed by intrusions which, in the year just ending, had kept him from doing his own work. According to the original agreement, he had been promised as much free time for his writing as he might choose to take, and to have no regular classes. He had not expected to be in demand for so many tea parties, formal dinners, entertainments, talks, conferences, readings. True, he had made himself available for more things than he had needed to do, but he was disappointed in the quantity and quality of the poetry he had written while at Ann Arbor. The president reassured him that if arrangements could be made for his return, Frost should consider himself free to disappear from the campus, or even from Michigan, whenever he liked, for sensible periods of time.[2]

Regardless of Burton's friendliness and sympathy, Frost had fled to his Vermont farm in an ugly mood, glad to escape from the academic by helping Carol with work in spraying the new orchards, hoeing in the small vegetable garden, splitting wood, caring for the newly hatched chickens, cleaning the fancy-stepping Morgan, and occasionally milking their one cow. His athletic daughter Lesley, at home for the summer, found another way to divert him. She had heard that the Green Mountain Club had nearly completed making a 261-mile "Foot-path in the Wilderness" across the longitude of Vermont, from Massachusetts to Canada. This "Long Trail," as it was usually called, appealed to Lesley as a supurb challenge for anyone who enjoyed packing blankets and food, sleeping on mountain tops, cooking meals over campfires, and enjoying kaleidescopic changes in scenic views. More than that, Lesley appealed to her father's fondness for quoting Coleridge's "We were the first who ever burst . . ." The Frost family—at least the mountain-climbers in it—could set a new record by being the very first to walk all the way along what was completed of the new trail, and she estimated that the expedition would take not more than two weeks.

Lesley's father was ready for such an outing, and he had anticipated her in one regard. At Ann Arbor, while talking with Morris Tilley about mountain-climbing experiences they had shared in the Franconia Range, he had learned of a cele-brated local cobbler—a Frenchman from Switzerland—who fashioned beautiful and expensive custom-made shoes con-sidered perfect for mountain-climbing. Unable to resist, Frost acquired from the Frenchman a fancy pair of handmade shoes. He wore them occasionally, in his walks around Ann Arbor, just to break them in, before he returned home. At first they seemed a bit snug, but he felt he could stretch them enough with a few more short walks, before tackling the Long Trail. If any record-breaking was to be done, he wanted to be in on the excitement. More than that, he was eager to escape from all the nervousness he had brought home with him. As plans developed, Carol promised to go if the others would wait until the middle of August, when he could best leave his farm work. Marjorie, also enthusiastic about the venture, gained permission to invite her friend Lillian LaBatt to join the hiking party. Carol, usually shy in the presence of strange girls, had already become sufficiently well acquainted with the lively and attractive Lillian to agree that she would make a good companion on the Long Trail. Their father suggested adding one more member to the group: a young man named Edward Ames Richards, who had just been graduated from Amherst. Richards, during his freshman year at Amherst, had been one of Frost's favorites because he had shown ability as a poet. He had visited the Frosts at South Shaftsbury often enough to be known and liked by all the Frost children, and they were pleased when he accepted the invitation to hike with them.

After elaborate preparations, six of them started for the Long Trail on Tuesday, the fifteenth of August 1922, each with a knapsack and blankets. Irma, who did not like to climb, was glad to stay at home with her mother. According to the revised plan, the hikers would cover 225 miles of the 261-mile trail—from the other side of Bald Mountain (the foot of which rose not far to the east of their own dooryard) to Smuggler's Notch in Johnson, Vermont, where the trail then ended. The "children" would return by train to South Shaftsbury, from there, in about seventeen days. Frost would go by train from Johnson, Vermont, to Littleton, New Hampshire, where he would meet his wife on Monday, the fourth of September, en route to Franconia, and they would stay there for the remainder of the hay-fever season.

Frost was amused to notice that as soon as the climbers began the ascent of Bald Mountain, he was the only one who settled into a slow and deliberate pace, content to let his children and their companions romp ahead. His private notions of mountain-climbing were based not so much on the fable of the tortoise and the hare as on his pleasure in botanizing with eyes and fingers and nose, as he went. He treated both sides of the path as though they were pages of an open book, as though he were there to read both pages as he walked, and even pronounce the names of old friends as he came upon them: dwarf cornel, checkerberry, goldroot, mianthemum. If nobody was near enough to make him embarrassed by eavesdropping, he did not hesitate to say "Hello," out loud, to any plant rare enough to deserve special greeting. The season was far enough advanced to make it unlikely he would find any of these little plants fresh in blossom, but it was part of his pleasure to notice flowers fading on the seed to come. When the woods grew too shaded for plants, he enjoyed reading the leaves of bushes and trees, enjoyed breaking off the newly grown twig-ends of the black birch and chewing the bark long enough to get the wintergreen flavor out of it. Then there was always the fragrance of trees, so strong on the mountainside that he could identify hemlock or white pine or balsam before he lifted his eyes to search for the source of the fragrance. Mixed in with all these pleasures came the intermittent songs of birds he cherished as affectionately as he did the plants, leaves, bark. One of his favorite songs was the clean, sustained and lingering melody of the white-throated sparrow, rarely seen even when perfectly heard. All these casual observations made mountain-climbing a special form of luxury for him. His lingering as he walked was merely a part of his cherishing.

Bald Mountain, in spite of its name, had long ago become so densely covered by trees that there was no chance to gain adequate vistas until the Frost party reached the top and climbed the sixty-foot lookout tower. From that vantage point they could look over into three other states: to the south, Massachusetts, and then the winding range of the Taconic Mountains, snaking up through Bennington, even up beyond the Frosts' Stone Cottage in South Shaftsbury, and on up to noble Equinox in Manchester. But the Taconics were low enough, directly to the west of Bald Mountain, to let these hikers see far over into New York State and even into the foothills of the Adirondacks. To the east and northeast, they had to look past the splendid obstructions provided by the nearby shoulders of Haystack Mountain and Mount Snow to catch even glimpses of foothills to the White Mountains of New Hampshire. Their immediate attention was directed to the northward, where they could see how the Long Trail would guide them: over Glastenbury Mountain and, to the left of that from their lookout, the tree-covered crests of Stratton, Killington, and Bromley.

For all of the Frosts, knowing the austere peaks of the White Mountains, with stone pinnacles thrust above the timberline, this panoramic view of the Green Mountains seemed so much more friendly that they were all eager to reach the Long Trail—on which they would not even start to walk until the next day. Their plan was to go down the eastern side of Bald Mountain to what was then the beginning of the Long Trail, in Hell Hollow, and spend the first night in (or at least near) a private camp owned by one of their neighbors. Down they went, and experienced considerable difficulty in locating the camp which none of them had previously seen. At last they thought they found it, but the key they had brought did not fit. Robert Frost impatiently solved that problem by breaking a pane of glass, so they could unlock the window and climb in. Before they left, the next morning, they made a temporary patch for the window. They had not yet reached the Long Trail, however, when they came on another cabin which so nearly fitted the description of what they had been looking for that Frost tried the key and found that it fit. Immediately, his children teased him for breaking and entering a stranger's camp, the night before. Ashamed of himself for his impatience, and always highly superstitious, he took this error as a bad sign, and started up the Long Trail with trepidation.

Secretly, he could admit to himself that he had already noticed another bad sign requiring no element of superstition to interpret. The day before, he was only halfway down Bald Mountain when he began to realize that his expensive hand-made mountain-climbing shoes kept pinching in ways he did not like. Unfortunately, he had placed so much confidence in them that he had not thought to put extra shoes or sneakers into his knapsack, and if these kept bothering him, he foresaw danger. Worst of all, he might be excluded from helping to set the intended record on the Long Trail, and that danger increased painfully before he had climbed to the top of Glastenbury Mountain, on the second day out. That night, after covering not more than fifteen miles in getting to the base of Stratton Mountain, near Grout Pond, just to the north of the Somerset Reservoir—and not far from the spot where Daniel Webster had made his celebrated Vermont address—Frost was glad to get his pretty shoes off.

His mood improved after he had eaten a supper the girls prepared, and after all of them had spread their blankets on the board floor of a shed which housed lumber sledges. Rain, or at least the threat of it, caused them to seek refuge under the roof of this long shed. To Frost, it was clear that the young people had taken these first two days of climbing far better than he had, but he did his best to conceal any hint that even the girls might be able to outwalk him. He was a little impatient with them, that second night, when they continued to chatter long after he was bedded down and trying to sleep. At last he made the fatherly suggestion that quiet was in order. They'd better get to sleep, and if anyone else began to talk after he finished, all the others should pay no attention, should give no answer. Silence, for several minutes thereafter. The only sound was that of summer insects talking in the grass and trees outside the shed. Then Frost had a happy idea which pleased him so much that he forgot his own order. He had scarcely begun to explain it, aloud, when his Amherst friend Ted Richard parodied his tone of voice in suggesting that quiet was in order and that they'd all better get to sleep. Annoyed by the interruption, Frost shouted: "Don't pay any attention to him!" He continued to explain his happy idea—and he was still talking when Richards fell asleep.[3]

When Frost woke up the next morning his feet were swollen just enough to make it hard for him to force his toes into the fancy boots. Cursing himself for having wasted so much money, he took his jackknife and furiously cut slits in each boot until he had given his toes plenty of room. Even this desperate remedy did not entirely relieve the pain. As they started climbing Stratton Mountain, the youngsters slowed down for him. They spent the whole day getting to the top of Stratton, and camped near the top for their third night. A day later, when they were approaching Bromley Mountain, at the point where the Long Trail crosses the road from Manchester to Londonderry, the clouds closed in so darkly that they decided to turn east and walk three miles to seek lodging in the town of Peru. Arriving there in the midst of a heavy thundershower, they were allowed to drip off in the kitchen of the Russell Inn, and nobody objected when Frost said that they would take rooms for this fourth night, right where they were, at his expense. By this time, his feet were bothering him so much that all the hikers accepted his invitation to spend another day and night at the Russell Inn. Sunday morning, August twentieth at breakfast, he announced that the youngsters should go on, without him: he would find conveyance to Manchester, take the train to Rutland, replace the slashed hiking boots with a pair of sneakers, and rejoin them. But where? And how soon? A study of the map and of distances suggested that in four days they would reach the Middlebury Pass, above the Bread Loaf School of English. Frost decided that he could stand a four-day rest, and he would somehow get conveyance to the Middlebury Pass in time to have supper ready for them at the Lake Pleiad shelter, on Thursday.

The plan was carried out. Richards deciding he had hiked far enough, accompanied Frost to Manchester, and went south. Frost, going north from Manchester to Rutland by train, hid in a hotel so that he could rest for two days. He bought sneakers, discarded his expensive boots, and hoped his sore feet would let him get back on the Long Trail. After going from Rutland to Middlebury by train on Wednesday, the twenty-third of August, he walked and hitchhiked to the Middlebury Gap, bedding down in the shelter at Lake Pleiad a day ahead of the time when the children were due to get there. He had chosen to circumnavigate the campus of the Bread Loaf School of English, on the way, and he had done so by hitting for the woods below the school and returning to the road, well above it, in order to avoid being seen by anyone who might recognize him. If his feelings had not been hurt so much, there, the previous summer, and if he had not refused Professor Davison's invitation to return during the summer session of 1922, he might have been welcomed with a measure of ceremony at nearly the time when he was sneaking out around the Bread Loaf School, more like a fugitive than a bard. The woods around tiny Lake Pleiad provided another excellent hiding place for him, until his hikers came into view along the Trail eager to see whether he had brought adequate supplies to replenish their dwindling larder. He showed them how thoughtful he had been: he had brought them one good steak for broiling over a campfire, and one two-pound box of chocolates, but nothing more. When they asked about his feet, he insisted that the new sneakers he was now wearing were far better than the boots he had thrown away in Rutland.

Unfortunately, those boots had done more damage than Frost was as yet willing to admit, and new complications developed. The next day, he had walked only a few miles along the skyline sacred to the memory of Joseph Battell—Battell Mountain, Bread Loaf Mountain (with Mount Ellen ahead)—when one of his knees began to bother him. Before he reached the Lincoln-Warren Gap, he decided that he might as well stop trying to keep pace with his youngsters, and he announced in a tone of martyrdom that they should leave him right where he was. He would get down into Warren slowly, he said, and they could forget about him. It seemed to him that his children took the news much too philosophically, and that their only concern was to be sure he gave them enough money for the cost of whatever food they might need to purchase in villages not too far off the trail during the next week or ten days, before they reached the end of the trail.

Abandoned, and feeling miserable, he limped down into the town of Warren not knowing whether he should go from there to South Shaftsbury or Franconia. If he went home, he would be ashamed to appear before his wife in his crippled condition. Having boasted of his prowess as a mountain-climber, he dreaded what Elinor might—or even might not—say. She had a scornfully silent knack for making him realize that he always took his sufferings with far more self-pity than she took hers, and he decided in Warren that her silence would be more punishment than he wanted to take. Anyway, he was in such a mood that he wanted to punish himself for his own failure.

Studying his map, he realized that he might get to Johnson before his children, if he could force himself to walk (or perhaps to accept rides from passing motorists) northward a distance of only forty-five miles along this valley road which ran through Moretown, Waterbury, Stowe, and Cady Falls to Johnson. Then he could wait for them at the end of the trail and participate at least vicariously in their record-setting triumph. His route, even if he took a week to walk it, would be over relatively flat ground, while his children would be ascending and descending some of the highest mountains in Vermont—including Camel's Hump and Mansfield. He would need to average less than seven miles a day to be in Johnson ahead of them.

During the next week, he alternated hours of resting and walking. Some nights he slept out, but on other nights he afforded himself the luxury of hotel comforts. He tried soaking his swollen feet in hot bathtubs and in cold mountain brooks. He tried walking in the cool of the night, barefooted. When tired of preparing his own meals, he gorged himself in out-of-the-way restaurants or in small hotel dining rooms, always dreading to be seen by someone who would recognize him. Successfully escaping such mortification, he continued to force himself onward until he was well north of Stowe and Mount Mansfield. Then he gradually felt that he might as well admit failure, even in this consolation game, because time was running out. Do his best or worst, he foresaw that the children would get down through Smuggler's Notch and on into Johnson before he could waylay and surprise them, near the end of the Long Trail.

His final choice, in this race, was made when he reached a road fork below Lamoille Lake. If he turned left, Johnson was only ten miles away. If he turned right, for the town of Wolcott, he could board a train, there, en route to St. Johnsbury and Littleton. Fearing that the children had already finished their record walk, and might be back in South Shaftsbury, he turned toward Wolcott. The decision itself was enough to cheer him up, and while he waited in Wolcott for the next train he tried to make calculations of how much ground he had covered. He estimated that he had done 65 miles on the Long Trail, and 50 more miles on the valley road from Warren to Wolcott—a total of 115 miles. That was farther than he had ever walked before, in one expedition, and good enough for the old man he suddenly felt he was. Entitled to boast, he wrote the second of two notes to Lesley's favorite instructor at Wellesley, Professor Charles Lowell Young, with whom he had walked across New Hampshire to Lake Willoughby, the previous summer:

"I went back on the trail on one leg and added fifty more miles to my sixty-five. But it was against nature. Here I am knocked out again with the same little toe. So you needn't feel the least bit my inferior in the legs or character.

"Those children though! Too much cannot be said for their grim forging. They had done their two hundred [miles] in fifteen consecutive days when they left me for a pitiable. May their deeds be remembered. . . ."[4]

There was time for another note, before the train came, and this one was written to Untermeyer, with poetic license and playful hyperbole. The heading was "Wolcott Vermont nr Canada," and the message:

"I walked as per prophesy till I had no feet left to write regular verse with (hence this free verse) and that proved to be just one hundred and twenty-five miles largely on the trail. Here I am stranded without Elinor's permission to go on or come home. I slept out on the ground alone last night and the night before and soaked both my feet in a running brook all day. That was my final mistake. My feet melted and disappeared down stream. Good bye."

Then a postscript:

"I should admit that the kids all did two hundred and twenty miles. I let them leave me behind for a poor old father who could once out-walk out-run and out-talk them but can now no more."⁵

Another mortification overtook him as he boarded the train at Wolcott for St. Johnsbury. His unshaved face, his bedraggled clothes, his misshapen and too-often-rainsoaked brown felt hat—not to mention the bedroom slipper on his right foot and the dirty sneaker on his left—made him look like a tramp: he seemed to be carrying all of his worldly possessions in the huge knapsack on his back or in the roll of blankets slung around his neck. The conductor, watching him suspiciously, protested when Frost dumped the dirty knapsack and blankets on the first empty seat he found, inside the door of the car, but a fellow-passenger who thought Frost must be a worn-out mountain guide, took his side in the argument and persuaded the conductor to leave him alone. Gratefully, Frost began to give his rescuer an entertaining account of his adventures and mishaps on and off the Long Trail. All the passengers within earshot were fascinated by this weird-looking creature who apologetically explained why he had boarded the train with one foot in a bedroom slipper. His defender introduced himself as Harold S. Gulliver, a teacher with a degree from Yale, now in these parts because he had just been visiting friends at the Bread Loaf Inn. That was enough to give the conversation another twist, and the disreputable-looking mountain guide gradually got around to admitting who he was. By the time the two men, seated together, had talked their way to St. Johnsbury, Frost asked Gulliver for another form of assistance. The poet wanted to spend the night at the St. Johnsbury hotel, but he was afraid the man at the desk might be just as suspicious of him as the conductor had been, unless someone like Gulliver could reassure the clerk. Gulliver explained that he had several hours to wait for a train, in St. Johnsbury, and that he would enjoy giving Frost the assistance, if needed. There was no difficulty at the hotel desk, and by way of gratitude Frost said he would like to invite his new friend to have dinner with him in the hotel dining room, but that he was low on cash. Gulliver had an answer for that: he would be glad to lend Frost five dollars, and he did. After dinner, Frost suggested that they retreat to his room, where they could talk. He added, "I always hate to go to bed." Their talk went on until Gulliver was forced to take his leave.[6]

After a long sleep, Frost again wrote to Untermeyer, this time using even more poetic license:

"Here I am out at St. Johnsbury . . . having for my part achieved peace without victory. The children made a record for the two hundred and twenty miles of Vermont from Mass. to Canada. I am content that it is all in the family though as for me personally the laurels wither on my brow as of course they were bound to sooner or later. I am beginning to slip: I may as well admit it gracefully and accept my dismissal to the minor and bush leagues where no doubt I have several years of useful service still before me as pinch hitter and slow coach. . . ."[7]

On Monday, the fourth of September 1922, he met his wife at the Littleton station, exactly as planned, but he was still wearing his bedroom slipper on his right foot, and he did not entirely escape the scornful teasing he had feared. Mrs. Frost was able to report that the children had reached Johnson on Friday, the first of September, and they had returned to South Shaftsbury the next day. All of them had survived very well, without even so much as a sprained ankle. But Carol was the one who had really surprised her by saying that during the expedition he and Lillian had fallen in love and that they were engaged to be married. Frost was not surprised. Having witnessed various phases of the courtship, on the Long Trail, he saw good reason why his farmer-son should choose to fall in love with a girl who was not only attractive and lively but also the knowing and capable daughter of a farmer. Carol's mother had the conventional reservations and jealousies. Faced with the prospect of losing her only son, she questioned his choice. But it was clear to both parents that nothing might come of this romance: Carol and Lillian were still children. Lillian, only sixteen, seemed very anxious to complete her high-school course at North Bennington. She stood at the head of her class, there, and she had already said she wanted to spend the next four years at the University of Vermont. Carol was twenty, and yet it seemed to his parents that he was still too boyish to talk of marriage. For the time being, it was enough that all four of the young people had come through the ordeal of their triumph in good health and in excellent spirits.

Lesley soon wrote an account of the adventure, and sent it to the Bennington *Banner*. It was published under the head-line, "LONG TRAIL, 225 MILES, YIELDS TO YOUTH AND VIGOR." The subcaption: "Entire Length Traversed in One Continuous Hike. The First Time on Record. Three Bennington County Girls and One Boy are the Conquerors."[8] Frost, not entirely happy over Lesley's way of dismissing him with brief mention, sent the article to Lincoln MacVeagh in a letter which again used just enough poetic license to improve and idealize his part in the story:

"The enclosed clipping will tell you what almost became of me in August and September. I don't feel that it does me personally quite justice. I did some hundred and twenty miles actually on the trail and pretty actually on one leg. In this damned newspaper account I am made to drop out and set off for Franconia on foot. Nothing is said of the privations I underwent after that. Nobody knew or asked what became of me. When I dropped in my tracks from a complication of gangrenous housemaids knee and old man's sore toe I was gone through for what money I had in my pockets that might be useful to the expedition and then left for no good. You'll notice nothing more is said of me. Yet as a matter of fact I survived to walk a hundred and fifty miles further all by myself and sleeping out on the ground all by myself to Franconia up a White Mountain or two and then around Willoughby Lake.

"I am sorry to have to admit that the Green Mountain Expedition proper was a success without me. It reached home with just one cent left over in its pockets after having wound up by sleeping one night in the graveyard for want of enough to pay for a nights lodging in the hotel at Johnson. . . ."[9]

Regardless of the exaggerations in his account, Robert Frost knew that this longest walking-venture of his life had been a major event for him, partly because it had enabled him to get so far away from all that was eating at him. He had gone into the Green Mountains with a congenial group of his own choosing and, although he had been forced to separate himself even from that much company, he had enjoyed traveling incognito, at the time when he had been punishing himself for being older than he wished. His double-edged retreat into the wilderness, with plenty of time for meditation and contemplation, had somehow purged all the rancor and bitterness he had brought back from Ann Arbor. By the time he returned to South Shaftsbury from Franconia, he had succeeded in finding not only the time but also the mood for at least a few tries at writing poetry, and he was now ready to arrange for more remunerative ways of supporting his family.

The prospect for returning to Michigan seemed dim. Although President Burton had written on the twenty-fifth of July 1922 to say he still hoped he would succeed in securing $5,000 for the continuation of the Fellowship in Creative Art, he had been forced to admit that he had not been successful, so far. Frost, hearing nothing further during August and September, had begun to protect himself against the apparent eventuality by accepting various invitations to give readings or talks, from Vermont to Texas. Unexpectedly, on the sixth of October 1922, he received a telegram from President Burton:

"Very happy to say that we have secured $5,000 for Fellowship in Creative Arts assuming that you can be with us as arranged last spring. We are hoping that both Mrs. Frost and you can be with us for our first reception Wednesday afternoon, October eleventh. In any case please wire assurances that the whole arrangement is agreeable to you. Warm personal greetings to Mrs. Frost and yourself."[10]

Frost hesitated, uncertain whether all of his newly made commitments would permit him to accept. Although the oral agreement with President Burton in the spring had nearly given him freedom to be on campus at the University of Michigan as much or as little as he chose, for the projected second year, he knew he could not be absent too much of the time. While still trying to decide, he received another telegram from President Burton:

"Our whole enterprise contingent on your acceptance. You will be deeply interested to know confidentially that unnamed donor is prepared seriously to consider permanent endowment of $10,000 in light of this second year's experience. You must come for the sake of cause. Students, faculty, regents and citizens unite in invitation. Please wire collect your willingness to come."[11]

That settled it, and Frost replied by telegram, "Arrangements most agreeable as you must know. Thanks for ourselves and whatever we may be supposed to represent. Happy to be with you at reception on Wednesday."[12] Knowing that he had less than a week to conclude preparations at home and to make the journey from South Shaftsbury to Ann Arbor, Frost was aware that he might be going alone. Carol bluntly said he would stay on the farm. The boy had obviously enjoyed running away from his father at Ann Arbor; now it was clear that not even Big Ten football could tempt him to run away from Lillian. Marjorie, planning her senior year of high school at North Bennington, proposed that she be permitted to commute from the Stone Cottage until winter weather set in, and that she might again live with Lillian in a rented room at North Bennington thereafter. Irma wanted to stay with Carol and help to keep house for him; Lesley had already made arrangements to work in a New York City bookstore. Mrs. Frost, reluctant to leave her children, and knowing that her husband's previously made commitments would require his return to New England soon after the reception, decided not to go until later. All of these decisions were made amicably, in ways that seemed to satisfy everyone. Just before leaving South Shaftsbury, Frost sketched his plans in a note to MacVeagh:

"I've had a hurry-up call to come to Ann Arbor in time to be at the President's reception on Wednesday. So the thing is settled for this year. I had an idea it would be by hook or crook.

"I shall be back East again right away for engagements at Rutland, Wellesley and Boston I had got myself in for for fear there mightn't be any Michigan money this year. I expect to be in New York early in November on my way South."[13]

A ROUND OF READINGS

Gee does anybody suppose I would lecture as badly as I do if I could find anybody to take the responsibility for my staying off the platform entirely?[1]

DURING the reception at the University of Michigan on the eleventh of October 1922, Robert Frost had no difficulty in explaining to President Burton that prior commitments would force the poet to be absent from Ann Arbor during the next few weeks. He stayed only two days in the home of Dean Bursley, meeting old friends and making plans for continuing the work he had begun so successfully during the previous year. Then he went back to South Shaftsbury, en route to his first engagement. It was a reading in Rutland, Vermont, under circumstances he regretted.

The Vermont State League of Women's Clubs, in solemn conclave assembled, had caused the circumstances. They had voted, in Springfield, on the seventh of June 1922, to name Robert Frost as their choice for the title of Poet Laureate of Vermont. Reactions had occurred quickly, even as far away as New York City. An editorial in the *Times* had noticed the event with mild sarcasms:

"If one of our states is to have a poet laureate, the natural expectation is that he would be a native or at the very least a long-time resident of that State. It is more than a little curious and an incitement to considerable thought, therefore, that the Vermont State League of Women's Clubs, in annual convention this week, selected Robert Frost to be Vermont's official representative of the Muse. To be sure, the choice does credit to the critical imagination of these women, for the man they chose to be their laureate is noteworthy. . . . But Mr. Frost was born in California, and his college days were spent partly at Dartmouth and partly at Harvard. He was a farmer for a while, or *Who's Who* says so, though one wonders, and then, after teaching in several New Hampshire schools he finally landed a post as Professor of English Literature in Amherst. His home is set down as Franconia, N. H., but he does have a summer place in South Shaftsbury, Vt., and that seems to be his only connection with the Green Mountain State. . . ."[2]

The editorial writer in the *Times* went on to make further mistakes, including the claim that Robert Frost, as a writer of free verse, should not appeal to such traditionalists as Vermonters. The first corrections were sent down to New York by Mrs. Halley Phillips Gilchrist, who had arranged for the Frosts to make their initial visit to Vermont. Writing from Arlington, she began by saying that the *Times* editorial had interested her because of its errors. Robert Frost had been able to vote as a citizen of Vermont for two years, she said, and he was certainly no mere "summer resident." She continued, "Here he maintains a farm for he is a good farmer in spite of your doubts." As for the mistake in calling him a writer of free verse, she answered that one by quoting "unofficially from Mr. Frost" as follows: "I know of no critic in America, England, France or Vermont who supposes me to have written any free verse."[3]

The next defender of the ladies of Vermont was Sarah Cleghorn, who wrote from Manchester to protest that the *Times* "paragrapher" seemed to be ignorant concerning Robert Frost's place of legal residence, his activities as a farmer, and his way of writing poetry. On the last point, she bore down with considerable scorn: "Blank verse, as Mr. Frost uses it, is so natural in its cadence and language that it is nothing strange if careless readers call it 'free.' But that is really a very free use of the word, 'free.' Look at the lines, and they will be found regular, according to the best traditions of English poetry." As for the decision made by the women of Vermont, Miss Cleghorn concluded, "I take a sentimental pleasure in the credit they have done themselves in formal recognition of the greatness of our best, I think, American poet."[4]

Although Robert Frost had been in Michigan when these little skirmishes had occurred, he acknowledged the honor by accepting an invitation from the Rutland Women's Club to give a reading at the Rutland High School on the evening of the eighteenth of October 1922. Even that occasion stirred up a local controversy: there were some Vermonters who jealously protected the reputation of an Edgar-Guest-like rhymer named Daniel L. Cady, author of a book of doggerel entitled *Rhymes of Vermont*. Some other opponents in this local controversary were snobbish Vermonters who scornfully rejected any literature which could be viewed as merely local. Not long after his reading in Rutland, Frost touched pleasantly on these matters in a letter to Untermeyer:

"In Detroit I was bidden to a feast with Eddy Guest; even so in Vermont I am bidden to a feast with Daniel Cady. Haply you never heard of Daniel Cady. Stop your ears with wax or you will hear. . . . I heard in Rutland Vt. that the wife of the President of the Rutland Railroad regarded Dorothy Canfield as local talent and as such refused to be interested in her. 'Why she hasn't a reputable publisher, has she?' was her question. Tell Harcourt that. The years we waste!"[5]

Next after Rutland in his autumnal round of readings came several Boston commitments made delicate by other jealousies there. Always above jealousy, however, was the unassuming Katharine Lee Bates, poet and professor, who had previously brought Frost to Wellesley College as often as she could. Each time, she successfully coaxed him to stay long enough to talk informally before at least one of her classes. This time, in making arrangements for another reading at Wellesley on the twenty-fourth of October 1922, she enlisted the help of another poet, Gamaliel Bradford, who had made most of his literary success with his prose "psychographs." Bradford had played host to Robert Frost in the fall of 1919, during Frost's first visit to Wellesley, and as a result of that meeting the two men had established an affectionate friendship. With the best of intentions, Frost had tried to help Bradford find outlets for his poems, his plays, and his novels.[6] Following the first of these attempts, Bradford had written him, "What strange perversity is it that induces a man to set his heart on doing those things which he has not succeeded in. . . . Yet the witchery, the infatuation of fiction and especially of poetry torments me in my dreams. I cannot let them rest, cannot resist the fascination of teasing words into all sorts of lovely and fantastic cloud-visions, which stray and wander out into regions altogether beyond the sober and prosaic limits of historical research."[7] Immediately under way was his research on such figures as P. T. Barnum, Aaron Burr, John Randolph,

Thomas Paine, and others, for phychographic treatment in a projected volume to be called *Damaged Souls*. Frost had already been shown an early draft of the chapter on Aaron Burr, and had written from South Shaftsbury on the eighteenth of January 1922, "I've just been reading your Aaron Burr. He's a beauty. On with the job. Don't spare to be a little wicked yourself over these wicked people. Not that I would have you make the judicious grieve, but you can afford to make the judicious guess. Tease us."[8] Bradford had replied on the twenty-first of January 1922:

"I am glad you liked the Burr. . . . when I get a man like Burr who throws the last wrapping off his soul, I am so grateful to him that perhaps I treat him with greater leniency than he deserves. Anyway, it has been a strange experience, living for a year with all these damaged souls. You tell me to yield to their wickedness a little. Great heavens, the difficulty is to keep from yielding to it altogether: they all somehow had such human charm, all made such a piercing, clinging appeal to my own human frailty, that when I got through I felt that I was the most damaged of the lot, and I feel so still.

"And then the charm of the women in it all. . . . And as for Sarah Butler. Well, you love human nature, New England human nature, and understand it as well as anyone understands anything in this utterly incomprehensible world. It would really pay you to turn over the vast accumulation of pages in Butler's correspondence and glance at some of those letters of Sarah Butler. If ever there was a tortured, tormented, enraptured, ecstatic, and above all self-revealing soul, it was hers. . . ."[9]

When the Frosts spent the evening of the twenty-second of October 1922 with the Bradfords in Wellesley there was a living woman, and a poet, known personally to all of them, whom the two men discussed with little sympathy. Amy Lowell, having published her *Critical Fable* anonymously, earlier that fall, was continuing to pretend that she was not the author of it. On the two-color title page she had described *A Critical Fable* as "A Sequel to the 'Fable for Critics' " in which James Russell Lowell had wittily balanced praise and faultfinding throughout his treatment of popular poets of his day, including Emerson, Longfellow, Holmes, Whittier, Poe, and himself. It seemed to Bradford and Frost that Amy Lowell, following her cousin's pattern even to the rhymed "Preface" set in prose, greatly lacked her cousin's critical insights and poetic gifts. She had fumbled and stumbled through her supposedly balanced appraisals of Frost, Robinson, Sandburg, Masters, Lindsay, and herself, and then had placed in a lesser category such authors as Sara Teasdale, the Untermeyers, Pound, Eliot, Wallace Stevens, and Edna St. Vincent Millay. She had offended Frost because she found so many nice things to say about herself and so many uncomplimentary things to say about him. Perhaps her most barbed criticisim was her treatment of him as an Emersonian poet-prophet who claimed a direct communication-line from the Source of all inspiration:

> . . . He's a foggy benignity wandering in space
> With a stray wisp of moonlight just touching his face,
> Descending to earth when a certain condition
> Reminds him that even a poet needs nutrition,
> Departing thereafter to rarefied distances
> Quite unapproachable to those persistencies,
> The lovers of Lions, who shout at his tail—
> At least so he says—when he comes within hail.
> Majestic, remote, a quite beautiful pose,
> (Or escape, or indulgence, or all three, who knows?)
> Set solidly up in a niche like an oracle
> Dispensing replies which he thinks categorical.
> No wonder he cleaves to his leafy seclusion,
> Barricading his door to unlawful intrusion,
> The goal of the fledgling, a god in a thicket,
> To be viewed only Tuesdays and Fridays by ticket.
> Yet note, if you please, this is but one degree
> Of Frost, there are more as you'll presently see,
> And some of them are so vexatiously teasing
> All this stored heat is needed to keep him from freezing.
> Life is dreadfully hard on a man who can see
> A rainbow-clad prophet a-top of each tree;
> To whom every grass-blade's a telephone wire
> With Heaven as central and electrifier.
> He has only to ring up the switch-board and hear
> A poem lightly pattering into his ear,
> But he must be in tune or the thing takes a kink,
> An imminent lunch-bell puts it all on the blink. . . .[10]

Frost didn't have to explain to Bradford why such mockery infuriated him. Bradford, agreeing with Frost that Amy Lowell was probably the author of this harshness, had his own reasons for being annoyed. His name had not even been mentioned in *A Critical Fable*, and yet he had received from Houghton Mifflin a prepublication copy with a note from Amy's editor, Ferris Greenslett, saying that several critics to whom advance copies had been sent had guessed that Bradford was the author. Whatever his weaknesses as a poet, Bradford was so fastidious in his conventional handling of meter and rhyme that he was horrified to have anyone try to dump this foundling on his doorstep. He had answered Greenslett curtly, "I could never possibly have been satisfied to write such shambling slouchy verse."[11] One of the first to penetrate Miss Lowell's masquerade was Louis Untermeyer, who had also received an advance copy and had quickly noticed that many of the critical attitudes were identical with those he had so often heard Amy Lowell make. More than a week before the book was published, he had sent his congratulations to her, hailing her as the anonymous author of *A Critical Fable*. She had promptly replied,

"I quite agree with you that 'A Critical Fable' is a good book. Ferris sent me an advance copy just as he did you. But, my dear Louis, you are mad if you think I wrote it; I wish to God I had. And permit me to offer you my congratulations on your excellent bluff. From the first moment I opened the book I said to myself: Louis is the only person I know of who would have been likely to write this book, and now you hastily forestall me by suggesting that I have done it, which is one of the neatest little side-steppings I have ever seen. . . ."[12]

Frost was given his own chance to unmask Amy Lowell during his visit to Boston in the fall of 1922. A year earlier, when he had played host to her in Ann Arbor, she had insisted that the Frosts must stay with her at Sevenels during their next visit to the "Hub of the Universe." Mrs. Frost, accustomed to serving as secretary for her husband in these matters, had written to Miss Lowell from South Shaftsbury, "Would you like to have Robert and me spend a day or two with you, coming to you either the 24th or 25th of October. We are to be at Wellesley for two or three days, and I am not quite sure which day we are expected to leave there."[13] As the arrangements worked out, the Frosts went from Wellesley to Brookline on the twenty-sixth of October to spend one night with Amy Lowell. Frost, having learned much about her foibles during her celebrated visit to Ann Arbor, thought he could use banter and irony as traps which would make her admit she was the author of *A Critical Fable*. He failed. Not long after his visit with her, he suggested to Untermeyer that the best way to make her confess her guilt might be to inform her confidentially that the author of the anonymous work was a so-called poet whose verses she detested:

"If you really want to find out who wrote A Critical Fable just follow my advice and proceed as follows with Miss Amy Lowell. Tell her you had it quite independently of me from a man named Ira Sibil that it was Nathan Haskell Dole the well-known-in-Boston punster. Say I seem to have heard the same thing from George Herbert Palmer the well-known-in-Boston widower of Alice Freeman Palmer. Be perfectly open and aboveboard if you want to get an appreciable rise out of her. Don't be funny. Station someone with a red flag two or three hundred yards on each side up and down the road to warn off the traffic before you touch this off.

"Gee some Boston this time.[14] And now a long jump from where John Stark licked the British in 1777 to where Andrew Jackson licked them in 1814. After that Ann Arbor. . . ."[15]

Robert Frost had been forced to lick a few of his own prejudices before he could be persuaded to go so far South as New Orleans. The stimulus had been provided by an extraordinary Browning devotee, A. Joseph Armstrong, who had been teaching a course in contemporary literature (among other courses) at Baylor University in Waco, Texas, since 1919. Having begun his graduate work at the University of Chicago, during the start of the "new poetry" movement, and having completed his doctorate at the University of Pennsylvania, Armstrong had carried to Texas a hope that he could attract from the North, to Baylor, a parade of visiting poets and lecturers. His method was to promise that he would arrange several well-paid performances for each prospective visitor so that the long trip would be financially profitable. In 1920 he had succeeded in bringing to Waco a cluster of poets: Amy Lowell, Vachel Lindsay, Edwin Markham, and Harriet Monroe. The next year, he scheduled many readings for Carl Sandburg in Texas and the Southwest. Frost had ignored Armstrong's many letters of invitation until one of them had prompted him to answer, from Ann Arbor on the twenty-eighth of December 1921, "You scare me. I could never think of being away from home anything like 'the greatest part of the year.' Poor Vachel has

[208]

thus far failed to get married, and so one place is unhomelike as another to him. I can boast of no such artistic detachment."[16] Given this much opening, Armstrong had used the assistance of Carl Sandburg, who had written to Frost:

". . . if you hear anything from A. J. Armstrong at Baylor University, you will make no mistake about co-operating with him on any plans he may have for bringing you south. I had some engagements under his direction last winter and found him just the kind of all round worker I believe you would enjoy taking up with. At Dr. Armstrong's own school they not only read a man's books before he arrives but they buy them in record-breaking numbers. His interest in you is a sure one and they have a way of looking after you that gets to your heart."[17]

Sandburg's encouragement came at the time when Frost was doubtful whether Michigan would be offering him a position for the academic year 1922-1923, and the double prospect of bunching several performances, and of increasing the sales of his books, had made him overcome his prejudices. He had let Armstrong arrange a schedule which was to begin with a reading at Sophie Newcomb College in New Orleans on Friday, the tenth of November 1922, continue with readings in Austin, Dallas, Fort Worth, San Antonio, and Waco, in Texas, and end with a reading in Columbia, Missouri, on the twenty-third of November—ten readings in fourteen days.

The trip from New York to New Orleans turned out to be a curious adventure. To save money, he had reserved an upper berth, and when the porter deposited his bags near his seat, part of it was already occupied by a man who had reserved the lower berth. The stranger looked up at Frost with obvious displeasure and asked why Frost hadn't reserved a lower. Hating to admit that he had been trying to save money, he answered that he had tried and failed. Well, the stranger would take care of that, if Frost was willing to spend an extra $10. Frost produced the money, the porter was called, and almost immediately Frost's bags were transferred to the seat immediately across the aisle. By this time the two men, seated next to each other, had begun to talk, and Frost was quickly fascinated. This odd character was clearly a tycoon, and the story of his life as it was gradually told was an account of one bold business adventure after another. Born in Massachusetts, he had moved to New Orleans at the age of fourteen, and completed his high-school education there. After he had earned enough money to go into business for himself, he had bought a small foundry and had successfully run it with a minimum of assistance. The business prospered, two partners were added, and the foundry became one of the largest in the South. There had been difficulties which required the spirit of a gambler, and yet many of the gambles had paid off handsomely. As the story unfolded, it contained good characterizations and subplots which delighted Frost.

The two men started their talk at four in the afternoon, they ate dinner together in the dining car, they returned to their seat and kept on talking straight through the night, neither one of them saying anything about going to bed. Toward morning, the stranger apologized for talking so much, and asked how his companion earned a living. Well, said Frost, he was also something of a gambler, but in an entirely different field. Every morning when he opened his mail he never knew whether the next letter would contain a big check or a little one or none at all. He continued his mystifications until the stranger grew impatient and cried,

"Shoot!"

"I'm a writer."

"What do you write?"

"Poetry."

"Hell, my wife writes that stuff."

They were still talking briskly as they disembarked in New Orleans, but even when they shook hands in saying good-bye neither man gave his name. That evening, when Frost dined with President and Mrs. Dean Pierce Butler on the campus of Sophie Newcombe College, he entertained them with a vivid description of the stranger, and wondered if they could guess who he might be. Of course. He was William Markus Bancroft, a wealthy benefactor of the college. As proof that they also knew the wife who wrote "that stuff," Mrs. Butler took down from a bookcase within reach of her chair an inscribed volume of poems written by Emma Putnam Bancroft.[18]

Frost's talk and reading at the regular assembly at Sophie Newcombe College on Friday, the tenth of November 1922, impressed his listeners in ways which amounted to a triumph for him. No longer did he permit his audiences to see the signs of that nervousness which had troubled Katharine Lee Bates, a few years earlier.[19] Now, and not for the first time, a reporter called particular attention to Frost's sense of humor:

"Not only did he give selections from his own works, but he also explained the origin and characteristics of modern poetry, including references to other modern poets, thus giving the audience an intimate glimpse of every contemporary in the art. And besides these things, and something which many will remember longer probably than the context of his lecture, his charming sense of humor."[20]

As he moved on from New Orleans to Fort Worth in Texas, in itself a journey of more than 500 miles, the change in the audience was as surprising to Frost as the change in the landscape. For the first time, he encountered a front-row heckler who upset him dreadfully, from the very beginning. The costume worn by the heckler suggested that he was an ancient Confederate soldier, and yet he seemed to dislike Frost for reasons other than that the poet was a Damnyankee. "Do you call that stuff poetry?" he asked in a plainly audible voice, before Frost had finished his first selection. Trying to ignore the questioner, Frost went on reading—through the sound of grunts and growls which came intermittently from his front-row critic. When the same question was asked again, even more audibly, Frost felt he had to answer it. "*I* call it poetry," he said, and tried to explain. When "the very old and well-known local character" continued his interjections, ushers appeared and escorted him out. But the damage had been done, and Frost was upset more than his audience realized.[21]

The next stop, in Dallas, where he was cordially received, renewed his confidence and prepared him for his more important appearance at Baylor. Dr. Armstrong had a flair for making elaborate preparations. As Sandburg had predicted, the bookstores in Waco had ordered extra copies of Frost's books, and the local newspapers heralded the event well in advance of Frost's arrival. The first undergraduate announcement in the Baylor *Lariat* quoted a special message from the chairman of the English department:

"Students, buy your tickets for Robert Frost at once. Get the best seats, so you can hear every word and see the expression of the poet. Reserved seats 50 cents for students, one dollar for the public. No student can afford to miss hearing one of the greatest American poets. Some critics claim he is America's greatest, the very greatest America has ever produced. If you want to get one of his books to be autographed—to keep as a lasting souvenir—there are still a few at the book store. Get either (or all three) 'A Boy's Will,' 'Mountain Interval,' or 'North of Boston.' Don't wait until all the good seats are taken. Remember there will be a great crowd and you may as well have the best. Frost is a great New England poet. He is much like the great English poet, Browning. He stands well in England, where he has been most cordially received."[22]

In his class on contemporary poetry, Dr. Armstrong made further preparations. He not only helped his students to become familiar with the poetry of Robert Frost but also coached a few of them to be ready with particular questions they might ask when the discussion period began at the end of the poet's reading. The build-up in publicity was continued with professional skill: ". . . advance sale of tickets has been good and all the books which were ordered for autographing have been sold. It is expected that the author will spend about one hour writing his name in the books that have already been sold to the students at the University and the citizens of Waco."[23] The article added the latest news: "Mr. Frost arrived this morning from Dallas where he spoke last night. He will be the house guest of Dr. and Mrs. Armstrong and will be tendered a dinner by them after the reading. At 9 o'clock a number of friends have been asked to call to meet the poet informally."[24]

The hundreds of students, faculty members, and townspeople who gathered for the reading were too many for the chosen hall, and the excitement became almost riotous when the announcement was made that the crowd would move to the University Chapel. By the time Frost was introduced, the atmosphere approached the gaiety of a carnival. He set the tone for his talk and his reading when he reminded them that one of their previous speakers, Miss Amy Lowell, had publicly accused him of having no sense of humor. After reading his poem about his own cow that almost jumped over the moon while elated with apple cider, he carefully pointed out that Amy Lowell seemed to think his cow must be a tragic cow, and the jump a tragic jump. Mixing with his readings gay reminiscences and caustic asides on other modern poets, the Yankee won his Southern audience completely. He kept returning to Amy Lowell's interpretations, and after he had read his blank-verse narrative concerning the irate farmer who dumped a load of hay on his boss, Frost reminded his listeners that Miss Lowell had called this one a "grim tragedy." The next day, the local newspapers devoted unusual space to praising his performance. One article began, "A sense of humor is almost requisite to the poet—and we are pleased to discover that Robert Frost possesses this attribute in a manner droll and spontaneous . . ."[25] Another said, "The impression that Frost left with most of us was one of inexpressible gentleness, with humor and strength and whimsical sincerity. . . ."[26]

After such a triumph, Frost found the remainder of his ten readings anticlimactic, at least for him. But before he reached Ann Arbor, where Mrs. Frost was waiting, he knew he would pay the price of another illness for all this gallivanting. To Lincoln MacVeagh, who had expected him to return to Ann Arbor by way of New York City, he wrote,

"I saw before I had gone many miles on the Katy that I wasn't going to last to get to New York. . . . If I had been absolutely sure I could have telegraphed 'Can't keep appointment. Expect to die November 25th. Sorry.' But one doesn't like to make gloomy predictions about one's health. It looks too cowardly. It furnishes the Christian Scientists with too much to go on. One just waits patiently in silence till one's worst fears are realized. Then one can't talk or telegraph.

"What I suppose I felt coming on was the dengue (pronounced dang you) fever from a mosquito bite I got on my first day at New Orleans (pronounced differently from the way I was accustomed to pronounce it). Or it may simply have been the influenza. I was fighting a bad sore throat when I got to Columbia [Missouri]—fighting it without medicine you understand. And now here I am at Ann Arbor in bed with a temperature. . . .

"I had many and various fortunes on the expedition. My best audiences were at New Orleans, Austin, Waco and Temple. These were large and seemed to know what I was joking about. In Fort Worth I was attacked by a Confederate veteran in a front seat. Though named after Robert Lee I dealt with him like Ulysses Grant. The Mexicans in San Antonio failed to attend my lecture. . . ."[27]

His letter of thanks to Dr. Armstrong, for having arranged the trip so carefully and for having served as host with such gracious hospitality, was genuinely warm:

"You surely gave me The Great Adventure down there toward Mexico, and I have only myself to blame if it was too fast and furious for my faculties to take in. . . . You are the master manager, and I was ready to say so with my latest breath, which was what I was about down to when I wound up in Missouri. . . . You are the friend indeed of wandering poets (I have no doubt, of poets fixed in their places). Browning is your presiding genius. Under him it is your life to think for poets and to provide for them. I am sure I understand so much from having been in Texas if I understand nothing else. Sometime on another visit more at leisure 'I shall desire more love and knowledge of you.' . . ."28

This round of lectures cooled his responses to those who were already asking him to make commitments. Among the requests awaiting him in his mail at Ann Arbor was an invitation to appear, next summer, at the Bread Loaf School of English. Professor Davison, having been rebuked by a previous refusal, this time made his approach through the services of Frost's former Amherst colleague, George F. Whicher. Responding impulsively, Frost agreed to give two lectures on successive days at Bread Loaf. On reconsideration he wrote again to Whicher:

"I shall have to take back what I said in my last letter. I wrote it without consulting Elinors wishes enough. I had promised her in a way, she had understood me to promise that there should be no more lecturing after April 1st this year. This was in my interest, in the interest of my writing. You know my slovenly way of spreading myself round in loose talk that gets neither me nor anybody else anywhere. She's right: it's time I shut up long enough to get my last poems written. At any rate right or wrong she is entitled to a voice in the matter. I'm going to do as she says for a while and see how I like it. It lets me out of having to think of money for the family as much as I was feeling I had to. It has that strong recommendation. And it is so heroic on her part that I should think it must silence criticism on yours and mine. Gee does anybody suppose I would lecture as badly as I do if I could find anybody to take the responsibility for my staying off the platform entirely?

"You can show this to Davison if necessary to save you from embarrassment.

"Forgive me my selfishness . . ."29

16

THE PULLS ON ME

I'm jaded with the pulls on me that I can't answer to. I've made up my mind that with a few people to abet me I won't do one single thing in verse or out of it or with it till I God damn please for the rest of my natural life.[1]

ROBERT FROST was so ill with influenza when he returned to the University of Michigan immediately after his round of readings in Louisiana, Texas, and Missouri that he was confined to his bed in his new home at 1432 Washtenaw Avenue for more than a week. His wife, having left all their children contentedly occupied with their separative activities, had been waiting for him when he arrived. Her thank-you note to Amy Lowell had begun, "Well, here we are back in Ann Arbor again. It was like coming to old friends this year, for I am really fond of some of these hospitable people. . . . We are in a smaller house, almost directly across the street from the other. It is more cheerful and homelike, and more easily taken care of than the other. . . ."[2] There was nothing cheerful about her husband's mood. Alternately enraged and depressed by his illness, he viewed it as a well-deserved punishment for his having once again frittered away so much time and energy on what he now viewed as trivialities. The requirements waiting for him would be deterrents to his immediate goal: writing enough, while at Michigan, to complete the manuscript for a new volume of poetry.

As soon as he did recover from his illness, he was pulled from one diversion to another, as Dean Bursley and President Burton invited the Frosts to teas and receptions which could not always be refused. Plays written and acted by the undergraduates were considered literary events which the Frosts were expected to attend. The *Whimsies* staff once again began to ask for help in making plans for another series of readings or talks by poets and novelists who might refuse to visit the campus unless he used his persuasion. Professor Cowden, carrying on the traditional evenings at his home, urged Frost to be present at each of them. He liked these evenings best, because he was always the star performer, and he enjoyed amusing his listeners with reminiscences which inevitably included gossip concerning the private lives of his friends and enemies.

That fall, an embarrassing scene was caused by an earlier indulgence of his pleasure in gossiping. A stranger arrived unexpectedly at Frost's door, in Ann Arbor, to discuss a malicious narrative frequently told by Frost concerning Joseph Warren Beach. Seven years earlier, when Beach was a young instructor at the University of Minnesota, he had made a pilgrimage to Franconia to express his admiration for the poetry of Robert Frost. Beach rented a room in a hotel not far from the Frost farm and spent several days walking and talking with Frost in the Franconia region. Although there was a puritanical austerity in the poet's attitude toward free love, he did enjoy listening to confessions made by those who were bolder than he in this regard, and Beach welcomed the opportunity to boast. A year later, when Beach arranged to have Frost give a reading at the University of Minnesota, Frost enjoyed the younger man's hospitalities and asked to be brought up to date on the new affairs of this Lothario. Quite eagerly, Beach confided that he was now devoting himself exclusively to a young lady who was his assistant in the graduate school, a girl so wonderful that she could walk on flowers without crushing them. Her name was Dagmar Doneghy. Frost was quick to challenge. If Beach was serious, why didn't he marry Dagmar Doneghy? He would marry her, Beach explained, if he could win her consent, but she seemed far more inclined toward matrimony with a local circus owner. Amused, and suspecting that this latest attachment was merely the latest, Frost wickedly urged that Beach should not let the circus owner steal Dagmar from him; Beach should kidnap her and force her to marry him. Frost even volunteered to serve as accomplice in the kidnapping and as best man at the wedding. Apparently inspired by the suggestion, Beach took Frost in an automobile, that same afternoon, and drove back and forth along a Minneapolis street until the girl came walking home. Beach introduced her to Frost, and the three of them went for a ride together. Very pleasantly, they drove into the country without any discussion of either kidnapping or marriage, but finally Beach stopped the car on an isolated back road and asked Frost to stay in the car while Beach and Dagmar took a brief stroll. Required to wait longer than he liked, Frost decided that something more than strolling must be the cause of their delay. He was surprised when the couple returned to announce that they were engaged to be married, and would be happy to accept his offer to act as best man at their wedding. Somewhat vindictively, Frost insisted that the wedding must occur immediately. Ah, that was impossible because Minnesota laws prohibited it. Then, said Frost, they would drive out of Minnesota into whichever neighboring state permitted the quickest arrangement for marriage, and which would that be? Well, Indiana, where marriages could be made within twenty-four hours. To Indiana they went, a license was obtained, a justice of the peace was found, and Frost served as a witness at the marriage. Before leaving the bride and groom, he gave them a splendid wedding dinner, with champagne.

Later, after Frost returned to New England from Minnesota he enjoyed telling how he had forced Beach to marry Dagmar. Before long, his embellished and ribald account was relayed to Beach, who wrote an angry letter of protest. The letter merely served to add new enrichments to the story as told by Frost, and he continued to tell it. In the summer of 1920, while in Franconia for the hay-fever season, he met a vacationing professor from the University of Minnesota, A. B. White, and assumed that White would especially enjoy the ribald account of how and why Frost had forced Beach into wedlock.

The stranger who now came to visit Frost at Ann Arbor in the fall of 1922 was a friend of Beach's, a physician who explained that Frost's story was hindering Beach's promotion in the Department of English at Minnesota. The stranger hoped that Frost would be willing to make amends, somehow, preferably by writing a letter to Professor White, clearing Beach of certain insinuative defamations. Why of course, Frost said, defensively. He was always glad to tell lies for a good cause. And he did write, somewhat ambiguously, to White from Ann Arbor:

"Explanations from J. W. Beach through a common acquaintance have convinced me that I did him a grave injustice in my talk to you about him last year. It all grew out of something he himself said at the time of his second marriage when I had been through a great deal with him and was out of sorts and ready to turn his own words against him. I now see that he was as far as possible from meaning what I had all these years taken him to mean. This is merely a hasty note to undo at once any harm I may have done him in your estimation. Sometime when we meet I will tell you more and go more fully into regrets. . . ."[3]

The explanation was accepted, the suspicions held against Beach were dropped, and he was promoted to permanent tenure at Minnesota. The friendship between Beach and Frost ended, however, as a result of this mutual embarrassment.

There were other embarrassments awaiting Frost during his absence from Ann Arbor for the Christmas vacation. He went back to his farm in Vermont eager to make it a retreat from any and every pull which might disturb him. But he had agreed to give a reading at Clark University in Worcester, Massachusetts,[4] on the fifth of January 1923, and then to go to New York City for several activities there. In preparation, he wrote from South Shaftsbury to Lincoln MacVeagh, on New Year's Day, thanking him for books sent as Christmas presents from Henry Holt and Company, and hinting at New York plans:

"The question was whether to go down this week and thank you for the really beautiful books or to stay at home and read them. I decided to stay at home and read them aloud to Carol to console him for the absence of his sisters who are in New York at the theatres.

"But I'm coming to New York next week early. Will you say which evening will suit you best for having me, Sunday the 7th or Monday the 8th. And can you produce [Carl] Van Doren for either?

"I've had a great time off here away from Ann [Arbor]. She doesn't mean to be, but she's a jealous paymaster or rather mistress. She wants to see something of me in person or in print (dedicated to her I suspect—the horrid thought!)[5] for her five thousand. I don't deserve any sympathy for my entanglement."[6]

He foresaw less pleasure than business during this trip to New York. Carl Van Doren had attracted him by requesting a new poem and a chance to interview him for a *Century Maga-*

zine article.[7] MacVeagh, as head of the trade department at Holt, had been trying for months to discuss with him plans for a volume of selected poems which might be published in England as well as in the United States. Without discussion, Frost had initially given his consent, and early in the fall of 1922 Holt had announced that Frost's *Selected Poems* would appear in the spring of 1923.[8] But some teasing reactions to this announcement had upset Frost. While still sick in bed at Ann Arbor following his return there from Texas in November 1922 he had written MacVeagh a somewhat grouchy note of protest:

"Please, please if you love me can this selected poems thing. Everybody is misunderstanding. The enclosed . . . is just a sample. I want the field clear for my new book. It is going to break my heart to have this old dead horse talked about and reviewed as if it were my present bid for notice. I'll write more when I feel less upset. I'm sure its a mistake. Of course if you've already spent good money to have it printed I shan't know what to say . . ."[9]

There were other pieces of unfinished business to handle in New York City. Ridgely Torrence, still serving as poetry editor for the *New Republic*, had asked for regular contributions of new poems, and it was therefore important to Frost to keep in close touch with Torrence. Untermeyer, on whom Frost counted most for favorable notices and reviews of anything he published, was planning to go abroad. He had urged Frost to visit him in New York City during this vacation, lest they should fail to see each other until after Untermeyer's return.

All of these visits were arranged and made, but Carl Van Doren apparently took Frost to one literary celebration which disgusted him. The affair was a raucous cocktail party, a sort of housewarming, given by Lawton Mackall in the new office of Mackall's magazine, *Snappy Stories*, and Frost had reason to feel out of place there. As part of the entertainment Christopher Morley read his own snappy parodies of a few modern poems, including "The Waste Land." Eliot's newly published poem had already created such a splash that Frost was made nervous and jealous by this newcomer's rapidly increasing fame. The literary controversy evoked by "The Waste Land" had been equalled only by that attending the appearance in Paris of Joyce's *Ulysses*, also published in 1922, and Frost quickly sided with those who found ways of trying to dismiss both Eliot and Joyce as pretentious fakers. Immediately after Mackall's party he fell into argument concerning Eliot and Joyce with a young reporter named Burton Rascoe, who wrote a weekly column for the book department of the New York *Tribune*. By the time Frost and Rascoe parted they had worked each other into animosities which were mutually infuriating. Rascoe, instead of dropping the matter, pursued it further in his literary column, and after Frost returned to South Shaftsbury, Untermeyer sent the article to him. Frost was particularly enraged by finding, therein, some direct quotations from his private conversation with Rascoe:

"Robert Frost in voice and demeanor reminds me much of Sherwood Anderson. He has the same deliberate and ingenuous way of speaking; he is earnest, earthy, humorous, without put-on, very real, likable, genuine. I admire him very much as a person. I regret that I find almost nothing to interest me in his poems. They are deft, they are competent, they are of the soil; but they are not distinctive.

"Frost and I left the party together and went to Grand Central Station, where we talked for half an hour about Ezra Pound, T. S. Eliot, Conrad Aiken, and Amy Lowell. He astonished me somewhat by telling me that Prof. John Livingston Lowes, author of *Convention and Revolt in Poetry* (an excellent treatise, insofar as it touches poets established by time), snaps his fingers in dismissal of T. S. Eliot, and that in doing so at a recent encounter at Miss Amy Lowell's house he had incurred the wrath of William Rose Benét.

"Frost himself has little sympathy with Eliot's work, but then he wouldn't naturally; his own aesthetic problem is radically different from that of Eliot's.

" 'I don't like obscurity in poetry,' he told me, voicing the familiar complaint. 'I don't think a thing ought to be obvious before it is said, but it ought to be obvious when it is said. I like to read Eliot because it is fun seeing the way he does things, but I am always glad it is his way and not mine.'

"I take it to be self-evident that those who talk of Eliot's 'obscurity' are using the word as a defense through an inability to derive any emotional response from it. But why should one defend himself, especially upon such unreasonable grounds? There is no law requiring one to read Eliot and like his work. . . .

" 'I have heard that Joyce wrote *Ulysses* as a joke,' said Frost to me, repeating what I have heard a dozen times from the credulous about both *Ulysses* and 'The Waste Land.'

"Dismissing for a moment the absurdity of the notion that a penniless man in ill health would spend four years writing a half-million-word novel without hope of adequate remuneration merely as a joke, whether he did or not would have nothing whatever to do with its artistic significance and importance."[10]

Frost immediately wrote a letter of reprimand. On occasions like this, his chronic vindictiveness caused the poet to hammer away at his opponent as though he were throwing words for punches, and this time he struck so furiously that when he showed the letter to his wife she urged him not to send it. Still angry, and unwilling to waste his long tirade, he sent it to Untermeyer with the following explanation:

"Elinor thinks perhaps I ought not to send a letter like this. You judge for us. If you don't think I'll live to be sorry just put it into another envelope and send it along to Burton.

"I came home [from New York City] with grippe. Everybody has had it in the house and Irma has had pneumonia—yes. But it's all right now. I ought to let one at Burton. If you'd like the fun of seeing me punch him I'll come down and punch."[11]

Untermeyer's response was one of dissuasion, and Frost accepted it:

"You and Jean think such wrath ill becomes me. I'm over it now anyway. We won't send the letter to Burton the rat. My grounds for wanting to let him have both fists in succession in the middle of the face are chiefly that he stated me so much worse than I know how to state myself. That is the greatest outrage of small town or big town—misquotation. It flourishes worst, it seems, among these smart cosmopolites. But never mind."[12]

The unsent letter, preserved by Untermeyer, did more than serve as a safety valve for rage. It contains glimpses of certain characteristics in Robert Frost never suspected by those who saw him only during his affable moods:

"You little Rascol:

"Save yourself trouble by presenting my side of the argument for me, would you? (My attention has just been called to what you have been doing in the *Tribune*.) Interview me without letting me know I was being interviewed, would you?

"I saw you resented not having anything to say for yourself the other day, but it never entered my head that you would run right off and take it out on me in print.

"I don't believe you did the right thing in using my merest casual talk to make an article of. I shall have to institute inquiries among my newspaper friends to find out. If you did the right thing, well and good; I shall have no more to say. But if you didn't, I shall have a lot to say.

"I'm sure you made a platitudinous mess of my talk—and not wilfully to be smart. I saw blood was ringing in your ears and you weren't likely to hear me straight if you heard me at all. I don't blame you for that. You were excited at meeting me for the first time.

"You seem to think I talked about obscurity, when, to be exact, I didn't once use the word. I never use it. My mistake with the likes of you was not using it to exclude it. It always helps a schoolboy, I find from old experience, if, in telling him what it is I want him to apprehend, I tell him also what it isn't.

"The thing I wanted you to apprehend was obscuration as Sir Thomas Browne hath it. Let me try again with you, proceeding this time by example, as is probably safest.

"Suppose I say: Of all the newspaper men I ever met, you most nearly resemble a reporter I once talked with casually on the street just after I had paid ten dollars in court for having punched a mutual friend. I talked to him exactly as I talked to you, without the least suspicion that I was being interviewed. He must have taken sides with the mutual friend, for he ran right off to his office and published everything I had said as nearly as he chose to reproduce it.[13]

"There you have what I call obscuration. 'I say no harm and I mean no harm,' as the poet hath it; but the stupider you are the more meaning you will see where none is intended. The really intelligent will refuse to listen to such old-wives' indirection.

"Or again, suppose I say: Just because you have won to a position where you can get even with people is no reason why you shouldn't perform face forward like a skunk, now is it?[14] I only ask for information. . . .

"Or to 'lay off' you personally for the moment, suppose I say: I learn that someone is bringing out an Anthology of the Best Lines of Modern Poetry. He proposes to run the lines more or less loosely together in a narrative and make them so much his own that anyone using them again will have to enclose them in double quotes, thus:

> " ' "What sayest thou, old barrelful of lies?" '
> " ' "Not worth a breakfast in the cheapest country under the cope." '
> " ' "Shall I go on, or have I said enough?" '

"These three lines are from Chaucer, Shakespeare, and Milton respectively. Please verify. . . .

"Or suppose I say: Good sense is plebeian, but scarcely more plebeian than any sense at all. Both will be spurned in aristocratic circles this summer. . . .

"I thought you made very poor play with what I said about the obvious. The greatly obvious is that which I see the minute it is pointed out and only wonder I didn't see before it was pointed out. But there is a minor kind of obviousness I find very engaging. You illustrate it, when, after what passed between us, you hasten to say you like me but don't like my books. You will illustrate it again if, after reading this, you come out and say you like neither me nor my books, or you like my books but not me. Disregard that last: I mustn't be too subtle for you. But aren't you a trifle too obvious here for your own purpose? I am told on every hand that you want to be clever. Obviousness of this kind is almost the antithesis of cleverness. You should have defended your hero's work on one Sunday, and saved your attack on mine for another. You take all the sting out of your criticism by being so obvious in the sense of easy to see through. It won't do me the good you sincerely hoped it would.

"You are probably right in thinking that much literature has been written to make fun of the reader. This my letter may have been. Do you remember what Webster said or implied about the farmer who hanged himself in a year of plenty because he was denied transportation for his grain?—or what Nemphrekepta said to Anubis?

"When my reports are in on your conduct, I may be down to see you again.

"I shall be tempted to print this letter some time, I am afraid. I hate to waste it on one reader. Should you decide to print it take no liberties with it. Be sure you print it whole."[15]

In spite of his resentment against Rascoe, Frost derived one major consolation from the New York visit. His discussions with MacVeagh concerning future publications clarified plans on both sides. The poet was eager to give primary emphasis to a projected volume of new poems, and MacVeagh assured him that if he had a new book ready for publication during the autumn of 1923 it could be sold alongside *Selected Poems* in such a way that each title would help the other. Frost immediately promised that the new book would be completed in time for such publication, and he returned to South Shaftsbury convinced that he could make a start in organizing the manuscript before he returned to Ann Arbor, late in January. Unfortunately, his illness spoiled those plans. By the time he got back to Michigan, feeling guilty for having been absent too long, he was again caught up in his own conscientious attempts to make amends. From Ann Arbor he wrote to Untermeyer:

"I'm back out here as you may judge from the fact that last night I entertained a couple of young non-smokers till ten, went out calling till after midnight, and read through a novel in MS by Lawrence Conrad between then and six this morning. That takes rank with my fourteen [ten] lectures in fourteen days ... I'm on a tear. Let who will be clever. Let's see when was your date to come again?"[16]

Keeping in mind the date when the Untermeyers were planning to go abroad, Frost insisted that they both should return to Ann Arbor to help him begin his new series of readings or talks by authors. The plan was carried through on a scale more modest than that of the year before. Untermeyer was the only poet whom Frost was able to obtain; then came two novelists who were actually persuaded only as a result of his urgings: Dorothy Canfield Fisher and Hamlin Garland. The success of these first two visitors was reported to Alfred Harcourt, Untermeyer's publisher:

"Your Louis Untermeyer (and mine) has just been here generously talking about everybody's poetry but his own and it would be no more than poetic justice if I bought some of his own and distributed it where it would do the most good among the Ann Arboreals. So if you will please, have sent me six copies of Roast Leviathian and the bill.

"I might have ordered these of your business department, but I wanted the chance to say hello to you personally and tell the farmer in you that I am this year setting out four hundred apple trees against my old age and am otherwise disporting myself on the land.

"Also I ought to say a word about Dorothy Canfield another of your first-string putters of it across. She recently made a speech here that will stand as a record for lovely till she herself surpasses it. She ought to be made to write it down and a whole book full like it. There is something she gives in such a talk that she has never yet been able to get into a book. It was an unpretentious wonder."[17]

Hamlin Garland's appearance was a disappointment to Frost and to the other listeners.[18] Under the circumstances, Frost decided to make amends by permitting the *Whimsies* staff to schedule him for a public reading on the Michigan campus. It was postponed, however, by the return of illness. On the second of March 1923 he wrote to a friend, "I've been sick out flat in bed for two weeks and dead to the world of education and refinement."[19] He recovered sufficiently to spend the spring vacation in South Shaftsbury, but was forced to stay there longer than he had planned. To Sidney Cox he wrote from South Shaftsbury on the thirtieth of April 1923, "I'm just returning to an interest in life after my fifth fluenza in one winter. What's come over me? . . . I've been fairly absent from Ann Arbor this year and not half the sensation in the Michigan papers I was last year. I don't know what I think of the berth now that I'm about to rub my eyes and climb out of it. The sleeping in it was only so-so."[20]

Returning to Ann Arbor early in May, he went through the necessary motions with indifference. Belatedly, he participated as a judge in a poetry contest conducted by the editors of *Whimsies*, and found little to interest him in the manuscripts submitted by the undergraduates. He gave two public readings from his poems, and was disappointed when he failed to draw audiences as large as those of his guests.[21] Some of his students rallied to thank him for the assistance and encouragement he had given them. Lawrence Conrad paid him tribute in a letter to President Burton:

"Before leaving the University I want to express to you my appreciation for the Fellowship in Creative Arts and to say something of what it has meant to me during the past two years. . . . the Fellowship has made it possible for me to come into contact with Robert Frost, and this contact has enriched my University career beyond any other single factor. I have seen, during my junior and senior years, a new, sound and praise-worthy spirit taking possession of the University, somehow touching every person in it, and, since this spirit is the one I value most highly, I have felt moved to call someone's attention to it. I know of no one to tell but yourself.

"I need not mention to you what a good thing it has been for the University as a whole to have a creative artist of high standing here on the ground for two years. Once tried, a University without one becomes unthinkable. I have often, looking back, asked myself: Where did this University stand before it started doing this. Looking ahead, I have grown a little fearful: the Fellowship is not a thing that advertises well; you can't get excited about any good poet. I have wondered if the thing might be given up. I appeal to you, sir, in all earnestness, to do all in your power to have it continued. Let me testify to its value.

"Since the Fellowship has been maintained there have come to Ann Arbor to give public lectures eight of the most prominent literary men and women of America, and one of England[22]— over and above the number of such artists as came before. Since I had charge of the arrangements for these people, I can tell you that they would never have been brought here had not the Fellowship assured them of a congenial reception and had not the Endowment first put the notion into the heads of the little band of students to which I belong. . . . I ought to add, too, that, owing to Mr. Frost's presence here, none of the lecturers showed any haste in leaving Ann Arbor, and it was possible in every case for a group of students (never less than twenty) to meet these men and women and profit by an hour or more of informal contact.

"I hesitate to mention the little magazine [*Whimsies*] to which you have graciously referred in some of your speeches and reports. It could hardly have been fully born and certainly would have wilted had not Mr. Frost appeared on the scene. Since it is partly mine, I shall say no more to recommend it than that Mr. Frost has made it the object of his lively interest ever since he arrived. It, in turn, has sought to catch and to spread the kind of interest in, and feeling for creative literature that Mr. Frost has. In an age of controversy and of criticism it has printed no word of either. . . .

"It has been my privilege to know Mr. Frost very well. I know that he cannot make any public statement concerning

[226]

the Fellowship without seeming to be urging himself forward. Without his knowledge and solely upon my own judgment, I should like to say that the fellowship has been on the whole a very acceptable thing for him. His lifelong struggle has been for the establishment of a few strong principles in art. Recognition of the establishment of those principles was never more certain than by the fact of this University's patronage. Publication of his work was only the first step. I know that he ranks the tender of the Fellowship along with his acceptance in England, as important steps in his career.

"As to his writing, I know that it has gone forward at its normal rate. He does not write many poems in the course of a year. He has written a number of poems recently. I know this because I was privileged to typewrite them for him (for the first time) from his original notebook. . . .

"Robert Frost has touched many more of your ten thousand students than you may realize. The students who know him are about us like apostles. I have felt him in classrooms when he was not there at all, curbing 'smartness,' checking rash judgments, warring against the cheap, the silly, the spectacular. Everyone who knows him has been given a turn toward a new appreciation of hard, honest effort, of sound, sane values, of honesty and simplicity and open-mindedness. I should like to see him adopted and continued here for the rest of his life. Everyone knows that he will never change except in the direction of growth. He could do for our ills what he is doing for the ills of American art."[23]

Robert Frost did not want to be adopted by Michigan—did not want to continue there for the rest of his life. The arrangement which had brought him back had promised nothing more than a single year, and he was glad when the year was ended. President Burton and many others were grateful to him for all that he had done, and the farewells were extremely cordial. But he returned to South Shaftsbury early in June 1923 wishing for nothing more than a chance to proceed with work on his new volume of poetry, as soon as he could get done with one final public commitment. Vermont University, in Burlington, had invited him to appear at their commencement to receive an honorary degree, and he had been so pleased by the precedent (the first bona fide offer of a degree, as he thought, because there were strings attached to those awarded him by Amherst and Michigan) that he had sent his grateful acceptance. Someone had apparently confided the news to the elderly Henry Holt, whose summer estate was not far from Burlington, and Holt had immediately written to request the privilege of playing host when the poet came north to receive the degree. Returning from that occasion, Frost reported to MacVeagh, "I had a good evening with your Mr. Henry Holt at his place between the [Green] mountains and the lake [Champlain] when I was in Burlington. . . ."[24] The elderly Mr. Holt showed enthusiasm for the news that Frost would have another book of poems in the fall, and this visit seemed to be the last engagement, social or academic, which stood between him and his intended work on the book—if nothing unexpected came along.

The unexpected had already happened, without his knowing it: President Meiklejohn had been dismissed by the Trustees of Amherst College, with startling local results. Fourteen of the faculty members hired by Meiklejohn—including Stark Young—immediately submitted their resignations, in protest. Another protest was made by thirteen seniors who refused to accept their Amherst diplomas on graduation day. Among the juniors, more than three-quarters of the class formally announced that they would not return to Amherst in the fall. Frost, when he heard the news, aligned his sympathies with the conservative elements on the faculty at Amherst. Because his enmity toward Meiklejohn had been openly expressed, and because his resignation from Amherst had been made in protest against Meiklejohn's policies, he was one of the first to receive a telegram from the trustees asking if he would accept a position as a member of the heavily depleted department of English. Again he was forced to reconsider all his arrangements for restricting his energies primarily to the writing of poetry. To MacVeagh he confided his quandary:

"They've asked me by telegram to come me back to Amherst. What do you know about that? Dont tell the Bristols. Dont tell anybody. Its going to be embarrassing to stay out of the row or to go into it."[25]

While he was trying to decide, he received a visitor. The newly appointed President, George Daniel Olds, elevated from his position as professor of Greek and Latin literature, drove up to South Shaftsbury from Amherst to persuade Frost that he could do much to help re-establish the college's traditional scheme. Attractive promises were made. If he came back, he could teach any two courses he might propose in the English department. Otherwise he would have no duties and could serve as a poet-in-residence. And President Olds also wanted his advice on possible candidates to fill gaps in the philosophy department. Frost, having strong feelings about what seemed to him the ways in which the teaching of philosophy had been botched at Amherst, immediately proposed that a guest lecturer such as Harvard's William Ernest Hocking might be persuaded to give temporary assistance. Before President Olds returned to Amherst he succeeded in winning more than Frost's acceptance of the offer. The poet even agreed to make a summer trip to Cambridge for the purposes of calling on Professor Hocking and of explaining to him the needs of the Department of Philosophy at Amherst. A few days after this visit, President Olds made public the names of those newly appointed to the faculty at Amherst College, including Robert Frost. Although some of the poet's friends sent letters of congratulation, Wilbur Cross at Yale wrote a note which was guarded and skeptical. Frost, answering, tried to defend his awkward position:

"You strike just the right dubious note in congratulating me about going back to Amherst. I ought to have been poet enough to stay away. But I was too much of a philosopher to resist the temptation to go back and help show the world the difference between the right kind of liberal college and the wrong kind. You were on my trail at Ann Arbor. You say you talked me over with the Lloyds and others there. I know what you said: that I concerned myself too much for my own good with what was going on around me. I never could keep out of things. But I can get out of them. That's my saving virtue. I *will* bite the hook if it is baited with an idea, but I never bit one yet that I couldn't wriggle off before it was too too late. . . ."[26]

In all this new and flattering excitement, Robert Frost did not quickly get back to the manuscript on which he had done much while at Ann Arbor. Determined to complete it for a publication date which would occur soon after he began his duties at Amherst, he tried again to ignore all the other holds on him. He had already decided that the book would be entitled *New Hampshire* and that he would give it a mock-scholarly subtitle: *A Poem with Notes and Grace Notes.*

17

YES I SUPPOSE I AM A PURITAN

Only the other day in New York he said, "Yes, I suppose I am a Puritan." Then he went on to define slowly, and as if he were thinking aloud, what a Puritan was to him.[1]

THE entire plan for Robert Frost's fourth book, entitled *New Hampshire,* grew out of an event which had occurred during the spring of his first year at Ann Arbor. Invited to give a talk before the local Rotary Club, and aware that he would be addressing businessmen, he decided to play figuratively with the subject of buying and selling. He could have made metaphors out of his own firsthand experiences as a merchant of eggs, back in the Derry days, or he could at least have entertained his listeners with some good stories about his own horse-trading on his Derry farm. Instead, he saw a chance to be playful and satirically amusing with a discourse on two opposed attitudes toward selling. One of these was the snobbishly aristocratic notion that a true lady or gentleman should never get hands dirty by working for money—or even by selling anything. There was nothing new about such a notion, and Frost liked to point out that the famous courtier Castiglione, three centuries ago, made the claim that anyone who works for gain is ignoble: "You know in great matters and adventures in wars the true provocation is glory: and whoso acts for lucre's sake . . . deserveth not the name of a gentleman, but is a most vile merchant."[2] In contrast, and relatively new, was what seemed to Frost another snobbish attitude toward buying and selling: the communistic complaints against bourgeois profits achieved through competitive capitalism.

Because his liberal friends, including Untermeyer, kept trying to educate him by sending articles from such periodicals as the *Liberator* and the *Nation,* Frost had become increasingly familiar with this latest snobbery. He had noticed that during the spring of 1922 a series of critical articles began to appear in the *Nation* on "These United States," apparently for purposes of explaining what was wrong with commercialism in state after state. Edmund Wilson had written one of these, describing what was wrong with New Jersey. Then, much to Frost's surprise, the *Nation* invited Frost to write a piece for the series, presumably to tell what was wrong with either Vermont or New Hampshire. Although he declined, he was tempted to accept, so that he could reverse the trend and praise one or both of his favorite states.[3] While still meditating what he might have written teasingly, with tongue in cheek, he received the Rotary Club invitation and decided to use in that talk some of those taunting observations he had dreamed of putting into a *Nation* article.[4]

The talk went well enough, although Frost belatedly realized he had pitched his playful remarks over the heads of the businessmen. His game had been to strike an ironic posture of claiming that New Hampshire is the purest noncommercial State in the Union: while it has a splendid variety of precious and admirable things for show, it does not have enough of anything to sell. He had supposed his listeners would recognize the ways in which he only pretended to make that claim, for the satirical purpose of mocking what he viewed as the two opposed categories of snobs: those among the pseudo-aristocratic capitalists, and those among the pseudo-aristocratic communists.

The most important gain derived from giving the talk was the exercise in manipulating a cluster of images and anecdotes which he viewed in retrospect as materials for a long poem quite different from any he had previously written. In some of Horace's satirical discourses, there was classical precedent for such a poem. The *Sermones* always scattered friendly banter through a rhapsody of anecdotes, exempla, dialogue, self-appraisal, self-disparagements, epigrams, and proverbs. Having decided to try writing his own Horatian poem, Frost was forced to postpone such a pleasant experiment: he was kept too busy in Ann Arbor during the remainder of his first year.

When he had returned to Vermont in the late spring of 1922 he was in no mood for writing, immediately, although he kept thinking about details he might use when he got around to it. At last, one July night after everyone else in the Stone Cottage had gone to bed, he sat down at the dining-room table knowing vaguely what the shape of the satirical poem would be. As a starting point, he pretended to admire and agree with a snobbish lady from the South who had implied that commercialism of any kind was disgraceful:

> *I met a lady from the South who said*
> *(You won't believe she said it, but she said it):*
> *"None of my family ever worked, or had*
> *A thing to sell." I don't suppose the work*
> *Much matters. You may work for all of me.*
> *I've seen the time I've had to work myself.*
> *The having anything to sell is what*
> *Is the disgrace in man or state or nation.*

Such a start was designed to be a deliberate parody of both those forms of snobbishness which annoyed him, and from this ambiguous beginning he went on to give three examples of individuals from states other than New Hampshire who had sullied themselves through different forms of salesmanship. Then he added,

> *It never could have happened in New Hampshire.*

Continuing, he admitted that he had once found a person "really soiled with trade" in New Hampshire, but this person "had just come back ashamed / From selling things in California." Then Frost stated the splendid ideal:

> *Just specimens is all New Hampshire has,*
> *One each of everything as in a showcase,*
> *Which naturally she doesn't care to sell.*

To illustrate, he gave examples within discursive contexts, ironically pretending to praise some details which were obviously not praiseworthy. Foreshadowing the last line of the poem, he boasted that New Hampshire was "one of the two best states in the Union." Vermont, of course, was the other, and he added,

> *Anything I can say about New Hampshire*
> *Will serve almost as well about Vermont . . .*

As he continued, he half-seriously and half-playfully defended New Hampshire against criticisms made by the Massachusetts poets Emerson and Amy Lowell:

> Emerson said, "The God who made New Hampshire
> Taunted the lofty land with little men."[5]
> Another Massachusetts poet said,
> "I go no more to summer in New Hampshire.
> I've given up my summer place in Dublin."
> But when I asked to know what ailed New Hampshire,
> She said she couldn't stand the people in it,
> The little men (it's Massachusetts speaking).
> And when I asked to know what ailed the people,
> She said, "Go read your own books and find out."

At this point in the poem, he teasingly pretended to explain his own position, using words which could, of course, be misleading if taken merely at face value:

> I may as well confess myself the author
> Of several books against the world in general.[6]
> To take them as against a special state
> Or even nation's to restrict my meaning.
> I'm what is called a sensibilitist,
> Or otherwise an environmentalist.
> I refuse to adapt myself a mite
> To any change from hot to cold, from wet
> To dry, from poor to rich, or back again.[7]
> I make a virtue of my suffering
> From nearly everything that goes on round me.[8]
> In other words, I know wherever I am,
> Being the creature of literature I am,
> I shall not lack for pain to keep me awake.
> Kit Marlowe taught me how to say my prayers:
> "Why, this is Hell, nor am I out of it."[9]
> Samoa, Russia, Ireland I complain of,
> No less than England, France, and Italy.
> Because I wrote my novels in New Hampshire
> Is no proof that I aimed them at New Hampshire.

At this time in his life, he was most often complaining about Russia, and even in the writing of this poem he was not actually making a digression when he made a few satirical thrusts at Russia:

> *The glorious bards of Massachusetts seem*
> *To want to make New Hampshire people over.*
> *They taunt the lofty land with little men.*
> *I don't know what to say about the people.*
> *For art's sake one could almost wish them worse*
> *Rather than better. How are we to write*
> *The Russian novel in America*
> *As long as life goes so unterribly?*
> *There is the pinch from which our only outcry*
> *In literature to date is heard to come.*
> *We get what little misery we can*
> *Out of not having cause for misery.*
> *It makes the guild of novel writers sick*
> *To be expected to be Dostoievskis*
> *On nothing worse than too much luck and comfort*
> *This is not sorrow, though; it's just the vapors,*
> *And recognized as such in Russia itself*
> *Under the new regime, and so forbidden.*
> *If well it is with Russia, then feel free*
> *To say so or be stood against the wall*
> *And shot. It's Pollyanna now or death.*
> *This, then, is the new freedom we hear tell of;*
> *And very sensible. No state can build*
> *A literature that shall at once be sound*
> *And sad on a foundation of well-being.*[10]

The next target for thrusts, in this discursive Horatian satire, was what he viewed as the cheap Greenwich Village talk to which he had been exposed repeatedly during his visits with the Untermeyers and others in New York City. Those who espoused sexual freedoms which they justified by means of Freud's writings were inclined to resent Frost's opinion that William James had done more than Freud for the cause of psychology and even of psychoanalysis. Some of Frost's critics viewed him as either immature in this regard or prudish—or both. In reply, here, he began his evasive and again teasing answer:

> *Lately in converse with a New York alec*
> *About the new school of the pseudo-phallic,*

I found myself in a close corner where
I had to make an almost funny choice.
"Choose you which you will be—a prude, or puke,
Mewling and puking in the public arms."[11]
"Me for the hills where I don't have to choose."[12]

Then he digressed long enough to bring under satirical criticism, from his genuinely puritanical viewpoint, some opposed notions concerning nature and human nature:

I know a man who took a double ax
And went alone against a grove of trees;
But his heart failing him, he dropped the ax
And ran for shelter quoting Matthew Arnold:
" 'Nature is cruel, man is sick of blood';
There's been enough shed without shedding mine.
Remember Birnam Wood! The wood's in flux!"
He had a special terror of the flux
That showed itself in dendrophobia.
The only decent tree had been to mill
And educated into boards, he said.
He knew too well for any earthly use
The line where man leaves off and nature starts,
And never overstepped it save in dreams.
He stood on the safe side of the line talking—
Which is sheer Matthew Arnoldism.
The cult of one who owned himself "a foiled
Circuitous wanderer," and "took dejectedly
His seat upon the intellectual throne"[13]

Although Frost's religious beliefs were extremely important to him, he was embarrassed by them to the extent that he often merely hinted at them through poetic ironies such as these. Even here, as he continued, he again struck a posture of pretending to praise and agree with what he considered to be false religious notions:

Agreed in frowning on these improvised
Altars the woods are full of nowadays,
Again as in the days when Ahaz sinned
By worship under green trees in the open.
Scarcely a mile but that I come on one,

A black-cheeked stone and stick of rain-washed charcoal.
Even to say the groves were God's first temples
Comes too near to Ahaz' sin for safety.
Nothing not built with hands of course is sacred.[14]

To Frost, nothing built with hands was sacred—not even poems—unless the creative act was performed with a devout awareness of continuities between the parts, in the divinely ordained scheme of things. He might confide to Untermeyer, privately, that the preacher in him would eventually triumph over the poet, but so long as he struck these equivocal postures of pretending to agree with views he was intent on satirizing, he hoped nobody would accuse him of preaching. He concluded the helter-skelter satire by returning to the demand of the "New York alec" that Frost characterize himself by deciding whether he would rather be childishly immature or prudishly puritanical:

> *"Come, but this isn't choosing—puke or prude?"*
> *Well, if I have to choose one or the other,*
> *I choose to be a plain New Hampshire farmer*
> *With an income in cash of, say, a thousand*
> *(From, say, a publisher in New York City).*
> *It's restful to arrive at a decision,*
> *And restful just to think about New Hampshire.*
> *At present I am living in Vermont.*[15]

Fatigued and yet elated, after finishing the rough draft of "New Hampshire" in one stretch of work, Frost was not immediately aware that he had written straight through the short June night. When he put his pen down on the dining-room table and stretched, looking out through the living-room window, he was surprised to see that there was light in the east and that the syringa bush at the edge of the front lawn was already coming out of darkness. With a sense of unusual excitement, he stood up, walked stiffly to the front door, opened it, descended the stone steps to the dew-heavy grass, and stood marveling less at the dawn than at his night's work. Never before, in all his years of sitting up late to write, had he worked straight through until morning. Even now, with the poem tentatively finished, he was not ready to stop. There was something else he wanted to write, or that he felt impelled to write, although he had nothing immediately in mind as a starter. Back into the house he went, moving through the living room to the dining room almost as though he were sleepwalking. He picked up his pen, found a clean page, and began a lyric which had nothing to do with the dawn of a June day. He seemed to hear the words, as though they were spoken to him, and he wrote them down as best he could, in his fatigue, even though they came so indistinctly at times that he was uncertain what he heard. In a short time, and without too much trouble, he completed a rough draft of these four quatrains:

> *Whose woods these are I think I know.*
> *His house is in the village, though;*
> *He will not see me stopping here*
> *To watch his woods fill up with snow.*
>
> *My little horse must think it queer*
> *To stop without a farmhouse near*
> *Between the woods and frozen lake*
> *The darkest evening of the year.*
>
> *He gives his harness bells a shake*
> *To ask if there is some mistake.*
> *The only other sound's the sweep*
> *Of easy wind and downy flake.*
>
> *The woods are lovely, dark, and deep,*
> *But I have promises to keep,*
> *And miles to go before I sleep,*
> *And miles to go before I sleep.*[16]

Pivoting on the word "promises," and therefore suggesting innumerable extensions, this new poem immediately seemed to him one of the best he had ever written.[17] The tensions between his promises to himself as artist and to his wife and family—and others who made demands he often resented—continued to make him feel guilty. Equally serious to him was the feeling that although he had promised himself, years ago, that he would do everything in his power to succeed as a poet, he often doubted whether he had the creative energy to keep adding elements of newness to his poetic performance. This night's accomplishment, no matter how faulty and incomplete, gave him new courage to face the miles he hoped to go before he slept. New in this experience was the odd juxtaposition of the tight lyric form, with its unusual rhyme scheme, and the sprawling, discursive conversational form of "New Hampshire." The incentive provided by the excitement of this night's work made him begin to think he could build around this doubly centered nucleus enough pieces to make a book more to his liking than *A Boy's Will* or *North of Boston* or *Mountain Interval*.

Unfortunately, he had another set of promises to keep during that summer of 1922, and his plans for the new book advanced no further until he returned to South Shaftsbury from Ann Arbor during the Christmas vacation of 1922. Even then, his commitments down-country hauled him away too soon, with results which were not all impertinent. On his way down to New York, one surprise which came to him after his reading at Clark University in Worcester, Massachusetts, suggested the possibility that his new book might be illustrated with woodcuts by J. J. Lankes. His host for the night, in Worcester, showed him a copy of *Mountain Interval* extra-illustrated with some appropriate Lankes woodcuts, including one directly inspired by Frost's poem, "After Apple-Picking."[18] Frost had already noticed and praised one woodcut made by Lankes, and as soon as he discovered that Lankes had already made an illustration for one of Frost's poems he was eager to arrange deliberate collaborations. When he reached New York and talked with Carl Van Doren about the plan for publishing "The Star-Splitter" in the *Century Magazine*, he suggested that Lankes (who had already done woodcuts for *Century*) would be just the artist to do an illustration for this new poem. The suggestion was accepted, and carried through. Then Frost had told MacVeagh that Lankes would be an appropriate illustrator for the new book. Again the suggestion was accepted. During the same visit to New York, he placed in the hands of Ridgely Torrence a fair copy of "Stopping by Woods," which appeared in the *New Republic* not long after the visit.[19] Returning to South Shaftsbury, from New York City, after talking there with Untermeyer about the still vague plans for the new book, Frost began to select and arrange poems. By the time he returned to Ann Arbor from South Shaftsbury, he had progressed far enough to confide to Untermeyer:

"It might be a good idea to call the explanatory poems Notes. I'm pretty sure to call the book New Hampshire. The Notes will be The Witch of Coos, The Census-taker, Paul's Wife, Wild Grapes, The Grindstone, The Ax-helve, The Star-splitter, Maple, The Witch of Grafton (praps), The Gold Hesperidee (praps), and anything else I can think of or may write before summer.

"I'll go further and say that I may even bring out a volume of lyrics at the same time and refer to it in New Hampshire as The Star in the Stone-boat. I'm in a larking mood. I'll do almost anything for the sake of contraption."[20]

In this larking mood, he did have fun with his academic relationships by adding to "New Hampshire" passages which served as undeveloped hints which needed explaining. These passages justified his use of mock-scholarly footnotes containing merely the titles of the so-called "explanatory poems." His next decision was to give the book a three-part structure: Part One would be devoted exclusively to the title poem, Part Two would be the "explanatory poems" grouped as "Notes," and Part Three would be lyrics which could be referred to on the title page as "Grace Notes" in the sense that they were added for pure ornamentation.

When he began to assemble the poems to be used as "Notes," he gave first place to "A Star in a Stoneboat." Obliquely this poem did provide extensions of the self-revealing and self-concealing equivocations, in "New Hampshire," concerning polarities in his religious beliefs and unbeliefs. The first image of the "star" poem is a meteorite which a laborer "picked up with stones to build a wall" and loaded on "an old stoneboat" or horse-drawn sledge built of heavy planks. After suggesting his own reasons for wishing he might find such a heaven-sent token, the poet concludes with hints concerning the acknowledged limitations of his own vision:

From following walls I never lift my eye,
Except at night to places in the sky
Where showers of charted meteors let fly.

Some may know what they seek in school and church,
And why they seek it there; for what I search
I must go measuring stone walls, perch on perch;

Sure that though not a star of death and birth,
So not to be compared, perhaps, in worth
To such resorts of life as Mars and Earth—

Though not, I say, a star of death and sin,
It yet has poles, and only needs a spin
To show its worldly nature and begin

To chafe and shuffle in my calloused palm
And run off in strange tangents with my arm,
As fish do with the line in first alarm.

Such as it is, it promises the prize
Of the one world complete in any size
That I am like to compass, fool or wise.

This poem, first published in the Yale *Review*, pleased him because it was a newly approached subject handled with a freshness of supporting imagery, and also because it reaffirmed his posture of standing apart from the ordinary run of those who "may know what they seek in school or church." He continued to enjoy casting himself in the role of rebel and skeptic, even though his actual position in matters of belief was far more conservative and orthodox than he permitted his public to guess.[21]

Closely related was the third poem which he presented as another "Note" to the following passage in "New Hampshire":

I knew a man who failing as a farmer
Burned down his farmhouse for the fire insurance,
And spent the proceeds on a telescope
To satisfy a lifelong curiosity
About our place among the infinities.[22]
And how was that for otherworldliness?

In the blank-verse poem serving as "Note" to this passage, and entitled "The Star-Splitter," the failed farmer is permitted to explain his motives philosophically:

"The best thing that we're put here for's to see;
The strongest thing that's given us to see with's
A telescope. Someone in every town

> *Seems to me owes it to the town to keep one.*
> *In Littleton it may as well be me.*"[23]

The poet, in his garrulous account of these transactions, describes his own experience in looking "Up the brass barrel, velvet black inside, / At a star quaking in the other end," and then concludes with sarcastic praise which gives way to questioning:

> *It's a star-splitter if there ever was one,*
> *And ought to do some good if splitting stars*
> *'Sa thing to be compared with splitting wood.*
>
> *We've looked and looked, but after all where are we?*
> *Do we know any better where we are,*
> *And how it stands between the night tonight*
> *And a man with a smoky lantern chimney?*
> *How different from the way it ever stood?*

With these lines, Frost balanced the two opposed assertions, "The best thing that we're put here for's to see' and "We've looked and looked, but after all where are we?" Again teasing, in his "Grace Note" entitled "For Once, Then, Something," he struck another posture of apparent skepticism.[24]

This game of poetically taunting—which he had played, years earlier, in his correspondence with Susan Hayes Ward—provided him with one way of triumphing over his opponents.[25] Nevertheless, he usually played this game in close relation to his need for affirmation. The Stoical-puritanical-Christian yea-sayings he had learned from his mother had been buttressed by his own ways of reading two other literary taunters: William James and Thoreau.[26] With an eye always on the lookout for accounts of heroic endeavors in which men had confronted and triumphed over hardships, when circumstance drove life into a corner and reduced it to its lowest terms, Frost had found some fine examples in the reports of Arctic explorers. Among these heroes, one of his favorites was the Danish Knud Johan Victor Rasmussen, born in Greenland of Eskimo ancestry on his mother's side. He had established his famous Thule station at Cape York, Greenland, in 1910, and had used it as the base for several expeditions which he led. Frost, during a splurge of reading about the boldness of Arctic explorers, had written playfully to Untermeyer, in 1915, that he was considering a retreat from literary controversy—a retreat to Hudson Bay in northern Canada:

"Can you drore pitchers? Let me do you one of our new home (not yet finished or begun) on the Shores of Hudson Bay. . . . The object with the long matted hair is me neglecting the fur business to go fishing on the immemorial sea incarnadine. . . . The boat is named the New Moon to put it in the moon series with Henrick Hudson's Half Moon."[27]

Imaginatively, Frost had gone further in this direction by writing a serious poem in which he represented a hardy individual talking, just at the moment when he returns to his isolated station on the shore of Hudson Bay, and just after he has been warned or threatened (by someone who has apparently brought him back there, presumably by dogsled) that death is all he can expect if he insists on staying there. The poem starts with the hardy individual's retort: "I stay . . ." As the poem continues, the same speaker describes what life is like when it is thus reduced to its lowest terms in such a seemingly Godforsaken realm. These are the last three stanzas of this poem entitled "An Empty Threat":

Give a headshake
Over so much bay
Thrown away
In snow and mist
That doesn't exist,
I was going to say,
For God, man, or beast's sake,
Yet does perhaps for all three.[28]

Don't ask Joe
What it is to him.
It's sometimes dim
What it is to me,
Unless it be
It's the old captain's dark fate
Who failed to find or force a strait
In its two-thousand-mile coast;
And his crew left him where he failed,
And nothing came of all he sailed.

> *It's to say, "You and I—"*
> *To such a ghost—*
> *"You and I*
> *Off here*
> *With the dead race of the Great Auk!"*
> *And, "Better defeat almost,*
> *If seen clear,*
> *Than life's victories of doubt*
> *That need endless talk-talk*
> *To make them out."*[29]

In spite of all his teasings, aimed at the doubts (or even the beliefs) of those whose opinions differed from his, Frost was essentially concerned with using his poetry for the purpose of affirming his own religious belief, and the element of dialogue, in his poems, sometimes reflected the conflicts in his own consciousness. In saying repeatedly that he was a dualist in his thinking and a monist in his wishing, he liked to stress the old truths that man has two natures, physical and spiritual; that there are two mutually antagonistic principles in the universe, good and evil; that the world is ultimately composed of, and explicable in terms of, basic entities such as mind and matter; but that he was at least emotionally sympathetic with anyone like Plato who made the leap beyond the dualism of the known to the all-controlling "One" of the unknown. Among the "Grace Notes" which he chose to add to the manuscript of "New Hampshire" was a mood-poem reflecting his emotionally sympathetic belief in oneness. He called it, "I Will Sing You One-O," and he used as a starting point the experience of lying awake in the middle of a stormy night, wondering what time it was; waiting for either of the town clocks to tell him, by striking the hour:

> *Then came one knock!*
> *A note unruffled*
> *Of earthly weather,*
> *Though strange and muffled.*
> *The tower said, "One!"*
> *And then a steeple.*
> *They spoke to themselves*
> *And such few people*
> *As winds might rouse*

From sleeping warm
(But not unhouse).
They left the storm
That struck en masse
My window glass
Like a beaded fur.
In that grave One
They spoke of the sun
And moon and stars,
Saturn and Mars
And Jupiter.
Still more unfettered,
They left the named
And spoke of the lettered,
The sigmas and taus
Of constellations.
They filled their throats
With the furthest bodies
To which man sends his
Speculation,
Beyond which God is;
The cosmic motes
Of yawning lenses.
Their solemn peals
Were not their own:
They spoke for the clock
With whose vast wheels
Theirs interlock.
In that grave word
Uttered alone
The utmost star
Trembled and stirred
Though set so far
Its whirling frenzies
Appear like standing
In one self station.
It has not ranged,
And save for the wonder
Of once expanding
To be a nova,
It has not changed
To the eye of man

On planets over,
Around, and under
It in creation
Since man began
To drag down man
And nation nation.[30]

He thought the intensity of that hymn to Oneness should offset any doubts raised in the minds of religious readers by his own teasing expressions of doubt in so many of his other poems. Just the variety of tones and meters, in all these new poems assembled for this prospective volume, pleased and encouraged him. He was content to let his readers notice the consistency with which he intermingled with the humorous or comical or satirical elements the serious hints of his physical and metaphysical affirmations.

The next task, after he had roughly completed the assembling, was to get the entire manuscript typed in time to meet the summer deadline set by MacVeagh. In Ann Arbor, throughout the spring of 1923, he worked on the manuscript with the aid of Lawrence Conrad, the young man who had been his favorite student the year before. This year, Conrad was serving as an instructor in the department of rhetoric. Because he hoped to make a career of writing either prose or verse, he was delighted to serve as a typist for Robert Frost.

Conrad, as he typed, was amused to have Frost sit at his elbow and make last-minute revisions. Occasionally the poet would invoke the services of his wife in helping him reach decisions concerning lines or stanzes which troubled him. While Conrad waited at the typewriter, Frost would carry a page to the bottom of the stairs and would call to Elinor, invisible above, to ask if she would listen while he read something aloud, so that she could give him her decision as to which of two passages was the better. Occasionally, the question shouted up the stairs would be, "Elinor, how did we decide to spell this word . . ."[31]

Elinor Frost, preferring to remain out of sight, took pride in the part she played as advisor to her husband—the part she had played ever since she herself stopped writing poetry.[32] Her strong admiration for his work found expression while Frost and Conrad were still preparing the typescript of the new book. When MacVeagh wrote to Frost, in Ann Arbor just prior to the publication of *Selected Poems*, adding to his business letter a special tribute to the poems themselves, Mrs. Frost assumed the responsibility for answering:

"I have wanted to write to you ever since your last letter came, to thank you for what you said at the end of it about Robert's poetry. Robert was greatly pleased, and I myself felt it deeply that you should realize how much there is in the poetry that those who have written about it either don't see at all, or touch on very lightly. There is in it all the truth, vigor and humanity that they emphasize, but there is also a clean beauty, and even 'glamour' in line after line, and poem after poem, which his own particular way of expressing seems to have blinded them to so far. . . ."[33]

One not blinded was the artist, J. J. Lankes, who was so delighted by Frost's choice of him to make woodcut illustrations for *New Hampshire* that he paid his tribute to Frost by sending a portfolio of proofs newly pulled from some of his earlier blocks. Until this time, the arrangements with Lankes had been made by MacVeagh, and Frost had not exchanged any words with Lankes, whom he had not even met. His warm letter of thanks for the portfolio began a lasting friendship between these two men:

"Just as most friendship is feigning, so is most liking a mere tacit understanding between A and B that A shall like B's work as much and as long as B likes his. In our case I have good and substantial evidence that there was no such sordid bargain. I liked your work before I knew you liked mine; you apparently liked mine somewhat before you knew I liked yours. Such a coincidence of taste can never be foreseen. It ought to settle it between us.

"I'm hoping Lincoln MacVeagh will arrange with you to do the three frontispieces for the three parts of my new book, New Hampshire. I mean I'm hoping you'll want to do it. I know he wants you to. I should tell you I've already seen some of your things used as illustration for my Mountain Interval in the library of a man in Worcester.

"About these pictures you've heaped on me. Woodcuts are a form of art I'm the absolute victim of, and yours are such beautiful examples of it. I shall treat them as they deserve, particularly the back side of a village in snow and the Deserted House and The Apple Tree. And so I might go on. Im not alone in this: my whole family thanks you. . . ."[34]

Justifiably, Frost was disappointed with the woodcuts which Lankes made for *New Hampshire,* and soon after he received proofs of them he confided his disappointment to MacVeagh: "The Lankes pictures are well enough. They haven't the distinction of some of those he gave me however. He's worked in too great haste and not done himself quite justice. I like the grindstone one best . . ."[35] When the book was published, on the fifteenth of November 1923, many of the reviewers wrote approvingly of the kinship between Frost's pleasure in handling black and white in his poems and Lankes's related handling of black and white in his woodcuts. Some of the reviewers considered *New Hampshire* the best of Frost's work, and John Farrar was ecstatic in parts of his review:

"It is difficult for me to write sanely of Robert Frost; for in my opinion he is one of the few great poets America has ever produced. . . . This volume marks so great an advance over his previous work that it should be hailed with any amount of hand-shaking and cheers. Perhaps this is the perfection of Frost's singing. Perhaps this is the fruit of his ripest powers. It is a book of which America should well be proud. . . ."[36]

An even more incisive statement was made by Cornelius Weygandt, whom Frost had mentioned anonymously in the title poem as the man who "comes from Philadelphia every year / With a great flock of chickens of rare breeds / He wants to give the educational / Advantages of growing almost wild / Under the watchful eye of hawk and eagle . . ." Weygandt made his best comments on the narrative poems:

"What he does with stories that others than himself may know, that may even be common property, is to isolate them from the chaos of life and recreate for them a little world all their own. The truth is that his human sympathy and divination of motive give him more knowledge of the people of New Hampshire than anybody else possesses. . . . [His dialogues are] as full of intimations of what has passed and what is to come as is that of Ibsen, say, in *Rosmersholm.* You have an intensity of present situation, but the past out of which the present intensity has come is always making itself manifest through the words and pauses between the words. So, too, is what is to come adumbrated, suggested, intimated in the charged speech. There is often the intimation of something, we know not what, about to happen that makes Turgenief[37] so thrilling. There is a power of condensed story-telling equal to that of Hardy. . . . He sticks to the drama of the moment, and leaves the outcome, generally, to the reader's imagination. . . ."[38]

The highest tribute paid *New Hampshire* occurred when the newly established Pulitzer Prize for Poetry was awarded to it as the best book of poems published in America in 1923.

18

IN THE COUNCILS OF THE BOLD

Safety first! But you mustn't expect me to have time for adventures in safety. Just because you are in the woods and mountains is no distinction to talk of. You've got to get into something deeper. . . . It's to be in the councils of the bold that I have been tempted back to Amherst.[1]

A FEW MONTHS before *New Hampshire* was published, Robert Frost carried out the first of the promises he had made to President Olds of Amherst College. He visited the philosopher William Ernest Hocking at Harvard, and tried to persuade him that Amherst needed his presence for at least one semester during the next academic year. Hocking, unable to be absent from his regular commitments at such short notice, nevertheless welcomed the poet whose friendship he had cherished since that extraordinary occasion in 1915, when Frost had arrived for tea and had stayed two days.[2] Sympathetic to the unusual Amherst problem, Hocking named several of his former graduate students who might be available and, he thought, might interest Frost as possible candidates for vacancies. One of them, on whom Frost later called, annoyed and amused him so much that he had to tell others:

"Meeting people who have developed separately is as much fun as anything. I inspected a young Harvard Ph.D. and found him of the opinions that there was no God and that we all ought to commit suicide. I dont mean that he developed those particular opinions separately from everybody (he probably picked them up in some course in the history of philosophy); only that he developed them separately from me; and so burst on me with them more or less as a surprise. I asked him at once if one followed from the other on the ground that it wasn't polite for his creature to exist when God the Creator didn't exist, just as it wouldn't be the thing to remain seated when a lady was standing. His face lighted with intelligence for a moment at the unexpected reinforcement. Such is the infant mind. . . ."[3]

Considering this young philosopher worthy of further description, Frost gave more details in a letter to Wilbur Cross:

". . . fortunately I missed my train and the evening was added to the afternoon and just before midnight and my next train he all came out: he was a Ph.D. of Harvard 1921 who believed in suicide as the only noble death and in no God. He said he classified in the census as a monist, but you could count on there being no moaning of the bar when he embarked. Now if I hadn't formed the habit of staying round after everything was supposed to be over, you can see what I would have missed. And by the way what a detached or detachable young man . . . [he] made himself seem."[4]

In his capacity as scout for President Olds and the Department of Philosophy at Amherst, Frost had in mind a particular type of teacher: one whose knowledge concerning the history of philosophy could be adapted to the limitations of undergraduate responses. Influenced by William James in this regard, the poet was willing to admit that for him there had to be a blend between the realms of philosophy and theology, hence his eagerness to seek the assistance of a man like Hocking, who had declared himself openly in the title of his first book: *The Meaning of God in Human Experience*. A professor who was an atheist would never serve to offer the philosophy course which Frost wanted for Amherst. After another futile search, this time in New York City, where he discussed the problem with Lincoln MacVeagh, Frost could not resist confiding to MacVeagh the outcome:

"I have to report having found the philosopher I was on the hunt for in myself. On my way home from our talks together I said Why not? And the next day being called on the telephone from Amherst to say what courses I would announce for this year in English, I proposed to give one in philosophy on judgments in History, Literature, and Religion—how they are made and how they stand, and I was taken on by the department like odds of a thousand to one. Well the debacle has begun. Here begins what probably won't end till you see me in the pulpit."[5]

Somewhat frightened by his own boldness in choosing to offer a course which would combine so many disciplines, he planned to use a few guest lecturers, including Untermeyer. Because Untermeyer was then in Germany, the best that Frost could do for the moment was to alert him:

"I'm going to give the first course I ever gave in philosophy next year on judgments (or less technically Verdicts) in History, Literature, and Religion—how they are made and how they stand. As you see I am on my way into the church. What did I tole you, Doctor, if you went away and left me with nothing to lean on but God? It is too late to do anything about it now (at any rate by mail). You may as well accept it. But I do wish you could come home and mitigate a little the complications that are sure to ensue. . . . wish you were where I could invite you in on the job at least once in the year. You could be of great assistance in a course run as this will be by the case method or, as I like to put it, the illustration-first method. . . ."[6]

Having received assurance that he would not be required to teach more than two courses, each of his own choosing, and having made up his mind to proceed with bold innovations, he announced that his English department offering would expose a selected group of seniors to an unusual assortment of forms, selected from American, English, and European literature. While making up his reading list, well in advance of the fall term, he concentrated on the writings of rebels. He would start the boys off pleasantly, he decided, by giving them as their first assignment Melville's more or less autobiographical— and highly romantic—narrative concerning a rebel who jumped ship in the South Seas and lived for a time among cannibals: *Typee: A Peep at Polynesian Life*. Frost decided that Thoreau was another American rebel who should be taken under consideration in such a course, and *Walden, or Life in the Woods* was placed early on the schedule of assignments. Thoreau could be used to pave the way for his older neighbor-rebel, Emerson, and the students would be asked to read all of *Representative Men*—essays on such bold adventurers-in-ideas as Plato, Swedenborg, Montaigne, Shakespeare, and Goethe. Wanting to make a few unusual selections from English authors, Frost selected George Henry Borrow, who imbibed infidel ideas before he became a Bible salesman, and the assignment from Borrow would be *Lavengro: the Scholar, the Gypsy, the Priest*. Another assignment would be the *Autobiography* of another rebel, Edward Gibbon, whose education was so irregular and independent that it made a special appeal to Frost. The only translation placed on the projected list of readings was another autobiography—that of the violently wrathful and vengeful genius, Benvenuto Cellini. The only author chosen to represent poetry was one of Frost's secretly cherished favorites, and by no means a rebel: Christina Rossetti, who found her own ways of blending mysticism with passionate sensuousness.[7]

The Frosts, in all their planning for the move back to Amherst, spent much time in company with their Thoreau-admiring real-estate friend, Warren R. Brown, who knew their domestic tastes and needs. They found, with his help, and quickly rented a brick house at 10 Dana Street, not far from the campus. Mrs. Frost, describing the arrangements, spoke of one travel plan which was crowded out:

"We *had* looked forward to a quiet year here [in South Shaftsbury], but the work at Amherst will be light, only four hours a week, and we have taken a large house, where Robert will have a very quiet study, and I shall try to get a good servant, who will take some of the responsibility of the house (is such a thing to be had nowadays?) so that I hope it may be a rather restful year. As Robert has to be there for the opening day of college, we gave up the idea of England for the hay fever season. President Olds is willing he should be absent for six weeks later, however, so we have planned to sail [for England] the 5th of November and reach home the 15th of December."[8]

Unfortunately, the projected trip to England had to be postponed indefinitely because many unexpected demands were made on the Frosts soon after the academic year began. They enjoyed the cordiality of the welcome given them by old friends on the faculty and in the town. President Olds even made a boast about the poet when he announced to the alumni that he and the trustees, in the process of filling seventeen vacancies, had persuaded Robert Frost to accept a "permanent appointment," and that Amherst would henceforth be the poet's permanent home.[9] Frost could not resist doing a little boasting, himself, when he discovered that the enrollments in his two courses proved he was among the most popular of the newly appointed professors. "Fifty tried to get into my seminar in Fill," he wrote to MacVeagh. "As a first exercise in it I sent them out with lanterns to find the originals in life of the half dozen philosophies we talk and write. Queer doings at Amherst. Plainly our philosophies are but descriptions of a few attitudes toward life already long since taken in living."[10] He might have added that he began this course on "Judgments" by expressing two of his own: A philosopher, he said, gets up one metaphor and spends all his life studying and amplifying it; a poet tosses off metaphors at the rate of one a day: the danger which should be feared most is imprisonment within one hard-and-fast metaphor.[11]

Part of his purpose, in both courses, was to decontaminate students who might have become infected by the disease he chose to call "Meiklejaundice." The boldness he prided himself on, as teacher, was partly that of provocation, achieved by knocking established ideas into cocked hats. By contrast, what he disliked most strongly was the conventional orthodox procedure of spoon-feeding facts and accepted ideas through the lecture method. In his English course called "Readings" he gave special emphasis to that title: he hoped that his own reading-aloud, in class, from an assigned text, and his original comments on inseparable relationships between what was said and how it was said, in a passage under consideration, might encourage freshness of insight on the part of his students. One cluster of insights, partly assembled through his articulations in the classroom he passed to Untermeyer in the form of a letter:

"Since last I saw you I have come to the conclusion that style in prose or verse is that which indicates how the writer takes himself and what he is saying. Let the sound of Stevenson go through your mind empty and you will realize that he never took himself other than as an amusement. Do the same with Swinburne and you will see that he took himself as a wonder. Many sensitive natures have plainly shown by their style that they took themselves lightly in self-defense. They are the ironists. Some fair to good writers have no style and so leave us ignorant of how they take themselves. But that is the one important thing to know: because on it depends our likes and dislikes. . . . I am not satisfied to let it go with the aphorism that style is the man. The man's ideas would be some element then of his style. So would his deeds. But I would narrow the definition. His deeds are his deeds; his ideas are his ideas. His style is the way he carries himself toward his ideas and deeds. Mind you if he is down-spirited it will be all he can do to have the ideas without the carriage. The style is out of his superfluity. It is the mind skating circles round itself as it moves forward. Emerson had one of the noblest least egotistical styles. By comparison with it Thoreau's was conceited, Whitman's bumptious. Carlyle's way of taking himself simply infuriates me. Longfellow took himself with the gentlest twinkle. I don't suppose you know his miracle play ['The Flight into Egypt'] in The Golden Legend, or Birds of Killingworth, Simon Danz, or Others."

So far, in his essay-like letter to Untermeyer, Frost had avoided making any direct comment on his own style, but as he continued he closed the focus gradually until he included himself in one important regard:

"I own any form of humor shows fear and inferiority. Irony is simply a kind of guardedness. So is a twinkle. It keeps the reader from criticism. Whittier, when he shows any style at all, is probably a greater person than Longfellow as he is lifted priestlike above consideration of the scornful. Belief is better than anything else, and it is best when rapt, above paying its respects to anybody's doubt whatsoever. At bottom the world isn't a joke. We only joke about it to avoid an issue with someone[;] to let someone know that we know he's there with his questions: to disarm him by seeming to have heard and done justice to his side of the standing argument. Humor is the most engaging cowardice. With it myself I have been able to hold some of my enemy in play far out of gunshot."[12]

With a mingling of humor, sarcasm, irony, and banter, Frost had tried to keep some of his enemy in play far out of gunshot range while writing "New Hampshire." But his own self-protective uses of irony sometimes blinded him to less complicated procedures. One of the "illustrations-first" which he took into his "Readings" class during the spring term of 1924 was a sonnet by Edwin Arlington Robinson entitled "New England." Because Robinson's stylistic game was to make ironic thrusts at those outsiders who wanted to view poets like Frost and Robinson as cold and lacking in any intense emotional response to experience, Frost should have had no difficulty in understanding the typically Robinsonian ironies:

> *Here where the wind is always north-north-east*
> *And children learn to walk on frozen toes,*
> *Intolerance begets an envy of all those*
> *Who boil elsewhere with such a lyric yeast*
> *Of love that you will hear them at a feast*
> *Where demons would appeal for some repose,*

Still clamoring where the chalice overflows
And crying wildest who have drunk the least.

Passion is here a soilure of the wits,
It seems, and Love a cross for them to bear;
Joy shivers in the corner where she knits
And Conscience always has the rocking-chair,
Cheerful as when she tortured into fits
The first cat that was ever killed by care.[13]

Soon after "New England" was published, G. R. Elliot at Bowdoin called Frost's attention to it by mailing it to him with newspaper clippings which reflected the growth of a controversy over how to interpret it. Because the sonnet first appeared in the London *Outlook*, one complaint made by a local poet, David Darling, in Robinson's hometown newspaper, the Gardiner (Maine) *Journal*, was that Robinson had played into the hands of the enemy: "The British find rocks to heave at us without our help, and are 'on target' often enough without our giving them the range." Darling, extending his complaint, added a poem of his own, in which he made a direct attack on those who belittled Yankees. Robinson, in reply to Darling, had written:

"Having read Mr. D's vigorous letter and still more vigorous poem in the *Journal* of last week, I find myself constrained to ask for a small amount of space in which to say a few words of explanation. If Mr. D. will be good enough to give my unfortunate sonnet one more reading, and if he will observe that Intolerance, used ironically, is the subject of the first sentence . . . he will see that the whole thing is a satirical attack not upon New England but upon the same patronizing pagans whom he flays with such vehemence in his own poem. As a matter of fact, I cannot quite see how the first eight lines of my sonnet are to be regarded as even intelligible if read in any other way than as an oblique attack upon all those who are forever throwing dead cats at New England for its alleged emotional and moral frigidity. As for the last six lines, I should suppose that the deliberate insertion of 'It seems' would be enough to indicate the key in which they are written. Apparently Mr. D. has fallen into the not uncommon error of seizing upon certain words and phrases without pausing to consider just why and how they are used. Interpretation of one's own irony is always a little distressing, yet in this instance, it appears to be rather necessary . . ."[14]

Here was excellent subject matter for a class discussion on style, but when Frost presented the sonnet and the letters to his students, he assured them that Robinson had contrived his letter as an afterthought, for the self-protective purpose of trying to conceal his intent. This interpretation was presented as a fact, a "judgment," not as a subject for discussion.[15] After he had used the poem and the clippings in his class, he forwarded them to Untermeyer with this comment: "Amusing to see Robinson squirm just like any ordinary person in a tight place trying to keep in with his neighbors. . . . Funny motions life makes. We must try to be comparatively honest."[16]

Frost had some difficulty of his own, in being comparatively honest, on and off the campus. "I'm rather blue over my teaching," he wrote to MacVeagh. "I don't like the boys as much as I ought to."[17] Off-campus, during the fall of 1923, he placed himself in an odd predicament when he went to Boston for a reading, registered for the night at the Parker House, and simply wrote in the register, "Robert Frost, Amherst, Mass."

"I am most sorry to trouble you, Mr. Frost," said the clerk, "but we must have your complete address—your street and house number, you know . . ."

"Nonsense," replied the poet. "I have traveled east and north and south and west, and I have never had to write any more than that; besides, I am here."

"But the law requires it," the clerk apologized. "We are required to get the full address of every guest."

"But I haven't any full address," angrily protested the man from 10 Dana Street. "I live in a house, I have a roof, I am not a tramp, you understand. But my street has no name and my house no number. On that account, am I to be denied lodging?"[18]

Not waiting for any further answer, Frost wrathfully picked up his bag, stormed out of the Parker House, and went to Young's Hotel. The next day, after being introduced to a women's club audience in Pilgrim Hall, he began by telling of his difficulties at the Parker House. Making a humorous story of it, he said that after he had been turned away, he went to another hotel where he fearfully explained that he lived in a rural district where the road was not named and his house was not numbered; that, much to his relief, he was welcomed, as though this hotel catered especially to countrymen.[19]

Such a boldly creative act of storytelling pleased Frost so much that he repeated it to Gamaliel Bradford, during that same visit to Boston. After Frost had gone back to 10 Dana Street in Amherst, Bradford wrote to the manager of the Parker House, explaining what had happened and suggesting that "a line of apology to Mr. Frost would not be a bad idea." He added, "If addressed simply Amherst, Mass., it will reach him, as a letter addressed to President Coolidge would be likely to be delivered in Washington."[20]

While Bradford was thus linking Robert Frost and Coolidge, the journalist Mark Sullivan was telling a story which linked them in another way. The death of President Harding on the third of August 1923 had elevated the then Vice President, Mr. Coolidge, and he had taken the oath of office from his father, a notary public, in Plymouth, Vermont. Amherst College was properly excited to have an Amherst graduate become the nation's chief executive. Frost had long admired the fact that Coolidge was descended from a modest, frugal, and unpretentious line of puritan farmers in Vermont; that as governor of Massachusetts he had broken the Boston police strike with such firmness; that he subscribed to much the same laissez-faire economic theories as did Frost. Because Coolidge was a classmate of Dwight Whitney Morrow, whom Frost knew well, there was the possibility that Frost might some day meet the laconic President from Vermont. Mark Sullivan, working independently, had his own reasons for trying to arrange such a meeting. President Coolidge had sent for Sullivan, in Washington, soon after Harding's death, and had asked for advice on certain policies involving news releases. Before the discussion ended, Sullivan made the suggestion that the new President ought to use his office to confer distinction on men eminent in their lines. Theodore Roosevelt had frequently brought authors, artists, and scientists to the White House. A President from Vermont would have good reason for honoring some of the outstanding poets.

"Just what poets do you have in mind?" the President asked.

"Oh, any of the New England ones—Robert Frost, Edwin Arlington Robinson, Edna St. Vincent Millay—she was born in Maine."

"Frost? Robinson?" asked Coolidge meditatively, as though searching his memory. "I never heard of them. There was a fellow in Boston when I was in the legislature that used to write poems—he was a newspaper man—his name was Denis McCarthy."[21]

The conversation ended there, but Sullivan was so amused by the Amherst-graduate President's ignorance of literary goings-on in Vermont and Amherst that he eventually passed the story along to Frost, who enjoyed repeating it.

Although Coolidge was not the only prominent Vermonter who had ignored Frost's move from New Hampshire to the Green Mountain State, one of his literary friends paid tribute to him and his family in the fall of 1923, when the Frosts went up to South Shaftsbury from Amherst for an important wedding. The engagment of Carol Frost to Lillian LaBatt, following the Long Trail hike, had not been taken too seriously by his parents. It was clear that Lillian wanted to continue her studies by going to the University of Vermont after she completed her high-school work at North Bennington. Carol had driven her to Burlington, early in the fall of 1923, and it seemed probable that he would not see her again until Christmas vacation. But Lillian, partially deaf, had so much difficulty in understanding lecturers that she quickly became discouraged and decided to drop out. Carol, informed of her decision, brought her back from Burlington, persuaded her to marry him at once so that they could attend a New York apple fair together, won the permission of Lillian's widowed mother, and went ahead with plans to hold the wedding in the small Congregational Church in East Arlington. Carol's abrupt boldness pleased his father, who gave the young man full support in all these plans. Aside from members of the immediate family, only a few guests were invited; Dorothy Canfield Fisher was among them, for Lillian had so often visited, and sometimes worked in, the Fisher home. Shortly after the wedding, Frost sent to MacVeagh an account of these developments:

"Carol's marriage was only a little of a surprise. He and Lillian had been engaged for some time. They were such children that I didn't want to commit them to each other by taking much notice of the affair or saying much about it. I doubt if I thought it would survive Lillian's first year at college. But it turned out in a way to show that I was no judge of the intensity of children. Lillian's first year at college it was that didn't survive. She quit, homesick, and Carol went right to her mother and got her. It was all done in a week. I may be frosty, but I rather like to look on at such things. And I like children to be terribly in love. They are a nice pair. Lillian is an uncommonly pretty little girl. She is pretty, quiet and unpractical. She has been a great friend of the girls in the family for some years. All she has done is transfer herself from the girls to the boy. We'll see how completely she deserts the girls."[22]

Frost demonstrated some boldness of his own during the fall of 1923. In spite of the demands made on him at Amherst College, he still found time to meditate wistfully on all that Wilfred Davison was trying to accomplish, by way of innovation and experiment, with his summer program at the Bread Loaf School of English. When Davison wrote Frost, asking whether Professor Walter Powell, in the Department of English at Amherst, might be a good man to hire for the Bread Loaf staff, Frost did more than answer the question by way of reply:

"You've done something with Breadloaf to make it different from the ordinary American school in more than location, but, as I look at it, not nearly enough. You're missing a lot of your opportunities up there to make a school that shall be at once harder and easier than anything else we have. I'd be interested to tell you more about it if you should come down for a visit overnight; and I'd be interested in coming up for longer than my stay of last summer . . . might even stay a week, if you would excite me with something rather more advanced in educational experiment.

"By all means have Powell if a good ordinary academic is all you want. That's all he is. He won't set your buildings on fire and he won't start anything you never heard of before. . . ."[23]

Davison accepted the invitation, went down to Amherst from Middlebury, visited the Frosts on the twenty-second of December 1923, and commemorated the event in a journal entry:

"I found him at 10 Dana St., in a house on the edge of the village with a beautiful western exposure and one of the gnarled appletrees, without which he cannot seem to get on, just outside his study window. Rather, Mr. Frost met me. I had stayed at 'The Perry' Friday night and telephoned him Saturday morning about nine that I was at his disposal at any time. He told me to start right out and that he would meet me. I saw him coming as I approached Dana St., and he recognized me with a wave of the hand when we were quite a distance apart. He was, as ever, genial and friendly, and fell to talking at once. . . .

"Mrs. Frost greeted me in the living room and asked me to remain for luncheon. Shortly afterward Mr. Frost and I went to his study and talked there until past noon. After dinner Mrs. Frost joined us again for a time. But whether we were alone or with Mrs. Frost, Mr. Frost kept up a steady stream of comment and anecdote. How he does like to talk! There were things I wanted to say, but there was little opportunity. I asked a few questions, answered a few, and listened. And such talk! It makes an average person despair. Mainly it was Mr. Frost's ideas about the teaching of English, but he digressed to discuss the Amherst situation, Eddie Guest, and the Parker House incident . . . which caused the Parker House people to send him an apology, which he said he refused to accept. . . .

"In general, I found Mr. Frost somewhat less unspoiled than when I first saw him four years ago.[24] He is feeling his oats a bit, I fear. He said he was vindictive, and the comments he made showed it. But his fighting blood is up, and for the most part, he is apparently in the right.

"He scored many things about teaching, especially the new notion that the students should teach themselves, which he called 'Nonsense.' He said he told his boys that if he should leave his left leg lying on the desk for them to use, they wouldn't know what to do with it. He thought it absurd to assume that students knew better than their teachers what they needed.

"But at the same time he has all his old zeal for reform. He said that English teaching is in a bad way generally and especially scored graduate work, which he called futile. He thinks we are too much bound to books. . . .

"For proper growth, there must be idleness. Mr. Frost said that idleness had been the making of him. He thought that in all our school work there was too much 'busy work.'

"Specifically regarding Bread Loaf, Mr. Frost's idea was that we should have there a Pastoral Academy, where freedom should abound. He would have no formal restraint, but he would feel free to send students home at any time when they failed to take advantage of their opportunities. He would have very few formal lectures and recitations. For these he would substitute conferences and discussions. Instead of final examinations of the usual sort, he would substitute various tests, for he said students even in graduate work must be checked up. He would assign ten students to every teacher and ask each teacher to form his estimate of them through informal association in walks, talks, and from those general observations by which we form estimates of people in ordinary life. In fact, he said he would always 'freshen' method by bringing into the schoolroom as much of the atmosphere of life outside as is possible. For tests to take the place of examinations, Mr. Frost would substitute oral examinations, pieces of creative work, lectures by students before the class, with an occasional written examination. . . .

"Dinner was interesting. We had baked potatoes, lamb chops, peas and carrots served together, and apple pudding. There was bread on the table and salted peanuts, as the daughter [Marjorie] did not eat meat. The table, like the house, bore witness to Mrs. Frost's lack of ability to make things homey, but Mrs. Frost was more cordial than when I saw her before. They plied me with questions about my home, and I told them about my recent visits to Plymouth, Concord, and Haverhill, in which they were mildly interested. Mrs. Frost asked what author my students liked best, and they tried to discuss Hawthorne. Mrs. Frost suggested that 'The Scarlet Letter' was the only important thing Hawthorne did. Mr. Frost thought we must not forget the short stories, but he couldn't recall any but 'The Great Stone Face' and 'The Snow Image.' These he thought rather mild. When I suggested 'Ethan Brand,' he informed Mrs. Frost that it was an Italian story!![25] Just then he had to fix the furnace; he fixed it twice during dinner, and the second time he didn't come back. He had let the fire in the study [fireplace] go out, and he was glad to lean against the radiator after dinner. I should never have got away, I guess, if we hadn't begun talking about Mrs. Conkling and I suggested seeing her. He called her up for me and arranged an appointment, and I caught the four o'clock car, by rushing. Mr. Frost was going to try to go with me, but said he had to slick up a bit first; he needed to.

"Sometimes I think Mr. Frost is a great man, and sometimes I think he is only a ne'er-do-well who has happened to find fame. When his gray eyes are upon you, you cannot get away from them. His mind is fertile in thought; his conversation was brilliant, but racy. He chose words with more precision than

I ever noticed before. But I believe his range of ideas is comparatively narrow; that is what I mean when I say he is not great. I doubt whether the spiritual makes any very deep appeal. Certainly he is not conventionally religious. He damned quite a few things, including 'those bloody papers.' But the way that mind unfolds idea after idea on the topic he is thinking about, is marvelous. He sees ideas from many angles, and he illustrates everything to himself as he thinks, in specific instances and anecdotes. His talk was full of digressions, as one thing suggested another to him. I came away with a somewhat confused impression of it all; I was mentally weary, in fact, from the strain. . . ."[26]

Davison was only one of the many who marveled at the ways in which Robert Frost unfolded his ideas, saw them from different angles, and illustrated them vividly with specific instances. These extraordinary exercises of mind, which the poet demonstrated in his best appearances, increased the public demand for him, to such an extent that President Olds was occasionally forced to let him be absent briefly from the Amherst duties. In late February and early March of 1924, he gave talks and readings in Baltimore, in Boston, and in Philadelphia. Next, he went out into western Pennsylvania, to give a talk and reading at Allegheny College, where his performance gave him an unexpected chance to combine muscular and mental gymnastics. He had just begun his talk in the Ford Memorial Chapel, on a mild and springlike evening, when he was interrupted by a bat which flew in through an open window. As the web-winged creature skimmed back and forth over the audience, the ladies screamed and pulled their coats over their heads. Someone suggested that the intruder might leave of his own accord if the lights were turned out, and the ruse was tried. When the lights were turned on, the audience was delighted to find that the farmer-poet-teacher had armed himself with a broom. The still-circling bat came near enough to let him take a few lusty swings, without any luck. At last, when the creature seemed weary, and settled on the side of an open window in the transept, Frost climbed to the highest row of the choir pews and, with a single sure motion of the broom, swept it out into the night. Then, holding the emblem of his victory over his head, he stood there long enough to acknowledge the applause of the spectators.[27]

He was required to perform an even bolder act of gymnastics, this time entirely mental and emotional, when he went back to the University of Michigan with Mrs. Frost, during the Amherst spring vacation. Somewhat mysteriously, he had been asked to spend a week on the campus as guest of the University. As the week progressed, he was honored and feted in some extraordinary ways by President Burton, by Dean and Mrs. Bursley (with whom the Frosts stayed), by the students, and by the faculty.[28] Finally, after all these attentions had been enjoyed, President Burton made the confidential revelation that he was empowered by the Regents of the University of Michigan to offer Frost a lifelong appointment at Michigan, as a poet in residence, with the title, Fellow in Letters. If Frost accepted, he would have absolutely no faculty duties on committees, no teaching duties other than those he might voluntarily arrange in the form of occasional conferences or seminars on writing. He was tempted to accept at once.

But he had promises to keep, at Amherst. The question he faced, inwardly, was how bold he could be in making this choice between the permanent appointment he had so recently accepted (with four hours of classes a week) and this even better offer of a permanent appointment at Michigan (with no hours of teaching required), and at a salary of $5,000. Perhaps he could escape from his moral obligation to President Olds by assuaging his conscience; perhaps he could convince himself that "Meiklejaundice" had ruined possibilities at Amherst for him to such an extent that the Amherst students did not respond as readily to his informal methods of teaching as the students at Michigan did. He might salve his conscience if he avoided pulling out of Amherst until he had taught for at least one more year there. After considerable exercise of mind, he informed President Burton that he would accept the offer, and would begin his duties as permanent Fellow in Letters at Michigan in the fall of 1925, provided no announcement be made until after he had begun the next year of teaching at Amherst. These terms were accepted, and Frost returned to the councils of the bold, after the spring vacation, feeling far more sheepish than leonine.

During the remainder of the term, he tried to justify his secretly made contract by finding local targets for disparagment. The senior class, having teased him in various ways,[29] unintentionally gave him a chance to complain when it elected former President Meiklejohn as one honorary member of its class and then elected Robert Frost as another. He took revenge by giving the seniors in his "Readings" course something to worry about at the time of the final examination. Instead of writing the usual questions on the blackboard, he instructed them to make up their own questions—or at least to do something that would please him. In concluding his instructions, he told them he wanted not more than four bluebooks full of answers. Few of the baffled seniors guessed that they could please their teacher most if they wrote nothing. He boasted, later, that he had all the information he needed, concerning their abilities, and didn't need to see how well or badly they did on the final exam.[30]

In the midst of his truculent mood, he was infuriated by news concerning two poets whom he viewed as competitors. Without asking Frost's advice, the trustees appointed to an instructorship in the Department of English at Amherst the young poet David Morton—and Frost was hurt.[31] Then Lincoln MacVeagh innocently called his attention to the success achieved by a newcomer, Marianne Moore, whose second book of poems, recently published by Holt, had just gone into a second edition. In answer to MacVeagh's question whether the news made Frost angry, he wrote:

"On the contrary I was thinking that Marianne Moore had been turning you against me. You undoubtedly sent me that little folder today to twit me on her having run into the second edition. The handwriting was your own personal. Be careful, or you'll make her a household word. Then where would she be?—at once rare and common? Like her for all of me. 'All those that change old loves for new, pray gods they change for worse.'[32] Speaking of worse, we drew off [from Amherst] rather worsted from our year's teaching and lecturing, Elinor worse worsted than I. I would have given anything for a baseball game anytime these three months. But what's a fellow to do that combines so many occupations and arts?"[33]

He had drawn off from Amherst to attend the graduation ceremonies at Middlebury, where he received an honorary degree; he had hurried from Middlebury to New Haven to be present at the Yale commencement, where he received another honorary degree. For one who combined so many occupations, he could easily be convinced that he was far more appreciated in other quarters than in the place where Meiklejohn had spoiled everything. When he found himself in the right mood for gathering his complaints and self-justifications, he piled them into a letter:

"The boys had been made uncommonly interesting to themselves by Meiklejohn. They fancied themselves as thinkers. At Amherst you *thought,* while at other colleges you merely *learned.* (Wherefore if you love him, send your only son and child to Amherst.) I found that by thinking they meant stocking up with radical ideas, by learning they meant stocking up with conservative ideas—a harmless distinction, bless their simple hearts. I really liked them. It got so I called them the young intelligences—without offense. We got on like a set of cogwheels in a clock. They had picked up the idea somewhere that the time was past for the teacher to teach the pupil. From now on it was the thing for the pupil to teach himself using, as he saw fit, the teacher as an instrument. The understanding was that my leg was always on the table for anyone to seize me by[,] [anyone] that thought he could swing me as an instrument to teach himself with. So we had an amusing year. I should have had my picture taken just as I sat there patiently waiting, waiting for the youth to take education into their own hands and start the new world. Sometimes I laughed and sometimes I cried a little internally. I gave one course in reading and one course in philosophy, but they both came to the same thing. I was determined to have it out with my youngers and betters as to what thinking really was. We reached an agreement that most of what they had regarded as thinking, their own and other peoples, was nothing but voting—taking sides on an issue they had nothing to do with laying down. But not on that account did we despair. We went bravely to work to discover, not only if we couldn't have ideas, but if we hadn't had them, a few of them, at least, without knowing it. Many were ready to give up beaten and own themselves no thinkers in my sense of the word. They never set up to be original. They never pretended to put this and that together for themselves, never had a metaphor, never made an analogy.[34] But they had, I knew. So I put them on the operating table and proceeded to take ideas they didn't know they had out of them as a prestidigitator takes rabbits and pigeons you have declared yourself innocent of out of your pockets trouserlegs and even mouth. Only a few resented being thus shown up and caught with the goods on them."[35]

As long as he could, he kept to himself the secret of the

arrangements with Michigan—and then he began to drop hints. On the twenty-sixth of July 1924, in a letter to Professor Elliott at Bowdoin, he prefaced the hintings with another back-hander: "One year more of little Amherst and then surcease of that particular sorrow. I like to teach, but I don't like to teach more than once a week now. I'm become a spoiled child of fortune. I may be drawn back to Michigan or I may take to the woods."[36]

There was another convenient way of justifying his decision: making derogatory remarks concerning any of his Amherst friends or colleagues whom he might represent as being disloyal to him. He found one such target, that summer, while at the Bread Loaf School of English to fulfill his obligations to Professor Davison. George F. Whicher, the Amherst specialist in American literature, and one of Meiklejohn's youngest appointees, had worshipfully admired Frost since the afternoon when the poet had given his first Amherst reading.[37] At Frost's suggestion, Davison had successfully added Whicher to the Bread Loaf staff, and he was there with his wife, his father, and his mother. Before Frost's week of associations with the Whichers at Bread Loaf had ended, he had made up his mind that they had all offended him. He said as much, and more, as he continued his retrospective letter of complaints:

"I went to Middlebury [Bread Loaf] and put the finishing touch on myself and my teaching for the year. I speak literally. I am sick to death almost with having gnothied so many people. It seems to have come hardest on my liver or kidneys this time: whereas in the old days the straight teaching I did, wholly unpsychoanalytic, only ruined my first and second stomachs, particularly the first, the one that I ruminated with. I wasn't happy at Middlebury, the scene of my rather funny failure last year with New Hampshire (the poem, not the book). The Whichers were there, the old man Poetry Societist, George, and the wives, and I was aware that for some reason they were not helping me much. George is his father's son. He's the petty sort of half-friend. I've found him out in several deceits and concealments I don't admire. He catches the germs of the people he's with. I left him a protective wash against Meiklejaundice when I came away [in 1920]. But he got the bug though in attenuated form, as is like him."[38]

Throughout the remainder of the summer, he continued to

brood over the boldness of his decision to break his contract
with Amherst by staying only one more year. President Olds,
having become aware that Frost was not happy with the way
things had gone for him at Amherst during the past year, tried
to smoothe his feathers by giving him additional freedom. The
arrangement was that Frost would drop his course on "Judgments," offered in the philosophy department and, instead,
would offer to a select group of twelve seniors a course in
advanced writing; a course which could be handled largely
in conferences, if Frost chose. As for the other course, entitled
"Readings," it would be offered again for upperclassmen: sixty
students had signed up for it. The poet had also been promised
more freedom to absent himself from the campus, for readings
in various parts of the country. The generosity of these
arrangements only heightened the discomfort caused by his
conscience, and forced him to transfer additional self-blame.
What he dreaded most was the unspoken reproach which
might await him when he told President Olds and others that
he was leaving Amherst for Michigan, that Michigan would
make the public announcement during the fall of 1924. On
edge, and almost sick with a case of nerves, he made two
hay-fever retreats with Mrs. Frost that summer, and used his
hay-fever illness as excuse for asking permission to return to
Amherst after the beginning of the term. Late in September,
Mrs. Frost wrote to a friend, from Franconia, "The summer
has passed very rapidly for us and now college is open again,
but we are staying on up here five or six days after the opening
of college, on account of hay fever."[39] What ailed him, inwardly, was far more distressing than hay fever, and when
he finally did return to Amherst, a full week after classes
had begun, he felt cross and ugly.

FREED FROM OBLIGATION

When Mr. Frost takes up his residence at Ann Arbor next fall as permanent Fellow in Letters at the University of Michigan, he will be officially freed from all obligation to conform to any of the rules of that educational community. Naturally, he is pleased. No regular classes to meet, no routine duties, social or academic; nothing but the spur of his own spirit to prod him. He is simply going to live in that college community and do whatever he pleases.[1]

ONE of the Amherst seniors who took Robert Frost's course in advanced writing, during the fall term of 1924, had already made enough progress in journalism to enable him to earn money as a newspaper reporter in his home city of Lawrence, Massachusetts. A few months after the course began, he wrote for his paper about the now-famous former Lawrence resident and how the work of the semester had started:

"My acquaintances with Robert Frost began one night early last October when I attended his first lecture (more accurately described, it was not a lecture but an informal talk) to 12 select members of the senior class at Amherst College. . . . It had always been my impression that poets are odd and uncompanionable, but in Robert Frost I soon came to know a man whose great characteristic is his companionable nature.

"At that meeting Mr. Frost told the group of budding authors that he would not blue-pencil their creations, that his course on 'advanced writing' would be conducted in discussions on their ideas of writing. Just before he dismissed this group in their first meeting as a class (since then he has been meeting the students in individual conferences) he said: 'I'm not interested in marks as marks. I'll give you A's and B's, whichever you please! Now that you know what you are going to get, let me see what you can do.' Hardly an afternoon in the week passes by which does not find some Amherst student sitting in the parlor of the poet's home which overlooks the beautiful Connecticut Valley and Mount Tom in the distance, discussing his poem, or play, or essay, or whatever else may be the nature of his creation with Mr. Frost."[2]

The idea of avoiding regular classes and of requiring the students in this course to come to him, separately, had seemed a good one in theory. In practice, it made Frost the victim of any boy who felt free to knock on the door at 10 Dana Street at any hour of the day or night and stay as late as he chose. Mrs. Frost became impatient with these worshipful intrusions even before her husband did, and she was even more concerned over how he was to find time for his own writing. The early developments of that fall at Amherst thus gave him new reason and means for justifying his decision to accept the Michigan offer. He was ready to say quite pointedly, to anyone who might accuse him of having broken his word to President Olds, that his primary obligation must be to his own writing and to his career as poet. His previous withdrawal from Amherst in 1920 had been made partly in protest against Meiklejohn and partly to isolate himself on his farm in Franconia, where he could get more poems written. He had been driven back into the academic simply because he could not support his family on the earnings from his writings. He had gone to Michigan from Amherst, the first time, because Percy MacKaye had assured him the demands on his time would be light. They had not been light, even in the second year of that experiment, and he had therefore withdrawn once again from the academic. He would not have returned to Amherst if he had not been promised that his four hours of teaching each week would give him the freedom he desired for getting more writing done. Again, the arrangement had not given him enough freedom. Nevertheless, the announcements Presidents Burton and Olds would soon make should spell out the fact that he had been offered, finally, a way to get a living through casual and occasional participation in the educational processes of a great university. Under the circumstances, he felt fully justified in breaking his connection with Amherst. This, at any rate, would be his form of defense, when his critics assailed him.

The announcement, made in November of 1924, placed stress on the new freedom thus made available to the poet, and the Amherst release went into particulars:

"Robert Frost, professor of English at Amherst College since 1923, has resigned, his resignation to become effective at the end of the present academic year, according to an announcement made public at the president's office this morning. . . . His fellowship at the University of Michigan has been created especially for him, and will exist for life. The fellowship entails no obligations of teaching and it provides for all living expenses. He will have entire freedom to work and write.

"In accepting the fellowship, Professor Frost feels that he will be able not only to write but also to carry on as he has done in this college his theory of 'detached education.' This theory of education is one in which the students are encouraged to do more and more work for themselves and to expect from the teacher more of guidance than of tutoring.

" 'It takes me one step further along to the kind of teaching I have done here at Amherst,' Professor Frost is quoted as saying . . . 'It might be described as no more than a slight interference with students in their self-teaching. I have never been able to care much about following boys up with detailed daily questions. I have wanted to sit where I could ask everything of them at once, where by a challenge I could ask them to go the whole length in some one of the arts, for example. . . .'

"Commenting upon his departure from Amherst, the poet declared that 'it will cost me something in broken ties to leave Amherst, but I haven't seen how I could refuse the advantages offered me at Michigan. Chief of these will be the freedom to get my writing done. The fellowship will give me practically all my time to do with it as I please.' "[3]

Frost was relieved to discover that as soon as the word was out the students and his colleagues on the faculty at Amherst were more inclined to congratulate than criticize. Eager to make amends for his planned departure, he threw his energies into his two classes with more liveliness and geniality than he had usually shown. Students who visited him at his home found that he was in a particularly affable mood, and willing to talk with them late into the night.

One evening an unexpected visitor was a reporter from the

Boston *Globe* who wanted to write a feature story on this man brought suddenly into the news by the Michigan appointment. Escorted into Frost's comparatively undecorated and somewhat disordered study, the reporter was quickly fascinated by the way in which Frost slouched down into an easy chair, stretched out his legs, and began to talk about himself as a rebel in educational communities. The poet wore a soft white shirt without a necktie. His deep-set blue eyes were merry, and chuckles bubbled in his conversation. Repeatedly he ran his long fingers through his gray hair and rumpled it into a new disarray without any concern for how he looked. He admitted that some of his colleagues on the Amherst faculty frowned on him because he sometimes failed to show up for his classes and because he ignored students in the classroom who wrote letters or played cards or whispered to each other while he was reading poetry. His particular concern, he said, was for the diffident undergraduates who, for one reason or another, were considered by the others to be outsiders. He thought a poet-teacher should serve as a rallying point for undergraduates who were "poets on the sly." The reporter, pleased with the story he got, wound it up with a description of the poet's manner in saying good-bye:

"As he stood on the step of his Amherst home bidding his guests farewell, the moon shone full upon him. His gray hair was tousled in the most grotesque manner, his hands were extended in a curious, generous gesture, and his voice carried across the yard a gentle invitation to come again. It was a picture not soon forgotten. It typifies one of the friend-liest spirits in the land, a spirit that refuses to attack, but refuses to conform. . . ."[4]

Although Frost liked to say he never read any articles about himself, he often peeked at them, and he may have been amused by a certain naïveté in the *Globe* reporter's story. He knew that if the young man did accept the invitation to call again at 10 Dana Street he might learn of the poet's darker belief that there is a time for enmity as well as friendliness. And the *Globe* reporter, in his article, had been a bit too sweeping when he had informed his readers that Frost at Michigan would be "freed from all obligation to conform to any of the rules of that educational community."

It often happened that the poet was irked by the obligations he cherished most. Nobody had a greater gift for infuriating him than his beloved wife. As for their four children, the older they grew the more often they annoyed him with the independence of mind he had helped them fashion. Carol's ridiculous talk about the need for a $35 rooster had been a case in point. In spite of all his father had told the boy, from firsthand poultry experience, Carol had gone right ahead and had bought that expensive rooster, as though to prove he was no longer under complete obligation to his father. Lesley and Marjorie, having decided to go into the bookselling business, on their own, had opened their store in Pittsfield in the spring of 1924, and had felt under no obligation to listen to their father's advice concerning titles they should stock. He sympathized with all these shows of independence even when he was annoyed by them. In the right mood, he entertained himself by noticing how different the same fact or object or person or idea might look when viewed from a different angle. His public audiences, charmed by his way of reading "Stopping by Woods," might be surprised if they could hear him say with great sarcasm, in a moment when things weren't going well at home, "But I have promises to keep."

At Amherst, during the fall term of 1924, things went well enough to make it relatively easy to keep promises, although he had already begun to worry about some which would overtake him in the spring. Amy Lowell was at the center of one such worry. Frost, having told the Amherst students he would give them a chance to hear and see this picturesque monster in action, tried to make arrangements for her to read there in November of 1924. Instead of extending the invitation himself, he turned the matter over to Mrs. Frost, urging her to assure Amy that they could offer adequate hospitalities for the night at 10 Dana Street. They both supposed she would prefer to reserve a large suite of rooms for herself and her servants in a hotel, but Mrs. Frost sincerely went through the motions:

"I hope your book [on John Keats] is coming on satisfactorily. We want you to come here for a reading or lecture sometime in November. Do you think you can? If you do, I wish Ada [Russell] could come here for a night beforehand, to see if she doesn't think you could be made comfortable in our house, instead of going to a hotel in Holyoke or Springfield. We have a large house, six bedrooms and three bathrooms and I could get in a good cook for a few days. Ada could assume charge of the house, and give her own orders for your comfort. I think it would be easier for you, and we should enjoy it. There is, you see, plenty of room for your maid."[5]

Miss Lowell replied that she wouldn't even consider the invitation until she had finished reading proof on her Keats biography, but it might be off her hands in late February of 1925, and she might come then. She appreciated the offer of hospitalities, and yet there was no need to bother: if she could be there for the reading, she would stay in the Kimball Hotel in Springfield. The plan was worked out very successfully. Miss Lowell arrived, from Springfield, in good spirits, talked to a capacity audience in Johnson Chapel, amused the students with her haughty mannerisms, and even pleased some of them with her poems. After the performance, she made another occasion of the reception given her at the Frost home. Mrs. Frost told Mrs. Fobes about it:

"Last Monday Amy Lowell came. She stayed at the Kimball in Springfield, but she was here for supper, and after the lecture I had a little party for her. About thirty people came in for an hour, and as she was in a particularly gracious mood, it went off very well. I had a caterer come in and serve chicken salad, rolls, coffee and ice cream and cake. . . ."

Mrs. Frost went on to tell Mrs. Fobes about Miss Lowell's plans for another event which promised to be far more spectacular:

"Some literary people in Boston are getting up a big dinner for her in Boston, just before she sails the first week of April, in honor of the Keats book, and Robert has got to make a ten minute speech in praise of her on that occasion. Robert and I and the Untermeyers are going to stay with her two or three days at that time, and I am sure we'll have a lot of fun. Robert and Louis will be joking about everything and everybody. . . ."[6]

The joking had already begun, and some of it involved plans for another "big dinner." Frederic G. Melcher, editor of *Publishers' Weekly*, had proposed to celebrate Robert Frost's so-called fiftieth birthday (actually his fifty-first) with a dinner in New York City on the twenty-sixth of March 1925—not much more than a week prior to Miss Lowell's dinner in Boston. Although Amy had permitted Melcher to use her name as a member of the committee sponsoring the Frost birthday party, she had insisted from the start of these preparations that because of her chronic ailments and the complicated plans not only for her own dinner but also for her impending departure for England, she could not get down to New York City on the twenty-sixth. Bantering, Frost had said that of course if she couldn't attend his party he wouldn't attend hers. Mrs. Frost, as though to make amends for such a threat—or at least to place the terms in a better light—wrote to Miss Lowell soon after her reading in Amherst:

"Robert says to tell you that he'll be on hand for your party if there is anything left of him by that time. He has twelve or thirteen reading engagements between now and then (which means a lot of travelling, as you know) besides keeping up his college work, and I just don't know how he is going to manage it. Then there is his own party on the 26th, which will, of course, be a nervous strain, though a pleasure at the same time. I wonder if anyone will come to *his* party. Please change your mind and come yourself.—I hope you reached home none the worse for the little trip to Amherst. It was a great pleasure to have you here. . . ."[7]

There was more malice in Frost's banter than was immediately apparent. During the decade since he had returned from England to find himself acclaimed (no matter how clumsily and imperceptively) by Amy Lowell, in her *New Republic* review, he had been polite and even obsequious to her. Several times, he and Mrs. Frost had enjoyed the hospitalities lavished on them during visits to Sevenels in Brookline. Frost admired her ruthless wit and sharp tongue. Nevertheless, he continued to hold her poetry in low regard, and he did not hesitate to tell others that she was a charlatan. He had said as much to Untermeyer, privately, nearly five years earlier:

"But I'll whisper you something that by and by I mean to say above a whisper: I have about decided to throw off the light mask I wear in public when Amy is the theme of conversation. I don't believe she is anything but a fake, and I refuse longer to let her wealth, social position, and the influence she has been able to purchase and cozen, keep me from honestly bawling her out—that is, when I am called on to speak! I shan't go out of my way to deal with her yet awhile, though before all is done I shouldn't wonder if I tried my hand at exposing her for a fool as well as fraud. . . ."[8]

It was also to Untermeyer that Frost had written, "I always hold that we get forward as much by hating as by loving,"[9] and now that he was placed in a position where there would be some competition over the question of whether more guests of distinction would gather for her dinner than for his, the envy and jealousy he felt soon turned banter into a renewal of his disgust for what he viewed as her charlatanism. While she continued to treat as a joke his claim that he wouldn't attend her party if she didn't attend his, he became increasingly serious. Next, he persuaded Untermeyer to join him in the plot to stay away from her party.

The Frost birthday dinner, held at the Brevoort Hotel in New York City, was a modest success. The master of ceremonies was Carl Van Doren, and one of the tributes which he read aloud was from the absent Miss Lowell. She gave an account of the start of her acquaintance with Frost and described it as "a friendship which, on my part, has been an ever-increasing admiration of his work, and a profound attachment to the man."[10] More playfully, the after-dinner speakers combined praise with teasing. They included Dorothy Canfield Fisher, Wilbur L. Cross, Walter Prichard Eaton, and Louis Untermeyer. Frost, in his reply, added to the spirit of playfulness by offering his listeners a little one-act drama inspired by John Lynch of Bethlehem: "The Cow's in the Corn."[11] The ladies among the guests included the novelist Willa Cather, the poet Jean Starr Untermeyer, the poet and novelist Elinor Wylie, the journalist Elizabeth Shepley Sergeant, Mrs. Frost, and the two daughters, Lesley and Irma. The atmosphere of the entire evening was thoroughly pleasing to the guest of honor. But the absence of Amy Lowell gave strength to his now vindictive decision that he would absent himself from her dinner. While the Frosts were still in New York City, immediately after his birthday celebration, he persuaded his wife to make excuses for him:

"My dear Amy,—

I am writing to say what we ought to have said decidedly in the first place—that it's simply out of the question for Robert to speak at your dinner. He just isn't able to. He is tired now, and has three lectures ahead of him this week, with much travelling. He is sorry, and we hope very much that is won't greatly disarrange your plans.

And we hope very much, too, that the occasion will be a happy and satisfactory one for you. I am sure it will be.

With love to you and Ada,

Faithfully yours,

Elinor Frost"[12]

Even without Robert Frost, the "Complimentary Dinner in Honour of Miss Amy Lowell," held in the ballroom of the Hotel Somerset, Boston, was a spectacular triumph. The two-volume *John Keats*, on which she had worked with so much devotion, had already gone through four large printings. The sponsors of this celebration were distinguished Bostonians—scholars and artists—including John Livingston Lowes (then the chairman of the English Department at Harvard), the famous American painter John Singer Sargent, the editor-in-chief of the *Atlantic Monthly*, Ellery Sedgwick, and author-critic M. A. DeWolfe Howe. After the cordial speeches had been made, praising Miss Lowell for her successful battle in behalf of Imagist poetry, and commending her scholarly achievement in her study of Keats, she responded briefly with a reading of "Lilacs" and "A Tulip Garden." Although she pronounced the party a "huge success," she was scarcely able to maintain her poise to the end of the evening. As her intimate friends knew so well, she suffered great pain throughout the evening, in spite of sedatives given her by her physician. The strain of the occasion was too much for her, and she became so ill that she was forced to cancel her accommodations aboard the SS *Berengaria*, scheduled to sail for England on the fifteenth of April 1925. A few weeks later, on the twelfth of May, she suffered a stroke and died.[13]

Frost, conscience-stricken, made the only amends possible. He immediately sent a telegram of condolence to Ada Russell, and Mrs. Frost wrote at length to her, saying in part,

"Robert and I are terribly shocked and grieved to hear of Amy's death. We have supposed from the newspaper reports of her condition that she was gaining strength rapidly, and was around the home again as usual. We did not dream it was anything serious.

"I have intended to write to her every day, but my heart and hands have been occupied with plans for our son's welfare. I went directly to the farm after Robert's birthday dinner in New York, while he went off on a lecturing trip, and I found

[276]

Carol in what seemed to me a serious condition. He had incipient tuberculosis nine years ago,[14] and it seemed to me that the same condition had returned, after a winter of too many colds and grippe attacks. Since then I have been at the farm most of the time, looking after his food and urging him to rest, but we are still worrying about him. Robert has been excessively nervous and overtired. I feel dreadfully that we didn't send any message to Amy, of sympathy for her illness and giving up the English trip.

"We shall miss her very much. We were fond of her, and were always delighted, when we saw her, with her lovable traits, and her liveliness of mind and spirit. . . ."[15]

Soon after Amy Lowell's death, President Olds called on Frost to make a commemorative statement, before the students, in chapel exercises. He could not refuse. In his remarks he discriminated precisely between what he admired about her "liveliness of mind and spirit" and what he did not like about her poetry. A day later, a reporter from the *Christian Science Monitor* appeared at 10 Dana Street to ask for a tribute to Amy Lowell which might be published in the *Monitor*. Made uneasy by the request, Frost explained that he would prefer to write out such a tribute rather than dictate it on the spur of the moment. If the reporter would be willing to wait a few minutes, he would try to gather his thoughts. Retreating alone to his study, he found paper and pen, still wondering what he could write that would not mock him when he saw it in print. He remembered a pair of thoughts he had recently formulated in conversation, and decided to put them down as part of his tribute, even though he had not previously associated them with Amy Lowell—or even with each other. As he wrote, he patched in a few additional statements which might be taken as praise, provided the reader did not look too closely.[16] What he gave to the reporter, a few minutes later, was adequate:

"It is absurd to think that the only way to tell if a poem is lasting is to wait and see if it lasts. The right reader of a good poem can tell the moment it strikes him that he has taken an immortal wound, that he will never get over it. That is to say, permanence in poetry as in love is perceived instantly. It hasn't to await the test of time. The proof of a poem is not that we have never forgotten it, but that we knew at sight that we never could forget it. There was a barb to it and a toxin that we owned to at once. How often I have heard it in the voice and seen it in the eyes of this generation that Amy Lowell had lodged poetry with them to stay.

"The most exciting movement in nature is not progress, advance, but expansion and contraction, the opening and shutting of the eye, the hand, the heart, the mind. We throw our arms wide with a gesture of religion to the universe; we close them around a person. We explore and adventure for a while and then we draw in to consolidate our gains. The breathless swing is between subject matter and form. Amy Lowell was distinguished in a period of dilation when poetry, in the effort to include a larger material, stretched itself almost to the breaking of the verse. Little ones with no more apparatus than a teacup looked on with alarm. She helped make it stirring time for a decade to those immediately concerned with art and to many not so immediately.

"The water in our eyes from her poetry is not warm with any suspicion of tears; it is water flung cold, bright and many-colored from flowers gathered in her formal garden in the morning. Her Imagism lay chiefly in images to the eye. She flung flowers and everything else there. Her poetry was forever a clear resonant calling off of things seen."[17]

Still conscience-stricken, partly because he did not immediately hear how Untermeyer had reacted to the news of Amy Lowell's death, and partly because he suspected that Untermeyer might hold him responsible for the awkwardness which had developed in their warm friendship, Frost let more than a month pass before writing to him:

"I suspect that what lies at the bottom of your *Schmerz* is your own dereliction in not having gone to her Keats Eats just before Amy died. She got it on us rather by dying just at a moment when we could be made to feel that we had perhaps judged her too hardly. Ever since childhood I have wanted my death to come in as effectively and affectingly.[18] It helps always any way it comes in a career of art. Whatever bolt you have shot you have still, as long as you are alive, that one reserve. But, of course, it always does the most good on a world that has been treating you too unkindly.

"I didn't rise to verse, but I did write a little compunctious prose to her ashes. And I did go before the assembled college to say in effect that really no one minded her outrageousness because it never thrust home: in life she didn't know where the feelings were to hurt them, any more than in poetry she knew where they were to touch them. I refused to weaken abjectly."[19]

Far more important to Frost was another death which had occurred while he and Amy Lowell were still bantering over who would or would not appear at whose dinner. On the nineteenth of February 1925 many newspapers throughout the country bore the announcement that Dr. Marion LeRoy Burton, President of the University of Michigan, had died the day before. Massachusetts papers gave particular space to the obituary because Burton had become President of Smith College in 1910, the same year when Coolidge had become Mayor of Northampton, and the two men had developed so close a friendship that Burton had been named to make the speech nominating Coolidge as candidate for President of the United States, at the Republican Convention in Cleveland in June of 1924. More important to Frost was Burton's leadership in arranging to bring Frost to Michigan. The support he had given during the two previous stays had provided impetus for the poet's decision that he would return in the fall of 1925. But the death of Burton raised questions whether his unnamed successor would have enough sympathy for a "Fellow in Letters," appointed for life, and yet "freed from all obligation." Not invited to the funeral, where attendance was limited to members of the family, Frost was asked to be the main speaker at a memorial service to be held in Ann Arbor on the first of May 1925. Accepting the honor, he chose that occasion to review for his listeners what he described as some of President Burton's ideas on education:

"Administration was never enough to satisfy the idealism of his nature. He brushed it aside in his mind for something beyond, which as I came to see was no less than the advancement of learning through magnanimous teaching. Building, discipline, entrance requirements, professional schools were but the spread and ramification of the tree. His heart was really in some slight branch away at the top by which alone the tree was gaining height. The height of teaching was what concerned him—how far it would be carried. We talked of nothing else the last few times I saw him. . . .

"Remember now that I am telling you almost his very words. No one was ready to give a name yet to the change that was coming over education. He preferred to describe it himself in terms of teachers. He built the future on teachers who would know how to get more out of a student than by throwing or by putting the screws on him. They would ask without asking. How? By implication, by challenge, by example, by presence.

"What would they ask? First of all that the student make his own trouble and not wait for teachers to make it for him. Second, they would ask a student to . . . [grasp] the idea that telling over a story he read last night, in nearly the order in which he read it, is no more good recitation than is polite conversation. And they would prejudice him against intruding with the sciences into art. They would prejudice him against putting a poem or book to any use except that it was intended to be put to by the man who wrote it. They would remind him that, in both the arts and sciences, a man shows the quality he is to be known by, strikes what is called his note, young, or, almost certainly, not at all. He has no time to waste dawdling with nothing but good marks for an excuse. Between 15 and 25 are the springing years. And last of all, they will turn their claim on him into his claim on them, and ask him, by implication, to use it. . . .

"President Burton's plan was just unfolding. It was all his own. Others will go on with it. But that will not be the same to his friends who sympathized with him in his ambition. Our loss may be great, but his loss was great, too, interrupted in what he could not help feeling was a great enterprise."[20]

Robert Frost hoped that none of his listeners at the memorial service would realize that he had placed so many of his own personal opinions concerning education in the mouth of the dead President Burton. The poet had stretched the truth considerably when he had assured these listeners, "Remember now that I am telling you almost his very words." In a sense, his primary theme throughout his address had been the justification of the unorthodox stance he had taken at Amherst and would take when he returned to Ann Arbor that fall, in his new post as permanent fellow in letters. If anyone saw through his machinations, and chose to view the address as an *Apologia Pro Vita Sua*, academically, Frost could at least say that he himself deeply believed in these notions, and that he had already talked them over with President Burton, who seemed to like them.[21]

In spite of his unorthodox methods as a teacher, Frost had already made several important contributions to the educational programs at Michigan and Amherst. Even before he attended the Amherst College commencement of 1925, a great many of the students, the faculty, and the townspeople found occasions for expressing their gratitude to him, personally. An editorial which had appeared concerning his plan to go to Michigan praised him warmly and made only one complaint: "The wish has been expressed from more than one source that such an opportunity had been created for Prof. Frost here at Amherst, so that we might have benefited by his progress in the kind of teaching he has been doing in Amherst College."[22]

As the academic year drew to its close, another important recognition served to delay the Frosts' return to the Stone Cottage in South Shaftsbury. President Sills had written to say that Bowdoin College would confer on him an honorary degree if he could attend commencement there. Frost, supposing that the initial suggestion had been made by his admiring friend George Roy Elliott, eagerly accepted the invitation. When it came time for him to set out for Bowdoin, however, he hesitated because Mrs. Frost had been ill for several weeks, and she still seemed too ill to be left alone. Blaming himself, he was distressed by his realization that he had dragged her through so many crises during the school year. On the very morning when he should have started for Maine, he abandoned the plan and sent an explanatory telegram of regret to President Sills. Then he wrote to Elliott:

"I'm sorry this had to happen, but we've been riding for it and I can't say it wasn't expected. Elinor had a serious nervous collapse early last week. I saw it wasnt going to do to leave her and I should have wired regrets then, but she hated to be the cause of my failure to keep an engagement and kept me waiting on from day to day to see if she wouldn't be better. I was actually on the point of setting out for Brunswick on Wednesday but at the last moment my courage failed me—she looked so sick. The amount of it is, my way of life lately has put too much strain on her. All this campaigning goes against her better nature and so also does some of this fancy teaching, my perpetual at-home charity clinic for incipient poesis, for instance. Time we got back into the quiet from which we came. We've had our warning. I'll tell you more about it when I see you if you make it worth my while by forgiving me first. . . ."[23]

20

SICKNESS AND SCATTERATION

All this sickness and scatteration of the family is our
fault and not our misfortune or I wouldn't admit it. It's
a result and a judgement on us. We ought to have gone
back farming years ago or we ought to have stayed farm-
ing when we knew we were well off.[1]

WHEN Robert Frost and his wife made the journey from
Vermont to Michigan by train in the fall of 1925, he knew
she was reluctant to go. "Neither Carol nor Lillian seem
well enough to please me," she had written to Mrs. Fobes a
few weeks earlier, "and I am rather worried and tired."[2] Still
fearful that Carol's respiratory ailments might be signs of
incipient tuberculosis, or worse, she would have preferred
staying to keep an eye on him. Her husband thought she
worried unnecessarily about their children, even about the
happy ways in which Marjorie and Lesley threw themselves
into long hours of work at their beloved bookstore in Pittsfield.
She had worried particularly about Irma during the past
summer. Irma was as much a hay-fever victim as her father,
and she was therefore taken to the Fobes guest-cottage in
Franconia, when her parents went there for the hay-fever
season. She had returned to New York City, however, to continue her studies in drawing and painting, at the Art Students
League, prior to the time when her parents set out for Ann
Arbor. The year before, Mrs. Frost had worried so much about
the advisability of letting Irma live alone in New York that
Mrs. Frost had twice visited her there. All these fears and
worries concerning the children were indeed debilitating. But
some of her nervousness and fatigue, now, stemmed from
the aftereffects of her serious illness during the previous June
—an illness which her husband had misrepresented, in his

excuse-making letter to Elliott, for reasons of delicacy. She had not suffered a nervous collapse, although the school year had indeed been difficult for her.[3]

Immediately awaiting Mrs. Frost in Ann Arbor was the problem of furnishing the attractive and small colonial house which friends of the Frosts had chosen and rented for them at 1223 Pontiac Road, across the Huron River from and not too close to the campus. Taking the life-appointment seriously, the Frosts had sent their furniture by freight from Amherst, and as they had been slow in making arrangements for its shipment, delivery would be late. Dean and Mrs. Joseph A. Bursley, two of their closest friends, insisted that the Frosts plan to be their guests until the house on Pontiac Road was ready for occupancy. Mrs. Frost could at least count on obtaining some rest while waiting for the furniture to arrive.

Almost as soon as the Frosts reached Ann Arbor, other friends were so quick to extend hospitalities which could not be refused that they were promptly caught up in too many social engagements. The poet at once discovered that during the past three years his stature as poet had grown in the eyes of these admiring people. Copies of *New Hampshire*, which he had dedicated to Vermont and Michigan, were often in evidence awaiting his autograph, and many people congratulated him on its having won him a Pulitzer Prize. New luster was provided by his having been given so unique a position as permanent Fellow in Letters at Michigan, and by his having served as the major speaker in the memorial service for the late President Burton.

One of the first social invitations came from Burton's successor, the newly arrived President, Clarence Cook Little, a New Englander who had specialized in biology and genetics while doing graduate word at Harvard and who had become a professor in the Harvard Medical School before serving as President of the University of Maine. When the Frosts went to the "White House" for dinner, they discovered that the attractive Mrs. Little was strongly sympathetic toward Frost's new appointment: she herself was a poet, and was eager to organize an informal group of nonstudents who might enjoy sharing their literary enthusiasms. Frost, trying to show more interest than he felt for such a plan, made and later kept a promise to meet with this group as soon as Mrs. Little could assemble it. Much of his conversation with President Little, on that initial evening they spent together, was tactfully directed to the subject of biology and to questions concerning the President's work in the field. To hold up his end of the conversation, Frost spoke with sincerity about his early delight in reading and re-reading Charles Darwin's book on the famous voyage of the *Beagle* to the islands of the South Seas. His host, impressed, later took from a shelf in his own library, and presented to Frost as a gift, the first English edition of Darwin's *Journal of Researches*. The rapport established seemed mutually gratifying, but Frost knew he could never develop with this cold-mannered scientist the same cordial friendship he had formed with the late President Burton.[4]

Another early invitation was a request that Frost be present at the first fall meeting, in Professor Cowden's home, of those students currently serving on the editorial board of the campus literary magazine, now called the *Inlander* instead of *Whimsies*. At this first meeting he recognized and named those seniors he had known as freshmen, on the *Whimsies* staff, when he had last met regularly with them in the spring of 1923. One of them was Mary Elizabeth Cooley, daughter of the world-renowned sociologist Charles Horton Cooley. As far back as the spring of 1922, when Frost had heard Mary's father give a Phi Beta Kappa address at Ann Arbor, the poet had been so much impressed that he had impulsively visited Cooley at his home, to give him a copy of *Mountain Interval*. During this call, he had met Mary and had been surprised to find that she, then a high-school student, owned *A Boy's Will* and *North of Boston*. In the fall of her sophomore year she had written him to say that while on a geological expedition in Wisconsin she had slept for two night in a barn, and had found that the wife of the farmer who owned the barn knew the poetry of Robert Frost. Later, Mary said, she sent the farmer's wife a copy of *New Hampshire*. Frost had answered:

"I shall surely never count it against you that you have scattered grains of my poetry to the uttermost parts of Wisconsin. I always say that the best criticism of a book is some story of something done with it . . . I shall soon be where I can see more of your poetry. You should still have a year to go after this, unless you are rushing through in three years. You musn't graduate the minute we get there."[5]

By the time he did get there, in the fall of 1925, Mary

Cooley and two other undergraduates—Dorothy Tyler, also a senior, and Sue Bonner, a junior—had established a little magazine of their own which they called the *Outlander* and for which they did all the writing and editing. Frost responded with particular enthusiasm to the literary enterprise of these three attractive girls, whom he later nicknamed "The Three Graces."

One of the boys who called on the Frosts soon after they moved into their new home at 1223 Pontiac Road was a young poet, Wade Van Dore, whom they had first met in New Hampshire several years earlier. Van Dore was not a registered student: a rebel, he had never gone further than the ninth grade in his formal education. Writing poetry was his primary concern, and he had consciously taken Thoreau's *Walden* as his gospel because it preached freedom and protested that the mass of men lead lives of quiet desperation, enslaved by dispensabilities. A husky six-footer, Van Dore had intermittently lived by himself in the woods of northern Michigan and Canada during all seasons of the year. He worked occasionally, but only when he needed money for clothing or food or shelter. In 1922 he discovered the poetry of Robert Frost, wrote the author to say he admired it, and went on to explain his Thoreauvian idealism. Then he asked for advice about where he might live and work (a little) in New Hampshire while getting acquainted with the Robert Frost country. Touched by unusual elements in the letter, Frost had replied:

"First about Thoreau: I like him as well as you do. In one book (Walden) he surpasses everything we have had in America. You have found this out for yourself without my having told you; I have found it out for myself without your having told me. Isn't it beautiful that there can be such concert without collusion? That's the kind of 'getting together' I can endure.

"I'm going to send part of your letter to a farmer [Willis Herbert] in Franconia N. H. where I lived and owned a small property until last year. The farmer is a friend of mine and will listen sympathetically to what I shall say about you. I don't know just what your plan would be. Would it be to camp out for a while on his land and then find a few boards and nails to build a shack for the winter? . . . I hope I tell you what you want."[6]

After this beginning, other letters were exchanged, and Van Dore was camping in Franconia when Frost had arrived there for the hay-fever season in the summer of 1922. Together they walked the Franconia countryside while getting better acquainted, but they had not again seen each other until Van Dore showed up at 1223 Pontiac Road. The visit was so important to the young poet that he recorded it in his journal:

"At the white cottage Mrs. Frost came to the door . . . and led me into the sitting room. A fire was burning in the fireplace and I warmed my hands before it while the poet was summoned. When he came I thought he was even more impressive-looking than he was three years ago in New Hampshire. In the firelight we talked first of the happenings at Franconia. . . . Mrs. Frost, pale in complexion and very mild in manner sat at one end of the davenport making quiet observations about the Franconia people. . . . Finally Frost said: 'Elinor, if you don't mind I'd like to speak to Mr. Van Dore alone.' Then when she was gone he slumped far down in his chair and started talking about the long poem I'd sent him in February, and about poetry in general. . . . Going on, he talked about colleges. 'The problem of colleges is a constant agony to me. I sometimes feel that I'll never be able to stay here, finish what I've undertaken. Last night at a meeting of teachers I quarreled with all of them. With one I tried to hold myself because I became too cruel and relentless with my questions. . . .'

"At last he said he would like to read the poems I'd brought, and coming beside me on the davenport he read several of them first to himself, and then aloud to me. . . . By this time it was four o'clock—I had been there two hours. Someone knocked on the front door and with feeling he exclaimed, 'That's too bad, spoiling our mood like this!' But he let Mrs. Frost go and kept on reading. Coming to my little poem 'Far Lake,' he was so delighted with it he called Mrs. Frost (who was entertaining the caller in the front room) so that he could read it to her. He repeated it several times, and then listed its 'felicities' as he called them, saying they were 'enviable'—strongly accenting like a rebel in grammar the word on its second syllable instead of the first as I would have done. Of course I was delighted that he was so pleased with the poem. But now since somebody else was waiting for an interview I got up and started into the hall. He detained me a moment while looking for a book—'Slow Smoke' by Lew Sarett. 'A few of the poems in here may interest you,' he murmured, handing it to me as a gift. Then, taking me to and outside the front door, he said, 'You must come back so we can talk more about poetry—and the other things.' "[7]

All of these pleasant contacts with the young people on or near the campus at Ann Arbor were interrupted by reports of illness from the children back home. Carol's pulmonary ailments had flared up so seriously as to interfere with his farm work, and his parents talked with him over the telephone, urging him to take the precaution of getting into a higher and drier climate, at Frost's expense. They were certain that the Bartletts in Boulder, Colorado, would help him and his family find a place to stay. Frost notified Bartlett, but Carol refused to budge, and when Bartlett wrote for further advice, Frost replied:

"Don't you get too ready to have him [Carol] for Christmas company. He will be moved to act slowly if at all. He's a good boy and faithful to what he sets his hand to, which is the same as saying not unamiably obstinate. It will come hard for him to break off and start all over. He has something of my father in him that won't own up sick. It's from no ideal of gameness either. He's just naturally self-disregardful. He rather despises frail careful people. . . ."[8]

Another interruption marred the newly established serenity of the Frosts in their attractive hideaway on Pontiac Road. Not long after they moved in, the poet made a considerable journey to give a series of readings, the first being in New Hampshire. Mrs. Frost went with him as far as Vermont so that she could visit with her children. From New Hampshire, he started southward: first to Philadelphia, then to Baltimore, and then to Chapel Hill, North Carolina. Within ten days he was back in Ann Arbor, where Mrs. Frost was waiting for him. The trip had been so arduous, however, that he was once again suffering from an ailment which threatened to be influenza, and he spent the next few days in bed regretting his attempts to crowd too many diversions into a period which was supposed to be a withdrawal from all that might interfere with poetry-writing.

Even on Pontiac Road he could not withdraw from newspaper reporters who sought him out and prodded him with questions which were often annoying. Fortunately, one of them pleased him by leading into a discussion of a favorite topic. The reporter asked whether the scalpel of modern science might have probed so deeply into the mysteries of earth, air, and water that there was no longer room enough for poetic genius to find free play in the imaginative explorations of the unknown. To Frost, the word "science" could be simultaneously fascinating and repulsive. He was always deeply absorbed by details concerning any new scientific discovery. At the same time he could be offended by any cocksure scientific manner which chose to use human revelations for purposes of mocking poetic and religious concerns for true mysteries. On this occasion, he answered the reporter in ways which hinted at how and where Frost took his position on the old-new battle line between science and religion:

" 'Science offers just compensation,' says Dr. Frost. 'Think of the great abysses opened up by our study of the atom.[9] Think of the strange and unaccountable actions of the hurrying winds experienced by our travelers of the skies. Think of the marvels of marine life lately brought to us by the explorers of the distant oceans, each more wonderfully wrought than ever mermaid or water sprite of which the poet dreamed.

" 'Life has lost none of its mystery and its romance. The more we know of it, the less we know. Fear has always been a great stimulus to man's imagination. But fear is not the only stimulus. If science has expelled much of our fear, still there is left a thousand things from which to shape our dreams.

" 'Keats mourned that the rainbow, which had been for him as a boy a magic thing, had lost its glory because the physicists had found it resulted merely from the refraction of the sunlight by the raindrops. Yet knowledge of its causation could not spoil the rainbow for me. I am so sure that it is not given to man to be omniscient. There will always be something left to know, something left to excite the imagination of the poet and those attuned to the great world in which they live.

" 'Only in a certain type of small scientific mind can there be found cocksureness, a conviction that a solution to the riddle of the universe is just around the corner. There was, for example, Jacques Loeb, the French biologist, who felt he had within his grasp the secret of vitality. Give him but ten years and he would have it fast. He had the ten and ten more, and in ten more he was dead. Perhaps he knows more of the mystery of life now than ever he did before his passing. . . .' "[10]

One cause of his immediate brooding over the tugs and pushes between science and religion, during the fall of 1925, was his uneasiness over the presence of the science-oriented

President Little, in the place of the religion-oriented President Burton.[11] As he had hinted to Van Dore, he had spent only a few weeks of his permanent appointment in this new atmosphere at the University before he began to doubt if he could last until spring. In a sense, he did not even last through the fall term: family illness again interfered. Early in December of 1925, Van Dore returned for a second visit and found the poet alone in the house on Pontiac Road. Mrs. Frost had gone east to Pittsfield because of disturbing news that Marjorie was in a hospital there with pneumonia. Although she had passed the crisis before Mrs. Frost arrived, she made a slow recovery. According to the doctors, she was also suffering from a pericardiac infection, from chronic appendicitis, and from a nervous breakdown. Her condition became so critical that Frost himself went to her bedside before the middle of December.

Other members of the Frost family gathered in Pittsfield, and braced for a somewhat forlorn celebration of Christmas. Irma came up from New York City, Carol and Lillian drove down and over from South Shaftsbury with their one-year-old son, Prescott. Lesley drafted her father to help deal with customers at the bookstore during the final Christmas rush, and New Year's Eve found him writing somewhat despondently to John Bartlett:

"I am not sure of hanging on long at Ann Arbor though the position is supposed to be for life. It's too far from the children for the stretch of our heart strings. Carol probably wont be budged. And heres Lesley and Marjorie in the book business in Pittsfield. We've just come on to be with Marj for an operation for appendicitis. She's been having bronchial pneumonia. We dont like to be scattered all over the map as long as we dont have to be. Elinor stands being separated from the children worse than I do. What I want is a farm in New England once more."[12]

He also reported to Bartlett that his browsing in the family bookstore, with plenty of leisure, had caused him to do considerable reading:

"One advantage of being here is it gives me a chance at all the brand new books without money and without price. I've just read Lord Grays Twenty-five Years (corker), Charnwood's Gospel of St. John (worth a look into if you want to know the latest higher criticism) the Panchatantra (the most ancient book of anecdotes, source of most now going) and Max Eastman's Since Lenin Died (in hopes of getting the truth at last from our fiercest American Communist). Gee they're all good books. Any book I cant let alone is a good book. . . ."[13]

During the same evening, and yet in an entirely different mood, he wrote to Sidney Cox. He began by scolding the young professor for trying to build a teaching method on a foundation of contentiousness, and gradually brought the letter around to that subject on which he himself was always contentious: modern science, in its opposition to religion.

"You're a better teacher than I ever was or will be (now). But I'd like to put it to you while you are still young and developing your procedure if you dont think a lot of things could be found to do in class besides debate and disagree. Clash is all very well for coming lawyers politicians and theologians. But I should think there must be a whole realm or plane above that—all sight and insight, perception, intuition, rapture. Narrative is a fearfully safe place to spend your time. Having ideas that are neither pro nor con is the happy thing. Get up there high enough and the differences that make controversy become only the two legs of a body the weight of which is on one in one period, on the other in the next. Democracy monarchy; puritanism paganism; form content; conservatism radicalism; systole diastole; rustic urbane; literary colloquial; work play. I should think too much of myself to let any teacher fool me into taking sides on any of those oppositions. May be I'm wrong. But I was always wrong then. Its not just old age with me. I'm not like Maeldune weary of strife from having seen too much of it. (See Tenn[yson]) I have wanted to find ways to transcend the strife-method. I have found some. Mind you I'd fight a healthy amount. This is no pacifism. It is not so much anti-conflict as it is something beyond conflict—such as poetry and religion that is not just theological dialectic. I'll bet I could tell of spiritual realizations that for the moment at least would overawe the contentious. That's the sort of thing I mean. Every poem is one. I have to guard against insisting on this too much. Blades must be tempered under the hammer. We are a political nation run on a two-party system: which means that we must conflict whether we disagree or not. School must be some sort of preparation for the life before us. Some of our courses must be in rowing. Dont let me oversay my position.

"They say time itself is circular and the universe a self-

winding clock. Well well just when it reaches the back country that the universe is a mechanism and what reason have we
to suppose we are anything but mechanisms ourselves the
latest science says it is all off about the universe; it isn't a
mechanism at all, whatever we fools may be. It will take fifty
years for that to penetrate to the Clarence Darrowsians and
Daytonians.[14] The styles start in Paris and go in waves, ten
years from crest to crest, to the ends of the earth. Let us
put in some of our time merely sawing wood . . ."[15]

Letting himself unwind through writing such a letter as
this to Cox was one of Frost's favorite ways of keeping his
mind off whatever worried him most. This time Marjorie's
slow recovery from nervous exhaustion and pericarditis caused
a postponement of the scheduled operation for chronic appendicitis. Her father, perplexed to know which of his responsibilities should be given priority, lingered in Pittsfield until the
middle of January and then departed alone to give three readings before returning to Ann Arbor. Mrs. Frost remained in
Pittsfield with Marjorie and Lesley.[16]

The most important of these three engagements was at
Bryn Mawr. In his talk there, before reading, he began by teasing his audience in a typically provocative way. He said the
current excitement over "the new poetry" had caused him to
look carefully at a few poems called to his attention by Sir
Arthur Quiller-Couch. (At this moment, he deceptively held
aloft, for all to see, a small fat volume to which he had added
a flamboyant dust jacket acquired in Pittsfield and cut to fit
the book: his old copy of *The Oxford Book of English Verse*,
edited by Quiller-Couch.) He wanted to share his discovery by
reading one of these poems. The first one he read from the
small fat volume (without naming author or title or book)
brought gasps of delight from the girls. Would they like to hear
another, by the same author? Oh they would! Again he read,
this time a gracefully cadenced lyric, and again there were
murmured sounds of approval. Just one more, from the same
author? Yes, please. When he had finished the third poem,
which everyone admired, he asked if anyone could name the
author. No, but it was plain they were breathless to hear, and
he told them: Henry Wadsworth Longfellow. Groans. When
the noise had subsided, Frost teasingly asked the girls to decide
for themselves when they had been correct in their evalua-
tions. Had their tastes and insights been wrong when they had

liked the poems without knowing who wrote them? Or had their prejudices been right when they had reacted to an unpopular name?

From this teasing start he went on to discuss his announced topic: "Metaphors." Praising Longfellow's fresh uses of metaphors in the poems he had read, and also honoring Longfellow's quiet refusal to snap metaphors like whips, he borrowed from his Amherst course in "Judgments" some examples of poor metaphors used by philosophers. Then he offered some examples of metaphors employed by critics and interpreters, in their attempts to describe the motives of poets. Some critics liked to say that some poets, trying to "escape" from life, wrote their poems as forms of retreat, after they had been wounded by life. Other critics claimed that the realistic poet deserved most praise because he used poetry as a means of "grappling" with what bothered him in his private or public experiences.

Escape? Grappling? He moved on, by offering a definition of poetry, with the aid of a metaphor borrowed from his recent reading in science. Poetry is tropism, he said, in the sense that the biologists use the word. He reminded them that tropism may be defined as an orientation of an organism, usually by means of growth rather than movement, in response to external stimulus. Tropism, then, may be growth-toward-light, an aspiration toward light. Poetry, considered in this way, might be defined as aspiration.

Having established this ambiguous definition, he invoked a homely image—the housefly—to suggest two different ways of looking at the word "escape." If you wish to rid a room of houseflies, he said, all you must do is darken it and let a small crack of light appear at an open window. The flies will go to and through that crack of light, not because they want to "escape" from the room but rather because the attraction of the light is too much for them: they aspire toward it.

His listeners, fascinated, were slightly bewildered, and he was ready to make his point. Aspiration, he said, is belief, faith, confidence. There are of course many different kinds of belief. First there is one's belief in one's self and in one's abilities, before any performance has justified such belief. Then there is the belief in someone else, as expressed when one falls in love. Beyond that there is the belief in others and in a society organized along the ideal of democracy. Finally, there is the belief in God. Poetry may deal metaphorically with any one or all of these beliefs. A poem may be an unfolding of an emotion which is at first purely implicit. It may begin merely as a vague lump in the throat, and out of that tension the images of a poem may be used for purposes of passing from the implicit to the explicit. The poem itself might be the quiver of the transition from belief to realization.

Having thus guided his Bryn Mawr listeners up a little flight of stairs which amounted to his own subtle version of Plato's ladder in the *Symposium*, he began to read some illustrative poems of his own, starting from images he himself had endowed with metaphorical hints of aspiration, in "Birches."[17] By the time he finished, the girls were captivated, although some of them were not exactly sure they understood the points he had tried to make.

At this stage in his career as a performing bard, Frost increasingly enjoyed teasing and tantalizing his audiences by making bold statements which meant much to him, and also by aiming his remarks just high enough over the heads of his listeners to make them stretch for his meanings. He had previously talked on Longfellow, in May of 1925, at an "Institute of Literature" held on the campus of Longfellow's alma mater, Bowdoin, and there he had used as topic his favorite subject, "Vocal Imagination." To illustrate it, he read to his audience a passage he particularly liked: "The Flight into Egypt" from Longfellow's *Golden Legend*. In the discussion, afterward, one of the Bowdoin professors had infuriated him by saying he wondered where Frost ever found that "slight thing" which Longfellow could have written when he was an undergraduate at Bowdoin. Irritated into sarcasms, Frost had replied, "You think it is slight, do you? That's a very fine poem and I'll tell you how I know. I found it in an anthology compiled by an Englishman."[18]

The schedule of readings led Frost from Bryn Mawr to Union College in Schenectady, New York, and then back to Amherst for a two-week stay. He had promised President Olds that he would not desert Amherst: he would return for two-week stays, occasionally, and would place himself at the disposal of professors who wanted him to talk in their classrooms —or even at the mercy of students who just wanted to talk. During this two-week stay, he gave one public reading in Johnson Chapel. He also renewed his acquaintance with Professor G. R. Elliott, whom Frost had pried away from Bowdoin by helping him obtain a position in the Department of English at Amherst. To Elliott, Frost confided that the permanent fellowship at Michigan was not working out as well as had been expected: he seemed to be too much of a Yankee to enjoy the prospect of living permanently in the Midwest, and he might resign from the University at the end of the year and offer his service at various colleges for a week or two, using his Vermont farm as home base.

By the time he returned to Ann Arbor, late in January of 1925, the second semester was about to begin. According to the agreement he had made with the late President Burton, Frost was to have only one formal obligation at the University of Michigan each year. He was to offer a second-semester course, intended chiefly for those students who would be writing even if they were not in the course. Having limited the enrollment to twelve students, and having arranged to have the applicants screened by a member of the English Department, he was not surprised to discover that the twelve included his favorites from the editorial boards of the undergraduate literary magazines, including Sue Bonner, Mary Cooley, and Dorothy Tyler. At first, he met the class in one of the seminar rooms in the library, and was tolerant of the uninvited. After three sessions he said there was no need to meet as a group any more, each of them should write something new and when ready to show it should telephone to make an appointment for a conference at his home. Those who accepted the arrangement were the serious ones; the others were merely eliminated by this Gideon's test.[19]

One advantage thus gained by Frost was that he could protect the hours he liked best for writing. As long as Mrs. Frost remained in Pittsfield with the slowly recovering Marjorie, he found that any hour of day or night (except the morning) was good for his own writing. Wade Van Dore soon learned of this aberration. Calling unexpectedly, at two o'clock in the afternoon, he was surprised to have Frost say he had just got out of bed: he had stayed up all night, "obeying a whim." An uninformed Boston reporter had asked him whether the "flat country" around Ann Arbor, presumed to be so different from New England, might have a bad effect on his writing poetry. His polite answer had been, "I never write about a place in New England, if I am there. I always write about it when I am away. In Michigan I shall be composing poetry about New Hampshire and Vermont with longing and homesickness better than I would if I were there, just as [I did when I was] in England."[20]

One night he sat alone before the fireplace in the house on Pontiac Road, feeding branch after branch of black walnut to the flames and enjoying the fragrance. The signs of spring in Ann Arbor reminded him of what must be happening back in Vermont and New Hampshire—reminded him in particular of images that asked to be caught in a poem. Truly homesick, he reached for pen and paper, and wrote:

SPRING POOLS

These pools that, though in forests, still reflect
The total sky almost without defect,
And like the flowers beside them, chill and shiver,
Will like the flowers beside them soon be gone,
And yet not out by any brook or river,
But up by roots to bring dark foliage on.

The trees that have it in their pent-up buds
To darken nature and be summer woods—
Let them think twice before they use their powers
To blot out and drink up and sweep away
These flowery waters and these watery flowers
From snow that melted only yesterday.[21]

Much of his loneliness and homesickness disappeared when Mrs. Frost returned to Ann Arbor from Pittsfield, bringing with her not only the slowly recovering Marjorie but also the strong-willed Irma, who had grown tired of studying art in New York. The presence of the girls in the household on Pontiac Road required a certain amount of social acivity for entertainment. One family of visitors, distantly related to Dorothy Canfield Fisher, brought with them an attractive young man, John Paine Cone, who had grown up on a wheat farm in Kansas, and who planned to return there. To the surprise of everyone, John Cone and Irma Frost so quickly fell in love that they were engaged to be married before Irma went back to Vermont and John returned to Kansas.

As the end of the term approached, another visitor brought another surprise. President Olds of Amherst had been informed by Elliott that there might be a possibility of persuading Frost to give up his attractive position at Michigan and go back to

Amherst, on a part-time basis. Olds appeared in Ann Arbor, found Frost amenable to such a prosposal, and completed the arrangements.[22] Frost was so relieved that the tone of his letter of thanks to Elliott gradually ascended to the almost-lyrical:

"The five thousand is a lot for ten weeks. I'm satisfied with the amount. What I am after is detachment and long times alone rather than money. Nobody knows how much less money I have taken in late years than I could have. Enough is enough. So say I and all my family fortunately agrees with me. For at least one or two of them less is enough than for me. There's where my real success lies, if I may be accused of having any, in being so uncursed in my family.

"Think of the untold acres I can spade up in the forty weeks of every year I am going to have free for farming. Suppose I live like Landor till ninety. That will give me one thousand six hundred weeks all to myself to put in at any thing I like. I hadnt thought of it before but by that calculation I have more freedom ahead of me than I have behind (and I have a good deal behind). . . . I came west on an impulse; I go back east on an impulse; and nobody says a word. I am simply indulged in everything regardless of my deserts. Where is there a case parallel? And over and above everything I have had the fun of writing a few poems."[23]

After the first excitement had worn off, Frost began to suffer his usual twinges of conscience over neglected promises: "I haven't put the least bit of interest into my duties here," he wrote. "I've practically done nothing for anyone and I feel like an ingrate."[24] To comfort himself, in such a situation, he could always find fault with others for having spoiled the original plan. President Little served as a convenient target for such reproaches, and with him were bunched all the scientists on the campus at Ann Arbor who did not appreciate either religion or the humanities. Frost attacked them scornfully in a letter to Cox:

"Nobody knows it here but the President: I'm not coming back next year. Going to have another aberration back to the land. You should have heard me standing off a club of scientists the other night on the subject of evolution. I'm not a good debater but they are so sure of themselves in evolution that they haven't taken the trouble to think out their position. All I had to do was ask them [Socratic] questions for information. The last one led up to was, Did they think it was ever going to be any easier to be good. I wouldnt call it an evolution unless there was hope of screwing virtue to the sticking point so it would cost less effort and vigilance than now to maintain. Amelioration was as much as they could make me see. The funny thing was their surprise at my unscientificalness. They made more awful breaks. Sometime I'll tell you about them. I believe I'll never forget them. They just jumped off the edge. Me, I didn't have to expose myself. I was just out for information. Tell me, I'd say."[25]

Still trying to justify himself in his arrangements for leaving his permanent appointment at the University of Michigan, and at the same time eager to let his friends know of the big decision he had reached, Frost found other ways of describing what had happened. The best summary of the year was sent to John Bartlett:

"We're going east again said the pendulum. This was no go this year, or rather it was too much go and what wasn't go was come. Marjorie's long illness (means more than sickness) kept Elinor with her in Pittsfield Mass and me commuting for months. Every week or so I would run the water out of the pipes and leave the house here to freeze. It wasnt exactly in the contract that I should be away all the time and I wasn't quite all. I'm not going to try to keep it up here with the children back there and such things likely to happen again. And anyway I want a farm. It's all arranged so you needn't exclaim a protest about such whiffling. Amherst, Dartmouth, Bowdoin and Connecticut Wesleyan are going to give me a living next year for a couple of weeks in each of them. The rest of the time I shall be clear away from the academic, feeding pigeons hens dogs or anything you advise for the pleasure or profit in it. The only thing that worries me is that Bennington College coming in on our pastoral serenity. I ran away from two colleges in succession once and they took revenge by flattering me back to teach in college. Now I am running away again and it looks as if they would come after me. I'll probably end with one of the ponderous things in bed with me on my chest like an incubus. . . ."[26]

SPEAKING OF CONTRARIES

"Speaking of contraries, see how the brook
In that white wave runs counter to itself. . . .
It is this backward motion toward the source,
Against the stream, that most we see ourselves in,
The tribute of the current to the source.
It is from this in nature we are from.
It is most us."[1]

CAROL FROST and his wife Lillian had set out a hundred dwarf Astrachan trees and sixty cultivated high-bush blueberry plants on their farm in South Shaftsbury before Robert Frost returned there in June of 1926. These young people had thrown their efforts into such a variety of experiments, and with such eagerness, that it was difficult to keep track of their plans. The summer before, they had added flower-raising to their farm-work, had put up a sign on a stand in front of the house, and sold to passing motorists enough sweet-pea blossoms to bring in approximately a hundred dollars. The newly established Bennington College, only four miles from the Frost farm, had led Carol to wonder whether it would be profitable to build a greenhouse so that he might sell flowers the year round. His father, boasting of Carol's earnestness, wrote: "He's such a worker as I was never suspected of being though I may have been."[2] Of course the poet never had been such a worker, but so long as he could be as lazy as he liked, offering assistance when in the mood for playing farmer, he took extraordinary pleasure in watching the farm prosper.

One drawback to this pleasure was that the family was getting too big for the Stone Cottage. Frost's grandson Prescott was just reaching the age when he could walk and talk well enough to charm and exhaust those who tried to protect him from his own garrulous boldness. Marjorie, slowly recovering

"New England's New Poet"
at Eaton's Studio in Littleton, N. H., 1915

The poet using his homemade writing-board
in his parlor, Franconia, N. H., 1915

The Frost family in Bridgewater, N. H., 1915
Lesley   Irma
Marjorie   Carol

The strolling bard in Troy, N. Y., 1921

The Stone Cottage in South Shaftsbury, Vt., 1921

The farmer-poet at the Stone Cottage, 1921

Fellow in Letters at Michigan in 1925

American visitor, Imperial Hotel, London, 1928

The Gully farmhouse in South Shaftsbury, Vt.,
after renovations were made in 1929

At the Bread Loaf School of English in 1935

15 Sunset Avenue
the Frost home in Amherst, 1931–1938

from her ailments, continued to require the worried attentions of her parents. Irma was buzzing with plans for her wedding to John Paine Cone. Then Lillian became unexpectedly ill and was hospitalized in Bennington, where she underwent major surgery early in July of 1926. The pressures thus placed on Frost as head of the family were enough to make him talk about getting away, and Mrs. Frost, writing to Mrs. Fobes, explained the plans for an unusually early departure for Franconia:

"Robert and I have decided to go up to the mountains next Monday the 9th [of August]. . . . Irma and Marjorie are going to stay here two weeks longer. Irma can do the house work and they can be company for Lillian during her convalescence. She is getting along splendidly. Robert has become very nervous, and it is necessary for us to be by ourselves, without the children, for a little while, so that he may recover his equanimity. . . . I think it would be pleasant to use the corner room downstairs for a bedroom. I am not sure. It depends on how nervous Robert is."[3]

The escape to Franconia, from the annoyances in the Stone Cottage, afforded so much relief that Frost soon found himself in the mood for writing new poems and revising old ones. The longest of his unfinished poems had been started in the spring of 1920 and had been inspired in part by Edward Ames Richards, the Amherst student who had subsequently gone part way with the Frosts on the Long Trail hike in the summer of 1922. Richards had published in the Amherst *Monthly* for March 1920 a poem entitled " 'Joe Wright's Brook,' " a meditative lyric in which two lovers talk briefly about the brook's name. In discussing the poem with Richards at the time of its publication, Frost had said that if he were to build either a lyric or a dramatic dialogue around the name of a brook he would make something quite different out of it. Richards, misunderstanding the remark, had given Frost permission to rework the poem.[4]

The only help needed or gained from Richards was a particular memory-jog. Back in his Derry days, Frost had often admired a stream which flowed westward, as though it were deliberately ignoring its eventual destination to the east: the Atlantic Ocean. On all the Derry maps, old and new, that stream was officially designated as West-Running Brook. Never before had Frost considered building metaphors around the contrary direction of that stream, but Richards had shown him possibilities, and a good start had been made. Returning now to this unfinished poem entitled "West-Running Brook," he brought to it a new stimulus afforded by the scientists with whom he had quarreled at the University of Michigan. He had boasted of his own Socratic contrariety in merely asking those men questions about the Darwinian theory,[5] but he had previously confided to Untermeyer something else concerning his artistic pleasure in reacting against more than evolutionary formulas:

"I . . . [am very] fond of seeing our theories knocked into cocked hats. What I like about [Henri] Bergson and [J. Henri] Fabre is that they have bothered our evolutionism so much with the cases of instinct they have brought up. You get more credit for thinking if you restate formulae or cite cases that fall in easily under formulae, but all the fun is outside[:] saying things that suggest formulae that won't formulate—that almost but don't quite formulate. I should like to be so subtle at this game as to seem to the casual person altogether obvious. The casual person would assume that I meant nothing or else I came near enough meaning something he was familiar with to mean it for all practical purposes. Well well well."[6]

What Frost liked, in addition, about Bergson and Fabre was that each of them had acquainted himself with the results of modern science and then had found his own ways to attack some of the most cherished scientific hypotheses. Fabre's distrust of evolution as a scientific theory had attracted new attention in America following the publication of one of his works translated under the title, *The Hunting Wasps*; Bergson's distrust of scientific reasoning, and of the scientific concept of time, had been admired by Frost since his first reading of *Creative Evolution*, soon after its American publication in 1911. One image in Frost's gradually developing poem, "West-Running Brook," owed far more to Bergson than to Richards. In *Creative Evolution*, Bergson had extended the Lucretian view of life as a river: the stream of everything that runs away to spend itself in death and nothingness except as it is resisted by the spirit of human beings. Bergson had added another analogy built around a wave-image:

"Life as a whole, from the initial impulsion that thrust it into the world, will appear as a wave which rises, and which is opposed by the descending movement of matter. . . . Our own consciousness is . . . continually drawn the opposite way, obliged, though it goes forward, to look behind. This retrospective vision . . . must detach itself from the *already-made* and attach itself to the *being-made.* . . . turning back on itself and twisting on itself. . ."[7]

To Frost, one of the most important elements in Bergson's highly poetic philosophy was the denial of essentially deterministic elements in the Darwinian theories. In his gently contrary manner, Bergson insisted that the human spirit has the freely willed power to resist materialism through creative acts which pay tribute to God. Frost, in bringing his poem to completion, made it a study in Bergsonian contraries.

"West-Running Brook" begins as a dramatic narrative in which a New England farmer and his wife notice similarities between themselves and the brook: "It must be the brook/Can trust itself to go by contraries/The way I can with you—and you with me . . ." Then they notice another contrariety:

> *The black stream, catching on a sunken rock,*
> *Flung backward on itself in one white wave,*
> *And the white water rode the black forever . . .*

Immediately, the noticing man and wife express pleasantly contrary views concerning whether the wave should be endowed with masculine or feminine symbolism, but the wife encourages the husband to say how he interprets it, and he does:

> *"Speaking of contraries, see how the brook*
> *In that white wave runs counter to itself.*
> *It is from that in water we were from*
> *Long, long before we were from any creature."*

Although the husband seems to be accepting the familiar evolutionary theory that man has ascended from lower creatures, he quickly carries his observations behind this theory or formula as he continues:

> *"Here we, in our impatience of the steps,*
> *Get back to the beginning of beginnings,*
> *The stream of everything that runs away."*

At this point, the husband seems to be expressing a purely materialistic view of biological devolution and of eventual annihilation. But the continuing motion of the poem is contrary to such a view, even as it is contrary to the Havelock Ellis view of life as dance.[8] The husband goes on:

> *"Some say existence like a Pirouot*
> *And Pirouette, forever in one place,*
> *Stands still and dances, but it runs away;*
> *It seriously, sadly, runs away*
> *To fill the abyss's void with emptiness."*

If the husband had stopped here, he would have expressed a decidedly pessimistic and evenly nihilistic view of extistence; but as he is allowed to continue he extends the meaning of the word "existence":

> *"It [existence] flows beside us in this water brook,*
> *But it flows over us. It flows between us*
> *To separate us for a panic moment.*
> *It flows between us, over us, and with us.*
> *And it is time, strength, tone, light, life, and love—*
> *And even substance lapsing unsubstantial;*
> *The universal cataract of death*
> *That spends to nothingness . . ."*

Again, if the speaker had stopped here, his view would still be nihilistic; but this time he continues by more clearly invoking the crucial Bergsonian notion of the *élan vital*:

> *". . . and unresisted,*
> *Save by some strange resistance in itself,*
> *Not just a swerving,[9] but a throwing back,*
> *As if regret were in it and were sacred."*

This particular "As if" makes the line a precise understatement: within the givens of this Bergsonian poem, the act of resistance is primarily motivated by sorrow or remorse over that which is happening, as all substance seems to be lapsing unsubstantial in the universal cataract of death. At the same time, the act of resistance is represented as being sacred in the sense that it is an assertion of belonging and dedication and consecration to the Source of the *élan vital*.

In his next statement, the husband seems to be manipulating, metaphorically, such Heraclitean-Lucretian-Pauline[10] contraries as that the death of the earth gives life to fire, the death of fire gives life to air, the death of air gives life to water, and the death of water gives life to earth—thus figuratively suggesting the endless cycle of birth, death, rebirth, and continuity, in nature and in human nature:

> "It [life, or existence] *has this throwing backward*
> *on itself*
> *So that the fall of most of it is always*
> *Raising a little, sending up a little.*
> *Our life runs down in sending up the clock.*
> *The brook runs down in sending up our life.*
> *The sun runs down in sending up the brook.*
> *And there is something sending up the sun."*

At this point, the motion of these metaphors is one of circling back to the beginning of beginnings, in the cautiously ambiguous statement, "And there is something sending up the sun." Such a statement might or might not be made to fit the Darwinian formula of evolution, but the husband's concluding lines endow the statement (and the entire poem) with religious overtones which are contrary to a purely scientific interpretation of evolutionary theories:

> "It *is this backward motion toward the source,*
> *Against the stream, that most we see ourselves in,*
> *The tribute of the current to the source.*
> *It is from this in nature we are from.*
> *It is most us."*[11]

Robert Frost knew that the metaphors he had borrowed and adapted to his own uses, in "West-Running Brook," had provided him with the most incisive and expansive poetic expression he had yet given his deepest religious belief concerning death, and the possibilities of eternal salvation after death. Nevertheless, he knew he had conveyed these beliefs with enough artistic indirection to let him escape from any self-conscious embarrassment. Perhaps it was his filing and sharpening of the lines in this poem, at Franconia in 1926, which so intensified his pleasure in the metaphors that he could not resist making other uses of them, elsewhere. Writing to a friend, before "West-Running Brook" was published, and mentioning his grief over the news that family affairs had become disastrous for his friends the Untermeyers, he further revealed his belief in his prophetic powers as poet—and his preoccupation with Bergsonian metaphors:

". . . still I can't say that I didn't always know it was coming. My prophetic soul told me I was in for it forty five years ago come yesterday on the cliff house beach at San Francisco. Is it not written in a poem of mine . . . ['Once by the Pacific']? I take nothing back. I don't even grow. My favorite theory is that we are given this speed swifter than any stream of light time or water for the sole purpose of standing still like a water beetle in any stream of light time or water off any shore we please."[12]

The same Bergsonian images of contrary resistance provided him with the central metaphor in a poem he wrote as a present for the bride and groom, Irma Frost and John Cone, on the occasion of their marriage in Franconia during the summer of 1926:

THE MASTER SPEED

No speed of wind or water rushing by
But you have speed far greater. You can climb
Back up a stream of radiance to the sky,
And back through history up the stream of time.
And you were given this swiftness, not for haste
Nor chiefly that you may go where you will,
But in the rush of everything to waste,
That you may have the power of standing still—
Off any still or moving thing you say.
Two such as you with such a master speed
Cannot be parted nor be swept away
From one another once you are agreed
That life is only life forevermore
Together wing to wing and oar to oar.[13]

The wedding, which occurred in the Fobes guest-cottage on the fifteenth of October 1926, was attended only by members of the family. Frost admired his new son-in-law, who showed so many interests and abilities that nobody expected him to remain long on the Kansas prairie wheat-farm where he had grown up. His plan was to return there with his bride and to stay for a year or two until he could fulfill his immediate responsibilities to his aging parents. As soon as the newlyweds started on their honeymoon, en route to Kansas, leaving only Marjorie and her parents in the Fobes cottage, the serenity of the place encouraged Frost to work further on the cluster of manuscripts which he was shaping toward a new book of poems.

Too soon, for the poet, he was forced to put aside his manuscripts and begin his next series of performances. His first commitment—a two-week stay at Wesleyan University in Middletown, Connecticut, early in December of 1926—was made particularly congenial by his host and hostess there, Professor and Mrs. Wilbert Snow. A poet of the Maine coast, Snow had served as a reindeer agent in Alaska and had taught in seven American colleges before he had been brought to Wesleyan. Frost so greatly liked the man and his poetry that he took Snow to New York City to attend a dinner given in honor of the seventy-year-old Baltimore poet Lizette Woodworth Reese, on the evening of 15 December 1926. There were special reasons why he wanted to be present at this dinner, not the least being his admiration for certain of Miss Reese's stubbornly puritanical qualities. He had described some of them to his daughter Lesley, two years earlier:

"I saw Lizette Reese in Baltimore. She had just been refusing to meet Edna Millais [Millay] at the Kinsolvings. She says she is about done with such Churchly toleration for prostitution and hard drinking as some people nowadays go in for. She says we have to be good. She dared to say that right in Knopf's office [in New York City] the other day before Heywood Broun and a lot of joyous hellbirds and what do you suppose they did? They burst right out laughing at her. She said she thought they were making fun of her. She gave them her opinion of Jurgening[14] since they would have it. She'll be seventy in two years. She's not afraid of them. She's not the only Puritan by all I hear tell. Johnny Farrar has been getting right up and walking right out of the theatre in protest against something said or done in the play, MacVeagh tells me. He has been roasted at the stake or column for it by all his friends. Of course you have to forgive some of them: they never heard of the cult of evil before. It is all so new to them. But you can't help being glad that some are sticking to the plain unmystical literal decencies. It leaves you free to tend to your farming. Dick Potter may go to jail for liberally attacking girls out hiking and telling them his name was Beagle. But the thought of Lizette way down below the Mason and Dixon line should reassure us. Something still stands fast."[15]

After paying his tribute to Miss Reese at her seventieth-birthday dinner, Frost went from there to the Stone Cottage in South Shaftsbury, nearly exhausted. The entire family, except for himself and Carol, succumbed to a siege of grippe, leaving Carol and his father to wait on the bedridden Lillian, Prescott, Marjorie, and Mrs. Frost. As Christmas approached, Frost wrote to John Bartlett, "Elinor has been about to send the enclosed to the [Bartlett] children every day for the last two weeks. The general family sickness has prevented her. Never mind what it all is. My sickness is with sickness. We'll all survive . . ."[16] Early in January of 1927, when he was scheduled to begin his promised ten-week stint at Amherst, he was able to take Mrs. Frost with him, but Marjorie had to be left behind. They had rented the Tyler house at 34 Amity Street, and as soon as Marjorie could make the journey she joined them. Her parents continued to worry over her ailments which continued to be as much psychological as physical. Mrs. Frost explained as best she could to Mrs. Fobes:

"I think Marjorie wrote you that she and I as well as Lillian and Prescott were quite sick with grippe just before Christmas. I couldn't myself seem to get over it for more than a month. I coughed and felt very weak and miserable, and as for Marjorie she has had one chill after another since then. She is now in the care of the doctor, who had charge of her for several years as a little girl, you know, and he is quite sure it is a case of nervous prostration, and that she probably had it before she had pneumonia last year. He says we must go very easy with her but that it is only a question of time and rest. She is so unhappy now, however, that she cannot rest. She seems to have reached the end of her endurance, and goes for days hardly speaking and she doesn't want to eat. I believe myself that there must be some obscure trouble in her intestines. She really ought to have been in some warmer climate for the winter.

"We have a large, comfortable house, with an oil heater. She has a very large sunny bedroom, and is as well fixed as anyone could be in this climate.

"I have a middle-aged colored woman helping me with the house work—a very good cook, and it has been a wonderful help.

"Robert has been very well all the winter, and his obligations here are really not tiring him at all. After we finish here, he goes to Ann Arbor for a ten days lecture-and-conference engagement, and then to Dartmouth, and then to Bowdoin, for the same kind of engagement. . . ."[17]

Marjorie's perplexing condition failed to improve, and Frost reluctantly took leave of his daughter and wife when he made his uneventful spring tour to Michigan,[18] to Maine, and to New Hampshire. Early in May of 1927, as the three of them returned to the Stone Cottage in South Shaftsbury, from Amherst, the parents tried to cheer Marjorie by discussing the possibility of a voyage to England and France that summer, but she remained so weak that the plans had to be abandoned. One innovation, made in the hope of providing more serenity for all three, was a retreat from the Stone Cottage to nearby summer quarters—a place which came to be known as the Shingled Cottage—on a back road in North Bennington, only a short distance from the summer-deserted campus of the new Bennington College. Another reason for this move was awareness that Carol and Lillian, given clear title to the farm at South Shaftsbury, as a wedding present, had been forced to share it with so many other members of the Frost family that the cumulative frictions had become unpleasant.

Carol's father, easily upset by distractions which kept him from writing poetry, longed for the isolation he needed if he were to recover his mood for playing with metaphors. His acts of spending so much time running errands for his family—including errands to the nearest grocery store for whatever items might be in immediate demand—did furnish him with one metaphor which he treated humorously to dramatize his ideal of making the best of any predicament, no matter how annoyingly trivial:

THE ARMFUL

For every parcel I stoop down to seize
I lose some other off my arms and knees,
And the whole pile is slipping, bottles, buns—
Extremes too hard to comprehend at once,

[307]

Yet nothing I should care to leave behind.
With all I have to hold with, hand and mind
And heart, if need be, I will do my best
To keep their building balanced at my breast.
I crouch down to prevent them as they fall;
Then sit down in the middle of them all.
I had to drop the armful in the road
And try to stack them in a better load.[19]

During the summer and fall of 1927, he wrote enough new poems to make him think about the shape he might give his next book. The structural problem, this time, was not unlike the one he had faced when he had tried to assemble a scattering of lyrics for his first book, *A Boy's Will*. There he had established a progression through moods of escape, retreat, doubt, denial, negation, to moods of pursuit, love, hope, and affirmation. This time, he chose to divide his latest assemblage of poems into six carefully arranged structural parts, each illuminating different ways of looking at "contraries." Centrally, as Part Three, he placed by itself the unifying study-in-contraries, "West-Running Brook"—the title-poem for the projected volume. Part One, containing eleven lyrics, was made to foreshadow the cumulative emphasis on contraries by carrying on its section-page this juxtaposition:

I

SPRING POOLS

From snow that melted only yesterday

At the close of Part One, he placed a sonnet built around contrary responses to darkness, a sonnet which gave metaphorical expression to the poet's firmly Stoical-puritan belief in the Christian doctrine of submission:

ACCEPTANCE

When the spent sun throws up its rays on cloud
And goes down burning into the gulf below,
No voice in nature is heard to cry aloud
At what has happened. Birds, at least, must know
It is the change to darkness in the sky.

Murmuring something quiet in her breast,
One bird begins to close a faded eye;
Or overtaken too far from his nest,
Hurrying low above the grove, some waif
Swoops just in time to his remembered tree.
At most he thinks or twitters softly, "Safe!
Now let the night be dark for all of me.
Let the night be too dark for me to see
Into the future. Let what will be, be."

He made Part Two continue this theme of responses to light and dark by using as the section-title for it a pair of words which might at first glance seem directly contrary to God's "Let there be light"; then as balance, he borrowed from the preceding poem a motto which set up another contrariety on its section-page, thus:

II

FIAT NOX

Let the night be too dark for me to see
Into the future. Let what will be, be.

He placed first, in Part Two, the darkly imaged poem entitled "Once by the Pacific," and followed it with nine other poems in which the moods were predominantly dark. Here again, however, he chose as concluding poem a meditative lyric calculated to convey further hints of metaphysical submission and acceptance:

ACQUAINTED WITH THE NIGHT

I have been one acquainted with the night.
I have walked out in rain—and back in rain.
I have outwalked the furthest city light.

I have looked down the saddest city lane.
I have passed by the watchman on his beat
And dropped my eyes, unwilling to explain.

I have stood still and stopped the sound of feet
When far away an interrupted cry
Came over houses from another street,

[309]

But not to call me back or say good-by;
And further still at an unearthly height
One luminary clock against the sky

Proclaimed the time was neither wrong nor right.
I have been one acquainted with the night.[20]

Here was one of his recurrent themes: ideally, he had been forced to confront some of the worst forms of darkness, and he liked to think he had coped with them in ways which enabled him to avoid the extremes of self-deceptive pessimism or optimism. In that sense, the "luminary clock against the sky/Proclaimed the time was neither wrong nor right." Immediately following this poem he placed his title-poem, "West-Running Brook," letting it stand alone as Part Three. In Part Four, entitled "Sand Dunes," he permitted six lyrics to extend the affirmations implicit throughout the title-poem. The first two quatrains of "Sand Dunes," for example, set up images which represent all the destructive powers of ocean—as reflected in sea waves and sea-made sand dunes. But the last two stanzas establish a contrary attitude, again as a form of affirmation:

She [the ocean] *may know cove and cape,*
But she does not know mankind
If by any change of shape
She hopes to cut off mind.

Men left her a ship to sink:
They can leave her a hut as well;
And be but more free to think
For the one more cast-off shell.[21]

Into Part Five, bearing the section-title "Over Back," he placed four brief rural poems which were the least useful to his design. Part Six was made up of seven much stronger poems, each manipulating contraries by further balancing attitudes of negation against attitudes of affirmation. The section-title and motto, here, were calculated to set the pace for this concluding parade of tantalizations:

[310]

VI

MY NATIVE SIMILE

"*The sevenfold sophie of Minerve.*"

Although he borrowed this motto, somewhat perversely, from an obscure sixteenth-century poet,[22] he enabled his readers to find the source of the section's title merely by turning the page and reading the playfully serious first poem in Part Six:

THE DOOR IN THE DARK

In going from room to room in the dark
I reached out blindly to save my face,
But neglected, however lightly, to lace
My fingers and close my arms in an arc.
A slim door got in past my guard,
And hit me a blow in the head so hard
I had my native simile jarred.
So people and things don't pair anymore
With what they used to pair with before.

Thus placed, as the first poem in the final structural unit of *West-Running Brook*, "The Door in the Dark" provided more than the source for the title of Part Six. It hinted that the poet had begun to approach the sevenfold wisdom of Minerva only after he had suffered through a jarring and a disillusioning experience; that this experience, no matter how painful, had given freshness and originality to all the subsequent poetic comparisons he made, all the implied or stated analogies between seemingly dissimilar things.[23] In concluding his arrangement of this manuscript, he chose to place in last position a poem satirically aimed at one of his favorite targets: man's arrogant quest for scientific knowledge.

This final poem, entitled "The Bear," had been inspired in part by events in the Franconia region. Long before writing it, he mentioned the immediate source of the central imagery. "We are enjoying a descent of bears upon this region," he had written from Franconia in August of 1925. "If we survive it there should be much to tell. . . . Six of the Fobes sheep have been eaten. A mother and two cubs went up the road by our house the other evening tearing down the small cherry trees along the wall. You could see where one of the cubs had wiped his bottom on a large stone and left traces of a diet of choke cherries and blueberries. I almost got one cornered in our pasture last night, but he lifted the wire and went under the fence."[24] If the Franconia bears provided one element of inspiration for the poetical satire he chose to use as a set piece for the conclusion of his new volume, Alexander Pope's "Essay on Man"[25] provided other elements—including the appropriateness of using mock-heroic couplets:

THE BEAR

The bear puts both arms around the tree above her
And draws it down as if it were a lover
And its chokecherries lips to kiss good-by,
Then lets it snap back upright in the sky.
Her next step rocks a boulder on the wall
(She's making her cross-country in the fall).
Her great weight creaks the barbed wire in its staples
As she flings over and off down through the maples,
Leaving on one wire tooth a lock of hair.
Such is the uncaged progress of the bear.

Having thus established the basic image for his analogizings, Frost moved into the satirical application:

The world has room to make a bear feel free;
The universe seems cramped to you and me.
Man acts more like the poor bear in a cage,
That all day fights a nervous inward rage,
His mood rejecting all his mind suggests.
He paces back and forth and never rests
The toenail click and shuffle of his feet,
The telescope at one end of his beat,
And at the other end the microscope,
Two instruments of nearly equal hope,
And in conjunction giving quite a spread.
Or if he rests from scientific tread,
'Tis only to sit back and sway his head
Through ninety-odd degrees of arc, it seems,
Between two metaphysical extremes.

He sits back on his fundamental butt
With lifted snout and eyes (if any) shut
(He almost looks religious but he's not),
And back and forth he sways from cheek to cheek,
At one extreme agreeing with one Greek,
At the other agreeing with another Greek,
Which may be thought, but only so to speak.
A baggy figure, equally pathetic
When sedentary and when peripatetic.[26]

The total manuscript of *West-Running Brook*, finally including thirty-nine poems, was as different from *New Hampshire* as that volume had been from *Mountain Interval* or
North of Boston or *A Boy's Will*. The range and variety of
forms was heightened by the freshness of metaphors in the
rhymed lyrics, by the metaphysical reach of the blank-verse
title poem, and by the mingled play and seriousness of the
couplets in "The Bear." Quite boldly, Frost had also combined
new and old by sprinkling throughout the manuscript a few
poems written so early that he could have included them in
A Boy's Will.[27]
He may not have realized that his new manuscript contained far more hints of his deep religious faith than any of
his other books had done. Although he remained self-consciously shy, and sometimes deceptively coy, in making direct
statements concerning his metaphysical beliefs, he could not
resist this artistic game of hinting at the importance to him
of his puritan heritage, which he sometimes mocked and sometimes defended. Priding himself on being a nonconformist
among nonconformists, he was still in the process of shaping
and fashioning his own homemade religious doctrine. In an
eclectic fashion, he had been making his private adaptations
from the writings of Henri Bergson and William James for
many years; yet never before had he tried to write a poem so
spiritually all-inclusive and self-revealing as "West-Running
Brook."[28] He knew that if some readers found this poem
slightly vague or even unorthodox, the same readers would
not be likely to see anything unorthodox in supporting poems
such as "Acceptance" and "Acquainted with the Night." Nor
would any of his older, Victorian readers object to the almost
consistent manner in which he continued his warfare against
science—particularly against Darwinian evolutionary theories.

From the beginning of his poetic career he had grown increasingly aware that one artistic gain made available to him from his religious belief was that it enriched and extended the ulterior meanings of his best metaphors, that it permitted him to talk about at least two worlds simultaneously. He had done more than hint of this awareness when he had echoed Emerson by telling his latest Bryn Mawr audience that poetry might be defined as aspiration; that aspiration implies belief, faith, confidence; that poetry makes its best progressions when it deals metaphorically with belief in self, others, love, and God.[29] "I almost think any poem is most valuable for its ulterior meaning," he had puckishly said, and then had added a mocking salute to Adler: "I have developed what you might call an ulteriority complex."[30]

Long before he completed the manuscript of *West-Running Brook,* he began to doubt whether he would give it to Henry Holt and Company for publication. His friend Lincoln MacVeagh, who had played such a valuable part in making *New Hampshire* an attractive book and a financial success, had resigned from the Holt firm late in 1923. As a consequence, there had been a cooling-off in Frost's relations with his publisher. At the same time, he had become so well acquainted with Frederic G. Melcher, editor-in-chief of *Publishers' Weekly,* that he had acquired an increasingly sophisticated attitude toward author-publisher relations. He had even decided that he should have driven a harder bargain over royalties prior to the publication of *New Hampshire.* In March of 1927, Melcher had written to say that the trade department at Holt was in the doldrums and that Frost should move on to a more enterprising publisher such as Charles Scribner.[31] Remembering the difficulties he had met when he had tried to leave Holt and go with Alfred Harcourt, he cautiously weighed possibilities during the winter of 1927–1928. He discussed the entire problem with his best-informed friends when he returned for his ten weeks at Amherst, and when he went back to Michigan for another one-week stay in April of 1928. Perhaps through no accident, word of these discussions reached his publisher, with the result that some hurried moves were made. Richard H. Thornton, successor to MacVeagh as the Holt representative, was sent to call on Frost in South Shaftsbury, late in May of 1928.[32]

In these negotiations, Frost knew that he had the advantage

of being a Pulitzer Prize winner with a new manuscript, and he drove a good bargain. His royalties on *New Hampshire* had been 15 per cent of the retail price; he asked and was promised 15 per cent royalties on the first 5,000 copies of *West-Running Brook*, and 20 per cent on all copies thereafter, the book to be illustrated with woodcuts by his favorite, J. J. Lankes. There would be a limited as well as a trade edition, and an advance of $2,000 would be paid on request.[33] Thornton also promised that a new and enlarged edition of *Selected Poems* would be published alongside *West-Running Brook* in the fall of 1928, and all five of Frost's books would be brought together in a *Collected Poems* to be published either in the fall of 1929 or the spring of 1930. Thornton carried back to Holt's office, and gained approval for, a proposal that Frost should be guaranteed a monthly payment of $250 throughout the next five years, with the understanding that he would also receive whatever royalties his books might earn above that annual amount of $3,000.[34] Having gained far more contractual advantages than he had expected, he was thoroughly satisfied to stay with Henry Holt and Company.

HELPING TO SHAPE AN IMAGE

I am sending the manuscript back with suggestions.
We want to get the fact part right for future reference.[1]

WHILE Robert Frost was carefully working on the revisions of his manuscript for *West-Running Brook,* he kept looking out of the corner of one eye at the progress being made on another manuscript: an incipient biography of himself. There was nothing stealthy or clandestine in his concern about the other manuscript. He had been told that a study of him was to appear in a series of monographs to be published by the firm of George H. Doran in New York City. The editor in charge of the series was the young Vermont poet John Chipman Farrar, who had been an undergraduate at Yale when Frost had first met him. Farrar, combining the talents of a businessman with those of a poet, had chosen to earn his living as a publisher. He had made a good start with Doran, and was honored in that firm; recently he had also been honored by Middlebury College. Asked to serve as director of Middlebury's new addition to the Bread Loaf School of English, he had conducted the first session of the Bread Loaf Writers' Conference in the summer of 1926. Frost, who had participated in the arrangements for this development, also attended the first session. At Bread Loaf, Farrar told him of the plan for the series of monographs, and asked him to help by naming an author who might acceptably write the Frost study in the series. Farrar may have made the mistake of anticipating the choice Frost would make, for they both knew that Wilfred Davison, Director of the School of English at Bread Loaf, was gathering materials for a biographical study of Frost. Nevertheless, the decision was to rest entirely with Frost, who was so completely caught off guard by the announcement that he asked for time to consider possibilities.

As it happened, another man named Davison—Edward Davison—called on Frost at Bread Loaf during the Writers' Conference in the summer of 1926. He was a young poet who had come to the United States from his native England in 1925, and he had sent to Frost letters of introduction from Walter de la Mare and J. C. Squire. These letters, addressed to Frost at Ann Arbor, had caught up with him in Pittsfield while he and his family had lingered there because of Marjorie's illness. In response to Frost's cordial invitation, Edward Davison and his wife had visited the Frosts at the Stone Cottage in South Shaftsbury, early in June of 1926. Frost had been much impressed by this young Englishman, who in turn showed a flattering admiration for Frost. As a consequence, Edward Davison was urged to stop briefly at Bread Loaf, where Frost somewhat impulsively asked him if he would like to write the book which Farrar wanted. No decision was immediately reached, but during a second visit with the Frosts in South Shaftsbury, shortly after the close of the Conference, Edward Davison provisionally agreed to write a trial chapter which he would submit to Frost, not to Farrar. In fact, Farrar had not yet been given any hint that Edward Davison was being considered for the assignment.

In the trial chapter, Davison made an introductory survey of the "new poetry" movement in America, and used it as background for Frost's belated entry, following his return from England in 1915. Davison also brought into the chapter a few references to Untermeyer, and they were sufficiently uncomplimentary to reveal that Davison had been in America long enough to develop a strong dislike for the poetry and the personality of Untermeyer. When the chapter was submitted, Frost was dismayed. He explained that there was no reason why Davison should like Untermeyer for Frost's sake, but there was an obvious reason why he should not express that dislike in a book on Frost. Davison took the criticism well, promised to rewrite the chapter, and assumed that Frost had forgiven him for the blunder.[2] But Frost had not forgiven him, and had secretly decided that someone else must be found to write this particular monograph.

While Davison was continuing to work on his revision, Frost went ahead to make other arrangements. His attention had been called to an essay in the *Saturday Review*, an essay built around these lines in "New Hampshire":

> *It seems a narrow choice the age insists on.*
> *How about being a good Greek, for instance?*
> *That course, they tell me, isn't offered this year.*

The essay began: "The purest classical poet in America today is Robert Frost." It continued by pointing out that while several of Frost's critics had mistakenly viewed him as a romantic poet of nature, nobody had paid sufficient attention to his being deeply rooted in Hellenism. The author of the article, Gorham B. Munson, could have made an equally strong case to support the claim that Frost was even more deeply rooted in puritanical Hebraism. Temporarily, however, Frost preferred to think of himself—and to have others think of him—as a classicist. If Munson could be persuaded to write the Murray Hill biography under Frost's guidance, Munson could also be helped to shape the classical image even more pointedly than he had already done.[3]

In moments of humorous self-deprecation, Frost liked to say that his own father's political career had rubbed off just enough to account for the son's pleasure in asserting backstage power and influence. Years earlier, he had jokingly pretended to let Untermeyer say of him, ". . . give you a field like poetry that calls to the pulling of wires and the manipulation of ropes, to the climbing of every black reviewer's back stairs for preferment, and you are there with a suit case in both hands 'like an old stone savage armed.' "[4] In addition, Frost enjoyed suggesting to his reviewers and critics what they might say in his favor, and nobody had been cultivated to serve better in this regard than Untermeyer. Under Frost's guidance, Untermeyer had strenuously attacked those who were inclined to view Frost as a romantic rather than as a realist. Frost had even helped to prepare the first prefatory note in Untermeyer's anthology, *Modern American Poetry,* which had contained this direct quotation: " 'There are,' he [Frost] once said, 'two types of realist—the one who offers a good deal of dirt with his potato to show that it is a real one; and the one who is satisfied with the potato brushed clean. I'm inclined to be the second kind. . . . To me, the thing that art does for life is to strip it to form.' "[5] Having assisted Untermeyer in the campaign to make the public view Frost as a realist, he was now eager to help Gorham Munson or anyone else heighten the stature of the Frost image as that of a "good

Greek."⁶ The next step was to meet and become acquainted with Munson.

In the autumn of 1926, Frost spent a few days in New York City, staying with the Torrences in the Greenwich Village apartment which belonged to Mrs. Moody. While there, he went around to Munson's quarters and, not finding him at home, left a note asking that he telephone the signer at Torrence's apartment the next day. During the telephone conversation Frost told this man he had never met that Munson was his choice for the writing of the monograph for the Murray Hill series, and when Munson showed interest he was invited to dinner at the Torrences' that evening. At this meeting, Frost began by explaining why he had never written to thank Munson for the *Saturday Review* article: "I was waiting for a chance to do something to show my appreciation."⁷ Munson said he would accept the invitation, and Frost promised to have John Farrar offer him a contract. The plan worked smoothly, and on the nineteenth of December 1926 Munson wrote to Frost,

"I had a very agreeable luncheon with John Farrar a short time ago. We agreed on terms and I am to sign a contract just as soon as my other book is out of the path—which will be in January. Farrar wishes to publish the biography in the early autumn.

"The other book which I'm calling *Since 1900 in American Letters* occupies me during lunch hours, evenings and weekends in a great effort to complete it soon, and that is why I appear slow in writing you. . . . I shall probably be free to come to Amherst at any time you suggest. I have a feeling that I shall be in a very good mood for doing the biography."⁸

As Frost became better acquainted with Munson, some reservations were felt concerning this hasty choice of biographer. Munson's literary and even political interests were in a state of flux at that time, as he himself admitted later: "Having been in rapid succession a liberal, a socialist, a supporter of the Soviets, I had called myself for a couple of years a philosophical anarchist. . . . In literature my taste was voraciously catholic: I ranged from George Moore to Blaise Pascal. Among living writers in my country Waldo Frank was most appealing, and *Our America* I regarded as the gospel of the oncoming generation."⁹ In 1921, while living in Paris shortly after his marriage to a professional dancer, Munson had aligned his sympathies with Dadaism and had even tried his hand at writing Dada literature in prose and verse. With two other exiles, Matthew Josephson and Malcolm Cowley, he had conspired to organize and edit a little magazine, *Secession,* deliberately "intransigent, aggressive, unmuzzled."[10] Soon after that short-lived publication came to a disastrous end, Munson became attracted to the poetry of Robert Frost through his discovery that the title-poem in *New Hampshire* was "a Horatian satire in a contemporary manner,"[11] containing Frost's confession that he had written "several books against the world in general." It was the quality of "secession" in this poet named after a secessionist which appealed most strongly to Munson. It soon became obvious to Frost, however, that Munson would need some careful tutoring before he could satisfactorily complete the Murray Hill biography.

At the same time, Frost was troubled by the awkwardness of his relations with Edward Davison, who had to be let down as gently as possible, now that Munson was about to sign a contract with Farrar for the book Davison thought he was writing. Frost made his next move. He confided to Davison that Farrar had made a serious mistake: when Frost had said Davison was his choice for the assignment, Farrar had supposed Frost meant Dean Wilfred Davison at Middlebury. Farrar, having approached the Dean, had subsequently resolved the confusion by signing a contract with a third author, Gorham B. Munson. Frost insisted, however, that Edward Davison should continue his work on his own version of the biography, for which he could easily find a publisher when he next returned to London. As a sign of his continuing friendship for Edward Davison, and as a way of salving his own conscience, he then made arrangements for Davison to earn some much-needed money by giving a lecture at Amherst College. Before the Amherst lecture occurred, Farrar sent Frost a tactful plaint which hinted at the predicament caused by Frost's artful dodgings:

"I find the Edward Davison situation is becoming a bit of a mare's nest, due largely to my failure to see at first glance that it would be rather strange to have two books about you by men of the same name. You must know I was far from planning anything that would 'hurt' Ted. That isn't the way I work. . . . It is, therefore, quite disquieting to me to have Ted Davison accusing me of a deep-laid-and-dyed-plot against him.

Lord knows what difference it would make to me anyway; and it is all a little like a ladies' social. . . .

"As far as Dean Davison is concerned, he is now all up in the air for fear somebody or other will think he has antagonistic motives. For the matter of that, he has been planning for years on this work, and his disappointment is great. . . . This is the first time I have been involved in a literary imbroglio and I don't like it any more than I imagine you do."[12]

It was easier for Frost to forgive Farrar than to forgive himself for the clumsiness with which he had played his part in the "imbroglio," and he was sure many delicate moves would be required before he could fully disentangle himself. He carried out his plan to cultivate Edward Davison's good will by obtaining fine preliminary notices for the Amherst lecture, and by continuing to provide biographical information for the book Davison was still writing.[13]

Less than two months after Davison's lecture at Amherst, Frost arranged for Munson to lecture there—on "New Movements in American Letters"—and did not enjoy having Munson devote the lecture to such upstarts as William Carlos Williams, Wallace Stevens, E. E. Cummings, and Kenneth Burke.[14] Nevertheless, Munson made satisfactory progress on the little biography. At Frost's suggestion, he wrote to several of Frost's oldest friends, asking for their reminiscences, and was somewhat surprised to have Cox refuse assistance: ". . . he tells of his plan some day to write a life of you and [of] his disinclination to anticipate himself by preliminary reminiscence."[15] In spite of such disappointments, Munson moved ahead so rapidly that he completed the manuscript before the first of June 1927. Writing to Frost, he announced that he had delivered one copy to Farrar and was mailing another to Frost in the hope that any mistakes could be caught and corrected before Farrar sent the manuscript to the printer.[16]

Not satisfied with the manuscript, Frost took the blame for certain mistakes. They amounted to faithful reportings, on Munson's part, of misrepresentations which Frost had somehow conveyed, in trying to give an impression of what life had been like on the Derry farm during the years from 1900 to 1909. These years were particularly important to Frost because he thought they provided the turning point in the whole story. Munson's account endowed the Derry venture with a sadness of deprivation, Frost thought, and such handling would give the wrong impression. He had not previously explained to Munson (nor did he now explain) that he and his family had been able to live almost casually on the Derry farm, with less and less concern for drudgeries, and with a far larger income than most of the neighbors, because Frost received the annuity which was regularly paid from his grandfather's estate.[17] Perhaps Frost felt that such a materialistic note, if acknowledged, might spoil the mythic idyll of self-regenerating isolation. Nevertheless, he did now try to give Munson a few more details which might convey the freshness and originality and luck of the cherished and (at least in retrospect) perfect hiatus on the Derry farm:

"I dont know how [my account of] the life on the farm grew into such a hard luck story unless it was as one thing leads to another. I probably started with what we lacked so as to clear the deck for what we had. But I got too much interested in what we lacked for its own sake and never got any further. It is true that we lacked friends. Only three people ever came the twelve miles out of our past to visit us, and they never more than once or twice a year.[18] No neighbors came calling.[19] I got acquainted with my neighbors when we "changed works," mostly in haying time. But lack of company means plenty of solitude. And solitude was what I needed and valued. I had days and days and days to think the least little thought and do the least little thing. That's where I got my sense that I have forever for accomplishment. If I feel timeless and immortal it is from having lost track of time for five or six years there. We gave up winding clocks. Our ideas got untimely from not taking newspapers for a long period. It couldnt have been more perfect if we had planned it or foreseen what we were getting into. It was the luck. It wasn't even instinct that carried us away—just the luck. We didnt even know enough to know how hopelessly lost we must have looked from the outside. We never can recapture that. It was for once in a lifetime. That's roughly what A Boys Will is about. Life was peremptory and threw me into confusion. I couldnt have held my own and done myself credit unless I had been a quitter. My infant industries needed the protection of a dead space around them. Everybody was too strong for me, but at least I was strong enough not to stay where they were. I'm still much the same. What's room for if it isn't to get away from minds that stop your works? And the room is the most noticable thing in the universe. Even in an atom there's more space than matter—infinitely. The matter in the universe gets together in a few terribly isolated points and sizzles.

"In arranging the poems in A Boys Will I tried to plot the curve from blinking people as if they were the sun to being able to face them with my eyes open. But I wasnt escaping. No escape theory will explain me. I was choosing when to deliver battle.—I'm just amusing myself with all this retrospection. It may help give you the spirit.

"We were poorer than anyone around us, but that kept us from taking a birds eye view of Rockingham County.[20]

"I botanized a lot. One of my favorite plays was making paths in the woods and bushes. We were showing the country things to the children as they came along. We had apples pears peaches plums cherries grapes black berries raspberries cranberries and blueberries of our own. I settled what was to be my writing. I got horses into my head. I was always afraid of them, but their ways caught me. We had three horses in succession.

"We never had more than one warm room in winter.[21] When I wanted to turn it into two, one of them a study for me to write in, I had E turn her back on me so she couldnt see my struggle and I couldnt see her stretching thread.

"Them were the days when we knew whether we really liked a book or not. Now we cant always be sure we dont like or dislike it because we know the author. We read whole books of poetry then. Now we peek at them.

"We'll look for you then weekend after next. I'll have poured some more on you before then. I am sending the manuscript back with suggestions. We want to get the fact part right for future reference.

"You'll be amused to hear that the classicist-scientist[22] I spoke of admiringly has been made president of Amherst. . . ."[23]

Frost was apparently slow in getting his suggestions down to Munson in New York City. Although the corrective information was gratefully received, Munson was forced to admit that the manuscript given Farrar had already been sent to the printer. Under the circumstances, Frost could only hope that the reviewers would be kind.

The little book was published on the first of November 1927, under the title *Robert Frost: A Study in Sensibility and*

Good Sense, and the reviewers made too much out of the last chapter. In his suggestions for revision, Frost had apparently failed to notice and comment on the fact that the last chapter, entitled "Against the World in General," amounted to an expanded version of the *Saturady Review* essay, and Munson, in his revised attempt to strengthen the claim that Frost was a classicist rather than a romantic, had invoked the support of the new humanist leader, Irving Babbitt. Munson was so sympathetic toward Babbitt's position in the current humanist controversy that he unintentionally encouraged critics to misrepresent Frost by viewing him as a disciple of Babbitt's.

Scornfully opposed to being called the disciple of anyone, Frost had even deeper reasons for wanting to separate himself completely from the new humanists, and if he could have foreseen the damage Munson might cause by associating the poet with Babbitt's version of humanism, he would have insisted that Munson make further revisions. The deeper reasons why Babbitt's humanism offended Frost were contained in Babbitt's controversial book, *Rousseau and Romanticism,* particularly in the first chapter entitled "The Terms Classic and Romantic." There offering a brief historical survey of meanings assigned to those very slippery terms, Babbitt claimed that a sensible corrective for imaginative unrestraint could be derived from the classical virtues of moderation and good sense. At the same time, he went beyond the terms "classic" and "romantic" to endow the word "humanism" with classical weight. He showed that while medieval Christianity had insisted that man's life on earth was significant only insofar as it affected the soul's expectation of God's mercy after death, the Renaissance humanists invoked classical ideals for purposes of resisting such a belittlement of man's natural condition, and of asserting that man fulfills the greatness of his potential in this life without reference to either God or immortality.

To Frost, such views were offensive because they contradicted his own cherished belief in the essentials of Christian teaching, especially the belief in God's mercy after death. As far back as 1914 Arthur James Balfour in his Gifford Lectures entitled "Theism and Humanism" had articulated the point which was to Frost the crux of this new controversy: "My desire has been to show that all we think best in human culture, whether associated with beauty, goodness, or knowledge, requires God for its support, that Humanism without Theism loses more than half its value."[24] Babbitt further offended Frost by dismissing William James and Henri Bergson, in arrogant and querulous ways, by insisting that they were pure romantics who inherited too much nonsense from Rousseau:

"According to Bergson one becomes spiritual by throwing overboard both thought and action, and this is a very convenient notion. . . . It is hard to see in Bergson's intuition of the creative flux and perception of real duration anything more than the latest form of Rousseau's transcendental idling. To work with something approaching frenzy according to the natural law and to be idle according to the human law must be accounted a rather one-sided view of life. The price the man of today has paid for his increase in power is, it should seem, an appalling superficiality in dealing with the law of his own nature. . . . For the adult to maintain an exclusive Bergsonian interest in 'the perpetual gushing forth of novelties' would seem to betray an inability to mature. . . ."[25]

Babbitt disliked, in Bergson, exactly what Frost liked: the creative uses of imagination, and the throwing overboard of at least certain categories of thought and action. Continuing, Babbitt had implicitly correlated Bergson and James as romantics, and then had added:

"It is equally significant that the humanist can agree with nearly every line of James's chapter on habit [in *Psychology*] and that he disagrees very gravely with James in total tendency. That is because James shows himself, as soon as he passes from the naturalistic to the humanistic level, wildly romantic."[26]

Such an approach to James and Bergson heightened Frost's distaste for those meanings which Babbitt assigned to the opposed terms, "romanticism" and "classicism." What Frost admired most about James and Bergson was that no matter how theologically heretical they might be, they did view life as God-centered; what he disliked most about Babbitt was the insistence that human life should be man-centered. Hence the misery in finding that some reviewers of Munson's book hailed Frost as a humanist while other reviewers damned him —for the same reason.

It was too late to make any protest to Munson, the man chosen to help improve the image of Frost as classicist. But just when it seemed that the less said the better, Munson made another unintentional mistake. He had given journalistic assistance to Babbitt from the start of the controversy between the new humanists and the theists, and he now tried to give additional support by publishing a *Bookman* essay entitled "Robert Frost and the Humanistic Temper." Further linking the names of Frost and Babbitt, he now wrote, "Not by theory but by practice as a poet is Mr. Frost truly a contemporary humanist. To illustrate: Mr. Babbitt says . . ." Then to clinch his point Munson analyzed "West-Running Brook" as evidence that "the poet's sense of contraries is not far from the humanist's declaration that in man there is a duality of consciousness, a struggle between his impulse to unify himself and his impulse to drift with the stream of life."[27]

That was too much for Frost to take without protest, and he wrote Munson a letter which combined reprimand with oblique self-explanation, beginning, "We know each other so well that it seems as if we ought to go on and know each other better."[28] In his reply, Munson tried to defend himself, but the harm done to their friendship was irrevocable, and thereafter Frost merely went through the motions of courtesy.

The other friend, Edward Davison, to whom Frost still felt obligated, was treated in a far more apologetic manner. New favors were heaped on him in attempts to make amends, the climactic gesture being a strongly written recommendation which enabled the Englishman to obtain a Guggenheim Fellowship for study in England. Davison thanked him warmly in a farewell letter, and Frost replied:

"You got away from this Hemisphere without giving me a chance to ask you what so much more than anybody else I had done for you over here, accepted the engagement at Penn State . . . written my books, stood my ground, been myself or got you deported with Guggenheim money to your own incontinent continent if only for the term of a year. The last is all I ask you to thank me for. . . ."[29]

This pleasant letter made no mention of the work Davison had done on a possible biography of Robert Frost, to be published either in America or England. Frost had already taken care of this very delicate matter in a letter tactfully sent to Davison just prior to the appearance of Munson's book, and the method of approach in that letter had been very gentle:

"I've been thinking of you lately—disinterested thoughts only. So dont be troubled in the conscience about that biography. Let's not have the biography between us always as our reason for meeting or avoiding each other. Let's consider it dropped. Then if you ever do write the thing, it won't be because I had you where you had to. It can be entirely of your own motion and I can be as surprised and pleased as a kitten is when a spool seems to show signs of life without being pushed or pulled. Is it a vote? . . ."[30]

It was a unanimous vote. The friendship between them continued, but Davison did not go on with the biography.

TO EUROPE FOR HEALTH

*We didn't dare to make this expedition with Marj as she
is and we didn't dare not to make it. The second fear won
and we are here. I doubt if we'll be able to stay. At most
I hope to see a few friends. Then for sea-sickness again
and home.*[1]

WHENEVER the Frosts talked about going abroad for Mar-
jorie's health, France was given special consideration because
Marjorie wanted to live there and learn to speak French.
Advice was sought from their neighbor, Dorothy Canfield
Fisher, who knew France almost as well as she knew Vermont.
For several months during the First World War she had lived
in Bellevue, near Sèvres, only a few miles to the southwest of
Paris, and she had remained on intimate terms with a family
in Sèvres. If Marjorie would enjoy living with this family for
a few weeks or months, Mrs. Fisher would make all the arrangements with Madame Marguerite Fischbacher. The offer
was accepted, and Mrs. Fisher kept her word. The only remaining drawback was the fear that Marjorie might not be strong
enough to enjoy staying with the Fischbachers while her parents left her there and went over to England to visit friends.
Frost, in his uncertainty about how to make plans for such a
precarious trip, had notified only one of his friends in England,
the barrister-poet-botanist-bookcollector John W. Haines, in
Hucclecote, near Gloucester. Responding with his persistent
friendliness, Haines assured the Frosts that he and his wife
would enjoy having the Americans stay with them as guests
as often and as long as possible during the proposed return
to England. Haines apparently notified their mutual friend
Walter de la Mare, who wrote to Frost on the fourth of July
1928: "I heard the other day that you are really and indeed
coming to England some time this summer. . . . Do be sure

to let me know when you are safely here. We should love to see you."[2] On the twenty-ninth of July, Frost replied to Haines,

"We have the tickets and that is nearer you and England than we have been for thirteen years. The only thing that can keep me from walking a path with you this year will be the failure of Margery to come up to the mark on sailing day. She is not right. We have a nurse in the house conditioning her for the trial by water. We will have to think of her a good deal while over. We plan to put her in charge of a nurse companion in France to see if the interest in picking up French and the society of some one young enough to laugh a lot wont help her case. So we are sailing, if we sail, directly for France. The ship leaves Quebec Canada with or without us on August 4th. Don't set your heart too much on seeing us . . . I will bring Elinor to your house inside of a few weeks, though, if it in me lies. You don't care how old we look. . . ."[3]

They did sail as planned, from Quebec to LeHavre, and the voyage was spoiled for them because all three of the Frosts suffered intermittently from seasickness. When they reached Paris, they lingered for a few days before going on to Sèvres, and Frost dutifully tried to enjoy the wicked city he was predisposed to dislike. For Marjorie's sake, he spent an afternoon with her in the Louvre, and an evening at the Opéra. When they moved out to Sèvres, Mrs. Frost was so fearful that Marjorie would have difficulty in making adjustments to the Fischbacher family that she insisted on taking up residence for a short time in a Bellevue pension. For several days, Marjorie's parents took her on brief sightseeing trips. They visited the famous ceramics museum which specialized in Sèvres ware; they even went to Versailles and peeked into the palace, the gardens, the park.

Frost was embarrassed by his inability to read or speak French, and feared that any Frenchman speaking to another in his presence must be making fun of his ignorance. At Versailles, his greatest enjoyment came when he found a portrait of George Washington in the palace gallery of noted generals. "Everything is American to him who looks with American eyes," he shamefacedly confessed.[4] In Bellevue, while walking alone to the lookoff point which gave the town its name, he saw again with American eyes. According to Marjorie's guidebook, this vantage point provided a splendid vista of the site where a palace had stood in which Madame de Pompadour "kept herself or was kept".[5] The guidebook also told him that the park from which he enjoyed this view was named for Woodrow Wilson.

There was far more provocation, for this traveler, in thinking of Woodrow Wilson than of the mistress of Louis XV. When Frost had left England, in 1915, eager to bring the United States to the aid of his British friends, he had hated what he still viewed as the sentimental sophistry in Wilson's saying, "There is such a thing as a man being too proud to fight." Even more repugnant to Frost had been Wilson's claim that nothing permanent was ever achieved by force. (History was useful, here: it seemed to Frost that what Rome had done to Carthage had been fairly permanent.) Yet he believed that Wilson possessed ideals as noble and vast as those of any politician or statesman who had ever lived—that he was a great something even if only a great mistake. Some might think his failure was in missing a mark which someone else would later hit, but Frost was more inclined to think that Wilson had missed a mark that simply wasn't there—in nature or in human nature.[6]

As an American in or near Paris, Frost could read enough names in French newspaper headlines to remind him that others were still trying to aim some leftover Wilsonian idealism at marks which, he was willing to prophesy, would also be missed. Frank B. Kellogg, the United States Secretary of State, was in Paris at this time, completing negotiations with the French premier, Aristide Briand. On the twenty-seventh of August 1928, they signed the Pact of Paris and invited other nations to add their agreement that the settlement of all conflicts, no matter of what origin or nature, which might arise among nations, should be done only by pacific means; that war was to be renounced as an instrument of national policy. Disgusted by what seemed to him a ridiculous dream, Frost was ready to leave France and start for England immediately, by way of protest.[7] What kept him, however, was Mrs. Frost's distress over Marjorie's recurrent depressions and physical weaknesses. Having expected to stay only a few days in France before crossing the Channel, he finally decided that he should explain the delay to Jack Haines, and he wrote:

"Thus far I have nothing to report of this expedition but bad. We came to France in the hope that it might improve our invalid Marjorie by awakening an interest in her to learn the French language. That hope has failed and the disappointment has been almost too much for Elinor on top of everything else she has had to bear for the last two years. I cant tell you how she has lost courage and strength as I have watched her. She is in a serious condition—much more serious at this moment than Marjorie. We ought by right to abandon our campaign and baggage and retreat to America. But that seems too cruel to contemplate with nothing done, none of our friends seen that we wanted to see and have been wanting to see so long. I have one last recourse. I am going to try to find a sort of travelling-companion-nurse for Marjorie to take her off her mother's hands for a few weeks. . . . Then I am going to ask you to help me about Elinor. She must be put on her feet again before we attempt any going around among people in England. . . ."[8]

Early in September, Marjorie's parents felt safe in committing her to the understanding care of Madame Fischbacher. They started for Gloucestershire, got as far as London, and stayed at the Imperial Hotel on Russell Square for several days while Mrs. Frost tried to overcome her own fatigue and depression. Frost, not immediately choosing to get in touch with any of his London friends, wrote letters. One of them, to Charles Monroe in South Shaftsbury, gave his retrospective impressions of Paris:

"Paris was no more than I expected, and, as you know, that wasn't much. We were constantly told it was at its worst in August. I suppose it has more monuments than any city I ever saw or shall see. If you went there young enough it would be a good place to get over any curiosity you might have about the human form divine. It is very widespread and as you might say ubiquitous and universal. There wasnt so much as a one of them that had had so much as the tip of a nose knocked off by the war apparently. They look as if they hadnt felt the war as they should have. The live people look sort of cross about having got so little out of a minimal victory. The ordinary ones look as if they had been cheated by us more than by the Germans. Only the better sort with brains know that we werent to blame either for their going into the war, their winning it or their getting nothing out of it.

"I'm really no traveller. One place is like another to me except that the one I left is if anything always better than the one I have come to. So you wont get any enthusiastic descriptive writing from me. Right now I am thinking best of the peak of Bucks Cobble [in South Shaftsbury] and the view from our old place in Franconia. Such am I. It is wasting good money to take me travelling or sight-seeing. . . . We left Marjorie in Paris and came over here in seven hours by train and boat yesterday. Dover Cliffs were all right."⁹

As soon as Mrs. Frost felt strong enough to continue the journey, they went on to Gloucester, were welcomed by the Haines family, and spent the next ten days there, in hiding. The affection of the Haineses had a salutary effect on Mrs. Frost. While she was regaining her strength, Haines and Frost walked those roads and footpaths of the Dymock region they had often explored with Edward Thomas, Lascelles Abercrombie, and Wilfrid Gibson. Botanizing as they went, they visited what had been Abercrombie's thatched cottage at Ryton, known as The Gallows, now neglected and falling into ruins; Gibson's former home, the thatched cottage called The Nailshop, at a crossroads just outside the town of Dymock; and the homely black timber and whitened brick cottage called Little Iddens, where the Frosts had lived.

The faithful, outgoing Haines still kept in touch with the Abercrombies and the Gibsons, but he could give no cheerful news about them. Lascelles and Wilfrid continued to write and publish verse without attracting any attention from the newcomers. The Abercrombies were living at Leeds and he was giving lectures at the University there. The Gibsons lived in the town of Letchworth, over in Hertfordshire. Frost, still bearing a grudge against Gibson for his failure to help Edward Thomas establish himself as a poet, could not make up his mind whether he would bother to get in touch with Gibson. Haines thought he should.

In tribute to Thomas, Haines and Frost made additional pilgrimages to several botanizing areas in the Cotswolds. They also climbed May Hill, again for his sake, to survey the panorama of countryside which reached from Brecon Beacons to Shropshire, from the northernmost Cotswolds to the Channel's rim, and far into the mountains of Wales. As Haines later wrote, concerning these walks and talks, "the wraith of that dead friend was ever before us 'and the tender grace of a day that is dead' . . ."¹⁰

While the Frosts were staying with the Haines family, encouraging letters came from Marjorie, strengthening their hopes that they had been correct in leaving her with strangers in France. Mrs. Frost, slightly buoyed by the prospect of remaining longer in England, returned with her husband to the Imperial Hotel in London, knowing that he was far more eager than she for the renewal of other friendships.

The best London clearing house for information concerning fellow poets was Harold Monro's Poetry Bookshop—which had been moved in 1926 from 35 Devonshire Street to 38 Great Russell Street, near the British Museum. Frost telephoned the dour Monro, with whom he had occasionally corresponded during the thirteen years since they had last seen each other, and was surprised at the warmth of Monro's response. Monro insisted that Frost should promise to give a reading of his poems, in a room at the back of the Poetry Bookshop, and when Frost hesitated, Monro sweetened the invitation: If Frost would promise to read, Monro would give him a stag dinner with his fellow American, T. S. Eliot. Both offers were accepted, the date of the reading was set for the eighteenth of October 1928, and Monro mailed announcements to his customers.

Other telephone calls prepared the way for several additional visits. The Frosts went up to Buckinghamshire to spend a night with the De la Mares at Taplow; they entertained Mr. and Mrs. John Gould Fletcher at the Imperial Hotel; they spent two nights in the home of the Georgian poet, John Freeman. This latter visit was marred somewhat by another Geogian poet, W. P. R. Kerr, whose aggressiveness had already been described to Frost by Haines. Later, when leisure was made available by a slight illness, Frost gave Haines an account of the little unpleasantness:

"I'm sick with a cold too. I grant at once, though, that yours is worse than mine. So don't be roused to jealousy and argument. Such is my indolence cowardice or both that I will grant anything you please rather than run the risk of argument. . . .

"Speaking of argument, I had an encounter with your papist friend Kerr that woke me from my lethargy at Freeman's the other night. He came at me hurtling. He defied me to doubt [that] lost causes and unread books were best. He blamed us puritans for having overthrown civilization in England and having established it in the southern states of America. There he delivered himself into my hands. But my work was still all before me[11] to bend the slippery muscular porpoise round so as to make the two ends of his argument meet and stick his tail down his throat. I'm afraid he surprised me into an unwonted severity,[12] bless his vigourosity. At this point I remembered your story of the way he had offended Abercrombie and [I] took a resolution not to mind him. And from then on I kept it through onslaught after onslaught on my country with weapons supplied chiefly by my fellow countrymen. His sentence [i.e., judgment] took the form of regret that we seemed to be what Men[c]ken and Sink Lewis said we were. My position[,] held fairly calmly after I got my balance[,] was that I didn't know what we were except that we had evidently grown so important that a really good country like England preferred our friendship and alliance to that of France. He knows a lot and if he doesn't know how to use it logically his intentions are of the best. We have to make allowances for all converts especially to Romanism."[13]

Another unexpected awkwardness developed when the Frosts called on the widow of Edward Thomas. She had recently shocked many of her friends by publishing some intimate autobiographical reminiscences in a volume entitled *As It Was*. The book had attracted international attention—it had even been suppressed in Boston—and it had greatly eased her financial difficulties. But the Frosts, during their one visit with her, severely expressed their regrets that she had gone into so much detail about her marital difficulties. They feared she might have injured rather than strengthened Edward's literary reputation. Now enjoying her own literary triumph, she graciously accepted all the criticism made by these American friends, and she wrote them the next day to say she appreciated their frankness.[14] Frost remained unforgiving for reasons hinted in his next letter to Haines: "We saw Helen Thomas and that ended one passage in our lives. I decided before I had listened to her long that Edward had worse enemies to his memory than poor old simple Wilfrid [Gibson]. It needed only that decision to make it easy to visit Wilfrid at Letchworth. . . ."[15] At the same time, needing another outlet for his disgust with Helen Thomas, he found it in writing Sidney Cox and in concentrating particularly on what he disliked about her book, *As It Was*:

"Its a good piece of work in a way, but it took a good [deal] of squirming on her part to justify it. I wondered if she wasnt in danger of making E. T. look ridiculous in the innocence she credited him with. Mightnt men laugh a manly laugh? E. T. was distinguished at his college at Oxford for the ribald folk songs he could entertain with—not to say smutty. Worse than *As It Was* are some other chapters in his life she has been undressing to the public since.[16] In one she has him invite to the house a girl he has met and come home full of admiration of. She gives herself away by calling the girl 'this paragon of women.' But she finds the minute she sees her (how homely she is) that she can conquer her with magnanimity, or conquer her jealousy of her with magnanimity. All women are sisters that the same man loves, she tries to make herself think. Once in the woods listening to a nightengale in the dark E[dward] says to the two of them We are knowing, but the nightengale knows all. Then he kisses his wife and to keep the score even his wife makes him kiss the other women. She pretends to think that is large and lovely but I happen to know it was a dose she was giving him and rubbing in. These things are hard to do sincerely. And unridiculously. In another chapter she has him carry her off to bed on his last leave of absence before going to the front. It reminds me of Schnitzler's Whatsername."[17]

While the Frosts were thus indirectly prompted by Helen Thomas to reconsider visiting the Gibsons, Frost felt guilty enough to hope he could make amends for the hostile ways he had ignored Gibson. As soon as Gibson had learned that Frost was in England he had written, "Dear Robert, I have just received a Poetry Bookshop announcement which says that Robert Frost is reading his own poems there on the 18th. . . . We are thrilled to think that may be a chance of seeing you again, at last! Even though you never answer letters, you do remember us, don't you, and those old days in Gloucestershire. I cannot tell you with what warm affection we always think of you and yours."[18] The visit was carried through with ease because both of the Gibsons crowded the conversation with their favorite recollections of events in Gloucestershire. Frost was glad the small talk enabled him to conceal his dislike for this man who specialized in sentimentalities. Within a few days after the visit, Gibson sent him thirty-three lines of blank verse commemorating their reunion; a poem in which, as Frost told Haines, "he stoutly excuses us all for looking so horribly old."[19]

There was one other comparable occasion when Frost was embarrassed and amused by being given a poem written in his honor. His call on the one-legged supertramp W. H. Davies was made entertaining by the old man's garrulousness, and yet the beginning of the visit was so quaint that Frost could not resist reporting it to a friend who could appreciate: "Davies was the same old Davies. The minute Elinor and I got there he rose and presented us with an autographed poem as a 'souvenir of our visit.' He hasnt aged a hair. Still harping on why he isnt read in America. Wants to come over lecturing."[20]

The saddest of these brief calls occurred one night when Frost went alone to a shabby Lincoln's Inn apartment to surprise John Cournos. This Russian Jew from Philadelphia had been struggling to establish himself as a literary figure in London, back in 1914, and he was still struggling.[21] Delighted to receive such an unexpected visitor, Cournos was in need of comfort. His wife was to undergo surgery the next day and there was the possibility, at least the fear, that she might not survive the operation. As usual, Cournos was also worrying about where he would find money enough to pay the expenses. The next morning, Frost enclosed a check for $50 with a note to Cournos, and took to the hospital a bouquet of yellow roses for Mrs. Cournos. "A thousand thanks," Cournos wrote. "I cannot tell you how handy your enclosure will come in at this moment. I will let you know how Helen is as soon as the ordeal is over. I too enjoyed our talk."[22] Mrs. Cournos recovered well from the operation, and attempts were made for further visits between Frost and Cournos, but they did not see each other again during this trip.

Long before the Frosts started for England and France, he had informed his Irish friends Padraic Colum and George William Russell ("AE") that he wanted to visit them in Ireland. Colum, who had sailed for Ireland from the United States not long before the Frosts sailed for Le Havre, had expressed his eagerness to be Frost's guide around Dublin, and Frost wrote him from London in an attempt to set up a mutually convenient time for the visit:

"You may be clear out of Dublin, you may even have gone back to New York; but I am not going to give you up without another trial. (I made one by telegraph a few days ago.) I dont want to miss the chance of being introduced to Ireland by the right person. . . . Nobody ever talked Ireland to me as intimately as you did that day lying by the side of a road in Pelham (near Amherst) ten years ago."[23]

Arrangements were soon worked out, and Frost went to Ireland for five days, leaving his wife alone in London at her request. Colum, about to sail back to America, could only begin to acquaint Frost with Dublin, but he left him in the care of AE, whom Frost had met and liked during one of AE's visits to America. Through the intercession of AE, the Irish poet Constantine P. Curran played host to Frost: he stayed four nights with the Currans at their home on Garville Avenue in the Dublin suburb of Rathgar, not far from where AE was living.[24] During one evening Frost was taken to a gathering of literary notables, including William Butler Yeats, who had been elected a senator of the Irish Free State in 1922, the year before he was awarded the Nobel Prize for Literature. Once again, however, there was disappointment for Frost in the way he was barely noticed by his favorite Irish author.[25]

Back in London, Frost soon realized that Harold Monro had done him a considerable favor. Even before the reading at the Poetry Bookshop on the night of the eighteenth of October 1928, the mailed announcements had spread the news to officers of the International P. E. N. Society (of which Frost had been made an honorary member, a few years earlier) and of the English Speaking Union. Each group began making plans to honor him. Those who gathered to hear him read at the Bookshop were mostly strangers, and he was disappointed to be told by Monro that T. S. Eliot had sent his regrets. The night after the reading, however, Monro kept his word and took Frost to dinner with Eliot, whom he had not previously met.

The two Americans entered into conversation easily by comparing notes on how their host had and had not assisted them more than a decade earlier. During the summer of 1914 while Frost was living in Gloucestershire, Monro had been given his first opportunity to help Eliot, and had failed him. Conrad Aiken, then a stranger, appeared at the Poetry Bookshop, offered Monro a manuscript entitled "The Love Song of J. Alfred Prufrock," and explained that the author of it was his former Harvard classmate, just then in Germany. After considering the manuscript for *Poetry and Drama*, Monro returned it to Aiken, dismissing it as being (according to Aiken's later telling of the story), " 'absolutely insane,' or words to that effect."[26] Aiken then showed it to Ezra Pound, who called it "the best poem I have yet had or seen from an American" and insisted that the reluctant Harriet Monroe publish it in *Poetry*, where it first appeared.[27] Immediately after the war, however, Monro had liberally encouraged poets as different as Eliot, the Sitwells, Herbert Read, Aldous Huxley, and Richard Aldington by publishing them in his *Chapbook* series. While Eliot was accepting this help, Pound was less forgiving, and when Monro tried to explain to him the "programme" for the series, Pound protested, "*HELL*—you never had a programme. . . . One always suspects you of having (and knows you have had) sympathy with a lot of second-rate lopp—and never knows when the ancient sin will break out again."[28]

Secretly, Frost could more easily forgive Monro for having disliked "Prufrock" than for having failed to help Edward Thomas in 1915, and having refused to publish the first volume of poetry offered anyone by Edward Thomas. At least Frost knew that after the death of Thomas, Monro had revised his opinion and had written to Helen Thomas offering to bring out an edition of his poems.[29] Eliot, of course, was no more interested in Thomas's poetry than he was in Frost's, at that time, and there was something strained about the entire evening. What annoyed Frost most was the way in which this native of St. Louis affected an English accent. Long before the evening was over, Frost decided to go on disliking Eliot as a tricky poet—and as a mealy-mouthed snob.[30]

Late in October of 1928, just as Frost was beginning to be noticed by individuals and groups who had belatedly learned of his presence in England, disturbing news came from Madame Fischbacher. Marjorie was not well. Mrs. Frost, knowing of her husband's many commitments in England, insisted on going alone to France. Frost promised to meet her there in a week or ten days, and they planned to sail home from Le Havre before the middle of November. In making his commitments, he had accepted an invitation from Lascelles Abercrombie to give a reading of his poems at the University of Leeds in Yorkshire. He had also promised to go as far north as Edinburgh, to visit the Spenser scholar, James Cruikshank Smith and his family, whom the Frosts had met at Kingsbarns in Scotland during the summer of 1913. Smith had cordially answered Frost's tardy announcement of their arrival in London: "Your letter gave me great pleasure—& relief: for I had heard that you were in Britain, and should have taken it very much amiss if you had gone back without coming to see us."[31]

Frost could guess how the Smiths had heard: Mrs. Smith's sister, Mrs. Jessy Mair, whom the Frosts had also met at Kingsbarns in 1913, had already arranged to have Frost give a talk and reading in London. Recently widowed, Mrs. Mair was serving as Secretary of the London School of Economics and Political Science, and was soon to marry the British economist, William Henry Beveridge, who had been the director of the School since 1919. She had invited the Frosts to dine with her and Mr. Beveridge at The Georgian House, 10 Bury Street, on the twenty-fifth of October, prior to Frost's talk before the Literary Society of the School, "a delightful group of young students who would regard it as a great honour to meet you."[32] Frost had to go alone, on that occasion, because of Mrs. Frost's absence in France, but the entire evening was a pleasant one for him, and the students were far more responsive than the more critical poets who had listened to him at Monro's Bookshop. Soon after his appearance at the School, he went alone to Edinburgh, spent a night with the Smiths, and then stopped off at Leeds to visit briefly with the Abercrombies.

Lascelles Abercrombie had been one of the first to help Frost gain a reputation in England, and out of his enthusiasm for Frost's poetry had grown the friendship which had caused the Frosts to move from Buckinghamshire to Gloucestershire in the spring of 1914. Much had changed since then, as Haines had implied. Because Abercrombie was now a chronic invalid, most of the talk at dinner centered around the scales he used for weighing his food, and the insulin he was taking for his diabetes. Frost was disappointed to find that so little ground for friendship seemed to remain, at least on Abercrombie's part. The well-meaning and motherly Mrs. Abercrombie made matters worse by saying that if Lascelles had had any luck he would have "beaten" Frost in reputation and fame. So far as Frost could see, there had never been any spirit of competition between them.[33]

Back in London, he found encouraging word that Mrs. Frost had decided to bring Marjorie over to England because she wanted to see some of the places she remembered as a child. The three of them would therefore sail for home from Southamton as soon as they could after Frost had met his obligations. Before the ladies returned from France, Frost seized one more chance to renew another old friendship. The poet F. S. Flint had helped Frost meet Ezra Pound, in 1913. Flint had attended the reading at Monro's Bookshop and had subsequently made arrangements for Frost to meet him on an appointed evening, near the post office where Flint worked: by the Washington statue in Trafalgar Square. Frost was on time for their meeting, but when he could not find a "Washington statue" anywhere near Trafalgar Square he suspected a practical joke. Flustered, he asked a policeman if there was any statue of George Washington nearby. For a moment, the bobby seemed ready to say no. Then his face lit up and he wondered if perhaps the gentleman was looking for that bit of a thing not much bigger than a thumb, over there. Flint was waiting for him, beside the little statue, and when Frost ended his apology for being late by saying the monument seemed unworthy of George Washington, Flint countered by asking where in America one might find any statue of George the Third.[34]

After dinner at the Garrick Restaurant, Flint took Frost to the apartment of the critic Edward Garnett, who was expecting them. No other critic in England had written of Frost's poetry more appreciatively or had been a closer friend of Edward Thomas, and there was every reason for assuming that Frost would enjoy this first meeting with Garnett. Unfortunately, Frost was in a grouchy mood, and he soon arranged to make sparks fly. He wondered if Garnett had ignored him, after one article, because he thought *Mountain Interval* a failure, made up of poems not good enough for *A Boy's Will* or *North of Boston*. When Garnett frankly answered that *North of Boston* was his favorite among Frost's four books, Frost took offense. Flint tried to change the subject by introducing names of other poets, and immediately Frost fell into disagreement with Garnett over what qualities were best in the "new" poetry. Although Frost's belligerence spoiled the evening, Garnett made a gracious and tactful gesture when his visitors were leaving. No matter what their differences of opinion might be, he said, he felt sure they could agree that Frost had written one nearly perfect pastoral poem which discerning people would not soon forget: "The Mountain." That was enough to mollify Frost, and the parting was friendly.[35]

By the time Mrs. Frost and Marjorie reached London, the two most important events remaining on Frost's immediate calandar were the separate dinners arranged for him by the P. E. N. Society and by the English Speaking Union. One of the prime movers in arranging each of these occasions was the Irish-American poet Norreys Jephson O'Conor, nearly ten years younger than Frost. Back in February of 1919, when Frost had been elected president of the New England Poetry Club, O'Conor had been elected vice president; in October of 1919, when the new president had made his first appearance at the monthly meeting of the Club, the meeting had been held in O'Conor's home, where Frost had met and liked O'Conor's wife Grace. Thereafter, while O'Conor was teaching at Mount Holyoke and then at Bryn Mawr, Frost had become quite friendly with him. By the time the Frosts reached London, the O'Conors were living there and were well acquainted with a wide literary circle. As a member not only of the P. E. N. Society but also of the English Speaking Union, O'Conor was eager to participate in honoring his fellow countryman.

It frequently happened, however, that when Frost set too fast a pace for himself and was forced to risk having his sensitivities scraped raw by too many contacts with friends and strangers alike, he became genuinely ill, and his illness usually took the form of a severe grippe cold. It happened again, just before the scheduled dinners, and the O'Conors were drafted to serve as liaison between the Frosts and the authorities. Both occasions had to be canceled, and the Frosts were planning to leave so soon for America that there was insufficient time to arrange later dates.[36]

At least a week remained, before the booked sailing, and when it became apparent that Frost was recovering quickly from his illness—that he had only one more call to make, on the Poet Laureate Robert Bridges in Oxford—the O'Conors asked for permission to arrange a small farewell party at their home on Sunday evening, the tenth of November 1928, the day after his tea with the poet laureate. Given permission to make her plans, Mrs. O'Conor soon telephoned the Frosts, to relay another invitation. Miss Edith Sitwell was not certain that she would be able to meet the Frosts on Sunday evening, and she did so want to make their acquaintance that she wondered if they would come to her home for dinner Saturday night, the ninth of November. She had already invited, for that dinner, Mr. and Mrs. T. S. Eliot and Mr. and Mrs. W. B. Yeats. Regretfully, the Frosts declined. "You should not be so popular and be making so short a stay," Mrs. O'Conor wrote to Mrs. Frost, in the midst of all this last-minute planning. "But we shall have a few people, anyway, at this short notice, and we are selfish enough to be glad you are coming to us even if we cannot do you the honor you deserve by bringing the great of the land to your feet."[37]

Frost went alone to Oxford to call on Bridges, whom he had met in England in 1913, just prior to the poet laureate appointment, and Frost had enjoyed discussing with Bridges the sharp differences between their theories of poetry. Again the two men had briefly seen each other at the University of Michigan in 1925. On the strength of these previous meetings, Frost had written to Bridges shortly after reaching London, and had said he wished to call just long enough to pay his respects. Answering graciously, Bridges had invited him to call at Chilswell, Boars Hill, Oxford. When he arrived, Frost was again disappointed. It was immediately apparent that this distinguished eighty-four-year-old gentleman who had published his first book of poems before Frost was born was in no mood to discuss poetic theories. The poet laureate did have much to say, somewhat pompously, about his immediate work on the long poem he was going to call "The Testament of Beauty," and about his brief stay at the University of Michigan. The conversation was too cold and formal to satisfy Frost. Taking his leave as soon as he dared, he was sorry he had not accepted the invitation to have dinner with the Eliots and the Yeatses, at Edith Sitwell's.[38]

After the farewell evening at the O'Conors', there was time enough to show Marjorie a few more of the scenes in London she remembered from childhood; then they sailed for home aboard the SS *Olympic* on the fifteenth of November 1928. In retrospect, Frost could not be sure that the trip to France and England for health had been at all successful for Marjorie. He was certain that Mrs. Frost had lost more than she had gained from all these adventures, that one serious cause of her suffering had been his insistence on making so many final social engagements when she would have preferred taking Marjorie home weeks earlier. "I've made Elinor unhappier keeping her on than I think I ever made her before," he guiltily wrote to Haines.[39] He was more philosophical in writing to Davison, "Some things have disappointed us as much as we were afraid everything might (we were prepared for the worst) . . ." This was a favorite posture of his: always expecting the worst and counting as pure gain anything better than that. But as the *Olympic* hammered through heavy rains and rough seas, all three of the Frosts were far more seasick than they had expected to be, and long before they reached New York they were sorry they had ever tried to seek health by going abroad.[40]

GOOD OLD FOLKWAYS

*. . . very few people that leave the good old folkways can
keep from getting all mixed up in the mind. We can make
raids and excursions into the wild, but it has to be from
well kept strongholds.*[1]

WHEN Robert Frost disembarked from the SS *Olympic* in New
York City on his return from England in November of 1928, a
series of previously scheduled engagements awaited him, and
so he could not accompany his wife and daughter to South
Shaftsbury. As soon as he had started them toward home, he
went to Baltimore to give a talk before a convention of teachers.
Then he journeyed even farther South to give a reading of his
poems at the North Carolina College for Women, in Greensboro.[2] On his return trip he stopped in New York City long
enough to autograph several copies of his newly published
West-Running Brook, so that they could be wrapped in the
office of his publisher and mailed to his friends. Early in December, when he finally reached South Shaftsbury, he was
forced to confront some extremely delicate family problems
involving the separate lives of his three daughters.

Marjorie had decided, not too suddenly, that she wanted to
leave home and start a course which would train her to become
a registered nurse. A year earlier, when she spent several
weeks as a patient in the Johns Hopkins Hospital, she was
impressed by the school for nurses there, and now she wished
to attend it.[3] Even as her parents hadn't dared to take her to
Europe and hadn't dared not to, so they now decided that her
persistent desire to undertake a strenuous nurse-training course
must be given more weight than their own doubts whether she
had the strength to stand under the requirements. They finally
gave their permission. She made application, and was admitted
to the Johns Hopkins Nurse Training School in February 1929.

Irma, married two years and the mother of a son, wanted a divorce from John Paine Cone. When the bride and groom had left Franconia for Kansas immediately after their marriage in the fall of 1927, they seemed so well suited to each other that her father had felt certain of the prophecy made for them in his poem entitled "The Master Speed." Irma, in the letters she had written from Kansas, had given no hint that she was expecting a child, but early in the spring of 1928 she suddenly appeared with her baby son at the Stone Cottage in South Shaftsbury. She had run away from her husband, vowing that she would never go back to that isolated wheat farm.[4] Her husband soon followed her, after making arrangements to secure other means of assistance for his parents. He was ready to take up life as a Vermonter if he could thus make Irma happy. For a time, the reconciliation seemed to be complete. Irma's father bought for them a small farm in North Bennington and they went into the poultry business. By the time Irma's parents returned with Marjorie from England, however, Irma was complaining that the marital tensions between herself and John were intolerable.

Lesley's problems were also marital. In Pittsfield, she had met an attractive and wealthy young man named James Dwight Francis, while she was managing her bookshop there. Francis had already been married and divorced, but he seemed ready to settle down. He and Lesley had been married almost secretly while her parents were in England, and her father had been pleased with the news.[5] Before the return from England, Lesley had decided that Dwight was too much of a playboy, and she was now asking for advice about permanently leaving her husband.

Irma and Lesley soon learned that their parents had strong prejudices against divorce, for reasons they explained at length. Frost was particularly sensitive on the subject because his volatile friend Louis Untermeyer had been dragging him through emotional strains of one marital crisis after another for many years. During Frost's visits to New York City he had stayed so often with the Untermeyers that he had suffered innumerable embarrassments caused by the ways in which the couple tortured each other in his presence. Blaming them both, he had sternly urged them to consider the effect their wrangling might have on Richard, their only child, who was an undergraduate at Yale. What annoyed Frost most was the

Greenwich Village manner in which Untermeyer went about his self-consolatory philanderings.[6] Trying at first to use playful banter which could be mixed with fatherly warnings, Frost had tucked one of his earliest warnings into an ambiguous postscript:

"I saw your wife in The Bookman the other day. I thought she was looking very unusual. You must take care of her . . . and she will take care of you. Believe me she has your best interests at heart. I'm sure of it. There, there. I didn't mean to strike the domestic note. You're not to cry. . . . We all know you are happily married. There's no call for a demonstration. It's not yourself as a husband but the institution of marriage you are anxious to make out a case for? I can well believe it, knowing you as I do know you and what you have come through and up out of. But never you worry about the institution of marriage . . ."[7]

Untermeyer, continuing to complain, may have excused his need for extramarital relations by claiming that a wedding ring could be used more cruelly than a ring in the nose of a bull. Sarcastically answering some such complaints, Frost built them into a little dramatic monologue, couplet-rhymed, which permitted the Untermeyer-like speaker in the poem to indulge some insinuatively erotic wordplay. Entitling the poem "The Nose-Ring," he sent it to Untermeyer with the quiet warning, "The Nose-Ring is for you, not particularly for anyone else."[8]

THE NOSE-RING

Honor's a ring in the nose that people give,
But it makes my sensitive nose more sensitive.
It makes me wince when I use my nose for a plow;
Where once I thought all thorns were on branch
and bough,
Every root in the ground is thorny now.
Henceforth it seems I am not to get my girth
By going below the surface of the earth.
But let me get down again to the roots of things
And I will dispense with my honor in rings.[9]

Knowing that Untermeyer was chafing beneath his promises to love-honor-and-obey, Frost nevertheless continued to defend the institution of marriage. Whenever he could find evidence to support his own views on the subject of monogamy he used it: "I recently ran across a biological fact that interested me, as facts go. It establishes exclusiveness much lower down in the scale than you would expect to find it. Exclusiveness in love. Way way down. Exclusively yours, Robert Frost."[10] In his next letter, he was bluntly reproachful:

"Honestly I hope you folks aren't going to pull anything boneheaded. It will be a poor advertisement of my philosophy if it won't keep my most intimate friends from getting unmarried. Think how any foolishness on your part is going to involve me and cut out the cheap talk. That is what I say unto you both."[11]

When Untermeyer informed him that the divorce was unavoidable and that he hoped Frost would forgive him, Frost answered, "Louis, Louis. Don't talk to me about forgiveness. I'm not Peter Rhadamanthus. I've simply felt my natural sorrow that two such good friends of mine as you and Jean should be winding up your affairs. As I said before, I wish I could see you for a day. It couldn't do you any harm. I wouldn't even try to ground you in my philosophy and religion. I'm long since past my confidence in meddling."[12]

Frost's genuine sadness was soon blended with amusement over the inconsistency of Untermeyer's attitude toward marriage. Hastening to Yucatan, for a quick divorce, Untermeyer took with him another poet, Virginia Moore, and married her in Yucatan as soon as he was freed from Jean Starr.[13] It seemed to Frost, however, that the next development in the story came as a tragic consequence of Untermeyer's failure to keep his promises. Approximately two months after the second marriage, Untermeyer's son Richard killed himself in his dormitory room at Yale. Frost, with typical austerity, viewed this death as a punishment the parents had brought on themselves through the self-pitying attempts of each to win Richard's sympathies without considering the effect that such a tug-of-war might have on the boy.[14]

Immediately after Richard's death, Frost and Untermeyer did not keep in touch with each other, but within a few months the newspapers carried the announcement that Untermeyer had divorced Virginia Moore, and reporters who interviewed him quoted his philosophical comments on what he had learned about life. Jean Starr, asking the Frosts if they had heard from Louis, seemed hopeful that they had completely broken their friendship with him. Her questions prompted

Frost to resume his correspondence: "Seems funny for Jean to be asking for you. How much married to you does she think she is? Women are too much for me." He continued, giving some reassurance—and further reproach:

"I was afraid my silence would begin to be misunderstood. If I was more silent with the pen than usual it was because I could think of nothing adequate to say: I was willing to leave consolation and advice to the author of the author of Elmer Gantry, I mean Alfred [Harcourt] the Sloganist. You would have only to call on him to comfort you with slogans and he would touch your various stops as skillfully as if you were the public and he were just what he is. Can't I just hear him inspiring what I see by the papers you have been free to say on the subject of faith in life. Honestly it sounds like office talk. Om Mani Padmi Hum. Which is to say the lotus flower has a center that means something. So has Eugene O'Neill's Great God Brown to anybody who prides himself on living in New York. Come to me if you want to hear some small part of the truth. You are not bad except in the sense that I am bad and a lot of others are bad. Don't mistake me as implying there is no such thing as goodness anymore. You will hear it claimed that esthetics is all there is of ethics. Nothing could be worse thinking, as I could explain to you in full if I had time. There is such a thing as badness. But as I say you are not bad. You are only in Dutch. You haven't been prospered. I'm sorry for that, and you hold my sympathy just so long as you keep from delivering *obiter dicta* to the newsmongers. Don't don't say things like that about faith in life where I can come across them because they simply bust me all up in the seat of philosophy. You are not responsible I know in the circumstances and I wouldn't want you to be responsible. I should think less of you if you were responsible. Only if you love me for Christ's sake find some more poetic way of going irresponsible than in dub sophistries. I'm hard on you—too hard. But you've got to stand this and more from me. . . ."[15]

Frost was the one who had to stand more, and it came in the form of the announcement that Untermeyer was remarrying Jean Starr, that they were going to Germany for their second honeymoon, that expenses would be covered through the process of writing a travel book on the Black Forest, and that when they returned they would move out of New York City to a farm in the Adirondacks. They returned from their second honeymoon before Frost could catch up with Unter-meyer and scold him again:

"How much better if you had been a staid orthodox Jew and never had run wild after a super-wisdom that doesn't exist. You are back now where you started from and not one bit improved in mind or spirit. The whole experiment has been a waste of time and energy. You haven't found out anything that you didn't know before, that we didn't all know before: and I won't listen to you if you say you have. That's the one thing I can't stand from a person in your predicament. For my sake, if you still care for me, don't talk about having been chastened or having profited in any way. You've lost—time, if nothing else. I've lost. We've all lost. . . ."

As he continued this letter, he tried to warn against the romantic notion of looking deep into the heart and writing poems from the profundity of personal sorrow:

"I'd impose it as a penalty on you that you shouldn't wax literary on what you have been through—turn it to account in any way. I won't if you won't. It must be kept away down under the surface where the great griefs belong. I don't mean you must stop writing, but you must confine yourself to every-thing else in the world but your own personal experience. I beg of you. Honestly. The thought would be too much for me of all three of you putting up a holler in verse about it all. The decencies forbid you should score off it. Write a court drama of the IVth Dynasty. I should think this was the point where you have almost got to leave off being a subjective poet. That is if you care of me."[16]

Back of this warning was Frost's knowledge that Unter-meyer and Jean Starr had already made literary capital of their marital anguish. In the first *Miscellany of American Poetry* Jean Starr had published a suicidal lyric beginning, "Take me under thy wing, O Death," and Untermeyer had fol-lowed it up, a few pages later, with five autobiographical quatrains of his own, entitled "A Marriage." Frost also knew that two of the three had subsequently put up "a holler in verse about it all," when Jean Starr and Virginia Moore had publicly conducted a poetic hair-pull, not long after Unter-meyer-as-husband had first changed hands. Frost had given his own version of this event in a letter to Edward Davison, who could be counted on to understand and enjoy it:

"I've just been telling old Carl [Sandburg] the Ballad-monger, that when he gets tired of collecting other peoples ballads and turns to writing ballads of his own, I have a subject for him right out of our own level of society that beats Frankie and Albert to a pulp. Three poets make the triangle. The girl he left behind him comes out in a poem in a book published by Macmillan (the best poem she ever wrote) and insults him with having no wool on the top of his head which is just where the wool ought to grow. The other girl comes right back at her in the poem in The Saturday Review of Henry Canby, the burden of which is that it may be true he has no hair on his head at his age, but anyway he has hair in his ears, a thicket of hair in his ears—so now! For a man of his sense of humor I should think such goings on would break any spell he was under. I should think it would kill him of laughter in the third degree. Poor man. God send that the worst is over for him."[17]

The worst may have been over, but there was plenty of unpleasantness ahead, for Untermeyer, in the realm of marital difficulties, and even before those developments occurred, he was subjected to further scoldings from his New England friend:

"My judgment on you is that you have wronged yourself in all this business of alternating between two wives. You have been acting against your nature under pressure of the bad smart talk you have listened to and learned to share in in the society you have cultivated in your own New York salons (so to call them). I've heard the mocking when I have been there and heard you lend yourself to it till I was ready to bet what would happen. None of it was right or wise or real. What I dread most now is that you will go on the assumption that, though it was folly and landed you in tragedy, it was on the way somewhere and somehow prepared you for the greater and fuller life. Shut up. To hell with such comforts. It was all time and energy lost, as I have said before.

"You have merely talked yourself out of your senses. I refuse to admit you were ravished out of your senses. You talked yourself out of them in your own parlor. For I heard you. Now you are yourself again by sheer weight of the honesty in your bones. Talk no more—unless you can talk unclever, unsophisticated, simple goodness. You tempt me to soak you in milk to renew your innocence. The funny positions people can talk themselves into in a lifetime of try-it-on talk."[18]

As further guidance and illumination, Frost offered a little parable drawn from life:

"Someone you know said to me in drink the other day:

"Dyou blieve im marriage? after miwife died I got mix tup with a woman wanted me tmarry her. Ver attractive woman y understan. Had a child by her. Wouldn't marry her. Didn't want to. Think I ought to marry her?

"Does she still want you to?

"Shdoes—innaway. D you think ought to have married her before?

"Has it caused her much pain—your not marrying her?

"Sidible.

"Well we have to consider whether decent marriage isn't a provision of the ages for causing the least possible pain between the sexes. The least possible is all I say.

"Shwants to marry someone elsenow.

"I thought you said she wanted to marry you.

"Shwants to marry me first. Then get a divorce n marry nother man.

"I don't understand yet.

"Marry me make tall reglar. Xplain it to him sos she won't have tell him. Thinks he'll like it better.

"Wants you to marry her for his sake.

"S bout it.

"Louis Louis very few people that leave the good old folkways can keep from getting all mixed up in the mind. We can make raids and excursions into the wild, but it has to be from well kept strongholds. I think you think so now. Let's drop the whole subject."[19]

This was a subject which Untermeyer could never drop. Within a few months, he had divorced Jean Starr for a second time—and he subsequently married two more women, with the result that Frost gradually became detached and humorous in his attitude toward his friend's quaint love life. Once, while passing through New York City, Frost had just enough time between trains to telephone Jean Starr and ask how she was. Miserable, and she did hope Louis's new marriage might not last long; she counted on Frost to help her in any way he could. Yes, he said, of course. In fact, he was already working on a scheme in her behalf: he thought he might be able to arrange that Louis would marry Jean Starr every other time.[20]

While these doings were still in process, Frost was in no

mood to sympathize with his daughters for their haste in having tied themselves to men they so quickly wished to discard. Once again he tried to advise, and this time it seemed as though his counsel would be of help, particularly when his views were strongly reinforced by those of Mrs. Frost. In the end, he failed again. The precarious marriages did last some years more—Irma's much longer than Lesley's—and yet each ended in divorce.

ENCOURAGING YOUNGER POETS

"I don't encourage them," he said, referring to the under-graduates of Michigan and Amherst, to whom he has been an elder companion. "Let them encourage themselves. If the thing isn't self-driven it will get nowhere."[1]

ON HIS WAY back to South Shaftsbury from Maryland and North Carolina, shortly after his return from England in the fall of 1928, Robert Frost was interviewed by a New York City reporter who asked him if he would be willing to predict which of the younger poets might achieve prominence. He named five: Robinson Jeffers, Raymond Holden, Archibald MacLeish, Joseph Moncure March, and Stephen Vincent Benét. Had he helped any of his own students to get a firm start as a poet? No, he supposed not. In fact, he was doubtful about the value of trying to ease the ordeal which youngsters had to pass through if they were to establish themselves. Nothing he had said or done, nothing he had failed to say or do, was likely to have any lasting effect on the making or unmaking of a poet. He supposed he had given some help merely by employing what might be called reverse encouragement. He had frequently challenged their powers of creativity and endurance:

"I would often tell them that their first work was rotten, and the only question was: Did they have the guts to go on? And they probably didn't have. They'd get a good job or get married and forget about their poetry. Most of them disappear. They can't take the punishment, they don't want to take the punishment. Many of them have a sense of enjoyment in being artistic at college, in feeling superior and Bohemian, and they get nowhere."[2]

But hadn't he received help from his own teachers when he was just getting started with poetry? No, he thought not:

"I never owed anything to a teacher and I don't want anyone to owe anything to me."[3]

He considered young Joseph Moncure March a good example of how any poet might get started. While he had been an undergraduate at Amherst, March had wasted some time in trying to write like Frost, and then he had gradually discovered his own idiom. His fresh narrative poems which had been published in books entitled *The Wild Party* and *The Set-up* had already made reviewers pay attention to him, and Frost was certain that March would continue to improve.[4]

A few weeks later, when Frost returned to Amherst following his various bouts with family problems at South Shaftsbury, he kept talking about his hopes for the future of Joseph Moncure March. Some undergraduates asked him to conduct one of the regular faculty-student poetry discussions, and he said he would give them a reading from "an Amherst poet," although he refused to name the poet in advance.[5] Those who mistakenly guessed that he would read from his own poems were surprised to hear him offer the entire text of March's narrative poem, "The Set-up." It is the story of a Negro prize fighter, Pansy Jones, whose ambitions and abilities are crookedly misused by his manager. In a match he is expected to lose, Pansy does not understand the arrangement and knocks out his opponent. The adherents of the loser, seeking revenge, pursue Pansy into a subway and push him under the wheels of an approaching express. Frost, in his comments, claimed that March had successfully invoked sympathy for this Negro who had chosen his own ways to aspire toward his own concept of noble heroism; March had thus found fresh wherewithal for dramatizing unfairness in human experience at any social level. Some of the students found the "grim reality" of the poem "almost overwhelmingly disagreeable," but they were convinced that this Amherst alumnus deserved special consideration among the new poets. Although Frost found fault with March's attempts to convert picturesque slang and profanity into poetry, he concluded by saying he believed March would eventually become an important literary figure.[6]

Frost had actually done much to help March with his poetry, and there were many other students at Amherst, Bowdoin, Dartmouth, Michigan, and Wesleyan whom Frost had assisted far more than he was willing to admit. Some of them continued to call on him, at his home, long after their graduations, and they always found him willing to stay with them in conversations about poetry late into any night. Many kept sending him manuscripts, only a few of which he read and acknowledged in letters which combined firmness with gentleness. Occasionally he encouraged a promising group of undergraduates to do more than contribute their poems to the campus literary magazines. Once he wrote an introduction to a volume of poems gathered and published by some of his favorite Dartmouth undergraduates, and his remarks therein were gentle:

"No one given to looking under-ground in spring can have failed to notice how a bean starts its growth from the seed. Now the manner of a poet's germination is less like that of a bean in the ground than a waterspout at sea. He has to begin as a cloud of all the other poets he ever read. That can't be helped. And first the cloud reaches down toward the water from above and then the water reaches up toward the cloud from below and finally cloud and water join together to roll as one pillar between heaven and earth. The base of water he picks up from below is of course all the life he ever lived outside of books.

"These, then, are the three figures of the waterspout and the first is about as far as the poet doomed to die young in everyone of us usually gets. He brings something down from Dowson, Yeats, Morris, Masefield, or the Imagists (often a long way down), but lifts little or nothing up. If he were absolutely certain to do as doomed and die young, he would hardly be worth getting excited over in college or elsewhere. But you can't be too careful about whom you will ignore in this world. Cases have been known of his refusing at the last minute to abdicate the breast in favor of the practical and living on to write lyric like Landor until ninety.

"Right in this book he will be found surviving into the second figure of the waterspout, and by several poems and many scattered lines, even into the third figure. . . .

"We are here getting a long way with poetry, considering all there is against it in school and college. The poet, as everyone knows, must strike his individual note sometime between the ages of fifteen and twenty-five. He may hold it a long time, or a short time, but it is then he must strike it or never. School and college have been conducted with the almost express purpose of keeping him busy with something else till the danger of his ever creating anything is past. Their motto has been, the muses find some mischief still for idle hands to do. No one is asking to see poetry regularized in courses and directed by coaches like sociology and football. It must remain a theft to retain its savor. But it does seem as if it could be a little more connived at than it is. I for one should be in favor of the colleges setting the expectation of poetry forward a few years (the way the clocks are set forward in May), so as to get the young poets started earlier in the morning before the freshness dries off. Just setting the expectation of poetry forward might be all that was needed to give us our proportioned number of poets to Congressmen."[7]

Among the contributors to this volume of Dartmouth verse was a student named Kimball Flaccus, who eventually abandoned poetry for scholarship, but while he continued to write verse he sent Frost occasional samplings, in and out of print. One of these offerings inspired Frost to give more than casual encouragements:

"The book has come and I have read your poems first. They are good. They have loveliness—they surely have that. They are carried high. What you long for is in them. You wish the world better than it is, more poetical. You are that kind of poet. I would rate as the other kind. I wouldn't give a cent to see the world, the United States or even New York, made better. I want them left just as they are for me to make—poetical on paper. I don't ask anything done to them that I don't do to them myself. I'm a mere selfish artist most of the time. I have no quarrel with the material. The grief will be simply if I can't transmute it into poems. I don't want the world made safer for poetry or easier. To hell with it. That is its own lookout. Let it stew in its own materialism. No, not to Hell with it. Let it hold its position while I do it in art. My whole anxiety is for myself as a performer. Am I any good? That's what I'd like to know and all I need to know. I wonder which kind of poet is more numerous, your kind or my kind. There should have been a question in the census-taking to determine. Not that it should bother us. We can be friends across the difference. You'll have me watching you. We must meet again and have a talk about poetry and nothing but poetry. The great length of this letter is the measure of my thanks for the book . . ."[8]

To Frost, there was always the delicate question of where to draw the line between too much encouraging and too much discouraging a beginner. He tried to make each student find his own way, to liberate him so that his education would provide enjoyment of his own artistic freedom to develop his own manner of excellence. He was sure that such an excellence had to begin with the simple process of discovering new analogies, new metaphors: putting two and two together, out of space and time, in ways nobody had previously thought of. He liked to call it a process of connecting the unconnected, and such insight depended on the ability of the individual to disconnect himself from others so that he could have the freedom of his own meditations, away from anybody's company. Frost tried to treat his poetically inclined students in such ways that they would gradually feel that his purpose was to leave them alone, even to force them into isolation: "Give him that terribly abandoned feeling, left to the horrors of his own thoughts and conscience."[9] These were the circumstances which, he knew from his own experience, forced the poet in on his own meditations concerning possibilities.

There were times when combinations of harshness and encouragement were calculated to have a healthy shock-effect. One of the Amherst students who showed promise was Clifford Bradgon, '28, who had scarcely left Amherst before beginning to doubt his capabilities. Frost answered:

"What you need is someone to be severe with you, someone intimate enough to know how much punishment you can take and still live.

"If you want my sympathy you shouldnt have told me you had written a good story and almost had it published. What more do you want so soon after getting loose? I want to see you fight it out where you are. Your good beginning gives me hope for you. You've got more chance in my opinion teaching some of the time than you would have reading bad manuscript for a publisher in New York. But literature takes courage and endurance. It takes foolhardiness. The wife of a distinguished British poet told me this summer it was not for married men. Their wives I suppose she meant cut off their hair so they couldnt carry gates. You have to stop to consider. Maybe thats what you are doing in your letter. The road ahead scares you. Well you know best what you can stand. But I should have thought you had done very well so far. You evidently have gifts. I should be inclined to bet on you. I dont set my heart on you, mind you. I can get all the disappointment I need in life setting my heart on myself. . . ."[10]

Sometimes a student who asked for advice was a complete stranger. One of these was Burrhus Frederic Skinner, a senior at Hamilton College, in the Class of 1926, who sent manuscripts of short stories with his request that Frost say whether he found enough promise in them to warrant Skinner's continuing. Even a stranger was honored with a reply if his writing showed something unusual, and young Mr. Skinner received one of Frost's best replies:

"My long delay with these stories has given you time to think of some things about them for yourself, alternating between doubt and confidence. It has probably done you good: so I won't apologize.

"You know I save myself from perfunctory routine criticism of ordinary college writing on purpose to see if I can't really help now and then someone like you in earnest with the art. Two or more times a year I make a serious attempt to get to the bottom of his work with someone like you. But it's all the good it does. I always come a long way short of getting down into it as far as the writer gets himself. Of course! You ask me if there is enough in the stories to warrant your going on. I wish I knew the answer to that half as well as you probably know it by heart. Right at this moment you are very likely setting your determination to go on, regardless of anything I say, and provided only you can find within a reasonable time someone to buy and read you. I'd never quarrel with that spirit. I've a sneaking sympathy with it.

"My attempt to get to the bottom of a fellow writer's stuff this time put this into my head: All that makes a writer is the ability to write strongly and directly from some unaccountable and almost invincible personal prejudice like Stevenson's in favor of all being as happy as kings no matter if consumptive, or Hardy's against God for the blunder of sex, or Sinclair Lewis's against small American towns or Shakespeare's, mixed, at once against and in favor of life itself. I take it that everybody has the prejudice and spends some time feeling for it to speak and write from. But most people end as they begin by acting out the prejudices of other people.

"There are real niceties of observation you've got here and you've done 'em to a shade. 'The Laugh' has the largest value. That's the one you show most as caring in. You see I want you to care. I don't want you to be academic about it—a writer of exercises. Of course, not too expressly, overtly caring. You'll have to search yourself here. You know best whether you are haunted with any impatience about what other people see or don't see. That will be you if you are you. I'm inclined to say you are. But you have the final say. I wish you'd tell me how you come out on thinking it over—if it isn't too much trouble—sometime.

"I ought to say you have the touch of art. The work is clean run. You're worth twice anyone else I have seen in prose this year."

Frost, ending the letter to Mr. Skinner with such praise, had scarcely signed his name to it when he thought of another way to explain his feeling about all "that makes a writer." He added it, in a postcript:

"Belief, Belief. You've got to augment my belief in life or people mightily or cross it uglily. I'm awfully sure of this tonight."[11]

Of all the students Frost met, one who augmented his belief mightily by showing a determined capacity for disconnecting himself from society for the purpose of cultivating poetic growth was that young man who had hung around the edge of the campus at the University of Michigan and yet had resisted the academic: Wade Van Dore. Modeling his life, more and more, after Thoreau's experiment as described in *Walden*, Van Dore sometimes stole away into the wilderness and stayed away for weeks and even months. Occasionally he sent Frost new poems, with accounts of his latest peregrinations, and Frost could rarely resist answering in ways such as this:

"Two of these last four you sent are thrust home, 'High Heaven' and 'The Seeker.' 'The Silence' and 'The Moment before and after Moonrise' are less merciless. You are finding out. You are going to do it—if you dont let up on yourself—if you dont get too conceited to watch yourself and everybody else who ever attempted it. Dont miss any tricks or arts, traits or ingredients. Look and then look some more. It's your funeral. Little I can do to help except say 'em and see 'em. I'm with you and I'm your friend."[12]

When Van Dore showed too much eagerness to get his poems into print, and wrote to tell of those who might give him a hand in finding a publisher. Frost tried to slow him down:

"It is pleasant to have those folks out there so kind to you. But remember nothing counts but the sheer goodness of your own thought and art. Weight is what you must achieve to make a place for yourself in the ruck of rhymsters. The visitors at the Bread Loaf School of English made a great fuss discovering a certain young Charles Malam last summer and already he is out with a book, the only really good poem in which I enclose. From that culture spot he might have spread out pretty far. Whats now to prevent his spreading out from his other and worse poems."[13]

As soon as Van Dore really had enough poems from which to select the makings for a first volume, Frost helped him select the best ones and found a publisher for him. When the book appeared, under the title *Far Lake*, it bore this dedication: "To the sunlight on the pines near Far Lake; to the sound of the aspen leaves at Shebandowan Lake; and to Robert Frost." Among the poems which Frost advised Van Dore to hold back was one entitled "The Echo," which the older poet criticized as being merely sentimental:

Made mellow by a wall of trees
My call came swiftly back to me.
My word the forest would not take
Came bounding back across the lake.
Through outer trees to shade grown black
I peered and saw, like strips of snow
That form in rocks the ages crack
The trunks of birches, half aglow.
Again I called, and now I stirred
A fearful bird to swiftly fly.
Far off I heard his angry scream,
But not a gladdened human cry.
It seemed I could not overthrow
The brooding barrier of the trees.
My voice grew swift, my call more keen,
But always backward came the word
Of it to me, that seemed to sigh
For him I sought, for all reply.[14]

Part of what seemed unsatisfactory and sentimental to Frost about "The Echo" and other poems by Van Dore was the recurrent unwillingness to accept the loneliness of that wilderness life he claimed to like best. Another poem of Van Dore's, entitled "Man Alone," contained these lines:

If he should loudly call, then stand and wait
Until the sound had traveled far and made
A voice reply, he'd know the forest held
No mate for him. An echo would reply,
Giving him back his lonely call and word.
A deer might start. . . .

*   *   *

. . . But the day would fade,
And the room too large for one man would dim
Before he could grasp with his working mind
One thought or dream to ease his troubled heart.[15]

Frost was occasionally inspired to answer, in a poem of his own making, a particular attitude he found annoying in the work of another poet. Van Dore apparently provided one such inspiration, in that Frost grew impatient with Van Dore's wistful attitude of asking nature for something nature could not give. One sought the solitude of wilderness, Frost believed, to make the most of it in terms of natural wonders, whatever they might be, without cultivating a "troubled heart" over such companionship as it would obviously fail to provide. His ironic reply to Van Dore was first entitled "Making the Most of It." Later, the title was shortened to "The Most of It":

He thought he kept the universe alone;
For all the voice in answer he could wake
Was but the mocking echo of his own
From some tree-hidden cliff across the lake.
Some morning from the boulder-broken beach
He would cry out on life, that what it wants
Is not its own love back in copy speech,
But counter-love, original response.
And nothing ever came of what he cried
Unless it was the embodiment that crashed
In the cliff's talus on the other side,
And then in the far-distant water splashed,
But after a time allowed for it to swim,
Instead of proving human when it neared
And someone else additional to him,
As a great buck it powerfully appeared,
Pushing the crumpled water up ahead,

And landed pouring like a waterfall,
And stumbled through the rocks with horny tread,
And forced the underbrush—and that was all.[16]

Such a poem, stimulated by the intensity of Frost's reaction against an attitude taken by someone else, in or out of verse, did not often occur to Frost. Usually, he found release in outspoken and sometimes vituperative complaints. Yet with undergraduates and former students who were still trying to establish themselves, he seemed to remember his own long years of apprenticeship and of neglect from others so strongly that he was inclined to give them support along with criticism. Lawrence Conrad, friend of Wade Van Dore's in Ann Arbor, and still a favorite of Frost's, had launched his literary career with the publication in 1924 of what Frost called a free-verse novel, entitled *Temper*, a story based on the young man's own experiences as a laborer in the Ford factory in Detroit. He became a teacher, moved from one school to another, continued writing, and then had difficulty in completing his second novel. Frost read the manuscript of it, tried to make suggestions for change, read the revision, and finally offered a new approach to Conrad's immediate literary problem:

"In my opinion you might make a mistake to care too much about this novel right now. Turn to something else for the moment and see if in picking it up again you wont see in a flash some day just the way through your material in a story's easy curve. You *must* know what I mean. I wont say this isnt a powerful book in many respects. But it has suffered too much from your mighty efforts to pull it together and into something. Maybe theres enough stuff in it, good thought, observation and writing to make up for the deficiency. You have to be the judge. And if you say so we will make our stand on the book as it is and I will use what influence I may have to jam it through with some publisher. The question is are we quite ready for the jamming tactics. Dont you get over-heroic about your predicament. You are all right. You have done some splendid work there. There are all sorts of makings shown. Only— only I want that easy rise and fall. And I want a little less invention still—or a little less implausible invention. You still will tell me something now and then that I just cant believe. Strip to the indubitable. You mustnt mind my insistence. Gee you can afford to listen—with all you have ahead of you."[17]

Just how much literary education Frost might manage to impart, in all these genuinely sincere and sympathetic efforts to be of help, he continuously refused to estimate. His only certainty was that if an undergraduate had been led, through the study of literature, to reconsider his attitude toward the important uses of analogy and metaphor in any form of human response to experience, such a student could use this knowledge to advantage in any profession he might later choose. He had tried to find different ways of talking about this topic, and of extending it, on many occasions subsequent to his talk on "Metaphor" at Bryn Mawr College.[18] When the Alumni Council at Amherst invited him to address them on any subject he liked, he entitled his talk "Education by Poetry."

He began by saying that he could name several colleges where the study of poetry was barred. He supposed that such a ruling took the onus off poetry completely by keeping it from being misused. In some schools and colleges where poetry was assigned it was used primarily for the study of syntax, language, or technique. To Frost, however, it seemed that it could better be read for purposes of discovering how beautifully enthusiasm could be brought under artistic control; enthusiasm "taken through the prism of the intellect and spread on the screen in a color, all the way from hyperbole at one end—or overstatement, at one end—to understatement at the other end. It is a long strip of dark lines and many colors. Such enthusiasm is one object of all teaching in poetry. . . . I would be willing to throw away everything else but that: enthusiasm tamed by metaphor. . . . I do not think anybody ever knows the discreet use of metaphor, his own and other people's, the discreet handling of metaphor, unless he has been properly educated in poetry."

Continuing, he tried to suggest the range and scope of metaphor, inside and outside formal poetic utterance:

"Poetry begins in trivial metaphors, pretty metaphors, 'grace' metaphors, and goes on to the profoundest thinking that we have. Poetry provides the one permissible way of saying one thing and meaning another. People say, 'Why don't you say what you mean?' We never do that, do we, being all of us too much poets. We like to talk in parables and in hints and in indirections—whether from diffidence or some other instinct. I have wanted in late years to go further and further in making metaphor the whole of thinking. I find some one now and then to agree with me that all thinking, except mathematical thinking is metaphorical. ..."

He would not make exception for scientific thinking, and to demonstrate his point he reviewed certain scientific uses of metaphor, starting with the Greeks and coming down to the Einsteinian theory of relativity and even down to Niels Bohr on the structure of the atom. Having mocked some of the scientific uses of metaphor, he went on to praise the uses of it in religion and philosophy:

"Greatest of all attempts to say one thing in terms of another is the philosophical attempt to say matter in terms of spirit, or spirit in terms of matter, to make the final unity. That is the greatest attempt that ever failed. We stop just short there. But it is the height of poetry, the height of all thinking, the height of all poetic thinking, that attempt to say matter in terms of spirit and spirit in terms of matter. It is wrong to call anybody a materialist simply because he tries to say spirit in terms of matter, as if that were a sin. Materialism is not the attempt to say all in terms of matter. The only materialist—be he poet, teacher, scientist, politician, or statesman—is the man who gets lost in his material without a gathering metaphor to throw it into shape and order. He is the lost soul."

He had warned his friends that as he grew older he seemed more and more likely to become a preacher, and at this moment he did not hesitate to say some things more openly than he had said them before, concerning the all-encompassing importance of poetry to him:

"The person who gets close enough to poetry, he is going to know more about the word *belief* than anybody else knows, even in religion nowadays. There are two or three places where we know belief outside of religion. One of them is at the age of fifteen to twenty, in our self-belief. A young man knows more about himself than he is able to prove to anyone. He has no knowledge that anybody else will accept as knowledge. In his foreknowledge he has something that is going to believe itself into fulfilment, into acceptance.

"There is another belief like that, the belief in someone else, a relationship of two that is going to be believed into fulfilment. That is what we are talking about in our novels, the belief of love. And the disillusionment that the novels are full of is simply the disillusionment from disappointment in that belief. That belief can fail, of course.

"Then there is a literary belief. Every time a poem is written, every time a short story is written, it is written not by cunning, but by belief. The beauty, the something, the little charm of the thing to be, is more felt than known. . . .

"Now I think—I happen to think—that those three beliefs that I speak of, the self-belief, the love-belief, and the art-belief, are all closely related to the God-belief, that the belief in God is a relationship you enter into with Him to bring about the future. . . ."[19]

The members of the Alumni Council at Amherst, watching Frost and listening to his thoughts concerning the importance to him of education by poetry, were more convinced than ever that Amherst College should continue to afford the luxury of having this man on campus not as a regular teacher but simply as a poet in residence; as a man whose attitudes toward the close relationship between art and life must have a fertilizing effect on the hearts and minds of the undergraduates. One of them began his praise by writing, "You did a most difficult thing last Saturday. You captured completely the people of your own Amherst family."[20]

A FARM FOR MYSELF

I bought a farm for myself for Christmas. One hundred and fifty three acres in all, fifty in woods. The house a poor little cottage of five rooms, two ordinary fireplaces, and one large kitchen fireplace all in one central chimney as it was in the beginning.[1]

THERE was a special fascination, for Frost, in any country real estate with a "for sale" sign posted on it. He always seemed to be looking for a new farm he could buy at a reasonable price, particularly if the house was attractively old and the view panoramic. He could be unintentionally flattering in the way he entered a farmyard on foot to ask the owner how much it would take to buy the place, what the total acreage was, how many acres were cultivated, how many tons of hay could be harvested, how many head of cattle the pasture would stand, and how reliable the water supply was. This game of exploring possibilities was never merely a game. He was always quite serious in imagining how he might renovate house and barn, on any good property that was available, so that the buildings would suit his needs.

In South Shaftsbury, one of his favorite walking companions who understood these curiosities about real estate was the bearded mail clerk and beekeeper Charles Monroe. The many articles which Monroe published in the Bennington *Banner* plainly revealed that he was well acquainted with the history of the region. He knew the owner of every outlying farm in the district, and he made it easy for Frost to meet and talk with people who were ready to sell, even though they had made no public statement of such intent. Usually, when these two men went walking, they headed up into the foothills of the Green Mountains, to the east of the village, knowng that before they went far they would have several choices of back roads. Or, if time was short and they were forced to settle for a quick view, they would go no more than two miles to the eastward of the village before climbing the bare dome of an isolated hill known as Buck's Cobble. The prospect from there to the northward, through the Battenkill River Valley, gave them a splendid chance to study a variety of forest-covered shoulders and peaks in the Taconic Range and in the Green Mountains, as far north and east as Equinox, in Manchester.

It seemed as though an authority like Charles Monroe ought to be able to say where Frost could buy a farm with a view almost as good as that. He could and did. Halfway back to the village from Buck's Cobble a little dirt road turned off to the left, and up that road perhaps a quarter of a mile stood a small eighteenth-century house built with an eye to the view up the valley and, westward, far into New York State. Or, if one wished to keep climbing hillside fields beyond the clutter of barns and sheds and corncribs surrounding that old farmhouse, one could gain other views to the south and west. There was also a pretty stand of paper birches right on the edge of one high field in the 150-odd acres of that farm. Was the farm for sale? Well, it might be. (The wrinkles around Charles Monroe's eyes always grew deeper and seemed to make his eyes twinkle whenever he implied more than he said.) It just happened that Charles Hawkins, brother of Monroe's wife and father of Wales Monroe Hawkins, had picked up that farm a few years ago in the settlement of a long-unpaid debt. Since then, Hawkins had sold it, but the chances were good that if Frost liked it well enough to offer maybe $5,000 for it, he could pick it up in a reasonably short time.

Frost and Monroe set a day when they could take a leisurely walk around the boundaries of that farm, tucked away out of sight in a high hollow or gully between two ridges of land— as though the original builder had thought of ways to protect himself from northeast and southwest winter gales. Frost liked the coziness of this little and ancient house, snuggling down in this hillside pocket without losing the best view of all. The two men walked the entire boundary of the property, all the way up behind the beautiful fieldside stand of birches, and before they had completed the circuit Frost was ready to buy.

He was serious, and he had reasons. Since the fall of 1923, when Carol had married and had brought Lillian to live at the Stone Cottage, Frost had really been without a farm of his own. He had given the bride and groom that farm as a wedding present, but without immediately realizing that something was wrong about continuing to live in a house one had given away. There was no need to feel crowded out, even after the birth of Prescott, but there had been a growing sense that the young people ought to have that home for themselves, without the interference or even presence of their elders. In addition, so long as the Stone Cottage remained the gathering place for the grown-up children—Marjorie, Lesley, Irma—the frequent noise and hubbub put a strain on Frost's nerves and made him want to find a farm of his own to which he could steal away. The newly considered farm was only a mile and a half from Carol's farm, if one went by road; only three-quarters of a mile distant if one walked crosslots through hillside fields and pastures. It was not nearly so far away as the Shingled Cottage in North Bennington, which the Frosts had rented in the summer of 1927, and which they rented again in the summer of 1928, staying there until they went abroad with Marjorie. As soon as Frost found that the owner of the farm in the hillside gully was willing to sell, and that he could give the tenants of the farm a six-month notice at any time, all that was needed was $5,000 in ready cash. Frost could count on much more than that from Henry Holt and Company, as royalty earnings from *West-Running Brook.* Moving rapidly, he was soon able to boast:

"I bought a farm for myself for Christmas. One hundred and fifty three acres in all, fifty in woods. The house a poor little cottage of five rooms, two ordinary fireplaces, and one large kitchen fireplace all in one central chimney as it was in the beginning. The central chimney is the best part of it—that and the woods. . . . We have no trout brook, but there is a live spring that I am told should be made into a trout pond. There is a small grove of white paper birches doubling daylight. The woods are a little too far from the house. I must bring them nearer by the power of music like Amphion or Orpheus. . . ."[2]

As soon as the property was his own, Frost made a new game out of going there as often as he could, puttering around while making plans to tear down useless outbuildings and to renovate the house. Not long after he went to Amherst, in January of 1929, he began to talk of his hope that he could make a mutually advantageous arrangement with his friend the poet Wade Van Dore, who had often worked briefly as a farm hand. Before the Frosts returned from Amherst, Van Dore stopped in at South Shaftsbury, surveyed the newly purchased farm, and learned from Carol what changes were planned. Frost wrote Van Dore on the third of April 1929:

"I wonder what you would say to taking charge of my farm for a year. You would have to keep house for yourself entirely and you would be alone up the gulch. The work could be as much or as little as you cared to make it. There would be tree-planting and tree-moving, there would be tearing down some of the old buildings we want to get rid of, there would be some trench digging and stream damming, there would be some repairing and doing over of the old house . . . and there would be some improving of the road in to attend to. There would be or could be; as I say you could decide for yourself how much of anything you cared to give time to. The first thing to do would be to fix up one room in the house homelike for you to live in. I dont mean the house is open to the weather. People are now living in it. But I expect them to leave it somewhat delapidated and anyway of course empty of furniture. I would pay you forty cents an hour (or more if you say so) for such time as you worked. You could take all the time you pleased for your writing. . . . I shall be around more or less, puttering and overseeing the carpenter's work on the house. (There will be a bathroom to put in.) We'll be living in our old house [the Shingled Cottage] when in S. Shaftsbury at all. Perhaps we might get round to spend a month in the house up the gulch in the late fall if I am not too buried in my own writing. I want a fearfully carefree year. . . ."[3]

Van Dore accepted the offer, and made plans to move in as caretaker and handyman as soon as the house was vacated. Before the Frosts could return to South Shaftsbury after finishing their duties at Amherst, in the spring of 1929, Frost made a different proposition to another fellow artist who needed help. J. J. Lankes, whose woodcuts had been used to illustrate *New Hampshire* and *West-Running Brook*, had twice visited the Frosts at the Stone Cottage in South Shaftsbury. Having moved from New York State to Virginia, he had recently complained that he needed to get away from tensions in his own home long enough to complete the cutting of twenty blocks already ordered. Frost wanted to give him assistance: "My notion would be for you to hang on there and come up and camp out on our land in the summer. You could build yourself a shack out of some of the material of the buildings we are going to tear down."[4] When Lankes showed enough interest to ask for more information, Mrs. Frost wrote at length, explaining that most of the carpentry and overhauling of the house would be completed by the first of July, that he could have rooms to himself if he were willing to rough it, that Van Dore would be there for company, and that the Frosts did not expect to move in until the first of October.[5] Lankes accepted, and shortly after the first of July he moved into what Frost began calling "The Gully House" where Van Dore was already living and working.

The two artists, not previously acquainted, soon began to annoy each other. Lankes, notoriously cantankerous and quick to complain, was not convinced that he could get his work done. After less than a week he wrote to his wife, "Just now 3 stonemasons are working, 1 teamster, two plumbers . . . then there is Wade. Altogether not a quiet place. I've been lending a hand . . . unloading stone, doing a little mowing— and sech. Frost comes every day (except Sunday—he does not show up at all). He always comes into the studio and work is impossible for the talk. . . ."[6] Frost, made uncomfortable by the tension between the two men, sketched the activities:

"My farm is fast going back to wilderness. . . . Give it a year or two more unpastured and I doubt if it will ever be overtaken. . . . Our barns are coming down little by little, a board at a time as the mood comes over Wade our poet in labour—at, I mean. And as the barns come down the view comes out. Our trickle . . . has held its own through the drought with pristine vitality. Some are in favor of calling the farm The Trickle. Marjorie wants it called Nine Barns in memory of the barns it once had. But Prescott has become accustomed to The Gully, and one hates to undeceive a child. . . .

"Lankes is over at the Gully camping out. But I am afraid we are not giving him just the company he wants in Wade Van Dore. Wade has a good deal of the Wobbly in him. He is burly, but he has a principled objection to work and the courage and ingenuity to dodge it. Lankes has a family of four to work for and Wade's emancipation rouses his wrath and jealousy. Also I'm afraid my moderate interest in Wade rouses his jealousy. It ought not to. My interest in Lankes is such a very different thing. Lankes is a woodcutter and no mistake. Poor Wade has his place all to make. . . . He will go back to

Kashabowie, his settlement north of Superior, in the fall and I shall have less to worry about."[7]

Frost, out of deference to Lankes, occasionally took him away from Van Dore long enough for a meal, either at the Shingled Cottage or at the Stone House, and for long walks. Some of these adventures were recorded in Lankes's journal-like letters to his wife. On 13 July 1929 he wrote her: "Went to Bennington to shop and Frost had various errands. We passed the foot of the Bennington monument—which moved Frost to remark on the atrocities all countries use as memorials. Carol had a sweet pea order for the Catamount Inn. Frost took in the flowers himself. Some gent yelled from the window to bring them in by way of the 'service' door. I'll bet that particular hostelry never had a guest nearly as important as Frost enter the main gate. Back to Carol's place where another order from a guest at the same place was waiting but Frost had had enough of it—so we wandered around the farm. It has grown up much. . . . After wandering about a good deal we sat on a bench under the trees . . . and talked and talked. Ambled slowly back to the house and Frost helped unload hay and helped make another load. . . ."[8]

This playful dabbling with hard work on Carol's farm was just the kind of outdoor game Frost liked. So long as he could quit after helping to empty one rack of hay in the barn and then build part of the next load, he was extremely happy. Even more to his liking was the game he played at his new farm up in the Gully, planting and transplanting trees while they were still seedlings. No good-sized trees shaded the little cottage-farmhouse there, and it was Frost's pleasure to study the terrain before driving stakes at exactly the sites where Van Dore should set out maple and elm shoots, in anticipation of the time when the shoots would become trees twice as high as the ridgepole of the house. A much larger job of transplanting, given Van Dore, was the setting out of 500 red pine seedlings purchased at a nominal price from the State of Vermont, and calculated to start a pine grove in an abandoned pasture. Always with an eye to the future, Frost liked to carry a few acorns in his trousers pocket whenever he walked up the road and into the woods beyond his new farm. If he found an open place in the woods, he would study overhanging branches carefully to see where there might be room, some day, for a good-sized oak tree. Then, using his thumb to punch a hole in the leafmould topsoil right there, he would drop an acorn into the hole, and tamp it with the heel of his shoe.

He had warned Van Dore that there might be some need to dig trenches for pipes. The trickle of water which flowed down out of the woods and through the gully to the westward of the house came from a good hillside spring several hundred yards uphill to the eastward. Carol's skill was drafted for building a cement tank around the spring, and this supply of water was piped down to the house, the pipe buried in a trench deep enough to keep it from even the deepest winter-freezings. The overflow from the spring was enough to keep the brook running, and Frost decided to dam it up near the house, just for the fun of it. He mentioned the project play-fully, in answering a friend's request for permission to visit the poet in South Shaftsbury:

"I ought to warn you if you come here you have to work digging out my fish duck dog and frog pond. You would go round New York sowing suspicion that my farm was the kind where there was no work done. There'll be some done by you all right. Other tools you may as well bring besides forceps are rubber boots and Dutch Cleanser. Also a manicure set and vanity kit. We have a looking glass—in fact we are a looking glass. As I look out my window this pleasant but torrid morn-ing my eyes rest peacefully on as many as ten bowed autograph hunters, my captives, spading hoeing and weeding in my garden."[9]

Part of the joke, here, was that Wade Van Dore had planted a vegetable garden, for his own use, if the corn and peas and beans ripened sufficiently for eating before the early frosts nipped them. "There was a light frost here on the night of July 3rd," Lankes wrote to his wife. "The fireplace is a-going and yet I am a-chilled." Anyone who needed exercise to keep warm could always lift and carry some of the stones being used to provide a retaining wall for a terrace along the entire front of the house. Before the summer was over, the wall was completed, and much fill was used to bring the level of the terrace even with the stone step outside the front door. Lankes helped the stonemasons complete this retaining wall, and even turned architect long enough to design two well-propor-tioned and attractive little dormer windows which Harrington, the carpenter, built into the roof on the front of the house. By the time the Frosts left for Franconia, late in August, most of the repairs, remodelings, and improvements had been completed. Before they returned, late in September, Lankes had gone back to Virginia and Van Dore was in Michigan.

There was still much work to be done when the Frosts moved into the Gully House from the Shingled Cottage around the first of October, but they were delighted with the lofty isolation of it. Long before they left, to take up their tasks in Amherst, early in January of 1930, they had firmly decided that their experiment in trying to arrange for mutual assistance with artists such as Lankes and Van Dore was nervously too exhausting to be acceptable for another summer. But they were grateful, and said so to both of their friends, repeatedly. Soon after they returned to South Shaftsbury in June of 1930, Frost wrote to Lankes:

"I look out your dormer window on the northwest every night and morning. I dont know whether I've told you the big barn is clean gone (except for the stone foundations), we have a good rush of water from the faucets—Carol built the spring all over and laid in iron pipes last winter, the north porch is floored with brick 24 ft by 9 ft and new tin-roofed, the road had an easy winter and came through in very decent condition, the house is all papered and painted inside and your two greatest pictures ["Winter" and "Deserted House"] are over the long mantel of the cavernous fireplace. Elinor and I are alone here with nothing but a black New Foundland pup—in breathless quiet after our stormy life. Having failed to educate my own children and other people's children I propose to end up as a teacher training a pup.

"The aim is to subdue to polite usages without breaking the pride or spirit. I know the idea all right. I want one last chance to see if I can't carry it out. Given a pup that comes all over you with affection and knocks you in the face with her teeth. In two months we'll see if I dont have her so she walks toward me with her pleasure all in her eye and tail, takes her place beside me as an equal uncowed by any sound of my voice or motion of my hand. If I fail with her I will resign my professorship at Amherst College."[10]

The Newfoundland puppy, a thoroughbred, had been purchased with the aid of Warren R. Brown, Frost's real-estate agent and friend in Amherst. The esoteric name on her papers which registered her pedigree was ignored and she was simply called Winnie. Frost did succeed in teaching her manners, with one exception: he failed to impress upon her that porcupines should be treated with scornful disregard. In her first meeting with a porcupine, Winnie came away with a mouthful of quills which had to be removed by means of pliers. Having obtained chloroform as the conventional anesthetic for such an ordeal, Frost nervously gave more than Winnie's heart could stand. "We have had a tragedy," he wrote to Brown. "The evening of the day your letter came about the new dog, we lost Winnie. She got her face and mouth full of porcupine quills and died under the c[h]loroform we had to give her for the really terrible operation of getting them out. No dog could ever take her place in our affections. No dog will have a chance to."[11]

FRIENDSHIP MEANS FAVOR

*Friendship means favor and I believe nothing can flourish
without favor not even justice and pure art.*[1]
*. . . jealousy is a passion I approve of and attribute to
angels. May I be guarded and watched over always by
the jealousy of a strong nature. It is better than arms
around the body. Jealousy alone gives me the sense of
being held.*[2]

IN HIS continuous process of campaigning on his own behalf,
Robert Frost kept forcing himself into complicated postures
which involved strange ramifications. Long before the appearance of his *Collected Poems*, in the fall of 1930, he began to
suffer dreadfully over his frightening belief that the reception
given this volume would bring his literary career to some kind
of turning point. If the critics were favorable in their reap-
praisals of such poems as he chose to save from the forty
years of effort which would be represented in his *Collected
Poems*, his immediate position would be strengthened; if not,
he might be swept into the discard, along with so many other
so-called "new poets" who were either fading or already forgotten. "I tremble and am never too happy at being exposed
to the public with another book," he confided to his publisher.
"I hope this one won't be badly received."[3]

Given the choice, however, of passively awaiting the verdict
or of trying to influence those who might help to make it, he
once again exerted himself. Privately, he was willing to admit
that during the fifteen years since his return from England
he had cultivated many friendships with an eye to favors.
Braithwaite and Untermeyer had rewarded the attentions he
had paid them, but Frost had wasted no more time with
Braithwaite after his usefulness ended. Untermeyer continued
to serve well, and the exceptional space he gave to Frost in

those anthologies which were by this time well known and widely used throughout the United States could be counted on to work favorably when the *Collected Poems* appeared.

Still dangerous were several other critics and reviewers whom Frost had already tried to win over to his side. One was H. L. Mencken, feared by many poets and novelists because his brutal witticisms in *American Mercury* were so popular. As early as 1921, Frost had written, "Isn't Men[c]ken the ablest rotter we have almost? He makes me think of nothing but flight. . . . I don't want to feel obliged to remember my sins everyday in fairness to such non-fur-bearing skunks as Men[c]ken and a few others I could name."[4] A few years later, however, Frost had been friendly and even obsequious toward Mencken on the occasion of their first meeting, in Baltimore. In August of 1930, when Marjorie, continuing her nurse training course down there, informed her father that Mencken was soon to be married and was planning to spend part of his honeymoon in New England, Frost wrote quickly to Mencken:

"The news warms me in my friendship for you. Our Baltimore daughter Marjorie tells us how particularly well you have done and we have other ways of knowing.

"I may not be supposed to have heard that your bridal tour is to be through New England and it will be seeing New England for the first time for both of you. But I wonder if you could be persuaded to look in on us for a night in your travels either in our camp near Franconia N. H. before September 15th or at our home here in South Shaftsbury, Vermont after September 21st. See us and you see New England. And we have been married ever since 1905 [1895]. We wouldn't talk dialect to you.

"Thanks for your kindness to my wood-chopper J. J. Lankes. You remember I said to you once you did more than all the teachers put together to find 'em out and help 'em up. Ruth Suckow sat on our porch the other day and acknowledged her debt to you. Always yours friendly Robert Frost."[5]

Similar gestures of friendliness had to be made toward literary radicals who shared the political views of Frost's "wood-chopper J. J. Lankes." In the copy of the *Liberator* which contained the first Lankes print Frost also noticed an inflammatory article claiming that Sacco and Vanzetti were being

given an unfair trial simply because they were anarchist idealists, and Frost was infuriated by any of his literary competitors
who joined in the Sacco-Vanzetti protests.[6] One was Edna St.
Vincent Millay, whose poems of protest included "Justice
Denied in Massachusetts"; another was Genevieve Taggard,
who published in 1925 a volume of radical verses entitled
May Day, containing selections from back numbers of the
Masses and the *Liberator*. Miss Taggard's reviews of newly
published volumes of poetry appeared in various periodicals,
and therefore when Frost was given an opportunity to try to
disarm her by making her his friend, he went out of his way to
do so. She made the first move by writing to him in August
of 1928 to say she was coming to Amherst to "see everything
that pertains to Emily Dickinson," and she added, "May I see
you, too?"[7] Frost was in England at the time, but he later sent
her assurances that he would be glad to see her.

When Miss Taggard did visit Frost in Amherst, she tactfully
expressed as much interest in his poetry as in Emily Dickinson's, and he responded so warmly that she gained several
important insights.[8] As soon as she explained that she was
gathering materials for a book about the love affairs in the
Dickinson story, she found that Frost was well informed about
only those which had occurred in the Dickinson family after
Emily's death.

Frost's delight in gossiping about the Dickinsons was heightened by his having been treated discourteously by Emily's
niece, Martha Dickinson Bianchi, on the only occasion when
he had been invited to her home. The visit had not been
prompted, he was told, by Madame Bianchi's desire to see
him. Instead, a guest of hers, Miss Mary Austin—who had
written and published much on Indian and Spanish cultures
in America—had asked to meet Frost. She had her own theories
about the importance of poetic rhythms in everyday speech,
and she was certain that Robert Frost's pronouncements about
"the sound of sense" would make him sympathetic. During
his visit with Miss Austin, in the splendid home next to the
house where Emily had lived, he had been treated with open
hostility by Martha, although he and the elderly Miss Austin
got along very well together and did find similarities between
their theories. After he had gone and Miss Austin had expressed her admiration for him, Martha Dickinson expressed
disgust. She assured Miss Austin that those who counted in

America had no use for Frost. They considered him merely a "clod-hopper."[9]

Miss Taggard, in talking with Frost about Emily, had to let him work backward through his hatred for Madame Bianchi. With obvious pleasure he reviewed events which had occurred long before he had reached Amherst; gossip about how Martha had gone abroad, year after year, intent on marrying a nobleman, and of how she had finally brought home a man who at least claimed he had a title. He had even shared that claim with her in marriage, and she continued to use the title even after the impostor had been unmasked and, as Frost liked to say, chased out of town by the sheriff.[10]

Frost insinuatively told how Madame Bianchi had shocked the Amherst villagers after her husband fled and after her mother died. In editing her aunt's poems, she had acquired the collaborative assistance of a young man named Alfred Leete Hampson, who moved in with her quite brazenly and stayed. When Frost had asked his landlady, the widowed Mrs. Tyler, whether she approved of such an arrangement for living, he had been shocked by Mrs. Tyler's sympathetic explanation: "Oh, but poor Martha was so lonesome."[11]

Miss Taggard was also required to hear the Frostian version of that other Dickinson scandal which had entertained Amherst many years earlier: the one involving Martha's father Austin and Mabel Loomis Todd, the attractive wife of the befuddled David Todd. Old Todd had been professor of either astronomy or astrology at Amherst—there were differences of opinion Frost said, as to whether he actually taught anybody anything. But Frost was certain that Mrs. Todd had deliberately seduced Austin Dickinson for the sole purpose of gaining access to the unpublished poems of his sister Emily. Anyway, Mrs. Todd had been able to edit, with the assistance of T. W. Higginson, the first three volumes of *Poems* by Emily Dickinson, and Frost had bought two of those volumes while he was a senior in high school.[12]

By the time Miss Taggard completed her researches in Amherst, Frost had charmed her so completely that she was apparently willing to ignore his lack of sympathy for the fate of Sacco and Vanzetti. Or perhaps, like others, she had not yet learned where he stood on the most notorious court case of the 1920s. Shortly before the *Letters of Sacco and Vanzetti* had been published, the *Atlantic* had made the mistake of inviting

Frost to write a review of that volume,[13] and before Frost had sent his refusal, further pressure was brought to bear on him. He explained to his liberal and ever-complaining friend Lankes:

". . . there always is something left to kick about. I just got a letter from Gardner Jackson an old boy of mine and late chairman of the Sacco Vanzetti Defense Committee calling on me in the name of Justice to review the Sacco Vanzetti Letters and register my kick against the way such obviously meditative thinkers were treated. . . . Will you illustrate my review if I write one. Justice is a very important thing and injustice is a very important thing to kick against. I wish there were no injustice and I should like nothing better than to join the crusade against it but it will be under the banners and transparencies of a greater than Sacco or even Vanzetti. . . ."[14]

While Frost was still waiting for the publication of his *Collected Poems*, the liberals embarrassed him further: the New School for Social Research, in New York City, invited him to give a series of lectures on poetry during the first three months of 1931. To Frost, this New School was a hotbed of radicalism-socialism-communism, and he feared that he might tarnish his public image if he permitted himself to be associated with it. Before making up his mind, he sought the opinion of a friend who had already given excellent advice on matters having to do with his career as a poet: Frederic G. Melcher, editor-in-chief of *Publishers' Weekly*:

"I am going to ask you very privately for a piece of advice. Do you think I would derogate from my dignity or aloofness or anything if I did a series of lectures (so to call them) on poetry this winter at the New School of Social Research. I'm not afraid of the radicals I should be thrown with nor of the Jews. I may be a radical myself and there is a theory that the Scotch were Jews and another that the Yankees were Jews. I am a Scotch Yankee. What I want to know is, do you think I would cheapen myself in some way. I'm half inclined to accept Alvin Johnson's invitation to lecture there if only to save myself from too much humanism."[15]

Frost's nervousness, just prior to the appearance of his *Collected Poems*, was heightened by his desire to protect himself from several of the "isms" then being touted in ways which annoyed him: humanism, humanitarianism, romanticism, socialism, communism, anarchism. When Melcher assured him that the opportunity to lecture at the New School would afford an excellent way of gaining a wider audience for his poetry, he accepted Alvin Johnson's invitation. He was determined that, before he finished giving these lectures, the radical humanitarians among his listeners at the New School would know more about him than just his theory of poetry. As for the humanists, they still kept moving in on him uncomfortably as a result of Munson's biography. In protest, Frost kept insisting that Babbitt's way of preaching the gospel of the new humanism made it no less sentimental than the gospel of humanitarianism. Frost had his own way of hurling the word "romantic" at anyone who crowded him too hard, and just at this time he was jealous enough of Robinson's recent success to take pleasure in condemning him as a romantic.

What infuriated Frost most about Robinson, now, was the way in which the commercial success of Robinson's *Tristram* had been assured, prior to publication, by a group of literary salesmen. Carl Van Doren, as editor of the newly organized Literary Guild, had hired a theatre for the Sunday evening nearest publication day; friends of Robinson's had persuaded the celebrated actress Mrs. August Belmont (Eleanor Robson) to come out of retirement and read, to a large audience of guests, passages from *Tristram*. The next day, newspapers across the country told the story of how America had at last found and honored a great poet. Even worse, for Frost, was the fact that the publicity thus gained was excellent, and the timing perfect. The Literary Guild distributed 12,000 copies of *Tristram*, and within a year Macmillan sold over 75,000 copies.[16] Then Macmillan brought out a volume of Robinson's *Collected Poems*, which won a Pulitzer Prize. Frost had already explained to Untermeyer that jealousy was a passion Frost approved of, and he had not needed to add that he approved of it only when others were jealous of him. In one of his ugly moods, he could not resist striking a few verbal blows at Robinson while worrying about the prospects for his own *Collected Poems*:

"Where have I been the last six months in abeyance? But where was I the eighteen years just preceding—the years I mean from 1912 to 1930? In no very real dream. The book of all I ever wrote, when it comes out this fall, ought to do something toward accounting to me for those false years. But I have seen it in proof and it looked like no child of mine. I stared at it unloving. And I wonder what next. I don't want to raise sheep; I don't want to keep cows; I don't want to be called a farmer. Robinson spoiled farming for me when by doubting my farm he implied a greater claim on my part to being a farmer than I had ever made. The whole damn thing became disgusting in his romantic mouth. How utterly romantic the enervated old soak is. The way he thinks of poets in the Browningese of 'Ben Johnson'! the way he thinks of cucolding lovers and cucold husbands in 'Tristram'! Literary conventions! I feel as if I had been somewhere on hot air like a fire-balloon. Not with him altogether. I haven't more than half read him since 'The Town Down the River.' I simply couldn't lend a whole ear to all that Arthurian twaddle twiddled over after the Victorians. A poet is a person who thinks there is something special about a poet and about his loving one unattainable woman. You'll usually find he takes the physical out on whores. I am defining a romantic poet—and there is no other kind. An unromantic poet is a self-contradiction like the democratic aristocrat that reads the Atlantic Monthly. Ink, mink, pepper, stink, I, am, out! I am not a poet. What am I then? Not a farmer—never was—never said I was. I've stayed your friend through several vicissitudes. A friend is something to be. Roy Elliott, the Humanist professional, asked me if I had written anything since I came home in April. Me! Write anything in two months! It used to take me ten years to write anything. And now that I have found myself out for an unromantic and so have no incentive, it should take me not less than twice as long."[17]

It was easier for Untermeyer to understand these signs of running scared than for Frost to explain to himself what anxieties drove him to such venomous pronouncements. He felt that he had dropped behind Robinson, in the race for public attention, and he was as angry at himself as at Robinson. But there was comfort in finding any target for rage, and another one was found. Not long after John Livingston Lowes published his Coleridge study, *The Road to Xanadu* (1927), Frost sat beside him at a Cambridge dinner party given to celebrate the dedication of the Amy Lowell Poetry Room in the Widener Library at Harvard. They knew each other moderately well, and they had once served as fellow judges in a poetry contest. It was easy enough for them to tease each other with pleasant banter at the dinner table, and even to entertain those who might be eavesdropping. At one point in these exchanges, however, Frost grew malicious. He had not read *The Road to Xanadu*, he said, but he had been told that Lowes had really introduced the scientific method to literary criticism.

"I supposed," Frost teasingly said, "poetry was least of all given to quotation."

"On the contrary," Lowes replied, "it is one texture of quotations. You write it out of all the books you have ever read, and it is my pleasure to come after you and trace it to its sources."[18]

Frost, silenced, took the retort as a personal insult, for reasons which were unknown to Lowes. Years earlier, the charge had been brought against Frost that some of the poems in *A Boy's Will* contained unacknowledged quotations from other poets.[19] Hurt by that charge, Frost resented what Lowes had said, and could not stop brooding over it until he had tried to find an answer, in satirical verse:

> *Lowes took the obvious position*
> *That all of art is recognition*
> *And I agreed. But the perfection*
> *Of recognition is detection*
> *That's why Lowes reads detective stories*
> *And why in scholarship he glories*
> *A poet need make no apology*
> *Because his works are one anthology*
> *Of other poets best creations*
> *Let him be nothing but quotations*
> *(That's not as cynic as it sounds)*
> *The game is one like Hare and Hounds*
> *To entertain the critic pack*
> *The poet has to leave a track*
> *Of torn up scraps of prior poets.*[20]

This first and incomplete draft of a possible answer did not satisfy Frost. Needing another way to strike back, he found it almost accidentally while writing a letter to a philosopher who may have been surprised to find Frost hauling Lowes into a discussion of philosophy:

"I have just one object in writing this letter and that is to warn you against being just one more philosopher like the three thousand (an average of three for every college, professor ass-professor and instructor) at the present moment in this country. Let me tell you a story. A friend of mine, a business man and a thinker, asked to join the American Philosophical Society or whatever it is called. They wanted to know if he was a professor. He couldnt say he was. Then he couldnt join. No philosopher, but only professors of philosophy need apply. And to show you the mentality of the professors of philosophy I heard a prominent one say: 'Let young men learn to quote philosophers. Who are they that they should set up to think?' How long oh Lord are we for this provincialism. The most conspicuous book in literary criticism with us at present has scarcely one thought of the author's own in it. It is a marvellous texture of quotations from everywhere. It is a professor's work and about as far as a professor can be expected to go. It is the height of the academic. The professor's name is John L. Lowes."[21]

Such a diatribe enabled Frost to do more than gain release from pent-up rage. It helped him to improve in his own eyes his ideal sense of being another Uriel, for purposes of offsetting self-doubt. Speaking with low tones that decide, he doubt and reverend use defied, with a look that solved the sphere, and stirred the devils everywhere. As he had said to Melcher, "I'm not afraid of the radicals . . . I may be a radical myself."

Another radical disturbed and annoyed him, indirectly, while he was still awaiting the publication of *Collected Poems*. A Vermont poet, Walter J. Coates, wrote to Frost's publisher to say he represented the Committee on Vermont Traditions and Ideals: with the aid of Professor Frederick Tupper of the University of Vermont, he was compiling a book of Vermont poetry and wished permission to include four of Robert Frost's poems. Richard Thornton asked for advice from Frost, and received more than advice in answer:

"It would relieve me of something distasteful if you would deal with this Committee of Vermont Traditions and Ideals (tell it to Men[c]ken!). Have I not put it in plenty good blank verse that the ideals will bear some keeping still about. The Walter J. Coates you mention is no friend of mine. I sat in an audience of twenty-five at Arlington, Vermont, two years ago and heard him read me out of the State and out of the ranks of important poets. Afterward ashamed of himself, he climbed all over me with adulation. I have become an issue in their local literary politics. It makes you laugh. They say I'm a foreigner because I came only ten years ago from New Hampshire. The leaders of this purging movement—I say leaders but should say cathartics—are this Coates, an unfrocked parson from New York State, a Rutland (Vt) editor from Ohio and the reformed-radical Welsh jew John Spargo. I don't know what their ideals may be, but possibly one of them is to stay black Republican, set the nigger free and elect Taft retroactively as of 1912. Vermont and Utah were the only states Taft carried in that election.

"I can barely stand such people. And still I must be careful not to get tarred and feathered and ridden on a rail by them some fine night lest I be suspected of doing it for the advertisement. If you act between us it will be all right probably. Tell them they can have the poems. I'll pretend not to know what's going on. If they send me their Anthology I'll burn it privately only in one of our three open fire places or the kitchen stove. All this sounds more like a mountain feud than it really is. I manage not to seem to notice most of the time.

"Let's think of something pleasanter, the book you have made of my Collected. I look forward to seeing it. . . ."[22]

When the first prepublication copy of *Collected Poems* arrived in South Shaftsbury, Frost was delighted by the format. Pronouncing it perfect, he immediately returned to his worries over what the reviewers might say. One of his worst fears was that some of the attacks made against *West-Running Brook* would be repeated and even elaborated. He was inclined to suspect that one of his own colleagues on the Amherst faculty had been the author of one of those attacks, an anonymous review which had challenged Frost's insights and outlooks:

"This construction of an adequate philosophy raises Frost above other contemporary poets, and it has given him, one suspects, a feeling that the outcry, raised by many poets, against this particular era or this particular country, is senseless. He has a poem entitled 'Acquainted with the Night,' which begins with a description of the experience of loneliness and recognition of suffering, and ends by telling of the clock which 'proclaimed the time was neither wrong nor right.' Frost evidently believes it is the artist himself that matters and not the time in which he happens to live. He may be right, but we must still remember that he has created the ordered world in which he lives only by the exclusions of many, many chaotic elements in the real world. Perhaps it is this fact that explains why Frost is, even at his best, a very perfect minor poet, not the major poet for whom America is looking."[23]

It seemed to Frost that such criticism failed to give him credit for trying to express, in his poetry, the perilous attempts he himself had made to cope with the immediate and chaotic elements of his own inner world; his desperate effort to assert order on that inner world for purposes of surviving well enough to meet his primary obligations from day to day. He knew just where he was vulnerable to attack, and just where his enemies —either humanistic or humanitarian—might take pleasure in scolding him. But if he were forced to do so he would quote Emerson in self-defense: "Leave this hypocritical prating about the masses. Masses are rude, lame, unmade, pernicious in their demands and influence. . . . I wish not to concede anything to them, but to . . . divide and break them up, and draw individuals out of them. . . ."[24]

The thing he feared came unto him. One of the first reviews of *Collected Poems* appeared in the *New Republic*, and it seemed to be a close paraphrase of the anonymous reviewer who had claimed that Frost had created his make-believe world only by excluding from his attention so many chaotic elements in the real world. The *New Republic* reviewer was Granville Hicks, one of Frost's communistic enemies, who also pounced on Frost's claim that the time was "neither wrong nor right." Then Hicks began to probe:

"This is vigorous doctrine in an age that has been fertile in self-analysis and self-commiseration. Frost's credo, however, runs counter to the consensus of opinion of the critics of all ages as well as to the temper of his own era. Matthew Arnold summarized the verdict of most students of letters when he said, 'For the creation of a master work of literature two powers must concur, the power of man and the power of the moment, and the man is not enough without the moment.' Wordsworth said something of the same sort, and perhaps came closer to the difficulties of our own time, when he pointed out that facts and ideas have to become familiar to mankind, have to become part of common human experience, before the poet can use them. . . . So much in modern life has not been assimilated to organized human experience, so many of our acts and thoughts are unrelated to any central purpose or unifying hypothesis, so

[385]

many obstacles stand in the way of the much-discussed modern synthesis, that the poet must grow desperate who looks for the order of ideas, the intellectual and spiritual atmosphere, that Arnold says he needs. It is no wonder that most poets and critics would say that a time may indeed be either wrong or right and that the present time is decidedly wrong.

"So strong is the case for this view of literature that we may omit the task of defending it in detail, and, instead, ask ourselves how it is possible for Frost to hold the contrary opinion. . . ."

Continuing, Hicks surveyed Frost's *Collected Poems* to discover that three important subjects were missing. He found in them "nothing of industrialism," nothing of "the disruptive effect that scientific hypotheses have had on modern thought," and nothing of "Freudianism." After admitting that Frost used less pertinent ways to exercise his poetic imagination, Hicks returned to his complaints in making a summary conclusion:

"There is one thing, of course, Frost cannot do: he cannot contribute directly to the unification, in imaginative terms, of our culture. He cannot give us the sense of belonging in the industrial, scientific, Freudian world in which we find ourselves. The very limitations that are otherwise so advantageous make it impossible. That is why no one would think of maintaining that he is one of the great poets of the ages. To that extent the time, even though he refuses to lay the responsibility at its door, is not right. . . ."[25]

Still pretending that he never read any reviews of his books, and yet rarely missing the important ones, he did not miss this one. Although he had written to Thornton, "I manage not to seem to notice," he immediately began to formulate his answer to Granville Hicks. Just when or where he would deliver that answer, he could not foresee, but he apparently watched for an occasion which might not be wasted. Some of his students at Amherst gave it to him, some time later, by sending him birthday greetings, and his answer to them was published in the campus newspaper. Starting with thanks to those who had shown "sympathy for me for my age," he went on to offer an essay on "ages" in another sense:

"But speaking of ages, you will often hear it said that the age of the world we live in is particularly bad. I am impatient of such talk. We have no way of knowing that this age is one of the worst in the world's history. Arnold claimed the honor for the age before this. Wordsworth claimed it for the last but one. And so on back through literature. I say they claimed the honor for their ages. They claimed it rather for themselves. It is immodest of a man to think of himself as going down before the worst forces ever mobilized by God.

"All ages of the world are bad—a great deal worse anyway than Heaven. If they weren't the world might just as well be Heaven at once and have it over with. One can safely say after from six to thirty thousand years of experience that the evident design is a situation here in which it will always be equally hard to save your soul. Whatever progress may be taken to mean, it can't mean making the world any easier a place in which to save your soul—or if you dislike hearing your soul mentioned in open meeting, say your decency, your integrity.

"Ages may vary a little. One may be a little worse than another. But it is not possible to get outside the age you are in to judge it exactly. Indeed it is as dangerous to try to get outside of anything as large as an age as it would be to engorge a donkey. Witness the many who in the attempt have suffered a dilation from which the tissues and the muscles of the mind have never been able to recover natural shape. They can't pick up anything delicate or small any more. They can't use a pen. They have to use a typewriter. And they gape in agony. They can write huge shapeless novels, huge gobs of raw sincerity bellowing with pain and that's all they can write.

"Fortunately we don't need to know how bad the age is. There is something we can always be doing without reference to how good or how bad the age is. There is at least so much good in the world that it admits of form and the making of form. And not only admits of it, but calls for it. We people are thrust forward out of the suggestions of form in the rolling clouds of nature. In us nature reaches its height of form and through us exceeds itself. When in doubt there is always form for us to go on with. Anyone who has achieved the least form to be sure of it, is lost to the larger excruciations. I think it must stroke faith the right way. The artist, the poet, might be expected to be the most aware of such assurance, but it is really everybody's sanity to feel it and live by it. Fortunately, too, no forms are more engrossing, gratifying, comforting, staying, than those lesser ones we throw off like vortex rings of smoke, all our individual enterprise and needing nobody's cooperation: a basket, a letter, a garden, a room, an idea, a picture, a poem. For these we haven't to get a team together before we can play.

"The background is hugeness and confusion shading away from where we stand into black and utter chaos; and against the background any small man-made figure of order and concentration. What pleasanter than that this should be so? Unless we are novelists or economists we don't worry about this confusion; we look out on it with an instrument or tackle it to reduce it. It is partly because we are afraid it might prove too much for us and our blend of democratic-republican-socialist-communist-anarchist party. But it is more because we like it, we were born to it, born used to it and have practical reasons for wanting it there. To me any little form I assert upon it is velvet, as the saying is, and to be considered for how much more it is than nothing. If I were a Platonist I should have to consider it, I suppose, for how much less it is than everything."[26]

To Frost, idealists like Granville Hicks were Platonists in that they measured the immediate realities of life against human perfection which would never exist on earth and then complained that there was something horrendously wrong about the present. In explaining his own attitude to his newly made friend, the leftist Genevieve Taggard, he had been so persuasive that her review of *Collected Poems* could scarcely have been more sympathetic to his position if he had written it himself. In a sense, it was made to his order in that he had converted her at least temporarily to a defense of his viewpoint. In the process he had apparently complained to her that Munson should not have tried to crowd him into a pigeonhole with humanists like Irving Babbitt and his followers. She began her review by explaining Munson's mistake:

"The humanists have been trying to pigeonhole Robert Frost. Long, long shall our humanists sit with their rubber bands in their hands ready and waiting to snap them around the quotations they want from his works. The rest of Frost they would undoubtedly discard. Texts from his book laid neatly on four sides of him may serve the two-dimensional critic and the literal-minded reader; but not even his own texts nicely dovetailed, can box the intelligence expressed here so sure of its goings-out and its comings-in. Frost is too cussedly non-conformist to trust even his own words as texts five minutes after he has uttered them. His mind is too seasoned, too humorous, to relish the owlish solemnity of dicta and dictations. He trusts his poems as poems, as metaphors spread to catch meaning, as words that have become deeds. He has given them speech that suggests not one meaning but many. Any effort, therefore, to strip Frost down to singleness of meaning in the interests of propaganda must be opposed. The wisest and most mature poet of our time should not be hacked at and shaved down to suit a pigeonhole. If, in their text-gathering, the humanists had paid more attention to Frost's behavior with his poems, if they had understood the meaning of tone and intention—if, in other words, they had known how to read poetry and not merely how to collect texts, they would have abandoned the attempt."

As she continued, Miss Taggard revealed that she had also listened carefully to Frost's boast concerning his own rebel attitudes and his abhorrence of systems:

"Toil has dignity in this poetry; it is universal human experience portrayed concretely, in locality, in Yankee accent. Then lest toil become a doctrine, Frost abandons it. Like Thoreau, he rebelled in his life, and he here and there rebels in his verse, from the morality of work-for-its-own-sake. He loafs. We see him insisting on leisure for meditation—rejecting toil for something better, and more active—creation. . . . Frost accompanied the swing of his scythe with the cast of his thought for many years. When the time came he knocked off work and called it a day. . . . Frost is a mature artist in a society of clever mechanical youngsters."[27]

As other reviewers lined up unevenly on the opposed sides represented by Miss Taggard's praise and Mr. Hicks's faultfinding, it quickly became apparent that the admirers were making the publication of Collected Poems the major triumph Frost had nervously hoped it might be. Even his British friend Hugh Walpole helped the cause by publishing a single sentence of evaluation, in which he said that Collected Poems "is for me more sure of immortality than any other book of the last five years, whether in England or America."[28] It was awarded the Pulitzer Prize as being the best volume of verse published during 1930 by an American author. An even more important honor, not unrelated to the appearance of Collected Poems, was Frost's election to membership in The American Academy of Arts and Letters. Among the five members who nominated him to this membership, he later learned, one was Edwin Arlington Robinson.[29]

NO ARTIST SHOULD HAVE A FAMILY

One sickness and another in the family kept us till I could have cried out with the romantics that no artist should have a family. I could have, if the idea hadn't been so stale and unoriginal.[1]

LATE in the autumn of 1930, when Robert Frost was beginning to relax under the praise given him for his *Collected Poems*, he received the frightening news that his daughter Marjorie had suffered a breakdown and was a patient in the Baltimore hospital where she had been training to become a nurse. Her work had gone so well there for nearly two years that she had gained much of the confidence she so desperately needed. If this new illness should cause her to lose that confidence, she might feel hopelessly discouraged. Her parents hurried to Baltimore in mid-December, and were distressed anew by the diagnosis of her condition. At first, the doctors thought she was again suffering from her previous ailment, pleurisy. A few days later, they said they had found definite evidence that she had tuberculosis: she ought to be placed in a sanatorium as soon as possible. She and her parents forlornly celebrated Christmas day in her hospital room.

After some groping and indecision, they remembered that John Bartlett had moved from New Hampshire to Boulder, Colorado, partly because of his asthma but primarily because of the fear that his wife had tuberculosis. The Bartletts had prospered in Boulder, and only recently Frost had agreed to spend a week at the Rocky Mountain Writers' Conference at the University of Colorado. Marjorie knew the Bartletts well, and if a place could be found near them, so that they might visit her occasionally, she would like that. A telephone call was made, and Mrs. Bartlett assured them that the Mesa Verde Sanatorium on a hill only three blocks from the Bartlett home would be the perfect place for Marjorie. Further consultation revealed that the Baltimore authorities supported Mrs. Bartlett's judgment in this matter. Arrangements were quickly made, and as soon as Marjorie was strong enough to make the long journey by train she went alone to Denver, where the Bartletts met her.

Frost, returning to his duties at Amherst and trying to carry on as casually as though he were not frightened by Marjorie's plight, went through his performances remarkably well. As soon as he completed his obligations at Amherst he followed his usual pattern of going the rounds of readings, but with a new sense of his need to earn more if he were to pay Marjorie's expenses in Colorado. He gave readings at Wesleyan, Yale, Harvard, Bowdoin, Bates, and Clark University; he carried out his promise to give six lectures at the New School for Social Research in New York City—and he was relieved to find that some of the "radicals" liked his poetry.[2] As usual, the strain of all this barding-about and socializing wore him down so much that he became ill. Then fell another unexpected blow: Carol's wife Lillian was also found to be suffering from tuberculosis. Elinor Frost, informing her friend Mrs. Fobes, reflected her own grief:

". . . since coming home [to South Shaftsbury] there have been a great many things to do, and besides that I have been much disheartened and sad. Not about Marjorie, for just lately the improvement has been very marked. . . . For quite a while, the gain in her condition was slower than with ordinary tuberculosis patients whose symptoms are worse than hers were, so they concluded that a partial nervous breakdown was complicating the case. She has felt from the first that it was just the right place for her to get strong in, and lately she is very happy and cheerful, I can see by her letters. . . .

"The reason I have been almost crushed with discouragement lately is that Lillian, Carol's wife, also has tuberculosis. . . . You know Marjorie and Lillian were intimate friends in High School. Isn't it extraordinary that they should both have the same thing at the same time, after being separated most of the time for several years?

"Well, Carol and Lillian have decided to sell their farm, and move to sunnier climate. . . . After getting information about a good many places, they have decided to go to San Bernardino, California. . . . You can imagine what a blow it is to me to have them go so far away. I have always wanted to watch Carol a little on account of his lack of vigorous health, and he is very dear to me, while Prescott has become very precious to us. . . ."[3]

Frost, for his part, tried to cheer the family with talk of compensations: now that his children were giving him an excuse to go West, even to the State of his birth, he hoped Carol would arrange his trip so that his father could be in California to meet him when he got there. Lillian's doctor had given her permission to make the journey by automobile, in slow stages, and Carol mapped out a route which would enable them to call on Marjorie in Boulder. Reports from Marjorie continued to be good, and her father cheerfully thanked Bartlett:

"Marjorie wrote in her last letter, Don't say our family never does anything right. In her opinion we did a big thing right when we sent her out where the John T. Bartletts live. . . . Between you and me (you mustnt tell her for fear of making her self-conscious) you folks and Colorado have changed her tune. You know where to come for thanks if you want any in words.

"She wants me to come out there and do the cooking for the sanatarium she intends to establish when she gets well and finishes training for a nurse. She says I am a good meat cook— that's where I would come in. Elinor could do the bread and pastry. Carol could run the dairy and kitchen garden. What dissipates that dream is your altitude. You live too high for us —about 2500 feet too high. . . .

"We mustn't think so far ahead. It will be something to have a few weeks out there with you this summer. We'll want to be sure of Elinor [because of her heart] of course. But if the doctors give her permission, I dont see why we shouldn't all have a gay time together. . . ."[4]

Before they could start West, the elder Frosts were called on to show solicitude for one of their married daughters, Lesley. Expecting her second child in June—at almost the same time she hoped to complete proceedings for her divorce—she was living near Montauk Point on Long Island. Her parents had agreed to delay their trip to Colorado until the child was born, and the wait proved longer than they had anticipated. Writing to Untermeyer from Montauk on the twelfth of June 1931, Frost hinted at his own state of mind: ". . . today particularly I am in no mood to estimate myself or anything I ever did. Lesley is at the hospital in Southampton (L. I.) in ineffectual

pain and has been for three days now. We don't understand
what's the matter. The doctors say nothing's the matter. We'll
be convinced of that after everything comes out all right.
All our children are an anxiety at once it happens. Marj gains
very slowly. . . . Carol must sell his farm just when it is coming
into productiveness. The orchards began blooming this year.
Irma is on the strain of having a husband at college. . . .⁵ And
here is Lesley in trouble too. Elinor just interrupted me to say
on the telephone that it is bad but the worst of it is it doesn't
get worse. . . ."⁶ Eight days later, Lesley gave birth to her
second daughter, Lesley Lee, and as soon as the elder Frosts
were convinced that the ordeal had ended successfully they
started for Colorado.

The Bartletts gave Rob and Elinor a cordial reception in
Denver, spoke reassuringly of Marjorie's progress at the Mesa
Verde Sanatorium, and insisted that the visitors must stay as
guests in the Bartlett home. The Bartletts had obviously
prospered since their arrival in Colorado. John had established
a flourishing journalistic enterprise, all his own, which he and
his wife conducted without any assistance.

The elder Frosts were delighted to discover that their
daughter was much better than they had dared hope. "Marjorie
looks beautiful—she weighs 120 pounds and her skin is clear
and firm," Mrs. Frost quickly wrote to Mrs. Fobes. "It was a
most fortunate decision—to bring her here."⁷ Marjorie's father,
as soon as he learned that she was well enough to be given a
brief change of scene, began making inquiries concerning a
mountain retreat, and was soon able to gain some firsthand
information. Following an afternoon-reading of his poems to a
good-sized audience at the University of Denver, he accepted
the hospitalities of the Denver poet, Thomas Hornsby Ferril,
who took him by car some thirty miles southwest of Denver to
consider a cottage for rent in the mountain town of Evergreen.
A few days later, Frost brought his wife and daughter there for
a ten-day stay. Still trying to carry his family responsibilities
as graciously as he could, he wrote from Evergreen one letter
which gave Untermeyer a chance to see beneath the surface of
the verbal gaiety:

"I am up here 8000 feet high, gasping for oxygen, my walk
slow and vague as in a world of unreality. Anything I say feels
as if someone else said it. I'm told it's not my heart but the size
of my lungs that's to blame. . . .

"We came here to give Marj a vacation from the sanitorium. We're having a fine time all to ourselves in spite of the uneases of altitude. (Marj and I are the sufferers as it turns out, though Elinor was the only one we feared for beforehand.) . . . I'm botanizing all over in an almost entirely different flora. Up one ravine today there were masses of larkspur and monks-hood. It's a very flowery country. . . . Three weeks ago I was settled for a month but as if forever in the sand-dunes of extreme Montauk. Such lengths our children drag us to. I'm glad none of the family are foreign missionaries or we should be snatched back and forward very likely from continent to continent instead of as now from state to state. I don't care if God doesn't care. . . .

"I, we all, go back to Boulder next Wednesday for my talks to the summer school. I may live to be sorry I got into those. Sometimes I do well and then again I get too tired from the strain leading up to a performance. I musn't complain . . . I don't manage myself very well. I don't care if God doesn't care. . . .

"Sometimes I almost cry I am afraid I am such a bad poet. But tonight I don't care if God doesn't care. . . ."[8]

The anxiety shared by Frost and his wife found more open expression in her letters to Mrs. Fobes. Writing from Evergreen on the second of August 1931, she began as pleasantly as she could: "We have a cottage on a hillside, with spruce and pine woods around us. It *seems* to be in the wilderness, but there are large estates on the hills about. . . . We have enjoyed the quiet here, and the beauty of the scenery. Marjorie is able to go about with us a little. . . . We have a fine view of Mt. Evans 1400 feet high, from our porch.

"Marjorie doesn't seem as well as I had hoped to find her. She must rest in the sanatorium several months longer, I think, before she goes about much or undertakes any mental or physical work. But she seems happy, and I know she will re-cover, if she cannot be considered already recovered.

"With Lillian it is different. I am afraid she may not live, and the great concern I feel for her, and for Carol and Prescott, stretches my endurance almost to the breaking point. Why are we so unfortunate? I have worked so hard for my family all these years, and now everything seems tumbling around me. I do not lament this way to everyone, of course. I am too proud, and with Robert I have to keep cheerful, because I mustn't drag him down, but sometimes it seems to me that I *cannot* go on any longer. Probably I have overworked these last six months, and will feel stronger after we reach home, and I shall have six weeks of quiet before we go to Amherst. . . ."⁹

Shortly after the Frosts returned to Boulder from Evergreen, Carol arrived from Vermont in his Model A Ford with his always-cheerful wife Lillian and their adventurous six-year-old son, Prescott. For Prescott and the men, mountain picnics were arranged, and the Bartletts knew where to find nearby lakes and streams which pleased their guests. Carol's schedule for continuing toward California was made with the assistance of the Bartletts, who recommended appropriate stopping-places. As Carol started on with his family, his parents assured him they would finish their duties in Boulder soon enough to reach San Bernardino on or near the same day he did.

When these duties began, at the Writers' Conference, Frost was caught up in more social obligations than he had anticipated, and before long he was sorry he had exposed himself to local jealousies. The five sessions of his writing course, conducted during the week which began on the eleventh of August 1931, went well enough to satisfy him. The crowds which turned out for his two evening lectures (one on "Modern Poetry" and the other simply a reading from his own poems) pleased him with their flattering responses. Bartlett, sympathizing with Frost's distaste for teas and cocktail parties, did his best to protect his guest from invitations which could be refused. The Frosts gladly spent their last night with the Ferrils in Denver, and developed a strong liking for the young poet. Early the next morning, the Ferrils put them on the train for Salt Lake City, en route to California.¹⁰

Before the elder Frosts reached San Bernardino, Carol and his family were already established at the California Hotel and had even begun to search for a house to rent. Frost, having paid Marjorie's expenses for the six months she had been at the sanatorium in Boulder, and having promised to keep supplying Carol with money to cover the costs of hospitalization for Lillian in California, began to wonder how and where he would earn or beg the money to make good these promises. He joined Carol in house-hunting, and they were not content until they had explored as far as the town of Monrovia, only eight miles from Pasadena. With some difficulty, they found a house which gave a superb view of the San Gabriel Mountain Range to the north. "It is in a good locality," wrote Mrs. Frost to Mrs. Fobes, "one of the older houses and lacks a coat of paint, but the inside has lately been put in good repair, and there are six good rooms, besides an unusually large and pleasant sleeping porch, and the rent is only $27.50 a month. There is a very large live oak tree in the yard, and several smaller trees, and enough land for Carol to have many flowers and some vegetables. And Monrovia has good T. B. specialists, and a particularly good sanatorium. . . . I feel greatly relieved to have them so favorably settled here. Robert and I like southern California so much better than we expected to."[11] The elder Frosts stayed for only a week, establishing contacts with recommended medical specialists, gaining assurances that the best care would be given Lillian, and then they started homeward by way of San Francisco.

There was an odd excitement for Frost in anticipating this return to his birthplace. On the train, as they approached, he drew for his wife an outline map of the city, putting in such names of streets and landmarks as he could remember, with special attention to those on and around Nob Hill. As soon as his wife lay down to rest in their hotel room, he went out alone to prowl streets changed so much that only their names were familiar. Using his map, he finally stood perplexed at the corner of Larkin and Broadway until the approach of an elderly gentleman gave him the courage to ask if this was the corner where the old Abbotsford House used to stand. With a distinct Scots accent the old man replied, "Yes and we called it 'Brogan's Folly.'" That well-remembered nickname was enough to start conversation, and when the stranger understood that Frost's sightseeing was purely nostalgic he insisted that they go to his nearby home and reminisce over an old scrapbook of ancient San Francisco scenes. That visit with the Scotsman was the best part of this lonely meandering about the city.[12] Mrs. Frost was not well enough to go with him. But before they were scheduled to take the ferry to the train shed in Oakland, he could not resist going all the way across the peninsula. His goal, this time, was to walk again on the beach below the old Cliff House—nearly four miles southwest of the spot which would soon anchor one end of the already projected Golden Gate Bridge. Several months later, back in South Shaftsbury, the poet celebrated these wanderings of the previous summer, in verses calculated to please his children and grandchildren:

MY OLYMPIC RECORD STRIDE

In a Vermont bedroom closet
With a door of two broad boards
And for back wall a crumbling old chimney
(And that's what their toes are towards),

I have a pair of shoes standing,
Old rivals of sagging leather,
Who once kept surpassing each other,
But now live even together.

They listen for me in the bedroom
To ask me a thing or two
About who is too old to go walking
With too much stress on the who.

I wet one last year at Montauk
For a hat I had to save.
The other I wet at the Cliff House
In an extra-vagant wave.

Two entirely different grandchildren
Got me into my double adventure.
But when they grow up and can read this
I hope they won't take it for censure.

I touch my tongue to the shoes now,
And unless my sense is at fault,
On one I can taste Atlantic,
On the other Pacific, salt.

One foot in each great ocean
Is a record stride or stretch.
The authentic shoes it was made in
I ought to see what they would fetch;

But instead I proudly devote them
To my museum and muse;
So the thick-skins needn't act thin-skinned
About being past-active shoes.

[397]

And I hope they're going to forgive me
For being as over-elated
As if I had measured the country
And got the United States stated.[13]

The writing of poetry at South Shaftsbury during the autumn of 1931 was interrupted by several trips to give previously scheduled readings in various parts of New England, and as far south as Philadelphia. More complicated interruptions were caused by decisions involving a major real-estate transaction. The Frosts had decided that they were tired of renting quarters in Amherst during their annual stays, and that they would prefer to purchase a house there if they could find one suitable to their tastes. Again they asked their friend Warren R. Brown to serve as agent, and again he showed them a place which was very appealing. A relatively small two-and-one-half-story building, typically Victorian in architecture, it was more elegant and expensive than any home they had previously owned, and it was said to have been designed by the celebrated Stanford White, formerly of the New York firm of McKim, Mead and White. The address was 15 Sunset Avenue, and the view to the west included the lower Berkshires, with Mount Warner in the near distance. It had been owned and occupied for many years by Dr. Henry H. Goodell, a former president of Massachusetts State College. The Frosts completed the purchase late in November of 1931, with the aid of a mortgage provided by Amherst College. Then they hired a decorator who was asked to advise them in making the furnishings appropriately Victorian. When finished, the living room was elegantly done with lace curtains and damask drapes, an Axminster rug, a horsehair sofa, and a chair to match.

The Frosts moved into their new home on the first of February 1932, just before he was to take up his duties at Amherst College. By that time, however, he had worn himself out with all the tasks of moving, and became seriously ill. His primary ailment, the doctor said, was influenza, complicated by inflammatory rheumatism and nervous exhaustion. Late in February he felt strong enough to unburden some of his discouragement by writing to Untermeyer:

"Jean [Starr Untermeyer] writes that where e'er you may roam you worry about me. You should. I'll tell you what we'll do: I'll worry about my family; you worry about me; and let

Hoover worry about you. Concerning you are all Hoover's expressions of hope and fear—concerning you and the proletariat you represent or used to when you were an editor of the Masses. Me and mine are below the threshold of legislative cognizance. Beyond participation of politicians and beyond relief of senates lie our sorrows: if any of the farm bloc (heads) chance to heave a sigh, they pity us and not our grief. And the chiefest of our sorrows is that the world should go as it does—that thus all moves and that this is the justice that on earth we find. What justice? Do I have to tell you? Why injustice, which we either have to turn on the other fellow with a laugh when it is called comedy or we have to take like a spear-point in both hands to our breast when it is called tragedy.[14] Laugh no more, gentles, laugh no more. For it is almost too hard for anything to succeed in being divine, though Lionel Johnson sware the opposite. But let what will be be. I am so deeply smitten through the helm that I am almost sad to see infants young any more. . . .

"Yet I refuse to match sorrows with anyone else, because just the moment I start the comparison I see that I have nothing yet as terrible as it might be. A few of our children are sick or their spouses are and one of them has a spouse still in college. I and my wife are not well, neither are we young: but we mean to be both better and younger for company's sake. That is to say we mean well, though we aren't well.

"I thought I'd just lay it on lugubrious this letter. I saw and heard what you said about me in Springfield, but it didn't cure my evil mood because it threw me into a superstitious fear that you would incur for me the jealousy of gods and men. I shall have to tell you some day just how great I can allow you to say I am—that is if Elinor will allow me to set you a limit. (But she says now if you don't go to extremes for me she will.) The gods I am afraid of are your God of Israel, who admits he is a jealous god, and Edna's goddess Venus, who can't deny the love she stands for is a 99 per cent adultery of jealousy. Never mind the names of the men I am afraid of. Now don't for goodness sake *ever* take me at my word and incontinently give up praising me altogether. . . . I seem slowly to be getting over what I imagined was the matter with me."[15]

While still in a dark mood, and depressed by his ailments, he hopefully shared with his wife the unexpected announcement from Marjorie that she had fallen in love with a student at the University of Colorado and that they were engaged to be married. "He is a dear, kind, and considerate man, another real Victorian, papa," she wrote, "with the beautiful ideals that I had feared no longer existed."[16] She had often mentioned his name, Willard Fraser, in her previous letters, and had told of how she had met him through one of Frost's students, Dwight Morrow, Jr., son of the distinguished financier and trustee of Amherst. Willard had been forced to delay his studies while earning his way through college, but he would be graduated from the University of Colorado in June of 1932, and he hoped to make a career either in archaeology or in newspaper work—or in politics. Marjorie had introduced Willard to the Bartletts and they liked him. Of course her parents would meet him when they returned to Colorado, that summer, for their promised visit with her. Before then, she planned to visit Lillian, Carol, and Prescott in California, now that the doctors had pronounced her so nearly well: "At any rate I promised Lillian and Carol I would come. Lillian is sick, and I can make her happy, and where is the use of a new love if you can't be true to your old ties? I may not stay more than three or four weeks."[17]

Marjorie's father managed to have a letter waiting for her when she reached California: "Just a word from Amherst to welcome you to Monrovia. Your last news from Boulder went to our hearts and imaginations. Willard sounds like a good boy in a sad world. Bless you both. Perhaps on our way out in June we'll see him and on our way back see him and you together."[18]

There were three important obligations to be attended to before any definite time could be set for the planned return of the Frosts to Colorado and California. Frost was at Columbia University on the twenty-fourth of May 1932, serving as Phi Beta Kappa Poet, and reading for the first time his new poem, "Build Soil." He was also present at the Columbia University commencement on the first of June to receive his ninth honorary degree, and later in the month he went to Williams College to receive his tenth. As soon as these events were behind them, the elder Frosts departed for Colorado.

Marjorie and Willard were waiting for them, at the station in Denver, when they arrived, and Marjorie's parents became increasingly impressed by their daughter's choice of this quiet and straightforward young man. When he had first written to Marjorie's parents, Frost had answered, "That was a fine letter. I know I couldn't have done half as well under the circumstances. . . . I am particularly glad you are bringing archaeology into the family. Archaeology is one of the four things I wanted most to go into in life, archaeology, astronomy, farming, and teaching Latin. . . ."[19] It was easy enough for these two men to talk about their common interests. Frost soon learned that Willard had spent a summer digging with the distinguished Colorado archaeologist Earl Morris at Chichén Itzá in Mexico, and he was to leave for another dig with Morris in a few days.[20] When Willard left Boulder for his summer work, Marjorie and her parents started for California.

In Monrovia, Carol had carried out instructions that he find a house his parents could rent inexpensively for several months. They particularly liked the place he had chosen—219 West Greystone Avenue—because it again afforded them a fine view of the foothills of the San Gabriel Mountains, rising steeply to the north, and because it was within walking distance of Carol's temporary home at 261 North Canyon Street. Carol and Prescott did much of the housework and cooking for the bedridden Lillian, who seemed to be making no progress. Marjorie, again offering her services as nurse, immediately began helping to care for Lillian, who courageously insisted that she was getting better.

The elder Frosts tried to stay in hiding throughout the summer of 1932, and they succeeded until an ardent Frost-collector gave away their secret.[21] Not too reluctantly, Frost let himself be persuaded to give three readings in the Los Angeles area, late in September: at Occidental College,[22] at the University of Southern California,[23] and at California Institute of Technology.[24] Then, early in October, they started for home,[25] with the understanding that Marjorie would stay with Carol and Lillian for a few weeks longer and that she would thereafter visit Willard's parents in Montana before she returned to Amherst.

Constantly worrying about the heavy expenses he had agreed to meet, in the attempt to restore his children to health, Frost had accepted several invitations to give lectures and readings on the way back across the continent. The first stop was with the Bartletts again, in Boulder, for a talk at the University of Colorado on the subject, "All Thinking Is Metaphor."[26] Next, he and Mrs. Frost went to Omaha, Nebraska, for another reading. From there they went to Ann Arbor and stayed with their friends the Bursleys long enough for Frost to talk before the assembled graduate students in English and to give one public reading of his poems.[27] By the time he and Mrs. Frost reached South Shaftsbury, late in October, he had completed arrangements for another miscellaneous group of readings and talks, all mixed in with unavoidable social engagements.

The most memorable of these engagements occurred as a result of Ferris Greenslet's invitation to attend a banquet in honor of T. S. Eliot at the St. Botolph Club in Boston on the fifteenth of November 1932. Eliot, having come over from England to spend the fall semester as the Charles Eliot Norton Professor of Poetry, at Harvard, had quickly become celebrated as an object of adulation. Other guests at the dinner included John Livingston Lowes and such younger Harvard poets as David McCord, Robert Hillyer, Theodore Morrison, and John Brooks Wheelwright. As the dinner started, Frost's initial reaction was one of disgust at what he viewed as the obsequiousness with which the younger men fed questions to Eliot, hung on his words, and bowed to all his pontifications without challenging any of them. If Scotland had not been slighted by Eliot in one of his comments, Frost might have managed to remain silent. With a British tone of superiority, Eliot announced that no good poetry had ever been written north of the Scottish border except, perhaps for one poem, William Dunbar's "Lament for the Makers" with its Latin refrain, *"Timor Mortis conturbat me."* Trying to conceal his indignation, Frost challenged that pronouncement by asking if an exception to it might be made for Bobby Burns. No, Eliot thought not. Then, said Frost, might it be said that Burns was at least a good songwriter? "One might grant that modest claim," Eliot acknowledged, in a tone which seemed deliberately condescending. Frost, disgusted, wanted to leave the table and not come back. Nothing about the affair pleased him until, over coffee and brandy, someone produced a copy of "The Hippopotamus" and asked the guest of honor to read it aloud. To Frost, the request seemed accidentally funny, for Eliot had already retracted the satirical attitude he had held when he had written that poem. Eliot graciously answered that he would read his poem if Mr. Frost would read one of his. Mischievously, Frost agreed to do more than asked: he'd write a poem while Eliot was hippopotamizing. The other guests were amused, and Frost made a show of collecting a few place cards, on which he immediately started to scribble. When Eliot's sepulchral droning ended, and attention turned to Frost, he stopped writing. He'd have to improvise the tail end of his poem, he said, because he hadn't quite figured out the last quatrain. Then he announced his title: "My Olympic Record Stride." None of his listeners knew he had actually completed the poem months earlier, that he had already said all nine quatrains of it, from memory, earlier in the fall, or that he had chosen it now for purposes of criticizing what he considered to be the pomposity of this visitor, this native of St. Louis, this son of a Boston girl, who had run away from the United States, and who had apparently worked hard to develop a British accent. Frost hoped some of his listeners would notice that one difference between his own poetry and Eliot's would be suggested in the final quatrain he would pretend to improvise:

> And I hope they're going to forgive me
> For being as over-elated
> As if I had measured the country
> And got the United States stated.

After he made a show of reading from his penciled place cards, and of finding the last quatrain on the ceiling of the private dining room, he was not prepared for the polite solemnity with which his listeners praised his accomplishment. He had hoped his game would be taken as a practical joke, and that someone would challenge his claim that he was improvising, but their seriousness deprived him of any chance to confess.[28]

This performance at the St. Botolph Club cost him more nervous energy than he could afford, and he had scarcely returned to Amherst before he became seriously ill with a condition the doctor called grippe. As Christmas of 1932 approached, he recovered sufficiently to be up and around the house before his daughter Irma came from New Haven with her husband, John Cone (now doing graduate work in architecture at Yale), and their obstreperous six-year-old, Jacky. Unfortunately, the noise and excitement of this invasion placed too much strain on his nerves. Even worse, almost everyone in the house came down with grippe. Mrs. Frost described the scene to Mrs. Fobes:

"Before Christmas, Robert and I were very miserable, off and on. . . . Irma and John and Jacky came up for the holidays.

We got through Christmas day very pleasantly, but two days later Marjorie and my maid came down with grippe and the next day John and Irma followed suit. My maid just comes in day times, so her husband took care of her at her home. I got hold of a good nurse to take care of Marjorie, John, and Irma, and then devoted myself to looking after Robert and Jacky, and protecting them from infection, also getting the meals for the crowd. Well, I *did* get exhausted and do not feel well yet. Marjorie has recovered nicely, much to my relief, and Irma and John and Jacky returned to New Haven."[29]

During the next few months, Frost carried on his public commitments at Amherst and elsewhere under the burden of another family tension. Marjorie, busy assembling her trousseau, raised questions hard to answer. Should her wedding be held in Amherst? Or in South Shaftsbury? In a church, or in her home? Indifferent to religion, and free from any church affiliation, she wanted a small wedding to which only relatives and closest friends would be invited. Because she was her father's favorite among the four children, she was quickly encouraged to make her own choice. Willard helped her by writing that his newspaper work had become so demanding that it would be difficult for him to come East in June of 1933—the month chosen for the wedding. After further correspondence with him, she announced that they would be married on the third of June 1933 in Willard's home in Billings; that she would leave for Montana in mid-May.

Her father was relieved by the announcement. Ahead of him lay an elaborate schedule of readings in Texas,[30] arranged to help his children pay their bills. If he was well enough to get to Montana for the wedding, he would go, but he doubted that he could. Mrs. Frost, wearied by all her efforts to help Marjorie, had her own doubts. She should immediately go to Texas with her husband, she felt, just to watch over him: he was always careless about his health. Although she did not start with him, she did join him in Austin when he was halfway through—and she found him near exhaustion. After they returned, he tried to meet other engagements and kept trying until he was again ill. His wife described their predicament as it existed late in May of 1933:

"We are still in Amherst. We have lingered here because of Robert's health. Two days after he was in New York, he came down with a bad cold. It was a queer cold, with temperature, and has been followed by a prolonged period of temperature and prostration. He has very little appetite, and is intensely nervous. The doctor is watching him, with tuberculosis in mind, and advises absolute quiet for an indefinite period, that is, an avoidance of whatever might be a physical or nervous strain. He stays in bed until dinner time, and then dresses and then wanders around the house, and if it is sunny, sits a little while outdoors. I expect that after we get up to the farm he will improve, as the air is really better up there, and probably his digestion and appetite will improve. I hope I am mistaken, but my opinion is that he is in for real trouble this time. His cough has settled into something that seems to me to have a permanent quality in it. He has been overdoing too much these last two years. . . .

"Marjorie is to be married in Billings on Saturday. The young man she has been engaged to for a year, has got a job on a weekly newspaper in Helena. He is business manager, and may work in as editor. He seems to be doing nearly everything [in the newspaper office] and cannot come east for a wedding. As Robert hates ceremonies, it is just as well not to have it in our house. It will be a very quiet affair in his father's house in Billings, and then they will drive to Helena. Marjorie is a lot stronger, and looks fine, but I am rather anxious about the effect of housekeeping on her."[31]

Intermittently, throughout the next twelve months, Frost was incapacitated by a series of ailments which depressed him and frightened his wife. During the summer of 1933, they were visited briefly by Carol and Prescott, who drove east from California and brought good news about Lillian's progress toward recovery. There was still talk that Frost himself might have contracted the disease. That fall, he suffered extremely from hay fever, ran a temperature for several days, and was forced to stay in bed for some time immediately after reaching the sanctuary of the Fobes guest-cottage in Franconia. Doctors had repeatedly urged him to protect himself against winter cold by spending the worst months in Florida, and there were times during the winter of 1933–1934 when he was tempted to go. But always there was the problem of whether he could afford such an expensive trip, and he was still needing all the money he could earn from such public readings as he could manage to give. Marjorie and Willard had urged the Frosts to visit them in Montana during the approaching summer of

1934, and in February Frost wrote to Willard, "We or I any-way read your Montana Year Book clean through every little while in preparation for our visit. . . . We shall be along bye and bye. I got out of three lectures I was supposed to give this month or next but to make up for it I shall have to preach the [Amherst] Baccalaureate sermon in June."[32]

These expectations were suddenly changed by frightening events. Mrs. Frost, knowing that Marjorie was expecting a child in mid-March, decided to go alone to Montana in order to be with her daughter during her confinement. On the six-teenth of March 1934, the child was born and was named Marjorie Robin Fraser. Eleven days later, Mrs. Frost thought her daughter was recovering normally, and she hurried back to Amherst because of word that Frost was ill again. She was home only two weeks when Willard telephoned from Billings to say that Marjorie was seriously ill with puerperal fever. The elder Frosts left for Montana by train as soon as they could, knowing that the dread ailment was frequently fatal. When they reached Marjorie's bedside, it was difficult for them to tell whether she recognized them: the fever made her delirious. Day after day, they lived in a confusion of hopes and fears which grew increasingly dreadful. On the twentieth of April 1934, Frost wrote to Roy Elliott at Amherst:

"Still the same desperate chance. The doctors tell us the length of time Marjorie has stood the fever is a favorable sign. She has been sick five weeks. She has been out of her mind most of the time and never completely in her mind for more than a week. Fatal as most of the facts of the case sound, we are determined to win—the same as we would be when our side was far behind in a game. I don't know what will become of Elinor if we lose. Or Willard either. . . .

"I wrote Stanley King [President of Amherst College] how ready I would be for anything and everything if we come out all right, but how utterly against the world and unwilling to face it if fate fails us. He must be the one to decide what to do about my taking part [at commencement] in June. I agree with you I am a pretty bad bet. I seem to find ways of getting out of all obligations this year. . . ."[33]

Frantically trying to learn whether there was any new way to combat the fever, Frost was told that the Mayo Clinic in Rochester, Minnesota, had developed a serum which was still in the experimental stage. Telephone calls were made, and the doctors at the Mayo Clinic urged that the patient should be brought from Billings to Rochester by private plane. These arrangements were quickly completed, and Willard drove the elder Frosts to Rochester in his car. On the twenty-ninth of April 1934, Frost wrote to Untermeyer, from Rochester:

"We are going through the valley of the shadow with Marjorie we are afraid. She had a baby in Billings, Montana, six weeks ago and most of the time since has hovered on the verge of death. The harm must have been done by her first doctor there of course. The infection was a terrible one. But once it was done her first doctor and the others we have called in have done everything possible for her. Three days ago we put her in a small airplane with a doctor and nurse to fly here. The thousand mile flight seems not to have set her back, and here we can expect the miracles of modern science. Rosenow, the great biologist, finds he has a serum for a close cousin of the organism diffused in her blood-stream. It would be better if it were for the exact organism. But that and blood-transfusions every other day and Marjorie's tenacity and Elinor's devotion and the mercy of God are our hopes. You will probably see us home again alive whatever the outcome, but it will be months hence and changed for the worse for the rest of our days. . . . My favorite poem long before I knew what it was going to mean to us was Arnold's 'Cadmus and Harmonia.' "[34]

For several days thereafter, terrible suffering continued for everyone involved. Marjorie died on the second of May, and her body was taken back to Billings for burial. It was not until Frost returned to Amherst with his wife that he could bear to express the anguish. On the fifteenth of May he wrote to Untermeyer:

"I told you by letter or telegram what was hanging over us. So you know what to expect. Well, the blow has fallen. The noblest of us all is dead and has taken our hearts out of the world with her. It was a terrible seven weeks' fight—too indelibly terrible on the imagination. No death in war could more than match it for suffering and heroic endurance. Why all this talk in favor of peace? Peace has her victories over poor mortals no less merciless than war. Marge always said she would rather die in a gutter than in a hospital. But it was in a hospital she was caught to die after more than a hundred serum injections and blood transfusions. We were torn afresh every day between the temptation of letting her

go untortured or cruelly trying to save her. The only consolation we have is the memory of her greatness through all.
Never out of delirium for the last four weeks her responses
were of course incorrect. She got little or nothing of what we
said to her. The only way I could reach her was by putting my
hand backward and forward between us as in counting out
and saying with over-emphasis *You*—and—*Me*. The last time
I did that, the day before she died, she smiled faintly and
answered 'All the same,' frowned slightly and made it 'Always
the same.' Her temperature was then 110, the highest ever
known at the Mayo Clinic where as I told you we took her,
but too late. The classical theory was not born out in her case
that a fine and innocent nature released by madness from the
inhibitions of society will give way to all the indecencies.
Everything she said, however quaint and awry, was of an almost straining loftiness. It was as if her ruling passion must
have been to be wise and good, or it could not have been so
strong in death. But curse all doctors who for a moment let
down and neglect in childbirth the scientific precautions they
have been taught in school. We thought to move heaven and
earth—heaven with prayers and earth with money. We moved
nothing. And here we are Cadmus and Harmonia not yet placed
safely in changed forms."[35]

It was even longer before Marjorie's mother could bring
herself to tell even her closest friends about the unacceptable
loss. On the twelfth of June 1934 she wrote to Mrs. Fobes,
merely giving the facts and then adding, "Poor darling child—
it seems too heart breaking, that after achieving good health,
and finding perfect happiness in life, she had to lose it all so
soon."[36] Mrs. Fobes, in reply, tried to console her, but she refused to be comforted:

"It is true that her two years in training at Baltimore were a
great satisfaction to her, and her marriage a great happiness,
but somehow the thought of all that does not help me. She
wanted to live . . . and yet she was so brave and noble. The
pathos of it was too terrible. I long to die myself and be
relieved of the pain that I feel for her sake. Poor precious
darling, to have to leave everything in such a cruel and unnecessary way. I cannot bear it, and yet I *must* bear it for the
sake of the others here."[37]

THINGS IN PAIRS ORDAINED

. . . it ignores so superciliously the strain we may have been under for years trying to decide between God and the Devil . . . between endless other things in pairs ordained to everlasting opposition.[1]

WHEN Robert and Elinor Frost returned to Vermont after the funeral service for Marjorie, in Montana, they were accompanied by their inconsolably bereaved son-in-law Willard Fraser and his baby daughter Robin. Although the Frosts felt they did not have enough strength to take charge of the child indefinitely, they knew that Willard needed such immediate help as they could give him, and they insisted that he leave Robin with them when he returned to Montana. Lillian, who had regained her health remarkably after her almost fatal siege of tuberculosis, offered her assistance. At her own request, she assumed the primary responsibility for taking care of the baby, at the Stone Cottage, during the summer of 1934, and the grandparents returned Robin to Willard early in the fall. The plan for this return was easily arranged because Frost had agreed to participate in ceremonies connected with the inauguration of Gordon K. Chalmers as president of Rockford College in Illinois, where Lesley had obtained a teaching position after getting her divorce from Dwight Francis. Willard and his mother were waiting for the Frosts, at Rockford, and took Robin from there to Montana.[2] By the time the Frosts returned to Amherst, near the middle of October 1934, it was plain that Mrs. Frost had overtaxed herself. Early in November she was prostrated by a severe heart attack, angina pectoris, and several days passed before she was out of danger.[3] Although warned by her doctor that she must carefully reserve what little strength she had, she seemed not to care whether she recovered; her husband, disliking the intrusion of a maid, was given no alternative.

The doctor urged that, because Mrs. Frost's condition was so precarious, and because Frost himself had suffered from severe pulmonary ailments throughout the previous winter, they should plan to escape the coldest months of the approaching winter by going to Florida as early as possible.[4] Lillian's doctor had given her similar advice, and therefore cooperative plans were developed. Just for the novelty and adventure of it, Key West was chosen as their joint destination. Early in December of 1934, the elder Frosts went to Miami and down across the Keys by train; Carol and his family drove approximately 1,700 miles from Vermont by slow stages, arriving in Key West shortly after Christmas. Frost, trying to keep his mind off griefs and fears, soon began writing letters in which he described the strangeness of this almost tropical retreat:

"Well, one hundred and fifty miles south of Miami, six hundred south of Los Angeles, three hundred south of Cairo in Egypt, and sixty miles at sea, we reached Key West by train over a string of keys and bridges. It is an island about ten times as big as your farm, and fairly dense with population, equal parts Negro, Cuban, and American, 12,000 now, which is a reduction from 25,000 since the cigar business went to Tampa a few years ago. There is no sanitation. The water is all off the roofs and after it goes through people I don't know where it goes. Everything is shabby and even dilapidated. There are as many stinks as there are nymphs who rule o'er sewers and sinks (Delete sewers). There are mosquitoes. But there is no Yellow Fever any more. There is no malaria. There has never, absolutely never, been a frost. The air is balm. . . . We are on the point of the island exactly between the Gulf of Mexico and the Atlantic Ocean. The waves break 20 feet from our door—Elinor's and mine. Carol, Lillian, and Prescott live down town by the Customs House and Post Office equally distant from the abandoned Navy Yard and the small Army Post. . . . Hemingway is said to be here much of the time. But he knows not me and I know not him. . . ."[5]

Trying hard to enjoy the oddity of Key West, Frost did whatever he could to keep his wife from brooding over Marjorie's death and over her own condition.[6] She remained so physically and nervously tired that even the least exertion was hard for her. Nothing seemed attractive to her in the picturesque shabbiness of the palm-shaded streets or in the quaintly varied architecture of the houses, built from coral limestone and whitewashed. The one place which interested her most during short walks around the town was the Old Island Trading Post where Spanish women made various kinds of apparel. The gracious and friendly owner, Mrs. Jessie Porter Kirk, was the granddaughter of Admiral David Dixon Porter who had been assigned the task of supervising the naval defense of Key West immediately after the Civil War. Almost daily, Frost helped his wife up the steps of the Trading Post and left her in the special care of Mrs. Kirk while he went shopping for groceries.[7]

Quite often, when troubled by a new cluster of worries, Frost made countermoves which were only indirectly related to his fears. Here in Key West a convenient target for verbal mauling happened to be the New Deal activities of the Federal Emergency Relief Administration. Knowing that Untermeyer's liberal attitude toward President Roosevelt and his New Deal was as sympathetic as Frost's was hostile, he warmed to the subject in his first letter to Untermeyer from Key West:

"The only thing at all socially disturbing is the presence in force of Franklin D. Roosevelt FERA. This has been one of the Administration's pet rehabilitation projects. No taxes had been paid on anything. Everybody was riding round in cars without silencers and without licenses. There was talk of transporting seventy five percent of the crowd. But nobody could think of anybody who would want them. So the author of a book called *Compulsory Spending* [Julius Stone] is here with a staff to put everybody at work on public improvements, some building, some tearing down, and some general cleaning up of filthy vacant lots. We had to get our rent thru them. They are mildly and beneficently dictatorial. Both the Mayor of the Town and the Governor of the State have abdicated in their favor. Their great object they say is to restore the people to their civic virtue. When in history has any power ever achieved that. You see how much I am interested."[8]

Another diversion to which he gladly devoted himself while doing next to nothing in Key West was the writing of an introduction he had promised for another rabid New Dealer, the humanitarian socialist-reformer-poet in Vermont, Sarah Cleghorn. His friendship for this neighbor of his had forced him into this awkward assignment and as a result he permitted the introduction to tell more about himself than about her. Always liking to define his own conservative position in terms of opposites, he this time built toward them through a seemingly playful start:

"Security, security! We run in all directions for security in the game of Pussy-wants-a-corner. I find security chiefly in proper names—the thought of certain people, I mean people I can be certain of at their posts or postoffices. I am like Childe Roland on his way to the Dark Tower: I need someone pleasant to think of. They that are against us should be more than they that are for us by all present-day accounts.

> 'May be true what I have heard:
> Earth's a howling wilderness
> Truculent with force and fraud.'[9]

It will not do to underestimate the relative strength of the enemy. But neither will it do to overestimate it. That, I take it, is one lesson of Grant's greatness as a general. It is necessary to keep in mind in a campaign just whom we can muster in an emergency. We in Vermont are taken care of on the north by three great ladies up the valley, three varieties who can be depended on to hold Vermont true to its winter self against all the summer comers. And one of these is wise and a novelist [Dorothy Canfield Fisher], one is a mystic and an essayist [Zephine Humphrey Fahnestock], and the third is saintly and a poet. This book is about them all, but principally (and charmingly and naturally) about the poet. It is her story of her life told with a beautiful unconsciousness of its beauty."

After this beginning, he expressed his opposition to the current fashions of reformers. Still smarting under the attempt to make him take sides in the warfare between humanitarians and humanists, he had recently been offended by a reformer-poet, Hermann Hagedorn, who had tried to convert him to humanitarian Buchmanism, as he hinted in his continuation:

"Saint, poet—*and* reformer. There is more high explosive for righteousness in the least little line of Sarah Cleghorn's poem about the children working in the mill where they could look out the window at their grown-up employers playing golf than in all the prose of our radical-bound-boys pressed together under a weight of several atmospheres of revolution. The reformer has to be taken with the rest of it. And why not? Some

of us have developed a habit of saying we can't stand a reformer. But we don't mean it except where the reformer is at
the same time a raw convert to the latest scheme for saving the
soul or the state. The last we heard of him may have been two
or three fashions ago as one of the ultra-arty insisting that we
join him in his minor vices at his wild parties. Now he turns
up at our door to ask without ceremony—You don't mean to
say you don't love God or you don't mean to say you don't love
humanity.—Don't you believe public confession [Buchmanism]
is good for the soul?—Don't you believe so-and-so [Sacco or
Vanzetti] died a martyr to the cause of humanity?—Let me recall you to your better self.—Have you given anything any
thought?"

While writing this preface to Sarah Cleghorn's autobiography,
Frost may not have realized that as his literary reputation increased he was growing bolder in asserting his prejudices concerning social, political, and religious matters. So far, however,
he had not published any prose statement which indicated so
clearly as this the close relation between his underlying puritan
bias and his social-political conservatism. As he continued his
comment on his distastes for any reformer who might be a raw
convert "to the latest scheme for saving the soul or the state,"
he went even deeper into self-revelation:

"I don't know what makes this so nettling unless it is that it
ignores so superciliously the strain we may have been under
for years trying to decide between God and the Devil, between
the rich and the poor (the greed of one and the greed of the
other), between keeping still about our troubles and enlarging
on them to the doctor and—between endless other things in
pairs ordained to everlasting opposition.[10] No, it is not the
reformer we object to. Nor is it yet the convert. The convert
has his defense. It is the rawness, the egotism, the gross greed
to take spiritual advantage of us. We have all had attempts on
our self-respect of the kind, and we cringe at the memory. I
have had four, one of them lately that would afford one scene
in a comedy. But a reformer who has all her life long pursued
the even tenor of her aspiration, is no one to resent. On the
contrary, she is one for me to claim friendship with and, if
permitted, kindred spirit with. Pride enters into it, as may be
seen."

After an ambiguous digression, touching briefly on Miss

Cleghorn's sympathetic concern for the predicament of the Negro, he concluded by returning once again to abstract opposites:

"A philosopher may worry about a tendency that, if run out to its logical conclusion, might ruin all; but he worries only till he can make out in the confusion the particular counter tendency that is going to collide with it to the cancellation of both. Formidable equations often resolve into no more information than that nothing equals nothing. It is a common question: What has become of the alarming old tendency to come to grief from each one's minding his own business? Oh, if I remember rightly, that bumped head on into the tendency to come to grief from minding each other's business. The philosopher values himself on the inconsistencies he can contain by main force. They are two ends of a strut that keeps his mind from collapsing. He may take too much satisfaction in having once more remarked the two-endedness of things. To a saint and a reformer like Sarah Cleghorn the great importance is not to get hold of both ends, but of the right end. She has to be partisan and even a trifle grim. I heard a clergyman say she is the kind we need most of to get the world forward. Well, here we have her, her whole story from the first dawning on her childhood of the need of goodness and mercy."[11]

Frost could count on the fact that many readers would misunderstand the subdued ironies and sarcasms in his tribute to the reforming zeal of this woman who was indeed "trying to get the world forward." He would have spoiled what was genuine in his tribute to this friend if he had openly stated his own doctrine of laissez faire, and his own belief that justice should always take precedence over mercy. And yet he knew from his own experiences how easily the impulsive responses of the heart could and did sentimentalize the more rigorous perceptions. His concern for opposites, in this regard, had provided him with the makings of a poem, recently written. It had grown out of his having seen from his Pullman window a "human pathetic light" in the darkness of the desert while he was traveling by train from Denver to Salt Lake City in August of 1931:

Something I saw or thought I saw
In the desert at midnight in Utah,
Looking out of my lower berth

At moonlit sky and moonlit earth.
The sky had here and there a star;
The earth had a single light afar,
A flickering, human pathetic light,
That was maintained against the night,
It seemed to me, by the people there,
With a Godforsaken brute despair.
It would flutter and fall in half an hour
Like the last petal off a flower.

So far, in this poem, he had represented the heart in control
of the imagination; the sentimental indulgence of pity and
sympathy for anyone living under such desolate conditions.
Continuing, he represented an opposed or balancing use of
the imagination:

But my heart was beginning to cloud my mind.
I knew a tale of a better kind.
That far light flickers because of trees.
The people can burn it as long as they please;
And when their interests in it end,
They can leave it to someone else to tend.
Come back that way a summer hence,
I should find it no more no less intense.
I pass, but scarcely pass no doubt,
When one will say, "Let us put it out."
The other without demur agrees.
They can keep it burning as long as they please;
They can put it out whenever they please.
One looks out last from the darkened room
At the shiny desert with spots of gloom
That might be people and are but cedar,
Have no purpose, have no leader,
Have never made the first move to assemble,
And so are nothing to make her tremble.
She can think of places that are not thus
Without indulging a "Not for us!"
Life is not so sinister-grave.
Matter of fact has made them brave.
He is husband, she is wife.
She fears not him, they fear not life.
They know where another light has been,

And more than one, to theirs akin,
But earlier out for bed tonight,
So lost on me in my surface flight.

This I saw when waking late,
Going by at a railroad rate,
Looking through wreaths of engine smoke
Far into the lives of other folk.[12]

Increasingly, during these days, Frost kept finding more detached and more philosophic ways of manipulating opposites, in his poetry and in his conversations. Invited up to Miami from Key West, to speak before the Winter Institute of Literature at the University of Miami, he talked about the outside extremes of a poem. In the creative act, he said, a certain impulse or state of mind precedes the writing of the poem. Next comes what Stevenson had called a visitation of style, a power to find words which will somehow convey the impulse. The subject matter is provided by a combination of "things that happen to us and things that occur to us." And gradually, out of this happy process the poem gets made, leaving something more implied than stated: "It is what is beyond that makes poetry—what is unsaid. . . . Its unsaid part is its best part."[13]

Not long after the Frosts returned to Amherst from Key West in April of 1935, he chose to make further extensions of his thoughts concerning opposites. President King felt that the Amherst students were not being given sufficient opportunity to become acquainted with their poet-in-residence, and he arranged to have Frost make three public appearances that spring. The first of these was devoted largely to a reading of his own poems; the second was more nearly a lecture on two different kinds of originality—good and bad—in modern poetry. He singled out for special attack those "children and grandchildren of Ezra Pound" who had been striving for what he called a bad form of originality. Pound had tried to achieve his originality by "imitating somebody that hadn't been imitated recently." Too many of the modern poets, he said, had been trying absurd methods to attain originality, such as taking away meter, taking away meaning, leaving out sentiment, and of generally following the lead of Archibald MacLeish, who had recently claimed, according to Frost, that "our object is to be untimely." Others had worked on the theory that poetry must be as good as prose and they had therefore tried to write their "poetry" in prose. The students were charmed by Frost's way of defining originality in terms of opposites. One undergraduate reporter wrote:

"This second talk had the same unique excitement and freshness as his first: he speaks out his thoughts as they come to him and gives us the feeling that we are attendant at the process of creation. That is probably why, at a Frost lecture, there is such an extraordinarily tense hush in between the waves of laughter."[14]

Frost's platform manner had undergone a remarkable change, and the first few "waves of laughter" helped him overcome his nervousness. A reporter for the Amherst *Record* made his own estimate of the response Frost achieved in both of these appearances during the spring of 1935: "The character, wit, and chatty informal style of address of Robert Frost delighted crowded halls . . . Mr. Frost's benevolent satire touched on many objects . . . [including] the 'moderns' in poetry, who received their usual roasting at the hands of America's premier conservative poet."[15]

The third and final public appearance which Frost made in Amherst, that spring, occurred when he addressed the seniors at their final chapel service at the opening of commencement week. His announced topic was "Our Darkest Concern," and this time he worked out his talk in terms of political or social opposites: the extreme left and the extreme right. Again his target was the New Deal, with its goal of achieving social improvement by protecting and directing the lives of its citizens toward what Frost viewed as a Utopian ideal of society. His darkest concern was that "Utopia may get us yet," and he offered as the opposite of Utopia his concept of freedom:

"True freedom is the privilege of meeting the emergencies of life by apt recalls from the past; enough of these good recalls, scattered and freely had, form future mental figures which lead to reason. Personal freedom has always been considered by the world as too remotely unsocial: this personal freedom has now vanished in favor of a new freedom of relationships, of social rights and contracts.

"Men have always dreamed of Utopia in the past; I suppose Utopia will get us yet. Life wastes away into death, insanity, poverty and crime. Utopia aims to alleviate or stop these sorrows. There are too many things to be done before Utopia can be attained, yet writers from Plato to Spenser and even later have crusaded in this seemingly hopeless cause. Our lives are an attempt to find out where we are standing between extremes of viewpoint; in politics and in education we are now shifting betwen the extreme left and the extreme right. Twenty years from now I shall expect to find education still leaning a bit to the left—but still human."[16]

As soon as Frost could escape from Amherst to his farm at the Gully in South Shaftsbury, he tackled another literary assignment by manipulating another variety of opposites. Back in the days when he had been trying to establish himself with his own countrymen, immediately after his return from England in 1915, he had considered Edwin Arlington Robinson his most serious competitor for honors. As the years passed, however, he became increasingly confident that he was displacing Robinson in public estimation as the foremost living American poet. Then the success of *Tristram* had been such a disappointment to Frost that he had wallowed in jealousies which, on one occasion, he had not even tried to conceal. A younger poet, Merrill Moore, having established himself as a practicing psychiatrist in Boston, and having made the acquaintance of Frost and Robinson, arranged to play host to them both at a private dinner. The evening began awkwardly, and Moore was made particularly unhappy by the ways in which Frost mocked Robinson for having wasted so much time reworking the Arthurian legend. Refusing to take offense, Robinson merely changed the subject and tone of the conversation by talking of his favorites among Frost's poems. Going even further, he said there was one quatrain which seemed to him the best in all modern poetry. In fact, someone who knew of his admiration for it had given him an appropriate woodcut with that quatrain printed beneath it, and Robinson had placed it in a frame over the head of his bed. Merrill Moore could corroborate: he had seen the woodcut-and-quatrain on the wall in Robinson's room. What were the lines? Frost asked. Robinson quoted them:

The woods are lovely, dark, and deep,
But I have promises to keep,
And miles to go before I sleep,
And miles to go before I sleep.

Immediately, Frost's harsh tone disappeared, and the remainder of the evening was completely amicable.[17] The first important news Frost heard, thereafter, about the Tilbury Town poet, was received in Key West: the rumor that Robinson was seriously ill and might not have long to live. Before Frost returned to Amherst from Key West, Robinson died, on the sixth of April 1935—just after he had completed reading proof on a new narrative poem which was to be published under the title, *King Jasper*.[18] A few weeks later, Robinson's publisher asked Frost to write an introduction for *King Jasper*, and he accepted the invitation with understandably mixed motives. In working on the first draft of the introduction, he used some of the ideas he had played with in his recent talks at Amherst and elsewhere. He began:

"It may come to the notice of posterity (and then again it may not) that this our age ran wild in the quest of new ways to be new. The one old way to be new no longer served. Science put it into our heads that there must be new ways to be new. Those tried were largely by subtraction—elimination. Poetry for example was tried without punctuation. It was tried without capital letters. It was tried without metric frame on which to measure the rhythm. It was tried without any images but those to the eye, and a loud general intoning had to be kept up to cover the total loss of specific images to the ear, those dramatic tones of voice which had hitherto constituted the better half of poetry. It was tried without content under the trade name of poesie pure. It was tried without phrase, epigram, coherence, logic, and consistency. It was tried without ability. I took the confession of one who had deliberately to unlearn what he knew. He made a back-pedalling movement of his hands to illustrate the process. It was tried premature like the delicacy of unborn calf in Asia. It was tried without feeling or sentiment like murder for small pay in the underworld. These many things was it tried without, and what had we left? Still something. The limits of poetry had been sorely strained, but the hope was that the idea had been somewhat brought out."

So far, Frost had conveyed his own prejudices against modern poetry without mentioning Robinson. As he began the next paragraph, he briefly digressed to include Robinson and then quickly turned to his own meditations concerning religious matters:

"Robinson stayed content with the old-fashioned way to be new. I remember bringing the subject up with him. How does a man come on his difference, and how does he feel about it when he first finds it out? At first it may well frighten him, as his difference with the Church frightened Martin Luther. There is such a thing as being too willing to be different. And what shall we say to people who are not willing but anxious? What assurance have they that their difference is not insane, eccentric, abortive, inadmissible? Two fears should follow us through life. There is the fear that we shan't prove worthy in ourselves. That is the fear of God. And there is the fear of Man: the fear that men won't understand us and we shall be cut off from them."

Having made this digression concerning his own fears, Frost seemed to forget he was preparing an introduction to Robinson's last poem, which he had not yet mentioned. Instead of mentioning it, now, he moved even deeper into a revelation of his immediate prejudices by attacking poets who were making poetry a "vehicle of grievances against the un-Utopian state." A distinction should be made, Frost said, between grievances and griefs. He preferred having grievances restricted to prose, and "leaving poetry free to go its way in tears." After saluting Robinson as one who understood this differentiation, and as one who was "a prince of heartachers amid countless achers of another part," Frost again returned to expounding his own prejudices:

"Grievances are a form of impatience. Griefs are a form of patience. We may be required by law to throw away patience as we have been required to surrender gold; since by throwing away patience and joining the impatient in one rush on the citadel of evil, the hope is we may end the need of patience. There will be nothing left to be patient about. The day of perfection waits on unanimous social action. Two or three more good national elections should do the business. It has been similarly urged on us to give up courage, make cowardice a virtue, and see if that won't end war and the need of courage. Desert religion for science, clean out the holes and corners of the residual unknown, and there will be no more need of religion. (Religion is merely consolation for what we don't know.) But suppose there was some mistake; and the evil stood siege, the war didn't end, and something remained unknowable. Our having disarmed would make our case worse than it had ever been before. Nothing in the latest advices from Wall Street, the League of Nations, or the Vatican inclines me to give up my holdings in patient grief."

After giving so much sarcastic airing to some of his own grievances, even at the moment when he was pleading that the poet should restrict himself to griefs, he concluded by placing in Robinson's mouth some more of Frost's often repeated opinions:

"There were Robinson and I, it was years ago, and the place (near Boston Common) was the place, as we liked afterwards to call it, of Bitters, because it was with bitters, though without bitterness, we could sit there and look out on the welter of dissatisfaction and experiment in the world around us. It was too long ago to remember who said what, but the sense of the meeting was, we didn't care how arrant a reformer or experimentalist a man was if he gave us real poems. For ourselves, we would hate to be read for any theory upon which we might be supposed to write. We doubted any poem could persist for any theory upon which it might have been written. Take the theory that poetry in our language could be treated as quantitative, for example. Poems had been written in spite of it. And poems are all that matter. The utmost of ambition is to lodge a few poems where they will be hard to get rid of, to lodge a few irreducible bits, where Robinson lodged more than his share."[19]

Frost was not sure Robinson's publisher would find such an essay appropriate to serve as introduction to the poem not even mentioned, but he was certain he had never before given so compressed a statement of his own position. Later, when someone asked him for a source of information about his views, he wrote, "The nearest I ever came to getting myself down in prose was in the preface to Robinson's *King Jasper*. That is so much me that you might suspect the application to him of being forced."[20] Macmillan did indeed feel that the essay was perhaps too much Frost, and politely asked him to bring Robinson in a bit more. He obliged by adding some quotations from "Miniver Cheevy," "Old King Cole," "Mr. Flood's Party," and "Dear Friends." But his most revealing addition was an expression of his own belief in the need for stylistically counterbalancing seriousness with its opposite, humor:

"The style is the man. Rather say the style is the way the man takes himself; and to be at all charming or even bearable,

[421]

the way is almost rigidly prescribed. If it is with outer seriousness, it must be with inner humor. If it is with outer humor,
it must be with inner seriousness. Neither one alone without
the other under it will do. Robinson was thinking as much in
his sonnet on Tom Hood. One ordeal of Mark Twain was the
constant fear that his occluded seriousness would be overlooked."[21]

To Frost, the entire experience of writing any tribute to his
friend-and-enemy Robinson had been an ordeal in itself, and
he suffered much over the various stages of revising it. Before
the summer of 1935 was over, however, he was caught up in
several other ordeals which were ever more painful. His puta-
tive biographer, the English poet Edward Davison, again in
the United States, had waylaid him in Miami early in the year
and had asked him to serve once more on the staff of the Rocky
Mountain Writers' Conference, which Davison would be supervising as program director, that summer. Frost agreed to go,
partly because his wife urged him to do so. She hoped they
could extend their travels by going from Boulder to Billings to
visit Marjorie's grave and see Robin again. He doubted
whether she was strong enough for the emotional strain such
a visit would entail. "Elinor is not fit for anything," he wrote.
"She is trying to save up energy for a melancholy journey to
the terrible scenes in Colorado and Montana. I am doing my
best to dissuade her from such a pilgrimage."[22]

A FURTHER RANGE

To E. F. for what it may mean to her that beyond the White Mountains were the Green; beyond both were the Rockies, the Sierras, and, in thought, the Andes and the Himalayas—range beyond range even into the realm of government and religion.[1]

ROBERT FROST was unable to dissuade his wife from starting on their westward pilgrimage. Late in July of 1935 they made the long journey together by train from South Shaftsbury to Colorado, and at Frost's invitation, Willard Fraser and his mother brought Robin down from Billings to Boulder for the reunion which meant so much to Mrs. Frost. "Marjorie's baby is in perfect health," she wrote to Lankes, "and an exceptionally bright, forward child."[2] While she took charge of caring for her granddaughter during the week the Frasers remained, her husband turned to his duties at the Rocky Mountain Writers' Conference.

He had done much to strengthen the popularity of the Conference during three previous summers, although he had not been there in person during the summer of 1933. Always liking to exercise his powers behind the scenes as much as on stage, he had persuaded the authorities to appoint his English poet-friend Edward Davison as program director, and in his first conversation with Bartlett after arriving, he asked particularly about the impression Davison had made. Bartlett, who had helped with the organization and management of the Conference since its establishment in 1930, said that Davison had caused hard feelings in his first talk before the conference: he had insisted that anyone who wrote for money was a fool and a rascal. Although Davison may have thought he was carrying out Frost's wishes when he attacked the commercialism already threatening to dominate the Rocky Mountain

Writers' Conference, Frost was annoyed by the Englishman's tactlessness. Hoping to avoid unpleasant involvements, Frost nevertheless felt that he must go to the lecture scheduled for the night after he arrived in Boulder. He explained to Bartlett that he rarely attended lectures given by others, and had composed a couplet to serve as rule of thumb in such matters:

> *I only go*
> *When I'm the show.*[3]

The speaker, that evening, was Robert Penn Warren, and his topic—"The Recent Southern Novel"—did not interest Frost. He supposed Warren would give first place to the bitter narratives of T. S. Stribling, whom Frost described to Bartlett with extreme disapproval. Stark Young's *So Red the Rose* would have to come in for consideration, and to Frost any mention of Stark Young was anathema. He explained sarcastically to Bartlett that Young preached nothing more than the old heresy that the finest American flowering had occurred in the Old South, and that an irretrievable loss had been caused by the destruction of the South by the North during the Civil War. As for the writings of Faulkner, Frost loathed them all— he had never been able to read through a single one of them, he said. Dutifully, he went to the lecture with Bartlett, received with pleasure the attentions of those who came to speak with him before the lecture began, complained that Davison's introduction was too long, and then nearly went to sleep while Warren extolled new achievements in Southern literature.

A few nights later, when Frost made the first of his three public appearances at the Writers' Conference, he talked on the announced topic, "What Poetry Thinks of Our Age." By the time he was ushered on stage for introduction, by Edward Davison, an overflow crowd of people jammed the Colorado University Theatre. Extra chairs placed in the aisles and even on the platform were filled, and people were standing at the back of the theatre. He had decided to express anew some of those conservative prejudices against the liberalism of the New Deal which he had previously articulated in one way through writing his preface for the autobiography of Sarah Cleghorn, in another way when addressing the Senior Class of 1935 at Amherst, and in a similar way when writing his "Introduction" to *King Jasper*.

Always enjoying opportunities for tantalizing his audience by using common words in uncommon ways, he this time exchanged the verbs customarily associated with the terms "liberal" and "conservative." "In order to know where we are," he began, "we must know opposites."[4] Then, instead of describing the conservative attitude as one which wishes to save, and the liberal attitude as one which wishes to spend, he turned the tables. The Utopian social reformer, he said, is always trying to save the proletariat from the wastes of social and industrial ills. By contrast, the conservative individualist is more inclined to be wasteful in his own extravagant "lust for life" and quest for happiness. "We are always shifting between these two extremes." The poet, as individualist, is more inclined to waste his time and energy while he is waiting for the proper creative mood. Although he always fluctuates between opposites, the true poet knows that the function of poetry is to deal with happiness and grief, rather than with grievances. The true poet should not devote himself to representing or weeping over the unchanging social and industrial evils: "A poet may be concerned with the jails, the poor-houses, the slums, the insane asylums, and wars; or, because he sees no possibility of change, he may try to find what happiness he can for himself and be cruelly happy." To some people, Frost admitted, such an attitude might be viewed mistakenly as one of escapism. "I have been asked if I consider myself an escapist, and I have been called a pursuitist. Well, a man may climb a tree and still not be an escapist. He may go up there to pick something." As for the present trend of the so-called "proletarian" writers expressing grievances and insisting on change, Frost bluntly disassociated himself: "It is not the business of the poet to cry for reform." So far as he was concerned, the poet should mind his own business, and to illustrate what he meant, he read to his audience a poem he had published only a few months earlier, "Two Tramps in Mud Time." The writing of that poem had been inspired by his memory of an incident which had occurred in his own New Hampshire farmyard, nearly twenty years earlier. Two lumberjacks, out of work and looking for a way to earn a living, had stopped at the edge of the road long enough to watch him splitting wood. He knew what they wanted, but he wasn't going to give it to them, for reasons he explained in the conclusion of his poem:

[425]

Nothing on either side was said.
They knew they had but to stay their stay
And all their logic would fill my head:
As that I had no right to play
With what was another man's work for gain.
My right might be love but theirs was need.
And where the two exist in twain
Theirs was the better right—agreed.

But yield who will to their separation,
My object in living is to unite
My avocation and my vocation
As my two eyes make one in sight.
Only where love and need are one,
And the work is play for mortal stakes,
Is the deed ever really done
For Heaven and the future's sakes.[5]

He may have annoyed some of his listeners by reading such a poem to clinch his argument concerning how to cope with the social and economic problems of the worker. Those who challenged his various oversimplifications, in his poems, frequently echoed the critic who had said, ". . . he has created the ordered world in which he lives only by the exclusion of many, many chaotic elements in the real world."[6] The subject-matter of this poem seemed to invoke the currently serious problem of "tramps" or migrant workers who were unemployed, but Frost's pious way of concluding this poem seemed to sidestep this part of the problem invoked.

The next evening, one listener scolded him for oversimplifying other matters, this time in his theory of poetry. The evening began with a round-table discussion of the topic, "Poetry and Intelligibility." On the platform, the participants included the poet-novelist Robert Penn Warren, the highly poetical novelist Thomas Wolfe, the Denver poet Thomas Hornsby Ferril, the poet and program-director Edward Davison, and Robert Frost. Before the discussion began, each man stated his own attitude toward the question—and there was enough difference of opinion to provide wherewithal for entertaining debate. Frost was in a jovial mood, and the comments he interjected during these preliminaries delighted the audience. When his turn came to make his own case for poetic intelligibility, he advanced his favorite theory: if the poet will only be careful in ordering his lines, so that they convey the sound of sense, he can make each poem completely intelligible: there will be only one correct way to read the poem, and it will be intelligible, in only that one way, to all intelligent listeners. None of the speakers challenged him during the discussion, but one of his listeners in the audience was a professional actress who waited for a more private chance to protest.

The actress was Florence Eldridge March, wife of the film actor, Fredric March, and she was playing at a repertory theatre in Denver that summer. Ferril had brought her up from Denver for the evening, and she went with him to the reception at Davison's home following the public discussion. As soon as she met Frost, she asked if he really believed there was only one way to read a good poem. Yes he did. Oh no, Mr. Frost, you must know better than that, for if that were true then all actors and actresses reading lines from Shakespeare's best plays would read them in much the same way—or at least in as nearly the same way as possible. But they never do that. Instead, they demonstrate in their performances that there are many different ways to read—and to interpret—one and the same poetic passage. Frost answered pleasantly by saying that if such ambiguities occurred in any of Shakespeare's plays, the fault must lie with Shakespeare as poet. You mean, said Florence Eldridge, that you can do with words what Shakespeare didn't do? Smiling, Frost answered, yes. Not amused, Miss Eldridge abruptly turned her back on the poet and walked away.[7]

The next evening Frost may have annoyed a few other listeners. He devoted most of this third public appearance at the Writers' Conference to reading from his poems—some old, some new. Among the new ones he included a satirical piece which he puckishly said he had been forced to suppress. It had been written a year or two earlier, he added, and it might have been publishable as soon as completed. Since then, so many dreadful things had come true, which he had prophesied in this poem, that he now hesitated to print it. Saying that the subject of the poem was political, he announced the title, "To a Thinker." Then he began reading:

> *The last step taken found your heft*
> *Decidedly upon the left.*

One more would throw you on the right.
Another still—you see your plight.
You call this thinking, but it's walking.
Not even that, it's only rocking,
Or weaving like a stabled horse:
From force to matter and back to force,
From form to content and back to form,
From norm to crazy and back to norm,
From bound to free and back to bound,
From sound to sense and back to sound.
So back and forth. It almost scares
A man the way things come in pairs.
Just now you're off democracy
(With a polite regret to be)
And leaning on dictatorship;
But if you will accept the tip,
In less than no time, tongue and pen,
You'll be a democrat again.
A reasoner and good as such,
Don't let it bother you too much
If it makes you look helpless, please,
And a temptation to the tease.
Suppose you've no direction in you,
I don't see but you must continue
To use the gift you do possess,
And sway with reason more or less.
I own I never really warmed
To the reformer or reformed.
And yet conversion has its place
Not halfway down the scale of grace.
So if you find you must repent
From side to side in argument,
At least don't use your mind too hard,
But trust my instinct—I'm a bard.[8]

The conservatives in the audience, seeming to recognize Franklin Delano Roosevelt in Frost's satirical apostrophe, applauded with such enthusiasm that Bartlett pronounced the poem "perhaps the largest hit of the evening." Afterward, Frost was elated by the enthusiastic response he had won, but he did ask Bartlett whether it might not be dangerous to indulge so much jesting and banter between poems. Was it possible that his listeners might not be able to sort out the seriousness from the fooling and the whimsicality? Bartlett reassured him on this point, even though Frost did not need the reassurance.[9]

As soon as he completed his work at the Conference, he left his wife with the Bartletts and made a brief trip southward to Santa Fe, where he had been invited by his fellow-poet Witter Bynner to give a reading under the auspices of a local group of literary figures. Frost and Bynner had known each other since 1921, and although the differences between them were sharp enough to make a genuine friendship unlikely, Frost had timorously ingratiated himself with Bynner through the writing of several letters. There was always the possibility that such a character might be harmful, Frost thought, unless befriended. Previously, he had found reasons to excuse himself from accepting the invitations, and only the present westward trip provided a convenient way to make amends.

The visit began pleasantly because Frost was soon given a chance to indulge his archaeological enthusiasms. On the morning after his arrival in Santa Fe, he went by automobile far enough into the desert, with some of Bynner's friends, to see the prehistoric cliff dwellings of the Pueblo Indians.[10] Unfortunately, this little expedition did cause him to be late for a special luncheon at Bynner's home, where the painter John Sloan was one of the waiting guests, and Frost had scarcely made his apologies when he became embroiled in a literary argument. It began when Bynner showed the assembled guests a recently published volume of poems entitled *A Book of Leaves*, by his Harvard classmate Horatio Colony. Holding the work aloft as though it were a newly found Pentateuch, Bynner announced that he had seen nothing like it "since I discovered A. E. Housman." Frost recognized the book. He had received an advance copy of it, and had read far enough to find in it what seemed to him a repulsively Whitmanesque glorification of homosexuality. That day he read no more. But as soon as Bynner began to praise it, Frost maliciously pretended to side with him by saying that he and Bynner were joint-discoverers. Of course they might not agree on which poem in the volume was the best, and so Frost would read one of his favorites aloud, if Bynner would give him the chance. Bynner, momentarily deceived, put the book in Frost's hands, and he selected what seemed to him a subtly insinuative paean to homosexuality. As he finished, he turned to Bynner and said,

"Of course, Witter, you wouldn't understand that because you're too young and innocent."

The jeer was taken as intended, and Bynner lost his temper. Seizing a full mug of beer, he shouted down at the seated Frost, "Colony is a better poet than either one of us," and poured all the beer over Frost's head. Instead of going into a rage, he remained serene: knowing that he had scored, he could afford to shrug off the beer. While some of the ladies in the party solicitously mopped him, he merely smiled at Bynner and said, "You must be drunk." There was no other incident. The public reading was attended by a large audience and was well received. But after he returned to Boulder and told Bartlett of his adventures with Bynner he concluded, "I shouldn't have gone down there."[11]

Not long after the Frosts returned to Vermont from Colorado in August of 1935, he began to think and talk about his own plans for a new book of poems. During the seven years since the publication of *West-Running Brook*, he had not even bothered to keep track of how many pieces he had scattered through various magazines, and yet he felt he must have enough to make a volume. How he would shape it, or what he would call it, he could decide after spreading out his manuscripts on floor or table and moving them around until some sort of pattern emerged. It was certain that his gradual play with the political scene, in his poetry, since the beginning of the New Deal, would add novelty to such a book. It might even force him to collect the more satirical ones into a section by themselves, apart from the lyrics. The most polemical was the "political pastoral" he had read as the Phi Beta Kappa poem at Columbia University in June of 1932: "Build Soil." He knew that anyone who looked at that dialogue would understand his social prejudices well enough. Emerson had helped to inspire "Build Soil" not only through his essay on "Self-Reliance" but also through writing such a passage as this:

". . . society gains nothing whilst a man, not himself renovated, attempts to renovate things around him. . . . It is handsomer to remain in the establishment . . . than to make a sally against evil by some single improvement, without supporting it by a total regeneration."[12]

If "Build Soil" owed something to Emerson, it owed even more to Frost's own experience as isolated poet and farmer in Derry. Less than a year before he had written "Build Soil," a reporter asked Frost's opinion about the increasing drift of country people toward the city—and got a better answer than he could have expected:

"Poetry is more often of the country than of the city. Poetry is very, very rural—rustic. It stands as a reminder of rural life —as a resource—as a recourse. It might be taken as a symbol of a man, taking its rise from individuality and seclusion— written first for the person that writes, and then going out into its social appeal and use. Just so the race lives best to itself—first to itself—storing a strength in the more individual life of the country—of the farm—then going to market and socializing in the industrial city. . . . We are now at a moment when we are getting too far out into the social-industrial, and are at the point of drawing back—drawing in to renew our- selves. . . . I think a person has to be withdrawn into himself to gather inspiration so that he is somebody when he 'comes to market' with himself. He learns that he's got to be almost waste- fully alone. . . ."[13]

Another inspiration for "Build Soil" had been provided by some of Frost's city friends who had recently made a posture of withdrawing into the country—for the wrong reasons. One of them was Untermeyer, who had purchased a large farm in a valley of the Adirondacks, and had tried to set himself up as a gentleman farmer. Frost, visiting him there, had found him so completely out of character that he had tried to send him some advice in the form of metaphors drawn from the act of farming:

"The land be your strength and refuge. But at the same time I say this so consonant with your own sentiments of the moment, let me utter a word of warning against the land as an affectation. What determines the population of the world is not at all the amount of tillable land it affords: but it is some- thing in the nature of the people themselves that limits the size of the globulate mass they are socially capable of. There is always, there will always be, a lot, many lots of land left out of the system. I dedicate these lots to the stray souls who from incohesiveness feel rarely the need of the forum for their thoughts; of the market for their wares and produce. They raise a crop of rye, we'll say. To them it is green manure. They plow it under. They raise a crop of endives in their cellar. They eat it themselves. That is they turn it under. They have an idea. Instead of rushing into print with it, they turn it under to enrich the soil. Out of that idea they have another idea. Still they turn that under. What they finally venture doubtfully to publication with is an idea of an idea. The land not taken up gives these stay-outers, these loosely connected people, their chance to live to themselves a larger proportion of the time than with the throng. There is no law divine or human against them when you come to think of it. The social tyranny admits of squatters, tramps, gypsies because it can't make itself tight if it wants to. It isn't rebellion I am talking. It isn't even literary and intellectual detachment. It is simply easy ties and slow commerce. Refuse to be rushed to market or forum. Don't come as a product till you have turned yourself under many times. We don't have to be afraid we won't be social enough. Hell, haven't I written all that in my first book? But the point is the unconsidered land makes the life I like possible. Praise be to the unconsidered land. That's all. . . .[14]

After playing with these ideas in these ways, he captured them in that even more poetic form which he adapted from Vergil's "First Eclogue." He directly borrowed the names Vergil there used in letting Meliboeus the farmer meet and discuss with the farm-loving poet, Tityrus, some ancient problems concerning the plight of the farmer. Thus he could "take a writing hand in politics" while still preserving his poetic concern for images drawn from the countryside. His pleasure in writing "Build Soil" had stimulated many of his further poetic excursions into social and political satire.

The risk in such adventurousness was obvious. Just how these attitudinizings would be accepted by reviewers of his new book would depend largely on which critics were chosen by which magazine editors. He kept reminding himself that the making or breaking of a book could depend on those choices, and again he was unwilling to leave such matters entirely to chance. If he cultivated the most important editors properly, they would be sufficiently on his side to choose favorable reviewers. Early in the fall of 1935 he began the first moves of this new campaign by writing to Untermeyer, who had recently placed several of Frost's poems with editors:

"Please make Henry Canby [editor of the *Saturday Review*] give you back that Lost in Heaven poem. I've got to have all the poems I can muster to meet the editorial demand there has

been on me since you published A Leaf Treader. Tell Henry
Canby I have promised Lost in Heaven somewhere else. Tell
him I say he has already had too much of my next book, and if
he hasn't he can say the word and I'll write him some more at
once. And another matter: I seem to have lost somewhere
one whole note-book with the poem in it about proposing to
supply the sorrow felt if the storm will supply the tears:
Dammit I wonder in whose house I left that privacy lying
round. But never mind that now. Can you let me have a copy
of the tears poem? The time draws near for going to press and
I must get as many editors as possible implicated in the book
beforehand. Ain't I wiley? You remember Amy Lowell the
author and poet? Well they's a life of her out and they tell me
it's a caution the wileyness she showed with editors and reviewers."[15]

For practical purposes, he also used some other strategies
than those of cultivating the good will of editors and reviewers.
His long trip northward to Miami from Key West, to take part in
the Winter Institute of Literature at the University of Miami,
had enabled him to establish new contacts which deserved
further cultivating. As a result, when his Amherst doctor advised him that he and his wife should again escape the New
England winter by going South in December of 1935—and
staying South until springtime—he accepted an invitation to
participate in the next Winter Institute. Shortly before Christmas of 1935, he and Mrs. Frost went South again, this time
staying in a cottage at 3670 Avocado Avenue, Coconut Grove,
near Miami. Eager to make a good impression, he avoided
saying anything which might offend prospective reviewers or
buyers. Asked about the group of young poets "who have
rocketed into public attention recently," he "could not be drawn
into anything more than moderate comment." (This was no
time to repeat any of the harsh comments he had made to
Untermeyer about these upstart crows.) The reporter quoted
Frost as saying, "They are all my young friends. They have
various stages to go through before the real person emerges.
The essential of any real personality is only reached by striking a balance." Paul Engle, one of the young poets who had
won acclaim in 1934, with his Whitmanesque affirmations in
American Song, had just published a new book, full of social
protest: Break the Heart's Anger. Frost mentioned Engle as

an example of a youngster swinging between extremes. "It seems rather a pity," he added, "for him to get a completely new bottle of ink—to throw away all his purple ink and write entirely with black." Asked about the lectures he planned to give at the Institute, he said he would be offering a three-day series to writers, under the title "Learning to Have Something to Say"; that another lecture would be on "The Uses of Ambiguity."[16]

Before he had even begun these talks—in fact, before he had even reached Miami—he received three invitations which overshadowed anything likely to happen in Florida. Each of them came to him from Harvard, partly through the influence of David McCord, a young Harvard poet who had previously shown his friendship in many ways.[17] The first two invitations would require the use of unpublished poems: he was asked to deliver an ode at the Harvard Tercentenary Celebration, in the autumn of 1936, and to be the Phi Beta Kappa Poet at ceremonies also scheduled to occur that autumn. The third and most important invitation, contained in a letter from his enemy-friend Professor John Livingston Lowes, was to deliver the Charles Eliot Norton lectures in the spring term of 1936. He accepted the first two, immediately; he hesitated over the third, for reasons which he explained in his answer to Lowes:

"As you may imagine, I should be most happy to be your Charles Eliot Norton Professor next spring; and that not alone for the honor of the appointment. I should value also the compulsion the lectures would put me under to assemble my thinking right and left of the last few years and see what it comes to. I have reached a point where it would do me good.

"But let me tell you my situation. Your letter overtakes me on my way to Florida, where, after my last bad influenza I promised the doctor I would spend a couple of winters sunning on the tennis courts. I might as well be in Florida as in bed. (No reflection on Florida intended. Even Florida is no doubt somebody's home. And nothing but good of any of these States ever out of me.) I have already served one of my half terms down there. I am superstitiously afraid I ought to serve the other. If I served it clear out, I could hardly be back before the middle of March. I might risk the first of March. But even that is too late for your purposes. Or is it? I don't suppose I should ask that a Harvard thing so important should be reshaped somewhat to fit a mere person. Nevertheless I am tempted to ask. I am going to be greatly disappointed to see this opportunity pass from me. . . ."[18]

There was another hitch, and it frightened him. The terms of the Charles Eliot Norton lectureship specified that the six talks he was to give should be presented ultimately to the Harvard University Press in a manuscript for publication. He never wrote out his talks, and yet he supposed that there would be no difficulty in arranging to have a stenographer take down a shorthand transcript he could revise for publication. Lowes handled both these matters for him, and the agreement was made that he would not be required to take up his duties as Charles Eliot Norton Professor until the first of March. As soon as details were settled, he could not resist boasting. From Florida he wrote to Roy Elliott at Amherst:

"I can tell you about Harvard's having asked me to give the Charles Eliot Norton lectures in poetry this spring because . . . you will understand and sympathize. . . . I shall be in comparison with the British subjects who alone have hitherto given these lectures. Of course I dread it. But you will appreciate the fact that I could hardly refuse the trial. I shan't hope too much of myself. But suppose I merely get by indifferently. There is still the name of having been the first American asked. It seems as if it must strengthen my position."[19]

Before this boast was sent to Elliott at Amherst, Frost had awkwardly secured from President Stanley King permission to absent himself once again from his Amherst duties. The awkwardness grew out of his contractual promise that during the three months he spent each year as poet in residence at Amherst College he would accept no invitations requiring him to be away from the campus for any considerable length of time. During each of the years since King had been president, Frost had violated the terms of that promise in ways which had caused some of the hardworking members of the faculty at Amherst to protest that their poet-not-often-in-residence was a luxury the College should not afford. President King himself had tried to defend Frost, and had even sought to tie him down with a few campus lectures scheduled well in advance of each annual residence, but through such unavoidable circumstances as illness Frost had failed to deliver most of these promised lectures. This time, it was easy to persuade President King that honor would accrue to Amherst if a member of her faculty was given leave to serve at Harvard. It was also easy to say that Frost could run away from his duties at Harvard often enough to attend the series of informal seminars he had agreed to hold with students in the Babbott Room of the Amherst College Library, that spring. President King's public announcement of the arrangement reflected the manner in which Frost had represented the Harvard arrangement. "Colleges are frequently exchanging such amenities," the President was quoted as saying, "and the Harvard appointment means that he will be away from Amherst for a month this spring to deliver a series of six lectures at Harvard."[20] Before King made his announcement, Frost had done his best to enlist faculty support at Amherst. To George Whicher he had written to say that he was trying to find a name for his new book of poems; then he continued,

"Another thing I have to have a name for brings me to my news of the moment. I have promised to give the Charles Eliot Norton lectures at Harvard this spring . . . Stanley [King] seems to be willing I should have the honor. . . . being asked to give them flatters me a little. Of course it scares me too. And it troubles me because of the conflict with Amherst obligations. But I can be in Amherst for my Babbott-Room salons. And I know you'll all want me not to miss the political advantage there obviously is in the appointment. Speak and say if I am wrong."[21]

At Miami, there were a few colleagues on the staff of the Winter Institute who would forgive him for boasting about all three of these Harvard offers. One of them was a friendly giant, Hervey Allen, who in 1933 had published a gigantic novel entitled *Anthony Adverse*. A half-million copies of that novel had been sold during the next two years. Allen had made another small fortune by selling the moving picture rights. Having purchased many undeveloped acres of pineland in South Miami, he was building a good-sized ranch there. The Frosts had been entertained by the Allens in their new ranch-home, not too far below the University of Miami, and there was reason to know that the Allens would be happy about the Harvard plans.

Another colleague at the Institute whom Frost had newly met was a part-time Harvard tutor, a maverick from Utah, named Bernard DeVoto. After his graduation from Harvard, with honors, Phi Beta Kappa, in 1920, DeVoto had returned to Utah and had begun his literary career as a novelist. He had

taught briefly at Northwestern—long enough to marry a freshman, Helen Avis MacVicar—and then had moved to Cambridge, partly in the hope of acquiring a position at Harvard.
Within a short time he was serving temporarily as an instructor in English and as a tutor in the Division of Modern
Languages, at Harvard, but his prospects were precarious.

Frost, having read and admired one of DeVoto's articles entitled "New England: There She Stands," went alone and unannounced to call on him at his hotel room in Miami, one evening,
ostensibly to discuss the westerner's flattering views of New
England,[22] and DeVoto was flattered. At the end of this visit,
Frost said they would soon be seeing each other in Cambridge,
and the disclosure of the Norton Professorship appointment
was news to DeVoto. "What's happened to Harvard?" he exclaimed. "They're doing something right, up there, for a
change." Immediately he offered to serve as handyman and
guardian for the Frosts as soon as they reached Cambridge,
and he offered to find a furnished house for them to rent. His
assistance was accepted. Frost was relieved to know that he
would now have another friend in the Boston region, where
he felt that he had several dangerous enemies. David McCord
had already warned him that the favorite modern poet among
students and faculty at Harvard was the previous Norton Professor, Thomas Stearns Eliot—against whom Frost had unpleasantly competed for attention, at the St. Botolph Club
in Boston.[23]

There were other reasons why Frost suspected he might find
more enemies at Harvard than friends. He had been out-
spokenly critical of the way some Harvard reformers had helped
to organize a strike of floor-scrubbing charwomen, a year
earlier. The subsequent fracas had seemed to Frost a typical
example of that sentimental humanitarianism recently brought
into fashion by the New Deal, and the incident had been
enough to inspire his bitterly sarcastic poem entitled "Provide,
Provide":

> *The witch that came (the withered hag)*
> *To wash the steps with pail and rag*
> *Was once the beauty Abishag,*
>
> *The picture pride of Hollywood.*
> *Too many fall from great and good*
> *For you to doubt the likelihood.*

Die early and avoid the fate
Or if predestined to die late,
Make up your mind to die in state.

Make the whole stock exchange your own!
If need be occupy a throne,
Where nobody can call you crone.

Some have relied on what they knew,
Others on being simply true.
What worked for them might work for you.

No memory of having starred
Atones for later disregard
Or keeps the end from being hard.

Better to go down dignified
With boughten friendship at your side
Than none at all. Provide, provide![24]

Having been made uncomfortable by those who criticized him for his laissez-faire attitudes, and his belief in the old doctrine of "every man for himself," Frost was more and more inclined to strike out poetically in self-defense, even if his taunts against the providers-for-others did make enemies. Irked by the popularity of New Deal slogans and programs, he had found in his own family a good example of the ease with which pity and sentimentality could becloud common sense. During previous summers at the Stone Cottage in South Shaftsbury, he had been simultaneously boastful and angry over the ways in which Carol and Lillian worked so hard to raise and sell sweet peas to passers-by, from a little stand placed at the edge of the front lawn. Such a botanical triumph was fine, but there seemed to be something pathetic about this way of asking for pennies. He saw it in other yards where crudely painted signs offered wild raspberries and blueberries and crook-necked squash, for sale, in a manner which offended his own Scottish pride as being too near to begging. Again in a polemical mood, he had written a poem in anapestic lines irregularly rhymed and entitled "A Roadside Stand." Not content to let the images and actions in it speak for themselves, he had concluded with observations (only apparently balanced and philosophical) concerning New Deal humanitarianism:

> *It is in the news that all these pitiful kin*
> *Are to be bought out and mercifully gathered in*
> *To live in villages, next to the theater and store,*
> *Where they won't have to think for themselves anymore;*
> *While greedy good-doers, beneficent beasts of prey,*
> *Swarm over their lives enforcing benefits*
> *That are calculated to soothe them out of their wits,*
> *And by teaching them how to sleep the sleep all day,*
> *Destroy their sleeping at night the ancient way.*
>
> *Sometimes I feel myself I can hardly bear*
> *The thought of so much childish longing in vain,*
> *The sadness that lurks near the open window there,*
> *That waits all day in almost open prayer*
> *For the squeal of brakes, the sound of a stopping car,*
> *Of all the thousand selfish cars that pass,*
> *Just one to inquire what a farmer's prices are.*
> *And one did stop, but only to plow up grass*
> *In using the yard to back and turn around;*
> *And another to ask the way to where it was bound;*
> *And another to ask could they sell it a gallon of gas*
> *They couldn't (this crossly): they had none, didn't it see?*
>
> *No, in country money, the country scale of gain,*
> *The requisite lift of spirit has never been found,*
> *Or so the voice of the country seems to complain.*
> *I can't help owning the great relief it would be*
> *To put these people at one stroke out of their pain.*
> *And then next day as I come back into the sane,*
> *I wonder how I should like you to come to me*
> *And offer to put me gently out of my pain.*[25]

Murder, and even the desire to murder for justice rather than for mercy, never stayed out of Frost's consciousness too long. He had thought of entitling this poem, sarcastically, "Euthanasia," but part of what bothered him as literary strategy was his recent tendency to let his new poems reflect too many of his murderous thoughts. The newness was all on the surface: he could remember how a San Francisco boy named Percy MacPartland had come so near to killing him that he had dreamed for days thereafter of ways to kill Percy.²⁶ He could remember a fight in Lawrence, Massachusetts, years later, when he had hammered (and would have enjoyed killing) a young man named Herbert Parker, who dragged him into a civil court, with the help of a policeman, and caused Frost to pay a fine.²⁷ In Derry, there had been times when he would gladly have killed clumsy Carl Burell before he found a sufficently cruel way to get rid of him.²⁸ In England, there came a day when he would have taken pleasure in murdering Ezra Pound. Not long after he returned to the United States, he had thought of killing his old enemy, Ellery Sedgwick, editor of the *Atlantic Monthly*.²⁹ As for Ernest Silver, for whom he had nurtured so much hatred for so many years, there had been one night in Plymouth after his return from England when he had used razor words in public to achieve a murderous revenge.³⁰ Now he was forced to consider strategies complicated by his literary reputation as a successful poet, and even though he still permitted his killer instincts to find expressions in only slightly veiled poems, the immediate problem was how to justify his new departure, in the eyes of those who liked to think of him as the personification of old-fashioned New England virtues.

If he had seemed to go beyond New England in the subject matter of his verse, part of the reason was that the lives of his children had drawn him away from the White Mountains to the Green, away from the Green Mountains to the Rockies, beyond the Rockies and even beyond the Sierras to his birthplace in California. Why not use as metaphor the fact that his experiences had caused him to look across all the ranges of mountains in the United States, and thus to endow his poetry with a further range of themes, even social and political. But he only hinted at these possibilities in a letter to Untermeyer before he and Mrs. Frost left Florida, en route to his one-term position as Charles Eliot Norton Professor at Harvard:

"David [McCord] writes he saw a picture of me in the N. Y. Times looking worried beside Hervey Allen and DuBose Heyward at the Pan American Airport [at] Dinner Key [in] Miami Florida. He thinks it was because of all I was in for at Harvard and I let him, as a Harvard man, think so. In reality what was worrying me, if anything, was having to be with too many literary people for too long a time at the risk of losing their respect by being found out; or if it wasn't that it was not yet having hit on a name for my sixth book. The latter defect has been remedied in the last twelve hours and I hasten to share the satisfaction with you. I have it as Archy the Mede [Archimedes] is said to have said[:]

A Further Range

"You and Merrill Moore put it into my head and perhaps it may seem immodest of me to say it for myself and let it for the moment it will take the reader to discover by turning a page or two [to the Dedication] . . ."[31]

New ways to advertise the new book were much in his thoughts as he and Mrs. Frost journeyed toward Cambridge from Miami. They stopped overnight in Baltimore to visit with Miss Mary Goodwillie, particularly to thank her for all she had done for Marjorie. As he was leaving the city, he found himself in the presence of a Baltimore newspaper reporter, and was ready for him. The poet had in his pocket a fair-copy manuscript of the rhymed political satire, "To a Thinker," which he had first read publicly at the Rocky Mountain Writers' Conference the summer before, and had published in the *Saturday Review* for the eleventh of January 1936 under the more pointed title, "To a Thinker in Office." During his conversation with the Baltimore reporter he hauled the manuscript out of his pocket and presented it as though the poem were unpublished. The reporter, building his story around this incident, printed article and poem in the *Sun* the next day with a rhymed headline: "Latest Poem by Robert Frost Versifies New Deal Is Lost." Even the subheading was rhymed: "New England Poet Strums His Lyre, And Says The Nation's Plight Is Dire As Projects Swerve 'Twixt Pan and Fire." The article began:

"Robert Frost has descended from the poetical Parnassus to the political arena. But the figurative lyre he strummed in the New England hills—strummed until he has become one of America's best-known poets and won two Pulitzer Prizes—is being lugged along to confuse and refute Administration lions.

"Pausing yesterday before catching a train out of Baltimore after a brief visit here, the versifier, whose home is in Vermont, asserted he was anti-Roosevelt. He declared he once had held high hopes for Henry Wallace but had lost them. He bitterly condemned an alleged Administration policy of regarding farmers as possessors of what he called submarginal minds. And with something of a flourish, he produced a new poem, 'To a Thinker.'

"The verse, he indicated, was written about the President. Mr. Frost smiled sardonically.

" 'I'm going to stay a Democrat if I have to push everyone else out of the party . . .' he said. 'I'm a pursuitist, not an escapist. And I'd rather cast an idea by implication than cast a ballot.' "

At this point in the article, the full text of "To a Thinker" was printed, and the reporter continued:

" 'Seriously though,' said Mr. Frost, 'I'm not horribly anti-Roosevelt. Henry Mencken bears down on the President pretty hard. Roosevelt is making his mistakes, just as we did. But I'm very much a country man, and I don't like to see city against country. And I can't stand coercion.' . . .

"The poet, white hair gleaming above ruddy face, looked dreamily into space. But he was not thinking of mending walls . . . nor of a New England countryside under snow. He had turned again to politics.

" 'Two lines from one of my earlier verses really sum up my whole viewpoint,' he asserted. 'The poem ran:

I never dared be radical when young
For fear it would make me conservative when old.' "[32]

Frost might have confided to the reporter that his playful jest at both radicals and conservatives was merely a pose, and he had actually followed a familiar pattern: after starting out as a young rebel against society, he had gradually become arch-conservative in his political views. But his immediate purpose was to advertise his wares prior to the forthcoming publication of *A Further Range,* and he was very successful. The day after the article appeared, the *Sun* carried an editorial entitled "Recruit Legislator," invoking Shelley's claim that poets are the unacknowledged legislators of the world, and going on with reminders that the poets of the moment were no longer content to see their legislative proposals pass unacknowledged. A day later the New York *Times* printed another editorial, "Poet in Politics," which began, "Waiting for a train in Baltimore Mr. Robert Frost was caught by a reporter of its *Sun.* Conforming to the custom of the place, he talked politics. He even produced a political poem. His first venture in a field new to him, so far as we know, is called 'To a Thinker.' Mr. Roosevelt is the addressee. . . . Mr. Frost is playful and benign. Not for him the absurd vehemence of Coventry Patmore, straying into politics, or the bitterness of William Watson. He winds up with a jest. . . ." The free advertising spread northward until it reached New England. In Massachusetts, the Springfield *Union* reprinted the full text of the Baltimore release, and other local papers were pleased to copy. Apparently as a result, Henry Goddard Leach wrote to ask if he might publish the new poem in the *Forum*. Answering, the poet enclosed a page proof of it, as set in type for use in *A Further Range,* with the words "in Office" deleted:

"Here is the offending poem. It is already in book form and about to be published. It first appeared in The Saturday Review. I am sorry you are too late. I should have liked you to have it in The Forum. You will see that it was only by restriction of meaning that it was narrowed down to fit the President. Changing the title from 'To a Thinker' to 'To a Thinker in Office' helped do the business. As a matter of fact it was written three years ago and was aimed at the heads of our easy despairers of the republic and of parliamentary forms of government. I encounter too many such and my indignation mounts till it overflows in rhyme. I doubt if my native delicacy would have permitted me to use the figure of walking and rocking in connection with a person of the President's personal infirmities. But I am willing to let it go as aimed at him. He must deserve it or people wouldn't be so quick to see him in it."[33]

There was more than humor in Frost's colloquial question to Untermeyer: "Ain't I wiley?" All this publicity served as good advertising not only for *A Further Range* but also for his arrival at Harvard—just when he was newsworthy as a political opponent of that prominent Harvard graduate, Franklin Delano Roosevelt.

A HARVARD YEAR

*Robert has consented to give the six Charles Eliot Nor-
ton lectures at Harvard this spring. He has been asked to
give the "Ode" at the 300th anniversary at Harvard in
September, and also the Phi Beta Kappa poem there in
September, and I think he will undertake to give them,
tho he hates to know that he must write. It will be a Harvard year for him. . . .*[1]

PROFESSOR John Livingston Lowes and his committee in
charge of the six lectures to be given by Robert Frost completely miscalculated the public appeal the white-haired and
Florida-tanned New England poet would make. Weeks in advance they announced that his lecture series on "The Renewal
of Words" would be given in the New Lecture Hall (which
would seat nearly a thousand). The first lecture was entitled
"The Old Way to Be New," and well before starting time on the
evening of the fourth of March 1936 over a thousand people
managed to crowd into New Lecture Hall. Some of them stood
in the side aisles, others sat in the center aisle, and the boldest
standees draped themselves along the edge of the platform.
Two seats, reserved near the front of the hall, were occupied
by President and Mrs. Conant. When Lowes and DeVoto escorted Frost up one crowded side-aisle to the stage, the bois-
terous applause of the audience seemed to frighten the poet.
As soon as he was introduced he began to speak in such a
nervously restrained voice that the listeners had to quiet down
if they were going to hear him. For several minutes he seemed
to grope for words and ideas, as though he were not sure of
himself. He used no notes, but he knew precisely what he was
going to say. The lecture as planned was a reworking of the
"Introduction" he had written for Robinson's *King Jasper*, except that he would illustrate his points this time by using his

own poems. As soon as he had made a few caustic remarks about some ways in which the present age sought new ways to be new, the laughter of the audience seemed to reassure him, and he soon established his winning platform manner.[2]

Like Mark Twain, Frost had learned to enthrall by deliberately interrupting himself with well-timed silences, and whenever he paused, the expectant hush of the entire audience was extraordinary. By the time he completed his performance —a truly professional piece of acting—he was called back repeatedly to read one more poem. Afterward, students pursued him backstage, requesting his autograph in copy after copy of his books.

Bernard DeVoto kept all the promises he had made in Miami. He did serve as guardian, and he had already arranged for the Frosts to rent a furnished home at 56 Fayerweather Street, not far from the Cambridge Common. DeVoto had also persuaded his close friends Mr. and Mrs. Theodore Morrison to hold a small reception for Frost after each lecture, in their home at 8 Mason Street. The Frosts had previously met the Morrisons. A tutor in English at Harvard, Morrison had been serving as director of the Bread Loaf Writers' Conference since 1932. His wife, formerly Kathleen Johnston, had been a leader in the small group of Bryn Mawr undergraduates who had brought Frost there to give a three-session writing course in 1920, and had also been editor-in-chief of the Bryn Mawr *News* during her senior year.[3] Mrs. Frost, because of illness, was unable to attend either the first lecture or the first reception. The sudden change from semitropical weather in Florida to the winter chill of Cambridge had been too much for her, and she was confined to her bed at 56 Fayerweather Street for several days immediately after their arrival in Cambridge.[4] Her husband, usually far more vulnerable than she, and frequently victimized by respiratory ailments, remained extraordinarily well. He seemed too excited to have time for illness.

All of Frost's Harvard lectures were attended by overflow audiences which were unusually sympathetic. The second one, entitled "Vocal Imagination—the Merger or Form and Content," was a concise summing up of what he had said during the past twenty years about his belief that the living part of a poem is the intonation entangled somehow in the syntax, idiom, and meaning of the sentences.

The third lecture was entitled "Does Wisdom Signify?" Frost

talked on both sides of this question, starting with the claim that the vividness with which the mood or viewpoint was conveyed, in poetry, was more important to the success of the poem than the question whether the poet's insights were wise. Such was his ideal posture, in moments of detachment. Privately, however, he was inclined to insist that whenever he came across a poem which reflected merely trivial insights on whatever subject might be under consideration, he grew impatient. Unfortunately, on this occasion, his talk became such a rambling and helter-skelter collection of thoughts that one Boston newspaperman had difficulty in seeing how they had anything to do with the announced topic, and his report, captioned, "1,000 Hear Robert Frost, Poet, Give Views on Life in Harvard Lecture," was disappointing. He began by saying that Frost "stood like a village philosopher" on the platform of the new lecture hall "and discussed with Parnassian humor some of the ills of writing and of the Universe." He went on to say that the poet, "grey-thatched and smiling, gently addressed his audience as though they were townsfolk of his adopted Vermont hills, gathered round the cannonball stove of the village store." The most revealing parts of this report were those which interwove direct quotations:

" 'The surest thing you know is that we'll never understand,' said Mr. Frost, referring to problems of the universe and wagging a lively forefinger for emphasis. 'And we'll never lack resources to stay here, to hang onto this globe. We'll never be shaken off. The two things go together.'

" 'Well, you know, God can count on me never to be disappointed in him,' he declared again, with one of those touches of earthly humor so apparent in his writings and so endearing to the listeners. . . .

" 'That means I am not an idealist. Of course, I have wished for things at times; for instance, an extra moon. But I haven't committed suicide about it—yet.'[5]

"The audience, seated and standing, chuckled with Mr. Frost as his tanned face beamed at them over a desk lamp . . . which the poet did not even bother to turn on. . . .

" 'What does the life in me want?' asked the poet, looking whimsically at the upturned faces before him. 'I must have life round me—violence. You know, we can stand lots of violence before we begin to talk like babies about security.'

"Mr. Frost indicated his skepticism concerning politics by

mildly questioning its importance. 'It seems as though those in it make an honest attempt to understand each other,' he declared, fingering his chin as though a beard grew there.

" 'This next election, now. T. S. Eliot has turned to poems about grief. And grief about what? Of our human bondage. Where does one turn then? To the church, to religion, to the Man of Sorrows, our sorrows. The next election doesn't turn on anything like that. I think it should be a humorous business to enter into a political campaign.[6] Just out of modesty, you know. For we can't tell what will come of it. . . .

" 'It's knowing what to do with things that counts,' is a last line of one of the poems inspired by his early residence in California. That last line, it was easy to imagine, pervades the poet's life, and helped make him the calm, easy-going humorist he seemed on the lecture platform. By no means did he indicate that he had ended his life question.

" 'I don't get offended by a poem just because it's utterly evil and bad for the state,' he declared during one of the periods, now and then, when he got round to talking of writing. 'I'd like virtue to be one point. I'd like a beautiful thing to be a good thing, too. Good for the state, good for the family, good for the soul.'

"Writers were interested, perhaps abashed, by Mr. Frost's reference to 'the evil search for synonyms.'[7] He also scolded in kindly manner the makers of 'book-end poems,' which he said started with the words, 'These are the things I like,' and which ended, 'Those are the things I like.'

" 'You can spread out as much as you want in between, and you might as well read an itemized bill,' he said, as his listeners roared."[8]

The fourth of the weekly lectures was entitled "Poetry as Prowess (Feat of Words)," and again Frost made it summarize much he had previously said—this time about how the words in a poem must become deeds, as flat and final as a showdown in a poker game. He had elaborated his views on this topic as far back as 1916, in an early letter to Untermeyer.[9] The fifth and sixth lectures, entitled "Before the Beginning of a Poem" and "After the End of a Poem," were largely repetitions of the talks he had given at the Winter Institute at Miami in 1931. All six were well received, and the steadily increasing crowd finally led the authorities to move everyone from the New Lecture Hall to Sanders Theater—which was filled to capacity.[10]

Frost received so many flattering attentions from President James Bryant Conant and from various members of the faculty that he began to believe Harvard was going to offer him a permanent appointment. As soon as Mrs. Frost recovered from her illness, the Conants invited the Frosts to dinner, and this gesture seemed auspicious, in itself. Unfortunately, Frost and Conant did not find ways to make science and poetry congenial. In addition, they quickly established sharp differences between their political views. Uppermost in the news for the moment was the preparation for the next national election campaign, and Roosevelt had already begun to make his tactical moves. Conant, admiring Roosevelt, praised him for bringing representatives of the Teamsters' Union to the White House to receive assurances that he would support their union. Frost, disgusted by this the latest sign of New Deal largesse, sarcastically suggested to Conant that a good title for that speech of assurances might be, "Every Man's Home His Own Poorhouse," because all of those Teamsters would eventually be living on government charity. Not amused, Conant answered gruffly: "You have a bitter tongue."[11]

Frost's newly made friend Bernard DeVoto had an even more bitter tongue, when speaking of Conant, for reasons which soon became apparent. Having served as tutor and lecturer at Harvard for six years, DeVoto still kept hoping for a permanent appointment. His most important plans were centered on continuing at Harvard. In the autumn of 1935, he had been offered the editorship of the *Saturday Review*, to replace Henry Seidel Canby, and he had tried to use that offer as leverage. Again he was told that because he lacked a doctorate he was not eligible for permanent appointment at Harvard. Still convinced that his friends might be able to help him get around this technicality, he turned down the offer from the *Saturday Review*. Six months later, when the same offer was made again, on even better terms, DeVoto went directly to President Conant and said he felt compelled to accept the offer unless he could get the Harvard appointment he preferred. Conant studied the matter for a few days and then wrote to say that the previous Harvard decision must stand; that if DeVoto really did have another offer he should accept it.[12] Enraged by the insinuation that he had not told the truth, DeVoto turned to Frost, who was genuinely sympathetic. Frost insisted that if DeVoto wanted to keep the respect of others and of himself he should immediately resign his lectureship at Harvard. Reluctantly, he did resign.

Strongly believing in his motto that friendship means favor, Frost achieved several favors from non-Harvard friends while at Harvard. Three whom he had purposefully cultivated were on the editorial board of the Book-of-the-Month Club, and in early spring of 1936 it was announced that *A Further Range* would be the Book-of-the-Month Club choice for June. The news came to Frost through his friend Richard Thornton, at Holt, together with the assurance that 50,000 copies of *A Further Range* would be distributed by the Club.[13] A few days later, Frost's wife confided to Thornton's wife:

"It is certainly *grand* about the Book-of-the-Month Club. I rather thought they would take it, because Henry Canby and Dorothy Canfield are always such staunch friends of Robert's work, and Christopher Morley has shown much friendliness the last year."[14]

There was another prize worth fishing for: the Pulitzer, for the best book of poems published by an American author in 1936. This award would not be made until May of 1937, but Frost already knew of one factor which would work in his favor. His friend Untermeyer had been appointed to the committee which would be making the award, and this might give him some advantage over other poets in the competition. It did.[15] In the previous year Untermeyer's volume of *Selected Poems and Parodies* had been in the running for a Pulitzer Prize, but he had lost out to R. P. T. Coffin. Frost, in Cambridge when this announcement was made, knew how disappointed Untermeyer must be, and therefore he tried to offer philosophical consolations:

"Just a word about the outcome. I know you were prepared not to mind it. So that if you do mind it you don't mind it so much. I hate this being automatically entered for prizes by the mere act of publication. I have suffered nervous collapse in my time from the strain of conscious competition and learned from it how to pretend at least that I am below or above it for the rest of my life. And I'm a good stout pretender when I set out to be. Nobody can catch me setting my heart on any rewards in this world. I'd as soon be caught breaking and entering. My days among the dead are passed. The only comparison I suffer gladly would be with them by them. Conflicting claims and the clamor that goes with these among our contemporaries are next to nothing to me. *Next* to nothing. I know too well the personal politics. So do you. We have our farms and our poems to cultivate. . . ."[16]

Untermeyer knew how to read between the lines of this "good stout pretender" who might suffer another nervous collapse if *A Further Image* should be mistreated too harshly by the critics. For the present, however, Frost's great fear was that some of his enemies at Harvard might have spoiled his chance to receive a permanent appointment there. He gave some hints of these fears, as he continued his letter to Untermeyer:

"I don't feel I made too big a hit with the dignitaries and authorities. There was a moment in March when I thought perhaps they were giving me back my father's Harvard. But probably I was fooling myself. I'm imperfectly academic and no amount of association with the academic will make me perfect. It's too bad, for I like the academic in my way, and up to a certain point the academic likes me. Its patronage proves as much. I may be wrong in my suspicion that I haven't pleased Harvard as much as I have the encompassing barbarians. My whole impression may have come from the Pound-Eliot-Richards gang in Eliot House here. I had a really dreadful letter of abuse from Pound in which he complains of my cheap witticisms at his expense. I may have to take him across my page like this: It is good to be back in communication with you on the old terms. My contribution was to witticisms: yours the shitticisms. Remember how you always used to carry toilet paper in your pocket instead of handkerchief or napkin to wipe your mouth with when you got through? Etcetera.—I suspect the same dirty sycophant of having reported me to him as reported me to Wallace Stevens. I think its Mattheson. Never mind. Peace hath her victories no less renowned than war."[17]

He had other reasons for worrying about the enmity between himself and Matthiessen, whose communistic sympathies were plainly reflected in his published writings. It was clear that the most dangerous criticism of *A Further Range* would come from such closely organized liberals as Matthiessen and his crowd. The anticipatory nervousness Frost felt in this regard was mixed up with his fright over the two poems he had promised to write for delivery at Harvard in September of 1936. When the first of these invitations had been received from M. A. DeWolfe Howe, he had responded by trying to explain the ambivalence of his reaction:

"I have never said anything but in telegraphic about the Phi Beta Kappa poem for September 17th. You knew very well what I would suffer from what you were letting me in for. I may not forgive you. All depends on how I come out with such a poem. It wont be absolutely the first I ever wrote [to order]. But it will only be the second. I wrote one for my class when I graduated from the high school. You knew how it would be: I should want to refuse, but couldnt refuse. All right then. No further fuss and throes."[18]

Unfortunately, his resolve was not so firm as his distaste for writing occasional verse, and he became nervously upset when he failed to find any inspiration for either of the promised pieces. Inseparable from that discomfort was his increasing sense of the danger to his literary position which the leftists might cause. When his socialistic friend Lankes had called his attention to some uncomplimentary things said about him in a *New Republic* article, Frost had partially explained his act of trying to pretend that such attacks had no effect:

"I thrive by not knowing what goes on in the newspapers and magazines and even when I do know, (when you *make* me know for instance) by pretending to myself and everybody else that I dont know. I'm a very artful dodger of unnecessary pains. I'll tell you what I'll do with you: I'll promise never to bring you word of anything unpleasant about you if you'll do the same by me. We'll conspire to make each other fool's paradises to live in. Why not? There's no sense in helping our enemies reach us: The New Republic might blaze away till its guns jammed and I would never know it except through you who are apparently one of the last remaining die-hard readers. Its subscription list has almost touched the vanishing point. You probably haven't observed, so I am going to confess to you I crave whole days weeks months unruffled by thoughts of either praise or blame. I manage to protect myself pretty well. You may ask if freedom from criticism is good for me. It may not be good for my art but it is good for my nature. I know from experience. I believe you need to know less about what the critics think of you than you have known. To Hell with all their unconsidered comment. It is unconsidered and it is not disinterested. I have seen enough of it to be sure their reasons for likes and dislikes are always other than what are given. I have decided to spend no more time fathoming their motives. Dont let them in on me if you want me to grow old gracefully."[19]

Such an ideal of self-defense in the face of criticism was often spoiled by Frost's eagerness to see and read at least the worst things said about him in print. The article to which Lankes referred was Newton Arvin's leftist review of *King Jasper*, beginning, "This last poem of E. A. Robinson and the prose preface of Mr. Robert Frost are two remarkable documents, full of disappointing implications to those who regard both writers as among the most honorable literary figures of their generation." After criticizing Frost's insistence that poetry should be built around griefs and not grievances, around "woes that nothing can be done for," Arvin continued,

"If the test of poetic woe is that no balm exists for it, then certainly the youngest writers [of our day] are unpoetical. But Mr. Frost used to complain that there were not enough woes of any sort about us: 'How can we write,' he once asked, 'How can we write/The Russian novel in America/As long as life goes so unterribly?' He asked the question with a certain facetiousness of course, but both that passage and the present preface have the effect of placing an astronomical distance between him and us. There is a cant of skepticism, a complacency of the pessimist, as well as their opposites, and it is profoundly disappointing to see distinguished minds succumbing to them."[20]

Frost had reason to fear reviewers such as Newton Arvin, and the strength of the leftist critics was becoming so unified that one could predict the savagery of the attacks they would make on such a poem as "Build Soil." Less than a month after the review of *King Jasper*, Arvin published an article entitled "A Letter on Proletarian Literature," in which he made some explicit exhortations: "All proletarian writers, I take it, are under a solemn obligation to fight tooth and nail against philistinism in all its nauseating forms; to rise above parochialism both of place and time; and to save from the black night of fascism all of the past that is really humane and of good report."[21] A month later, the *Partisan Review* carried an article which tried to define the change which poets should make if they would serve well in the class struggle:

"Undoubtedly the most vital (perhaps the only) contribution being made today to the art of poetry is the shift from the romantic-personal, individual consciousness to a collective mass-identification with a universal consciousness. The true 'revolutionary' poet is one who has grown beyond self-love sufficiently to discount the importance of his personal survival, and who is not only intellectually in sympathy with Marxian, or socialistic, beliefs, but is also emotionally identified with the class struggle."[22]

Considered within such a hostile framework, *A Further Range* would not get far, Frost knew. As it happened, the first attack on it was made by Newton Arvin, himself, in the *Partisan Review*. He began by saying with obvious disparagement that the poems of Robert Frost gave a precise rendering to one aspect of New England:

"It is the New England of nasalized negations, monosyllabic uncertainties, and non-committal rejoinders; the New England of abandoned farms and disappointed expectations, of walls that need mending and minds that need invigoration, of skepticism and resignation and retreat. How well one knows it!—that New England of so many unpainted farm-houses and so many frostbitten villages and so many arid sitting-rooms. . . . It exists, and Robert Frost is its laureate . . . that perfect cadence for that Yankee renunciation which, whatever else it is, is certainly what the Buddhists would call his own *dharma*. Everyone remembers the poem about the oven bird:

> *The question that he frames in all but words*
> *Is what to make of a diminished thing.*

Everyone remembers the poem about the bird at nightfall:

> *At most he thinks or twitters softly, 'Safe!*
> *Now let the night be dark for all of me.*
> *Let the night be too dark for me to see*
> *Into the future. Let what will be, be.'*

And—since no one expects that, even in a day when this philosophy seems as profitless as a dried-up well, Robert Frost will change his tune—everyone will be prepared to find the sentiment recurring, as it does more and more quaveringly, in this sixth volume of his. . . ."[23]

Apparently, part of Newton Arvin's purpose in writing the review was to deflate the current literary reputation of Robert

Frost. His article, entitled "A Minor Strain," contained the clarifying statement that Frost's poetry, instead of giving the true essence of the New England spirit, is "expressive much more of the minor than of the major strain in Yankee life and culture; or of a strain that perhaps seemed almost the major one in a late, transitory and already superseded period." The next attack, by Horace Gregory, in the *New Republic*, continued this further attempt at deflation:

"For the past five or six years, Mr. Frost's critics have done him a curious disservice. They have insisted, both by implication and emphatic reassertion, that his poetry is the work of a major poet; they have assured us that Mr. Frost must take an embarrassed stand as the inheritor of a New England tradition which at its best includes the names of Emerson, Whittier and the recently rediscovered metaphysical poet, Jones Very. I doubt if Mr. Frost pretends to any such eminence, for to do so would place his work at singular disadvantage. If he were to step at any point crossing the paths of Emerson and Whittier he would be forced to carry an unwelcome load of social responsibility—and even, God save him!—give up forever 'My own strategic retreat' and an obscure desire for a 'one-man revolution.' . . .

"Perhaps the title of his new book, 'A Further Range,' is half ironic; if not, I believe that he has heard too clearly the siren call of his unwise critics. It has always been Mr. Frost's particular virtue to make molehills out of mountains, to dig sharply, clearly and not too deeply into New England soil; so far as he has done this well, his integrity remains unquestioned. Beyond this range, however, he becomes self-defensive and ill informed; I refer to 'Build Soil,' 'To a Thinker,' 'A Lone Striker' and those thinly disguised platitudes in 'Ten Mills'—all included in the present volume. If Mr. Frost sincerely wishes to identify himself with 'A Drumlin Woodchuck' (one of the better poems in the book) to be 'more secure and snug,' why does he trouble his head about further ranges into politics, where his wisdom may be compared with that of Calvin Coolidge?"[24]

Another harsh criticism appeared in the *Nation*, where Richard Blackmur, in reviewing *A Further Range*, borrowed his epithet from the last line of "To a Thinker." Frost was not a true poet, he said, but rather a modern bard: one who is "at heart, an easy-going versifier of all that comes to hand, and

hence never lacks either a subject or the sense of its mastery."
In the old bards, Blackmur continued, we look mostly for
history, but in Frost we look for and find the recurrent theme
of escape.[25] The harshest of all these assaults occurred in the
New Masses, where Rolfe Humphries entitled his review "A
Further Shrinking." In the first sentence he invited his readers
to count the dashes representing the epithets he wanted to put
in print:

"There is an aspect of Robert Frost which criticism can dismiss
with objuration; when you call him a reactionary ———————, or
a counter-revolutionary ——— —— — —————, you have, in essence,
said it all. (Nor would Frost, who plays for it, care if you said so:
he might be more het up if you were to denounce his poses and
posturings in the presence of the young, for Frost, who professes to think Eliot a charlatan, has, for a long time, been
getting away with a good deal in this regard.) Still, underneath the obduracy and all the affectations of homeliness we
were content to recognize something real, something racy and
local, a tang and a twist, a combination of old Adam and New
England (with more of old England than met the eye), a
shrewd observation (though considerably less rustic than it
liked to make out) of the foibles of beasts and men. And this
(we thought at the time) was quite valuable.

"Unhappily, the art of being sedentary is difficult to cultivate.
You can't set indefinitely without running the risk of seeming
paralytic, yet heightened reputation does not necessarily attend
the act of getting up and going places. The man who, seated
on his kallipyge, looks like Olympian Zeus, turns out, when
he stands, to be of much less impressive stature, and when he
strides the hustings, to be ridiculous and unimportant of gait.

"So here. The further range to which Frost invited himself
is an excursion into the field of the political didactic, and his
address is unbecoming. . . . *A Further Range?* A further shrinking."[26]

In the midst of these attacks was one which Frost did not
want to ignore. It came in a personal letter from an attractive
young scholar and liberal named Ferner Nuhn—an Iowan
who had done graduate work in English at Columbia University and had married a fellow Iowan, the novelist Ruth Suckow.
Frost had met them both while they were living in Dorset,
Vermont, a few years earlier, and a warm friendship had
developed. On the strength of this friendship Nuhn had asked

for and received Frost's support of Nuhn's application for a Guggenheim Fellowship, to complete a volume which (as it turned out) would be called *The Wind Blew from the East: A Study in the Orientation of American Culture*. The fellowship was denied, but Nuhn, just returning to his manuscript after doing research and writing for two years in Washington —for the New Deal, in the Department of Agriculture—continued to discuss his proposed study with Frost. While again living for a brief time in Dorset, Nuhn sent Frost a sketch of the work in progress, explaining that Frost did not come within the scope of this study of two opposite-pulling forces acting upon the American character. Going on to suggest, however, where Frost might fit into such a scheme, Nuhn apparently could not resist trying to show what he viewed as the vulnerability of Frost's views under present circumstances:

"You will, I think, not feel misused in being labelled a 'survivor.' . . . Survival, toughness, 'come what may' . . . [in opposition to] sensitiveness, capacity to be overwhelmed. . . . Survival is something else again, and badly needed. To wait for the return wave, suffer eclipse for a while, lodged though not dead. . . . Of course it is a balance, with much on both sides, and a matter of balancing strength against sensibility. You feel that sensibility is a bit on the loose at present, too many young susceptibles ready to be martyred or do some martyring. Granted, and granted that waves come and go, times repeat themselves, and survivors wait for form and a return of common sense. But human will is part of nature and helps tip the scales the way the times go; the return of good is not inevitable without this extra fillip. So, may not survival lose its virtue if it is not so much strength as insulation?"

Nuhn, in thus challenging Frost's self-styled toughness, was taking more risks than he realized. Most of Frost's close friends were so familiar with his becoming furious when crossed or criticized that they timidly avoided differing with him. Unaware of this danger, Nuhn continued his letter by challenging the way in which Frost had misused Meliboeus as foil in "Build Soil":

"Poor Meloebeus (if I have his name right), I do feel he got rather talked down, and went away not so much convinced as subdued, and when *he* got by himself again, much *he* had to say came back to him, and he grumbled at not being as articulate as he might have been. I am moved to help his tongue a little, or anyway, use mine on his side. . . ."

Nuhn, as he continued his letter, wrote in defense of that New Deal liberalism which favored more social cooperation than Frost could stand. Although there are always tides in human affairs, Nuhn said, there are also transitions from one mode to another: an old mode becomes outmoded because life won't be contained fully in it any more—even as feudalism became outmoded. The problem, then, is to decide whether an upset is caused by the tide rocking the boat or by a real change of mode:

"Moelebeus and his fellows must be allowed their prophecy that it's the latter. They stand on it; I stand on it, and feel 'inside in' in it: that, as once we changed modes from monarchy to democracy, so now we are changing modes from individual to corporate economics. . . . If any large proportion of farmers took the advice given Moloebeus and 'dug in' and ate and wore their own products and didn't go to market to buy and sell more than a little dribble of excess, city people and easterners including poets and homilizers would pretty quickly be starved out, by the millions. . . . You'll excuse this finger-counting arithmetic, but you know, a westerner, a corn-belter, some times has to stand up and talk western farm arithmetic to Vermonters with their hankering for self-sustaining mountain farms which, however excellent as a way of life, are not sustaining the United States at present. . . . Farmers and poets and machine-tenders, we've all got beyond self-containment economically; the mode has passed; the emphasis is misplaced. . . ."

Nuhn was willing to grant that Tityrus (or however he spelled his name) was not entirely wrong:

"I know, of course, that Tyrtaeus isn't against 'cooperation'; I think he wants to apply a corrective to the times rocking and teetering and losing its balance. . . . But in the process, I don't want to give comfort to the crowd that rocks the other way, the real surplus-grabbers, who want to see all the Moelebeuses stay contented and quiet. They, the fat boys, the cashers-in on the system as it works now, would be very pleased to have the Moelebeuses and his fellow 'surplus' people in the cities go off quietly and grub out subsistence and keep out of sight. Tyrtaeus, defending the essential rightness of the time, is I really feel in danger of finding himself having to defend them,

and saying like Doctor Johnson that no one is more innocently occupied than in making money, no matter how and
how much. This other crowd wins by default, if Moelebeus
and all his fellows accept Tyrtaeus's corrective—so I feel that
Moelebeus didn't have his say out, and I want to come to his
support. . . ."[27]

Frost could not ignore such well-intended criticism of his
social-economic-political conservatism. Although Nuhn was
tied in with the New Deal crowd, and was even a close friend
of Henry Wallace's, Frost liked him and wanted to keep his
friendship. Indeed, through the Nuhns, Frost had recently met
Henry Wallace in Washington, and had found he rather liked
Wallace, too.[28] To answer Nuhn's arguments without damaging the friendly relations involved was a delicate task, and
Frost proceeded cautiously by writing the first draft of a possible reply, revising occasionally as he wrote. His first move
was to take refuge in a detached philosophic position:

"That was a frank and noble letter. I knew there was something on your mind and I think I partly get it. As you say the
rest can be done in conversation. There's no hurry there any
more than there is anywhere else. Time is long and theories
are fleeting. By the time we came to an understanding on the
present state of affairs we would be in the middle of another
state of affairs. Fortunately. I love change and I love personal
prejudice. From those two things I do my reasoning. In one I
seek the thread of what persists, in the other any common substance there may be of pure justice. The thread should be silk
and the substance radium."

So far, Frost had not invoked any serious ambiguities, other
than to say he loved change and personal prejudice. Had he
wanted to be more precise, he might have made a nice differentiation between the changes he loved—such as those which
came with weather's alternations—and the changes he ab-
horred. Years earlier, when he had tried to defend his conservatism against Untermeyer's socialistically inclined liberalism, he had written, "In the general rush of change with
almost everything going, I should think there would be danger
that some things would be carried away that even the wildest
revolutionary would be sorry to see carried away. Well then
that's where I come in. . . . I am interested in what is to stay
as it is; you are interested in what is not to stay as it is. . . .
You want to blow the candle to see if it won't give more light.

All right, let me hold the candle so you can give all your attention to blowing it carefully so as not to blow it out. And let me hold the matches too so that if you should blow it out we could form a society to relight it."[29] Nuhn also wanted to make the candle give more light, and as Frost continued his defense he added a playfully humorous note:

"I don't mind being called a survivor or anything else that doesn't reflect on my mother. I must have been called a survivor by every member of the department of social and economic sciences I ever spent the evening with. But excuse me if I don't think the name quite covers me. A better epithet would be survivalist. I believe in survival. That is my fundamental doctrine. I argued in a monologue lately that the fact of our race's having survived should be enough for others as it is for me. It proves those for us must be more than those against us —in nature and human nature. The blood stream is the one unbroken logic. . . ."[30]

His next defensive move was one of verbal Indian wrestling, in which he only seemed to place himself at a momentary disadvantage:

"Albert J. Nock, Editor [Paul] Palmer of Mercury and H. L. Men[c]ken are survivors in your invidious sense of the word. They survive from the individualistic unsocialistic days of Herbert Spencer. Strict justice their minds ran on. And of course strict justice is basic. It is primarily for government to preside with the strictest justice over the free-for-all struggle to win. It must pick the winners with no half-rewards. But the very next thing after it has rewarded the winners it must do something for the losers. It must show them mercy. Justice first and mercy second. The trouble with some of your crowd is that they would have mercy first. The struggle to win is still the best tonic. We like it. Many are game enough to say nothing against it when they lose. But never mind all that. The point is that mercy, which is another word for socialism, wouldn't mean anything till there had been a distinction made between winners and losers. All that is said in my Political Pastoral—if you will be careful not to read it in the light of this campaign. It was written before the New Deal was heard of. All I had heard of was the Old Deil (sp).[31] Albert Nock would leave the performance of mercy to the winners. Not so I, if you look again at my Pastoral. Mercy is a function of government. I believe in taking from the rich to keep the poor at school. My grandfather didn't. Herbert Spencer didn't. Herbert Spencer believed in private armies. I believe in parole and even pardon, but not until after trial conviction and sentence. . . ."

One way to ease the conflict, here, was to use certain words ambiguously, so that each side could find a comfortable meaning. As he continued, Frost manipulated the word "mercy" in a highly ambiguous and deceptive manner: "As long as you use socialism and mercy as interchangeable I am with you into the future." Such a posture of reconciliation was not supported, however, by what he had scarcely finished writing: that in his view justice must come first and mercy second, or that the "trouble with some of your crowd is that they would have mercy first." Even as he went on, he returned to his attack on the proponents of socially ameliorative mercy:

"The question of the moment in politics will always be one of proportion between mercy and justice. You have to remember the people who accept mercy have to pay for it. Mercy means protection. And there is no protection without direction. A person completely protected would have to be completely directed. And he would be a slave. That's where socialism pure brings you out. But you don't want it pure. You merely want a little more of it than I do. You may take my poetic play seriously but please not grimly. . . ."

Having provided this basis for reconciliation, Frost invited sympathy by going on to make an extremely attractive psychological explanation of his Political Pastoral:

"Both those people in the dialogue are me. I enjoyed having one part of me impose on the other. The fun of the imposition was what kept me writing. I like to know I am imposing on someone now and then. I distrust myself so (my prejudice in favor of myself so) I like to come right out into the open with my faults where I can't fail to see them with my own eyes. You take the greed to indoctrinate. I like to catch myself in it. Or the greed to benefact. All the forms of self-assertion are so hidden from the self. Show yourself up to yourself now and then for health, say I. There is an inclusive thought in my pastoral, but neither speaker owns it. Remember I am a survivalist. Perhaps that's the clue. I don't want to know too well myself. . . ."[32]

Such a confession was genuine, and yet perhaps not entirely candid. It was true that Frost had been fashioning poems, for years, out of the dramatic conflicts between the opposed sides of his own nature, but by the time he wrote "Build Soil" his inner sympathy for any form of socialistic idealism had weakened so much as to become practically nonexistent. He had gone as far as he could to win the sympathies and hold the friendship of Nuhn, yet he knew that their positions were almost diametrically opposed. Lapsing once more into whimsicalities, as a possible way of concluding the letter, he did not even try to conceal his awareness that Nuhn's views differed sharply from his own:

"I've said about everything, but have I said, I wonder (I don't want to look back) that your crowd had better treat me with respect because my poetry (while it lives) will keep alive the sentiments from which their theories spring. I describe a more classless society than they will bring to the world again in a thousand years of trying. Maybe it can't be gone back to. Maybe the only way to it is forward the thousand years. All right. Better hang on to my verse as a thousand-year plan. I'm descended from the Puritan who had both his ears cut off twice for equialitarianism. They grew again I suppose like tonsils."

Frost was apparently dissatisfied with this first-draft letter to Nuhn, and neither revised nor sent it. Instead, when he next saw Nuhn, some time later, Frost did go so far as to say that Nuhn's letter was so good that it deserved a good answer. Then he added, congenially, that perhaps Nuhn would better understand "Build Soil" if no attempt was made to apply it too closely to the present situation, particularly to the New Deal.[33]

There was nothing more difficult for Frost than to be as pleasant as he had been to Nuhn-as-critic, and he usually compensated for similar difficulties by finding some other target for attack, immediately after such an ordeal. This time, however, he found himself enmeshed in another one. Not long after he wrote the letter not sent to Nuhn, the poet gave a reading at the Bread Loaf Writers' Conference, stayed there over a weekend, and suffered abnormally from the good intentions of those who commiserated with him over the unpleasant reviews *A Further Range* had been receiving. Such a display of sympathy was enough to make him suspect that he was surrounded by jealous enemies. Theodore Morrison, in his sixth year as director of the Conference, was far too liberal in his political leanings to please Frost. Back in 1928, when the *Letters of Sacco and Vanzetti* had been published, Morrison was serving as book-review editor of the *Atlantic*, and had been the one who had written asking Frost to review the book on the basis of its literary merits.[34] Morrison had further offended Frost, unintentionally, in 1933, by offering to pay him only $50 for a possible talk or reading at the Conference—and had heightened the offense by adding that another distinguished guest-lecturer would be John Farrar.[35] Frost, after an unpleasant battle with Farrar at the Conference in 1929, had restricted his visits to the School of English, and there were various reasons why he had not often attended the Writers' Conference.[36] But the Morrisons had been so hospitable while the Frosts were in Cambridge that it was impossible to refuse the invitation to the 1936 session. He and Mrs. Frost had made their annual retreat to the Fobes cottage in Franconia, early in August, and the trip to Bread Loaf was made from Franconia. By the time he returned to the White Mountains he was far more disturbed and upset than he had been before. Now he was even more worried that he might not be able to settle in and write the two poems he had promised to read at Harvard in September. Earlier in the summer he had shown this worry, in a letter of complaints:

"And another thing to complain of is that ode to o[r]der (sp.) for Harvard and please don't you add to my misery by asking every once in so often how about it. Let's not talk about it. Let's not look as if we were thinking about it. Dave [McCord] should worry; because he cares for me and he cares for Harvard. What a position that puts him in if I should fail, as Macbeth said. To Hell with these baubles gewgaws kickshaws. I'll write 'em a poem the last night before I face the mike. . . ."[37]

At Franconia, Mrs. Frost began to fear that neither one of the Harvard poems would ever get written. "Robert is awake so late at night," she wrote to the travelling Mrs. Fobes, "and is apt to feel like a walk even after midnight, so he values the freedom to roam around the cottage very much. Especially this year, when he is having difficulty in even getting started on the poems. At least I am afraid he has hardly made a beginning."[38] She knew how deeply he had been hurt by the leftist attacks on *A Further Range*. When he became ill, she was not surprised—and Frost was actually relieved by the doctor's insistence that he send telegrams to the Harvard authorities. Mrs. Frost explained to Thornton, at Holt,

". . . he came down with a severe attack of shingles on his

face. Shingles is a nervous disease, you know, and the doctor here said he was suffering a nervous exhaustion and that if he didn't stop trying to work, he would get into a condition that might take a year to recover from. He *couldn't* work, anyway, the pain in his head was so acute. So he had to give up doing the Harvard poems. . . ."[39]

He also had to give up his promise to be at Amherst College when the fall term started, and he knew that President King had already grown impatient with him for dodging responsibilities at Amherst, year after year. Although the Frosts did return to the College late in September, he was quickly overtaken by another illness and was again bedridden. On the twenty-fifth of November 1936 he reviewed his difficulties:

"Away back early in September I swore off on letter-writing till I should get well entirely. But I begin to think if I wait till then I shall wait forever. So here I am writing again though from bed.

"Don't imagine I haven't been up all this time. I have been up and down. At one stroke I cut out all duties away from Amherst, I left Harvard to the English[40] and I left the American Academy[41] to Billy Phelps. I dropped all the pay engagements. From that moment I was a different man. It dawned on me that all this I had been imperceptibly getting deeper and deeper into wasn't the life of my choice and liking. What a relief to have the spell broken. . . . None of my friends would back me to backing down. They probably couldn't bear to see me with my bravery off. It would disillusion them. They left it to God, and God saved me with a charge of bird-shot in my right bump of ideality where all could see my incapacitation. I was in great agony of countenance when I was with you at Bread Loaf, but my stigmata hadn't yet shown on the surface. When it did come out I thought it smallpox and as such something I had better keep still about if I didn't want to start a panic. It was quite a malady. . . ."[42]

While the malady lasted, he began plotting revenge against his proletarian enemies. Bernard DeVoto, already flexing polemical muscles as editor-in-chief of the *Saturday Review*, had offered to slaughter Frost's critics with a murderous counterattack, and Frost could not resist encouraging him. Shortly before Christmas of 1936, he felt well enough to read his poems before students and faculty at the New School for Social Research in New York, and he there began to take revenge. Assuming that some of his leftist critics were in his audience, he reviewed some of the epithets hurled at him, and singled out the one used by Rolfe Humphries in the *New Masses:* "counter-revolutionary." If such cheap name-calling was in order, he said, he could easily cap that one: his opponent was merely a "bargain-counter revolutionary." Most of his listeners seemed to enjoy this retort, but as Frost was leaving the New School that night, he was stopped by an excited, long-haired, scraggly bearded creature who said he happened to be a friend of the man Frost had called a bargain-counter revolutionary, who also had a sense of humor. Maybe Frost didn't know what a firecracker was, but if he didn't he'd soon find out.

Frost laughed off the threat, without forgetting it. Shortly after he returned to Amherst, he received through the mail a crudely wrapped package bearing no return address—and the poet was immediately suspicious. The package felt as though it contained a cigar box, and Frost knew that homemade bombs were often concealed within cigar boxes. Suspicion was heightened by the fact that none of his friends would be sending him cigars because they all knew he didn't smoke them. Wouldn't it be safer, he asked his wife, to take the unopened package back to the post office, and just call attention to the suspicious lack of a return address? She tried to reassure him by saying it was so light it couldn't possibly contain a bomb, and she disliked attracting public notice by letting anyone learn of his fear. Thus restrained, he didn't know what to do. Perhaps there would be no danger in cautiously removing the string and wrapping. As soon as he had unwrapped it his suspicions were confirmed: it was a cigar box, the tax-stamp seemed to be deliberately broken, and the cover was held down by what seemed to be an oddly shaped tack. With reproachful boldness he said that if his wife disliked attracting public attention he would appoint himself to serve as a one-man demolition squad, no matter how great the risk. He'd carry the bomb into the backyard, tie a stone to it, and hurl it against a tree. He did—and scattered cigars all over the yard.[43]

32

PRIDE OF ANCESTRY

*... Descend from Owen Glendower as much as you please
but before you condescend to me give me time to find out
if I may not descend from Bruce or Wallace. By the time
you get here I may have a real ancestry worked up.*[1]

ON THE twenty-fourth of May 1936, only a few days after
the Frosts returned from Harvard to their farm in South
Shaftsbury, they were privately informed that their friend Edward Morgan Lewis, president of the University of New Hampshire, had died of cancer, the previous night. The funeral
service was to be held on the morning of the twenty-sixth and
would be attended by only the immediate family. A public
memorial service would also be held, in the University gym-
nasium on the afternoon of the same day, and the President's
widow hoped Robert Frost would read one or two of her husband's favorite poems at the memorial service.

Because Frost and Lewis had developed an exceptionally
warm friendship during the past nineteen years, such an invitation could not be refused. They had first met in the home
of President Meiklejohn, in Amherst, early in the winter of
1917, under circumstances which were simultaneously amusing and embarrassing for all three men. Back in those days
when Frost was a newcomer to Amherst, Meiklejohn occasionally invited a few upperclassmen to his home immediately
after the Sunday chapel service, to discuss any topic which
might be suitably controversial, and for one of these gatherings
he arranged a session which was to be conducted by a famous
outsider. He would start the discussion by saying anything he
chose about the "new poetry." The outsider was the forty-five
year old Welshman, Edward Morgan Lewis, who had first
distinguished himself twenty years earlier as a record-setting
pitcher for the baseball team later known as the Boston Braves.

Currently he was not only a professor of English but also an extremely popular dean of students at the nearby Massachusetts Agricultural College. Meiklejohn also invited Frost to attend this gathering and to participate in the discussion. Not knowing that Frost would be present, Lewis had decided to talk about and read from the works of only one modern poet— Robert Frost—and he stuck to his plan.[2]

After this pleasantly awkward meeting, Frost and Lewis built a substantial friendship on their mutual interests of baseball and poetry. As a boy, Frost had been the best pitcher on his school team in Salem, New Hampshire, and had dreamed he might some day be a pitcher in one of the big leagues.[3] Even after he awoke from this dream, he demonstrated his continuing passion for the game by studying newspaper accounts of big league standings, batting averages, and pitching records. In the fall of 1898, when he entered Harvard as a special student, the Boston papers were giving special attention to "Parson" Lewis, who was a twenty-five game winner that season, and he went on, that fall, to help the Boston Nationals (not yet called the Braves) win the pennant for a second consecutive year. Frost and Lewis, in their first conversations, spent as much time talking baseball as poetry, and Frost kept asking questions until he had obtained the life story of Edward Morgan Lewis.

The story would have served well as a plot for a novel by Horatio Alger. Lewis, only eight years old when he emigrated from Wales with his parents, suffered through boyhood humiliations and poverty in the city of Utica, New York. Although he quickly learned how to play "the great American game," his devout parents were so sternly Calvinistic that they never permitted him to waste much time at baseball. It was their wish that he might educate himself to become a minister or a teacher, and they succeeded in helping him develop an ambition to go to college. While he was working his way through his first two years of study at Marietta, in Ohio, he nevertheless found time to earn a position on the baseball team there, and he showed so much ability as a pitcher that he attracted notice far beyond the campus. In the summer of 1893, he accepted a scholarship at Williams College and transferred from Marietta to Williams in the fall. His record as a pitcher during these years of study earned him a contract offer from the Boston Nationals. When he signed with them immediately after his graduation from Williams in June of 1896, he insisted that his contract include the written statement that he would under no circumstances play on Sunday. His teammates therefore nicknamed him "Parson" Lewis, but he soon won their admiration. Determined from the start of his big-league career not to devote too much of his life to baseball, he continued his studies at various places between seasons, obtaining a master of arts degree from Williams in June of 1899 and insisting that he would resign as a ball player as soon as he could obtain a good teaching position.[4]

Lewis spent his fifth and last baseball season with the Boston Americans (later known as the Red Sox), and in the fall of 1901 he began teaching at Columbia University. From 1903 to 1911 he taught public speaking and oratory at Williams; in 1911 he went to Massachusetts Agricultural College as an assistant professor of literature and as associate dean of the college. By the time Frost met him, he had become a hero in the estimation of the "Mass Aggies." Among the courses he offered, his favorite was in Victorian poetry, and among the Victorians his favorite authors were Browning and Tennyson.

Frost was charmed by Lewis's story of how, as a boy in Utica, he had developed an enthusiasm for poetry. With his white-bearded father, he had attended an American-Welsh Eisteddfod, a contest in poetry, where a bard newly arrived from Wales sat in judgment while the original poems of the unknown contestants were read aloud. At the end of the reading, the boy heard the judge give the title of the prizewinning poem, and was amazed when his father stood up to accept the prize. Frost, telling this anecdote repeatedly, in later years, concluded on one occasion: "So poetry to him was prowess from that time on, just as baseball was prowess, as running was prowess. And it was our common ground. I have always thought of poetry as prowess—something to achieve, something to win or lose."[5]

Another bond between these two men was their pride in comparing notes on their Celtic ancestry, and in discussing the similarities of their religious backgrounds. Frost may have boasted that his great-grandfather in Scotland had the gift of second sight and—just before he died—saw angels opening the gates of Heaven to receive him. Lewis could match that; at least he made the claim that he was descended from Owen

Glendower who, according to Shakespeare, could call up spirits from the vasty deep. Recognizing the joke in the boast, and responding as skeptically as Hotspur, Frost playfully replied that if Lewis was going to insist on tracing his ancestry back to Glendower, then Frost would try to demonstrate his descent from either Wallace or Bruce.

Each of these Amherst residents had such a quick sense of humor that there was usually playfulness in their manner when they met on the street and stopped to talk. Once, after Frost stepped off a train which Lewis was hurrying to catch, in nearby Northampton, they almost passed without seeing each other in the dimly lit passageway underneath the tracks. Frost stopped only when he felt a staying hand on his coat-sleeve, and turned to find Lewis quoting with mock intensity the first lines from Browning's "Memorabilia":

> *"Ah, did you once see Shelley plain*
> *And did he stop and speak to you,*
> *And did you speak to him again?*
> *How strange it seems and new!"*

Frost always enjoyed the chance to cap one quotation with another, and he knew by heart as many of Browning's lines as Lewis did. This time, without hesitation, he answered by quoting the start of "Time's Revenges":

> *"I've a Friend, from over the sea;*
> *I like him, but he loves me.*
> *It all grew out of the books I write . . ."*

That was all they said, but Lewis gave a vanquished wave of his hand as he hurried toward the train.[6]

These two men were usually so busy that they could do little more than salute each other briefly while going their opposite ways, and the friendship between them did not develop rapidly. They were still addressing each other by last names in 1927 when Lewis, after serving for several years as the acting president of Massachusetts Agricultural College (and for one year as president) resigned in order to become president of the University of New Hampshire. Nearly three years later, he wrote to ask whether Frost would accept an honorary degree, would bring his wife with him for the occasion, and would stay for a few days thereafter, in the home of the Lewises. In his grateful reply, Frost mentioned the time and place of their first meeting:

"I always like to have something very pleasant and important happen to me in March as a sort of birthday present from Fortune. Your letter is it this year with your promise to give me the highest honorary degree in your command if I will come to visit you on June 16. Will I? I will. I shall be doubly honored in any honor I may receive at your hands. Your remembering me this way makes me remember you the first time I ever saw you—it was at another President's house—and the last time I saw you—it was in this house, in this very room in fact: you had called to tell me something grand about the University of New Hampshire. . . ."[7]

Both of the Frosts did go to Durham for the ceremonies, and were persuaded to linger for several days in the President's home. Time was found for sessions of pitch-and-catch, just between the two men, in the President's back yard, and Frost asked some serious technical questions. Remembering all he had learned from his own pitching experiences, he wanted to see just how and where Lewis placed his fingers on the seam of the ball when he threw his most deceptive curve. "He let me into the secret," Frost later wrote, "of how he could make a ball behave when his arm was just right. It may sound superstitious to the uninitiated, but he could push a cushion of air ahead of it for it to slide off from, any way it pleased."[8] Lewis, in response to Frost's praise for his prowess as a baseball player, kept insisting that Frost had established a far more enviable record for prowess, valor, skill, and ingenuity—as a poet. During the commencement ceremony, President Lewis took obvious pleasure in finding another way to salute his friend: he formally read, before the commencement audience, the citation he himself had written to accompany the hood representing the honorary degree of Doctor of Letters. It included this:

"Today your name is one of the foremost in American letters —a style unique and original among the poets. We rejoice to recall that, in verse both powerful and lovely with the magic of the cadence and rhythms of everyday speech, you have revealed to the whole world for all time not only the majestic glory of our north country, but also the distinctive and wholesome life of the rugged folks of our countryside."[9]

Frost was so profoundly touched by the warmth of the reception given him and his wife by the Lewises during this visit that he tried to convey more than gratitude in an unusual letter soon after he returned home:

"You don't know what ideas you were putting into my head as you apostrophized me on the platform last Monday. One dangerous one was that I ought to be ashamed to live anywhere but in New Hampshire. You watch the idea work. I predict that it will land me back in the state where my father was born and three fourths of my children and practically all my poetry.

"The degree you gave me was different from any other I have ever had; the hood will be the one I wear if I ever have occasion to wear a hood. You made me realize that your friendship had in it an element of personal affection: it went beyond a mere admiration for what I have done. I deserve a little friendship of that warmth in a life mostly subject to cold criticism. At any rate it goes to my heart, and whether I deserve it or not, I am going to cling to it. We must see more of each other in the years to come than we have in the last few. I am coming for the visit in the fall and you must come for a visit here when you can. . . . "[10]

Neither one of the plans for a quick reunion worked out. Recurrent illnesses made it impossible for Frost to accept various invitations to read his poems at the University of New Hampshire during the next two years. By coincidence, however, each of them was asked to be in Williamstown, Massachusetts, on the twentieth of June 1932 to receive an honorary degree, and Frost pleasantly began to make serious plans by writing Lewis: "The last time we played an exhibition game you pitched and I caught. This time we'll both be on the receiving end and it will remain to see who catches it the worse. You can show your freedom from professional jealousy by bringing your wife up to visit us at our farm if only for a night."[11]

This plan was carried out, and the Lewises visited the Frosts immediately after the ceremonies at Williams College. During their walks and talks and games of pitch-and-catch, Frost repeatedly expressed his disgust with those narrow-minded academics at Lewis's Alma Mater who had omitted from the citation any reference to his achievements in professional baseball. A better example had been set by Amherst College, in giving Lewis an honorary degree in 1927, with a citation which contained this: ". . . alumnus of our dearest foe; an undergraduate whom as a person we loved but whose speed, control and curves from the pitcher's mound we dreaded . . ."[12]

Poetry, not baseball, became the subject under consideration when the two men next corresponded. In the spring of 1934, Lewis wrote to say that Miss Shirley Barker, a senior at the University of New Hampshire, had won a prize in the Yale Series of Younger Poets. One of the judges had praised her poems about New England by saying that she seemed to have a literary kinship with Robert Frost, and for this reason Lewis had asked Miss Barker to send Frost a copy of her recently published book entitled *The Dark Hills Under*. Frost answered Lewis sympathetically:

"You wrote me in the spring that your young poetess would send me a book she was just having with the Yale Press. I was pleased for you that one of yours was having the honor of having a book. The book never turned up. . . . I wish I might meet the poetess. If she were to be numbered among the many who go riding round in the summer she might well look in on me for a talk unless she is more shy than I believe I am formidable. You say she seems too unassertive for teaching. That's too bad. I should think teaching would be better for a poet's poetry than editorial or clerical work in a publisher's office. I have heard Lincoln MacVeagh (late proprietor of the Dial Press, now ambassador to Greece) say the nearer the book, the further from literature. He meant the nearer the business of books. A lot of young writers get the notion that if they could be where manuscripts are being read and judged it would make them authorities and so authors. At best the jobs are critical (that is when they rise above the clerical) and lead nowhere but to more criticism—possibly for the Times Supplement, [the New York *Herald Tribune*] Books, or the Saturday Review—and so on up by a series of toe and finger holds till the nails are all worn off. I make it as bad as possible. The better the poet the more I should like to scare her off the publisher's premises. But tell me more. Her own wishes must be considered. . . ."[13]

Before Lewis could say more, Frost received a copy of *The Dark Hills Under*—and was infuriated by all of it. Having been led to expect that this young woman was following more or less in his own footsteps, he found that she seemed opposed to everything he stood for. Her interests were so different from his that he wondered whether his friend Lewis had given any care to the reading of these verses. Particularly annoying to Frost was her way of insinuating that the genuine New Englander must be opposed to passion, and must be governed habitually by smug repressions:

> A thousand maple-shaded streets there are,
> Veining New England like a withered leaf;
> A thousand picket fences, gates ajar;
> A thousand strips of lawn, close-cut and brief;
> A thousand houses, small and smug, and white,
> With bleakly shining panes where women sit,
> Turned from the heresy of April night
> To a bright hearth, and quietly hating it.[14]

This was bad enough, Frost thought, but even more annoying was the girl's pleasure in belittling a word he had been trying to defend, indirectly, throughout his life as a poet: Puritan. She began to disparage it in the first line of her first poem, a sonnet entitled "Old Voices":

> No Puritans can die. Their manner still
> Lives on, and must, till all their kind are clay.
> Restraining hands reach out from Burial Hill
> To quiet the sunset, and to draw a gray
> And pallid shadow down on all their land;
> To tear the scarlet leaves away too soon;
> To wall the gardens where their daughters stand,
> And fling cold fog between them and the moon.
>
> When I am gay because some lad has smiled,
> Beneath my quickened pulse they stir and move.
> A Great-aunt Prudence whispers, "Caution, Child."
> A Grand-dame Martha asks, "Would God approve?"
> But louder speaks some shameless Kate or Flo—
> "Rejoice, but do not let the Elders know."[15]

Particularly offensive to Frost was a poem entitled "Portrait" in which the speaker implicitly identifies herself with some characteristics of a great-grandmother whose picture is framed and prominently displayed. Nobody in the family seems to know much about this ancestor, but the speaker apparently guesses much from the passionate lips and the luxuriant hair.

Frost maliciously decided that Shirley Barker must be so romantic and sentimental as to suppose she inherited all her own gifts from one unstated marital aberration of the ancestor thus portrayed.[16] Gradually, he worked himself into such a state that he could relieve his emotions only through a characteristic act of poetic retaliation which he called "Pride of Ancestry":

> *The Deacon's wife was a bit desirish*
> *And liked her sex relations wild,*
> *So she lay with one of the shanty Irish*
> *And he begot the Deacon's child.*

> *The Deacon himself was a man of money*
> *And upright life and a bosom shirt;*
> *Which made her infidelity funny*
> *And gave her pleasure in doing him dirt.*

> *And yet for all her romantic sneakin'*
> *Out the back door and over the wall*
> *How was she sure the child of the Deacon*
> *Wasn't the Deacon's after all?*

> *Don't question a story of high eugenics.*
> *She lived with the Deacon and bedded with him,*
> *But she restricted his calesthenics*
> *To the sterile arc of her lunar rhythm.*

> *And she only had to reverse the trick*
> *And let the Irishman turn her turtle*
> *When by his faith as a Catholic*
> *A woman was almost sure to be fertile.*

> *Her portrait hangs in the family gallery*
> *And a family of nobodies likes to think*
> *That their descent from such a calorie*
> *Accounts for their genius and love of drink.*[17]

Such an act of retaliation against what he hated in the poetry of Shirley Barker might have been sufficient for Frost if he had not been infuriated further by another recurrent theme he thought he found in *The Dark Hills Under*. This girl seemed to take pleasure in mocking religious belief: "And since upon whatever gods I call, / Or call on none, my fortune is the same, / Better some lost delight I should recall / Than sit a vestal virgin by this flame."[18] Frost may have thought he found the same theme extended through the wording of a question at the heart of another poem: whether the speaker's admiration of a birch tree should seem "idolatrous" and "not so fair" as worshiping "whitened vestments in a somber church" or "spirits conjured" through the heat of prayer.[19] No matter how mistaken he might be, Frost could easily find personal affronts in anyone's mockery of religious belief—unless he was mocking a belief distinct from his own. Nor would he let anyone else say anything against God, although he permitted himself to be hilariously blasphemous. Having made up his mind that Shirley Barker was a disparaging despairer who had lost her belief in God, Frost scolded her in a tight riposte called "Not All There":

> *I turned to speak to God*
> *About the world's despair;*
> *But to make bad matters worse*
> *I found God wasn't there.*
>
> *God turned to speak to me*
> *(Don't anybody laugh);*
> *God found I wasn't there—*
> *At least not over half.*[20]

It was always easier for Frost to forgive someone for offending him, if he could wait until after he had found a way of striking back at the offender. But he did not want to hurt his friend, President Lewis, by letting him know that nothing in *The Dark Hills Under* deserved Frost's praise. Not sure what to say to "Parson" Lewis, Frost simply avoided writing to him during the next few months after he received the book from Shirley Barker—and when he did write he simply made no mention of her. He did accept an invitation to read at the University of New Hampshire, but he used illness as an excuse for canceling the engagement. His last letter to Lewis, written in the fall of 1935, contained protests that his immediate schedule was crowded, and he could not tell when he might be able to give a reading in Durham. He did end this letter, however, by implying that Shirley Barker had sent him some new poems which he liked: "I've just been reading some fine stuff of Shirley Barker's in manuscript. She's one unmistakably. Your institution has something to be proud of there."[21] The next important word he received about President Lewis was the news of his death.

When the Frosts arrived in Durham for the memorial service he had not yet learned which poems he was expected to read for his part in the program. He was told, however, that some verse had been used at the funeral service that morning: a fifty-line rhymed eulogy, written for the occasion by Shirley Barker and entitled "This Man My Friend."[22] At the afternoon service, attended by the faculty, the trustees, and hundreds of students, the invocation was given by one of Lewis's classmates from Williams College, and the opening address was made by the president of the Board of Trustees of the University of New Hampshire. There followed a tribute given by a lawyer who, having been a year behind Lewis at Williams, had looked up to him as much for the warmth of his friendliness on the campus as for the success of his accomplishments on the mound. Frost was permitted to bring the ceremonies to an end by reading two poems selected by Mrs. Lewis. Each had to do with the immortality of the soul, and the sentiments in them were congenial to Frost's own religious belief: Whitman's "On the Beach at Night" and the six stanzas from Tennyson's "In Memoriam" beginning:

> Strong Son of God, immortal Love,
>   Whom we, that have not seen thy face,
>   By faith, and faith alone, embrace,
> Believing where we cannot prove;
>
> Thou wilt not leave us in the dust:
>   Thou madest man, he knows not why,
>   He thinks he was not made to die;
> And thou hast made him: thou art just.[23]

STRIKE THAT BLOW FOR ME

*I am going to have you strike that blow for me now if you
still want to . . . I am not above asking favors, but principle
if not delicacy forbids that it should be too soon in a
friendship.*[1]

IN THE autumn of 1936, when the Frosts were advised by their
Amherst doctor that they should once again make plans to
escape southward before the arrival of winter, they decided
against going back to Florida. The two winters already spent
there had been spoiled by too many intrusions, and even Key
West had not provided the isolation they desired. Their enjoyment of California during their previous visits encouraged
them to consider the possibility of finding a place to hide somewhere below Los Angeles—perhaps near Long Beach—but
there again they knew they would be within reach of possible
intruders. The southern part of Texas was discussed because
they had enjoyed the countryside around Austin and San
Antonio in 1933, and after much talk about it, they finally
decided to gamble on a winter in San Antonio.

Hating to be separated from their children and grandchildren at Christmas time, the elder Frosts proposed a family
reunion in San Antonio on Christmas Day and offered to pay
expenses. Although Lillian had recovered well from her long
siege with tuberculosis, her doctor continued to advise that
she escape New England winters as much as she could. It was
therefore easy to persuade Carol, Lillian, and the twelve-year-
old Prescott. Irma was not interested. Living in Hanover, New
Hampshire, where her husband was establishing himself in a
successful architectural firm, she was still threatening to obtain a divorce, and she got along no better with her father than
with her husband. Lesley, divorced, had already decided to
spend the winter near Mexico City, in company with her two

daughters. She arranged to reach San Antonio en route to Mexico by car on or before Christmas Day. Willard Fraser was invited to bring his daughter Robin from Montana to Texas and to leave her under Lillian's care during the winter. These arrangements were so nicely coordinated that Lillian was able to boast in a letter to a friend, "On Christmas day we all—Father, Mother, Lesley, Elinor, Lee, Willard, Robin, Carol, Prescott, and I—had dinner together at our hotel, the Saint Anthony, here in San Antonio."[2]

A few days later, after Willard had started back alone to Montana and Lesley had continued with her children toward Mexico, Carol and his parents began house-hunting. A furnished apartment was rented for Carol and his family at 947 West Agarita Avenue, on the edge of the city. Less than two miles away, at 113 Norwood Court, the elder Frosts found and rented an apartment to their liking. The real-estate agent who helped them was almost successful in persuading Frost that he should buy property on the edge of a little canyon wilderness not too far outside San Antonio, but Mrs. Frost dissuaded him.

In no mood to write poems after the fiasco caused by his failure to produce those poems he had promised for Harvard, Frost entertained himself by writing letters, and the most serious of these was to his friend-of-a-year, the new editor-in-chief of the *Saturday Review*, Bernard DeVoto. Frost had not forgotten DeVoto's offer to write and publish in the *Saturday Review* an essay which would at least rebuke those critics who had attacked *A Further Range* and its author so harshly in the *Nation*, the *New Masses*, the *New Republic*, and the *Partisan Review*. DeVoto, having developed a satirical two-fistedness of his own while writing some of his earliest pieces for H. L. Mencken's *American Mercury*, could obviously throw verbal uppercuts and punishing body blows. His almost worshipful admiration of Frost had been cultivated by Frost not entirely without ulterior motives since he had sought DeVoto in Miami, and their friendship had increased rapidly during the Norton lectureship at Harvard. Shortly after Frost had returned to Amherst from Cambridge he had written laudatory thanks for DeVoto's newly published volume of essays entitled *Forays and Rebuttals*:

"Not just the two or three essays I had seen before—I like the whole damned book. I have read most of it more than once and most of it to Elinor aloud as if telling her something out of my head. You and I without collusion have arrived at so nearly the same conclusions about life and America that I cant seem to figure out how we came to vote different tickets at the last election. . . ."³

Frost had not given himself to such outpourings of enthusiastic praise since the days when he had begun to seek favors from Untermeyer. Part of his strategy, back there, had been to provide information which could be used in articles about Frost. In similar fashion he continued his letter to DeVoto:

"Someone said all my writing was about the poor. Was it because I had no sympathy with them? I am tempted to answer: I never would have written about the poor, if I had thought it would lead to anything's being done about them. Or better: I wrote about the poor as the most permanent subject to hitch onto. I took Christ's word for it that poverty wouldnt be abolished. But now we're asked to join the W. C. T. U. and do away with poverty prostitution drink and death. The great politicians are having their fun with us. Theyve picked up just enough of the New Republic and Nation jargon to seem original to the simple. . . ."⁴

Returning to *Forays and Rebuttals,* Frost added more praise:

"To go back to your essays. I cant get over my not having realized you were on earth. You don't know your power. No one else has your natural sensible and at the same time embracing thoughts about life and America. And the way you lay into the writing with your whole body like an archer rather than a pistolman. Neither perverse precious nor international. I wasn't marked off from the other children as a literary sissy like Yates and Masters. Maybe thats whats the matter with me. Theres consolation in the thought that you werent marked off either. . . ."⁵

Frost had subsequently carried this campaign further by arranging to have DeVoto give a lecture at Amherst College in the fall of 1936, by playing host to him, and by giving a reception for him after the lecture. DeVoto had brought to Amherst some news which tied him more closely to the controversy between Frost's friends and enemies. One of those friends, Robert Hillyer, had published in the *Atlantic Monthly* for August 1936 an embarrassingly fulsome poem entitled "A Letter to Robert Frost"—over 200 lines, in couplets. In answer, Granville Hicks sent to the *Saturday Review* a parody entitled

"A Letter to Robert Hillyer." As editor-in-chief, DeVoto rejected the manuscript, returning it to Hicks with the explanation that it was bad art. There were several more obvious reasons for rejecting it, one being that Hicks had satirically attacked Hillyer for praising the editor-in-chief:

> *The Eliots and Cranes you damn* in toto
> *But speak with vast respect of one DeVoto*
> *The Howells of our age—God save the mark!—*
> *Who's bid his sad farewell to Durgin Park,*
> *To swanboats, Pops, and other Boston joys,*
> *And now laments the humbug and the noise*
> *Of Mannahatta, though there's some suspicion*
> *He's well equipped to furnish competition.*
> *He's versatile at least, and swiftly shuttles*
> *From co-ed tales to forays and rebuttals.*
> *(His forays fill the women's clubs with awe,*
> *And his rebuttals slaughter men of straw.)*

Hicks had also mocked Hillyer for listening to no modern poet except Robert Frost, whom Hicks characterized:

> *You will not hear. Your practiced ears refuse*
> *All but the Pomfret Cambridge Bread Loaf muse,*
> *A muse experienced but not mature,*
> *Meticulous but not exactly pure*
> *Through indolence good-natured but not kind,*
> *A little deaf, more than a little blind,*
> *Self-satisfied and yet at times regretful,*
> *Profoundly smug but growing rather fretful.*[6]

During his Amherst visit, DeVoto had explained that Hicks and all the others who had attacked Frost deserved exactly the punishment he himself would like to inflict. Frost had demurred, but by the time he was settled in San Antonio for the winter of 1936–1937, he changed his mind and wrote to DeVoto:

"I am going to have you strike that blow for me now if you still want to and if you can assure your wife and conscience you thought of it first and not I. The Benny-faction must be beyond suspicion of procurement on my part or I will have none of it. All depends on the sequence of events; which I leave to your memory. I am not above asking favors, but principle if not delicacy forbids that it should be too soon in a friendship. In a Harvard lecture I based a whole theory of art on my particularity there. In about twenty-five years I may make an important death bed request of you.[7] Meanwhile give me only the Christmas presents you can get most pleasure out of for yourself.

"I have decided to let you make the English Selected Poems[8] your occasion rather than the prospective [publication of the] Harvard essays because I dont want any more depending on those essays than already depends. I am inhibited badly enough over them as it is. Damn the essays. . . ."[9]

Whiling away the winter in San Antonio, and waiting for DeVoto to "strike that blow" for him, Frost had leisure to follow an entirely different controversy. Edmund Wilson had published in the *New Republic* some complaints against DeVoto. One was that DeVoto seemed to enjoy writing primarily to combat somebody else's views rather than to present his own; another was that he always "seems to approach his subjects with a chip on his shoulder"; another, that he seemed to have "the Westerner's grudge against the Easterner"; another, that he seemed to show "the peevishness of the literary professor against the writer outside the academic enclosure."[10] DeVoto answered him in the *Saturday Review,* and began with double-edged self-definition: "I distrust absolutes. Rather, I long ago passed from distrust of them to opposition. And with them let me include prophecy, simplification, generalization, abstract logic, and especially the habit of mind which consults theory first and experience only afterward. . . . I have attacked a lot of people whose ideas seemed to me out of touch with known facts and common experience. People who prefer the conclusions of logic to the testimony of their senses. People who do not recognize that the behavior of the human race cannot be accommodated to a syllogism." He went on to attack Wilson as a Marxist who had shilly-shallying doubts about his own cause; doubts which had made his own comrades attack him. He added, "You tell me . . . that Marx and Engels exploded Utopian socialism almost a century ago. Oh, my dear Wilson! They merely asked us not to apply that label to their gospel. Is not Russia resolutely demonstrating to us that the dictatorship of the proletariat is no more than a Utopian vision?"[11] Frost, troubled at the prospect of getting mixed up in this controversy, wrote to DeVoto three days after the publication of the answer to Wilson:

"On third thought and after reading what you did to Edmund Wilson I have decided to have you leave me out of it a while yet, so that my enjoyment of your editorship may be unmixed with self-interest. You go ahead and let me applaud under no obligation. Dont think I dont realize what I am fore-going.

"I believe you came into the world to save me from trying to write social moral and aesthetic criticism by making me feel a failure at it before I got started. You can see the temptation I have been trembling on the verge of in my old age. I have caught myself in time. I draw back. You write the criticism who can really write it."[12]

DeVoto protested against this restraint. Because of illness, he had not yet been able to write what he had in mind on Frost and his critics, but he briefly outlined the article for Frost and asked for permission to continue. Frost answered, "All right, let's hear how good a poet I am. Perhaps it was to tell me and the world your flu spared you. The article as you block it out is too much for me to deny myself, especially the block for the head of [Horace] Gregory. I have never read a word of that ganglion's regrets about me in prose, but I suspect they are to be explained by his not unwarrantable if intuitive sus-picion that I hate his obscratulations of the muse in verse. There is no baser form of hypocrasy than a false air of dis-interestedness."[13]

There was nothing disinterested about the way Frost con-tinued to work on behalf of DeVoto through the spring of 1937. He had already used his influence with President Moody of Middlebury College to secure the promise of an honorary degree for DeVoto that June.[14] He had also arranged to have DeVoto rent the Shingled Cottage on the Bennington College campus as a temporary summer home. Answering DeVoto's account of developments, and pretending at least partial ignorance, he wrote to him early in May 1937:

"You're going to take a degree somewhere—you don't say where. That sounds as if your thrusts had gone home with some one. People are bound to be impressed with your great pen. You say I dont know how good I am. You dont know how good you are. We are two modest men. I'm getting the degree I missed in the conclave of unification last year [at

Harvard]. Thought by some to be my reward for not having done the two poems I was down for.

"There's a lot to talk about. I hope I haven't made you too unhappy by having thrown my weight into your decision to leave teaching. Nothing is momentous. Nothing is final. You can always go back if back is where you can best strike from. Some like a spear, some like a dirk. The dirk is the close-in weapon of city streets. Anybody can take his choice of weapons for all of me. I suspect you're an all round handiman of the armory. I had no idea of sacrificing you to the job down there—or letting you sacrifice yourself. You're there to lick em for us. To Hell with their thinking. That's all I say. I wish I were any good. I'd go up to the front with you. As it is—as I am—I must be content to sick you on. Results is all I ask.

"Fine to have you in Vermont. I'll be there just ahead of you. . . . I have one lecture to give. Its at Oberlin for commencement. Heaven is My Destination. My self assigned subject: What Became of New England? Then for some much needed self-indulgence. For a person who set out to have his own way in the world I am ending up a horrible example of duteous unselfishness. Dont tell anybody in that article—which by the way I really ought not to see till it's in print if I dont want to feel guilty of having written it myself. . . ."[15]

Frost had a special reason for wanting to use as the subject of his commencement address at Oberlin College, "What Became of New England?" He knew that the area of Ohio surrounding Oberlin had been settled by New Englanders; in 1786 the newly formed State of Connecticut, in ceding to the federal government its claims to most of its western land, had tried to keep half a million acres on or near the south shore of Lake Erie, and had called those acres the Western Reserve. He also knew that coeducational Oberlin College had been opened in 1833 with a faculty made up largely of New England Congregationalists, many of them preachers, and that the so-called "Oberlin Theology" had been a modified form of Calvinism, emphasizing the doctrine of free will. All these historical details would help him to claim that New England had thus given to this part of Ohio a certain puritan moral fibre which it still retained, and he was eager to make a defense of the broader puritan heritage. Part of his claim would be that, even as the whole function of poetry is to refresh and renew the meanings in words, so the function of puritan culture remained to purify some fundamental meanings. As he progressed, in his commencement address, that June, there were moments when he sounded more like a preacher than a poet:

"We hear today about the conquest of fear; and we speak lightly of that old thing, a 'God-fearing man.' Fear? Banish fear from your mind. What kind of a God is it that you should fear? One might forget God in a lull of faith. One might forget God, and talk about the highest in himself.[16] I can't imagine any honest man without the fear of finding himself unworthy in the sight of someone else. It might be something you didn't care to call by name.[17]

"I don't give up New England too easily. I don't give up these words that I've cared for—these phrases. I long to renew them. I seek to renew them. Another one: 'a jealous God.' In Greenwich Village I've heard two words dismissed: 'fear' and 'jealousy.' And that makes all the excitement in Greenwich Village. What is jealousy? It's the claim of the object on the lover. The claim of God is that you should be true to Him, and so true to yourself. The word still lives for me."

Continuing, he explained how the puritan tradition, spreading outward from New England, had given itself to this cause of stubbornly clinging to meanings which needed purification:

"New England, now—what has become of it? It's not necessarily to be found in a literature restricted to New England. The little nation that was, and was to be, gave itself, as Virginia gave herself, westward, into the great nation that she saw coming, and so gave help to America.[18] And the thing New England gave most to America was the thing I am talking about: a stubborn clinging to meaning—to purify words until they meant again what they should mean. Puritanism had that meaning entirely: a purifying of words and a renewal of words and a renewal of meaning. That's what brought the Puritans to America, and that's what kept them believing: they saw that there was a meaning that was becoming elusive."

Never before had Robert Frost made such an extraordinary confession of his own deeply rooted sympathies with Puritanism. In the process, he reached back across forty years for an illustration; back to his undergraduate days at Harvard, when he had sat in a lecture hall and had heard Santayana mock Puritan-Christian doctrine by saying insinuatively that anyone should be permitted to believe, at his own risk, any form of myth or illusion he liked. Frost told his Oberlin audience,

[483]

"You can get up a theory that meanings go out of things. You can call it disillusionment. You can get disillusionment of a phrase, such as 'fearing God' and 'equality.' And then you can form a religion, like George Santayana. He lets you see that there is nothing but illusion, and it can just as well be one kind as another: there is the illusion that you are conscious of, and there is illusion that you become conscious of, later. But you should go right on anyway, because there's no proof: all is illusion. You grow to be a sad person.

"Some people pity a person who loses his hero. Who suffers the worse, the person who loses his hero, or the lost hero? You must seek reality forever in things you care for. Witchcraft was an illusion, wasn't it? And so is all this Industrialism. And so is the New Deal. You can make it all illusion with a little help from Santayana. He says right out in his philosophy that there are two kinds of illusion, two kinds of madness: one is normal madness, the other is abnormal madness!"[19]

Santayana was just then receiving new attention: his satirical novel entitled *The Last Puritan* was a best-seller. But Frost, as though he had surprised and embarrassed himself by devoting too much time to Santayana, plunged abruptly away from him to an unexpected conclusion. Choosing one final word, in order to show how poetry could and did refresh meaning, he used as illustration a pair of stanzas from one of his favorite poems, "A Song to David" by the so-called abnormally mad Christopher Smart—without naming either the poem or its author:

"Let's take one more: prayer. I'll tell you one of the poems which comes out of the eighteenth century, and ought to be dead by this time:

> *Strong is the lion—like a coal*
> *His eye-ball—like a bastion's mole*
> *His chest against the foes:*
> *Strong the gier-eagle on his sail,*
> *Strong against tide, th' enormous whale*
> *Emerges, as he goes.*
>
> *But stronger still, in earth and air,*
> *And in the sea, the man of pray'r;*
> *And far beneath the tide;*
> *And in the seat to faith assign'd,*

Where ask is have, where seek is find,
Where knock is open wide."[20]

Although this commencement address at Oberlin College did amount to one of Frost's most outspoken public utterances concerning his religious belief, many of his intimate friends could remember occasions when he had privately expressed himself concerning explicit details. Sidney Cox later recalled a time when Frost had challenged a vaguely liberal attitude toward religion:

"Mr. Frost frankly calls himself superstitious; by which he means that he accepts no explanation of mystery.[21] He is religious. One memorable night, in 1916, he rejected my convenient disposal of God as the summation of Most High Things, and of religion as care for things spiritual. God, he said, is that which a man is sure cares, and will save him, no matter how many times or now completely he has failed. We have talked of religion repeatedly since then, and he has never recanted."[22]

At moments when Frost was made self-conscious by his awareness that he was addressing a nonbeliever, he frequently dropped guarded hints concerning relationships between his religious belief and his poetic strategies. One tantalizing hint was given to the infidel Untermeyer in 1915: "If I must be classified as a poet, I might be called a Synedochist, for I prefer the synecdoche in poetry—that figure of speech in which we use a part for the whole."[23] Two years later, after Untermeyer and others had described him as a "Yankee realist," Frost protested ambiguously: "I wish for a joke I could do myself, shifting the trees entirely from the Yankee realist to the Scotch symbolist."[24] In these two remarks he was implying that he had more than family kinship with those New England puritan poets (on the one side) and those earlier Scottish poets (on the other side) who liked to spiritualize temporal things by making physical images represent such metaphysical values as were central to their consoling religious beliefs.

Just ahead of him waited something for which he could find little consolation either in his poetry or in his religious belief. After an unusually busy summer he returned to Amherst College with his wife and learned that she needed immediate surgery for cancer. He took her to a hospital in nearby Springfield and was advised by the surgeon that her heart was so weak that she might not be able to survive an operation. The desperate decision was made, and she went through the surgery. The next day, Frost wrote to Untermeyer:

"I tried two or three times yesterday to tell you that Elinor had just been operated on for a growth in her breast. I doubt if she fully realizes her peril. So be careful how you speak in your letters. You can see what a difference this must make in any future we have. She has been the unspoken half of everything I ever wrote, and both halves of many a thing from My November Guest down to the last stanzas of Two Tramps in Mud Time—as you may have divined. I don't say it is quite up with us. We shall make the most of such hope as there is in such cases. She has come through the operation well, though there was delay over her for a day or so at the Hospital for fear her heart wouldn't stand the ether. Her unrealization is what makes it hard for me to keep from speaking to somebody for sympathy. I have had almost too much of her suffering in this world."[25]

Since the early days of their marriage, Frost and his wife had differed in their attitudes toward suffering. She had often chided him for acting like a spoiled child when he was ill, and he admitted that she was much braver than he. But in writing, "I have had almost too much of her suffering in this world," he had betrayed himself to such an extent that he regretted the confession almost as soon as he had mailed the letter. The next day he wrote asking Untermeyer to destroy it.[26]

After Mrs. Frost recovered sufficiently to return home to 15 Sunset Avenue in Amherst, she insisted that her husband must keep his promises to give readings in various parts of New England, that fall. On the first of November she wrote to Mrs. Richard Thornton, "I am gaining strength quite rapidly now, and have been out for a few drives, and a few very short walks. It seems grand. Robert has been very busy through October, but he seems very well. He hasn't many engagements during November and I am thankful. I hope he will escape taking cold, or grippe, before we leave for the south."[27]

Having been disappointed with their winter in Texas, and still hoping to find a congenial atmosphere in which to hide as much as they liked, the Frosts had already chosen to spend the coldest months of the approaching season in Gainesville, Florida. Plans had also been made for Carol and his family to drive down from Vermont; for Lesley and her children to join them when she could. The Frosts left for Florida early in December, stopping in Baltimore long enough for Mrs. Frost to consult a doctor recommended by their friend Miss Goodwillie. In Gainesville, and staying temporarily in the Brown Cottage at the Thomas Hotel, they began the leisurely process of hunting for a house to rent. The one chosen, at 734 Bay Street, North, had two furnished apartments, and Lesley insisted that she and her children should take the upstairs apartment so that her mother would not have to exert her weak heart by climbing the stairs. Mrs. Frost insisted that the downstairs apartment would never do for her husband: he would be constantly annoyed by the sound of the children's busy feet, overhead. The arrangement was carried out, as she wished, and a house nearby was found for Carol and his family. "We had our tree and our Christmas dinner altogether, over at Carol's, and everything went smoothly," she wrote to Mrs. Thornton. "The children played all day without quarreling. We have all been very well so far. I rest a great deal of course. The nights here are cool, almost cold, even after warm days, and one needs two or three cotton blankets for covering, which helps me to sleep well. . . . I hope the next three months will be as good as December, but of course they very likely won't be."[28]

Soon after Christmas, Frost received from DeVoto the long-awaited article entitled "The Critics and Robert Frost," already set in type and scheduled to be published in the issue of the *Saturday Review* for the first of January 1938. As soon as Mrs. Frost had read it aloud to her husband, he wrote to thank DeVoto:

"I sat and let Elinor pour it over me. I took the whole thing. I thought it couldnt do me any harm to listen unabashed to my full praise for once in a way. I said to Sidney Cox years ago that I was non-elatable. While I wasn't actually fishing I suppose I hoped he might see I wanted to be contradicted. All I got out of him was 'That's a serious thing for a poet to confess.' He was plainly by his tone crediting me with courage of self-betrayal. After hearing all you said in my favor today, I tried it at the wistfullest I could command on Elinor. 'What a lie,' she answered. 'You can't talk in public or private without getting elated. You never write but from elation.' Well I trust I am at least heavy-hearted enough to keep my feet on the ground no matter how personally successful I may seem to myself as for instance at this moment. I should like to think I had consideration and considerateness enough to hold myself down and didn't need to be held down by someone else like the triumphant balloon giants in a Macy's Halloween parade up Broadway. Elinor gave me permission to be as depressed as I pleased in emergencies. This is a hard world and it becomes us to pay our respects to its hardness some of the time. But some of the time I was free to bask self-consciously in being generously understood. You may recall the poem I wrote in those stormy March days at Harvard. I named it 'Happiness makes up in height for what it lacks in length.' "[29]

DeVoto's article was ostensibly a review of *Recognition of Robert Frost*,[30] a collection of notices, reviews, tributes to Frost, chronologically arranged under subject headings. Using as his point of takeoff Amy Lowell's review of *North of Boston*, and calling it the worst early piece of criticism, DeVoto added, "When Miss Lowell reworked her piece in *Tendencies in Modern American Poetry* she brought it down from the higher to the middle strata of the inane, but in the review you get the pure stuff and it is one of the most idiotic pieces written about poetry in this generation. It is screamingly silly. Nothing approached it until the publication of *A Further Range* impelled a group of muddled minds to tell us about Mr. Frost without bothering to read him. At that time Newton Arvin and Horace Gregory crowded Miss Lowell hard, only to lose in the end to Mr. Blackmur. His piece in the *Nation* may not be quite the most idiotic review our generation has produced, but in twenty years of reading criticism—oh, the hell with scholarly reservations, Mr. Blackmur's is the most idiotic of our time. It is one of the most idiotic reviews since the invention of movable type. The monkeys would have to tap typewriters throughout eternity to surpass it, and Mr. Blackmur may regard his immortality as achieved."

In the continuation of his article, DeVoto summarized the various interpretations which the critics had made of Frost's work. One third of them "see Mr. Frost escaping from reality into nature or idea or distance or the unknown." Another third "assert that he never escapes but instead holds fast to the fact which is the sweetest dream that labor knows." An English critic "says that he has a larger share of the English tradition than any other American of his time." Miss Lowell finds that he has no sense of humor. "To Mr. Munson he is the purest classicist of our time, to Mr. Lewisohn a pure specimen of the naturalistic revolt." The left-wing critics of Frost seemed to think that "the only right way to write poetry now was to revolt in it against private ownership of the means of production and saturate it with emotions, experience, and aspirations of the workers of the world." If it mattered, a case could be made for Frost as "a complete proletarian" poet. In fact, "Mr. Frost is, as he once outraged a group of literary feeble-minds by admitting, the only pure proletarian poet of our time. His is the only body of poetry of this age which originates in the experience of humble people, treated with the profound respect of identification, and used as the sole measure of the reality and value of all experience."

One of DeVoto's defensive points, in his essay, was that many readers misunderstood Frost's poetry because they failed to notice the various uses Frost made of the comic mode, and he quoted Frost as saying, "I want one to go with me only so far as he will go playfully." DeVoto added, "Much of the impatience that one kind of critic feels for him comes from his antic willingness to make jokes about the verities. The pure literary thinker will permit truth no handmaiden but solemnity—recall what horrid pain has been voiced in rebuke of Mark Twain. Yet God may be worshipped with conundrums, the Church was founded on a pun, and truth accepts familiarities from her familiars. It is besides a traditional habit of Yankees to say less than they mean, to say it lightly, and to let any fool go uncorrected who therefore takes them for fools."[31]

Some of Frost's friends were delighted with DeVoto's ways of thumping all enemies. Sidney Cox wrote to DeVoto, "I am grateful for your discerning disposal of major silliness concerning Robert Frost. It makes one too active to stay on a merry-go-round of aesthetic or political formula to go anywhere near all the way with him. If only your whacks might warm through the breeches of poets gone stiff on their bobbing gazelles and zebras!"[32] Ridgely Torrence wrote that he didn't see how Arvin, Blackmur, and Gregory "would ever get up from the slaughter house floor."[33] Others were not so pleased with the almost apoplectic manner in which DeVoto had thrown his punches. Theodore Morrison felt that another kind of defense should be written. Frost answered Morrison:

"I wish you could see that by lingering over them too long we make those fellows more important than I for my part like to think they are. I have read not one of their criticisms, but I can't pretend not to know what they think of me. This Blackamur you seem to fear—he says I simply don't know how to write. Hicks says I'm an escapist. Someone else whose name escapes me, says I'm a resignationist. The New Masses says I'm a counter-revolutionary. Who is Blackamur anyway? A Harvard professor? Abuse from The New Massess mass or mess comes particularly hard in that I have twice been approached by them in private to come in and be their proletarian poet. Though a countryman I would be eligible on the new People's Front theory. People's behind! There is more I know against myself. A high churchman says I am the last sweepings of the Puritan latrines. Don't look him up. Let's leave him nameless. As you may imagine I hate all this. It is a vexation of the spirit that cant help me write any more prose or verse. I should think Benny had dealt with it sufficiently for the time being. . . ."[34]

Another friend and poet, R. P. T. Coffin, planning to lecture on Frost, wrote to him in Gainesville and asked for any self-definition Frost had written or published. Coffin had made notes on a talk Frost had given at the annual dinner of the Poetry Society of America in New York City on the first of April 1937, and hoped that Frost might be able to send him a transcript of it. In his reply, Frost explained that he could not even remember the subject of his remarks at the Poetry Society. He added:

"The nearest I ever came to getting myself down in prose was in the preface to Robinson's *King Jasper*. That is so much me that you might suspect the application to him of being forced. It was really no such thing. We two were close akin up to a certain point of thinking. He would have trusted me to go a good way in speaking for him particularly on the art of poetry. We only parted company over the badness of the world. He was cast in the mold of sadness. I am neither optimist nor pessimist. I never voted either ticket. If there is a universal unfitness and unconformity as of a buttoning so started that every button on the vest is in the wrong button hole and the one empty button hole at the top and the one naked button at the bottom so far apart they have no hope of getting together, I don't care to decide whether God did this for the fun of it or for the devil of it. (The two expressions come to practically the same thing anyway.) Then again I am not the

Platonist Robinson was. By Platonist I mean one who believes what we have here is an imperfect copy of what is in heaven. The woman you have is an imperfect copy of some woman in heaven or in someone else's bed. Many of the world's greatest —maybe all of them—have been ranged on that romantic side. I am philosophically opposed to having one Iseult for my vocation and another for my avocation; as you may have inferred from a poem called Two Tramps in Mud Time. You see where that lands me on the subject of Dante's Beatrice. Mea Culpa. Let me not sound the least bit smug. I define a difference with proper humility. A truly gallant platonist will remain a bachelor as Robinson did from unwillingness to reduce any woman to the condition of being used without being idealized. . . ."[35]

Coffin wanted more, and he got it by reminding Frost that he had talked on "Crudities," before the Poetry Society of America. That was enough to evoke another self-defining summary:

"Your letter brings back my animus of that April 1st. I was gunning for the kind of Americans who fancied themselves as the only Americans incapable of crudity. I started off with some crudity I knew they could join me in laughing at and I ended up with some they might not be so incapable of themselves. But I protested all the way along my love of crudity. I thank the Lord for crudity which is rawness, which is raw material, which is the part of life not yet worked up into form, or at least not worked all the way up.[36] Meet with the fallacy of the foolish: having had a glimpse of finished art, they forever after pine for a life that shall be nothing but finished art. Why not a world safe for art as well as democracy. A real artist delights in roughness for what he can do to it. He's the brute who can knock the corners off the marble block and drag the unbedded beauty out of bed.[37] The statesman (politician) is no different except that he works in a protean mass of material that hardly holds the shape he gives it long enough for him to point it out and get credit for it. His material is the rolling mob. The poet's material is words that for all we may say and feel against them are more manageable than men. Get a few words alone in a study and with plenty of time on your hands you can make them say anything you please. . . ."[38]

Coffin had done well to approach Frost when he had plenty

of time on his hands to express himself on his attitudes toward crudities and on his non-Platonic attitude toward woman. Shortly after he had explained himself in this manner, he was agonizingly forced to reconsider.

34

AND I THE LAST . . .

All in all it has been such a lucky and original life that I can't understand my ever being for a moment cross or difficult or dissatisfied or cast down. . . . I came out so well by luck when there were nothing but reasons for failure. Theoretically I was doomed and crossed off from the start.[1]

ROBERT FROST and his wife were so much pleased by their stay in Gainesville that they decided to buy a small house they could occupy annually during their winter retreats. Carol used his car to drive them through the countryside near Gainesville, and Frost was particularly happy with his wife's encouragement to indulge once again his game of prospecting for property. At last they found a house which all of them liked, and on Friday afternoon, the eighteenth of March 1938, they went with Carol to make one final inspection before concluding the transaction. As they returned and were climbing the stairs to their second-floor apartment at 743 North Bay Street, Mrs. Frost suddenly complained of her chronic ailment. She had suffered so many minor heart attacks, before, that no immediate fear was felt, but a doctor was called. He listened to her heart and pronounced her condition alarming. Privately he told Frost that she was too ill to be moved. Within a few hours a more severe attack occurred, and she became unconscious. The doctor, happening to be present, quickly revived her. He told her husband, however, that her condition was precarious, and she would almost certainly have another attack which might be fatal.

Frost's anguish was inseparable from his guilt: it was his own fault, he told himself. He was to blame for dragging her about the countryside, house-hunting, when he should have been more considerate of the weakness she had shown since her cancer operation. He should never have permitted her to insist that they take the second-floor apartment, should never have let her climb those stairs day after day. All he could do now was blame himself. He was so distraught that the doctor ordered him out of the bedroom and closed the door.

If she was going to die, there was so much he must say to her. He had to ask forgiveness for all the wrongs he had done her since the days of their high-school courtship. She had nearly died when their first child was born, and her physician had then told Frost her heart was so weak she might not be able to stand the strain of giving birth to another child. When that first child had died at the age of four, something in her spirit had seemed to die. Now, remembering that his own passionate demands had brought six children, he felt that in a sense he had killed her.

But she was not dead, and it would be like her to disprove the doctor's prophecy. When she lived through the night, there seemed to be hope that she would recover. Frost, intermittently pacing the narrow corridor outside her bedroom, could occasionally hear her answering the doctor's questions. Certainly she would ask to see him as soon as she was permitted. He wanted her to say at least with her eyes that she forgave him; that all the pain and suffering he had caused her had been more than offset by the joys and triumphs of their forty years together. But she did not ask to see him, and as the hours of the second day passed he began to wonder if she had perhaps found her ultimate way of punishing him for what was unforgivable.

She did suffer additional heart attacks, one after another—seven in all—and after each one she grew weaker. He could hear her hoarse breathing as he returned to his pacing outside her door, and there were moments when all breathing seemed to stop. He would stop, until the breathing began again, and each time new anguish would rise in him. When finally he was admitted to her room, she was either asleep or unconscious, and all he could do was hope she would recover long enough to look at him. On Sunday afternoon she simply stopped breathing.

At first, the most painful element in her death was that she had gone without giving him the chance to ask and receive her forgiveness. Throughout their life together she had continued to refine her extraordinary capacity to reprimand or tease him with eloquent silences. Always, before, he had found ways to achieve ultimate clarifications of those silences, no matter how long or how mysterious they had been. What remained now was an irrevocable silence on which his imagination worked to perplex and torture him with uncertainties whether she had deliberately refused to say anything to him or had been unable to speak. His ever-present sense of guilt provided the answer which hurt most, and the longer he brooded over her final silence the more certain he became that he deserved it as punishment.[2]

While the final rites were being arranged, Frost was so ill that he could not immediately participate. He had been suffering from a sore throat and cold even before Mrs. Frost was stricken, and the pain in his throat had become worse during the two days she had lingered. The doctor, quickly realizing that he had another potentially serious condition confronting him, insisted that if Frost did not go to bed and stay there for some time there was serious danger of pneumonia. From his bed he talked with his children about the necessity for postponing any funeral arrangements, but he knew what Elinor wanted him to do. For years she had said she would rather be cremated than buried; she wished her ashes might be taken back to the farm in Derry, New Hampshire, and scattered along the bank of Hyla Brook in that little grove of pines where she had spent so many idyllic hours with her young children. Because the doctor would not permit Frost to attend the formalities of the cremation, Lesley and a friend accompanied the body to Jacksonville, Florida. During the identification ritual, there, Lesley was granted permission to place in the casket an envelope given her for that purpose by her father.[3]

Lesley, almost overcome by her own grief immediately after the cremation, unintentionally revealed a habit of vindictiveness she had acquired from her father. When he asked if he could make his home with her during the remainder of his life, she bluntly said no. Then she burst into an almost hysterical accusation which further amazed him: she said she had seen him cause so much injury to the lives of his own children— particularly to Irma, Carol, and Marjorie—that she would not permit him to move into her home, where he might also injure the lives of her two daughters. Her rage increased as she went on to insist, through her tears, that she could not forgive him for his having ruined her mother's life. It was his fault, she said, that her mother was dead, for it was his own selfishness which had forced her mother to climb those stairs to the upper quarters, repeatedly. Lesley had pleaded that she and her children should live up there, so that her mother wouldn't need to climb. But her father hadn't wanted to hear the children's feet over his head, and that was typical of his selfishness, Lesley cried. Then she hurt him most by concluding that he was the kind of artist who never should have married, or at least never should have had a family.[4]

Frost was so deeply wounded by these accusations that he could not answer. Lesley's hysterical outburst simply increased the pain caused by what he had said to himself, and what Elinor had not said. But what he needed now was someone who might contradict him by saying that his own self-condemnation was far too harsh. He could excuse Lesley for being more cruel than she realized, and yet even while he winced before the hostility in her tear-filled eyes he kept telling himself he deserved this as punishment.

There were no comforters in his family, however. Irma, far away in New Hampshire, would have given him no help if she was present. She had disagreed and argued with him so bitterly during the past few years that it was better for her to stay in Hanover and keep her silence, now, than to journey to his bedside and go through false motions of being sympathetic. Carol was less hostile than his sisters only because he was less articulate. There had never been any sustained affection between him and his father, and on many occasions each had antagonized the other in ways which had built up lasting enmities. He had been his mother's special care and he had leaned on her so completely that he suffered his own collapse when she died. Needing so much more comfort than he could find, Carol was unable to give any. As soon as he could leave, after his mother's death and cremation, he made haste to start North, with Lillian and Prescott, to whatever consolation the farm in South Shaftsbury might give him.

During the several days that Frost was confined to his bed in Gainesville, he kept going back over the spoken and unspoken reproaches. Although he had long ago rejected the trite saying that an artist should never have a family, Lesley's bitter use of it forced him into reconsiderations. Repeatedly he had said in moments of impatience that his devotion to his art had been spoiled by his devotion to his family, but he had been genuinely attentive to his wife and children. Most of his poems had been written for Elinor, first, and all his books had been dedicated to her. As for the children, he wondered how many fathers had spent as much time with their children as he had with his. Back on the Derry farm where three of them had been born and where all of them had learned to walk and talk, he had certainly given more of himself to them than to his farming or his writing. Before they could walk, he had carried each of them, again and again, to every boundary-corner of that farm. His goal had been to share with them sheer morning gladness at the brim. He had joined them in their games, outside or inside the house. He had taught them to name the wildflowers and to share with him a series of wonder-filled botanizing expeditions, each spring. He had helped them marvel at the stars, and at the northern lights. When he and his wife had decided that their own experiences as teachers qualified them to keep their children out of public schools, he had enjoyed his parts of the teaching. Throughout all of these activities, playfully treated as games, he had also tried to help them understand the differences betwen right and wrong.

Now he wondered whether Lesley had any justifiable reason for saying she would not permit him to injure her children as he had injured his own? He hoped not, and yet he knew some of the specific charges she might make. All four of his children had been taught by him to write poetry, and in later years Elinor had scolded him because he had failed them by refusing to help them get their poems published even in magazines. His defense had been that if they were to succeed as poets they must make their own way among editors and publishers without leaning on such influence as he might exert. There was one way in which he had unintentionally failed them, and as a former teacher of psychology he was particularly unhappy about it. From their early childhood he had tried to develop in them the courage needed to overcome the fears which had beset him in his own childhood, but it did seem that he had accidentally taught them more fear than courage.

Each of them had grown up somehow victimized by a peculiar set of fears. The succession of nervous breakdowns which had overtaken Marjorie after her graduation from high school might be explained, he thought, by fears not unlike those which had ruined the life of his sister Jeanie. Marjorie's pure idealism had made the evils in the world seem so intolerable that she had cringed in her attempts to make adjustments. Carol's oddities, apparent since boyhood, had expressed themselves in his cumulative suspicion that everyone (including his father) was trying to take advantage of him, or persecute him. Many of Irma's difficulties, not easily understandable until after her marriage, seemed traceable to a prudish notion that the sexual act was bestial. Her father was unwilling to take the blame on himself for that distortion. Lesley's bundle of fears were not unlike Carol's, and yet she had plunged into a variety of experiences with more courage and boldness than any of the other children. If he had injured them by communicating his fears to them, such an act had been just the opposite of what he had intended.

He was willing to grant that Lesley or anyone else could make a case for the claim that the artist should never have a family: it was obvious to him that there must always be a conflict between a man's devotion to his art and his devotion to wife and children. He could remember discussing this problem with his Amherst students while they had been reading Cellini's *Autobiography*. To set up the problem, he had read aloud to them the vivid little chapters in which Cellini described emergencies in casting his bronze statue of Perseus holding high the head of Medusa. Cellini, working in the studio just outside his own home, had been forced to strip his home of certain furnishings in order to protect his unfinished work from a driving rain: he had commandeered carpets, hangings, and anything else he could use. When the fierce heat of the furnace fire had consumed so much alloy that the molten metal began to cake, he had plundered his home of "all my pewter platters, porringers, and dishes, to the number of some two hundred pieces," and had tossed them into the vat, a few at a time, until the bronze achieved a "most perfect liquefaction." As a result of these plunderings, the mold filled perfectly, and when the statue had cooled he had uncovered it slowly to discover that his work of art was a success: "everything had come out in perfect order." It was true that Cellini's home had suffered in the process of this achievement, but that was the way it had to be with any artist, Frost believed.[5]

Visitors began arriving in Gainesville to express condolences before he had recovered from his illness. Among the first was the poet and novelist Hervey Allen who had written to his publishers soon after Mrs. Frost died, "Am running up [from

Miami] for a day or two to Gainesville, Florida—about a day's run—because of the serious condition in which Robert Frost is. You know his wife died. She has been sent to Jacksonville to be cremated and there will be a funeral at Amherst later. I talked to the University of Florida people this morning, where Frost has been lecturing,[6] and they say he is in a state of complete collapse. They seemed to have the jitters themselves and almost fell on the telephone when I mentioned I might come up. I don't know just what I can do, but I may be able to help and as Frost is really so great a person and we all have an enormous feeling of gratitude and affection for him I am taking a little time off just on the chance of being helpful. . . ."[7] Allen was a good listener, and he helped most by giving Frost a chance to pour out his own self-condemnations, against which Allen made the needed protestations. After his visit in Gainesville, he received from Frost a brief note of thanks made up largely of two quotations from Tennyson. The first was from Sir Bedivere's speech to King Arthur after surviving the last battle:

> "Ah! my Lord Arthur, whither shall I go?
> Where shall I hide my forehead and my eyes?
> For now I see the true old times are dead,
> When every morning brought a noble chance,
> And every chance brought out a noble knight.
> Such times have been not since the light that led
> The holy Elders with the gift of myrrh.
> But now the whole Round Table is dissolved
> Which was an image of the mighty world;
> And I, the last, go forth companionless,
> And the days darken round me, and the years,
> Among new men, strange faces, other minds."

The other quotation was from the first part of "In Memoriam":

> Let Love clasp Grief lest both be drown'd,
>   Let darkness keep her raven gloss:
>   Ah, sweeter to be drunk with loss,
> To dance with death, to beat the ground,
>
> Than that the victor Hours should scorn
>   The long result of love, and boast,

"Behold the man that loved and lost,
But all he was is overworn."

Hervey Allen, a quarter of a century younger than Robert Frost, and perhaps not aware of Frost's high regard for Victorian poetry, particularly that of Tennyson, had reason to be surprised at the note he received:

"Dear Hervey:
   And I the last go forth companionless
   And the days darken round me.
But it is written also by the same hand,
   Let darkness keep her raven gloss.
I shall never forget your coming to me with such sympathy.
Ever yours
Robert"[8]

Another visitor who came unexpectedly with sympathetic offers of assistance and consolation was Stanley King, President of Amherst College. Frost had written King, as soon as he could, to say that his illness following Mrs. Frost's death had made him realize once again the need to beg off from his Amherst obligations; under the circumstances he wished to tender his resignation from Amherst College. He had also asked for permission to arrange a memorial service in the Johnson Chapel, some time in April of 1938. President King responded by going directly from Amherst to Gainesville, and offered whatever assistance he could give in making arrangements for the memorial service. Shortly after King's visit in Gainesville, Frost wrote to his son Carol, in South Shaftsbury:

"Well, you're hard at work up there and that must be some comfort. I hope you have an interesting summer. You'll be getting new trees and baby chicks and I suppose putting on the dormant spray. There was nothing Elinor wanted more than to have you take satisfaction out of that home and farm. I wish you would remember it every day of your life.

"We plan to have the funeral either on Friday April 15th or on Monday or Tuesday of the week following. Something will depend on when the minister can come. I am going to ask Sidney Snow of Chicago to read some poem or two that she liked and some not too religious verses from the Bible. Stanley

King says we can use either the College Church or the Chapel.
. . . The Chapel means more to me. It is a beautiful room and
the pulpit has been one of my chief speaking places. I don't
know if she ever heard me there, but she was always waiting anxiously at home to hear how my talk came out. The
Chapel has had so much to do with our position at Amherst
that my sentiment is for it. . . .

"Lesley is getting Rosa down from New York to take care
of the children while she comes north with me for the funeral.
After the funeral we can all drive over to Derry and scatter
the ashes out in the alders on the Derry farm if the present
owner will let us. By all I mean just the family and perhaps
one or two of our closest friends. . . ."⁹

Some of the most practical assistance was provided by another visitor, Louis Untermeyer, who went to Gainesville from
New York City as soon as he could, and stayed long enough to
help address envelopes containing the formal printed announcement of the plan for the service at Amherst. Bernard
DeVoto's expressions of sympathy evoked this reply:

"I expect to have to go depths below depths in thinking
before I catch myself and can say what I want to be while I
last. I shall be all right in public, but I can't tell you how I
am going to behave when I am alone. She could always be
present to govern my loneliness without making me feel less
alone. It is now running into more than a week longer than I
was ever away from her since June 1895. You can see how I
might have doubts of myself. I am going to work very hard in
May and be on the go with people so as not to try myself solitary too soon.

"I suppose love must always deceive. I'm afraid I deceived
her a little in pretending for the sake of argument that I didn't
think the world as bad a place as she did. My excuse was that
I wanted to keep her a little happy for my own selfish pleasure.
It is as if for the sake of argument she had sacrificed her life
to give me this terrible answer and really bring me down in
sorrow. She needn't have. I knew I never had a leg to stand
on, and I should think I had said so in print.

"All the same I believe a lot of mitigating things, and anything I say against the universe must be taken with that quali-
fication. I always shrank from hearing evil of poor little Edgar
Allen Poe and my reason was when I come to search it out of

my heart, that he wrote a prose poem out of those lovely old lines

> *Stay for me there I will not fail*
> *To meet thee in the hollow vale.*

What is more he used a cadence caught from the Exequy to make the whole of his poem The Sleeper. Never mind that he couldn't be tender without being ghoulish. You have to remember he was little Edgar Allen Poe.

"We are to have a funeral over the ashes I bring home at Johnson Chapel Amherst College at three o'clock in the afternoon of Friday April 22. Perhaps I wish a little that my friends who can easily will come. I dont know how you feel about such things. I am uncertain. Of course there is no question of her honor. You and I and others will take care of that in more important ways wont we?"[10]

At Amherst, Mrs. Frost's closest friend had been the wife of Professor George Roy Elliott, and just before Frost started North from Gainesville he wrote to the Elliotts:

"I am coming back to Amherst on Tuesday or Wednesday for some more of the finalities I haven't yet learned to accept with the flesh. Otto and Ethel [Manthey-Zorn] have asked me to their house since I don't seem to want to see the inside of my own. It will be good of you if you will do as you said about John [Cone], Irma and Jack. I *wish* the whole family could be together, but we can be later. I shall probably wander round among them for a while till I can decide who I am now, and what I have to go on with. Some of the old ambitious resolutions may come back to me in some form. The danger will be that they may too openly concern her. Pretty nearly every one of my poems will be found to be about her if rightly read. But I must try to remember they were as much about her as she liked and permitted them to be. Without ever saying a word she set limits I must continue to observe. One remark like this and then no more forever."[11]

The entire family gathered for the service in Amherst. Sitting directly behind them, in the Johnson Chapel ceremonies, were the nineteen men he had invited to attend as honorary bearers.[12] Frost was more attentive to these men who had come long distances at his request to honor Elinor than he was to the service itself. He knew that she as a nonbeliever would have scoffed at having any memorial for her in a house of God. So did many others, including the Manthey-Zorns, who gave a reception at their home for the members of the Frost family and for the honorary bearers immediately after the service.[13]

Before the children left that afternoon, Frost called them into brief and private conclave. He had been unable to complete the plans for carrying out the final pagan ritual Elinor had requested. All of them had heard their mother say more than once that she wanted her ashes scattered alongside Hyla Brook, but that ritual would have to be postponed, he said, until he could make preliminary arrangements.[14] He would go alone to Derry and request permission of the present owner, whoever he was, so that when they gathered there at a later time their appearance would not seem to be an act of trespassing. He had come close to making that request back in 1911 when he had written especially for Elinor his poem "On the Sale of My Farm" ending,

> . . . Only be it understood,
> It shall be no trespassing
> If I come again some spring
> In the grey disguise of years,
> Seeking ache of memory here.[15]

There was no need to tell his children, now, that he had other and more personal reasons for wanting to go to the Derry farm alone, ahead of them. He merely assured them that soon after he could find the time for making those arrangements he would notify each of them, and together they would choose a suitable day for meeting at Derry. For the present, he must remain in Amherst long enough to make his formal resignation from the College and to sell the Sunset Avenue house into which he had not yet been brave enough to venture. His plan was accepted: Carol and Lillian returned to South Shaftsbury, Lesley went back to her children in Gainesville, Irma and John drove back to Hanover.

Frost's decision to resign from Amherst College had been taking shape for several years, and was not precipitated hastily by his wife's death. Unpleasant frictions had been developing with various faculty members who resented his being paid a salary for doing next to nothing, and he knew there were other complaints against him. When President Olds had brought him back to Amherst from Michigan, the understanding had been that he would spend ten weeks of each academic year in residence at Amherst, that he would have no formal teaching duties, and that he would be paid an annual salary of $5,000. During the first few years of this arrangement, there had been times when Frost himself had felt that his services did not justify the payment he received. When Stanley King became president, he and Frost had established cordial and friendly relations. King, after learning that Frost's salary was drawn in part from the Simpson Lecture Fund, had expressed his desire for Frost to gain more public attention at Amherst, and had proposed that the poet should give three or four public readings or talks each year. The proposal was accepted, but for various reasons Frost had failed to carry out many of the scheduled appearances, and some of his late cancellations had been embarrassing. Several members of the faculty had complained to President King that Frost had not even tried to live up to his terms of contract. Others complained that he used the treasury of Amherst College as a source for unearned gifts to friends whom he brought to Amherst for trivial lectures. Just recently, in 1937, he had arranged to have Untermeyer deliver four lectures on "Play in Poetry." Some in the English department considered Untermeyer's critical approach to literature far too shallow to be worth listening to, and they had deliberately rebuked Frost by staying away. He had expressed his own counter-resentment in a letter written to DeVoto from Gainesville on the sixth of March 1938—just two weeks before Mrs. Frost died:

"I'll be home soon now. I want to hear more of your plans for the future. You'd better go up into Vermont and write for a while. I have more than half a mind to do that very thing myself [instead of returning to Amherst]. Wait till I tell you all that has been happening at Amherst to make me sick of the smallness of academic ways. I dont blame the professors too much for their hostility to the writers out in the world. They have their own positions to magnify and defend. I have to remember the college is the whole of their life whereas it is only a very small part of mine. But my English department werent very good to me about the incursion of Louis [Untermeyer]. George Wicher attended all four lectures; none of the others, even for my sake, would show the least interest. It was all right, but deliver them from my friends. It is not enough consolation that Louis had a triumph with the house-full that came. I say Love me love what's mine. And I am in a position to enforce that rule. What puts me in that position and keeps me there is my recklessness of consequences."[16]

Mrs. Frost's death, making him even more reckless of consequences, had given him excuse enough to resign. In the days immediately following the funeral service, he talked informally with President King about his wish not only to resign but also to sell his Amherst home. The President expressed his genuine regret and urged him to reconsider before making his formal request. He said that if Frost was certain he wanted to sell the house, the College would buy it from him. Arrangements were made for that purchase, and Frost began the sad task of packing. "Closing myself out of Amherst has taken more time than I expected," he wrote to Dorothy Canfield Fisher. "The college is buying my house; so I have had to empty it."[17] There were other obligations, including scheduled talks and readings which he made, just to keep busy. He mentioned some of them to Richard Thornton, in a letter written from the Lord Jeffery Inn on the fourteenth of May 1938:

"Busy business alone keeps me from getting down for our talk together. Be patient with me. I shall manage to get clear soon. Meanwhile if you are particularly anxious to hear or tell anything you could come up for a night to this hotel where I am started on my new life (for what it is worth). I should enjoy your company. The dates to avoid would be the night of the seventeenth when I shall be at Wilbraham Academy, the weekend following when I believe I shall be at Phillips Exeter and the twenty fourth-fifth and sixth when I shall be at Dartmouth and with Irma and John at Hanover. It seems rather shot to pieces doesn't it. But thats the way I like my time for the time being. It does me good to be run to a frazzle. If there is anything that won't easily wait, catch me in an interval.

"It is going to take quite a number of my books to satisfy the courtesies before I close up this passage in my career entirely. Will you have sent to me at this hotel as soon as possible (by express it had better be) a dozen of the Selected Poems, a half dozen of the Collected Poems and a half dozen of A Further Range. . . ."[18]

On the third of June 1938, Amherst College completed the

transaction of purchasing the Sunset Avenue house, giving one third more than Frost had paid for it.[19] The next day he wrote to President King a not too formal letter of resignation, in which he tried to justify his record as poet in residence at Amherst College:

"On consideration of our recent talks I have decided that I shall be happier in not trying to prolong what is already done, if none too well done: and I beg to be permitted to terminate my professorship at Amherst at the end of this college year. Amherst has had something of me. She would have had more of a better poet and a better person. I for my part have had much from Amherst besides money. Elsewhere I began my educational life as a full-time teacher. At Amherst I have had the chance to taper off into a part-time teacher and at last into a no-time teacher—a no-time teacher and yet as I should like to think a teacher, specializing in the kind of teaching every teacher does more or less of. A teacher who influenced me most I never had.[20] A book that influenced me most I never read.[21] The mere name of it carried in mind for years did the work. There has been ample time (twelve years) to carry out the idea of detached attachment. I have felt that the point of it all was sharpened by the Desert Fellowship you founded to my description and in my honor and on which you permitted me to make one appointment.[22] Enough for the idea and symbol is all I ever ask. If your experiment with me has been something less than successful, you and I would agree that it was because neither of us thought soon enough to connect me more visably with the institution on public occasions. The fault is much more mine than yours as the regret must be: for whereas you might have thought, it was not even in my nature to have thought. Informality was to have been expected of me. But I am just naturally too informal. Nevertheless I can see with pride that there has been much that I shall be interested in writing about more fully some day, and for this I am yours gratefully . . ."[23]

President King wrote two answers to Frost's letter of resignation, and sent them both. The first was formal. The second was personal and affectionate:

"I want you to know the genuine personal sense of disappointment I feel that you have decided to sever your formal connection with the College. I think I understand the reasons which have led you to present your resignation. And as President of the College I have accepted your resignation with regret. You have had a long and unique relationship with the College which speaks for itself. No comment of yours or mine at this time will add to or subtract from its significance in the field of education.

"Personally, I shall miss you keenly as a member of our college family. I have often said that in the field of human understanding you are one of the wisest men I have ever met. Our talks together at your house and at our house are one of the happiest memories of the six years I have spent at Amherst. I have learned from you many things which I cannot put on paper.

"And so I hope that we may continue to see each other whenever you are in Amherst and that you will come to Amherst as frequently as possible."[24]

After Frost had completed the many details of what he had referred to as "closing myself out of Amherst," he went to his home in South Shaftsbury, knowing that if at any time he found the farmhouse at the Gully too lonesome he could always move down to the Stone Cottage and stay with Carol and Lillian. But he had not forgotten his promise to visit that other farm, in Derry, and make arrangements for spreading Elinor's ashes among the alders alongside the bank of Hyla Brook. He went alone, both wanting and dreading "the ache of memory" there. Over and over again he had said to Elinor and others that the days they had spent on that farm were in retrospect the most sacred in his entire life. He had kept the images of house and barn and orchard and pasture and mowing-field so vivid in his consciousness, during all the years since he had last seen it, that he was not prepared for the shock of finding everything changed. As he walked into the farmyard and saw nothing familiar, he could not resist the sense that the owner was the trespasser.

As the side door opened to his knock, he introduced himself to the woman of the house and could plainly see that she neither knew nor cared who he was. When he explained why he had come, she listened with an expression of puzzlement and indifference. She supposed what he asked would be all right, but she'd have to consult her husband and he was not at home. To his request that he be permitted to walk down through the alders to the brook, and up through the mowing-field to the orchard, she said that would be all right. Then she closed the door.

Already, this woman's indifference had spoiled the ritual in ways he had not anticipated. It seemed to him that Elinor, if she could have overheard that chilly conversation, would have changed her mind about wanting her ashes scattered where such a stranger might tread. As he walked down the stone steps in the retaining wall near the front of the barn he instinctively set his course toward the little corduroy bridge he had built across the brook—and suddenly knew the bridge could no longer be there: it must have rotted out years ago. The alders, obviously neglected, had been permitted to grow without any trimming, and when he tried to find the footpath he and she and their children had worn clean, he wasn't exactly sure where it had been. There was one way to tell. Just above the place where the bridge had stood, they had built a little dam of rocks so good-sized that even spring freshets could not have carried them far. Beyond that little dam would still be the opening among the pines. The carpet of brown needles had served as picnic ground for the Frosts even when the youngest child had to be carried to it on the father's shoulder. She had cherished all this isolation so much that she had inspired his mock-serious lines:

> They leave us so to the way we took,
>   As two in whom they were proved mistaken,
> That we sit sometimes in the wayside nook,
> With mischievous, vagrant, seraphic look,
>   And try if we cannot feel forsaken.

As he pushed through the leaves and branches of the alders he remembered lines of other poems which included her. This path which was no more a path, down to this bridge which wouldn't be there when he got there, had been where he and she had walked alone so many times in going for water when the well went dry. The pool made by the dam was always full enough to send a little water trickling over the edge of the dam, and if they came by moonlight they always stopped to listen:

> Each laid on other a staying hand
>   To listen ere we dared to look,

And in the hush we joined to make
  We heard, we knew we heard the brook.

A note as from a single place,
  A slender tinkling fall that made
Now drops that floated on the pool
  Like pearls, and now a silver blade.

Getting through the rank growth of the alders, he found where the bridge had been; he even found part of the dam still holding back water. He looked into the branch-cluttered opening made by the pines and saw the piece of plank he had wedged and nailed between the forked trunks of two pines as a special seat for her. Picking his way beyond the grove, along the bank of Hyla Brook, and studying blossoms as he went, he noticed wild orchises still growing there. He had transplanted rose pogonias, for her, into a wet marshy spot among the alders farther down, and he knew just how far up the brook he would need to go if he were to reach the best station of rose pogonias. She was in his poem about that station: that "saturated meadow, sun-shaped and jewel-small," which had just enough of an opening among the trees overhead to let the sunlight drench the plants:

There we bowed us in the burning,
  As the sun's right worship is,
To pick where none could miss them
  A thousand orchises . . .

On other occasions, when he had left her with the children and had gone bog-trotting alone, the orchises were the flowers she specially noticed in whatever bouquet he brought back. One of her favorites was a rare one hereabouts: the showy orchis with the white face of each blossom capped by a purple hood.

They are yours, and be the measure
Of their worth for you to treasure,
The measure of the little while
That I've been long away.

He turned at the stone-wall boundary mark and climbed the hill into the mowing field so that he could look through and over the orchard at the backsides of barn and house. The apple trees were past their prime now and nobody had bothered to trim them for years. Often, when he had come home this way from his botanizings in apple blossom time, he had broken off a small branch of them for her. (*"For this is love and nothing else is love . . ."*) Now, working his way through the orchard toward the set of buildings, he noticed the forlorn appearance of weather-beaten clapboards on the back of the barn. He knew what knocked paint off like that. Not flakes of snow but wind-driven sleet and hail, often followed by snow. (*"Those of us not asleep subdued to mark How the cold creeps as the fire dies at length,—How drifts are piled, Dooryard and road ungraded . . ."*) As he came alongside the barn he looked across the road toward the pasture gate and remembered how many times he had coaxed her out of the house for twilight walks through that gate and into the pasture. (*"I'll only stop to rake the leaves away, And wait to watch the water clear, I may. I shan't be gone long. . . ."*) It never took much coaxing, at any time of year, because she cherished signs of fall as much as those of spring.

> *My Sorrow, when she's here with me,*
>   *Thinks these dark days of autumn rain*
> *Are beautiful as days can be;*
> *She loves the bare, the withered tree;*
>   *She walks the sodden pasture lane.*

*   *   *

> *Not yesterday I learned to know*
>   *The love of bare November days*
> *Before the coming of the snow,*
> *But it were vain to tell her so,*
>   *And they are better for her praise.*

Now, as he climbed back up the stone steps and into the yard, he knew he still owned everything he wanted of this farm. What was left was merely a profanation, a desecration, of what was his. He also owned the urn of ashes, and he now knew he could never scatter those ashes in this desecration. He couldn't bear to bring his children here, to see their disappointment.[25]

When he got back to South Shaftsbury, and told Carol and Lillian the story of his visit to the Derry farm, he was relieved to find that they quickly accepted his decision.[26] There still

remained the problem of what to do with the ashes, and the
urn. There was a good-sized empty cupboard in the Stone
Cottage bedroom made available to him as soon as he found
he could not sleep in the ghost-filled farmhouse up at the
Gully. Because he didn't know where else to keep the urn, he
put it in the cupboard. Then he tried to think of other things.
Occasionally he offered help with daily chores around the
farm, always feeling that he was in the way even when Carol
tried to be kind. For many days he wasted daylight walking
up through the fields and woods of the Gully farm, then wasted
sleepless nights in his Stone Cottage bedroom writing letters
to those who might understand his loneliness enough to share
some part of it. One of these letters went to his fellow artist
J. J. Lankes:

"I was over at the Gulley Gulch today trying to get used
to it enough to use and keep it; and there I found myself prop-
ping the barndoor open with a board off the box you made
to ship yourself some pear wood in. . . . The place is bad with
good memories, but so's the whole world. I suppose you saw
no one ever got far into my affairs and friendship that didn't
succeed with Elinor. Her favor was the final test. I did a few
things she was opposed to, but that was only because she
wasn't seriously opposed to them. You can bet I didn't vote
the Democratic ticket this last election and shant this next.
It was an actual characteristic with her that she liked our
house-full of your work. From the day when I picked you out
of the Old Masses [*Liberator*], I didnt have to press her at all
there. You see I am going over in my mind the special places
where we were at one. There are a good many of them fortunately to console me for the suffering I must have caused her
sometimes. I'm afraid I dragged her through pretty much of
a life for one as frail as she was. Too many children, too many
habitations, too many vicissitudes. And a faith required that
would have exhausted most women. God damn me when he
gets around to it. I refused to be bowed down as much as she
was by other deaths.[27] But she has given me a death now that
I cant refuse to be bowed down by. Here I am brought up short
when in every way you can name I was still going full tilt.
I'm not behaving very well. I shall have to look for examples
of good behavior in my predicament. And then I dont know
about my ability to follow them. I have been relatively prospered in an outrageously self-indulgent life. I have been given

absolutely my own way. You might not notice it from the outside, but such are the facts. If I havent committed murder or frequented the movies it is simply and entirely because I havent wanted to commit murder and frequent the movies. Probably I'll have thought this all out and worked it off before I see you in the fall. So we can talk of ordinary things then. . . ."[28]

He kept trying to talk of ordinary things with Carol, with Lillian, and with their nearly fourteen-year-old son Prescott; also kept trying to find a satisfactory way of rearranging his life. Much as he had talked about stealing away and staying away from other people, he was now convinced by his loneliness that he could never live alone unless friends or relatives were near. Having cut himself off from Amherst, he could have greater freedom to devote more of himself to writing, but since Elinor's death he felt paralyzed. He was not sure he could ever again write a good poem, and he was almost sure he didn't care. He could at least earn his living with his talks and readings. But where would he live? Carol and Lillian talked about building an el for him on the northwest side of the Stone Cottage, and yet it seemed that Carol might not want him underfoot that much.

To Carol and Lillian he continued making excuses for his disappearances. Day after day he set out alone, aimlessly walking the boundaries of Carol's farm, or his own. He botanized enough to discover that in the grove of red pines he and Carol had set out as seedlings, seventeen years earlier, some wild orchises were beginning to grow. Down on one side of this grove he found one showy orchis and picked it. Without saying anything to Carol or Lillian about his find, he took it to his bedroom in the Stone Cottage, placed it in water in a thin vase, and stood it next to the urn on the closet shelf—as though he were trying to make amends for his failure to carry out her wish. He supposed he would stop this guilty brooding after a while and could get back into something like his old form, at least in public. Just now, there were moments when he felt so completely crushed by loneliness that he wished the urn in the cupboard held his ashes, with hers.[29]

NOTES

❧❁❧

TABLE OF CONTENTS
FOR THE NOTES

In the Notes, whenever a last name or a short title is given as a reference, the Index will serve as a convenient guide to the first reference and the full citation.

	Introduction	515
1 ·	Homecoming	517
2 ·	From Nowhere up to Somewhere	522
3 ·	My Own Strategic Retreat	524
4 ·	Return to Boston	526
5 ·	Making Friends—and Enemies	532
6 ·	My Voice and Manner	536
7 ·	Death of a Soldier-Poet	544
8 ·	The Amherst Idea	550
9 ·	Jeanie	557
10 ·	Trouble in Franconia	559
11 ·	Transplanted: A New Start	564
12 ·	Explorations	570
13 ·	The Michigan Fellowship	575
14 ·	The Long Trail	581
15 ·	A Round of Readings	583
16 ·	The Pulls on Me	589
17 ·	Yes I Suppose I Am a Puritan	592
18 ·	In the Councils of the Bold	602
19 ·	Freed from Obligation	611
20 ·	Sickness and Scatteration	616
21 ·	Speaking of Contraries	623
22 ·	Helping to Shape an Image	631
23 ·	To Europe for Health	634
24 ·	Good Old Folkways	640
25 ·	Encouraging Younger Poets	641
26 ·	A Farm for Myself	643
27 ·	Friendship Means Favor	647
28 ·	No Artist Should Have a Family	652
29 ·	Things in Pairs Ordained	663
30 ·	A Further Range	668
31 ·	A Harvard Year	672
32 ·	Pride of Ancestry	687
33 ·	Strike That Blow for Me	690
34 ·	And I the Last	698

[513]

When the physical location of a previously unpublished letter or manuscript is cited, one of the following abbreviations may be used for the library collection:

AAAL	The American Academy of Arts and Letters
ACL	Amherst College
ASCL	Agnes Scott College
BMCL	Bryn Mawr College
CUL	University of Chicago
DCL	Dartmouth College
HUL	Harvard University
JHUL	Johns Hopkins University
JLA	The Jones [public] Library, Amherst, Mass.
LC	The Library of Congress
MCL	Middlebury College
MUL	University of Michigan
NYUL	New York University
PSCL	Plymouth State College of the U. of N. H.
PUL	Princeton University
SUL	Stanford University
TCL	Trinity College
TUL	University of Texas
VaUL	University of Virginia
VtUL	University of Vermont
WCL	Wellesley College
WUL	Wesleyan University
YUL	Yale University

When the physical location of a previously unpublished letter or manuscript is cited from a private collection, one of the following abbreviations may be used:

PEMR	Mrs. Elizabeth Monroe Riley
PHBL	Miss Helen B. Lawrie
PHGS	Mr. Howard G. Schmitt
PJBL	Mr. Junius B. Lankes
PJMC	Mrs. Jane Monroe Curcuruto
PLFB	Mrs. Lesley Frost Ballantine
PLHC	Mr. Lawrence H. Conrad
PLLF	Mrs. Lillian LaBatt Frost
PMCB	Mr. Madison C. Bates
PMEC	Miss Mary E. Cooley
PWEF	Mr. Willard E. Fraser
PWES	Mr. William E. Stockhausen
PWPF	Mr. William Prescott Frost

NOTES

INTRODUCTION

1. Sylvester Baxter, "Talk of the Town," Boston *Herald*, 8 March 1915, p. 9.

2. This sentence contains a close paraphrase of elements in an undated journal entry made by RF not long after he arrived in England. For the text and context, see Lawrance Thompson, *Robert Frost: The Early Years* (New York, 1966)—hereafter cited as *The Early Years*—p. 427.

3. Sylvester Baxter, op. cit., p. 9.

4. RF was quoting the first line of Kipling's poem entitled "M.I." The subtitle is, "(Mounted Infantry of the Line)." For the circumstances of this quotation, see Note 10 of Chapter 28.

5. The importance to RF of the religious beliefs taught him by his mother cannot be overemphasized. In later life, however, he made so many coy and puzzling references to his own religious position that many of his interpreters mistakenly tried to represent him as either an agnostic or an atheist. (See, for example, the opinion of Joseph Warren Beach, quoted in Note 3 of Chapter 16.) Because such mistakes need to be corrected, and also because RF's life and art were saturated with his peculiar religious obsessions, various aspects of the subject are given extended scrutiny in some of the notes which follow. To suggest a configuration, a selected list of such notes is here given under topical headings:

(a) RF's humorous and misleading allusions to religious matters. Note 13 of Chapter 10; Note 4 of Chapter 19.

(b) His deliberately deceptive accommodations of his style, at times, to defensive concealments of his religious belief. Note 12 of Chapter 18.

(c) Evidences that his belief was deeply and seriously rooted in puritanism. Note 15 of this Introduction; Note 15 of Chapter 11.

(d) His puritanism is clarified by his way of interpreting a passage in *Paradise Lost*. Note 14 of Chapter 28.

(e) His puritanical attitude toward change. Note 30 of Chapter 17.

(f) His attitude toward the doctrine of right reason, in relation to his self-confessed anti-intellectualism. Note 14 of Chapter 8; Note 24 of Chapter 17; Note 5 of Chapter 31.

(g) His hints at the religious significance of his self-applied epithet, "Synecdochist." Note 23 of Chapter 33.

(h) His way of correlating his belief in God with his attitude toward form-giving in art. Note 19 of Chapter 25.

(i) His Puritan-Victorian ways of carrying on the warfare between evolutionary science and religion. Note 13 of Chapter 17; Note 14 of Chapter 20; Note 23 of Chapter 21; Notes 5 and 8 of Chapter 27; Note 24 of Chapter 28.

(j) His belief in a life after death, and in universal salvation. Note 22 of Chapter 33.

(k) His fear of death, considered as being perhaps the strongest motivation for his religious belief. Note 13 of Chapter 10; Note 15 of Chapter 11; Notes 9 and 10 of Chapter 21; Note 34 of Chapter 33; Note 27 of Chapter 34.

6. For source, see *The Early Years*, pp. 76–77.

7. For source, see Lawrance Thompson, ed., *Selected Letters of Robert Frost* (New York, 1964)—hereafter cited as *Selected Letters*—p. 55.

8. For source, see ibid., p. 202.

9. Quoted from "Afterflakes," *The Poetry of Robert Frost*, edited with notes by Edward Connery Lathem (New York, 1969)—hereafter cited as *The Poetry*—p. 303.

10. RF's confidences about Amy Lowell are here placed in context on p. 274 of Chapter 19.

11. For source and context, see Note 29 of Chapter 4.

12. For source and context, see p. 450 of Chapter 31.

13. For source, see *The Early Years*, p. 481, Note 3.

14. For source and context, see p. 134 of Chapter 9.

15. One of RF's most revealing defenses of hating occurred during a conversation with his close friend and summer-neighbor, Rabbi Victor E. Reichert, in Ripton, Vt., in July of 1960. The conversation, as first told to LT by RF, and then as corroborated by Reichert, was recorded in July of 1960. Reichert, knowing that RF liked to call himself "an Old Testament Christian," began by assuring RF that the best passages in the New Testament were merely quotations from the Old. This exchange followed:

"What's the best?"

" '. . . thou shalt love thy neighbor as thyself.' " [Leviticus 19:18; Matthew 5:43]

"That's not good enough," RF protested. "We need something higher than that, don't we?"

"What would it be?"

" 'And thou shalt hate thy neighbor as thyself.' "

When Reichert seemed puzzled, RF explained:

"It's only when we hate ourselves and our shortcomings that we can love and need God. All religions are based on that one: 'And thou shalt hate thy neighbor as thyself.' "

RF's mother, raised in Scotland as a Calvinistic Presbyterian, may have taught to her son, when he was relatively young, this idea which occurs as an element of Calvinistic doctrine. Essentially, RF's statement to Reichert amounts to a sympathetic paraphrase of a passage which may be found in Calvin's *Institutes*, Book One, Chapter One:

"Thus a sense of our ignorance, vanity, poverty, infirmity, depravity, and corruption, leads us to perceive and acknowledge that in the Lord alone are to be found true wisdom, solid strength, perfect goodness, and unspotted righteousness: and so, by our imperfections, we are excited to a consideration of the perfections of God. Nor can we really aspire toward him, till we have begun to be displeased with ourselves." (Quoted from *A Compend of the Institutes of the Christian Religion*, by John Calvin, edited by H. T. Kerr, Jr. [Philadelphia, 1939], p. 4.)

1. HOMECOMING

1. Quoted from "The Death of the Hired Man," *The Poetry*, p. 38.
2. RF to Ernest L. Silver, 8 Dec. 1913; *Selected Letters*, p. 103.
3. The furniture taken to England included a rocking chair for Mrs. Frost, a leather-upholstered Morris chair which was a favorite of RF's when he was in a mood for writing, two floor rugs, many books, and a few framed pictures. See *The Early Years*, pp. 392, 583.
4. *The Early Years*, pp. 590–591. A harmless example of RF's myth-makings which romantically improved or idealized autobiographical facts may be found in RF's saying repeatedly that until he reached New York City on Washington's Birthday 1915 he did not know he had an American publisher. As an illustration, consider an accurate reporting of this claim, as paraphrased by Gorham B. Munson in *Robert Frost: A Study in Sensibility and Good Sense* (New York, 1927), p. 69: "Passing down a side street in New York as he came away from the steamer . . . Robert Frost's eyes saw the *New Republic*. . . . a page appreciation . . . signed by Amy Lowell. But more arresting still, the book appeared to be published by Henry Holt and Company. An American publisher. He did not know he had one." The truth is that RF, more than four months prior to his arrival in New York, began to inform his friends and relatives that Henry Holt and Company had made arrangements to publish *North of Boston* in America. As evidence, see *The Early Years*, pp. 469–470.
5. Amy Lowell, "North of Boston," *New Republic*, Vol. II, No. 16 (20 Feb. 1915), pp. 81–82. Miss Lowell's reference to "this modest little green-covered book" supports her later claim (see Note 11 of this chapter) that she based her review on an English edition of *North of Boston*. The first English issue was bound in green buckram; the first American issue was bound in light tan paper-covered boards, with a brown cloth backstrip and with white paper labels on cover and spine. This first American issue of *North of Boston* was published on 20 Feb. 1915; the second American issue (the first one actually printed in the United States) was published

late in April 1915 and was bound in blue cloth. Uniform with the latter in binding was the first American edition of *A Boy's Will*, also published late in April 1915.

6. A statement reflecting the differences between Amy Lowell's and RF's responses to New England was made by the poet John Gould Fletcher in his autobiography, *Life Is My Song* (New York, 1937), p. 204, where he compared Amy Lowell's early praise of RF with Ezra Pound's praise: "I understand the cause for this praise of hers better in her case than in the case of Ezra. . . . It was because Frost stood in her mind for unfamiliar New England, not the New England of the cultivated and the affluent, among whom she had always lived, but the remote, shy, hermitlike New England of Thoreau and the backwoods farmer . . ."

7. These details, drawn from RF's conversations with LT, were corroborated (at least in part) by Charles C. Burlingham in two of his letters to LT. In one, dated 15 Oct. 1946 (PUL), he wrote, "I remember the episode but not very clearly. Robert Frost came into my office and told me that the boy was on Ellis Island, and detained as I recall because there was no one to be sponsor for him so that he might not become a public charge. I thought Frost came to me because either he or the boy knew Mrs. Mildred Minturn Scott. . . . Mildred, who has since died, I knew well. I don't remember exactly what I did, but it was easy enough. I probably telephoned to the Commissioner of Immigration Fred Howe and the boy was admitted. . . ."

Mervyn's troubles at Ellis Island were apparently treated by him with casual ease, at least retrospectively, in his letters to his relatives. The incident is mentioned in a letter from Edward Thomas to Eleanor Farjeon, 25 March 1915: "My mother had such a good letter from Mervyn about his detention and his whist playing with fellow prisoners. Now he is bored with Scott though." (Eleanor Farjeon, *Edward Thomas: The Last Four Years* [London, 1958], p. 128.)

8. The story as given in the text is LT's summary, based on documentary evidence as cited. The version given RF by Harcourt on 22 Feb. 1915 was repeated, in essentially the same form, by Harcourt, for LT's benefit, in Sept. 1941, with RF listening. Harcourt, sharing with RF a tendency to improve on the facts, made the story give more credit to himself than the facts justified. He said Mrs. Holt frequently returned from summer trips abroad with some newly published English books which she placed on Harcourt's desk for his consideration, and she came into Harcourt's office after her return from England in the summer of 1914 to give him a copy of the English edition of *North of Boston*. [LT's comment: Mrs. Holt did not go abroad in the summer of 1914, but she did have a copy of *North of Boston* when she wrote to RF from Stowe, Vermont, on 7 Aug. 1914. See *Selected Letters*, pp. 130–131.] Harcourt further said that because he had little respect for Mrs. Holt's literary judgments he initially tossed her copy of *North of Boston* into the wastepaper basket without even opening it.

[LT's comment: Because the Holt file of interoffice correspondence (PUL) shows that Harcourt knew this copy of *North of Boston* was highly prized by Mrs. Holt, it does not seem probable that Harcourt risked having it discarded with the wastepaper.] Harcourt, continuing, said that during the course of the same day an editorial conference at Holt brought forth the suggestion that the firm needed a few more books of poetry on its list of publications. Harcourt, remembering the book in the basket, went back to his office and rescued it; he took it home to read and returned the next day enthusiastically insisting that Holt must publish *North of Boston*.

Harcourt's dependence on the judgment of Mrs. Holt and others, however, seems to be expressed clearly in the letter he wrote to the firm of David Nutt and Company, 2 Sept. 1914: ". . . Mrs. Henry Holt, who is very enthusiastic over Robert Frost's NORTH OF BOSTON has very kindly loaned us her copy. The two readers we had look at these poems found them uncommonly interesting and, while we cannot see a paying market here for this particular volume, still we are so interested in this author's work that if you have some later book of his for which you would care to offer us the American rights, we would be most happy to consider it. . . ." (*Selected Letters*, p. 133.) Further evidence is provided by a carbon copy of a note from Alfred Harcourt to Henry Holt, 2 Aug. 1915 (Holt Correspondence, PUL): "I enclose a letter from Robert Frost which Mrs. Holt will like to see. From the attention Frost is receiving it looks as if we should thank her for the most distinctive addition to our list this year."

9. As a reader, Dorothy Canfield Fisher apparently shared her experiences with her close friend Sarah N. Cleghorn, whose autobiography, *Threescore* (New York, 1936), p. 173, contains the following: "Spending a summer evening at Dorothy's early in 1914 I listened while she read one poem after another from *North of Boston*, beginning, I well remember, with 'Mending Wall.' What first delighted me was their cool, heart-refreshing naturalness. Soon I saw the depths of meaning dawning beneath them. After Dorothy had ceased to read each one, I began to feel its unforced intensity of feeling rising round me in the silence. I never before had seen a body of poetry at once so faithfully plain and so delicately, thoughtfully beautiful. They reminded me of the few seventeenth century poems I knew well; but these sounded cooler, fresher, more natural and out-of-doors than those; closer, too, to the common lot, and the 'marvelous hearts of simple men.'"

10. RF told LT, on 27 Dec. 1941, that the sum paid him by the *New Republic* for "The Death of the Hired Man" was $40. In telling the same story to LT at several different times thereafter, RF always gave the same figure: $40. Elizabeth Shepley Sergeant, in *Robert Frost: The Trial by Existence* (New York, 1960), p. 153, quotes Harcourt as saying that the sum paid was "$80 or $90." Jean Gould, thus given the freedom of choice, states in *Robert Frost: The Aim Was Song* (New York, 1964, p. 151) that the sum paid was $90.

Harcourt's version of the story, which he told to RF in 1915, and which Harcourt told to LT in RF's presence in 1941, omitted the fact that his first letter to Nutt (quoted in part in Note 8, above) asked merely for a chance to take RF's next volume. His second letter, dated 12 Sept. 1914, continued to be cautious: "Following our letter of September 2nd in regard to Frost's 'North of Boston' we are inclined on further consideration to take a small edition of this book, say 150 copies in sheets, if it has not already been placed in the American market, and if you can supply them at a reasonable price. Of course, while we admire this book, it would not, we fear, be worth our while to take it up unless you could assure us that we can have the refusal of the American market on the author's next book." (*Selected Letters,* p. 134.) Nothing in these two letters supports Harcourt's claim that, from the moment he first read it, *North of Boston* aroused his deep enthusiasm.

11. RF to LT. In S. Foster Damon, *Amy Lowell: A Chronicle, with Extracts from Her Correspondence* (Boston, 1935), p. 289, Miss Lowell is quoted as follows: "When I returned to America, I brought the volume with me, and at once (unauthorized ambassador that I was) suggested its publication to various publishers with whom I was in relation. . . . They would not listen to me, and bitterly have they regretted it since. With the publication of the book by Messrs. Henry Holt and Company I had nothing to do. However, when I saw it announced here, I at once wrote to 'The New Republic,' then in its infancy, and asked—nay, demanded—to review the volume in the columns of that paper. My request was granted, and I believe I was the first to proclaim the book's amazing quality on this side of the water." (Ezra Pound was the first; see *The Early Years,* p. 598. For the first unfavorable American review of *North of Boston,* see Note 4 of Chapter 3.)

Alfred Harcourt, in *Some Experiences* (New York, 1949), pp. 47–48, further mixes fictions with facts concerning his claim that he was the first to praise *North of Boston* in America: "One day in September [1914], I went to lunch with Harrison Smith and Sinclair Lewis at the old Park Avenue Hotel. They asked for news from Holt's office, and I said we were going to publish a book of poems by a new American writer that would sell at least 10,000 copies in its first season. There was a hoot of disbelief, and they wouldn't listen when I wanted to read some extracts from a set of sheets I had in my pocket. As I started back to the Holt office, I ran into Francis Hackett [literary editor of the *New Republic*] in front of the old Holland House. We adjourned to the bar and he started talking about the *New Republic,* the first issue of which was rapidly taking shape. I asked him if they would print poetry. He said, 'Of course, if it is good enough.' I pulled the sheets of *North of Boston* out of my pocket and said, "Here it is. You would be smart to print a selection from this book in your first issue. We haven't any claim to magazine rights, but I'll take a chance on its being all right if you'll pay your usual rates for an extract.' The next day he telephoned me that he and Philip Littell had read the poems and wanted to make a feature of 'The Death of the Hired Man' in their first issue."

There seems to be a discrepancy between Harcourt's writing Nutt, in the Sept. 1914 letter already cited, ". . . we cannot see a paying market here for this particular volume" (of which he later ordered only 150 sheets) and his retrospective claim that in Sept. 1914 he was boasting that Holt would sell 10,000 copies of it. Another Harcourt error is easily corrected. The first issue of the *New Republic* appeared on 7 Nov. 1914, but "The Death of the Hired Man" appeared in the issue for 6 Feb. 1915.

12. The recording secretary was Jessie Belle Rittenhouse, whose account of the meeting held in December 1914 appeared in the untitled folder or bulletin of the Poetry Society of America issued in January 1915. The account also contained this: "Among our out of town guests were the Misses Ticknor of Boston and Mrs. Ernest B. Filsinger (formerly Miss Sara Teasdale) and Mr. Filsinger of St. Louis." Apparently the Filsingers were not among those who disliked RF's poems. Under date of 24 April 1915 (DCL), Ernest B. Filsinger wrote to RF, "Your work has gripped us as the work of no other contemporary writer of either poetry or prose has done. The naked power, the ease, the economy of words—greatest of all, the sympathy for all life and the subtle simplicity in revealing it— these have put you among the world poets." RF's attitude toward Schauffler was hostile, although he briefly tried to conceal it. In a letter to Sidney Cox, who had corresponded with Schauffler, RF wrote on 2 March 1915 (*Selected Letters*, p. 156), "I ran spank on to your S[c]hauffler (pronounced Shofler) in New York and made him a friend. I think we can like each other despite the irreconcilability of what we write. You must meet him." A little more than two months later, after RF again talked with Schauffler—at the first meeting of the New England Poetry Club—RF wrote to Cox, in a letter dated 16 May 1915 (*Selected Letters*, p. 174), "S[c]hauffler didn't pan out very well. He showed jealousy of my British made reputation. I suspect you didn't tell me all he said in his letter to you. I found him a treacherous second-rate mind."

13. RF to John Bartlett, 25 Dec. 1912; *Selected Letters*, p. 57.

14. Florence Taber Holt to RF, 7 Aug. 1914; *Selected Letters*, p. 130.

15. Mrs. Holt had sent to RF, in England, a copy of the book, *Stowe Notes* written by her brother Robert Taber (first husband of Julia Marlowe). After reading the sketches, RF gave the book to Edward Thomas, who was apparently appreciative. Writing to Thomas from Bethlehem, N.H., 17 April 1915 (*Selected Letters*, p. 164), RF obliquely mentions Thomas's comment on *Stowe Notes* and RF's plan to look for a farm in Vermont: "What you say of Taber I shan't fail to pass along to his sister. I am going to Stowe tomorrow at her invitation to see if I can find a farm there."

16. The proposed "Introduction" is mentioned in a letter, Mrs. Holt to RF, 11 March 1915 (DCL): "Ever since you've been here I have been ill with neuritis, and cannot use my right hand, so I'm

not getting on very quickly, I'm sorry to say, with arranging the Ms. to send you. But I shall peg along, and it will go to you in a week or so. However, the Ms., of which you saw a little, is almost in shape. . . . I know you'll remember our compact. . . . I'd be mighty proud if you would write a little introduction to it!" In another letter from Mrs. Holt to RF, 25 Sept. [1915] (DCL), the following occurs as a postscript: "I don't need to tell you how I appreciate all the trouble you've taken for me."

2. FROM NOWHERE UP TO SOMEWHERE

1. Quoted from "The Fear of God," *The Poetry*, p. 385.

2. Quoted from a letter, Jeanie Frost to Wilbur E. Rowell, South Fork, Pa., 25 Dec. 1914 (PUL).

3. Soon after her brother's visit with her, Jeanie Frost began to review and extend her knowledge of Latin, German, and French in preparation for college entrance examinations. She applied for admission to the University of Michigan in Ann Arbor, but her application was made too late for admission in the fall of 1915. She entered Michigan in February 1916 after successfully passing several entrance examinations. (For more details, see Chapter 9.) The best source of information concerning all of her activities, from 1912 until her death in 1929, is contained in her letters to Wilbur E. Rowell (PUL), usually written to explain why she is requesting advance payments from the annuity provided her from the estate of her grandfather. This account of RF's visit to his sister in 1915 is based in part on RF's conversations with LT, concerning it, and in part on the letters of Jeanie Frost to Wilbur E. Rowell (PUL).

4. The receipt which RF signed for the $200 advance made to him by Rowell in Lawrence is dated 3 March 1915; it is in the RF-Rowell papers, PUL.

5. The circumstances of the loan made by Ernest Jewell to RF are given in *The Early Years*, pp. 280–281, 552–553.

6. Quoted from memory by RF to LT, and recorded, 23 Feb. 1940. The same wording is reported in *The Trial by Existence*, p. 115.

7. Sedgwick, in a letter to Edward Garnett, 26 May 1915, mentioned the circumstances under which he met RF and took him home for dinner: "I feel a genuine obligation to print an appreciation of Frost. A few weeks before you wrote, he happened to come into my office. I found him quite delightful—as unspoiled as when he left his Vermont plough for his quite extraordinary adventures in poetical England. I took him home with me to dine and we had much talk about his theories of poetry which seem to me intelligent and genuinely distinctive. . . ." (Edward Connery Lathem, *Robert Frost: His "American Send-off"—1915* [Lunenburg, Vt., 1963], p. [9].)

8. Quoted from the title poem in John Boyle O'Reilly's *In Bohemia* (Boston, 1886), pp. 14–15.

9. William Stanley Beaumont Braithwaite (1878–1962) started to serve as a literary editor on the Boston *Evening Transcript* in 1904, and began to make his annual surveys of American poetry in the *Transcript* in 1906. His first *Anthology of Magazine Verse* appeared in 1913, and these volumes appeared in unbroken sequence through 1929. He also edited several other anthologies. He published three volumes of his own poetry: *Lyrics of Life and Love* (1904), *The House of Falling Leaves* (1908), and *Selected Poems* (1948). In his autobiography, "The House Under Arcturus," Part One (*Phylon: The Atlanta University Review of Race and Culture*, Vol. II, No. 1 [First Quarter 1941], pp. 9–26), he discusses his ancestry at length, and there traces the paternal side of his Negro ancestry to well-educated and distinguished citizens of that West Indies island, Barbados. He also offers convincing evidence, there, that his father's mother was white, and that his mother's father was white.

For assistance in gathering information on the complicated relationships between RF and Braithwaite, gratitude is here expressed to the poet and biographer Margaret Haley Carpenter, co-editor with Braithwaite of *Anthology of Magazine Verse for 1958*.

10. RF kept his word and sent Braithwaite a long letter, 22 March 1915 (*Selected Letters*, pp. 158–160), beginning, "I've got as far as finding you the copy of Book I [*A Boy's Will*], I promised you." In a follow-up letter, 4 April 1915 (*Selected Letters*, p. 164), RF wrote to Braithwaite, "I trust you got the small book. I want to be sure to have that right. You bought the other in my presence with such a friendly little flourish."

11. This conversation, quoted by RF to LT, is corroborated in a letter from William Ernest Hocking to Charles R. Green, 7 July 1951; JLA.

12. Idem.

13. The description of Amy Lowell's library was given by RF to LT, but it is here supplemented by the description which occurs in Damon, *Amy Lowell*, pp. 154–155.

14. Amy Lowell to Harriet Monroe, 15 Sept. 1914; ibid., pp. 238–239.

15. Fletcher, *Life Is My Song*, p. 204: "And Frost himself, as I recall him at that first meeting, seemed to me to have all the qualities to be expected from a man of his type. I was struck by the Celtic dreaminess of his eyes, his quiet unworldliness, his serene detachment of manner. He sat on her sofa and said little."

16. Damon, *Amy Lowell*, pp. 280–281.

17. Sylvester Baxter, "Talk of the Town," Boston *Herald*, 9 March 1915, p. 9.

18. RF to Sidney Cox, 13 and 22 March 1915; *Selected Letters*, pp. 156, 162.

3. MY OWN STRATEGIC RETREAT

1. Quoted from "A Drumlin Woodchuck," *The Poetry*, p. 282.

2. RF to Susan Hayes Ward, 4 Nov. 1907; *Selected Letters*, pp. 41–42.

3. RF to N. H. Dole, 26 March 1915; *Selected Letters*, p. 162. A brief account of RF's stay with the Dole family in March 1915 was given by N. H. Dole in an article entitled "A Migration of Poets," the *Bellman* (24 April 1915), p. 532. Braithwaite, in an unpublished MS, "The Reminiscences of William Stanley Braithwaite" (Oral History Research Office, Columbia University, 1959), p. 141, makes a passing reference to this visit, and to his meeting RF at Dole's home on this occasion: "Frost first stayed with Dole in Jamaica Plain. When he arrived, Dole invited me out to meet Frost. I was delighted, because an interview article for the *Transcript* could be important." (Gratitude is here expressed to the daughter of N. H. Dole—Mrs. Margaret Dole McCall—for her assistance in providing information about this visit, and the friendship which resulted from it.)

4. The reference is to all the editors who rejected RF's poems, but at this time Ellery Sedgwick was the only one who had shown a change of opinion. Years later, RF seemed to learn that Sedgwick was not the guilty party on the *Atlantic* board of editors. Louis Mertins (*Robert Frost: Life and Talks-Walking*, Norman, Oklahoma, 1965, p. 106) claims to be quoting RF's remarks on the same subject: "During the years on the [Derry] farm I had given all the good magazines a chance at my work. The office readers were dead set against me. One will never know just what good poetry the damn fool manuscript readers keep from ever being printed. There was an old bitch on the *Atlantic* staff who kept my verse out of the magazine for ten years. Once I sat by her at a dinner given by the Poetry Society of America. She confessed that she had read poetry sent to the *Atlantic* for years. My books were already famous when she told me this. I didn't tell her she had done her best to keep me down. I didn't think it worth the effort."

Another editor (relatively young) whom RF considered an "old bitch" because she rejected his first offering to *Poetry* magazine was Mrs. Alice Corbin Henderson, an associate of Harriet Monroe's until spring of 1916. For details, see *The Early Years*, p. 588. Mrs. Henderson also wrote the first harsh American review of *North of Boston*. Published in the *Dial* magazine, Vol. LVII, No. 679 (1 Oct. 1914), p. 254, it contained the following strictures:

". . . one is led to think of it as a new novel rather than as a book of verse. . . . Doubtless there will be many readers who will find Mr. Frost dull, and who will object to his verse structure. There is no denying that his insistent monosyllabic monotony is irritating, but it may be questioned whether any less drab monotony of rhythm would have been so successful in conveying the particular aspect of life presented."

5. The reference is probably to Sylvester Baxter's article de-

scribed in Note 17 of Chapter 2, but no photograph was used with that article. Baxter reworked and extended the materials of that article, in writing "New England's New Poet," which appeared with a photograph in the *American Review of Reviews*, Vol. LI, No. 4 (April 1915), pp. 432–434.

6. Braithwaite's first article on RF, "A Poet of New England: Robert Frost, A New Exponent of Life," appeared in the Boston *Evening Transcript*, 28 April 1915, Part 3, p. 4. A photograph of RF was reproduced with Braithwaite's second article, "Robert Frost, New American Poet: His Opinions and Practice—An Important Analysis of the Art of the Modern Bard," ibid., 8 May 1915, Part 3, p. 4.

7. The reference is to the two articles cited in Note 6 of Chapter 4.

8. RF to Bartlett, c. 20 April 1915; *Selected Letters*, p. 168.

9. *The Early Years*, p. 416.

10. Ibid., p. 417. Bartlett did help RF achieve revenge against their enemies in Derry, and in expressing thanks RF added parenthetically, "Christ forgive me the sin of vengefulness: from this hour forth I will have no more of it. Perhaps I only say so because for the moment I am sated."

11. Ibid., p. 93

12. Carl Burell to RF, from Manchester, N. H., 17 May 1915; DCL. The article which Burell mentions is "Current Poetry," *Literary Digest*, Vol. 5, No. 20 (15 May 1915), p. 1165, where use is made of quotations from the dust jacket of the second American edition of *North of Boston*.

13. There is only circumstantial proof that Burell received no answer to his letter dated 17 May 1915, even as there is only circumstantial proof that the correspondence between these two men was terminated with the same letter. However, see *The Early Years* (pp. 337–338) for a description of the many manuscripts and poems sent by RF to Burell and preserved by him. Further circumstantial proof is contained in a letter from Burell to Mrs. Edna Davis Romig, dated 5 March 1935 (the original owned by Frederick B. Adams, Jr., to whom gratitude is expressed for permission to quote the following excerpt): "I have lost touch with [Ernest] JEWELL long ago and active touch with Frost since the time HE went to ENGLAND but I am a good friend all the same and I am trying to give you a picture of HIM as he was 40 years ago. I liked him as he was then better than as he is now."

14. RF to Edward Thomas, 17 April 1915; *Selected Letters*, p. 166.

15. This version of the first encounter between RF and Willis E. Herbert was given to LT by Herbert's widow, in Franconia, N. H., on 20 July 1940. Mrs. Herbert was aware that RF frequently told another version of the story, and she was anxious to correct it. Among RF's idealized accounts of the incident, perhaps the earliest-known occurs in his poem entitled "New Hampshire," written seven years after the event (*The Poetry*, pp. 163–164).

4. RETURN TO BOSTON

1. Quoted from "Birches," *The Poetry*, p. 122.

2. RF's statements, paraphrased in this paragraph of the text, and in the next, were made repeatedly by RF to LT and others. Although these statements obviously represent RF's view of his wife's responses, there seems to be no way of comparing them with statements of her own. Sources of information about her own opinions, in this regard, are extremely limited.

3. RF to Braithwaite, 22 March 1915; *Selected Letters*, pp. 158–160.

4. RF to LU, 22 March 1915; *The Letters of Robert Frost to Louis Untermeyer* (New York, 1963)—hereafter cited as *Letters to Untermeyer*—p. 3. Gratitude is here expressed to LU for his generous act of providing LT with copies of all the letters in this volume, years before publication. There is no other single source of information concerning RF which is so valuable and so self-revealing as this group of letters.

5. A larger context for this reference to Wordsworth, by RF, is given in *The Early Years*, p. 428.

6. LU, "Robert Frost's 'North of Boston,'" Chicago *Evening Post*, 23 April 1915, p. 11. On the same page appears an editorial entitled "Robert Frost," by the literary editor, Llewellyn Jones.

7. RF to LU, 30 April 1915; *Letters to Untermeyer*, p. 4, where the letter is misdated 3 April 1915.

8. The Boston visit actually included a brief side-trip to Lawrence, Mass., where RF consulted with his lawyer, Wilbur E. Rowell, about two important matters. First, he obtained another advance of $200 on the $800 annuity due him in July 1915 from the estate of his grandfather. (Receipt in the Frost-Rowell file, PUL.) Next, he proposed to Rowell that the $1,000 needed to pay for the Herbert farm in Franconia might be made available to him as a loan from the principal in the same annuity trust fund. Preliminary terms of this proposal were worked out, and a formal search of title was begun soon thereafter. Matters dragged for more than a year, however, because no clear title could be established. On 13 July 1916, Rowell sent RF a check for $800 "in payment of the annuity due from the estate of William P. Frost" (PUL). Five days later, RF wrote to Rowell, "We are just as grateful as if you had done everything for us we know you have wanted to do. We have come to understand your position and we trust you understand ours in not having released you from your promise sooner. We *can* release you now. You will be pleased for more reasons than one to hear that we are going to be able to buy the farm with our own money." (RF to Rowell, 18 July 1916; PUL.) New Hampshire's Grafton County Records, as given within the Register of Deeds at Woodsville (Haverhill), reveal (Book 538, p. 110) that Willis E. Herbert formally conveyed the Franconia

farm to RF on 21 July 1916. (Gratitude is here expressed to Edward Connery Lathem for finding and sharing this documentary information.)

9. Josephine Preston Peabody—Mrs. Lionel Marks—(1874–1922) was so popular at the time that in one record of the occasion, a letter from the novelist Basil King to RF, 12 May 1915 (DCL), she is uncritically praised: "I was unable to stay long enough at the Authors Club on Friday afternoon to tell you how keenly I enjoyed your new & wonderful analysis of sound, which to me had something of the force of a bit of revelation. After the beautiful tapestry spread before us by Mrs Marks it was as if you were showing us . . ."

Mrs. Marks counted among her enemies not only Amy Lowell but also Miss Lowell's ally, John Gould Fletcher. Although RF deliberately cultivated the attentions of Mrs. Marks, after this first meeting, and wrote her polite letters, his attitude toward her was very similar to Fletcher's. In *Life Is My Song*, pp. 228–229, Fletcher describes Mrs. Marks as seeming to him "from the outset as being . . . false. She was a Victorian sentimentalist to the core, having been reigning queen of Boston poetry circles back in the days when Amy [Lowell] herself was a struggling novice; and her poetry, to my eyes, revealed only an arch-prettiness of phrase akin to the achievement of the well-bred ladies of the '80s who specialized in china painting. She had nonetheless jealously guarded her supremacy as America's great woman lyricist down to the days of the War; but she was now, I could see, a waning star, so consumed by envy at the thought of Amy's growing public following as to be ready to attack her on any provocation that offered."

10. W. S. Braithwaite, "Robert Frost, New American Poet," cited in Note 6 of Chapter 3.

11. For an account of how RF's jealousy of Rupert Brooke developed, see *The Early Years*, p. 454.

12. Quoted from the Tufts *Weekly* in Patricia Hanley, "A View of Robert Frost on the Hill," the *Tuftonian*, Vol. 16, No. 1 (Dec. 1959), p. 30. Another account of the occasion appeared on the "School and College" page of the Boston *Evening Transcript*, 6 May 1915, p. 16, under the caption, "Tufts College: Phi Beta Kappa Initiates New Members and Elects Officers." Excerpts: "The literary exercises were held in Goddard Chapel directly after the business meeting . . . Mr. Robert Frost, the poet of the occasion, read three short nature poems of the strikingly distinctive quality that characterizes the verse of 'North of Boston' and 'A Boy's Will.' The poems were 'The Sound of Trees,' 'The Road Not Taken' and 'Birches.'" A third account of this occasion was given to LT by N. H. Dole's daughter, Mrs. Margaret Dole McCall, during an interview on 9 Nov. 1969.

13. RF, in telling this anecdote many times throughout the remainder of his life, introduced no important variations. One version, placed in the best possible context of supporting information,

occurs in Edward Connery Lathem, *Robert Frost: His "American Send-off"—1915*, pp. [4]–[5]. A garbled version occurs in *The Trial by Existence*, pp. 165–166.

14. Garnett to Sedgwick, 24 April 1915; *Selected Letters*, pp. 169–170. Sedgwick, in a letter to Garnett already cited (see Note 7 of Chapter 2) mentions this second visit of RF to the *Atlantic* office: "By an odd accident, your enthusiastic letter concerning Frost had just reached my desk and I was in the very act of opening it, when Frost, who had once again returned from his farm, came in to see me. I bade him sit down and then read judicious extracts from your note. His blue eyes opened very wide, and, of course, he is enormously keen to have me print your appreciation . . ."

RF was not quickly convinced that part of Sedgwick's posture in regard to Garnett's article was one of counterteasing, but in his letter to Garnett (12 June 1915; *Selected Letters*, pp. 178–179), RF acknowledged the teasing and explained:

"I have tried two or three times to answer your letter but everything I started to say ran off into the unpatriotic. You see I was still fighting American editors—I hadnt heard that peace had been declared and I had quite believed Sedgwick when he told me he didn't see how he could use your article because he had already handed me over for review to some single-bed she professor with a known preference for the beautiful in poetry. I knew I should never have such another piece of good luck as your help at this moment and I was discouraged. Sedgwick was teasing me: he meant all the time to publish the article; and I should have known as much, but it has been a long fight with editors, my rage has gathered considerable headway and it's hard to leave off believing the worst of them."

15. In later years, RF told the latter part of the anecdote with some variations. On 15 Aug. 1947, when he first told LT of this telephone conversation, RF implied that his tone and manner were identical with the pleasantly teasing tone and manner he employed when he told of his offering the poems to Sedgwick in the *Atlantic* office. The circumstantial evidence, which does not support such a claim, strongly indicates that RF actually feared Sedgwick would reject all three of the poems and the Garnett article, and RF expressed this fear to LU during the evening of the telephone conversation. RF, not long after his return to Bethlehem from Boston, wrote to LU under date of 16 May 1915, "Contrary to what I thought was the understanding, Ellery Sedgwick is still hanging on to Birches." Later, when RF wrote to LU that all three of the poems had been accepted and would be published in the *Atlantic* with Garnett's article in the August issue of the *Atlantic*, LU replied, under date of 19 July 1915 (DCL), "I'm glad that the Eminent Ellery had the good sense & decent tho' belated taste to take 'Birches' & the two lyrics. And that's good news about Garnett's article. I'll watch for it." Sedgwick must have realized, from the start, that in obtaining three excellent poems from RF he had

managed to scoop all his competitors; he was the first editor to get any poems from RF since his return from England.

16. A typical example occurs in one of LU's early letters to RF, dated 24 Aug. 1915 (DCL): "I wish I had some of your cool caution. But my semitic ancestors neglected that virtue along with most of the other careful and christian ones."

17. Quoted in LU's autobiography, *From Another World* (New York, 1939), p. 47.

18. RF to LU, 1 Jan. 1916; *Selected Letters*, p. 199.

19. RF to Bartlett, 8 May 1915; *Selected Letters*, p. 173.

20. An account of this first meeting of the New England Poetry Club is given in Braithwaite's "Reminiscences," op. cit., pp. 121–123. At the second meeting, convened on 18 May 1915 for the postponed election of officers, the following results occurred: President, Amy Lowell; Honorary President, Josephine Preston Peabody; Vice-president, Sylvester Baxter; Secretary, William Stanley Braithwaite; Treasurer, Edward J. O'Brien. Although RF did not attend this second meeting, he sent from New Hampshire an ambiguous jingle of congratulations to the triumphant Amy Lowell, under date of 21 May 1915 (*Selected Letters*, p. 175):

> *Hail first President of the*
> *Poetry Society of New England!* (bis)
> *If I liked your poetry before*
> *You may imagine how much more*
> *I shall like it after this.*

21. RF to Braithwaite, 22 March 1915; *Selected Letters*, p. 51.

22. Braithwaite, "Reminiscences," pp. 135–136.

23. Ibid., p. 135. RF, writing from England on 17 July 1913, expressed to Thomas B. Mosher in Portland, Maine, a desire to meet Robinson: "I wish sometime if you know Robinson you could put me in the way of knowing him too—*sometime*, if it comes right. Not a month ago I was asking Miss [May] Sinclair if she shouldn't have put him ahead of Moody and Torrence in her article of a few years back in the Atlantic. She said that Robinson was the only one of the three she still cared for." (*Selected Letters*, p. 84.)

24. Braithwaite, "Reminiscences," pp. 136–137.

25. RF to LT, 5 July 1954.

26. "There were Robinson and I, it was years ago, and the place (near Boston Common) was the Place, as we liked afterward to call it, of Bitters, because it was with bitters, though without bitterness, we could sit there and look out on the welter of dissatisfaction and experiment in the world around us." (RF, "Introduction" to Robinson's posthumously published *King Jasper* [New York, 1935], p. viii.)

27. See the chapter entitled "Dismal Swamp" in *The Early Years*, pp. 173–189.

28. RF to Robinson, 13 June 1915; *Selected Letters*, pp. 180–181.

29. Of RF's letters to Robinson, only two seem to have survived, although there is circumstantial evidence (cited in Note 18 of Chapter 29) that one other was written. The complete texts of the two known letters are given in *Selected Letters,* pp. 180–181 and 190. According to RF, in conversation with LT, Robinson had already read *North of Boston* before he and RF met, and during their conversation Robinson expressed his admiration for the quality of distinction in several of the *North of Boston* poems. RF therefore sent to Robinson a copy of his earlier book, *A Boy's Will,* and Robinson acknowledged it in a letter which exists in a mutilated form: the first paragraph (together with the heading and salutation) has been torn away. That first paragraph may have contained some comment on RF's interpretation of *The Porcupine.* The surviving fragment (which provides internal evidence that it was written in June 1915 [DCL], after Robinson had received RF's letter) reads as follows:

"I like your second book so thoroughly, and in so many ways, that I don't mind telling you I am glad that I read it first. I think I might not know just how to tell you that your first seems to be what it is—your first. There is much good stuff in it and the good line is almost always authentic, but it hasn't quite the force or the distinction that I told you of in 'North of Boston.' This objection ought not to trouble you much, for you have shown beyond any doubt what you have in you. And your first book has one great advantage over mine, in that it contains nothing for which you need ever be sorry. Some of the juvenile things in my 'Children [of the Night]' makes me groan and roll in my sleep—or if they don't, they should. I am surely as much indebted to Braithwaite as you for his bringing us together and I hope sincerely that our meeting of a month ago may not be our last."

The next known opportunity for a meeting occurred approximately seven months later, on the evening of 25 Jan. 1918, when Robinson was among those who attended the sixth annual dinner-meeting of the Poetry Society of America, at which RF was one of the speakers. (An account of this occasion is given in Chapter 6, pp. 73–74.) Apparently the two men did not converse, during the evening, except perhaps in brief greeting. As though to make amends, Robinson sent a copy of his new book, *The Man Against the Sky,* to RF soon after it was published on 16 Feb. 1916, and wrote to RF from New York City on 22 Feb. 1916 (DCL):

"I was sorry not to see you again after that dinner, but somehow I oozed out slowly with the crowd and was in the street almost without knowing it. I wished also to meet Mrs. Frost, and to tell her what I thought of you. I'm sending you my new book."

There is no discovered record that RF acknowledged receipt of either the letter or the book. However, one anecdote in Braithwaite's "Reminiscences" (p. 137) seems to have a pertinence. After describing how he introduced RF to Robinson in 1915, he tells of a later occasion when Robinson asked if Braithwaite had

recently heard from RF. No. Robinson then explained his reason
for asking:

"He said, 'I was curious to know if you had seen him and talked
with him, because I sent him a copy of my latest book [*The Man
Against the Sky*]. That's been months ago, and I haven't had a
word of acknowledgment from him. I wondered if he was in any
way sensitive about that introduction that you made when we
met?' . . . I know that Robinson was quite disturbed about it, because he was so punctilious himself."

RF did make one gesture of acknowledgment, by sending to
Robinson a copy of *Mountain Interval* when it was published, late
in the fall of 1916. Robinson acknowledged it in a letter dated 2
Feb. 1917 (*Selected Letters of Edwin Arlington Robinson* [New
York, 1940], pp. 99–100):

"Let me thank you for your book, which came to me the other
day by way of the Macmillans. I don't know how long they have
had it, but I do know that they are sinners in such matters.

"In 'Snow,' 'In the Home Stretch,' 'Birches,' 'The Hill Wife,' and
'The Road Not Taken' you seem undoubtedly to have added something permanent to the world, and I must congratulate you. I like
everything else in the book, but these poems seem to me to stand
out from the rest; and I fancy somehow that you will not wholly
disagree with me. Please give my best regards to Mr. [Stark] Young
[at Amherst] and believe me Yours always, sincerely . . ."

Again, there is no discovered record that RF acknowledged receipt of this letter, and his refusal to maintain communication
with Robinson obviously spoiled the possibility of developing the
friendship. A further cause for estrangement is suggested by an
anecdote told by Wilbert Snow (in "The Robert Frost I Knew,"
Texas Quarterly, Vol. XI, No. 3 [Autumn 1968], p. 17):

"When Robinson was fifty years old in 1919, his publisher sent
out a request to poets and critics for letters to make up a brochure
that would tell of his great contribution to poetry. Almost everyone
responded and sang E. A.'s praise. Frost put the letter in the waste-
basket and did not answer. I [much later] asked him why not? He
replied, 'I thought it was merely an advertising dodge.' 'What of
it?' I said. 'It was advertising a good product.' Robert's refusal to
answer offended Robinson and his admirers. . . . From that time
on a coolness developed between them. Frost once said to Mark
Van Doren, 'There can be only one heavyweight champion at a
time.' And he himself apparently wanted to be that champion."

Percy MacKaye, not Robinson's publisher, was the prime mover
in gathering these tributes. Eighteen poets responded, and their
statements were published in an article (not in a brochure) written
by Bliss Perry: "Poets Celebrate E. A. Robinson's Birthday," New
York *Times Review of Books*, 21 Dec. 1919, pp. 765–766. RF gave
his own account of this event, in a letter to the poet John Holmes,
19 Aug. 1937 (*Selected Letters*, p. 447):

"My being solicited for Robinson some years ago went near to destroying our friendship. I got one letter asking me in on a symposium. He knew how much I thought of him. I had put it into a personal letter. I threw the demand (it was from someone named Marsh) into the waste basket. Then I got a second: 'Surely you won't fail to be in on this extraordinarily spontaneous outburst of admiration for E. A. Robinson.' I stayed out and looked ungenerous. It took Robinson some years to forgive me for behaving so Cordelierly."

Obviously far-fetched is RF's analogy, here, between himself and the youngest of King Lear's three daughters—the only one who remained faithful. For an account of another "personal letter" which RF wrote belatedly to Robinson, in December of 1935, see Note 18 of Chapter 29.

5. MAKING FRIENDS—AND ENEMIES

1. RF to LU, 1 Jan. 1916; *Selected Letters*, p. 22.

2. RF to LU, 3 Dec. 1915; *Letters to Untermeyer*, p. 19.

3. RF to Bartlett, 20 May 1915; Margaret Bartlett Anderson, *Robert Frost and John Bartlett: The Record of a Friendship* (New York, 1963)—hereafter cited as *Frost and Bartlett*—p. 92.

4. RF to LU, 16 May 1915; *Letters to Untermeyer*, p. 7. The price finally paid was only $1,000.

5. Edward Thomas to RF, 22 April 1915; DCL.

6. RF to LU, 20 July 1915. In an earlier letter to LU, 8 July 1915, RF had mentioned his "couple of cows that have to be anchored at both ends as a boat ought to be when you fish for perch and pout." *Letters to Untermeyer*, pp. 12, 11.

7. RF to Bartlett, 8 June 1915; VaUL.

8. RF to LU, 8 July 1915; *Letters to Untermeyer*, p. 11.

9. RF to Bartlett, 9 Sept. 1915; *Frost and Bartlett*, p. 100.

10. "Fish-leap Fall," first sent by RF to LU from Franconia in a letter dated 30 June 1919, was first published in *Letters to Untermeyer*, pp. 90–91.

11. RF to LU, 8 June 1915; *Letters to Untermeyer*, p. 9. RF was apparently paid $55 for the three poems: "Sedgwick has just written me a beautiful letter and sent me fifty-five beautiful dollars for poetry." (*Selected Letters*, p. 179.)

12. Edward Garnett, "Some Remarks on American and English Fiction," *Atlantic*, Vol. CXIV, No. 6 (Dec. 1914), pp. 747–756.

13. The reference is to a review of *A Boy's Will* by Norman Douglas in *The English Review*, Vol. 14, No. 56 (June 1913), p. 505; reprinted in Norman Douglas, *Experiments* (New York, 1925), pp. 162–163.

14. The reference is to RF's former friend, Wilfrid W. Gibson, against whom RF made other jibes at this time. In a letter to Edward Thomas, 17 April 1915 (*Selected Letters*, p. 165), RF wrote, "I have had one note from Wilfrid in which he says Ellery Sedgwick writes that he had a pleasant talk with me on English traits peculiarities idiocyncracies etc. Wilfrid wishes he could have heard

that talk! I wish he could. It was all about Wilfrid's nice feeling for country society *and* the Albrights [a farmer and his family who lived near the Abercrombies' cottage, known as The Gallows]. . . . Sedgwick said Wilfrid rather invited himself over here—asked Sedgwick outright if he couldn't arrange him a tour. That is not as I had it from Wilfrid. He was under the delusion that he had been urged to come over and save the country." In a letter to LU, 8 July 1915 (*Letters to Untermeyer*, pp. 10–11), RF wrote, "Take it easy and don't upon any consideration look for copy—as dear old Wilfrid Gibson does wherever he goes. Once we were coming home from some country races, what they call point-to-point races, when he asked me uneasily 'I didn't see a thing there I could use, did you?' He counted the day lost and only asked consolation in learning that I had lost it too. Those troubles rather told on me in my last six months in England."

15. RF to Garnett, 12 June 1915; *Selected Letters*, p. 179.

16. Edward Garnett, "A New American Poet," *Atlantic*, Vol. CXVI, No. 2 (Aug. 1915), pp. 214–221.

17. For source, see Note 6 of Chapter 3.

18. Llewellyn Jones, editorial, "Robert Frost," Chicago *Evening Post*, 23 April 1915, p. 11.

19. Jessie B. Rittenhouse, "North of Boston," New York *Times Book Review*, 16 May 1915. p. 189.

20. RF to Cox, 16 May 1915; *Selected Letters*, pp. 173–174.

21. Edmund J. Wheeler, "Discovered in England—A Real American Poet," *Current Opinion*, Vol. 58, No. 6, p. 427.

22. Quoted from D. D. Paige, ed., *The Letters of Ezra Pound, 1907–1941* (New York, 1950), pp. 62–63. Harriet Monroe apparently scolded Pound for having written the letter, and Pound replied to her under date of 1 Dec. 1915 (ibid., p. 66): "Re Frost: I must again insist that I did not send that letter to *The Transcript* but to the editor as a private citizen. I think however that the charge of my being jealous of Frost ought to be nailed, perhaps even at the disclosure of state secrets. . . . However, I am sorry if it annoyed you." (The four dots here shown after "secrets" were made by Pound in the original letter; CUL.)

23. Details of RF's motives for breaking away from Pound in England in 1914 are given in *The Early Years*, pp. 419–423, 437. Early in 1915, as RF was preparing to sail for America, he wrote Pound a farewell note, apparently saying he was sorry he had been unable to call on Pound prior to departure. Pound answered in a thoroughly friendly letter dated 16 Feb. 1915 (DCL): "Dear Frost: Sorry not to have seen you, still I'm not in London but in Sussex so it would have been no use your calling. Enclosed from Current Opinion just arrived same post your letter. You might note that H. L. Mencken (Smart Set) 454 Fourth Ave New York has just become editor . . . & is well disposed. You might send him stuff & say that I told you to—if thats any use. I sent you two copies of my review of you in Poetry—which I dare say you dislike. Good luck to you & the family. Yours, Ezra Pound."

24. RF to Braithwaite, 24 Aug. 1915; *Selected Letters*, p. 188.

25. Untitled editorial, New York *Times Book Review*, 8 Aug. 1915, p. 28.

26. RF to Harcourt, 12 Aug. 1915; Holt file, PUL.

27. RF to Amy Lowell, 13 Aug. 1915; *Selected Letters*, p. 186.

28. RF to Braithwaite, 14 Aug. 1915; ibid., p. 187.

29. RF to Amy Lowell, 13 Aug. 1915; ibid., p. 186.

30. RF to Braithwaite, 24 Aug. 1915; ibid., p. 188.

31. Howells, "Editor's Easy Chair," *Harper's*, Vol. CXXXI, No. 784 (Sept. 1915), p. 635.

32. RF told LT the details of this brief relationship. RF and Howells never saw each other again after this one visit.

33. For source, see Note 5 of Chapter 1.

34. RF to Thomas, 17 April 1915; *Selected Letters*, pp. 165–166.

35. For context involving Pound, see *The Early Years*, pp. 410–411. RF hinted that LU might help to correct the notion that RF had no sense of humor. In a letter dated 7 Aug. 1916 (*Letters to Untermeyer*, p. 40), RF wrote, "I have been counting and I find that seven out of fifteen of the poems in N. of Boston are almost humorous—four are almost jokes: The Mountain, A Hundred Collars, The Code, The Generations of Men. It won't do to go into all of that. But something saving could be said."

36. Mark Sullivan, ed., *National Floodmarks: Week by Week Observations on American Life As Seen by Collier's* (New York, 1935), p. 92.

37. In his *Tribune* column, "The Conning Tower," 11 June 1915, p. 9, F. P. A. [Franklin Pierce Adams] wrote, "We confess to disappointment in Robert Frost's 'North of Boston.' Intellects broader and riper than ours have acclaimed it as fine poetry. Mr. Frost begins his lines with capital letters just the same as the poets we greatly admire. One test of poetry is to set it as prose. Here is a piece at random from 'North of Boston' set that way . . ." After arranging as prose the opening lines of "The Death of the Hired Man," F. P. A. concluded, "There is, to our constricted notion, as much poetry in a boxscore or a weather forecast."

38. Editorial, "Short Stories," New York *Evening Post*, 11 June 1915, p. 14.

39. For source, see Note 16 of this chapter.

40. This version of the incident was told by RF to LT. A slightly different version was told by RF in his talk entitled "Poverty and Poetry," at Haverford College, 25 Oct. 1937; this talk was published in a quarterly issued by the Friends of the Princeton University Library: *Biblia*, Vol. IX, No. 1 (Feb. 1938), pp. [9]–[15].

The producers of these dramatic representations of "The Death of the Hired Man" and "Home Burial" were Helen Archibald Clark and Charlotte Endymion Porter, editors of *Poet-Lore* and prime movers in The American Drama Society. The broadside announcement (DCL) sent to members stated that the production would be given at the Huntington Chambers Hall (Huntington Ave., off Copley Square), on Saturday evening, 27 Nov. 1915; that the part

[534]

of Mary would be played by "Miss Shull" and of Warren by "Mr. Watson"; that the same pair of actors would play the parts of wife and husband, respectively, in "Home Burial"; that these two productions would be followed by a reading (by Mr. Watson) of "A Hundred Collars" and "The Code"; that RF would then read "Mending Wall."

41. RF to LU, 16 May 1915; *Letters to Untermeyer*, pp. 6, 7. In his headnote to this letter, LU incorrectly explains the reference to the *Masses* here by stating, "I took Frost . . . to meet my associates [in New York City]. He liked them. He refused to think of them as revolutionists; he considered them romantic rather than radical. It was more or less the way he considered himself." (Ibid., p. 6.) LU here makes two mistakes. RF did not go to New York City and meet LU's associates prior to the writing of his letter of 16 May 1915. RF did view revolutionists and radicals as romantics, but not "in the way he considered himself" a radical. He was particularly offended by the attempts of the *Masses* to condemn war.

42. RF to LU, 11 Nov. 1915; ibid., p. 18.

43. RF to LU, spring 1915; ibid., p. 5.

44. RF to LU, 8 July 1915; ibid., p. 11.

45. RF to LU, 20 July 1915; ibid., pp. 11–12.

46. RF to LU, 9 Sept. 1915; ibid., p. 14.

47. RF to LU, 24 May 1916; ibid., pp. 32–33.

48. RF to LU, 11 Nov. 1915; ibid., pp. 17, 18.

49. RF to Abercrombie; *Selected Letters*, p. 192.

50. RF to Abercrombie; ibid., p. 197.

51. RF to LU, 3 Dec. 1915; *Letters to Untermeyer*, p. 19.

52. Braithwaite's own discussion of his genealogy is cited and evaluated in Note 9 of Chapter 2.

53. The two letters, RF to LU, 22 Dec. 1915 and 1 Jan. 1916, are both in the Library of Congress. In the printed version of the first letter (*Letters to Untermeyer*, p. 19), the word "Braithwaite" is delicately substituted for the word "niggers." In the printed version of the second letter (ibid., pp. 21–23), the first paragraph is omitted without any indication of omission. Earlier (ibid., p. 9) LU as editor makes a comment which is pertinent here: "Frost was overly conscious of 'enemies.' Most of these were fancied and his animadversions were not to be taken too seriously. Any poet identified with 'the new poetry' was a potential rival and, hence, an enemy." Again LU (ibid., p. 31): "At this time his letters sounded many variations on the theme of foes and friends. I was, of course, touched by the evidences of a friendship which grew continually closer and warmer, and I was also amused by his mock fulminations against his enemies."

54. RF to LU, 1 Jan. 1916; ibid., p. 22. Jealous of all contemporary poets, RF had a knack for manipulating words ambiguously whenever he had to praise poems by his friends. One convenient ploy, a favorite of his, was to say he liked a certain poem because it "says something." For example, in praising LU's book of poems entitled *Challenge*, sent by LU to RF before they had met, RF said

of it in his letter of 8 June 1915 (ibid., p. 9), "The beauty of your book is that the poems in it all get together and say something with one accord. . . ." In his letter of 1 Jan. 1916, he praises a poem of LU's in Braithwaite's *Anthology:* "I read yours and liked it because it *says* something . . ." RF apparently failed to notice that three of LU's poems appeared in this volume of Braithwaite's *Anthology.* If he had noticed, however, he could have applied the same conveniently safe remark to each of them.

RF's jealousy of rival poets became a subject for conversation with Alfred Kreymborg during their first meeting in Amherst in the fall of 1917. Kreymborg, describing that conversation, quoted RF as saying, "I wonder do you feel as badly as I do when some other fellow does a good piece of work?" (Alfred Kreymborg, *Troubadour: An Autobiography* [New York, 1925], p. 336.)

6. MY VOICE AND MANNER

1. RF to Bartlett, [12 Feb. 1916]; *Frost and Bartlett,* p. 110.
2. Carl Wilmore, "Finds Famous American Poet in White Mountain Village," Boston *Post,* 14 Feb. 1916, p. 16; reprinted in Edward Connery Lathem, ed., *Interviews with Robert Frost* (New York, 1966), pp. 9–15. The passages here selected for quotations—particularly RF's conversational responses—seem accurate and in character.
3. Letter to the Boston *Post,* published in the *Post,* 17 Feb. 1916, under the caption, "Franconia Comes Back at *Post* Staff Visitor"; reprinted in Lathem, *Interviews,* pp. 15–17.
4. Ibid., p. 17.
5. An account of this episode is given in *The Early Years,* pp. xviii, 411–412.
6. RF to LU, 28 Feb. 1916; *Letters to Untermeyer,* p. 26.
7. Lathem, *Interviews,* p. 17; Wilmore to RF, 29 Feb. 1916; DCL.
8. See Note 15 of Chapter 2.
9. K. L. Bates to W. H. Dole, 30 Nov. 1915; WCL.
10. Although RF may have had difficulty with his performance at Abbot Academy on 13 Jan. 1916, it was well received—according to the report under "Abbot Academy Notes" in the Andover *Townsman,* 14 Jan. 1916, p. 4:

"The school thoroughly enjoyed the reading by Robert Frost last evening in Davis Hall. Mr. Frost read several of his shorter lyrics: 'Reluctance,' 'Flower-gathering,' 'Going for Water,' and 'Mowing,' the last his favorite of these earlier poems. He read also a humorous little poem, the Story of Brown and the Winter Wind. The most powerful thing he read was 'A Servant of [to] Servants,' a study of the tragic life of an overworked woman in the country. He read one or two unpublished poems and 'Mending Wall,' to illustrate his theory that 'tone' is the essential quality of poetry. It is a pleasure to listen to a poet who does not use the vernacular and yet makes real and natural our New England country life. He read as if he loved to do it, and at once gained the sympathy of his audience by his humor, frankness and very interesting personality. . . ." (Gratitude is here expressed to Edward Connery Lathem for gleaning and sharing this item.)

These "Abbot Academy Notes" contain the first-known reference to RF's public use of the "humorous little poem, the Story of Brown and the Winter Wind," later entitled "Brown's Descent, or, The Willy-Nilly Slide." This newly written poem was based on an actual incident told to RF by George H. Browne. According to Browne, the long slide over crusted snow had been made by a man named Goss, years earlier, in Ashland, N. H. For a description of the Frost material in the papers of George H. Browne, see "Plymouth State College Library Given Early Robert Frost Documents, Photos and Poetry," *Conning Tower Gleanings* (a publication of the Plymouth State College Alumni Association), Vol. XIX, No. 1 (Winter 1969), pp. 4–8. (Gratitude is here expressed to Thomas E. F. McNamara for his assistance in gathering information from these papers, particularly on the various associations of RF and Browne.)

11. RF's reading and talk in Lawrence, Mass., on 19 Jan. 1916, was reported in the Lawrence *Telegram*, 20 Jan. 1916, p. 1. The title of the article contains an obvious mistake: "Lawrence Born Poet Lectures: Robert Frost Talks on 'The Sound of Poetry' in White Fund Course."

12. Before RF gave a reading from his poems at Dartmouth College on 22 Jan. 1916, he talked on "New Sounds in Poetry." His visit was recorded in the personal diary of Harold G. Rugg, who was a member of the Dartmouth library staff and largely responsible for arranging this visit (DCL).

13. RF's reading at Exeter, N. H., on 26 Jan. 1916, was given a preliminary announcement in the Exeter *News-letter* for 21 Jan. 1916, p. 1, and was briefly reported in the *News-letter* for 28 Jan. 1916, p. 1.

14. For the Dartmouth alumni, RF read his New Hampshire poem, "Brown's Descent, or, The Willy-Nilly Slide." He and it were barely mentioned in the Dartmouth *Alumni Magazine* account, Vol. 8, No. 4 (Feb. 1916), p. 231.

15. An account of this unpleasant evening in New York City was given in the untitled bulletin of the Poetry Society of America, Feb. 1916, pp. 5–6: "The sixth annual dinner of the Society, held on January twenty-fifth, was in every respect a delightful occasion. . . . We have never given a dinner where a more genial spirit prevailed nor where the guests were more enthusiastic as to the speakers of the evening and the general work of the Society. . . . In the absence of Edgar Lee Masters, who was detained in Chicago by professional engagements, Josephine Preston Peabody spoke, in her always charming and interesting manner, amplifying the subject of 'Free Verse' . . . Gutzon Borglum, the sculptor, made a tell-

ing plea for the American spirit, the national note, in art, and Robert Frost, whose own work so well illustrates Mr. Borglum's idea, gave a thoughtful and suggestive talk upon Tone Quality of Poetry and its imaginative value. The evening closed with a reading by Louis Untermeyer of several of the parodies of contemporary poets from his volume [—*and Other Poets*] now in press. Those upon Edwin Arlington Robinson, Edgar Lee Masters, Robert Frost, Amy Lowell and Vachel Lindsay were given, and created no end of merriment. . . ."

16. RF to LU, 3 Feb. 1916; *Frost to Untermeyer*, pp. 24–25.

17. RF to LU, 21 March 1916; ibid., p. 27.

18. RF to Bartlett; *Frost and Bartlett*, p. 110.

19. Miss Jeannette Marks wrote to EWF, 18 March 1916 (DCL): "Mr. Frost arrived safely. He met with great enthusiasm despite the stormy night. And there was a splendid audience. He was good enough to come to my 19th Century Poetry Class the next morning and the girls had another opportunity to enjoy him."

20. This summary of the talk, "Having a Literary Moment," is based on two sources. First, RF's review of it, given to LT and recorded on 23 Feb. 1940. Second, George H. Browne's five pages of hastily made notes entitled, "R. F. Mar. 18 1916 N. E. Assoc. Tea. of Eng. Boston Pub. Lib." (Browne Papers, PSCL; source more fully described in Note 10 of this chapter.)

21. Source cited in Note 17 of this chapter.

22. For background, see *The Early Years*, pp. 203–209.

23. Unsigned article, "Poetry of Axe Handles Urged by Robert Frost: Sentiments True to Nature's Grain Are Advocated by Yankee Versifier Who 'Recently Arrived,'" Philadelphia *Public Ledger*, 4 April 1916, p. 11; reprinted in Lathem, *Interviews*, pp. 18–21. RF's talk at the University of Pennsylvania was entitled, "The New Sound in Poetry." It was also reported in the *Public Ledger*, 4 April 1916, p. 4, under the caption, "Other Work for Poets than Book Lore—Frost."

24. RF's reading and talk at Amherst College on 8 April 1916 was reported in the Amherst *Student*, 10 April 1916, p. 1, under the caption, "Well Known Poet Gives Reading of His Verses." An excerpt: "Robert Frost, the most recent of the prominent New England poets, gave a reading of some of his poems before a large audience in Williston Hall Saturday afternoon. Mr. Frost . . . showed a very real sense of humor and a poetic ability appealing strongly to an appreciative gathering. The author was brought to Amherst under the auspices of the Mitre and through the kindness of Professor Young. . . ."

25. Alfred Harcourt to RF, 13 April 1916; DCL.

26. This telegram has not been located, but RF repeatedly told LT and many others that the two quoted words were the essence of it.

27. Notice that RF made changes and adaptations, here, to suit his mood of discouragement and depression. The original lines occur as the first stanza of Browning's "A Serenade at the Villa":

That was I, you heard last night
When there rose no moon at all,
Nor, to pierce the strained and tight
Tent of heaven, a planet small:
Life was dead and so was light.

28. This is the earliest-known mention of "Mountain Interval" as the title for the projected third volume of RF's poems. RF's friend George H. Browne challenged the use of the word "interval" and urged RF to change it to "intervale." Weygandt defended RF's choice, and so did the distinguished geologist Charles P. G. Scott, who wrote to RF from Yonkers, N. Y., 7 Aug. 1916 (DCL): "The original word was interval." Later, RF wrote his own comments across the foot of Scott's letter as follows: "My old friend George Brown[e] of Brown[e] and Nichols School started all this by disputing my right to use the word Interval in the title of my book. He said the word was a vulgarism, of the 'Natives.' I wanted it, for its double meaning. I believe Emerson and Thoreau wrote no other. My neighbors spoke no other. . . . The dedication of Mountain Interval is but part of the controversy."
The dedication, to Mrs. Frost, is as follows:

TO YOU

WHO LEAST NEED REMINDING

that before this interval of the South Branch under
black mountains, there was another interval, the
Upper at Plymouth, where we walked in spring beyond
the covered bridge; but that the first interval of all
was the old farm, our brook interval, so called by the
man we had it from in sale.

Misleading, in this dedication, is RF's claim that he acquired his first farm—the "old farm" in Derry, N. H.—"in sale." He did not buy that farm. It was bought by his paternal grandfather, who eventually bequeathed it to RF. For details, see *The Early Years*, pp. 260–264, 275–276, 367–368, 573–575.
29. RF to LU, 4 May 1916; *Letters to Untermeyer*, pp. 28–30. It should be obvious that RF, in the gloomy self-lacerating mood which prompted the writing of this letter, counted on LU to sort out fact from fiction. RF did not have a "fourth book, 'Pitchblende'" completed in manuscript, and did not have "a fifth unnamed as yet."
30. Weygandt drove down to Plymouth to transport the Frost family to Wonalancet as soon as RF finished his week of giving classroom "lessons" and one public reading of his poems at the Normal School. The Plymouth *Record*, 15 July 1916, p. 1, carried the following announcement: "Several lectures by Mr. Frost, with readings from his poems, will be open to the community the last

week in July. To welcome back upon its teaching force a man whom many consider the distinctive living American poet, would be a unique privilege for any community, of whatever size, and we hope we are not too big to get into Livermore Hall when we get Mr. Frost back with us in Plymouth." The *Record,* 29 July 1916, p. 4, carried this further statement: "Throughout the week, Robert Frost, foremost American poet of this generation, is giving a series of lessons to Normal students upon the general topic, 'How to Get Good English into Pupils and Out of Them.' On Tuesday evening, Mr. Frost rendered readings of his poems. On Thursday evening he lectures on 'English Folks and Other Folks.' " (Gratitude is here expressed to Edward Connery Lathem for finding and sharing these two news items.)

RF, writing to Ernest L. Silver, 22 Aug. 1916 (DCL), mentioned both visits: "We've been home from Wonalancet long enough to have done something. But besides putting a few poems into a bundle for the next book we have done nothing. Lesley has done most of the work on the book. She's the only one of us who uses the typewriter well. I clarified a few ideas when I was talking at Plymouth. A book some day on a few such subjects as 'The Waiting Spirit,' 'A Literary Moment,' 'Composing in Things' and 'The Better Part of Imagination.' "

The best summary of the friendship between Weygandt and RF (including a good description of this visit to Wonalancet in 1916) may be found in Cornelius Weygandt, *The White Hills* (New York, 1934), pp. 231–254.

31. *Mountain Interval* was published on 1 Dec. 1916—later than Harcourt had planned. Of the thirty-two poems in *Mountain Interval,* at least twelve were written (or begun) before *A Boy's Will* was published in 1913—as the following itemized notes indicate:

"The Road Not Taken," discussed in Chapter 7, was relatively new: RF had begun writing it in England, perhaps in 1914, and had completed it in Franconia prior to his first public use of it on 5 May 1915.

"Christmas Trees" was written in Franconia on Christmas Day of 1915: "The poem was written, he said, on Christmas morning, and it was written on the spur of the moment." (For the source of this quotation, see the newspaper article cited in Note 11 of this chapter.) RF said this poem was written for use on a handmade Christmas card, each card to be decorated with marginal illustrations which the children were to make. They did not get far with the project. Perhaps the only copy completed in this form was the one sent to LU; see *Letters to Untermeyer,* pp. 20–21.

"An Old Man's Winter Night" was begun in Derry during the winter 1906–1907, perhaps inspired by a famous local character named Charles Lambert who lived for years as a hermit. For an account of him see the Derry *Enterprise,* 3 Aug. 1906, p. 3.

"A Patch of Old Snow" occurs in a preliminary form in a letter, RF to Bartlett, 22 Feb. 1914; see *Selected Letters,* p. 111.

"In the Home Stretch" was written in Derry, probably prior to 1909, and was first published in the *Century Magazine*, July 1916.

"The Telephone" was probably written in Derry between 1900 and 1910; it belongs with such a poem as "Wind and Window Flower." It was first published in the *Independent*, 9 Oct. 1916.

"Meeting and Passing" was inspired by an event which occurred in 1895 (see *The Early Years*, p. 205); it was probably written in 1906–1907 when RF was concentrating on the sonnet-form.

"Hyla Brook" was written, according to RF, on the Derry farm at some time between 1900 and 1910. It was probably written in 1906 or 1907; another sonnet-variant (fifteen lines).

"The Oven Bird" was written, according to RF, on the Derry farm at some time between 1900 and 1910. It was probably written during the sonnet period, 1906–1907.

"Bond and Free" was written, according to RF, at some time between 1896 and 1900.

"Birches" already discussed, was written in Beaconsfield, Buckinghamshire, England, 1913–1914.

"Pea Brush" was begun in Derry. It first appeared under the title "Pea-sticks" in the typewritten magazine compiled by the Frost children and called the *Bouquet* (July 1914), pp. 32–33. (See Note 8 of Chapter 10.)

"Putting in the Seed" was probably written during RF's sonnet period, 1906–1907; it was first published in England in *Poetry and Drama*, Dec. 1914.

"A Time to Talk" was written in Franconia in 1915 or 1916; it was first published in the *Prospect* (New Hampshire State Normal School, Plymouth), Vol. 11 (June 1916), p. 21.

"The Cow in Apple Time" was written in England and was first published in *Poetry and Drama*, Dec. 1914. (See *The Early Years*, p. 605.)

"An Encounter" fits into the bog-trotting days which produced "The Quest of the Purple-fringed" in 1896; it was first published in the *Atlantic* for November 1916.

"Range-Finding" was written in Derry, early enough to be sent to Susan Hayes Ward at Christmas 1911.

"The Hill Wife." In The Library of Congress is a copy of *Mountain Interval* which contains dates given by RF to indicate when he wrote each of the separate poems in this sequence: "Loneliness" 1905; "House Fear" 1906; "The Smile" 1913; "The Oft-Repeated Dream" 1916; "The Impulse" 1913.

"The Bonfire" was written in Franconia prior to June 1915; it was first published in *The Seven Arts*, November 1916.

"A Girl's Garden" was written in Franconia, 1915–1916.

"The Exposed Nest" recalls an event in the Derry period, but according to RF it was written in Franconia, 1915.

" 'Out, Out—' " was based on an accident which occurred in Bethlehem, N.H., in March 1910; but according to RF it was not written until 1915–1916. It was first published in *McClure's*, July 1916. (For background, see *The Early Years*, pp. 566–567.)

"Brown's Descent," written in Franconia, 1915, was based on an actual incident. See Note 10 of this chapter.

"The Gum-Gatherer," written in Franconia, 1915, was first published in the *Independent*, 9 Oct. 1916.

"The Line-Gang" is an experimental thirteen-line sonnet which seems to fit into RF's sonnet period, 1906–1907.

"The Vanishing Red" was written in Franconia, 1915–1916; it was first published in the *Craftsman*, July 1916.

"Snow" was written in Franconia, 1915–1916; it was sent to *Poetry* magazine on 8 March 1916 and was there published, November 1916.

"The Sound of Trees" was written in England, 1914; it was first published in *Poetry and Drama*, December 1914; then in the *Atlantic*, August 1915. (See *The Early Years*, p. 472.)

In summary, the thirty-two poems in *Mountain Interval* were written over a period of approximately twenty years. The earliest is "Bond and Free" (1896–1900). Eleven were written (or at least begun) in Derry (1900–1911): "An Old Man's Winter Night," "The Telephone," "Meeting and Passing," "Hyla Brook," "The Oven Bird," "Pea Brush," "Putting in the Seed," "An Encounter," "Range-Finding," "Loneliness," "The Line-Gang." Seven were written (or at least begun) in England (1912–1915): "A Patch of Old Snow," "Birches," "The Cow in Apple Time," "The Smile," "The Impulse," "The Sound of Trees," "The Road Not Taken." Thirteen were written in Bethlehem and Franconia (1915–1916): "In the Home Stretch," "A Time to Talk," "House Fear," "The Oft-Repeated Dream," "The Bonfire," "A Girl's Garden," "Brown's Descent," "The Exposed Nest," " 'Out, Out—,' " "The Gum-Gatherer," "The Vanishing Red," "Snow," and "Christmas Trees."

32. Obviously revealing is RF's hedge, "I don't want to antagonize anyone whose friendship won't hurt us." A good example of such hedging may be found in his earlier and later relations with Braithwaite. A few months after RF heaped on Braithwaite so much rage and insult, Braithwaite invited him to contribute a poem to a projected commemoration (in the *Transcript*) of the 300th anniversary of Shakespeare's death. Still bitterly hostile, and yet not wanting to antagonize anyone whose friendship might be useful, RF replied in a letter dated 21 March 1916 (MCL):

"You shall have the poem on Shakespeare if I can write it—and nothing said of pay. You rather scare me by asking for anything I haven't written. My faculties scattered like a brood of young partriges the minute you spoke. I'm ashamed of myself for being like this. Don't lay it up too much against me. I may be able to come to [in] time. Other redoubtable fellows will anyway from Maine to Indiana; so that Shakespeare shan't lack for praise nor you for material to fill your space. I heard good word of you at Mount Holyoke. These are piping times and surely you are one of the pipers." (RF did not write the poem on Shakespeare. For an example of an even more ambiguous letter to Braithwaite, see Note 16 of Chapter 11.)

RF accurately diagnosed his own hedging tendencies when he wrote of and to himself as follows: ". . . but give you a field like poetry that calls to the pulling of wires and the manipulation of ropes, to the climbing of every black reviewer's back stairs for preferment, and you are there with a suit case in both hands 'like an old stone savage armed.'" (*Selected Letters*, p. 229.) In a letter to Bartlett, 7 April 1919 (VaUL), RF returned to his favorite epithet for Braithwaite: "I have gone rather easy on the writing for the two years last past. Breath-weight had no choice in the matter of taking or leaving any poetry of mine for his anthology. There was none. . . . So that lets the nigger out. . . . Not that Ive absolutely stopped writing. I do a little and let it lie around where I can enjoy it for its own sake and not for what some nigger may think of it." (See Note 53 of Chapter 5.)

33. RF to Harcourt, Dec. 1916; *Selected Letters*, pp. 207–208.

34. RF to Sidney Cox, Oct. 1914; ibid., p. 138.

35. "The Amherst Idea," *Literary Digest*, Vol XLIII, No. 4 (22 July 1911), p. 140.

36. "'Dogmatism' as a Virtue," *Nation*, Vol. 94, No. 2448 (30 May 1912), p. 534.

37. In 1905 Eva Tanguay, a New York music-hall favorite, scored an exceptional success with her dramatic gestures of abandon made while putting across a song entitled "I Don't Care." Thereafter she became known affectionately as the I-Don't-Care Girl. RF became familiar with the song in 1906, and frequently intoned the chorus of it on various occasions when he cared more than he wanted to admit.

38. During the First World War, German shells hit Rheims Cathedral and destroyed almost all of the stained glass windows which gave it special fame. RF's use of this analogy may seem harsh, but it is characteristically puritanical.

39. The wordplay is made available through RF's deliberately phonetic spelling of the colloquial north-of-Boston pronunciation given to "unprincipled."

40. RF to LU, 24 May 1916; *Letters to Untermeyer*, p. 32. RF's pride in his own rebelliousness was best idealized for him by his way of admiring and interpreting Emerson's rebel-poem entitled "Uriel," from which he often quoted. Perhaps the best hint concerning the importance he attached to it may be found in "A Masque of Reason" (*The Poetry*, p. 485, l. 344), where the character named Job is permitted to paraphrase a line from "Uriel" and then to describe it as "the greatest Western poem yet." (See also Wilbert Snow, "The Robert Frost I Knew," op. cit., p. 14: "Of all Emerson's poems the one he [RF] cherished most was 'Uriel.' 'The greatest poem written in America,' he asserted. . . . To him it was a probe into the problem of good and evil expressed, as Frost liked to see things expressed, in 'low tones that decide.'")

Under oblique attack, in "Uriel," is dogma in general, and theological dogma in particular. Emerson, apparently identifying himself with the angel named Uriel, seems to dramatize his attitude toward what occurred as a result of the so-called heresies he uttered when he delivered the famous Divinity School Address at Harvard. He represents as noble and heroic the way in which Uriel boldly contradicts the conventional views of the listening dogmatists.

Even as one function of any true angel is to speak for and explain (or reveal) the divine plan, so Uriel is represented as one who corrects false notions concerning the natural laws of God. RF, viewing himself as a "sayer" who was at once poet and prophet, liked to place himself in opposition to the conventional blindness of man, and also liked to speak with Uriel's voice of haughty scorn, against those who misunderstood that punishing God in whom RF believed. (For later references to Emerson's "Uriel," see Note 35 of Chapter 13, and Note 6 of Chapter 21; for references to RF's fondness for viewing himself as a poet-prophet, see Note 33 of Chapter 8, and notes 12 and 13 of Chapter 21.)

41. The source of RF's familiarity with this statement by Woodberry is explained in *The Early Years,* pp. 474–475.

42. Ibid., p. 475.

43. Idem.

44. Ibid., p. 474.

45. RF to Bartlett, c. 5 Feb. 1916; *Frost and Bartlett,* p. 110.

46. RF to Harcourt, 29 June 1916; PUL.

47. RF to Bartlett, 8 Aug. 1915; *Frost and Bartlett,* p. 98.

48. Meiklejohn to RF, 16 Dec. 1916; *Selected Letters,* p. 209. The public announcement appeared in The Amherst *Student,* Monday, 18 Dec. 1916, p. 1, and contained the following: "Mr. Frost will take over two courses already begun by Prof. Churchill, a special Senior seminar on the theory of poetry and an elective for Juniors on the rise and development of the English drama. He will also work with a Freshman section in composition."

7. DEATH OF A SOLDIER-POET

1. Quoted from RF's poem, "To E. T.," *The Poetry,* p. 222.

2. RF to Edward Thomas, 17 April 1915; *Selected Letters,* p. 164.

3. Edward Thomas to RF, 23 May 1915; DCL.

4. RF, quoting himself, in reminiscent conversation with LT, 16 Aug. 1947.

5. The quotation is from the earliest known manuscript version: the manuscript sent to Thomas late in April or very early in May of 1915. This manuscript was purchased from Thomas's widow by Howard G. Schmitt, and remains in his collection.

6. Although RF apparently did not preserve Thomas's letter which first used the word "staggering," he did keep the one in which Thomas subsequently tried to explain and defend his use of this word. RF's letter which apparently challenged the implications of this word, as used by Thomas, seems to have contained the new title, first publicly used when it was read at Tufts College

on 5 May 1915: "The Road Not Taken." Thomas used both titles interchangeably in his defensive letter of 13 June 1915 (DCL), which contains this: "I ought to write about The Road Not Taken. I ought to search for the poem first among your letters. But I shan't yet. I am pretty tired. I must own though that it wasn't a very honest remark that of mine. For whether it was that I was deaf or that you didn't quite speak in verses I got the idea somewhat apart from the words. That is to say I thought I did,—the fact being that I got the idea as much as if I had skimmed the words, which I don't think I did. So at the time I was content to deceive you by referring to the poem when it was really to that idea not yet in the form of poetry which existed in my head after reading. The word 'staggering' I expect did no more than express (or conceal) the fact that the simple words and unemphatic rhythms were not such as I was accustomed to expect great things, things I like, from. It staggered me to think that perhaps I had always missed what made poetry poetry if it was here. I wanted to think it was here. I don't know what an honest man would have said under the circumstances. . . ."

(So far, in the letter, it is clear that Thomas is groping for ways to satisfy the request that he say more about the poem. Near the end, Thomas returns in a fashion which further implies his failure to understand that RF intended that the speaker in this dramatic lyric should be taken as Thomas or as anyone given to sighing over anything spilled.)

"I have found 'Two Roads.' It is as I thought. Not then having begun to write I did not know that is how it would be done. It was just its newness, not like Shelley or de la Mare or anyone. I don't pretend not to have a regular road & footpath system as well as doing some trespassing. On looking at it again I complain only of a certain periphrastic looseness in 'the passing there had gone to them both about the same.' [RF later revised the poem and displaced this "periphrastic looseness."] Also I hope that so far [you] have not found that you had to sigh on realising it had made all the difference, though it had. You don't wish you had been Drinkwater. Another trifle—the lack of stops I believe put me off a little. There. If I say more I shall get into those nooks you think I like. . . . I read 'The road not taken' to Helen just now & she liked it entirely, & agreed with me, how naturally symbolic it was. You mustn't go & exaggerate what I say about that one phrase."

7. Edward Thomas to RF, 11 July 1915; DCL. In spite of the cited evidences that Thomas did not get the intended point of "Two Roads" ("The Road Not Taken") until RF explained it to him, RF could never bear to tell the truth about the failure of this lyric to perform as he intended it. Instead, he frequently told an idealized version of the story. He told LT, for example, that Thomas immediately replied, after receiving the poem, "Stop teasing me." Some other pertinent remarks (by RF and by others) are here presented in the order of their reference to the chronological events connected with the writing and the reception of this poem:

(a) "One stanza of 'The Road Not Taken' was written while I was sitting on a sofa in the middle of England; was found three or four years later, and I couldn't bear not to finish it. I wasn't thinking about myself there, but about a friend who had gone off to war, a person who, whichever road he went, would be sorry he didn't go the other. He was hard on himself that way." (RF, Bread Loaf Writers' Conference, 23 Aug. 1953; tape recording made by George W. Smith, Jr., who lent the tape to LT.)

(In making this statement, RF apparently forgot that his Gloucestershire walks with Thomas occurred in the summer of 1914; that in less than a year thereafter—prior to the reading of it at Tufts on 5 May 1915—he sent an early version of the poem to Thomas from New Hampshire; that Thomas did not enlist until 14 July 1915.)

(b) "I wrote this one ['The Road Not Taken'] in England on a big fluffy sofa in a big house that belonged to a game-keeper. . . . You have to be careful of that; it's a tricky poem, very tricky." (RF, Bread Loaf Writers Conference, 26 Aug. 1961; recorded at the time by LT.)

(Although the discrepancy between "this one" and "one stanza" is apparently accidental, and although Abercrombie's rented home [The Gallows, in Gloucestershire] never "belonged to a game-keeper," there was a strong association between RF, Thomas, a gamekeeper, and Abercrombie. As context for that association, see *The Early Years*, pp. 446, 459, 467–468.)

(c) "Frost said that he wrote the poem 'The Road Not Taken' for his friend [Edward Thomas] and sent it to him in France, getting the reply, 'What are you trying to do with me?' " (Louis) Mertins, *Robert Frost*, p. 135.)

(d) "Thomas said about it ['The Road Not Taken'], 'What are you doing with my character?' And that was much more his character than mine." (RF. Poetry Center, New York City, 25 March 1956; recorded at the time by LT.)

(These two questions, not supported by anything in the preserved letters from Thomas to RF, seem to be variants of RF's idealized claim, made to LT, that Thomas wrote to RF, "Stop teasing me.")

(e) "Even here I am only fooling my way along as I was in the poems in The Atlantic (particularly in The Road Not Taken). . . . I trust my meaning is not too hidden in any of these places. I can't help my way of coming at things. . . . The best of your parody of me was that it left me in no doubt as to where I was hit. I'll bet not half a dozen people can tell who was hit and where he was hit by my Road Not Taken." (RF to LU, 9 Sept. 1915; *Selected Letters*, pp. 189, 190.)

(f) "The thing that delights me most in Frost's poetry is Robert Frost. It is his gesture & his slightly wry smile that lights up such a poem as 'The Road Not Taken.' " (LU to RF, 13 Sept. 1915; DCL.)

(Notice that LU's perceptiveness, here, occurred after RF explained to him the element of parody in the poem.)

(g) "You see, this is another of the issues: when shall you take a hint, at home in family life. Should you take a hint when none is intended? Or should you, with more sensitive nature, only take hints when they *are* intended? And that's so in reading my poetry. That poem ['The Road Not Taken']: there's a hint intended there. But you ought to know that yourself. One of the things I suffer from, you know, is being taken as intending a double meaning when I don't. Sometimes I do, and sometimes I don't. And I can't mark 'em [the hints]—there's no way of marking them. I have to leave it to nice people to know the difference." (RF, Wofford College, Spartanburg, S. C., 14 March 1950; tape recording, Wofford College Library.)

(h) "On one occasion he [RF] told of receiving a letter from a grammar-school girl who asked a good question of him [concerning one line in 'The Road Not Taken']: 'Why the sigh?' That letter and that question, he said, had prompted an answer. End of the hint." (Quoted from the "Introduction" to *Selected Letters*, p. xv, where RF's entire strategy of carrying himself dramatically, in a poem or in a letter, by assuming a posture not his own, is considered within a broader context.)

(i) One of RF's biographers, given the usual hints on "The Road Not Taken," fumbled them: "This was the cottage where Robert Frost wrote one of his most noted poems, 'The Road Not Taken,' which, at his public readings, as I have said earlier, he often introduces as 'more about Edward Thomas than about me.' Rightly enough, for Thomas, all his life, lived on the deeply isolated, lonely and subjective 'way less travelled by' which Frost had chosen in youth but had half deserted through the fate that gave him recognition at forty. At that point he faced, and wanted to, the more double and complex destiny of traveling both roads." (*The Trial by Existence*, p. 143.)

(j) "Sometime early in 1915 . . . Frost, although a married man, nearly forty years old, was then faced with an agonizing decision: whether or not to enlist in the British Army. He wrote a poem, 'The Road Not Taken,' which ended in a sigh at having chosen the more difficult course: resisting for his family's sake the passionate temptations of battle." (Robert Graves, "The Truest Poet," London *Sunday Times*, 3 Feb. 1963.)

(A more accurate reflection of RF's attitude toward the war, while he was in England, may be found in his letter to Sidney Cox, 20 Aug. 1914 [*Selected Letters*, p. 131]: "You must think I have been and gone to war for the country that has made me a poet. My obligation is not quite as deep as that. If I were younger now and not the father of four—well all I say is, American or no American, I might decide that I ought to fight the Germans simply because I know I should be afraid to. The war is an ill wind to me. It ends for the time being the thought of publishing any more books.")

(k) "Sir,—With reference to Robert Graves' tribute to Robert Frost, the poem 'The Road Not Taken' had nothing to do with, as Graves maintained, Frost's 'resisting for his family's sake the passionate temptations of battle' during the first world war. Five years ago, Frost allowed me to film him reading this poem for use on television. He then prefaced the poem with talk of when and how he came to write it. He said it was not autobiographical, that the 'I' in the poem was his friend Edward Thomas, and that the poem was prompted by the manner in which Thomas would weigh decisions before making them. That explanation by Frost exists on film and is in the possession of the Columbia Broadcasting System in New York." (Elliott Baker, letter to the editor, published under the caption, "Tribute to Frost," London *Sunday Times*, 10 Feb. 1963.)

8. Edward Thomas to RF, 15 June 1915; DCL. The atheistic views of Thomas, here hinted at, were frequently opposed in mild and teasing ways against the theistical views of RF and other "believers." See *The Early Years*, pp. 455–456.

9. RF to Edward Thomas, 31 July 1915; *Selected Letters*, pp. 184–185. Shortly after Thomas enlisted, he began to make arrangements for his son Mervyn to return from the United States to England. The boy visited the Frosts in Franconia during the summer of 1915, and Edward Thomas wrote to RF under date of 3 Oct. 1915 (DCL), "Mervyn likes Franconia." He wrote again concerning Mervyn, under date of 12 October 1915 (DCL), "I wish he could have another long turn with you. . . . Helen was willing for him to stay after December, but I might well be going out to France soon after Christmas & I should like to see him first." Mervyn was back in England shortly before Christmas of 1915. Edward Thomas mentioned Mervyn's return in a letter to Gordon Bottomley dated 24 Feb. 1916: "Mervyn returned just before Christmas. . . . We were very glad to see him safe at home." (R. George Thomas, ed., *Letter from Edward Thomas to Gordon Bottomley* [London, 1968], p. 262.)

10. John Moore, *The Life and Letters of Edward Thomas* (London, 1939), p. 243.

11. "Not to Keep" was first published in Yale *Review*, Vol. 6, No. 2 (Jan. 1917), p. 400; *The Poetry*, pp. 230–231.

12. RF to Harriet Monroe, c. 7 Jan. 1917; *Selected Letters*, pp. 209–210.

13. Helen Thomas to RF, begun 2 March 1917; DCL.

14. RF to Helen Thomas, 27 April 1917; *Selected Letters*, p. 216.

15. RF to Edward Garnett, 29 April 1917; ibid., p. 217. The affection between RF and Edward Thomas was indeed mutual. Eleanor Farjeon (*Edward Thomas*, op. cit., p. 38), in mentioning their first meeting, early in October of 1913, points out that Thomas wrote her saying, "I have an appointment of uncertain time with an American . . ." She goes on to point up the irony that Thomas, in this first reference, "did not name the American who was to become the greatest friend of his life."

16. RF wrote, under date of 18 Feb. 1918, to Wilbur Cross, editor of the Yale *Review*, "I wonder if you would let my friend George Whicher of our faculty write a paper for you on Edward Thomas.

Whicher is a writer of experience and a poet of quality himself who knows and cares for Thomas's work. I should do what I could to help him make the paper somewhat personal. Some time I shall have something of my own to show you about Thomas (it will probably be in verse), but not right away. These are overwhelming times. I feel as if my poetry and pretty much all the rest of me underneath a heap of jarring atoms lay." (YUL.) Cross accepted the offer. Under date of 13 Dec. 1918, Elinor Frost wrote to Cross (*Selected Letters*, p. 232): "Here is the essay which Mr. Frost promised you. He would write to you himself about it, but he is just beginning to regain strength after a very severe attack of influenza. He wants me to say that he has hoped to have a poem of his own to send with it, but certain lines in the poem are unsatisfactory and seem to him likely to remain so. But as he is greatly pleased with this essay, he hopes you will print it now, and not let his friend's memory suffer for want of the poem. This is the time for people to see it, while there is still some interest in Thomas' little volume of poems, and while there is so much interest in soldier poets in general. . . . I hope you will like the essay as much as I myself do. I think it has something of Thomas' own exquisiteness." Whicher's article, "Edward Thomas," appeared in the Yale *Review*, Vol. IX, No. 3 (April 1920), pp. 556–567, immediately following RF's poem, "To E. T.," which appeared on p. 555.

17. RF mentions LU's essay on Edward Thomas in a letter dated 17 Feb. 1919 (*Letters to Untermeyer*, pp. 81–82): "I can't say that I am not satisfied with the Thomas article. In our hearts we both wanted you to write it as you saw it. I'm credibly told that there's something about me the British prefer not to have mentioned in connection with Thomas. If so you will have bothered them by what you have written. They seem to think it must diminish their poet to have him under obligations to an American. And yet he knew and freely and generously said that it was not only in verse-theory but in inspiration that he was my debtor. Of course it is all nothing. But no harm in bothering them in their conceit."

RF had been "credibly told" by John W. Haines that the distinguished author and editor John Freeman had sharply rebuked Haines for saying in print that Thomas became a poet under RF's inspiration. Later, Freeman was persuaded that Haines was right.

LU's article, "Edward Thomas," appeared in the *North American Review*, Vol. 209, No. 2 (Feb. 1919), pp. 263–266.

18. "To E. T." was first published in the Yale *Review* (see Note 16 of this chapter). It was reprinted under the title "To Edward Thomas" in *American and British Verse from The Yale Review* (New Haven, 1920), p. [16]. It occurs in *The Poetry*, p. 222, under the title first used: "To E. T." Two remarks made by RF about his difficulty in writing this poetic tribute may help to throw light on his attitude toward using his private griefs as direct materials for poetry. In a letter to Wilbur Cross, 22 Nov. 1917 (*Selected Letters*, p. 225), RF wrote: "I have wanted to say a word to you to explain my failure to do anything about Edward Thomas. I find

he was too near me. Some time I shall write about him. Perhaps it will come to me to write in verse. As yet I feel too much the loss of the best friend I ever had. And by that I don't mean I am over-whelmed with grief. Something in me refuses to take the risk—angrily refuses to take the risk—of seeming to use grief for lit-erary purposes. When I care less, I can do more."

RF finished "To E. T." during the early summer of 1919. In a letter dated "July 1919" (ACL), to George Whicher, he wrote: "I am going to send you the E T poem to show you that it is some-thing more than a mere project. The truth is it is probably as complete as it will ever be. I'm not keeping it back to go on with it. Perhaps I can tell you why I have hesitated over it. Edward Thomas was the closest friend I ever had and I was the closest friend he ever had; and this was something I didn't wait to realize after he had died. It makes his death almost too much to talk about in The Yale Review in the hearing of Wm. Lyons Phelps even at two years distance. Just one little poem however ought not to do any harm if I'm sure of my motives in printing it—and I think I am. They are practical, non-sentimental and sufficiently removed from my impulses (not motives) in writing it. I'm one person in writing and I'm another or if cornered can become another for purposes of publication. I've about reached the point where I am willing to wrong whatever may be wronged by publishing this poem. Some part of an ideal is sacrificed to some god in every deed done and the old formal sacrifice of one child out of so many to Moloch was no more than symbolic recognition of the fact."

These austere prejudices are quite distinct from, and actually opposed to, Wordsworth's famous statement in the "Preface" to *Lyrical Ballads:* "I have said that poetry is the spontaneous over-flow of powerful feelings; it takes its origin from emotion recol-lected in tranquillity: the emotion is contemplated till, by a species of reaction, the tranquillity gradually disappears, and an emotion, kindred to that which was before the subject of contemplation, is gradually produced, and does itself actually exist in the mind." By contrast, RF's puritanical heritage, from both his parents, is re-flected in his insistence that the heat of passion and the anguish of grief could not provide him with the raw materials of art until after time and the artistic process itself had somehow cooled, refined, objectified the passion and the grief. Nevertheless, for evidence that he became justifiably impatient with anyone who claimed that his poetry revealed an essential frigidity in his nature, see Note 14 of Chapter 9.

8. THE AMHERST IDEA

1. RF to LU, from Amherst, 8 Feb. 1917; *Selected Letters*, p. 212. In this passage, RF twists words and phrases borrowed from Ecclesiastes 12:1 to help him mock a writing formula which was employed, he said, by other instructors at Amherst.

2. George F. Whicher, *Mornings at 8:50* (Northampton, 1950), pp. 34–35. RF's first visit to Amherst, here described, occurred on 8 April 1916. See Note 24 of Chapter 6.

3. Perhaps the most detailed source of information concerning RF's early years at Amherst is contained in a "Robert Frost issue" of the Amherst undergraduate literary magazine, *Touchstone*, Vol. 4, No. 4 (Feb. 1939). The description of the room in the Beta Theta Pi house is based on an article by Henry A. Ladd, Amherst '18, "Memories of Robert Frost," in that issue of *Touchstone*, p. 13, and on an article by Owen S. White, Amherst '18, "What the Lizard Learned," pp. 14, 31.

4. Henry A. Ladd, op. cit., p. 13.

5. Owen S. White, op. cit., p. 14

6. The Amherst *Student*, 26 March 1917, p. 6, carried among its news "Briefs" this announcement: "An innovation has been introduced into Prof. Robert Frost's course in pre-Shakespearean drama. Several plays have been abridged by members of the class for dramatic use and will be presented in College Hall. Prof. Frost concedes that this feature will aid the class in their study of the drama of the past. Among the plays to be given are: 'The Four P's,' 'Gammer Gurton's Needle,' 'Othello,' 'The Spanish Tragedy,' and 'Faustus.' " (For references to abridgements of Marlowe's *Doctor Faustus* and Jonson's *Silent Woman,* made by RF years earlier for use by his students at Pinkerton Academy, see *The Early Years,* pp. 360–364.)

7. "The Reminiscences of Gardner Jackson" (manuscript, Oral History Research Office, Columbia University, 1959), p. 73.

8. For source, see Note 1 of this chapter.

9. RF to G. W. Whicher, 23 May 1919; ACL. Although RF, in this letter, complains about the Amherst students and their subservience to conventional views, he elsewhere complained humorously about young men so immature that they refused to accept common-sense guidance offered by their parents and teachers. Repeatedly he said that his little farm fable entitled "The Runaway" (first published in the Amherst *Monthly* for June 1918) was inspired by students at Amherst; that it cast oblique light on one problem in education.

10. RF's account of this meeting was given to LT in conversations, and was essentially corroborated by a letter from Miss Mary Goodwillie to LT, 21 Oct. 1946 (PUL): "But now to Mr. Frost! I saw him first in the late summer of 1916—just after I had read North of Boston and had been greatly excited by it. I was at Peckett's-on-Sugar-Hill a few miles from Franconia. I walked down to the Frost house and said I was a friend of his poetry. They were all very friendly and I went back for the second time. I discovered that Mr. Frost was to read in Baltimore that winter before the Contemporary Club of which I was a member, so I asked him to stay at my house. Father and mother were living then, and they became great friends of his. The meeting of young girls of which he spoke was that same year. . . ."

11. Quoted from RF's talk entitled "Poverty and Poetry," *Biblia*, art. cit., p. [10]. Some closely related information concerning RF's extremely conservative social views may be found as context for his poem entitled "Good Relief" in *The Early Years*, pp. 593–594.

12. Henry A. Ladd, op. cit., p. 13.

13. John Erskine, *The Memory of Certain Persons*, p. 229.

14. John Erskine, *The Moral Obligation to Be Intelligent* (New York, 1915), pp. 3–10. The term "right reason" is here invoked because it conveys a weight of theological meanings which help to explain the motives beneath RF's anti-intellectualism. As used theologically, the term represents the individual act of placing self in accord with the belief that the world is reasonably ordered, and that the divine plan or design for it is benevolent. The term further implies that the virtues of submission and obedience to this reasonably ordered plan include a willingness "not to explore the secrets," a willingness to keep the "desire of knowledge within bounds" (*Paradise Lost*, VII, 95, 120).

Pope, in echoing Milton's usage of assumptions implied by the term "right reason," found his own ways of trying to "vindicate the ways of God to man" by disparaging intellectual curiosity and by asserting his so-called "one clear truth." These two phrases occur in Pope's *Essay on Man*, which begins,

> *Awake, my St. John! leave all meaner things*
> *To low ambition and the pride of kings.*
> *Let us, since life can little more supply*
> *Than just to look about us, and to die,*
> *Expatiate free o'er all this scene of man;*
> *A mighty maze! but not without a plan.*

RF found his own way to echo, in his own poetry, this Christian theme of right reason. His poem entitled "Acceptance" (*The Poetry*, p. 249) ends:

> *Now let the night be dark for all of me.*
> *Let the night be too dark for me to see*
> *Into the future. Let what will be, be.*

Another poem entitled "A Prayer in Spring" (*The Poetry*, p. 12) concludes:

> *For this is love and nothing else is love,*
> *The which it is reserved for God above*
> *To sanctify to what far ends He will,*
> *But which it only needs that we fulfill.*

RF's most extended poetic dramatization of his belief in the doctrine of right reason occurs in "A Masque of Reason" (*The Poetry*, p. 475) where God and Job hold a post-mortem in Heaven, and God is represented as praising Job for assistance:

I've had you on my mind a thousand years
To thank you someday for the way you helped me
Establish once for all the principle
There's no connection man can reason out
Between his just deserts and what he gets.
Virtue may fail and wickedness succeed.
'Twas a great demonstration we put on.

The pivotal word in this passage is "reason," and the word behaves properly, there, only when it is given heavy emphasis: "There's no connection man can *reason* out/Between his just deserts and what he gets." In this context, of course, the opposite of "reason" is "faith," and to the unsympathetic outsider the gospel of right reason may seem to be a doctrine of unreason. In defense, the insider may answer that it is a doctrine of accepting the divine reason, and of trying to place one's self in accord with it.

RF, having first learned the doctrine of right reason from his mother's teachings, permitted it to shape many of his attitudes toward the limitations of human reason. He also used this doctrine for purposes of buttressing his version of laissez faire, and of saying piously, "Whatever is, is right," or "Let what will be, be." By extension of these Christian notions, he could make a virtue of deriving various sermons from his Baltimore texts, "Let not man bring together what God hath set asunder" and "Let the rich keep away from the poor for all of me . . . I need them [the poor] in my business." (A convenient historical summary of the doctrine of right reason may be found in Douglas Bush, *Paradise Lost in Our Time* [Gloucester, Mass., 1957], pp. 37–41.)

15. Gardner Jackson, op. cit., p. 70.

16. Ibid., p. 66.

17. RF told LT, repeatedly, that RF gave to Meiklejohn enough information to justify the dismissal of Young, but that Meiklejohn, considering Young so valuable as a teacher, was not willing to dismiss him because of any peculiarities in his private life. RF's very strong prejudices against Meiklejohn seem to have been built on the foundation provided by this conflict over Stark Young.

18. Gardner Jackson, op. cit., pp. 70–72.

19. Details of this event, together with the titles of poems read by RF, are drawn from the unsigned article, "Professor Frost at C[hristian] A[ssociation]," Amherst *Student*, 5 Nov. 1917, pp. 1, 3. By this time—in the fall of 1917—RF was living in what was known as the Frank Wood house on Pelham Road. Another glimpse of the occasional ways in which RF gave hints of his deep religious preoccupations may be found in Walter R. Agard's article, "Frost: A Sketch" (*Touchstone*, op. cit., p. 9), "He taught me, more than anyone else I have known, how to enjoy the music of poetry. A group of us would spend the evening in his house on the Pelham road, before a blazing fire, listening to him as he read. 'Poetry is never poetry until it is *read aloud*,' he said. There was no display in

his reading, no attempt to create effects. He read as simply as he talked, with quiet emphasis; his 'tones of voice' were deep, caressing the words as if they were good friends; the music of the vowels flowed by, a strong, full current. One of his favorite poems I shall always associate especially with him: the 17th century 'Preparations,' in the *Oxford Book of English Verse*." The anonymous "Preparations," containing five six-line couplet-rhymed stanzas, begins and ends as follows:

Yet if His Majesty, our sovereign lord,
Should of his own accord
Friendly himself invite,
And say 'I'll be your guest to-morrow night,'
How should we stir ourselves, call and command
All hands to work! 'Let no man idle stand!'

* * *

But at the coming of the King of Heaven
All's set at six and seven;
We wallow in our sin,
Christ cannot find a chamber in the inn.
We entertain Him always like a stranger,
And, as at first, still lodge Him in the manger.

20. Jackson, in his "Reminiscences," p. 74, contrasts the attitudes of Meiklejohn and RF concerning enlistment: "Alexander Meiklejohn didn't want me to [enlist], argued strongly with me against it, as he did with others of my class, and other classes. Frost was very actively for it, urged me to go, and I did leave before the end of junior year, soon after we declared war, to try to get into the Army."

21. RF to C. L. Young, 8 Aug. 1918; WCL.

22. RF to G. F. Whicher, 21 June 1918; ACL.

23. RF to LU, 1 April 1917; *Letters to Untermeyer*, p. 52.

24. RF was always sheepish in telling to LT different versions of this incident. In the frequent quarrels between RF and his wife, indifference—or at least the posture of indifference—was one of her most effective weapons, according to RF, even to the day of her death. For an early example, and RF's comment on it, see *The Early Years*, pp. 232–233, 538.

25. RF to LU, 22 April 1917; *Letters to Untermeyer*, p. 53.

26. "A Way Out," *The Seven Arts*, Vol. 1, No. 4 (Feb. 1917), pp. 347–362. The first production of "A Way Out" occurred in the Northampton (Mass.) Academy of Music, on the evening of 24 Feb. 1919, together with two other one-act plays. The various phases of this production were covered in the Amherst *Student*, 3 Feb. 1919, p. 1; 17 Feb. 1919, p. 1; 27 Feb. 1919, p. 3.

27. RF to Bartlett, 13 Feb. 1917; *Selected Letters*, p. 213.

28. RF to Amy Lowell, 24 May 1917; HUL.

29. RF to Harcourt, 20 April 1917; *Selected Letters*, p. 215.

30. RF to Bartlett, 13 Aug. 1917; ibid., p. 218.

31. RF was so fond of Brown's cow story that he used it for purposes of analogizing in the "POSTSCRIPT" to one of his late poems entitled "Lines Written in Dejection on the Eve of Great Success"; *The Poetry*, p. 463.

32. There is no available evidence of when RF may have "neighed at night in the woods," but there is some provisional and circumstantial evidence that he may have behaved in such an odd manner during one of his many courtship-quarrels with Elinor White. See *The Early Years*, pp. 149–153.

33. RF to LU, 27 Oct. 1917; *Letters to Untermeyer*, pp. 58–59. The tug-of-war between RF's conservatism and LU's liberalism, at this time, caused RF to make a prophecy which is illuminating, even though incorrect. LU, in a headnote to this prophecy (ibid., pp. 56–57) gives an accurate setting for it: "Shortly after the United States declared war on Germany, April 6, 1917, President Wilson sent Elihu Root to Russia. Root's mission was to persuade the so-called revolutionary but actually moderate Kerenski government to wage war more vigorously than before. For a while it seemed that he had succeeded, but Root's efforts came to nothing when the Bolsheviks under Lenin took over the government by a coup d'etat in November, 1917. Within a month the new regime offered the Germans an armistice, and by the end of the year withdrew from the war." Then LU quotes RF's prophecy, written under date of 18 Aug. 1917:

"Let me not argue with you as to what Root saw in Russia to inspire confidence, but let me instead tell you what I think he thinks will happen in Russia and not only in Russia but in every other country in the world. I have very little in common with Root, but, though I come at things from almost an opposite direction from him, still my guess is his guess on this war. Middle class government, which is to say liberal democratic government, has won a seat in Russia and it is going to keep its seat for the duration of the war and share with us in the end in a solid out-and-out middle class triumph such as the Germans enjoyed when they marched into Paris. The lower class seeing nothing in all this for itself may do its worst to create diversions, but it will fail. This may be the last war between bounded nations in the old fashioned patriotism. The next war may be between class and class. But this one will be to the end what it was in the beginning, a struggle for commercial supremacy between nations. I will not guess further ahead than that. The lower class will kick a little on street corners and where it can find a chance in journalistic corners. But it will be suppressed—more and more brutally suppressed as the middle class gains in confidence and sees its title clearer. We are still surer of nationality than we are of anything else in the world—ninety nine million of us are in this country. I don't say this to discourage you—merely to define my position to myself. Live in hope or fear of your revolution. You will see no revolution this time . . ."

LU, commenting on RF's mistaken guesses, here, concerning what would happen in Russia, adds, "Robert was not given to prophecy . . ." LU would have been more accurate if he had said that RF was obsessively given to prophecy and to his belief that he had a gift for prophecy, but that his prophecies rarely came to pass. Another closely related example occurs in a letter, RF to Bartlett, c. 2 June 1915 (*Selected Letters*, p. 177):

"I think the war may end in five years in favor of the Germans. In that case Canada will join us to save herself, and all the British will steal away over here to live. North America will become the larger island of the English-speakers of the world. Maybe you don't see it as I do. But the prophecy stands. I wish I had been able to do it in ink, so that it would be more permanently of record . . ."

For some correlations between RF's fondness for prophecy and his poetic theories (including his theory that the poet is new priest and prophet), see Notes 12 and 13 of Chapter 21; see also the index-entries under the Frost subhead, POETIC THEORIES, in *The Early Years*, p. 626.

34. RF to Amy Lowell, c. 22 Oct. 1917; *Selected Letters*, pp. 219–220.

35. RF to LU, 7 Nov. 1917; *Letters to Untermeyer*, pp. 62–63.

36. Charles Lowell Young (1865–1937) became a pioneer in the teaching of American literature. For several years after his graduation from Harvard in 1893 he was an instructor in English at Harvard and Radcliffe. In 1901 he was appointed to a professorship in the Department of English at Wellesley. There he developed a course in American literature, years before the subject was instituted in any of the larger colleges. He specialized in the writings of Mark Twain, Emerson, Thoreau, Walt Whitman, and of his ancestor James Russell Lowell. His appeal to RF was heightened by his being a well-informed admirer of RF's poetry before the two men met.

37. RF's letter to Miss Fletcher, which has not been found by LT, is mentioned in RF's letter to C. L. Young, 7 Dec. 1917, quoted in the text.

38. The lecture was given at Plymouth Normal School during the summer session of 1916. See Note 30 of Chapter 6.

39. Professor Alfred D. Sheffield. For background concerning RF's difficulties with Sheffield in English A, at Harvard, see *The Early Years*, pp. 234–236.

40. RF to C. L. Young, 7 Dec. 1917; WCL.

41. RF to G. F. Whicher, 21 June 1918; *Selected Letters*, p. 230.

42. RF to LU, Aug. 1918; *Letters to Untermeyer*, p. 76.

43. Amherst *Student*, 6 May 1918, p. 1.

44. Ibid., 4 June 1918, p. 10.

45. RF to LU, 28 Oct. 1918; *Letters to Untermeyer*, pp. 77–78.

46. RF to LU, 4 Jan. 1919; ibid., p. 79.

47. One use of this saying, and elaborations, may be found in a letter from RF to LU, Aug. 1918; ibid., p. 75.

48. This version of the event, told by RF to LT, seems to ring true.

49. RF to Robert S. Breed, 2 Feb. 1920; *Selected Letters*, pp. 242–243.

50. Any detached and objective reader should be inclined to feel that RF must have put these words in the mouth of President Meiklejohn. They are completely at odds with the lofty idealism expressed in Meiklejohn's published writings, which reflect his strong prejudices in favor of state, home, church, and morality. RF's insistence that Meiklejohn espoused pacifism, during the war, can be corrected by means of a brief quotation from an address he made to the students at Amherst on Sunday 23 Sept. 1917, at the Chapel exercises which opened the fall term:

"Our people have gone to war. Why? Is it because they hate another people or would destroy them? It is not. Is it because of a desire to take something that other people have and keep it for their own? It is not. The reason for our fighting is a sense of danger; it is a threat against the kind of living which we think worth while. We fear a certain way of handling human affairs, of dealing with men. Our time for war came when that way of doing things came close to us, so we resolved to do our part in thwarting it, in thrusting it back.

"Fighting is negative; its meaning lies not in itself, nor even in the thing it would destroy, but rather in the thing to make a place for which the evil thing must be destroyed. Have we then kinship with our soldiers? Are we their comrades in a common cause? Yes, if we love the things because of which they fight. They would destroy the creed that Might makes Right . . . They would tear down a code by which a few, by cruel and mean deceit, can use their fellows for selfish ends. Are we their comrades? Yes, if with all our strength we try to see that justice is done and men are given fair play in human living." (The Amherst *Student*, 24 Sept. 1917, p. 1.)

51. The reader may speculate that the "immorality" RF was "in favor of," for his immediate purposes, could have been either slander or murder.

52. RF to Wilbur L. Cross, 15 May 1920; *Selected Letters*, pp. 250–251.

9. J E A N I E

1. RF to LU, 12 April 1920; *Selected Letters*, p. 248.
2. Rowell to RF, 29 March 1920; ibid., p. 245.
3. RF to Rowell, 31 March 1920; ibid., pp. 245–246.
4. L. Merriam to Rowell, 29 March [1920]; DCL.
5. The details concerning the terms of the annuity provided to RF and to his sister are given in *The Early Years*, pp. 274–275.
6. M. P. Tilley to RF, 12 Oct. 1916; DCL.
7. Quoted from Jeanie Florence Frost's account, in a letter to Rowell, 8 Dec. 1918; PUL.
8. Idem.

9. RF to LT, 21 Feb. 1940.

10. For source, see Note 3 of this chapter.

11. The West Pownal doctor was S. A. Bosmus; the other doctor was G. L. Sturdivant, of Yarmouth, Maine.

12. RF to LT, 21 Feb. 1940. RF further said that during this visit to Maine he spent one night in the home of the famous printer and publisher Thomas Bird Mosher, with whom he had corresponded for several years (see *Selected Letters*, pp. 46–47, 55–56, 74–75, 83–84, 96–97, 109, 129, 137, 139) and whom he had first met, in Boston, through their mutual friend Nathan Haskell Dole, on 10 Jan. 1916, after RF gave a reading at the Vendome Hotel.

13. There is no other evidence that Jeanie, hating her brother at this time, would have expected aid from him. Notice RF's later statement in this letter: "She has had very little use for me." See also *The Early Years*, pp. 518–519, for the context of RF's statement, "She and I always had unhappy times together, poor thing."

14. RF to LU, 12 April 1920; *Selected Letters*, pp. 247–248. It would be easy to misinterpret RF's attitude toward himself, his sister, and others, as expressed in this letter. From one viewpoint, his attitude might seem to reflect an inexcusably "cold and heartless" indifference for any sufferings other than his own. From that same viewpoint, it would be easy to pass inappropriately harsh judgments on related themes in two of RF's early poems, "My Giving" and "Good Relief" (see *The Early Years*, pp. 380–381, 429–432). It is true that he did possess the self-centeredness generally associated with the artist, but his motives for trying to be detached, here and elsewhere, were complicated by several factors which should arouse sympathy. As artist, he had developed his imagination to such an extent that his sensitivities—so much like some of Jeanie's—forced him into various protective strategies of retreat and of rationalization whenever certain forms of excruciation endangered or seemed to endanger his own precarious psychological balance. These strategies were closely related to those of his artistic theories which he had tried to explain in connection with the difficulty he had in writing his poem to Edward Thomas, following the soldier-poet's death. (See Chapter 7 and especially Note 18 of Chapter 7.) These theories, in turn, were tied in with what Theodore Maynard had misunderstood in calling RF the "Poet of Frost." (See "The 'Poet of Frost,' " *Literary Digest*, Vol. 66, No. 3 [17 July 1920], pp. 32–33.)

Just how much this problem of sympathy versus detachment bothered RF at this time is revealed in the similarity between the quoted letter from RF to LU, 12 April 1920, and the following letter to George F. Whicher at Amherst, also dated 12 April 1920 (ACL):

"I had rather you heard it from me than in round about ways from other people that my sister has at last gone clearly insane. She took the Portland police who picked her up on the streets for German officers who wanted to carry her off for immoral use. She didn't know me when she saw me. It seems as if the poor girl had tried being everything, pro-German, pacifist, internationalist, draft-obstructor, and seditionist as a protest against the war; only to decide in the end that nothing would do her feelings justice but going insane. I dont know that I blame her. I admire the courage that is unwilling not to suffer everything that everyone is suffering everywhere. She has always been a sensibilitist and has now gone the way of the sensibilitist to the bitter end. It is a coarse brutal world, unendurably coarse and brutal, for anyone who hasn't the least dash of coarseness or brutality in his own nature to enjoy it with . . ."

15. RF to LT, in conversation, 10 Jan. 1947.

16. RF to Rowell, 16 July 1920; PUL.

17. RF to Rowell, 27 June 1925; PUL. RF never did become legal guardian of his sister. In discussing his hesitation to become her guardian he later wrote to Rowell (4 July 1926; PUL), "As I see it the best use the money can be put to is to give her the comfort of feeling that she is not altogether dependent. Such comfort as it might be! Isn't it a wretched business? I haven't the courage to take hold of it nor the conscience (or whatever you call it) to let it alone."

18. RF to Rowell, 27 June 1925; PUL. Rowell handled the payment of Jeanie Frost's bills at the State Hospital, using funds provided by the annuity until it was exhausted. Thereafter, she became a charge of the State of Maine.

19. Elinor Frost to Rowell, 3 Sept. 1925; *Selected Letters*, pp. 317–318.

20. The visit to Napa is described in *The Early Years*, pp. 32–33.

21. Jeanie Frost to RF, c. Sept. 1925; the complete text occurs in *Selected Letters*, pp. 318–322.

22. RF was in Franconia, for his hay fever, at the time of his sister's death. Informed by the State Hospital in Augusta, he telephoned his son Carol in South Shaftsbury. Carol drove to Franconia and took his father to Augusta by automobile. They arranged to have the body sent to Lawrence, Mass.; they went from Augusta to Lawrence and stayed there until the interment took place. Jeanie was buried beside her mother in the Bellevue Cemetery.

23. John T. Bartlett, "Notes from Conversations with Robert Frost," c. 27 June 1932 and c. 8 April 1934; typewritten MS, VaUL.

10. TROUBLE IN FRANCONIA

1. RF to LU, 12 July 1920; *Letters to Untermeyer*, p. 111.

2. Details concerning this visit to New York City are given in *The Early Years*, pp. 284–286.

3. RF to Susan Hayes Ward, 6 Aug. 1907; *Selected Letters*, p. 40.

4. See *The Early Years*, pp. 341–346, 350–354, 567–568.

5. RF to Susan Hayes Ward, 13 May 1913; *Selected Letters*, pp. 73–74.

6. RF to Bartlett, 8 Aug. 1915; *Frost and Bartlett*, p. 98.

7. EWF to Margaret Bartlett, ibid., p. 95.

8. The Frost children were encouraged to begin writing when each was very young. Lesley started keeping a sort of journal, under the supervision of her parents, when she was approaching her sixth birthday. During the next three years she wrote more than 500 journal pages. All four of the Frost children collaborated in writing and illustrating several issues of their typewritten magazine called *The Bouquet* while they were living in England, and the last issue was completed in Franconia in 1915.

During the Franconia years, however, Mrs. Frost became increasingly critical of her husband because she thought he did not help his children with their writing as much as he should. Holden, in his "Reminiscences" (cited in Note 14 of this chapter) gives his own impressions on this point:

"Both Carol and Lesley, and later Marjorie, tended not unnaturally toward poetry. Perhaps Irma, too, although I never knew it if she did. Robert did his best to crush the poetic instinct in Carol and Lesley, perhaps for reasons which were not entirely clear to him, but which must have been in part a desire to believe that as his children they couldn't stand on their own feet as poets and therefore should leave poetry to him. There may also have been a feeling that he didn't wish competition from his family."

Belatedly, RF tried to make amends to Carol, on this score. For evidence, see *Selected Letters*, pp. 390–391, 398.

9. RF's jealous reaction against Elinor White's writing of poetry resulted in an obscure set of circumstances which are described in *The Early Years*, pp. 108, 504–505.

10. "Good-by and Keep Cold" (*The Poetry*, p. 228) was first published in *Harper's*, Vol. 141, No. 842 (July 1920), pp. 198–199.

11. Soon after RF gave Holden a manuscript copy of "Good-by and Keep Cold" he sent another copy of it to his friend Warren R. Brown in Amherst and asked whether the pomological details were correct. Brown, living near the Massachusetts Agricultural College and knowing Professor Fred C. Sears, Chairman of the Department of Pomology—also an amateur poet—sent the manuscript to him. Sears returned the manuscript to Brown with a note to the effect that while the pomological details were indeed correct the metrical handling of some lines was faulty, and that Sears had therefore taken the liberty of improving them. RF, instead of being angry, was amused, and often told this anecdote before or after he gave a public reading of the poem.

12. The two poems: "Stars" and "Home Burial." For more details, see *The Early Years*, pp. 258–259, 399, 546–547, 571–572, 597–598.

13. RF to LU, 21 March 1920; *Letters to Untermeyer*, p. 101. RF's humorous references to matters of religious belief were often misleading, and perhaps Mrs. Frost's irreligious taunts caused him to develop a self-protective habit of joking about such matters. One oblique explanation of this defensive manner was given by RF himself in a letter to LU (10 March 1924; *Selected Letters*, p. 300):

"Belief is better than anything else, and it is best when rapt, above paying its respects to anybody's doubt whatsoever. At bottom the world isn't a joke. We only joke about it to avoid an issue with someone[,] to let someone know that we know he's there with his questions: to disarm him by seeming to have heard and done justice to his side of the standing argument. Humor is the most engaging cowardice."

He might have added that he simply did not relish participating seriously in any "standing argument" between believers and non-believers, on religious matters. On this point, one of his often-repeated statements was actually a direct quotation from one of his early poems: "What counts is the ideals, / And those will bear some keeping still about." ("The Generations of Men," *The Poetry*, p. 80, lines 197–198.) He touched on the same point, obliquely, while writing to Sidney Cox in 1926. After urging Cox to transcend the argumentative, in classroom discussion, RF added (*Selected Letters*, p. 325):

"Mind you I'd fight a healthy amount. This is no pacifism. It is not so much anti-conflict as it is something beyond conflict—such as poetry and religion that is not just theological dialectic. I'll bet I could tell of spiritual realizations that for the moment would overawe the contentious."

Nobody was quite so contentious with him, however, on what he could or could not tell of spiritual realizations, as Mrs. Frost. Sometimes he tried to answer her and others, indirectly, in verse form, and one of these answers—a half-serious and half-playful countertaunt—pleased him because of its subtlety. Written in Franconia around 1917, in hendecasyllabics and unrhymed, it was at first entitled "Well" and then "Wrong to the Light" and finally "For Once, Then, Something." Under the second of these titles, it was sent by RF to LU from Franconia in 1919, in the following form (*Letters to Untermeyer*, p. 90):

> *Others taunt me with having knelt at well-curbs*
> *Always wrong to the light, so never seeing*
> *Deeper down in the well than where the water*
> *Gives me back in a shining surface picture*
> *Me myself in the summer heaven god-like*
> *Looking out of a wreath of fern and cloud puffs.*
> Once *when trying with chin against a well curb*
> *I discerned, as I thought, beyond the picture,*
> *Through the picture, a something white, uncertain,*
> *Something more of the depths—and then I lost it:*
> *Water came to rebuke the too clear water:*
> *One drop fell from a fern, and lo, a ripple*
> *Shook whatever it was lay there at bottom,*
> *Blurred it, blotted it out. What was that whiteness?*
> *Truth? A pebble of quartz? For once then something.*

In this deliberately ambiguous poem, the metaphorical overtones begin to accumulate with "taunt" and "knelt" and "wrong to the light." In the first six lines, the speaker implies that he has been taunted with the familiar insinuation that man creates God in man's own image: God is placed in heaven by the imagination. In the end, the speaker's use of the question, "Truth?" implies that he has also been taunted by someone's use of the skeptical saying attributed to Democritus: "Of truth we know nothing, for truth lies at the bottom of a well." In making his countertaunt, the speaker tells of an experience during which he caught a glimpse of something "beyond the picture, through the picture . . . / Something more of the depths." While describing this interrupted vision, he makes it accord with the Christian (and the Frostian) doctrine that heaven gives its glimpses only to those not in position to look too close: the word "rebuke" holds particular weight when tested within the framework of Christian doctrine. (For reference to the biblical imagery used elsewhere by RF to illustrate this element in his belief, see Note 24 of Chapter 33, where consideration is given to his metaphorical and metaphysical uses of his self-assigned epithet, "Synecdochist.")

Closely related to the playfully serious conflict between RF and his wife over questions of religious belief was his own inner conflict, caused in part by the skeptical side of his nature. Although his skepticism was genuine, it was often invoked as another means of protecting his religious belief from the criticism of others. Even his last book of poems, bearing the metaphorical title, *In the Clearing*, contained the opposed topical headings, "Cluster of Faith" and "Quandary," but his faith never had much difficulty in overcoming the temporary quandaries caused by his skepticism. That which apparently gave strongest motivation, and major support, to his religious belief was his obsessive fear of death. For evidence on this point, see Note 9 of Chapter 21; see also the subhead, DEATH, in the Index to *Selected Letters*, p. 621, and in the Index to *The Early Years*, p. 620.

14. Gratitude is here expressed to Raymond Holden for much information used in this chapter. The immediate quotation is drawn from his tape-recorded "Reminiscences of Robert Frost" (DCL). The event described in the text inspired Holden to write a poem entitled "Interval between Felled Trees," which he chose not to publish until after RF's death. (See Raymond Holden, *The Reminding Salt*, second edition [New York, 1964], pp. 108–110.)

15. The male guest then visiting with the Holdens was the sculptor, Aroldo du Chêne, whose associations are summarized in Holden's "Reminiscences":

". . . we invited to Franconia an impecunious sculptor named Aroldo du Chêne and his wife, a Scot named Eiley Hamilton. . . . [He] spent the entire summer [of 1919] with us doing heads of me and my children. The du Chênes returned the following summer and lived in a tent near my house. Aroldo had become interested in Robert and wanted to do a head of him. I paid Aroldo $100 to do it. . . . Robert used to walk up from his house almost every day and sit for Aroldo, with conversation coming out of him like a running brook. Robert liked Aroldo . . . a charming outgoing fellow and no trouble at all to anyone so long as he was provided with food, lodging and cigarettes. . . . Aroldo's bust of Frost—it was only a head—was done in built-up plaster on an iron core—an old piece of barn-door-hanger found in Robert's barn. It was a good head. Henry Holt and Company used a photograph of it as a frontispiece to a special edition of *Mountain Interval* [published in April 1921]."

16. "The Pauper Witch of Grafton" was first published in the *Nation*, Vol. 112, No. 2910, Spring Supplement (13 April 1921), p. 549. The inspiration, by way of Holden: William Little, *The History of Warren; A Mountain Hamlet, Located among the White Hills of New Hampshire* (Manchester, N. H., 1870), pp. 461–466, wherein Chapter II of Book VII tells of "a great lawsuit about Mrs. Sarah Weeks, whom foolish people called a witch." (As a pauper, she was chargeable to the town of Wentworth, where the counter-claim was made that she had once lived in Warren, which might therefore be chargeable.) RF's dramatic monologue, representing the self-characterizing speaker as a pauper "witch" in Grafton County, makes a minimal use of the story as told in Little's *History of Warren*. When Holden first read "The Pauper Witch of Grafton" in print, he could have found several reasons for pausing and brooding over these three lines in it:

> *Right's right, and the temptation to do right*
> *When I can hurt someone by doing it*
> *Has always been too much for me, it has.*

RF's various mountain-climbings with Holden provided the raw materials for another poem which is as oddly discursive as its title: "A Fountain, A Bottle, A Donkey's Ears and Some Books." In his "Reminiscences" (op. cit.), Holden gives the following information about the background for this poem:

"I recall walking with Robert through the valleys of Grafton County and over its mountains, he stopping often to look at and identify for me some plant or tree or bush that would send him off reminiscing about what someone had told him about the plant in question, or enlarging upon what it reminded him of. He would often go from the vegetable world to the world of human history, fascinated by the half-known, half-forgotten relics of New Englanders of an earlier day. We often searched—though without any positive direction—not particularly caring whether or not there was any reason for looking where we did—for the silver candelabra which Major Robert Rogers's Rangers were reported to have brought back from the sack of St. Francis and buried somewhere in the vicinity of Mount Moosilauke. . . . Robert often told me of the legend he had heard when he lived in Derry to the effect that the Mormons had once built a stone temple in the forest somewhere in New Hampshire, the ruined altar or font of which was sometimes stumbled upon by hunters. It could be said that Robert and I never took a walk without the sometimes spoken and sometimes tacit understanding that we were looking for that altar. We never found it. . . . The only reference to this romantically elusive spot in Robert's work is, so far as I know, in the poem, 'A Fountain, A Bottle, A Donkey's Ears and Some Books,' which appeared in the volume, *New Hampshire*. There, the Mormon temple is referred to as on Mount Kinsman, overlooking the eastern valley a little to the northeast of Moosilauke. I never heard Robert in conversation be as definite [on this point] as he is in the poem. In any case, neither we nor anyone else have ever found it."

17. Raymond Holden, "Reminiscences."

18. Ibid.

19. The association of these poems with this particular syrup-making occasion is based on RF's recollections as told to LT, also on the following statement in Holden's "Reminiscences":

"He had the habit, when he had finished a new poem, of writing out a copy of it in longhand, signing it, and giving it to me. I remember particularly the appearance of one called 'Evening in a Sugar Orchard,' and of another entitled 'A Hillside Thaw,' both of which were written in the early spring of 1920, after he and I had sat up all one night tending the fire and keeping the sap flowing . . ." Of these two poems, the first one published was "A Hillside Thaw," which appeared in the *New Republic*, Vol. 26, No. 331 (6 April 1921), p. 161. The other, "Evening in a Sugar Orchard," first appeared in print in *New Hampshire* (1923).

20. RF to LU [3 June] 1920; *Letters to Untermeyer*, p. 107.

21. RF to LU, 12 July 1920; ibid., pp. 110–111.

22. Raymond Holden, "Reminiscences."

23. Idem.

11. TRANSPLANTED: A NEW START

1. RF to LU, 11 Oct. 1920; *Letters to Untermeyer*, p. 118.

2. Dorothy Canfield Fisher to RF, 14 Jan. 1916; DCL.

3. RF to Mrs. Halley Phillips Gilchrist, 29 Aug. 1919; *Selected Letters*, pp. 239–240.

4. Unsigned article, "Robert Frost Reads Poems," Bennington *Banner*, 26 Sept. 1919, p. 3.

5. Madison C. Bates gave his recollections of house-hunting for the Frosts (in a letter to LT, 7 Feb. 1947; PUL) as follows: "In the summer of 1919 when the Frosts were planning to come to Vermont to live, it fell to my lot (I don't remember why—probably at the request of Mrs. Gilchrist) to take Mrs. Frost around in a car one afternoon to look at several farms for sale in the neighborhood of Manchester. (From all I could tell, Mr. Frost left the choice of a home to his wife.) My efforts as a realtor came to nothing; shortly thereafter the Frosts chose the little stone house in South Shaftsbury—Dorothy Canfield being largely responsible, I think, for the choice."

6. Again Madison C. Bates (in a letter to LT, 5 April 1947;

PUL): "The poetry Society of Southern Vermont was organized in the latter part of 1919. . . . In a letter I dictated in Manchester on January 12, 1920, this: 'Last summer we got Robert Frost to come over from New Hampshire and read from his verse, which he did very interestingly. . . . The latest news is that Robert Frost has recently been up here again looking for a house in the Fisher (Dorothy Canfield) neighborhood. However, he went back without either buying or renting.'"

7. RF to LU, 19–20 June 1920; *Letters to Untermeyer*, p. 109.

8. RF to LU, 18 Sept. 1920; ibid., p. 117.

9. RF to Lincoln MacVeagh, 16 Nov. 1920; JLA.

10. RF to Harriet Moody, 28 Dec. 1920; CUL.

11. RF to G. R. Elliott, 23 Oct. 1920; *Selected Letters*, pp. 255–256.

12. During 1917, RF published "Not to Keep" in the Yale *Review* (Jan.), "Locked Out" in the *Forge* (Feb.), and "The Ax-Helve" in the *Atlantic* (Sept.); during 1918, he published "The Runaway" in the Amherst *Monthly* (June).

13. RF to G. R. Elliott, 23 Oct. 1920; *Selected Letters*, p. 257.

14. "Fire and Ice" (*The Poetry*, p. 220) clearly represents deliberate compression. One example of how RF worked for compression, at this time, is provided by his way of arriving at the final version of his eight-line lyric entitled "Nothing Gold Can Stay" (*The Poetry*, pp. 222–223). Of the six known variant versions, the earliest was sent to G. R. Elliott, apparently with the letter dated 20 March 1920 (ACL). It contains three eight-line stanzas entitled "Nothing Golden Stays." The third of these stanzas was eventually adapted into the poem entitled, "It Is Almost the Year Two Thousand" (*The Poetry*, p. 361). The other two stanzas were compressed into the final version.

15. G. R. Elliott, "The Neighborliness of Robert Frost," the *Nation*, Vol. 109, No. 2840 (6 Dec. 1919), pp. 713–714. This article marked the beginning of the friendship between RF and Elliott, based in part on the fact that they shared religious views deeply rooted in puritanism. Elliott revised this article, and combined it with his others on RF, to make them one chapter in his book entitled *The Cycle of Modern Poetry* (Princeton, 1929). His unusual thesis is that John Milton set a pattern to which the cycle of modern poetry should return if it would redeem itself from its besetting weaknesses. (The last chapter is entitled, "Milton and the Present State of Poetry.") Because Elliott found in the verse of RF some exceptional puritan elements which he admired, one brief passage from p. 113 of his chapter entitled (with his native Canadian spellings) "The Neighbourly Humour of Robert Frost" is important here:

"Our poets should no longer allow the worn-out imaginings of the past hundred years to blur for them the supreme poetic vision of the seventeenth century. Whitman chanted at the close of our Civil War: 'Be not disheartened, affection shall solve the problems of freedom yet.' Milton wrote at the close of the English Civil War:

'Instead of fretting with vexation, or thinking that you can lay the blame on anyone but yourselves, know that to be free is the same thing as to be pious, to be wise, to be temperate and just, to be frugal and abstinent, and lastly, to be magnanimous and brave.' The first passage is the theme of nineteenth-century poetry; its social unreality is now glaring; it is a worn-out imagining. The second passage speaks to us, in our post-War era, like the voice of destiny close to our ear. Moreover, it is the theme of the greatest single poem in our language, *Paradise Lost.*" (For a glimpse of RF's admiration for *Paradise Lost,* see Note 14 of Chapter 28.)

RF privately subscribed (at least in theory) to the puritan ideal of conduct which Elliott there quoted from Milton. During his first conversation with Elliott, RF seems to have said that he was working on a poem which would reflect some aspects of his own puritan belief. As though continuing this part of his conversation, he wrote to Elliott on 23 Oct. 1920: "I am writing my Puritan Poem so to speak and expect to finish it by—and by." (*Selected Letters,* p. 256.) Although he seems to have made no further reference to his "Puritan Poem," he later sent to LU two essentially identical versions of an eight-line poem which does indeed reflect the ascetic puritan idealization of self-blame, self-abasement, and self-mortification. The first of these versions was placed in an epistolary confession (dated 7 July 1921; *Letters to Untermeyer,* pp. 270–271) which amounted to an apology for RF's recent display of self-centeredness during one of LU's visits with the Frosts in South Shaftsbury:

"No one put it into my head: I thought of it myself: there's that much good in me still, [—] thought [—] that's all there is. I mean there's that much thought for other people. The rest of me is swallowed up in thoughts of myself. All the time you were here [in South Shaftsbury] I read and read to you from my own works. You were partly to blame. You let me, to try me to see how far I would go in my self-assertion. You were stringing me, so to speak. You gave me all the line you had on the reel. And I took it. But there's this redeeming consideration. It did occur to me of my own motion though not until too late that you also may have had works to read from and were only diffidently waiting to be asked like the decent person you are. I'll be damned. It shows how far we can get along in our egotism without noticing it. I'm a goner—or almost a goner. The terrible example of others I could name I haven't profited by any more than I have by the terrible example of people I have seen die.

> *To prayer, to prayer I go—I think I go—*
> *I go to prayer*
> *Along a solemn corridor of woe*
> *And down a stair*
> *In every step of which I am abased;*
> *A cowl I wear,*
> *I wear a halter-rope about the waist,*

I bear a candle-end put out with haste.
I go to prayer.

"I shouldn't wonder if my last end would be religious; I weary so of cutting back the asparagus bed of my faults. I wonder what it is about prayer. I have half a mind to try it. I'm going to try to be good, if it isn't too late. . . ."

RF's "last end" was indeed religious, even as (with the influence of his mother) his early years had been religious. In fact, there was no period in his life when one side of his divided consciousness was not privately religious—even while the other side was very strongly inclined toward a self-indulgent and sensuous paganism.

His second use of the same puritanical self-abasement poem was made in another letter to LU written within three months of the first, but long enough after it to let RF forget, apparently, that he had already quoted it. His motives, this time, were provided by one of LU's poems which RF had recently seen and admired:

"Do a whole lot of poems like that[,] far from the question of love and labor. Leave the evils that can be remedied or even palliated. You are of age now to face essential Hell. Cease from the optimism as much that makes good as that sees good. Come with me into the place of tombs and outer darkness. When I say three begin gnashing your teeth.

"I'm in earnest. Just as the only great art is inesthetic so the only morality is completely ascetic. I have been bad and a bad artist. I will retire soon to the place you wot of [the grave]. Not now but soon. This is my last, my ultimate vileness, that I cannot make up my mind to go now where I must go sooner or later. I am frail.

To prayer, to prayer I go . . .

"Well, this was waiting for me to get on at this corner. Today was on the calendars a thousand million years before they were printed. I seem to smile." (26 Sept. 1921; *Letters to Untermeyer*, p. 136.)

These two letters and the repetition of the poem reveal the conflict between RF's puritanical idealism and his self-acknowledged egoism. This conflict is partially reflected in the self-protective interplay of seriousness and joking; in his juxtaposition of such statements as "When I say three begin gnashing your teeth" and "I'm in earnest" and "I seem to smile." But there are deeper self-revelations worth considering in these letters.

A different glimpse of RF's puritanism is provided by the sentence, "Just as the only great art is inesthetic so the only morality is completely ascetic." His use of the word "inesthetic" suggests some of the reasons beneath or behind his choosing to descend, in his poetry, to what he referred to as "an everyday level of diction that even Wordsworth kept above." (*Selected Letters*, pp. 83–84.) To RF, when in an austere mood, the only great art (as he here

[567]

defines it) is one which abjures the sense of the beautiful; abjures the purely emotional and sensational, in order to be more concerned with fact as emblem of the spiritual and the mystical. (See Note 23 of Chapter 21; see also Note 23 of Chapter 33.) His assertion that the only morality is completely ascetic provides a further glimpse of his puritanism. His context, here, makes the word "ascetic" mean an attempt to give effect to the quest for a purification of the soul and an atoning for sin by means of renunciation, self-denial, and self-mortification.

The same inner conflict may be found in RF's ambivalent attitude toward prayer as expressed in these two letters and elsewhere. Even in the poem itself, a hesitation is provided by the qualifying phrase in the first line. The ambivalence is heightened by his adding, after his first use of the poem, "I wonder what it is about prayer. I have half a mind to try it." Under stress, of course, he did try it, although there were times when he pretended that he did not. "I never prayed except formally and politely with the Lord's prayer in public," he wrote to LT in 1948. "I used to try to get up plausible theories about prayer like Emerson. My latest is that it might be an expression of the hope I have that my offering of verse on the altar may be acceptable in His sight Whoever He is." (*Selected Letters*, p. 530.) The same hope (expressed in almost the same words, which are adapted from Psalm 19, verse 14) occurs as the central element of theme in his poem, "A Masque of Mercy." That hope, as placed by him in that context, reflects his essentially self-abasing belief that wormlike man is so evil, at all times, that he cannot escape the deserved and eternal punishment of God, except by means of that eternal salvation which is provided only through the mercy and grace of God.

In later years, the pagan side of RF's divided consciousness caused him to react harshly against Elliott's cumulatively formalistic religious obsessions. (See *Selected Letters*, pp. 459–460.) On his deathbed, however, RF addressed his last letter to Elliott, and it contains this:

"Why will the quidnuncs always be hoping for a salvation man will never have from anyone but God? I was just saying today how Christ posed Himself the whole problem and died for it. How can we be just in a world that needs mercy and merciful in a world that needs justice. . . . It seems as if I never wrote these plunges into the depths to anyone but you. I remember our first walk to Harpswell together. . . . If only I get well . . . I'll go deeper into my life with you than I ever have before." (*Selected Letters*, p. 596.)

Anyone puzzling over RF's inconsistencies as they involved his religious belief might do well to start by working backward from this last letter. His fear of death, and his consequent "hoping for a salvation man will never have from anyone but God" would seem to lie at the heart of his need for religious belief. He liked to call himself an "Old-Testament Christian," and he clung to the almost primitivistic notion that God's wrath and jealousy could be placated through sacrificial offerings. Salvation from the fear of death, and salvation in a life after death, seemed all tied up in his thoughts with his hope that his own offering of poetry might be acceptable. Because RF subscribed to the puritan belief that we sinned all in Adam's fall, and that salvation did indeed depend entirely on divine grace, it sometimes seemed to others that he could easily accommodate the faults or weaknesses in his moral conduct by assuming these occasional and convenient postures of abasement, guilt, and self-mortification. His inconsistencies in these matters did not trouble him, however, as much as they troubled and puzzled others.

16. RF to Braithwaite, 4 Sept. 1920; MCL. The latter had written to ask for permission to use two of RF's poems in the projected *Anthology of Magazine Verse*, 1920—"To Edward Thomas" and "Place for a Third." RF begins his letter, "My dear Braithwaite: Of course I shall be glad to have you take the two poems for your book. . . ." Unable to resist adding a few prejudiced sentences of criticism, he continues, "It's a long time since I saw you or last heard what you were up to. I suppose you have been busy hailing English poets as fast as they come ashore. Still try to see an occasional American poet if you can in honesty—let me beseech you. That is to say, don't Medize [associate with the Medes] any more than you have to to keep up with the times. I say no harm and I mean no harm, as the song says in an anthology of yours I was looking over the other night." Then he added, in a third paragraph, the reference to Elliott's article and insinuated that it was more understanding than anything Braithwaite ever wrote about RF.

17 The first group of poems appeared in *Harper's* for July 1920; the second in Dec. 1920.

18. RF to Wilbur L. Cross, 15 May 1920; *Selected Letters*, p. 251.

19. This group of poems appeared in the Yale *Review* for Jan. 1921.

20. RF to G. R. Elliott, 20 March 1920; *Selected Letters*, pp. 243–244.

21. RF to G. R. Elliott, 27 April 1921; ibid., p. 248. In concluding this letter, RF added, "My chief object in writing this is to say I am to be in Augusta [Maine] Saturday [1 May 1921] and may call you [at Brunswick] by telephone." This was to be RF's first visit to his sister Jeanie after he had committed her to the State Hospital in Augusta. Instead of calling Elliott by telephone, RF simply went to Elliott's home in Brunswick. Elliott gave the following retrospective account of their first meeting:

"My memory is poor; but my wife helps. We think around May 1, 1920 was our first meeting. Characteristically he did not let me know beforehand that he was coming. I was holding a class in Bowdoin College. My wife was in our yard, at 254 Maine Street, when she saw him coming in the gate. When I came home, he and I talked shyly at first. After a while he said: 'So we two have found each other in the world.'

"He mentioned Jeanie at Augusta, but did not go into her case with me till we got to know each other better.

"I remember he wore a long brown overcoat; which he insisted on wearing when I took him for a long walk, despite my offer of lighter wraps—a sweater. The weather was quite mild. We walked to Mare Point [in Harpswell], some four or five miles from my house, on Casco Bay. There he saw [what he later called, in a letter to Elliott] the 'surfless shores,' for the Bay is protected by islands across its mouth. Only small waves would come up around the base of Mare Point—we did not go out far. The overcoat made him warm, and he opened it wide, letting it flop about. Thus, unintentionally, he looked Whitmanesque, or like The Romantic Poet. He seemed in excellent physical trim; robust; but of course you know how scared he always was of getting cold. . . .

"When I talked to him in a vein of Emersonian pantheism or rather immanentism, he thrust an arm up and out, saying decisively, 'No—God is outside all this.' I think he thus unwittingly gave me a boost towards orthodox Christian theology, which I was returning to, gradually, in those years. While loving Emerson, he ALWAYS criticized Emerson's lack of perception of evil and sin." (GRE to LT, 16 March 1949; PUL.)

(A similar account of this first meeting occurs in Elliott's typewritten and unpublished autobiography, "Deity and Teacher: Confession of a College Professor," pp. 194–195; ACL.)

22. The dates of these three private seminars at Bryn Mawr: 9 Dec. 1920, 17 Feb. and 10 Mar. 1921.

23. RF to Alfred Harcourt, 21 May 1919; *Selected Letters*, p. 238.

24. RF to Alfred Harcourt, 4 July 1919; quoted from Charles A. Madison, *The Owl among the Colophons: Henry Holt as Publisher and Editor* (New York, 1966), p. 123.

25. Ibid., p. 125.

26. Lincoln MacVeagh to RF, 10 Nov. 1920; carbon copy, Holt files, PUL.

27. RF to Lincoln MacVeagh, 16 Nov. 1920; *Selected Letters*, p. 226.

28. RF, in commenting on his poverty, and on the romantic wonders of his making a living from "nothing but poetry," frequently gave his accounts additional mythic qualities. To do so, however, he had to conceal (as he here conceals from Elliott) the fact that, since 1898, he had been protected from poverty by his paternal grandfather. See Note 20 of Chapter 22.

29. RF to G. R. Elliott, 16 Nov. 1920; *Selected Letters*, p. 259.

12. EXPLORATIONS

1. RF to Wilfred E. Davison, 19 Dec. 1920; *Selected Letters*, p. 261.

2. Ridgely Torrence to Harriet Moody; ibid., p. 236 (headnote).

3. RF to Harriet Moody, 21 April 1919; ibid., p. 236.

4. RF to Ridgely Torrence, 26 Oct. 1920; ibid., pp. 257–258.

5. Walter Havighurst, *The Miami Years: 1809–1959* (New York, 1959), pp. 190–192.

6. RF to Percy MacKaye; here quoted from ibid., pp. 195–196.

7. RF to Wilfred E. Davison, 19 Dec. 1920; *Selected Letters*, p. 261.

8. RF to Wilfred E. Davison, 27 Dec. 1920; ibid., p. 261.

9. A transcript of Davison's diary-like record of this visit was made and preserved by Professor Reginald L. Cook; MCL. The original seems to be lost.

10. RF to LU, 19 Jan. 1921: "Will you lend me exactly $150 for approximately three months? I believe you will, you generous soul; so I would be safe in thanking you in advance . . ." (*Letters to Untermeyer*, p. 125.)

11. RF to Harriet Moody, 20 Jan. 1921; *Selected Letters*, p. 262.

12. RF (Lesley Frost acting as amanuensis) to LU; original, Library of Congress. (See *Letters to Untermeyer*, p. 126, where "Braithwaite" is substituted for "Nigger.")

13. RF to LU, 8 Feb. [1921]; *Letters to Untermeyer*, p. 96.

14. RF to Hamlin Garland, 4 Feb. 1921; *Selected Letters*, pp. 265–266.

15. *The Early Years*, p. 476.

16. Ibid., p. 475.

17. RF to Harriet Moody, 21 April 1919; *Selected Letters*, p. 236.

18. RF to Harriet Moody, 20 Jan. 1921; ibid., p. 262.

19. An article in the New York *Times* for Wednesday, 2 March, 1921 (p. 8, col. 8), entitled, "HOWELLS EULOGIZED AS MAN AND AUTHOR," begins, "William Dean Howells was eulogized as a man and a writer at a meeting yesterday of the American Academy of Arts and Letters and the National Institute of Arts and Letters in the Stuart Gallery of the New York Public Library, which was attended by some of the best-known figures in national artistic life. . . ." The article is devoted largely to a tribute sent from England by Rudyard Kipling. No reference to RF occurs in the article, and there is no certain evidence that he did attend the meeting.

20. For nine days, from the 16th through the 24th of Feb. 1921, RF and EWF stayed at the apartment of Mrs. Harriet Moody, 107 Waverly Place, New York City; from there, RF went to Bryn Mawr College to give the second of his three seminars on writing, on the 17th of Feb.

21. On 9 March 1921, RF gave a talk at Princeton University; on 10 March, he gave his third seminar at Bryn Mawr.

22. Mr. Robert W. Cumberland of Collins Bay, Ontario, Canada, in five letters to LT, written in 1967, was extremely helpful in providing information concerning the two weeks RF spent at Queens University, Kingston, Ontario, in March of 1921. The following passage is quoted from one of these letters, with the permission of Mr. Cumberland:

"When I was a freshman in 1921 at Queens University . . . Robert Frost was the guest of the University and spent some time with the students discussing his theories concerning poetry. I was

NOTES

especially interested in this because he seemed to be succeeding where Wordsworth had failed. He puzzled and fascinated me also because in that part of rural Ontario where I had grown up there were many people of New England origin. He used the same idiom, and, knowing then very little of his background or degree of sophistication, I did not realize what a complicated person he was.

"In the spring of 1921 I was fortunate enough to win the University Poetry Award. Robert Frost was one of the judges and the circumstance of the award was of interest to me later when I learned more about his poetry . . .

"Before the award was made, Robert Frost discussed several of the poems which he had already read and I enjoyed the secret of knowing that . . . [my poem] seemed to have his strong support. . . .

"The winning of the award had a lasting effect on my future; for, though I did not write much more verse, it brought me important University contacts with staff and students, which led to much that I had not anticipated as well as to lasting friendships . . . if it had not been for Robert Frost, I would probably have gone back to raising chickens instead of becoming a teacher. 'Men work together . . . Whether they work together or apart.' "

23. Paul Elmer More to Alice More, 10 March 1921; Arthur Hazard Dakin, *Paul Elmer More* (Princeton, 1960), pp. 192–193.

24. Paul Elmer More, *A Century of Indian Epigrams, Chiefly from the Sanskrit of Bhartrihari* (Boston, 1898), pp. 14–15.

25. Monist and dualist are terms used by RF in ways which imply his remembering them from a philosophy course he took at Harvard, under George Santayana, in the fall of 1898. (See *The Early Years*, pp. 243–246.) RF said repeatedly that he was a dualist in his thinking and a monist in his wishing.

26. One of the largest and most useful collections of primary and secondary materials on the life and works of RF is still being formed and is in the process of being given to the Middlebury College Library by Mrs. Corinne Tennyson Davids, of Manchester, Vt., "to commemorate the friendship of Robert Frost and Wales Monroe Hawkins (1897–1928)." Over a period of thirty-one years, Mrs. Davids has been of much help to LT in the task of gathering information especially on RF's years in South Shaftsbury, and has often been thanked by LT for being one of his collaborators.

27. Grateful acknowledgment is here made to three members of the Monroe-Hawkins families for information concerning the friendship between RF and Charles A. Monroe (1876–1943): to his daughters, Mrs. Jane Monroe Curcuruto and Mrs. Elizabeth Monroe Riley, who jointly provided clippings and copies of twelve letters from RF to their father; to Mr. Anson S. Hawkins, nephew of Charles Monroe, who generously devoted much time to searching the files of the Bennington *Banner* to find and share with LT articles by Monroe and articles about RF.

28. "Frost is fond of bees, and he had a hive supported on a window-ledge just outside one of his living-room windows. The side of the hive nearest the house was walled with glass, and I

remember standing in the room with him watching the bees at work and listening to him talk about them." (Professor Madison C. Bates, Rutgers University Branch in Newark, New Jersey, to LT, 7 Feb. 1947; PUL.)

29. RF to LU, 8 Aug. 1921; *Letters to Untermeyer*, p. 133.

30. RF, sharing his wife's dislike of Sinclair Lewis's *Main Street*, mentioned the novel repeatedly in letters to LU at this time. For example: "Honestly now I'll bet you have kidded yourself into thinking the Foreword to Main St. an ironic delicacy. Out here in the country we think the illusion to Cannibal invading Carthage to enthrown the Corner Grocer on the Sugar Barrel is the Sage Cheese. For Gods sake don't *you* set up next as an authority on what ought to be done to protect small towns from the ravages of sympathetic measles. . . . Small towns do buy books: so what in Hell are the writers kicking about? Count me as in favor of reforming a whole lot of things downward. I keep hearing of Lewis wanting to better small town people. I'm for bettering or battering them back where they belong. Too many of them get to college [to their detriment]. . . . I went free from the Little Collegers like Sinclair Lewis ages ago." (15 April 1921; *Letters to Untermeyer*, pp. 127–128.)

31. Paul Waitt, "America's Great Poet Revels in Beauties of Old Vermont," Boston *Traveler*, 11 April 1921, p. 6.

32. RF to Raymond Holden, 17 July 1921, *Selected Letters*, p. 273.

33. The letter of 17 July 1921 also contains this: "In New York last week it came to my knowledge that Madam Nutt's receivers on representation of hers had made a claim to all the royalties I have ever had from Henry Holt and Co. It is at most a joke or a formality, I think I can say. We are perfectly safe. The law has been covered. Still for fear there should be an attempt made on me for what could be scared out of me I should like it better if the property you bought of me last year stood properly in your name. It would put us all in an awkward position to have them attach it. So please have Mr. Parker make out the deed for me to sign. That's what I sent you the old deed for. (You got it all right, I think you said.)"

When RF states, in this letter, "The law has been covered," he is referring to the manner in which Henry Holt and Company acquired legal copyright of *A Boy's Will* and *North of Boston* from the firm of David Nutt and Company. On 19 Feb. 1915—the day before the actual publication date of *North of Boston*—the firm of Holt sent the firm of Nutt a cable ordering 200 additional sheets of the English edition of *North of Boston*. (The first order had been for 150 sheets.) Nutt made no immediate reply.

On 17 March 1915, Alfred Harcourt wrote to RF, ". . . we have been out of 'North of Boston' practically ever since the day of publication, February 20th. We have had no reply to our cable of February 19th to David Nutt ordering a further supply or to our letter of the same date to them. In this situation, in order to protect your interests from piracy, rumors of which we hear, we are proceeding to set up 'North of Boston' and 'A Boy's Will' and hope to be able to have our edition of this on the market by the first of April." The same information was sent to Nutt by Holt in a letter dated 23 March 1915, together with an offer to pay Nutt 10 per cent royalty on the net price of $1.25 for all copies printed and sold in the United States. Nutt made no reply.

On 4 Aug. 1915, a legal advisor for Holt reported that a study had been made of RF's contract with David Nutt and Company, for *A Boy's Will;* that the contract stated that Nutt would print 1,000 copies of *A Boy's Will* and would pay a royalty of 12 per cent on all copies sold after the sale of the first 250 copies; that accounts would be made annually to 31 December, and rendered within two months of the date of make up, and the balance paid six weeks later. The legal advisor for Holt stated that because the firm of David Nutt and Company had never rendered any account to RF and had never paid him any royalties on *A Boy's Will* (for which there was this contract dated 16 Dec. 1912) or on *North of Boston* (for which there was no contract) RF was under no further obligation to Nutt.

A letter to Nutt was prepared for RF's signature, under date of 28 Sept. 1915, and it contained the following: "You have failed to render any account to me, and to pay any royalties due to me from the publication of my books . . . In the event of your failure to comply with this request within 60 days from date, I shall consider myself discharged from any further obligations under my agreement." No account was rendered by Nutt.

Another letter to Nutt was prepared for RF's signature, under date of 7 April 1916, as follows: "In view of the fact that you have failed to comply with the demands for an accounting and payments due me contained in my letter to you dated September 28, 1915, with reference to my books 'A Boy's Will' and 'North of Boston' you are hereby notified that all my obligations under my contract with you dated December 16, 1912 and also your rights thereunder are at an end." RF added a postscript, and the letter was retyped for his signature, with this addition: "P. S. I don't like writing this sort of letter. Won't you return my contract and I'll waive my claims for royalty on copies you've sold? Perhaps I'd even let you sell, free of royalty, the stock you now have on hand if you will tell me just what it is[,] naming the number of sheets and bound [copies] separately." The matter ended here. Mrs. M. L. Nutt was "adjudged bankrupt" on 8 June 1921. (Documents here cited are in the copyright file of Holt, Rinehart and Winston, New York City, and are here used with the permission of Alfred C. Edwards, to whom gratitude is here expressed for this and other assistance. For details on what happened, eventually, to the remainder copies of the English editions of *A Boy's Will* and *North of Boston,* see Note 14 of Chapter 15.

34. This summary of RF's first talk at Bread Loaf School of English, in July of 1921, is a close paraphrase of his own sum-

mary, written to George F. Whicher, 8 Feb. 1922; *Selected Letters,* pp. 275–276.

35. RF to LT, repeatedly. The record bears out this part of the story: RF was indeed absent from the Bread Loaf School of English in 1922, although he passed (or by-passed) it during an aberration from his Long Trail hike that summer. See Chapter 14, p. 194.

36. Unsigned article, "Frost Goes West of Boston," *Christian Science Monitor,* 4 Oct. 1921, p. 4. With this article is a panoramic photograph with the caption, "The Franconia Mountains, the view from Robert Frost's New Hampshire home."

13. THE MICHIGAN FELLOWSHIP

1. RF to Percy Mackaye, 16 July 1921; *Selected Letters,* p. 272.
2. Idem.
3. The Honorable Chase Salmon Osborn, a former governor of Michigan, donor of the fellowship honorarium of $5,000, was a member of the Board of Regents at the University of Michigan.
4. RF to M. L. Burton, 7 July 1921; *Selected Letters,* pp. 269–270.
5. M. L. Burton to RF, 29 July 1921; *Selected Letters,* p. 273.
6. Unforeseen by RF, in these calculations, were the demands made on him from beyond the campus. Before the fall term ended, he gave readings and talks in Oshkosh and Madison, Wisconsin, at several gatherings in Chicago, and in Detroit. Early in January of 1922 he gave readings at Ohio State University in Columbus, and before a women's club in Terre Haute, Indiana. Terre Haute was known to RF as the home town of the socialist leader and presidential candidate, Eugene Victor Debs, jailed in 1918. He was pardoned by President Harding on Christmas Day of 1921— shortly before this visit, concerning which RF gave the following public account:

"I don't suppose women's clubs know how poor they are in the estimation of some of my friends. They think just about the same of women's clubs as they think of Rotary Clubs—I'm betraying them to you. When I get with that kind of people, I feel like telling them about what happened to me in 'Terre Hut.' (That's what the conductor called it. . . .) Well, I went to Terre Hut. Once on a time I knew only the poor farmers in New Hampshire; lately I've sort of travelled. Before I read to the club there, I was asked what I'd like to see before sentence was pronounced on me by the women's club. I said I'd like to see Eugene Debs. (I thought that would blast them; they were all bankers' wives and such.) They looked at each other regretfully.

" 'Why, you must see him. But you know, he's very ill.'

"I said, 'I wouldn't want to disturb him. My idea was to disturb you.'

"And they said, 'Disturb us?'

"I said, 'I supposed he was an enemy of society.'

"And they said, 'Why, I suppose so.'

"And I said, 'I suppose he ruined your city.'

"They said, 'Well, he has done a good deal of harm, but he's such a nice person. We've just been singing carols to him.'

"There you are again—just as much blended generosity and largeness as you'd want to see anywhere—in Terre Hut, in the poor Middle West. One of my friends [Untermeyer] jokes, 'East is East and West is West, but the Middle West is terrible.' There's no argument to it. You can't generalize." (RF, "Poverty and Poetry," *Biblia,* art. cit., p. [13].

7. An early reflection of Tilley's admiring visits with RF in Franconia may be found in M. P. Tilley, "Notes from Conversations with Robert Frost," the *Inlander,* Vol. 20, No. 1 (Nov. 1917), pp. 3–8; reprinted in Lathem, *Interviews,* pp. 22–26.

8. "The children (bless their bobbed heads) are on our side and only need a little encouragement . . ." (RF to LU, 20 March 1922; *Letters to Untermeyer,* p. 145). One of the editors of *Whimsies,* the poet Ruth Lechlitner (later Mrs. Paul Corey), correctly noticed in a reminiscence that RF responded to the attractiveness of some of these girls with bobbed hair. Describing an unexpected visit she paid, with a classmate, at the Frosts' home, she wrote:

"We timidly knocked at the door of the Frost residence. Robert, in a well-worn grey sweater, opened it to us. He greeted me cordially, but his interest was obviously in Dee, an unusually pretty girl, and one of the first to have her hair cut in a short, curled 'bob.' Moreover, she had fastened her knickers well above the knee, displaying a pair of very shapely legs. I saw Frost's swift downward glance, and an elfish glint in his eye. At this, I think I liked him better than I had at any time before. In the livingroom, he introduced us to Mrs. Frost, a slim, handsome, unsmiling woman, who sat apart and said almost nothing during our brief visit. Frost addressed himself mostly to my good-looking friend. He asked her about Campus social life: dating, what the boys she went out with were like, etc. He talked about football—did we think Ann Arbor had a winning team this year [1921]? We did, especially because of Harry Kipke, Michigan's 'sensational' halfback. . . ." (From a letter, Mrs. Ruth Lechlitner Corey to Dorothy L. Tyler, 29 Nov. 1963; quoted with permission from sender and recipient, to both of whom grateful acknowledgment is here made.)

9. Unsigned article, "Robert Frost Outlines Artistic Aims before Audience at Union Reception," Michigan *Daily,* 16 Nov. 1921, p. 1. This article, in summarizing the most serious part of RF's talk at the reception, quotes him as follows: "The poet said, 'I have been hunting all my life, through all the years when I have visited. A friend of mine, J. C. Squire, the editor of England's foremost literary magazine, the *Mercury,* will be in Ann Arbor next week and he will be looking for what I have long been searching for: an intellectual enterprise among the rising generation of America that will make our great cities the intellectual and artistic centers

of the world. The great test of a college student's character is found when we know the sort of work for which he will neglect his studies. When we have in our colleges an intellectual enterprise rightly directed and of ever increasing force, America may hope to attain a position in philosophy and the arts equal to that now held in science.' "

J. C. Squire came to Ann Arbor, as planned, and through arrangements made by RF, gave a public lecture on the campus.

10. Unsigned article, "Robert Frost's Opinion of a Merciful God. He Looks upon Pestilence, Disease and Wars as Interpositions of Divine Providence," Washtenaw *Post*, 27 Oct. 1921, p. 1. For another view of RF's attitude toward the doctrine of acceptance, considered within a larger context, see Note 14 of Chapter 8. Closely related was his application of the laissez-faire doctrine, considered in *The Early Years*, pp. 378–381, 429–432, 579, 581–582.

11. RF to Amy Lowell, 22 Feb. 1922; *Selected Letters*, p. 276. Witter Bynner did visit RF at Ann Arbor, that year, and did meet with the *Whimsies* editors, but he did not give a public reading or talk.

12. Lois Elisabeth Whitcomb, member of the *Whimsies* editorial staff, "Padraic Colum at Ann Arbor," Michigan *Daily*, 30 March 1922, p. 1.

13. Lois Elisabeth Whitcomb, "Tea—with Padraic Colum," Michigan *Sunday Magazine*, 12 April 1922, p. 3.

14. Lois Elisabeth Whitcomb, "Sandburg States New Poets Fail in Over-nicety," Michigan *Daily*, 6 April 1922, p. 1.

15. RF to Lincoln MacVeagh, undated; *Selected Letters*, p. 277. There is unavoidable sadness in the knowledge that Sandburg believed he had established a lasting friendship with RF. In 1917, shortly after their first meeting, Sandburg wrote to Alfred Harcourt, "Met Frost; about the strongest, loneliest, friendliest personality among the poets today; I'm going to write him once a year; and feel the love of him every day." (Madison, *The Owl Among the Colophons*, p. 169.)

16. Lois Elisabeth Whitcomb, "Untermeyer Wins Audience in Talk," Michigan *Daily*, 21 April 1922, p. 1.

17. Quoted in Lois Elisabeth Whitcomb, "Mr. Untermeyer Talks —Some," Michigan *Daily*, 23 April 1922, p. 1.

18. Idem.

19. Lois Elisabeth Whitcomb, "The Poet Series: IV. Amy Lowell," Michigan *Sunday Magazine*, 7 May 1922, p. 1.

20. Damon, *Amy Lowell*, p. 602.

21. RF, in sending an account of this vaudeville act to LU (*Letters to Untermeyer*, pp. 141–142), blamed Miss Lowell for upsetting the lamp and the pitcher:
"Amy upset a lamp and a water pitcher and was in turn herself upset when I told her what you said about the lumber-yard on her shoulder. She called the janitor fool and damn fool to his face— this was out back before she went on—and she called [Lawrence]

Conrad (of the Whimsies) 'boy' in the sense of slave. She and I were ten minutes before the whole audience, disentangling the lengthener wire on her lamp. As a show she was more or less successful. After it was all over she described Straus [Louis A. Strauss, Chairman of the English Department] to some ladies, among them Mrs. Straus, as the fussy old professor who stood around and didn't help. Straus says she must have meant me. She laid about her. And in that respect she disappointed nobody. She only failed to live up to the specifications when she stole away from a house full of guests and came to my house to smoke her cigar in private. Her speaking and reading went well considering the uproarious start she made with the lamp and water. I never heard such spontaneous shouts of laughter. Out in front she took it all well with plenty of talk offhand and so passed for a first class sport."

22. Lois Elisabeth Whitcomb, "Amy Lowell Here on Poet Series," Michigan *Daily*, 11 May 1922, p. 1. Miss Lowell's deprecatory reference to Edgar Guest is quoted directly, in a letter from Mrs. Lois Elisabeth Whitcomb Bohlig to LT, 29 Feb. 1948; PUL.

Edgar A. Guest (1881–1963), born in Birmingham, England, had for years contributed a daily poem to the Detroit *Free Press*. These daily poems, widely syndicated, were extremely popular with those readers whom he called "folks." He was mercilessly ridiculed by such critics as William Rose Benét, Mencken, and Untermeyer, but his poems earned him considerable wealth, partly through royalties from collections of them in such books as *Heap o' Livin'* (1916) and *Just Folks* (1917). In his adopted state he was known as "the uncrowned poet laureate of Michigan."

Much to RF's chagrin, there were those in Michigan who claimed that RF was almost the equal of Edgar A. Guest. One of these admirers was a wealthy lady in Detroit who arranged a surprise party for RF. Only after he arrived at her home for a gala dinner was he informed that he was sharing honors with Detroit's favorite poet. The next day, RF gave LU an account of the occasion:

"Edgar Guessed of Detroit and I the Guessed of the University were brought together in public on the field of the cloth of gold yesterday and I wish you could have seen how happy it made the onlookers and the committee of burghers, who had arranged for our meeting. Eddie said significantly he knew Sylvester Baxter. I didn't know what to answer, so I didn't take my thumb out of my mouth. Eddie asked me to call Bill Benet off him. I sullenly refused to interfere. I confess I didn't make a very good appearance. . . ." (RF to LU, 23 Nov. 1921; *Letters to Untermeyer*, p. 139. See also Note 31 of this chapter.)

23. T. S. Eliot is thus quoted, by John Gould Fletcher, in the following passage from *Life Is My Song*, p. 281:

". . . here he [Lindsay] was in London, having momentarily and successfully turned the tables on all the English lecturers who were then swarming through America. [John] Cournos rather naively enjoyed him as a modern version of the old troubadours. Pound declared before the large audience at Central Hall that

Lindsay's poems were in reality libretti, needing the charm of Lindsay's personality and the special quality of his voice to be transmitted into art. Eliot, who had just met him, curtly replied to my eager questions with, 'I am appalled at Lindsay.'"

24. This inscribed copy of *The Congo* is now in the possession of RF's grandson, William Prescott Frost.

25. This parody may be found in *Letters to Untermeyer*, pp. 65–66.

26. Unsigned article, "Vachel Lindsay Talks to Members of Poetry Club," Bennington *Banner*, 25 April 1921, p. 1:

"The presence of Vachel Lindsay . . . who arrived in town today, brought together at the Y. M. C. A. this afternoon a rather remarkable gathering. It included Dorothy Canfield Fisher of Arlington . . . Robert Frost . . . Mrs. Grace Hazard Conkling, head of the English Department at Smith College, and her daughter Miss Hilda Conkling, aged about eleven years . . . [who has recently won] a prize at a monthly competition held by the Poetry Society of [America, in] New York."

27. Lois Elisabeth Whitcomb, "Lindsay Shows Whimsical Humor in Talk Here Ending Poet Series," Michigan *Daily*, 25 May 1922, p. 1.

28. As told by RF to LT, 29 June 1951.

29. Unsigned editorial, Michigan *Daily*, 21 April 1922, p. 2. Perhaps the best glimpses of RF, through a student's eyes, during his first year at the University of Michigan, were written by Frances Swain in the spring of 1922, and first published under the title, "The Robert Frost of the *Whimsies* Evenings," in the *Inlander*, Vol. V, No. 4 (April 1925), pp. 24–28. The following are excerpts from that article:

"'*Whimsies* Evenings,' for those who do not know, have been at the Cowdens'. Beforehand we always set a big wicker chair directly under the reading lamp for Mr. Frost, then he comes and selects some unpretentious, dim corner far distant from the throne, and we are ready to begin—talking, and more, listening to him talk. Although he speaks lightly enough, with a whimsical, skipping surface over his comments, there is a lasting tang of significance in the stuff of them that puts one remotely in mind of that earlier luminary, Dr. Samuel Johnson. Except for that note of rugged sincerity, however, the two are extremely unlike. The most trivial remarks of Johnson have the reputation for a quality of inkiness even though they escaped formal print; the conversation of Frost sparkles, more lightly, more elusively, and is at its best in the pauses—when it is in his eyes, between words.

"His talk proceeds so deliberately and informally that you might wonder, were you not too absorbed for wonderment, where it was leading anyway. When he was still a newcomer and a curiosity here, he launched his bolt against the academicians with the statement, 'I like to see a woman take a sixty-foot dive in the Hippodrome—and break her neck. . . . I like to be at a football game where five men are carried out on stretchers.' There are successive strata of illumination. Rambling he interpreted: 'I like to see the literary artist dare to risk his whole literary *life* just to say what he wants'—audacity, sincerity, tenacity! Then after an interval, his trick of making a clean breast of things forced him to add, 'I know you're not all in sympathy with me. I'm glad—because I don't mean half of what I say.' You conclude that he would perhaps not enjoy severed necks then; but as for the rest, his severity may be earnest. He makes you do the testing.

"He is humorous and ruthless. Occasionally he mentions professorial days at Amherst. . . . Fearlessness and conviction and honesty—I seem continually to be having to enumerate for him those virtues that are really most 'bark and steel.' Of free verse he remarks that the *difference* of it as a whole from the verse that preceded it is obvious, but that critics need hardly make much over eccentricities in its individual writers, because when they enter the ranks as vers librists they assume an obligation of nonconformity. 'Let's be honest with ourselves!' He is guilty of trifling statements that you suspect of hyperbole or irony, but his actual sturdy intent is seldom obscured.

"But, before sufficient temptation, he can be frail. When our Evenings were impending we discussed the advisability of refreshments. Mr. Frost was opposed to them; then we tried them despite him, and he countenanced and disposed of ** glasses of punch and ** cookies. . . . For one thing, there would have been Mrs. Cowden to propitiate had he refused. But we chortled in private. As for his laugh, he has a contagious chuckle mellowed into semi-dignity.

"After he moves the chair out of the light, and we begin to limber up, he chats about all sorts of things, and people, in his offhand way. Frost is an excellent gossip. . . .

"He told an anecdote about a minister who had written him testifying to eternal respect and admiration, and would not Mr. Frost just please criticize the enclosed original epic frankly? The servant of God would be grateful beyond words if the great hero among mortals would but condescend to give him the truth about this one piece of literature. The epic, by the way, had for a title some abstraction. Mr. Frost obliged, replying that in all probability the clergyman's sermons surpassed his poetic compositions. Shortly thereafter, current periodicals began featuring invectives against the adored and admired luminary, suffixed with the name of the minister. " 'Well, finally,' Mr. Frost confided, 'I sat down and wrote that chap a letter that simply finished him—just the littlest, meanest letter you ever read.' After a sufficient number of seconds had elapsed for us to have finished picturing the worst—'But I never sent the letter.' "

30. RF to Harriet Moody, 26 May 1922; CUL.

31. Quoted in an unsigned article, "Degrees of High Distinction Given to Eleven Today," Michigan *Daily*, 19 June 1922, p. 1. It is possible that part of RF's disappointment over being awarded only an honorary Master of Arts degree from the University of Michigan

was not unrelated to his knowledge that, a few days earlier, his unworthy rival Edgar A. Guest had been given an honorary Doctor of Letters degree by nearby Albion College. The following news item is quoted from the Detroit *Free Press*, 16 June 1922, p. 7: "Albion, Michigan. Edgar A. Guest, Detroit *Free Press* Poet, was given an enthusiastic ovation here, Thursday, at the sixty-first commencement exercises of the college. He was one of the speakers. The entire audience rose to its feet and applauded for several minutes. Later, the honorary degree of Doctor of Letters was conferred upon the poet." (See Note 22 of this chapter.)

32. RF to Harriet Moody, 21 Feb. 1922; CUL.

33. Mrs. Carol Frost (Lillian LaBatt Frost) told LT the details here used concerning the reasons for Carol's disappearance from Ann Arbor. She added that he did buy the $35 rooster.

34. RF to John Bartlett, c. June 1922; *Selected Letters*, pp. 279–280.

35. RF to LU, 8 July 1922; *Selected Letters*, p. 281. In the last two sentences quoted from this letter, two literary echoes are worth noticing. When RF writes, "I believe I will take example of Uriel and withdraw into a cloud . . ." he is paraphrasing a line from his favorite Emerson poem. (See Note 40 of Chapter 6.) Even as RF liked the haughty manner of the angel Uriel, so he liked the blend of haughty pride and resignation in Landor's "Finis," and was fond of quoting the entire quatrain:

> *I strove with none, for none was worth my strife.*
> *Nature I loved and, next to Nature, Art:*
> *I warm'd both hands before the fire of life;*
> *It sinks, and I am ready to depart.*

In the spring of 1944, RF quarreled with Howard Mumford Jones over the meaning which Landor implicitly assigned to "Nature" in the second line of this quatrain, and their quarrel was continued in RF's poem entitled "Lucretius Versus the Lake Poets" (*The Poetry*, p. 393).

14. THE LONG TRAIL

1. RF to John Haines, 20 Sept. 1922; DCL.

2. An informal statement of these terms, apparently obtained from RF, appeared in the Detroit *Free Press*, 25 June 1922, p. 7: "The poet was to be benefitted as well as the community. He was to be freed for creative work. But what happened? Ann Arbor turned Mr. Frost into a social lion. To us Mr. Frost seems a retiring man with simple tastes. We would imagine that tea parties and full dress dinners would be an abomination to him, unless they occurred upon rare occasions, or that he would be just as happy if they never happened at all. But the social whirl has kept up for him ever since he arrived in Ann Arbor and we surmise that he has had but little time to devote to his own work.

"But Mr. Frost is willing to repeat the experiment. We asked him what it was that made him look favorably upon returning next year. 'Well, for one thing, I've had a good time here,' he answered. 'I like to sit around and talk. I've done a lot of it here and made a lot of friends. And then, too—and this is my serious reason —I want to give the creative fellowship further trial. I have some ideas for making it more successful next year. . . . I would like to make my duties more definite in order that I might be more free—when I am free. I have a plan for combing all departments for people who are interested in writing, for forming these people into groups and having them meet at my house evenings or afternoons for two or three months each semester. There would be no credit given for their work. Their participation would be entirely voluntary, thus we'd get only those who were really interested. We'd read. We'd talk. It would be an informal gathering of people interested in literature.

" 'Then I would try to arrange my time so that I might be more free to do my own work. I cannot work unless I am utterly free. I would like to plan things so that if I felt like writing I could go off to some quiet spot where interruptions could not possibly occur, because when I sit down to write I must see before me a few days of undisturbed concentration.' "

3. This anecdote occurs in a copy of a letter written by Edward Ames Richards, 31 Jan. 1963, addressed to "Dear Family and Friends," containing an account of his friendship with RF, starting when he entered Amherst in the fall of 1917. The copy was sent to LT by Joseph Blumenthal, to whom gratitude is here expressed. In this chapter, the account of the hike on the Long Trail (and off it) is based on the following additional sources of information: RF's various accounts of the hike, as told to LT; Lesley Frost's account, as told to LT; Lillian LaBatt Frost's account, as told to LT; the contemporary printed account cited in Note 8 of this chapter.

4. RF to C. L. Young [1 Sept. 1922]; WCL.

5. RF to LU; *Letters to Untermeyer*, pp. 150–151. Although this letter is dated "January 1" (as though RF were playfully implying the end of one phase of his life and the beginning of another, with new resolutions), LU offers convincing evidence (ibid., p. 150fn) that the letter was written on 1 Sept. 1922.

6. In a letter to LT, 19 Aug. 1967, Harold S. Gulliver, Sr., Professor Emeritus, Valdosta State College, Valdosta, Georgia, enclosed seven mimeographed pages, without title, explaining, "A friend has suggested that I send the inclosed story of my friendship with Robert Frost to you. Use any part of it or none of it as you see fit." The "story" contains the anecdote here used, and adds that RF later sent to Gulliver an inscribed copy of *Mountain Interval* with a $5 check laid in. The "story" also quotes the full text of a letter, RF to Gulliver, 6 Feb. 1934, which begins as follows: "It is fine and warming to get such a long letter out of the friendship we formed that night in northern Vermont when you

took my side against the bad conductor and made me respectable to the clerk at the desk in the St. Johnsbury hotel."

7. RF to LU [2 Sept. 1922]; *Letters to Untermeyer*, p. 151.

8. This unsigned article appeared in the Bennington *Banner*, 13 Sept. 1922, p. 1.

9. RF to Lincoln MacVeagh [c. 15 Sept. 1922]; *Selected Letters*, p. 285. RF's various comments on this expedition—in his letters to Untermeyer, Young, Haines, MacVeagh—are so humorous and playful that the discrepancies are of minor importance. Nevertheless, they do provide another amusing illustration of his creative tendency to build fictions and myths around facts in order to fulfill his ideals—at least in fantasy. Notice the consistency with which he increases his claim concerning how far he walked. He tells Young he walked 115 miles; he tells LU he walked 125 miles; he tells Haines (in the letter cited in Note 1 of this chapter), "I did something like 200 miles most of them painful to the feet but all beautiful to the eye and mind." To MacVeagh he writes that he walked 270 miles, but then he goes on to make his exaggeration so preposterous that he can count on MacVeagh to see the entire boast as a joke: He walked all the way from the Long Trail in Vermont to Franconia in New Hampshire, and "up a White Mountain or two and then around Willoughby Lake [in Vermont]."

10. M. L. Burton to RF, 6 Oct. 1922; copy, MUL.

11. M. L. Burton to RF, 7 Oct. 1922; copy, MUL.

12. RF to M. L. Burton, 8 Oct. 1922; MUL.

13. RF to Lincoln MacVeagh, c. 8 Oct. 1922; Holt file, PUL.

15. A ROUND OF READINGS

1. RF to George F. Whicher, c. 1 Jan. 1923; ACL.

2. "Did Vermont Have No Candidate?" Editorial, New York *Times*, 9 June 1922, p. 14.

3. "Mr. Frost of Vermont," letter to the editor, from Halley Phillips Gilchrist, New York *Times*, Sunday, 18 June 1922, Section 7, p. 8.

4. "Mr. Frost, Vermont and Free Verse," letter to the editor, from Sarah N. Cleghorn, New York *Times*, 24 June 1922, p. 12.

5. RF to LU, 5 Nov. 1922; *Letters to Untermeyer*, p. 153. Another Vermont poet whom RF later treated more generously and tactfully than he did Daniel Cady was Walter Hard of Manchester. Margaret Hard, writing of her husband (in *A Memory of Vermont*, New York, 1967, p. 46), gives one version of RF's response to the Manchester poet:
"Robert Frost came in to talk to him. 'May it rightly be called poetry, Mr. Frost?' asked my husband. 'It troubles many people. It doesn't rhyme and it seems to fall into no conventional verse form—free or otherwise.' 'Assuredly, *it is poetry*,' Robert Frost declared. 'You have done a creative, poetic thing. You've created a true verse form to suit your need for the actual poetic expression

and speech of the people and region of which you are writing . . . the essence of Vermont.' Presently Mr. Frost was paying him the honor of talking about him and his poetry on his own programs; even reading from Walter's poems along with his own. . . ."

The other side of the same coin is shown by RF's response to Alfred Harcourt's request that RF write an introduction to Walter Hard's volume entitled *A Mountain Township*. After a considerable delay, RF answered under date of 6 June 1933:

"I have been in bed for three weeks with some kind of fever (it was on me the night I saw you last [4 May 1933]), and am just up around and permitted to do things again. As I lay with nothing to do but think, it came to me pretty clearly I would be making a mistake to write a preface for Walter Hard. There are two chief considerations. The first, multiple, is all the other people I have refused to write prefaces for, many of them as good authors as Walter Hard and true friends of mine. They all died of broken hearts, but their ghosts thronged round me in my deleriums with reproachful shakes of the head as much as to say they wouldn't have believed I would weaken. The second is my not knowing what to call Walter Hard's pieces. Good as they are and good as I have said they were to many audiences, I doubt if I think they are poems. They are not enough made (as the word is) except in the finals which is quoted. Why not call them hard pieces? They are certainly that. They are meant to bite like genuine coin. The day we encountered you in Madison Ave, I talked it up with Louis [Untermeyer] to call them readables. But both hard pieces and readables are evasions, subterfuges, tricks, which neither Walter Hard nor anyone else concerned would thank me for. They might pass in a review; they would amount to sabotage between the covers of the author's own book. There the author has a right to have his things called what I'm sure he thinks they are and what good judges like Homer Woodbridge have said they were. From the beginning I find I haven't wanted to write the preface except for you; and though you are a good reason and have given me long pause, I question at last whether even you would think yourself reason enough."

6. On 24 Jan. 1921, Lincoln MacVeagh had written to Bradford that Holt could not take for publication Bradford's manuscript-novel entitled "Her Own Way," even though RF had praised it in words which MacVeagh quoted as follows: "I'd publish a book like this in spite of Death and Hell, if I thought I could get my publicity department to be enthusiastic about it. Mr. Bradford knows what he is about. He is clever, knowing, spirited, and accomplished." Van Wyck Brooks (ed.), *The Letters of Gamaliel Bradford (1918–1931)* (Boston, 1934), p. 57.

Several months later, RF secured from Bradford six poems for LU's anthology, *American Poetry, A Miscellany* (New York, 1922). LU rejected them all. Not knowing about the rejection, Bradford wrote to RF on 26 July 1931, "It would be convenience to me to know which, if any, of the half dozen little poems I sent you last year you made use of. Or rather it is quite an inconvenience not to know. . . ." (HUL.) In an unusual posture of apology, RF replied, "I had hoped to get down to Boston to see you before you could demand an accounting of me. Perhaps you wouldn't have been as hard on me if you could have had by word of mouth what you now insist on having by letter. My aversion to letter-writing this time is altogether cowardly.

"With the best intention in the world (as I trust you know) I have simply done you a disservice by asking for your poems for Untermeyer's Miscellaney. I was assuming too much authority. I had no right to invite you in, and so you aren't in and I am sufficiently rebuked for an officious fool.

"You'll wonder on what grounds I so far mistook myself. Well, no one I ever heard of was consulted when I was invited in and no one I ever heard of passed on poems I contributed. I never was consulted about the admission of anyone else or the acceptance of anyone else's poems. That seems something to go on.

"I supposed I was complying with every form in telling Untermeyer I meant to ask you for poetry for the Miscellaney and getting his permission to go ahead. I thought that settled it. But not so. All he meant to grant me was permission to submit your poetry to the judgment of the other contributors as a sort of board of consent. Both you and I were only submitting your poetry for approval if we had but known it, and it has been rejected as not up to your mark.

"I'm an unpardonable mess-maker. But forgive me for the admiration I bear your work. Really you *must* forgive me. I'm wretched.

"I don't believe in the buck-passing way the Miscellaney is run and shall get out of it—if I may be considered in." (HUL.)

7. Gamaliel Bradford to RF, 26 Jan. 1921; *The Letters of Gamaliel Bradford*, p. 57.

8. RF to Gamaliel Bradford, 18 Jan. 1922; *Selected Letters*, p. 288, where the year-date is incorrectly given as 1923. RF is hinting at some of his own stylistic procedures when he urges Bradford not to spare being "a little wicked yourself over these wicked people," and when he adds that Bradford should tease his readers just enough to "make the judicious guess." In an essay of his own, published in 1924, RF demonstrated such a procedure. The opportunity occurred after he persuaded Lincoln MacVeagh to reprint a juicy volume of scandal to which RF had been introduced by his friend and real-estate agent in Amherst, Warren R. Brown. The reprint was entitled *Memoirs of the Notorious Stephen Burroughs* (New York, 1924). Having volunteered to write a preface for this reprint, RF there found several amusing ways to be wicked, himself, in praising this entertainingly notorious scoundrel. The essay is reprinted in *Selected Prose of Robert Frost*, edited by Hyde Cox and Edward Connery Lathem (New York, 1966), pp. 81–84.

9. Gamaliel Bradford to RF, 26 Jan. 1922; *The Letters of Gamaliel Bradford*, p. 58.

10. Amy Lowell, *A Critical Fable* (second edition, Boston, 1924), pp. 21–22. In the first edition, 1922, the title page stated that the work was written by "A POKER OF FUN, Witt. D., O. S., A. 1." On the title page of the second edition (1924), however, Amy Lowell acknowledged her authorship by allowing her name to appear. One reason why RF may have been so deeply offended by her satirical thrusts was that she came too close home when she teased him for trying to use a blade of grass, or any other object in nature, as "a telephone wire" to connect himself with "Heaven as central and electrifier." This particular witticism would seem to be her way of getting back at him for his saying that instead of being an Imagist or Vorticist he was a Synecdochist. (See Note 23 of Chapter 33, where consideration is given to RF's profoundly serious belief in Emerson's "telephone wire" concept that "there is no fact in nature which does not carry the whole sense of nature.")

11. *The Letters of Gamaliel Bradford*, p. 64.

12. Damon, *Amy Lowell*, pp. 612–613.

13. EWF to Amy Lowell, 11 Oct. 1922; HUL. RF's reading at Wellesley College was on 24 Oct. 1922, and was reported in an article, Wellesley *News*, 2 Nov. 1922, p. 2, beginning, "As a preface to the usual program of readings, Mr. Robert Frost, at his recital . . . gave a brief talk to young writers on the importance of tone in sentences. . . ." Implied, here, is the fact that RF's "usual program of reading" previously was given prior to his "brief talk" on poetic theory.

14. Two other significant events involved RF during this visit to the Boston area. First, he talked and read some of his unpublished poems before the members of the New England Poetry Club on 23 Oct. 1922. One record of that evening:

"The Club entered upon an active season in the fall of 1922 with a meeting at the College Club [in Boston] on Oct. 23. In spite of a regular tempest, a goodly group gathered to hear S. Foster Damon's interesting paper on the lyrical poet, [Thomas Holley] Chivers, who so directly influenced the work of Poe and others. After this paper and a lively discussion, Robert Frost talked with his delightful informality about what he conceived to be the poet's function, and method of work, especially about the contrasting value of 'narrative' and 'static' poetry. He also read several new poems in manuscript." (Abbie Farwell Brown, *The New England Poetry Club: An Outline of History, 1915–1923* [privately printed, 1923], p. 16.)

RF rarely attended the meetings of the Poetry Club. He was present at the first meeting on 11 May 1915, described in Chapter 4, pp. 42–43; he was not present at any other meetings during the next four years, although he was elected vice president (with Mrs. Josephine Preston Peabody Marks, President) at the meeting on 8 Feb. 1917, and although he was elected president (with Norreys J. O'Conor, Vice President) at the meeting on 24 Feb. 1919. For his reaction to the honor of being elected president, see his letter to Mrs. Margaret Perry, 3 April 1919; *Selected Letters*, pp. 234–235. The history of the Club contains a record of what was apparently his first appearance at a meeting held after he was elected president:

"In October [1919], at the house of Mr. O'Conor, the Club met to hear the President, Robert Frost, talk about his method of teaching Poetry, a very delightful and stimulating experience." (*The New England Poetry Club,* p. 11.)

RF was re-elected president of the Club (and Norreys J. O'Conor was re-elected vice president) at a meeting held on 22 Jan. 1920. Miss Katharine Lee Bates was elected president at the meeting on 29 April 1921, and RF then became an honorary president, in company with Miss Lowell and Mrs. Marks.

The other important event which involved RF, during this visit to the Boston area, occurred when he visited the Dunster House Bookshop and made arrangements with the owner, Maurice Firuski, to perform the odd task of selling large numbers of two scarce books.

Back of this proposal was the fact that when the firm of David Nutt and Company went into bankruptcy, in the spring of 1921, RF's friend J. W. Haines wrote to him from Gloucester, England, explaining the situation. He said that some bound copies of the first editions of *A Boy's Will* and *North of Boston* were in danger of being reduced to pulp, together with several hundred unbound sheets of each book, and that Haines had found ways to protect them until RF expressed his wishes in the matter. Several months later, on 20 Sept. 1921, RF wrote to Haines (copy, DCL): "I'm going to send you in a few days all the money I can raise to buy in those poor old first editions of mine with David Nutt. I may ask you to store some of the books somewhere until I think what exactly to do with them. Some of my friends think they might be worth something here."

Lincoln MacVeagh apparently suggested that Firuski, at the Dunster House Bookshop in Cambridge, might handle the entire matter for RF; hence the visit to Firuski in Oct. 1922. Haines, hearing nothing from RF during the next few months, bought all the bound copies and sheets of both books, and notified RF of what he had done. On 14 Dec. 1922, RF wrote to Haines (copy, DCL): "I have found a bookseller in Cambridge, Mass named Maurice Firuski who thinks he can undertake to handle all the North of Bostons in stock over there and all the Boy's Wills too." The arrangement was carried out, after considerable correspondence. As a result, some extremely complicated bibliographical points were created for those who chose to collect the various issues of the first editions of *A Boy's Will* and *North of Boston*. (A partial description of this transaction, and of the issue points, is given in W. B. Shubrick Clymer and Charles R. Green, *Robert Frost: A Bibliography* [Amherst, Mass., 1937], pp. 20–30.)

15. RF to LU, c. 5 Nov. 1922; *Letters to Untermeyer,* p. 152.

16. RF to A. J. Armstrong, 28 Dec. 1921; Lois Smith Douglas, *Through Heaven's Back Door: A Biography of A. Joseph Armstrong* (Waco, Texas, 1951), p. 134.

17. Ibid., p. 135.

18. RF to LT, 19 March 1962; the names were confirmed by Mrs. Dorothy Whittemore, Reference Librarian, Howard-Tilton Memorial Library, Tulane University, to whom grateful acknowledgment is here given for this and other assistance. An obituary of William Marcus Bancroft (1871–1928) occurs in the New Orleans *Times-Picayune*, 27 Jan. 1928, p. 3.

19. See the discussion of these traits, in the letter from Katharine Lee Bates to N. H. Dole cited in Note 9 of Chapter 6.

20. Unsigned article, "Robert Frost, Poet, Newcomb Speaker Friday," Tulane *Hullabaloo*, 17 Nov. 1922, p. 1. The same article contains this: "As a professor in the University of Michigan, Mr. Frost is, to quote him, first a teacher, then a philosopher, then a poet. Perhaps this accounts for his wide appeal to all in the audience—professors, students and patrons." (It should be clear that the undergraduate reporter failed to recognize the sarcasm in RF's description of the order in which his attributes were honored at the University of Michigan.)

21. RF to LT, repeatedly, in accounts generally supported by the following version:

"Just after the poet had begun his lecture and was reading some of his verse, a masculine voice from the front seat of the audience heckled: 'Do you call that stuff poetry?' The poet paused, ignoring the question, then proceeded with his reading. Again the voice of the very old and well-known local character came: 'What would Shakspere say of that stuff?' Mr. Frost stopped his reading and very kindly answered the taunt: 'I call it poetry, and it is the best that I can do. . . .' Hastily ushers reached the disturber and removed him from the audience. The incident unnerved the speaker; however, he continued his lecture calmly and charmed his hearers. The newspapers made no mention of the disturbance in their very fine handling of the performance, but the poet himself told Dr. Armstrong that he could not sleep [that night] because of it." (*Through Heaven's Back Door*, pp. 135–136.)

22. Dr. Armstrong's statement is quoted in an unsigned article, "Robert Frost, New England Poet, Here Thursday, Nov. 16," Baylor *Lariat*, 11 Nov. 1922, p. 1.

23. Unsigned article, " 'Second to No U. S. Poet of Today' A Waco Guest," Waco *News-Tribune*, 16 Nov. 1922, p. 1.

24. Idem.

25. Dixon Wecter, "Robert Frost Gives Reading . . . Proves That Some Poets Do Possess a Delightful Sense of Humor," Baylor *Lariat*, 18 Nov. 1922, p. 3.

26. Dorothy Renick, "Frost Reads Own Poems at Baylor," Waco *Times-Herald*, 17 Nov. 1922, p. 4.

27. RF to Lincoln MacVeagh, 28 Nov. 1922, *Selected Letters*, p. 287.

28. RF to A. J. Armstrong, c. 28 Nov. 1922; *Selected Letters,* pp. 286–287. RF's closing quotation is from Shakespeare's *As You Like It,* Act I, Scene 2, line 297.
29. RF to George F. Whicher, c. 1 Jan. 1923; ACL.

16. THE PULLS ON ME

1. RF to LU, 12 Aug. 1924; *Letters to Untermeyer,* pp. 171–172.
2. EWF to Amy Lowell, 12 Dec. 1922; HUL.
3. RF to A. B. White, 14 Dec. 1922; DCL. Here again the creative act performed by RF in transmuting the facts of the story about Joseph Warren Beach may help to illuminate RF's chronic need to triumph, vindictively, over those who offended him—no matter how unintentionally. What seems clear is that Beach had advanced so far in his courtship of Miss Dagmar Doneghy that they would have been married without any encouragement from RF. (The marriage was successful; it continued until Beach's death in 1957.) Nevertheless, RF repeatedly implied that he was the prime mover who forced it. One of his earliest boasts in this regard was made to his daughter Lesley while she was a freshman at Wellesley. To her he wrote, on 13 May 1918 (PLFB), giving this account of one event in his recently completed Western trip:
"I personally conducted the elopement of Joseph Warren Beach that awful sinner with an assistant of his in the graduate school. I never saw craziness so near the surface as it is in Beach. He's a darn fool but he makes me laugh when I'm near him—laugh and cut up. It was cruel of me to marry him off, but I had to do it— I was cutting up. It was like some Shakespearean confusion."
Nearly eight years after making these claims to Lesley, RF reviewed them in a letter to LU, and gave further hints of motives:
"I'm no authority on trouble for all the success you ascribe to me in settling Joseph Warren Beach's troubles in the day of them. . . . J. W. really seems to have been serious in that marriage. I made up my mind he should be as serious as lay in me to make him. He rather played it on me the day he used me for a chaperone to sit in his Ford car for respectability while he stole off in whatever takes the place of alders in Minnesota. I could see he thought it was funny to be so romantic at my expense. So to be equally funny and romantic at his I went straight on from that moment and inside of two days had him sewed up in marriage for the rest of his life. I bought 'em the only champaign I ever blew any one to either epi or prothalamial. I wanted to know who the laugh was on at last. Really I'm glad now if it was on no one. But you mustn't play lascivious tricks on me for a literary man. I help hasten the consequences. One practical joke deserves another. Of course mine was the more serious of the two. I can be rather unthinking. One of my faults is a love of the excitement of putting a thing through —or a person." (RF to LU, 11 Feb. 1926; *Letters to Untermeyer,* pp. 178–179.)

If the estrangement caused by RF's gossip had not occurred, Beach might have become well enough acquainted with RF, later, to avoid making one gross misinterpretation of RF's art and thought. Beach concluded his 600-page study entitled *The Concept of Nature in Nineteenth-Century Poetry* (New York, 1936) with brief references to several twentieth-century American poets. He there misrepresents RF as follows (pp. 551–552):

"Robert Frost is a refined modern agnostic in religion and philosophy, a clear-headed and fastidious realist. He has retained the aura of New England transcendentalism without a trace of its philosophy. . . . his poems show none but conscious and fanciful indulgence in the pathetic fallacy. In *A Boy's Will* he quietly and bluntly states his persuasion that 'there is no oversight of human affairs.' No American poet is more feelingly—if quietly—attached to earth as 'the right place for love.' None has more exquisitely displayed the spiritual refinements possible in human life. None is more acutely aware of the metaphysical dilemmas in which man finds himself. . . . But none of our poets has more steadily declined to formulate his thought in philosophic terms. His references to 'nature' are extremely rare." (See, as correctives, Notes 13, 14, and 24 of Chapter 17.)

4. This seems to have been the occasion when RF first saw woodcut illustrations of his poems made by J. J. Lankes—the occasion which later caused him to request that Lankes be paid to illustrate *New Hampshire*. For more details, see Note 18 of Chapter 17.

5. RF's *New Hampshire* was dedicated "To Vermont and Michigan."

6. RF to Lincoln MacVeagh, 1 Jan. 1923; JLA. (A postscript to this letter reads, "I lecture at Worcester on Friday [5 Jan. 1923].")

7. This response to Carl Van Doren further illustrates the fact that RF, having suffered neglect until nearly forty years old, could never thereafter obtain as much notice and praise as he hungrily desired. The interview was arranged, and Van Doren's article entitled "The Soil of the Puritans. Robert Frost: Quintessence and Subsoil" appeared in the *Century Magazine*, Vol. 105, No. 4 (Feb. 1923), pp. 629–636.

8. *Selected Poems* was published on 15 March 1923.

9. RF to Lincoln MacVeagh, undated; JLA; written either late in Nov. or early in Dec. 1922, from Ann Arbor.

10. Burton Rascoe, "A Bookman's Day Book," New York *Tribune*, Sunday, 14 Jan. 1923, Section VI, p. 23. The quoted passage occurs under Rascoe's entry, "Saturday, January 6." The entire article is reprinted in Lathem, *Interviews*, pp. 40–42.

11. RF to LU, 20 Jan. 1923; *Letters to Untermeyer*, p. 154. Earlier, in a letter postmarked at South Shaftsbury, 18 Jan. 1923, RF had written to MacVeagh,

"One after another we went to bed with grippe when we got home until finally Irma went down with pneumonia. It was terrible. We should have all died with her if she had died. But luckily she proved a mild case and is now pronounced out of danger. Yesterday Carol froze an ear and a toe sawing with a cross-cut out in a zero [temperature] wind. Irma has just given us such a scare however that nothing else will seem very terrible for some time to come.

"Except with you folks and with Ridgely Torrence I don't believe I had a very good time in New York. I was trying too hard to do my duty, a thing that never pays.

"I'd like to make you a list of the people I met and rather detested. It would be too long. . . ." (JLA.)

12. RF to LU, 23 Jan. 1923; *Letters to Untermeyer*, p. 156.

13. The occasion when RF talked with a reporter just after paying "ten dollars in court for having punched a mutual friend" is described in *The Early Years*, pp. 224–227, 533–536.

14. A skunk can "perform face forward" in that the animal is said to spray forward, while the tail is held flat against the top of its back.

15. RF to Burton Rascoe, undated [c. 20 Jan. 1923]; *Letters to Untermeyer*, pp. 154–156.

16. RF to LU, 5 Feb. 1923; ibid., pp. 157–158.

17. RF to Alfred Harcourt, 23 March 1923; files of Harcourt, Brace and Co., New York City; copy obtained through the courtesy of Charles A. Madison, to whom grateful acknowledgment is here made for this and other assistance.

18. The Michigan *Daily* gave no account of what Hamlin Garland said in his talk on Thursday, 3 May 1923. The issue for 1 May 1923, p. 1, had announced that he would speak on "Meeting with Famous American Authors."

19. RF to Wilfred Davison, 2 March 1923; MCL.

20. RF to Sidney Cox, postmarked 30 April 1923; DCL.

21. RF's only known comment on these two readings occurs in a letter written to MacVeagh from Ann Arbor on 28 May 1923 (JLA): "I read to all who would come last night and shall read again Thursday. I'm fighting my way out." He left the campus shortly after the second reading, and returned to South Shaftsbury on 9 June 1923, prior to the commencement exercises at Michigan.

22. The "one from England" was J. C. Squire, conservative editor of the London *Mercury*, who was making a lecture tour in the United States and who happened to be available, unexpectedly. He was not considered as a lecturer in the formal series. See RF's reference to him, as given in Note 9 of Chapter 13.

23. Lawrence H. Conrad to M. L. Burton, 22 May 1923; Administration files, MUL; here quoted with the permission of Conrad.

24. RF to Lincoln MacVeagh, undated, but written soon after RF was awarded the honorary L.H.D. by the University of Vermont on 18 June 1922; JLA.

25. Idem. One of the best contemporary analyses of "the row" at Amherst was written by Walter Lippmann: "The Fall of President Meiklejohn." (New York *World*, Sunday, 24 June 1923, Editorial

Section, p. 1.) Lippmann started his article, "When he fell, Alexander Meiklejohn had lost the support of all his trustees, of two-thirds of his faculty and probably of most of the alumni who had never studied under him. Of those who had been graduated during the ten years of his leadership of Amherst College, the overwhelming majority are his thick and thin supporters. From the present student body he elicits a kind of devotion which I have never seen before among college men. . . . they talk of Meiklejohn as only the greatest of teachers are talked about." Tracing the early antagonism to Meiklejohn's indelicate ways of trying to be a reformer by placing his newly hired faculty members above the older and more conservative professors on the staff, Lippmann used Robert Frost's attitude to represent the conservatives: "What the old Amherst feeling is like and how it reacted to President Meiklejohn is well illustrated by the following letter by Robert Frost, one of the leading American poets and at the time of this letter professor of English at Amherst. Mr. Frost, as it happens, was a Meiklejohn appointee. But this letter expresses what is in the hearts of the older faculty and the older alumni." (Then Lippmann quoted the full text of the letter cited in Note 49 of Chapter 8.)

26. RF to Wilbur L. Cross, 17 Aug. 1923; *Selected Letters*, p. 293. Alfred H. Lloyd, who had been a neighbor of RF's on Washtenaw Ave., was dean of the Graduate School.

17. YES I SUPPOSE I AM A PURITAN

1. RF to John Farrar; quoted in Farrar's review of *New Hampshire*: "The Poet of New England's Hill-men," *Literary Digest International Book Review*, Vol. 1, No. 12 (Nov. 1923), p. 25.

2. Baldassare Castiglione, *The Book of the Courtier*, Sir Thomas Hoby's translation, 1561 (London, 1900), pp. 83–84. (To clarify meanings in the passage quoted, a few modernizations have been made by LT.)

3. The series of articles in the *Nation* bore the genetic title, "These United States." It began with "Kansas: A Puritan Survival," by William Allen White, in the issue for 19 April 1922. H. L. Mencken contributed an article on Maryland, which appeared in the issue for 3 May 1922. Wilson's article on New Jersey appeared in the issue for 14 June 1922. The fourth article was "Vermont: Our Rich Little Poor State" by Dorothy Canfield. Although RF always gave the impression that these articles were devoted to fault-finding, Dorothy Canfield's article was pure praise. RF also gave the misleading impression that these articles were written by either socialistic or communistic radicals.

4. RF to LT, repeatedly; see also John Farrar (op. cit., in Note 1 of this chapter): "The long poem 'New Hampshire' . . . Mr. Frost credits its inception to *The Nation*. He had grown weary of reading criticisms of states. . . ."

5. RF is quoting from Emerson's "Ode Inscribed to W. H.

Channing," where the thrust is aimed at Daniel Webster. Emerson's far more explicit attack on Webster occurs in his "Address to the Citizens of Concord, 3 May 1851, on the Fugitive Slave Law," collected in *Miscellanies*.

6. RF's twenty lines beginning "I may as well confess . . ." may be misinterpreted unless approached with caution. He had not yet articulated his belief that style in prose or verse indicates how the writer carries himself toward his ideas and deeds, that many sensitive natures stylistically take themselves lightly in self-defense, that irony is simply a form of guardedness, and that any use of humor may show fear and inferiority. (His articulation of these points is discussed in Note 12 of Chapter 18.) Nevertheless, these later statements of his, on style, may serve to clarify the artistic game he is playing in these twenty lines immediately under scrutiny. Because he is being deliberately ambiguous, here, in permitting his outer humor to cover his inner seriousness, he forces the reader to differentiate between the apparent and the actual meanings. In a literal sense he is not justified in saying he is the author of several books against the world in general: None of his three previous books contains a single poem which, like "New Hampshire," is essentially critical and satirical. But these twenty lines may serve as a reminder that the training he received from his mother in religious matters caused him to sympathize (ideally, if not practically) with the notion that he should be against the world, the flesh, and the Devil. If considered in this light, perhaps he was the author of several books against the world in general. The point here emphasized (and expanded in subsequent notes for this chapter) is that the poem "New Hampshire" provides any reader with opportunities to acquire some extraordinary glimpses of RF's puritanism, and of his reasons for stealthily opposing so many modern trends which he viewed as being hostile to puritanism.

7. Deliberately misleading is RF's sarcastic statement, "I'm what is called a sensibilitist / Or otherwise an environmentalist," and his adding, "I refuse to adapt myself a mite . . ." If clarification is needed, notice the use made by RF of the word "sensibilitist" in his letters to LU and Whicher (quoted in Chapter 9, pp. 129–130, and in Note 14 of Chapter 9, respectively).

8. Again the ironies and ambiguities: two opposed meanings are operative within the lines, "I make a virtue of my suffering / From nearly everything that goes on round me." These lines, when viewed within the larger satirical context of this poem, may be interpreted as pretending to honor, while intending to satirize, anyone who takes a sentimentally masochistic pride in suffering. If, however, the same lines are viewed within the even larger biographical context, they may be seen as reflecting ways in which RF actually did "make a virtue" of suffering. Schooled by his mother, RF accepted the Christian belief that suffering is divinely inflicted for purposes of punishment or purification. (Remember Paul's letter to the Hebrews, 12:6–9 passim: "For whom the Lord loveth he

chasteneth . . . for our profit, that we might be partakers of his holiness. . . . Shall we not much rather be in subjection unto the Father of spirits, and live?") The trial by pain can thus be viewed as an act of endowing stoical submission with qualities of virtue which will bring the cherished reward or profit of life after death. RF spells out this belief in his early poem which he never repudiated, "The Trial by Existence" (*The Poetry*, pp. 19–21).

9. Considered within the context of "New Hampshire," RF's way of saying his prayers is pertinent: "Why, this is Hell, nor am I out of it." RF is quoting from Marlowe's *Doctor Faustus*, Scene III, line 19, but his use of the line seems to echo the following passage which also occurs in *Doctor Faustus* (V, 157–162):

> *Hell hath no limits, nor is circumscrib'd*
> *In one self-place; for where we are is hell;*
> *And where hell is, there must we ever be;*
> *And to conclude, when all the world dissolves,*
> *And every creature shall be purified,*
> *All places shall be hell that are not heaven.*

RF made a compressed version of *Doctor Faustus* for his Pinkerton students, who used it for one of their formal stage productions. (See *The Early Years*, p. 61.) No copy of this version is known to have survived.

10. In the passage here noted, RF makes a sarcastic thrust against the Russian claim that the changes they were making were signs of progress toward the perfect political state. In satirizing the "Pollyanna" element of this claim, however, RF unintentionally places himself in an odd position. He himself is able to play Pollyanna in his attitude toward political and social conditions in the United States, at exactly the moment when he is protesting that the Russian people are being given the choice between getting shot or playing Pollyanna. Insisting that "life goes so unterribly" in the United States, with "nothing worse than too much luck and comfort," Frost was characteristically closing his eyes to some social facts. The administration of Warren Gamaliel Harding was currently developing a notorious reputation for graft, corruption, scandal; widespread poverty helped cause more than 3,000 strikes involving some 4,000,000 workers in 1919 and 1920; the coal-mine strike at Herrin, Illinois, cost 36 lives on 22–23 June 1922— a date very close to the night when RF wrote the first draft of "New Hampshire." Also, protests were continuing to accumulate concerning the announced outcome of the murder trial of Sacco and Vanzetti, in Massachusetts. Obviously, social and political conditions in the United States did not justify RF's claim that in his own country, "We get what little misery we can / Out of not having cause for misery." Literary attacks on RF, repeatedly made by critics who resented his callous remarks, began immediately after the publication of *New Hampshire*, in 1923, and continued with increasing justification throughout the remainder of his life.

11. RF borrows this line from the familiar "Seven Ages of Man" passage in *As You Like It*, Act II, Scene 7, line 143.

12. RF is obviously teasing his challenger when he says, "Me for the hills where I don't have to choose." Nevertheless, his humorous answer gives an unintentional hint of a chronic weakness. A few lines later, he writes, "I'd hate to be a runaway from nature." Even as he could shut his eyes and play the Pollyanna game when confronted with social problems, so he could and did frequently run away to nature, as a means of escape from unpleasantness. Aware of the advantages and dangers of these runaway tendencies, he had considered both sides while arranging the poems for *A Boy's Will*. (See *The Early Years*, pp. 397–400, 621.) During the remainder of his life he defended himself as well as he could against the charge, made by many of his critics, that he was a runaway. One of his last poems was self-defensively entitled "Escapist [?]—Never."

13. In the passage cited, the subject under consideration is opposed attitudes toward nature, particularly as those attitudes reflect the nineteenth-century conflict between science and religion; between the concept of "Nature, red in tooth and claw" and the concept that "The heavens declare the glory of God, and the firmament sheweth his handywork." At different times, and in different moods, RF permitted his poems to reflect both sides of this controversy, but he was primarily committed to the Christian belief that the laws of nature mysteriously express the laws of God, and that man should therefore place himself in harmony with nature. (See, for example, his poem entitled "A Prayer in Spring.") In "New Hampshire," his attack on Matthew Arnold seems to be motivated primarily by his resentment against Arnold's rejection of this Christian belief. The quotation, "Nature is cruel, man is sick of blood," is taken from Arnold's sonnet sarcastically entitled "In Harmony with Nature" and subtitled "To a Preacher":

"In harmony with Nature?" Restless fool,
Who with such heat dost preach what were to thee,
When true, the last impossibility—
To be like Nature strong, like Nature cool!

Know, man hath all which Nature hath, but more,
And in that more lies all his hopes of good.
Nature is cruel, man is sick of blood;
Nature is stubborn, man would fain adore;

Nature is fickle, man hath need of rest;
Nature forgives no debt, and fears no grave;
Man would be mild, and with safe conscience blest.

Man must begin, know this, where Nature ends;
Nature and man can never be fast friends.
Fool, if thou canst not pass her, rest her slave!

RF, making his counterattack, lets the man who "ran for shelter" paraphrase Arnold's "Man must begin . . . where Nature ends" by knowing too well "where man leaves off and nature starts." RF borrows and twists other lines from Arnold to mock him further as "one who owned himself 'a foiled / Circuitous wanderer, and as one who 'took dejectedly / His seat upon the intellectual throne.'" RF knew he was quoting out of context to achieve these satirical thrusts. At the end of "Sohrab and Rustum" (a poem studied by RF's pupils at Pinkerton Academy), Arnold represents the Oxus River as a "foil'd circuitous wanderer," straining along "Through beds of sand and matted rushy isles" toward the Aral Sea. In "The Scholar-Gipsy," Arnold makes passing reference to Goethe as "one, / Who most has suffer'd" and who "takes dejectedly / His seat upon the intellectual throne." Pertinent here is the discussion of RF's anti-intellectualism, in Note 14 of Chapter 8.

14. RF's equivocations in these nine lines must be cautiously approached. Still under attack is Arnold's implied assertion that it is impossible to achieve a harmonious relationship between man and Nature, or, thereby, between man and God. RF's artistic strategy, now, is to pretend, playfully and teasingly, that he agrees with the attitude he is attacking.

15. RF gave to the Jones Library, in Amherst, the paper-covered notebook containing his first draft of "New Hampshire."

16. RF was extremely inconsistent in his various accounts of how he wrote "Stopping by Woods." His often-repeated assertion that it "just came" to him, complete, so that he wrote it all "with one stroke of the pen," is taken under scrutiny in *The Early Years*, pp. 594–597. But even as the incomplete first-draft manuscript of it (in JLA) reveals some of his hesitations and difficulties in writing it, so his first extended comment reveals some others. In a letter to Sylvester Baxter, in 1923, he made the following remarks on his use of the repetend in the fourth stanza:

"I'm surprised at you that you should be the one of all my poetical friends to miss the reason for the repetend in Stopping by Woods. There should be two reasons[,] one of meaning and one of form. You get the first and fail of the second. What the repetend does internally you come very near: what it does externally is save me from a third line promising another stanza. If the third line had been dead [i.e., without a rhymed ending] in all the other stanzas your judgement would be correct. A dead line in the last stanza alone would have been a flaw. I considered for a moment four of a kind in the last stanza but that would have made five including the third in the stanza before it. I considered for a moment winding up with a three line stanza. The repetend was the only logical way to end such a poem." (Quoted from R. C. Townsend, "In Defense of Form: A Letter from Robert Frost to Sylvester Baxter, 1923," *New England Quarterly*, Vol. XXXVI, No. 2 [June 1963], p. 243.)

This early, in his remarks on "Stopping by Woods," RF is implying that the problems involved in writing it were merely "considered for a moment" before they were resolved. During the next twenty years, and more, he very consistently slipped into the posture of claiming that he wrote the entire poem "with one stroke of the pen." (Elizabeth Shepley Sergeant, in her *Fire Under the Andes* [1927], quotes him as saying he thus wrote this poem and three others: "The Mountain," "Birches," and "Two Look at Two.") However, in 1946, when Charles W. Cooper and John Holmes requested RF's permission to reproduce a facsimile of the first-draft manuscript (or at least what remained of it, as previously given by RF to JLA), the poet discussed at length with Holmes the difficulties confronted in the writing of it. This discussion was published by Cooper and Holmes in their *Preface to Poetry* (New York, 1946), p. 604. Even so, on many occasions thereafter he repeated his idealized version of the event. After RF's death in 1963, John Ciardi accurately reported, "Time and again I have heard him say that he just wrote it ["Stopping by Woods"] off, that it just came to him, and that he set it down as it came." ("Robert Frost: The Way to the Poem," in *Dialogues with an Audience* [Philadelphia, 1963], pp. 156–157.) But on one occasion in 1950, RF's friend since Michigan days, Charles Madison, challenged the claim that many of his best poems were written with one stroke of the pen, and RF self-consciously replied:

"I won't deny I have worried quite a number of my poems into existence. But my sneaking preference remains for the ones I carried through like the stroke of a raquet, club, or headman's ax. It is only under pressure from friends that I can consent to come out into the open and expose myself in a weakness so sacred and in the present trend of criticism so damaging. When I look into myself for the agony I am supposed to lay claim to as an artist it has to be over the poems that went wrong and came to grief without coming to an end; and they made me less miserable than I deserved when I discovered that though lost they were not entirely lost: I could and did quite freely quote lines and phrases of them from memory. I never wrote a poem for practice: I am always extended for the best yet. But what I failed with I learned to charge up to practice after the fact. Now if I had only treasured my first drafts along with my baby shoes to bear me out in all this I should be more comfortably off in a world of suspicion. My word will be more or less taken for it that I played certain poems through without fumbling a sentence: such as for example November Days, The Mountain, After Apple-Picking, The Wood-Pile, Desert Places, The Gift Outright, The Lovely Shall Be Choosers, Directive. With what pleasure I remember their tractability. They have been the experience I couldn't help returning for more of—I trust I may say without seeming to put on inspired airs.

"Then for a small chaser of the low-down under the head perhaps of curiosa I might confess the trade secret that I wrote the third line of the last stanza of Stopping by Woods in such a way as to call for another stanza when I didn't want another stanza and didn't have another stanza in me, but with great presence of mind and a sense of what a good boy I was I instantly struck the line out and made my exit with a repeat end. I left the Ingenuities of Debt lying round nameless for forty years because I couldn't find a fourth line for it to suit me. A friend, a famous poet, saw it in 1913 and wasn't so much disturbed by my bad fourth line as he was by the word 'tessellation' further on. The same famous poet [Ezra Pound?] did persuade me to omit a line or two from the Death of the Hired Man and wanted me to omit the lines Home is the place where when you have to go there they have to take you in. The last three lines of Nothing Gold Can Stay were once entirely different. A lady in Rochester, N. Y., has, I think, the earlier version. I haven't. Birches is two fragments soldered together so long ago I have forgotten where the joint is." (Quoted from Cleanth Brooks and Robert Penn Warren, *Understanding Poetry*, Revised Edition [New York, 1950], pp. 603–604.)

The first draft of "Stopping by Woods" shows that the first three lines of the fourth stanza were initially:

> *The woods are lovely dark and deep*
> *But I have promises to keep*
> *That bid me give the reins a shake*

RF, having rhymed "shake" with "mistake" and "flake" in the previous stanza, reconsidered the third line, here, and came up with this one, provisionally:

> *That bid me on, and there are miles*

After these two tries, he apparently saw a better solution suggested by "and there are miles."

17. RF repeatedly named "Stopping by Woods" as his favorite among all his lyrics. As early as 1923 he called it "my best bid for remembrance." (*Letters to Untermeyer*, p. 163.) It may have had a special significance for him because he could read so many private extensions of meaning into and out of it. He could have endowed the word "promises" with his most cherished religious beliefs concerning the significance of fulfilling moral obligations. Also, he could have endowed the same word with his ambitious decision to achieve a lasting reputation as a poet.

18. Professor Loring Holmes Dodd, who played host to RF after the reading at Clark University on the night of 5 Jan. 1923, gave the following retrospective account of how RF discovered that Lankes had already made at least one illustration for one of RF's poems:

"Up to the time of his coming to read his poetry in the Fine Arts Course at Clark University . . . Robert Frost had published his books without illustrations of any sort whatever. Yet here I was asking him, teasingly of course, 'Have you seen the illustrated edition of your works the publishers are bringing out?' I held before him and opened up *North of Boston* and *Mountain Interval*, each illustrated with a half-dozen wood engravings by the artist J. J.

Lankes. For just a second he was puzzled. He examined the engravings seriously. Then, with a twinkle in his eye, he looked up at me from the chair in which he was sitting. 'You did that!' he said. He was right. Extra-illustration has long been a hobby of mine. Where I had obtained these woodcuts to insert in *North of Boston* and *Mountain Interval* I cannot now recall. But they fitted the poems as though drawn for them. For instance, the famous 'After Apple-picking' . . . in the Lankes engraving the moon, just over the horizon, outlines the 'two-pointed ladder sticking through a tree,' and the apples 'two or three' left 'upon some bough.' Lankes did draw the illustrations for the poems, as he admitted later, not upon commission but for the sheer love of the thing. The poems inspired him." (Quoted from Loring Holmes Dodd, *Celebrities at Our Hearthside* [Boston, 1959], pp. 234–235.)

RF, in his first letter to Lankes (c. 20 Aug. 1923; TUL), wrote, "I should tell you I've already seen some of your things used as illustration for my Mountain Interval in the library of a man in Worcester." When *Mountain Interval* was first published, in 1916, Julius John Lankes (1884–1960) was living in Gardenville (near Buffalo), New York. Born in Buffalo, he attended the Art School of the Boston Museum of Fine Arts, and worked in oils and water colors; for a time he earned his living as a mechanical draftsman. His father was a cabinetmaker, and Lankes obtained his first blocks for woodcutting from the excellent small pieces of hardwood discarded by his father. He made his first woodblock in 1917; his record-book shows that his first Frost-inspired woodblock was entitled "October (Moonlight and Apple Tree)" and that it was completed on 26 July 1921. The political views of Lankes were strongly socialistic, and some of his early woodcuts appeared in the *Masses* and the *Liberator*. RF first noticed his work and name in January of 1922 when LU sent to Ann Arbor a copy of the *Liberator* which contained one of the best woodcuts Lankes ever made: "Winter," described by RF as representing "the back side of a village in snow."

19. "Stopping by Woods" appeared in the *New Republic* for 7 March 1923. A fair copy of the poem, in RF's handwriting, signed, and with the inscription, "For Ridgley / January 8 1923," is in the Torrence Papers, PUL.

20. RF to LU, 5 Feb. 1923; *Letters to Untermeyer*, p. 157.

21. For a discussion of this ambivalent and Uriel-like posture, see Note 40 of Chapter 6.

22. Among the many books on astronomy into which RF looked during the early days of his lifelong preoccupation with the subject, the one which made the greatest impression was entitled *Our Place Among Infinities*. (See *The Early Years*, pp. 90–92.)

23. RF usually based some parts of his narrative poems on actual experiences. For the evidence that he knew a man who burned his hotel down for the insurance (but with no plan to use the insurance money for buying a telescope), see a Frost anecdote given in *The Early Years*, pp. 343–344. According to RF, the actual hotel-burning incident occurred not far from the Lynch farm in Bethlehem; the

NOTES

setting for "The Star-Splitter" is in the adjoining town of Littleton. An early draft of this poem, sent to LU from Ann Arbor on 12 Feb. 1923 (see *Letters to Untermeyer*, pp. 159–160), contains the following insinuative passage which RF later deleted:

> *After such loose talk it was no surprise*
> *When he came stumbling in the frozen ruts*
> *One night and shouting "Help my home's on fire!"*
> *Some threw their windows up, and one at one said*
> *"Let them that set the fire put out the fire."*
> *One at another, "Them or else their sons*
> *Or sons' sons to the seventh generation."*
> *Mean laughter was exchanged between the windows*
> *To let him know we weren't the least imposed on*
> *And he could wait: we'd see to him to-morrow.*

24. The full text of "For Once, Then, Something" is quoted in Note 13 of Chapter 10, and the suggestion is there made that RF's skepticism, while genuine, was often displayed merely for purposes of protecting his religious belief. Reference was made (in Note 3 of Chapter 16) to those who mistakenly assume RF's skepticism provides hints that he was an agnostic, or even an atheist. He actually hated the postures implied by both of these terms.

The present consideration of the poems in *New Hampshire* makes it possible to see clearly that he made various uses of his own skepticism; that, at times, he enjoyed striking a skeptical note merely to indicate that he set himself apart, heretically, from the orthodox religious believer. As has already been suggested (in Note 40 of Chapter 6) one aspect of his skepticism coincided with his fondness for casting himself in the heretical role of an Emersonian Uriel.

Consider a more orthodox way of viewing RF's skepticism. Whenever a devout believer (such as RF) asserts that the ways of God are mysterious, and that any true believer must therefore accept the inscrutabilities, such a person can be genuinely skeptical toward the notions of anyone who claims to know and understand not only the laws of God but also God's motives for causing, ordering, designing, the universe. RF frequently boasted that his mind could rest in the middle of a process. This boast fits his belief that he could and did believe in God, even know God, and yet not know (or at least not understand, even while accepting) the inscrutable benevolence implicit in God's causing-designing-ordering. (For another approach to RF's attitude of not knowing, see Note 14 of Chapter 8.)

25. RF's poem entitled "Design" (Originally called "[A Study] In White") may be considered as a companion piece for his later study in "whiteness" called "Wrong to the Light" before it was called "For Once, Then, Something." (A background for an interpretation of "Design" is given in *The Early Years*, pp. 383–387.)

26. On RF's responses to James and Thoreau, in this regard, see *The Early Years*, pp. 231–232, 272, 294–295.

27. RF to LU, 11 Nov. 1915; *Letters to Untermeyer*, pp. 17–18, with RF's facetiously drawn picture reproduced on p. 18.

28. In this stanza, RF again invokes his belief in the Christian concept of a divine plan or design which is benevolent in terms of "trial," no matter how much demand it places on the courageous individual.

29. This stanza, indeed the whole of "An Empty Threat," is best understood when considered within some such religious context as that described in Note 6 of this chapter. In saying, "Better defeat almost, / If seen clear, / Than life's victories of doubt / That need endless talk-talk, / To make them out," RF is placing the word "defeat" in a frame of reference previously suggested by such of his earlier poems as "The Trial by Existence" and "A Prayer in Spring."

30. Again, in "I Will Sing You One-O," RF's ulterior meanings are best understood after the poem is seen as reflecting his belief in those unchanging and interpenetrative elements in a divine plan which binds together all space and time: "They spoke for the clock / With whose vast wheels / Theirs interlock." These unchanging elements are further stressed in the conclusion: "It has not ranged, / . . . It has not changed / To the eye of man / On planets over, / Around, and under / It in creation / Since man began / To drag down man / And nation nation."

Change, or at least that form of change associated with improvement or progress, has no significant place in the most austere puritan concept of God's plan for earthly nature or human nature. Keeping in mind the poem, "I Will Sing You One-O," consider RF's statement quoted in Chapter 27, p. 387: "Whatever progress may be taken to mean, it can't mean making the world any easier a place in which to save your soul." And consider the passage quoted in Chapter 8, p. 116: "Now I get my punishment . . . for letting myself believe . . . that there is any such thing as progress. Mea culpa." Consider also, in this connection, these two lines from "The Black Cottage" (*The Poetry*, p. 58):

> *Most of the change we think we see in life*
> *Is due to truths being in and out of favor.*

In one aspect of puritan doctrine which RF admired, change-for-the-worse is the basic pattern of human response, hence RF's question about "what to make of a diminished thing" in "The Oven Bird" (*The Poetry*, p. 120). In puritan doctrine, all diminishment begins with Adam's disobedience to the divine plan in the perfect Garden of Eden, the Earthly Paradise, and it was as a consequence of this original sin or depravity that man began to drag down man, and nation began to drag down nation. According to RF's view, significant change for the better will occur only in the Heavenly Paradise, and there only through divine grace. Hence the appropriateness of RF's line in "New Hampshire" about life on earth: "Why, this is Hell, nor am I out of it."

31. Quoted to LT by Lawrence Conrad, to whom grateful

acknowledgment is here made for information about RF's years at the University of Michigan.

32. For an account of how and why Elinor White [Frost] stopped writing poetry, see *The Early Years*, pp. 504–505.

33. EWF to Lincoln MacVeagh, 15 March 1923; JLA.

34. RF to J. J. Lankes, c. 20 Aug. 1923; TUL.

35. RF to Lincoln MacVeagh, 29 Sept. 1923; JLA.

36. For source, see Note 1 of this chapter.

37. Weygandt could have derived from RF this hint of analogies between the story-telling art of Turgenief and RF. Just how early RF became exposed to Turgenief, there is no known record, but when RF was a seventh-grade student in Salem, N. H., with his mother as teacher, one of his textbooks was *The New Franklin Fourth Reader*, edited by Loomis J. Campbell, and it contained Turgenief's sketch, "The Sparrow." RF's first mention of Turgenief, in his correspondence, seems to occur in a letter to Walter Prichard Eaton, 15 July 1915 (*Selected Letters*, p. 182):

"Far be it from me though to regret that all the poetry isn't in verse. I'm . . . glad of all the unversified poetry of Walden—and not merely nature-descriptive, but narrative as in the chapter on the play with the loon on the lake, and character-descriptive as in the beautiful passage about the French-Canadian woodchopper. That last alone with some things in Turgenieff must have had a good deal to do with the making of me."

M. P. Tilley, in his "Notes from Conversations with Robert Frost," in the *Inlander,* op. cit., p. 6, reports this:

"He [RF] felt that he wanted to get the qualities of intimate conversation into his poetry. Next to this influence, Wordsworth (who to him is a very great poet), Turgenief, in his *Sportsman's Sketches,* and the *Odyssey* have influenced him most."

38. Cornelius Weygandt, "Frost in New Hampshire." *The White Hills* (New York, 1934), pp. 244–245.

18. IN THE COUNCILS OF THE BOLD

1. RF to Wilfred Davison [c. Dec. 1923]; MCL.

2. See Chapter 2, pp. 15–16, for an account of RF's first visit with the Hockings.

3. RF to Charles L. Young, 24 Aug. 1923; WCL.

4. RF to Wilbur Cross, 17 Aug. 1923; *Selected Letters*, p. 293. In this letter, RF begins his account, "I went to enquire into a young philosopher yesterday. I meant to spend the afternoon over him." The visit to Hocking was apparently made nearly a month earlier. RF wrote to MacVeagh on 22 July 1923, "I've bitten off the Amherst chew. Tomorrow I'm going to look up Hocking to see if he wont help us part of the year in philosophy." (JLA.)

5. RF to MacVeagh [c. 13 Sept. 1923]; *Selected Letters*, p. 238, where a probably less accurate approximation of the date is given.

6. RF to LU, 13 Sept. 1923; *Letters to Untermeyer*, pp. 164–165.

7. The only known list of readings for this course occurs on two sheets of paper on which the following notations occur in RF's handwriting (ACL):

Melville's Typee — November 5
Borrow's Lavengro — November 12 and so on at the rate of about one a week.
Hazlitt's Table Talk
Thoreau's Walden
Plutarch's Life of Coriolanus and Shakespeare's Play — In one book of Oxford Press.
Cellini's Autobiography
Christina Rossetti's Poems — World Classics
Emerson's Representative Men
Gibbon's Autobiography
Sheridan's School for Scandal
O'Neill's Moon of the Caribbees — Modern Library
Stevenson's Essays — *Selections* Scribner's
Ben Johnson's Silent Woman
Trelawney's Last Days of Shelley and Byron
Any good collection of British Ballads
Prescott's Conquest of Mexico
White's Natural History of Selbourne
Dryden's All for Love
A volume of good criticism
    Hazlitt's Eng. Comic Writers
    or Brownell's American Prose Masters
    or James' Notes on Novelists
    or Bagehot's Literary Studies
    or Coleridge's Lectures on Shakespeare
    or Dryden Essays on Dramatic Poesie
Gilbert's Babb Ballads
Ibsen's Lady from the Sea

(On the back of the second sheet is the notation, "Robert Frost's reading list for his students at Amherst, 1923–4." The notation seems to be in the handwriting of Miss Marion Dodd, bookseller in Northampton, Mass.)

8. EWF to Mrs. Von Moschzisker, 13 Aug. 1923; ACL.

9. Newspaper article entitled, "ALUMNI OF AMHERST WILL SUPPORT OLDS / Told Robert Frost Keeping Teaching Post There," Boston *Globe*, 4 Nov. 1923, p. 5.

10. RF to MacVeagh [c. 20 Sept. 1923]; *Selected Letters*, p. 295.

11. "It is interesting to see the things poets find to die away into.

They die into self-imitators, into virtuosos, and they die into philosophers. The last is the best death. You haven't heard the joke I
based my course in philosophy on last year: that a philosopher
strikes a simile and uses it all his life, but a poet tosses off similes
at the rate of one a day. But it's time we let up on the philosophers.
. . ." (RF, "A Literary Dialogue," Amherst *Writing*, Vol. XXXIX, No.
4 [May 1925], p. 4.) In the report of a talk given by RF at Bryn
Mawr College on 15 Jan. 1926, the following closely related paraphrase occurs: "All the philosophers had metaphors, but a philosopher is a person with one metaphor who lives all his life studying
and amplifying it. A poet dashes off a new one every hour, and
leaves it for the next." ("Robert Frost Talks on Metaphors," Bryn
Mawr *College News*, 10 Feb. 1926, p. 1.) This uncomplimentary
way of comparing a philosopher with a poet was one of RF's
favorites, and he often buttressed it by calling attention to Emerson's manner of taking exception to Swedenborg's unpoetic freezing of metaphors:

"He fastens each natural object to a theologic notion;—a horse
signifies carnal understanding; a tree, perception; the moon, faith;
a cat means this; an ostrich that; an artichoke this other;—and
poorly tethers every symbol to a several ecclesiastic sense. The
slippery Proteus is not so easily caught. In nature, each individual
symbol plays innumerable parts, as each particle of matter cir-
culates in turn through every system. The central identity enables
any one symbol to express successively all the qualities and shades
of real being. In the transmission of the heavenly waters, every
hose fits every hydrant. Nature avenges herself speedily on the
hard pedantry that would chain her waves." ("Swedenborg; or, The
Mystic," in *Representative Men*.)

12. RF to LU, Amherst, 10 March 1924; *Letters to Untermeyer*,
pp. 165–166. Because this epistolary essay on "style" is one of RF's
most self-revealing statements, some parts of it may reward further
consideration here:

"Many sensitive natures have plainly shown by their style that
they took themselves lightly in self-defense." The implication is
that an author easily hurt, and therefore inclined to guard himself
from attack, may employ a stylistic posture which is apparently
humorous, casual, gay, in the hope that he will thus deceive any
dangerous opponent. RF, after his return from England, increasingly developed this form of self-defense—in his poems, in his
letters, and in his public talks.

"They are the ironists." That is, such very sensitive natures may
also make stylistic uses of witty and sarcastic expressions in which
the intended meaning of a word, as used, may be the opposite of
what might be expected or considered appropriate. The goal is, in
part, to escape hurt by striking out at the weaknesses of others.
RF's ironic postures through his satire entitled "New Hampshire"
may serve to illustrate such a procedure.

"I own any form of humor shows fear and inferiority. Irony is
simply a kind of guardedness. So is a twinkle. It keeps the reader

from criticism." These four statements would not be acceptable to many other stylists who employ humor and irony, but RF is here confessing his own uses.

"Belief is better than anything else, and it is best when rapt, above paying its respects to anybody's doubt whatsoever." For RF, this is the heart of the matter under consideration. He places his own religious belief highest in his total scale of values because all his other values depend on it, and he envies the rapture of Emerson's idealism because it seems to be "above paying its respects to anybody's doubt whatsoever." By contrast, he finds that his own religious belief is constantly being disturbed by his inner doubts and by the irreligious challenges of others. (For evidence, see Note 13 of Chapter 10.)

"At bottom the world isn't a joke. We only joke about it to avoid an issue with someone[;] to let someone know that we know he's there with his questions: to disarm him by seeming to have heard and done justice to his side of the standing argument." This is a further articulation of what he implied when he said many sensitive natures take themselves lightly in self-defense. Joking, thus used, can provide another way to escape from injury, another way to "disarm" the always-dangerous opponent in the "standing argument."

"Humor is the most engaging cowardice. With it myself I have been able to hold some of my enemy in play far out of gunshot." Now RF is back where he started, in this extraordinary self-revelation. If he had tried to arrange these factors in a cause-and-effect sequence, he might have had difficulty in deciding which came first: fear (the feeling of anxiety or agitation caused by the actual or imagined presence of danger and pain) or sensitivity (the capacity for being easily hurt or offended—particularly in the pride) or inferiority (the sense of being brought low by the fear that one is inadequate). Taken together, these three factors did cause RF to view anyone as potentially "my enemy" and to seek for "self-defense" through trying to "disarm" such an incipient opponent. The essential factors to be defended were (as is said in those parts of "Education by Poetry" which are quoted in Chapter 25, p. 365) "the self-belief, the love-belief, and the art-belief . . . all closely related to the God-belief." RF implies, however, that because of his own sense of inadequacy he views these stylistic weapons of self-defense—humor, a twinkle, joking, and irony— as being more suitable for use by a coward than by a hero.

(Parts of this important epistolary essay are used to illuminate other and yet closely related postures, in Note 13 of Chapter 10, and in Note 6 of Chapter 17.)

13. Robinson's "New England" was first published in the London *Outlook*, Vol. LII, No. 11 (3 Nov. 1923), p. 335. Apparently for purposes of sharpening the ironies, following the criticism of this sonnet, Robinson subsequently revised line 3 to read,

Wonder begets an envy of all those

and changed line 10 to read,

We're told, and Love a cross for them to bear . . .

14. Robinson's letter appeared in the Gardiner *Journal* on 14 Feb. 1924; it is quoted entire in Charles Beecher Hogan, *A Bibliography of Edwin Arlington Robinson* (New Haven, 1936), pp. 179–180.

15. RF to LT, repeatedly; but on only the first occasion did LT try to persuade RF that the sonnet was obviously and intentionally ironic. Because an article entitled "The 'Poet of Frost' " (cited in Note 14 of Chapter 9) had described RF as being cold, and had thereby infuriated RF, he should have been more sympathetic toward Robinson when the critics misunderstood this particular sonnet. He never was, and perhaps his mistaken interpretation of this sonnet was caused by his reflexive attempt to measure it with his own inapplicable yardstick: "Irony is simply a kind of guardedness. . . . Humor is the most engaging cowardice. With it myself I have been able to hold some of my enemy in play far out of gunshot." It is more probable, however, that the blindness of his response was caused by jealousy. One fact is clear: RF enjoyed the misery and embarrassment caused to Robinson by those who attacked the sonnet.

16. RF to LU, 12 March 1924; *Letters to Untermeyer*, p. 169. LU's note (pp. 168–169) describes the clippings, quotes briefly from them, and concludes, "In any case, it is obvious that Robert did not like the way the Northeast Corner was characterized by his fellow New Englander." Such a conclusion seems to miss the point of RF's remark, and of Robinson's sonnet.

17. RF to MacVeagh, 24 Nov. 1923; JLA. RF might have been less hostile toward the Amherst students at this time if some of them had not resisted and mocked him. For an example of undergraduate satire and parody aimed at RF, see Note 29 of this chapter.

18. The direct quotations here given occur in an article entitled, "Turned Away from Big Boston Hotel, Says Robert Frost," Boston *Herald*, 18 Oct. 1923, p. 6. The article begins: "Robert Frost, one of the most distinguished of living American poets, is telling women's clubs a joke on Boston so utterly unfair that for the city's good name he must be exposed before he immortalizes his experience in imperishable verse." The article concludes: "Strangely enough, the second hotel is under the same management as the first, although Mr. Frost did not know it at the time."

19. Boston *Herald*, 18 Oct. 1923, p. 6.

20. Gamaliel Bradford to Manager, Parker House, 14 Oct. 1923; carbon copy, Bradford Papers, HUL. After receiving Bradford's letter, the manager of the Parker House wrote to RF saying he wished to apologize "for any discourtesy which you may have received at the hands of the clerk. . . ." (Carbon copy, Bradford Papers, HUL.) The guarded wording, "which you may have received," suggests that there may have been no actual discourtesy

on the clerk's part. In such circumstances, RF was so quick to take offense that he may have walked out before the clerk could make amends for the misunderstanding.

21. The quotations are taken directly from Mark Sullivan's version of the story, in *Our Times: The United States, 1900–1925,* Vol. VI: *The Twenties* (New York, 1935), pp. 438–439. Denis Aloysius McCarthy, born in County Tipperary, Ireland, was present with RF at the first meeting of the New England Poetry Club (see Chapter 4, pp. 42–43), and remained an active member up to the time of his death in 1931, at the age of 60. He published five books of poetry, none of which attracted much attention beyond Boston.

One hint of how Mark Sullivan apparently teased RF with the Coolidge anecdote, before telling him the details of it, may be drawn from RF's letter to Sullivan, 15 Aug. 1926 (PWES):

"Some time we must convene and then after you have given me three guesses as to what Calvin said about putting me on the map you will tell me the answer. I can foresee now what my first guess will be: 'How'd I look asettin up as an arbiter poetarum?' All the same I am in favor of Calvin. On the fur side of the Green Mountain (sing), that is, in Western Vermont where I live we have a word for the nigh side (reckoning always from Boston) that I like to use on Calvin. We speak of an overthemountain smock, an overthemountain wagon, an overthemountain hayrack. Well he has an overthemountain nature."

22. RF to MacVeagh, 19 Nov. 1923; *Selected Letters,* p. 296. (Of necessity, Lillian became the most practical member of the Frost family.)

23. RF to Wilfred Davison [c. Dec. 1923]; *Selected Letters,* p. 298.

24. Davison's first visit with RF is described in Chapter 12, pp. 161–162.

25. Hawthorne's well-known short story with an Italian setting is "Rappaccini's Daughter."

26. Davison's journal-like record entitled "Visit to Robert Frost" was transcribed by Reginald L. Cook, at Middlebury, shortly after Davison's death, and the transcription was made available to LT through the courtesy of Professor Cook.

27. Paraphrased from "Frost, Broom and Bat Fight Bizarre Battle," Allegheny College *Campus,* 25 March 1924, p. 1; copy provided to LT through the courtesy of Philip M. Benjamin, Librarian, Allegheny College. (A less accurate reminiscence of this incident, containing the claim that RF hit and killed the bat in flight, occurs in a letter written by an Allegheny alumnus which was published in *Life* magazine, 14 Oct. 1957, p. 22.)

28. The first published announcement concerning the visit appeared in the Michigan *Daily,* 27 March 1924, p. 1: "Robert Frost . . . will arrive in Ann Arbor Sunday morning with Mrs. Frost. While in the city, Mr. and Mrs. Frost will be the guests of Dean Joseph A. Bursley. Their stay in Ann Arbor will probably be limited to two or three days." Previously, Professor M. P. Tilley seems to

have written RF to say he had heard of the intended visit and that he would like to arrange for RF to give a public reading of his poems. RF wrote to Tilley, 20 Feb. 1924 (MUL): "I see no great need of my reading again so soon at Ann Arbor. Neither I nor the University will have changed enough to make me a novelty to it. Why do you bother to try to get me an audience? Let's just spend the time in friendly talk about who the five greatest moderns are. But if you are committed to getting me an audience, know that my time with you will extend from Sunday afternoon March 30 to early Thursday morning April 3, and you may act upon me accordingly. It will be fun to see several of you again. I got to be a good deal more Ann Arboreal than I should suppose I could have at my age. A few people and streets and a lot of the outlying landscape are pretty well incorporated in me. . . . Of course I must sit with the Whimsies an evening."

The Frosts arrived on Sunday, as scheduled; RF was interviewed by an undergraduate reporter the next day, and the interview appeared in the *Daily* for 1 April 1924, p. 1. It contained the announcement that RF would give a reading of his poems at 4:30, Tuesday afternoon, 2 April 1924, in Sarah Caswell Angell Hall. The *Daily* for 2 April 1924, p. 4, carried a brief notice entitled, "Present Frost's Play," as follows: "The Ann Arbor Playmakers are presenting an invitation performance of Robert Frost's one-act tragedy, 'A Way Out,' in honor of the poet's visit, this evening, in the Dodo Playshop. The audience will be composed of the members of Whimsies and the Writers' Club as well as several other guests." The reading was given in the afternoon, the play was given in the evening, and after the play RF met with the Whimsies and others at Professor Cowden's home.

RF's visit may have been scheduled by President Burton to coincide with the arrival of England's Poet Laureate, Robert Bridges, who reached Ann Arbor on Friday, 4 April 1924, to serve for two months as poet in residence. An article in the *Daily* for Saturday, 5 April 1924, entitled "Bridges Arrives To Assume Chair," contained this: "Last night, Dr. Bridges and Mrs. Bridges were in attendance at the special performance of 'Captain Applejack' given by the Comedy Club in honor of the visiting schoolmasters. Mr. Robert Frost and Mrs. Frost and Prof. Stuart P. Sherman were also present as guests of the Burtons." (For an account of RF's previous acquaintance with the poet laureate, in England in 1913, see *The Early Years*, pp. 442–443.)

29. One of the most pointed teasings, apparently made by the senior editors of the Amherst *Student* just prior to their formal relinquishment of the paper to the newly elected staff, took the form of parody. The issue of the *Student* for 7 Jan. 1924 (p. 2.) contained this editorial announcement:

"This issue is dedicated to alumni who don't understand what it's all about; also to worthy professors who may not appreciate our good natured but rough-hewn satire. May the dedication preserve the peace."

The parody-article which was aimed at RF (and which contained a parody of his then-most-popular-poem) bore this caption and subcaption:

FLEAS AND MORES CLOSE
KIN AVERS LOCAL POET

Vaudeville Acts at Recital Bring
Down House. Frost Likes His
Own Stuff and Kipling's.

One reference in the parody-article needs explanation: the Irish poet and dramatist Padraic Colum had been a guest speaker in RF's course on "Readings," on 14 Nov. 1923, and the following parody implies that some students thought Colum looked more like a bartender than a poet:

" 'No good poet can afford to ignore the growing prevalence of heredity and environment' said Robert Frost, noted poet, in a song and dance recital of his poems at Amherst today.

" 'I know the mores well,' he continued, 'and everyone has them. But without a keen recognition of the mores there can be no clear cut reaction of the individual to them. They are like fleas. If you don't know that they are troubling you, you can't get rid of them. I am for the critical attitude always. All I ask of my classes is whether a poem or a story is good or bad. Of course if they say it is good, I know it is bad.'

"Here Mr. Frost paused to interpret with suitable steps a few stanzas of Kipling. 'I like his stuff,' said the 'old man from the hills' as he is affectionately dubbed by his boys. 'It is so sweet, so innocently demure; not unlike Mencken's in that respect.'

"Here Mr. Frost again paused to impersonate a hypocrite but was not very successful, not yet having learned from his English class, in spite of two exams, what one really is. At this point Mr. Padraic Colum rose saying, 'Ha, I'll best you there,' and stepping up on the platform impersonated a bartender. The impersonation was most realistic.

" 'That reminds me,' then said Mr. Frost, 'of one of my late poems.' He recited it amid salvos of applause. Entitled 'Shopping in Woods on a Snowy Evening,' it goes as follows:

> *Whose woods these are I think I know.*
> *His house is in the village though;*
> *This is his still that I see here*
> *From which the goodly liquids flow.*
>
> *My little horse must think it queer*
> *That I don't jump to get the beer*
> *He does not know the game is up—*
> *Police are closing in the rear.*
>
> *He gives his harness bells a shake.*
> *Thank God there must be some mistake!*

[609]

They do not come to pull me in,
My thirst once more I now can slake.

"The audience here retired to Holyoke."

(This parody was written in prohibition days when, presumably, the best speakeasies were in the not-too-far-distant city of Holyoke, Mass.)

30. RF told many versions of this incident, all of them much the same. Here is one:

"I recently was compelled to give an examination, since such must be. In my classroom at the appointed time I said, 'Do something appropriate to this course which will please and interest me.' (It was a course in literature. There had been a wide choice of books.) I left the room.

"I thought probably three or four would get up and go home, thinking I already knew them well enough, that I already had their grades ready anyhow to hand in at the office. I thought others would come to me, a little later, and take it out in talk. I placed a limit upon them of four bluebooks, and you know perfectly well no one ever wrote four bluebooks in Amherst College; but I hoped some poor boy might write four in order to convince himself he was doing everything he should.

"I went away, upstairs. Presently one after the other, 'the whole kit and caboodle,' came ambling upstairs and waited their turns to say something pleasant to me in parting. That's the way they understood the word 'please' in my leading question. You never can tell what you have said or done till you have seen it reflected in other people's minds." (Lathem, *Interviews*, p. 71.)

A strikingly different account of this episode, written by Sargent B. Child, '24, appeared in the Amherst *Student*, 13 June 1964, p. 2.

31. RF to LU, 12 Aug. 1924: "Morrow is certainly intelligent and so liberal, he tells me, as to have sat in until very recently anyway at the councils of the *New Republic*. Mrs. Morrow is a member of the Poetry Society of America. Between them they have just put David Morton on the Amherst faculty, I am told over the telephone. The question of David Morton was worrying President Olds when I came away. He could have wished him a poet he knew more about. I couldn't help him much because I didn't know much myself. The Morrows pressed for Morton as the winner of some sort of Poetry Society prize. President Olds is not young. I have seen him worn out with running to New York all year for instructions and permisions." (*Letters to Untermeyer*, p. 169.)

32. RF is quoting "Cupid's curse" from *Fair and Fair* by George Peele. See *Oxford Book of English Verse*, p. 150, where the text is slightly different:

"My merry, merry, merry roundelay,
Concludes with Cupid's curse,—
They that do change old love for new
Pray gods they change for worse!"

33. RF to MacVeagh [c. 24 June 1924]; *Selected Letters*, p. 301.

34. For other references to RF on metaphor and analogy, see Note 11 of this chapter.

35. RF to LU, 12 Aug. 1924; *Letters to Untermeyer*, p. 170.

36. RF to G. R. Elliott, 26 July 1924; ACL.

37. For an account of RF's first reading at Amherst, see Chapter 8, p. 97.

38. RF to LU, 12 Aug. 1924; LC. In editing this passage (*Letters to Untermeyer*, pp. 170–171), LU made unacknowledged expurgations.

39. EWF to Mrs. Von Moschzisker, undated, but written in Sept. 1924; ACL. This letter contains the reference to the two hay-fever retreats: "We have been visiting Mrs. Fobes [in Franconia, N. H.] about two weeks and a half, and return to Amherst next Tuesday. Before coming up here we stayed ten days in a little hotel at Woodford City—which is a tiny village way up on one of the Green Mt. ridges. It is only 9 miles from Bennington but is 2300 ft. high—and Robert thought it might be sufficiently high for him to be free from hay fever there. He was pretty well there, but still had it a little. . . ." Earlier, in a letter to Mrs. Von Moschzisker from South Shaftsbury and dated 5 July [1924], Mrs. Frost had given other information about RF's condition: "Robert and I came up to the farm [from Amherst] the 1st of June and I had looked forward to having time to write to you at once, but Robert has been quite wretched all the time with a sort of nervous indigestion (the nervous strain of this last year has been almost too much) . . ."

19. FREED FROM OBLIGATION

1. Gardner Jackson, " 'I Will Teach Only When I Have Something To Tell,' " Boston *Sunday Globe*, 23 Nov. 1924, Editorial Section, p. 3; Lathem, *Interviews*, p. 54.

2. James A. Batal, "Poet Robert Frost Tells of His High School Days in Lawrence," Lawrence *Telegram*, 28 March 1925, p. 14. Batal in this article also gives a glimpse of how the students responded to the other course which RF taught at Amherst in the academic year 1924–1925: "It was after the poet had dismissed a class of 60 students in a course on English literature (the largest number of students to elect a course in Amherst College) that I met him and got this interview. Robert Frost likes to live life unhurried, but his many engagements, his duties at Amherst, and his never-ending conferences with his ambitious student authors keep him busy."

3. "Robert Frost, Poet, Leaves Amherst To Go To Michigan," Boston *Evening Transcript*, 4 Nov. 1924, p. 11. Another example of RF's myth-making is provided by the many claims he made while at Amherst in the fall of 1924 that he would be freed from all teaching obligations at Michigan. By contrast, the newspaper

NOTES

release made by President Burton implied that RF could not legitimately spend almost all his time doing whatever he pleased:

"Robert Frost, New England poet, at present a member of the faculty of Amherst College, will come to the University of Michigan next fall as permanent university fellow in letters, according to an announcement by Dr. Marion L. Burton. . . . The idea of a permanent fellow in letters is an innovation at Michigan. It means Frost will have time to teach a few classes but not enough to interfere with his writing. He will be a member of the faculty of the Literary College, but will have ample time to come into contact with and assist those students who show special ability in writing." (New York *World*, Nov. 3, p. 19.)

Specific details concerning how this plan was to be carried out were described in the following "Notice" which the Michigan *Daily* carried for several days in Oct. 1925:

"English 186:

"In the second semester Mr. Robert Frost will offer a course designed especially for students actively engaged in writing (prose or poetry). The class will necessarily be limited in number. Those interested in the course will please leave their names with the Secretary of the Department of English, Room 2209 Angell Hall, not later than October 24th. Opportunity to confer with Mr. Frost will be provided for other students through members of the Departments of Rhetoric and English, whose names will be announced later. L. A. Strauss."

RF did conduct this course, English 186, during the second semester of the academic year 1925–1926, but he "soldiered" through it so casually that he disappointed some of the students. For more details, see Note 19 of Chapter 20.

4. For source, see Note 1 of this chapter. The *Globe* reporter had also mentioned other members of the Frost family: "Mr. Frost's children are all working. His son, Carroll [who had informally changed the spelling himself because, he said, Carol was a girl's name], is on the farm at South Shaftsbury. His two eldest daughters, Lesley and Margery [a variant spelling which RF seemed to prefer], have a bookshop at Pittsfield, and during the summer they drive a book truck around the many camps of New England. The youngest daughter, Irma, is studying drawing in New York. They have been reared under Mr. Frost's philosophy of hands off as far as possible. He and Mrs. Frost have let their children learn for themselves, and have not impressed formal education or religion upon them."

Anyone who sets out to make a detailed analysis of RF's educational theories and practices might start by noticing that many of them were largely attempts to excuse or conceal or justify his frequently acknowledged laziness. He never seemed to notice how frequently he contradicted himself, in trying to describe precisely what he did consider to be the best teaching method. When Davison visited him on 22 Dec. 1923, Davison reported as follows:

"He scored many things about teaching, especially the new notion that the students should teach themselves, which he called 'Nonsense.' " (See p. 260 of Chapter 18.)

A few months later, RF again scoffed at the same notion:

"They [the Amherst students] had picked up the idea somewhere that the time was past for the teacher to teach the pupil. From now on it was the thing for the pupil to teach himself . . . So we had an amusing year." (See p. 265 of Chapter 18.)

In November of 1924, however, RF is making the odd claim that he himself fostered this theory of pupil-teach-thyself, at Amherst:

"In accepting the fellowship, Professor Frost feels that he will be able . . . to carry on as he has done in this college his theory of 'detached education.' . . . 'It might be described as no more than a slight interference with the students in their self-teaching. . . .' " (See p. 270 of Chapter 19.)

RF had one good reason for making this quick change in his theory and practice: it did work to the advantage of the lazy teacher to have the students teach themselves. He often repeated the story of how he once held aloft, before a Pinkerton class, a batch of themes just handed in, of how he asked if anyone wanted his theme back; whether anyone had put into his theme anything so important to the student that he wanted to save it. The students were obviously puzzled by the questions, and nobody knew how to answer him. There was silence. Very well, then, if they didn't care enough about their themes to want them back, he wasn't going to waste his time reading them. Having made that pronouncement, he said, he dropped the batch of themes into the wastepaper basket. End of story. Such a procedure, considered as a method of teaching, had one decisive gain: it did avoid some drudgery for the lazy teacher.

One of RF's most extraordinary utterances concerning education occurs in an undated letter to his daughter Lesley, written in the fall of 1924, not long after the birth (on 15 Oct. 1924) of his grandson William Prescott Frost (PWPF). Although the subject under consideration in this letter is the inevitable mistakes in any educational procedure, the following passages from it also throw light on the peculiarities of RF's self-styled heretical and nonconformist beliefs, which were sincerely devout even when they seemed to be irreverent:

"Couldn't we lay down the general rule that where education goes wrong just there is it most educative. But again I don't know. I'll never forget the day when a dozen of us were telling each other[,] exactly as if we knew[,] what was the proper training of a child in the way he should go and I was suddenly aware and by something in my manner made everybody else aware that we had Mrs. Patterson in our midst whose highly educated son had just broken an uncommon family pride by jumping into the ocean from a liner and drowning himself to rectify the mistake of his second marriage. From sheer embarrasment before God I said for all of us, What are we talking about all so self-assured?

"Mama was saying she hoped no mistakes would be made in the education of such a cute little fellow as Prescott [the newly born grandson]. Amen say I. You hear that, God? We are saying we hope no mistake will be made in the education of Prescott Frost, South Shaftsbury, Vermont, U. S. A. on the Earth. A word to the All-wise should be sufficient. There's nothing we can do about it if you ignore the hint. We are not threatening to stop going to church. (We've pretty well stopped already.) We were just discharging any responsibility we might be supposed to have in holding you to what we admit is almost entirely your own business. No disrespect intended. We believe in you. Go in and win. At any rate do the best you can. We are with you at every opening. We are in your fight against the Older God—I mean Chaos Chronos Column (Newspaper) Saturn Satan or whatever alias he turns up under."

(Underneath the facetiousness, here, something serious is implied by these two sentences addressed to God: "Go in and win. At any rate do the best you can." RF subscribed to the notion that God's power became limited when He gave to human beings those opportunities for choice implicit in man's freely willed thoughts and actions. RF's puritanism was thus heretical in the same sense that Milton's was: Arminian, rather than Calvinistic, at least in regard to the doctrine of the freedom of the will.)

5. EWF to Amy Lowell, 30 May [1924]; HUL.
6. EWF to Mrs. Edith Hazard Fobes, 1 March [1925]; DCL.
7. EWF to Amy Lowell, 27 Feb. [1925]; *Selected Letters*, p. 307.
8. RF to LU, 14 May 1920; *Letters to Untermeyer*, pp. 106–107.
9. RF to LU, "August Something" [1918]; ibid., p. 75.
10. Extended excerpts from Amy Lowell's birthday "Tribute to Frost" may be found in Damon, *Amy Lowell*, pp. 234–235, 289.
11. The full text of "The Cow's in the Corn" is given with bibliographical data in *The Early Years*, pp. 565–566. The important friendship between RF and the poet Wilbert Snow began at this birthday dinner. Here are excerpts from Snow's account of their meeting (op. cit., pp. 9–11):

"I first met Robert Frost at his Fiftieth Birthday Dinner. The letter of invitation was signed by Amy Lowell, Frederic Melcher, Louis Untermeyer and Irita Van Doren. The real inspirer and begetter of the dinner was Melcher . . . [who] wrote and asked if I would write [for *Publishers' Weekly*] an article on "New England in the New Poetry in America," with special emphasis on the contribution of Robert Frost. I agreed to carry out the assignment. . . . That tribute was a favorable one, as birthday greetings ought to be. But it was not altogether uncritical. . . . In spite of this, and before the postprandial speeches had begun, Frost came over to my table and introduced himself. (I was seated at a table with Willa Cather, whom he had already met.) He and I liked each other from the start. He took me by the arm and led me to the back of the room where he said, 'Now Louis will be jealous of you but we don't care.' I did not know the significance of that remark until much later. He said he liked what I had written in the *Publishers' Weekly*, but I had not in this opinion paid enough attention to his longer poems. . . . I insisted that 'Home Burial,' 'The Fear,' 'Mending Wall' and 'After Apple Picking' were still my favorites in that book [*North of Boston*]. He laughed and said, 'We'll let it go at that, but I want to see more of you. For we have much in common.'"

12. EWF to Amy Lowell, 29 March [1925]; HUL.

13. Damon, *Amy Lowell*, p. 701.

14. See Chapter 6, p. 85, for reference to Carol's ailment, nine years earlier.

15. EWF to Mrs. Ada Russell, 12 May [1925]; HUL.

16. RF to LT, 22 Feb. 1940; much the same account was told by RF to LT, in more detail, on many occasions thereafter.

17. RF's statement was published under the title, "The Poetry of Amy Lowell," *Christian Science Monitor*, 16 May 1925, p. 8; the original MS is in JLA.

18. The sentence, "Ever since childhood I have wanted my death to come in as effectively and effectingly," and other parts of this entire paragraph, will be found closely related to certain of RF's spoiled-child attitudes toward suicide, considered in *The Early Years*, pp. xvi-xvii, 175–180, 196–198, 266–268.

19. RF to LU [20 June 1925]; *Letters to Untermeyer*, p. 174.

20. RF's address was published under the title, "In Memoriam: Marion LeRoy Burton," in the *Christian Science Monitor*, 29 May 1925, p. 11.

21. To demonstrate that RF, in his address, did attribute to Burton many of RF's own self-justifying ideas on education, one might compare many of RF's sentences in this address with other statements he made to reporters shortly before and after this address. For such matchings, two of the best sources are the newspaper article cited in Note 1 of this chapter and "Robert Frost Interprets His Teaching Method," *Christian Science Monitor*, 24 Dec. 1925, p. 11. Each of these articles is partly reprinted in Lathem, *Interviews*, pp. 54–58, 67–71.

If, on the other hand, President Burton's own less vague and more practical views on education are placed against RF's statements, the difference is obvious. For example, Burton's last published article contained these two sentences: "In America, our whole future depends upon the high level of intelligence in every community. I have no hesitancy in stating that Detroit and Michigan have been so successful in leading in the manufacture of automobiles because of the primacy of the University of Michigan, and the existence here of a college of engineering which has been helping men to understand the fundamental principles of the internal combustion engine." (Quoted from the Michigan *Daily*, 17 Feb. 1925, p. 2, where it is explained that these two sentences are derived from President Burton's article, "That Mind of Yours," published in *Kiwanis Magazine*, Feb. 1925, and that the materials in the article were drawn from convocation addresses given by President Burton in Hill Auditorium.)

Occasionally, RF's chronic habit of attributing his own ideas to someone else, and then of saying something like, "Remember now that I am telling you almost his very words," caused him acute embarrassment. Perhaps the most painful consequences occurred when he put some of his own words into the mouth of Premier Khrushchev. A compressed account of this incident, and President John F. Kennedy's indignant reaction, is given in *Selected Letters*, pp. 591–592.

22. Editorial, Springfield *Republican*, 9 Nov. 1924, p. 19.

23. RF to G. R. Elliott, June 1925; *Selected Letters*, p. 312. For more details on this condition of EWF, see Note 3 of Chapter 20.

20. SICKNESS AND SCATTERATION

1. RF to LU, 11 Feb. 1926; *Letters to Untermeyer*, p. 178. Notice the hints implied by his remark that this sickness and scatteration, in his immediate family, "is our fault and not our misfortune or I wouldn't admit it." Closely related is the next sentence: "It's a result and a [divine] judgement on us." RF thus implied his belief that these consequences and sufferings were the reproofs of a displeased God.

2. EWF to Mrs. Fobes, 15 July 1925 (DCL). In this letter, EWF mentioned for the first time the Fobes guest-cottage (purchased in 1924 from Louis M. Cadarette) which became such an important hay-fever retreat for the Frosts during so many later summers. In a letter to Mrs. Von Moschzisker, 17 Aug. 1925 (ACL), EWF gave a brief description of the house and its surroundings: "We are now in the old 'Cadaret[te] place' on Toad Hill near the Fobes farm [in Franconia, N. H.]. Mrs. Fobes bought it a year ago, as she wanted the land to pasture her sheep, and afterward decided to fix up the house. She had made it thoroughly comfortable and homelike, with fireplace and bathroom, and we are enjoying it very much. . . . Behind the house are woods, and a little way in are two lovely meadows, encircled by woods, and with a really good view of the mountains."

During the three summers immediately previous to 1925, the Frosts had made other arrangements for spending the hay-fever season in Franconia. In 1922 and 1923, they stayed as guests in the farmhouse they had sold to Raymond Holden, in Franconia. In the summer of 1924, they were guests of Mrs. Fobes at the main house on the Fobes estate in Franconia. EWF mentioned that visit in a letter written from there to Mrs. Von Moschzisker, early in Sept. 1924: "We have been visiting Mrs. Fobes about two weeks and a half. . . . Mrs. Fobes' place is so beautifully quiet, too, way off from automobiles. . . . Grace Holden is living alone with the children and servants on her place this summer. We haven't seen her. I have heard that she expects to get her divorce in October. . . . Our little house [the farmhouse sold to Raymond Holden] has acquired a new piazza and is rented to a Hindoo writer."

3. RF's delicacy on this occasion may have been prompted in part by his feeling that if he told the truth Elliott would not believe him. Mrs. Frost had confided to her husband and to her doctor, early in the winter of 1924, that she had been suffering so consistently from morning sickness that she thought she must be pregnant. She was fifty-three years old, and the doctor was initially amused by her diagnosis. Gradually, however, it became apparent that her diagnosis was correct. Early in June of 1925 she became ill, and during this illness she suffered a miscarriage. The doctor, after examining the embryo, reported that she had indeed been pregnant for approximately five months. After the miscarriage, she remained so ill that RF concluded he could not leave her alone; hence the cancellation of his plan to go to Bowdoin to receive the honorary degree awaiting him there. A degree was awarded to him by Bowdoin in June of 1926. (RF to LT, June 1947.)

4. RF to LT, 14 Sept. 1946. This copy of Darwin's so-called "Voyage of the Beagle" is now in the Frost collection, NYUL. It bears the flyleaf inscription, "Robert Frost with the affectionate regards of C. C. Little, 1926."

5. RF to Mary E. Cooley, 10 Nov. 1924; PMEC.

6. RF to Wade Van Dore, 24 June 1922; *Selected Letters*, p. 278.

7. Wade Van Dore, journal entry, 19 Nov. 1925; permission to quote granted by Van Dore, whose assistance here and elsewhere is gratefully acknowledged.

8. RF to John T. Barlett, 11 Dec. 1925; VaUL.

9. RF's scientific interest in the structure of the atom was greatly stimulated by his having heard and talked with the distinguished Danish scientist Neils Bohr at Amherst in the fall of 1923. Bohr gave two lectures on the atom while at the College—lectures reported at some length in the Amherst *Student* 15 and 18 Oct. 1923. RF met Bohr and had dinner with him in the home of President Olds, who subsequently said that RF's questions addressed to Bohr were far more penetrating than those asked by the professorial scientists in the dinner group. (Mrs. G. D. Olds to LT, interview, 29 March 1947.)

The following passage may serve to illustrate the literary, philosophical, and religious uses which RF made of his constantly acquired and steadily accumulating knowledge concerning scientific facts and theories:

"You know that you can't tell by name what persons in a certain class will be dead ten years after graduation, but you can tell actuarially how many will be dead. Now, just so this scientist says of the particles of matter flying at a screen, striking a screen: you can't tell what individual particles will come, but you can say in general that a certain number will strike in a given time. It shows, you see, that the individual particle can come freely. I asked Bohr about that particularly, and he said, 'Yes, it is so. It can come when it wills and as it wills; and the action of the individual particle is unpredictable. But it is not so of the action of the mass. There you can predict.' He says, 'That gives the individual atom its freedom, but the mass its necessity.'" (Quoted from "Education by Poetry," a talk delivered by RF at Amherst College on 15 Nov. 1930; cited in Note 19 of Chapter 25.)

10. Quoted from Allen Shoenfield, "Science Can't Dishearten Poets, Says Robert Frost," Detroit *News,* 11 Oct. 1925; Lathem, *Interviews,* pp. 63–66.

11. Burton, son of a Congregational minister, earned his degree of Bachelor of Divinity at Yale in 1906, became pastor of the Church of Pilgrims in Brooklyn, N.Y., in 1908, and published his first book entitled *The Problem of Evil: A Criticism of the Augustinian Point of View* in 1909.

12. RF to John Bartlett [c. 1 Jan. 1926]; *Selected Letters,* pp. 323–324.

13. Ibid., p. 323.

14. In the celebrated "Monkey Trial," *Tennessee v. John Thomas Scopes,* held in Dayton, Tennessee, from 10 to 12 July 1925, Clarence Darrow as lawyer for the defense was instructed to make the trial a test case for the purpose of challenging Tennessee's Butler Law. That law forbade any teacher in a publicly supported school or college "to teach any theory that denies the story of the Divine creation of man as taught in the Bible, and to teach instead that man has descended from a lower order of animals." William Jennings Bryan, as lawyer for the prosecution, had long been thundering against the Darwinian theory of evolution, and had repeatedly said, "It is better to trust in the Rock of Ages than to know the ages of the rocks." Although RF aligned his deepest sympathies with Bryan (see Note 23 of Chapter 21), he could and did joke self-defensively about the trial: "Captain Mattison, our postmaster [in South Shaftsbury], and a man who has been to France, wanted to know of me what they had gone into court out in Tennessee for, to settle it once and for all who we were descended from, monkeys or the Virgin Mary?" (RF to LU, 20 June 1925; *Letters to Untermeyer,* p. 175.)

15. RF to Sidney Cox [c. Jan. 1926]; *Selected Letters,* pp. 324–325.

16. Retrospectively, on 28 Oct. 1926, EWF wrote to J. J. Lankes (TUL) a summary of what had happened to Marjorie: "Marjorie (the youngest) has been a great care since the 1st of last December, when she was taken with pneumonia. A serious heart infection [actually, pericarditis] followed, and then in March, before she had begun to sit up at all, the doctors advised that her appendix be taken out, as they thought she had chronic appendicitis. I think she was really too weak for the operation, as it seemed as if she would *never* get strong enough to walk around after it. Now she has got strong enough to walk about two miles a day, but she is still a great anxiety as her heart action is unstable, and her

throat is delicate. It is hard for her to keep from taking cold."
(Much of Marjorie's psychological depression during and after
this period was caused in part by physical debility: the two conditions were obviously synergetic. RF repeatedly told LT that
Marjorie's idealistic and easily offended sensibilities were similar
to those of her aunt, Jeanie Florence Frost. See Note 14 of
Chapter 9.)

17. This account and summary of RF's talk given at Bryn Mawr
on 15 Jan. 1926 is derived from two sources: an unsigned article,
"Robert Frost Talks on Metaphors," Bryn Mawr *College News*, 10
Feb. 1926, p. 1, and RF's summary of the talk, in retrospective
conversation with LT on 5 April 1940. The three Longfellow poems
which he used from *The Oxford Book of English Verse* were "The
Galley of Count Arnaldos," "Chaucer," and "Dante."

This Bryn Mawr talk, which grew in part from his Amherst
course on "Judgments," might be considered a trial flight for his
closely related and more successful "Education by Poetry" cited in
Note 19 of Chapter 25.

18. RF thus quoted himself when telling the anecdote to LT on
5 April 1940. Prior to his Bowdoin appearance, RF had made an
even more pointed defense of Longfellow:

" 'One of the real American poets of yesterday,' he said, 'was
Longfellow. No, I am not being sarcastic. I mean it. It is the
fashion nowadays to make fun of him. I come across this pose and
attitude with people I meet socially, with men and women I meet
in the classrooms of colleges where I teach. They laugh at his
gentleness, at his lack of worldliness, at his detachment from the
world and the meaning thereof.

" 'When and where has it been written that a poet must be a
club-swinging warrior, and a teller of barroom tales, a participant of
unspeakable experiences? That, today, apparently is the stamp of
poetic integrity. I hear people speak of men who are writing today,
and their eyes light up with a deep glow of satisfaction when they
can mention some putrid bit of gossip about them. "He writes such
lovely things," they say, and in the next breath add, half worshipfully, "He lives such a terrible life."

" 'I can't see it. I can't see that a man must needs have his feet
plowing through unhealthy mud in order to appreciate more fully
the glowing splendor of the clouds. I can't see that a man must fill
his soul with sick and miserable experiences, self-imposed and
self-inflicted, and greatly enjoyed, before he can sit down and
write a lyric of strange and compelling beauty. Inspiration doesn't
lie in the mud; it lies in the clean and wholesome life of the
ordinary man.' "

(Quoted by Rose C. Feld, in "Robert Frost Relieves His Mind,"
New York *Times Book Review*, 21 Oct. 1923; here quoted from
Lathem, *Interviews*, p. 47.)

19. Through correspondence with Mrs. Sue Bonner Wolcutt,
Miss Mary E. Cooley, and Miss Dorothy Tyler, LT gathered many
different impressions about how RF taught this course. Miss Cooley

wrote that RF never criticized her poems except to say he liked them. Mrs. Wolcutt, going into more detail, wrote a passage here quoted with her permission:

"I have been asked a number of times by various people writing on Mr. Frost, to describe his teaching methods. They were, of course, non-existent. He merely talked about poetry; sometimes he talked about the technique, sometimes about fashions in poetry. As always with Mr. Frost, what he said today he might contradict next week. I remember one class period he talked about metaphor in poetry, and how the new fresh image was the essence of poetry. He read us that evening Humbert Wolfe's poems, 'The Grey Squirrel,' 'The Lamb,' 'Tulip' and 'Iliad.' I had never read them before—they still sound like pure magic to me. A propos of 'Iliad,' he read a poem of Louis Untermeyer's, also an experiment in assonance. I haven't thought of it for over twenty years, and I can't remember the title, but it is about the seventh son of the widow, waiting in the forest to slay the dragon. Mr. Frost remarked that Louis was trying a little *too* hard with his assonance, but Humbert Wolfe's came naturally. Another evening he teed off in high spirit on a poem of mine in the *Inlander*, which he said I didn't mean. (I didn't.) From that he read us Swinburne's 'Itylus' which he said was very lovely poetry, but that Swinburne didn't *really* feel the least bit sorry about Itylus. Another time he talked a little about fashions in poetry and remarked that today (1926) no poet felt he was really writing poetry unless he used the word 'Malechite.' We were supposed to show him our poetry for his criticism, but he never criticized it very much one way or the other. Just among ourselves we secretly believed that he wasn't much interested in our poetry, and for some reason we didn't mind at all."

Miss Cooley remembered that RF was asked to be a judge in a poetry contest sponsored by the *Inlander* in the spring of 1926. The contestants were required to use pseudonymns, and RF seemed more interested in trying to guess who wrote what, than in evaluating the quality of the poems.

Miss Tyler found less to criticize and more to praise. In one of her several published articles on RF, she made the following references to this course: "Robert Frost's teaching methods, unique, heterodox, but also memorable, are known to many. . . . Probably they would not serve for an entire curriculum with a degree at the end . . . but certainly some of his students would not have exchanged his classes for all the other courses in the big book." ("Remembering Robert Frost," *Among Friends* [a quarterly publication of the Friends of the Detroit Public Library], No. 29, Winter 1962–1963, p. 3. Special gratitude is here expressed to Miss Tyler for sharing with LT, over many years, detailed information about RF's various activities at the University of Michigan.)

20. Quoted by John Hurd, Jr., "Poets and Writers Flock to Bowdoin for the Round Table of Literature," Boston *Globe*, 10 May 1925, Editorial Feature Section, p. 12. For references to poems

which, according to RF, were inspired by his homesickness for New England while he was living in England, see *The Early Years*, pp. 432–433.

21. "Spring Pools" (*The Poetry*, p. 245) was first published in the Dearborn [Michigan] *Independent*, Vol. 27, No. 27 (23 April 1927). This poem was the second of three contributions he made to the Dearborn *Independent*. First was "The Same Leaves" (later entitled "In Hardwood Groves"), which appeared in the issue for 18 Dec. 1926. Third was "The Cow's in the Corn," which appeared in the issue for 18 June 1927. While at Ann Arbor during the spring of 1926, RF was approached by William J. Cameron, then serving as editor of the Dearborn *Independent*, and was asked to help in getting contributions from some of the best modern poets. RF resisted, saying he would have nothing to do with this magazine of Henry Ford's because it had been notoriously anti-Semitic. Assured by Cameron, however, that the policy of the periodical had undergone a radical change, and that it aspired to be literary rather than polemical, RF softened. He said that soliciting manuscripts was not his work, but that his two daughters, Lesley and Marjorie, might be willing to do it for pay. They did do it, with their father's help. In a letter written to Dorothy Canfield Fisher from Franconia, during the hay-fever season of 1926, RF wrote (VtUL),

"I meant to tell you I have been telling the editors of the Dearborn Independent that you were the one to help them turn their magazine literary, as is now their ambition since they have exhausted the Jew. They seem fearfully in earnest about doing something for the arts with a slight pardonable emphasis on the American as distinguished from the New York arts. I shall do what I can for them. Wouldnt it be splendid if they could lead off with a set of short stories from you. . . ."

22. Details of this arrangement have been gleaned from several sources, starting with LT's conversations with RF and with G. R. Elliott. President Olds made the terms clear in his first release, thus reported:

"The most important announcement made by President Olds at the Alumni Dinner [noon, Saturday, 19 June 1926, at Amherst] was that Robert Frost would return to Amherst next year as professor of English. Under the terms of his appointment, Mr. Frost will not be in residence throughout the year, but will spend one term or its equivalent at college. He will conduct no classes, but will lecture and meet students in conference with entire informality. Whatever is done under his inspiration and guidance will be done as he would have it, as a labor of love without academic credit."

("Robert Frost Returns to Amherst," Amherst *Graduates' Quarterly*, Vol. XV, No. 4 [Aug. 1926], p. 271. At this time, the Amherst year was divided into three terms; RF's obligation was for ten weeks only, in each academic year.)

Corroboration of President Olds's visit to Ann Arbor, and of other details, may be found in a letter to "My dear Robert," signed,

"George D. Olds," dated 12 Jan. 1928 (DCL). Enclosed was a letter of the same date written by Olds to his successor, President Arthur Stanley Pease, containing this:

"A letter just received makes it evident that Robert Frost is troubled because of a misunderstanding of the terms under which he accepted the call to Amherst. It was implied in my early communications with him and definitely stated in the conference I had with him at Ann Arbor two years ago next Spring [i.e., spring 1926] that he was to have the rank of full Professor receiving a salary of $5,000 in consideration of which he was to be in residence at Amherst for the Winter term for the purpose of informal conferences with students and teachers; but that he was to have no regular classroom work. It was the further understanding that while it was obligatory upon him to meet certain engagements at other colleges already made for last Winter [i.e., 1926–1927] which would affect the residence noted above, no such engagements would be made in the future. I am very sorry that I failed to speak to you of this arrangement in the course of our many talks about the college. . . ." (DCL, together with a letter from President Pease to RF, 6 April 1928, clarifying the terms of RF's contract with Amherst.)

23. RF to G. R. Elliott [10 May 1926]; ACL. At the bottom of this letter Elliott wrote retrospectively, "I urged Pres. Olds to bring R. F. back to Amherst."

24. RF to LU, 17 May 1926; *Letters to Untermeyer*, p. 184.

25. RF to Sidney Cox [c. 17 May 1926]; DCL.

26. RF to John Bartlett, 26 May 1926; *Selected Letters,* pp. 329–330. Another brief summary of RF's predicament, caused by the almost fatal illness of his daughter Marjorie, deserves inclusion here. In 1925, Witter Bynner had asked RF to write a preface for a volume of Bynner's poetry, and RF had promised to do so provided Bynner was not in too much of a hurry. Bynner waited for a year, then wrote to say that he could use the preface only if he received it soon. RF answered, in an undated letter bearing the postmark cancellation date, 5 April 1926 (HUL):

"For my part, my daughter, the best poet in the family, has been dangerously ill for twelve weeks now, my wife is prostrated, and my heart undisposed to prefaces. Jesus Mary what a year you have chosen to get cornered and to corner in. In the last homecoming to roost, the exigencies of the irresponsible are more ruthless than the most military of law and order. But I forgive you them even as I hope to be forgiven a murder I once did. The question is what am I going to do for you. I'm damned if I see in my confusion. I haven't had a metaphor for months. This is the twilight of the mind—before God it is. I'll go out to grass at a word in the wrong key. Aren't we in a terrible mess? Yours (and have mercy on me) Robert Frost."

By the time RF wrote this letter, Marjorie was out of danger and Mrs. Frost was not prostrated: the entire letter invokes a past crisis for the convenient purpose of excuse-making. Also, some clarification can be made of what RF mysteriously implied by the statement, ". . . even as I hope to be forgiven a murder I once did." During another crisis, when his first child was ill, RF failed to summon a doctor until too late. The doctor reproached RF for this failure, and RF blamed himself for the child's death. In that sense, he accused himself of being a murderer, and the feeling of guilt was a lasting one. For more details concerning this very important event in his life, see *The Early Years*, p. 258.

21. SPEAKING OF CONTRARIES

1. "West-Running Brook," *The Poetry*, pp. 259, 260.
2. RF to John Bartlett [26 May 1926]; *Selected Letters*, p. 329.
3. EWF to Mrs. Fobes [c. 1 Aug. 1926]; DCL.
4. E. A. Richards, "'Joe Wright's Book,'" the Amherst *Monthly*, Vol. 34, No. 6 (March 1920), pp. 210–211. In his reminiscences, mentioned in Note 3 of Chapter 14, Richards implied more similarity than there actually is between the two brook-poems: "Its virtue as a piece of writing was scant, indeed, but Frost said, 'If I had that idea, I know what I'd do with it.' To which I replied, 'It's all yours if you want it.' As you may guess, the result was the poem that eventually appeared under the title, 'West-Running Brook.'"
5. For reference to RF's Michigan session on Darwin, see Chapter 20, pp. 296–297.
6. RF to LU [1 Jan. 1917]; *Letters to Untermeyer*, p. 47. This passage has so much bearing on some of RF's motives for striking self-protective postures (see Note 12 of Chapter 18) that it may reward further consideration. Reference has already been made to his admiration for Emerson's poem "Uriel," which one character in *A Masque of Reason* is permitted to describe as "the greatest Western poem yet." (See Note 40 of Chapter 6.) The angel Uriel had his own way of knocking theories into cocked hats. But the theories under consideration, here, are those connected with evolution, and RF likes the fact that Bergson and Fabre have "bothered our evolutionism . . ." One of RF's favorite Uriel-postures was to attack any scientific position which offended his own essentially orthodox Christian religious position. Nevertheless, he liked to make these attacks so subtle that the artistry of his attacks would be witty, teasing, and deceptive. After pointing out that one gets more credit for his thoughts if one restates formulas or cites cases that fall in easily under formulas, he adds that he gets his fun through saying things which fall outside formulas; things which won't quite fit: ". . . things that won't formulate—that almost but don't quite formulate." Notice that he adds, "I should like to be so subtle at this game as to seem to the casual person altogether obvious. The casual person would assume that I meant nothing or else I came near enough meaning something he was familiar with to mean it for all practical purposes."

As has been shown (Note 7 of Chapter 7), he was too subtle at this game when he wrote "The Road Not Taken," about which he commented to LU, "I trust my meaning is not too hidden . . . I can't help my way of coming at things." He was also too subtle at this game (and was forced to explain) in his writing to Sidney Cox (*Selected Letters*, p. 435): "Look out I don't spoof you. About five years ago I resolved to spoil my correspondence with you by throwing it into confusion the way God threw the speech of the builders of the tower of Babel into confusion." (See ibid., p. xvi, where this passage is considered within a context of some other stylistic deceptions.)

7. Henri Bergson, *Creative Evolution* (New York, 1911), pp. 269, 237. For background on RF's first reading of and admiration for *Creative Evolution*, in 1911, see *The Early Years*, pp. 381–382, 579–581.

8. RF mentioned Havelock Ellis—and Bergson—in his talk, "Metaphors," given at Bryn Mawr College on 15 Jan. 1926, but the undergraduate reporter apparently missed some of the essential points in her attempt to paraphrase RF, as follows (*College News*, 10 Feb. 1926, p. 1):

"Bergson, more a poet than a philosopher, said that the vapor was composed of the same atoms as in the beginning [perhaps as described by RF in referring to the atomic theory propounded by Lucretius], but that a new something [*élan vital*?] was added. Freud's metaphor is that life is nothing but appetite, alimentary or sexual. A less hopeful metaphor is that of Havelock Ellis, who calls all life a dance. To Mr. Frost, at least, this is unsatisfactory. . . ."

9. RF, in a public performance at Rutgers University on 5 Oct. 1949, read "West-Running Brook." LT, present at this occasion, was particularly interested to notice that when RF was reading the line which contains "Not just a swerving . . ." the poet paused after "swerving" and said parenthetically to the audience, "As in Lucretius." (His reference was apparently to Book II, lines 216–293, in *De rerum natura*.)

Because RF frequently mentioned his admiration for Lucretius, those of his friends who mistakenly claimed he was an agnostic were inclined to cite this admiration as reflecting his agnosticism. Others, who correctly knew that RF held devout religious beliefs (and who also knew that Lucretius, a rigorous materialist, dismissed as illusions such concepts as the immortality of the soul and the existence of Divine Providence), were puzzled by this admiration.

One relevant fact, here, is RF's habit of reading into and out of any literary work only such notions as were congenial to his own prejudices. His obsessive fears probably caused him to like best, in Lucretius, the attempt to persuade human beings that many of their fears (including the fear of death) could and should be overcome. One translator of *De rerum natura* makes a prefatory statement concerning Lucretius which might be applied to RF with some accuracy:

"He was oppressed at times by the unfriendliness of the world and the thought of its impending dissolution. We may suspect that the childish terrors, of which he speaks so feelingly, were not so much banished by his philosophy as diverted into other channels. Yet the great attraction of Lucretius is undoubtedly his defiant conviction that he has honestly faced these fears and trampled them underfoot." (Ronald Latham, tr., *Lucretius: On the Nature of the Universe* [London, 1951], p. 14.)

10. In *Creative Evolution,* Bergson repeatedly echoes not only Lucretius but also St. Paul, both of whom RF liked to re-read. The following example of a restrictively naturalistic Lucretian life-through-death metaphor is quoted from Ronald Latham's prose translation of *De rerum natura* (op. cit., pp. 38–39):

"Lastly, showers perish when father ether has flung them down into the lap of mother earth. But the crops spring up fresh and gay. . . . Visible objects therefore do not perish utterly, since nature repairs one thing from another and allows nothing to be born without the aid of another's death."

Perhaps the most famous of St. Paul's physical-metaphysical life-through-death analogizings occurs in his First Letter to the Corinthians, Chapter 15, here quoted from the Revised Standard Version:

"What you sow does not come to life unless it dies. And what you sow is not the body which is to be, but a bare kernel, perhaps of wheat or of some other grain. But God gives it a body as he has chosen, and to each kind of seed its own body. . . . So is it with the resurrection of the dead. What is sown is perishable, what is raised is imperishable. . . . When the perishable puts on the imperishable, and the mortal puts on immortality, then shall come to pass the saying that is written [Isaiah 25:8]: Death is swallowed up in victory. O death, where is thy victory? O death, where is thy sting?"

There is a special pertinence in correlating this passage from First Corinthians with RF's themes in "West-Running Brook." As was suggested in Note 15 of Chapter 11, he took pleasure in claiming that his religious stance was original and heretical, but he was sufficiently orthodox to center his faith around fear of death and hope for salvation in a life to come. ("Now faith is the substance of things hoped for . . ." Hebrews 11:1.) Fear of death is also the thematic center around which the images in "West-Running Brook" are built. One part of existence is there represented as being a "universal cataract of death / That spends to nothingness . . ." Another part of existence is there represented as being resistance to death, through a "backward motion toward the source." For RF, and perhaps for Bergson, this entire concept of "creative evolution" was of ultimate importance because it could be used to preach anew the gospel of triumph over death. Bergson came nearest to echoing the Pauline affirmation when he described the boldly willed struggle, on man's part, as "an overwhelming charge able to beat down every resistance and clear the most formidable obstacles, perhaps even death." (*Creative Evolution*, p. 271.)

11. The concluding lines of "West-Running Brook," not quoted here, round out this poetic study in contraries by implying that the husband and wife have helped each other through their act of sharing contrary views of the same thing; that they have thus collaborated to achieve fresh insights concerning existence.

12. RF to E. S. Sergeant, Aug. 1926; *The Trial by Existence*, op. cit., p. 143. RF's claim that God had given him prophetic insight, on the Cliff House beach at San Francisco, "forty five years ago come yesterday," and that he had written the prophecy into his poem, "Once by the Pacific," might be taken as merely a humorous remark—if RF had not seriously made similar claims for the same poem on many other occasions. Conveniently, there is so much vagueness in the prophecy that "a night of dark intent" is coming, "and not only a night, an age," that RF could and did later apply it to any circumstance he chose to view as calamitous. In the letter quoted, the immediate calamity is that Louis and Jean Starr Untermeyer are getting a divorce. By contrast, RF sometimes called the poem a prophecy of all the calamities associated with the two World Wars.

Although RF was usually shy about confessing his belief in the Romantic-Victorian concept of the poet as prophet, with powers of second sight, he was exposed to this concept early through his mother's teachings. (See *The Early Years*, pp. 4, 35, 488–491, 525–526.) Later, in his own reading, he found and admired this concept in the writings of Shelley, Wordsworth, Carlyle, Emerson, Tennyson, and Browning. One need go no further afield, however, than Emerson's famous essay, "The Poet," to find one major source for many of RF's hints concerning his belief in the poet as prophet.

13. There is an element of prophecy in "The Master Speed." (*The Poetry*, p. 300.) These two lovers cannot be parted or swept away from each other, now that they are "agreed" concerning the oneness achieved through their marriage. Presumably they were indeed "agreed," on the occasion of their marriage, but that agreement did not last. Eventually the prophecy itself was spoiled by their divorce. RF did not publish "The Master Speed" in *West-Running Brook*, perhaps because the metaphors in it were too closely related to some of those in the title poem of that book. The poem first appeared in the Yale *Review*, Dec. 1935.

14. James Branch Cabell had shocked many readers with his erotic dream-romance entitled *Jurgen* (1919), and attempts were made to suppress it on charges of obscenity.

15. RF to Lesley Frost [c. Oct. 1924]; PWPF. Wilbert Snow (op. cit., pp. 13–17), gives a detailed account of RF's visit to Wesleyan University and his attendance at the dinner for Lizette Woodworth Reese in Dec. 1926.

16. RF to John Bartlett, 23 Dec. 1926; VaUL.

17. EWF to Mrs. Fobes, 22 Feb. 1927; DCL.

18. On his way to Ann Arbor, RF went to Toledo, Ohio, and gave

a reading "before a capacity audience" in the Toledo Museum of Art on the evening of 25 March 1927, spending the night as guest of Mr. and Mrs. Lyman Spitzer. At Ann Arbor for approximately a week (24 March through 2 April), he was guest of Dean Bursley. The Michigan *Daily* gave him considerable coverage.

19. "The Armful" (*The Poetry*, pp. 266–267) was first published in the *Nation*, Vol. 126, No. 3266 (8 Feb. 1928), p. 151; the newly appointed poetry-editor of the *Nation* was then RF's admirer and friend Mark Van Doren, who had attended RF's fiftieth birthday dinner in New York City.

20. "Acquainted with the Night," *The Poetry*, p. 255. RF was so constantly a Bible reader, and so familiar with so many famous Bible passages, that the recurrence of the word "acquainted" and the full title of this poem may be considered as echoing Isaiah 53:3: ". . . a man of sorrows, and acquainted with grief . . ."

21. Again there would seem to be a deliberate echo, this time from "The Chambered Nautilus" by Oliver Wendell Holmes:

> *Build thee more stately mansions, O my soul,*
> *As the swift seasons roll!*
> *Leave thy low-vaulted past!*
> *Let each new temple, nobler than the last,*
> *Shut thee from heaven with a dome more vast,*
> *Till thou at length art free*
> *Leaving thine outgrown shell by life's unresting sea!*

22. Only because of his ability to lean with gratitude on the assistance of his erudite colleagues, Carlos Baker and Thomas P. Roche, LT can observe that RF borrowed this motto from a poem entitled "The Death of Zoroas, an Egiptian Astronomer, in First Fight, That Alexander Had with the Persians," by Nicholas Grimald (1519–1562). This poem first appeared in *Tottel's Miscellany* (1557), and RF owned a reprint of *Tottel's Miscellany*. His copy of it is now in the Frost collection, NYUL.

23. In *West-Running Brook*, one of RF's most tantalizingly ambiguous manipulations of analogies between seemingly dissimilar things may be found in the poem entitled "Sitting by a Bush in Broad Sunlight" (*The Poetry*, p. 266). RF's preparations for writing this poem provide further examples of his continuous involvement with the Victorian warfare between evolutionary theory and religious belief. He apparently began his preparation by making five exploratory notes in one of his notebooks (DCL) in 1925:

"Analogies for God
"Working hypotheses
"Axiom
"Spoke once and not since
"So did heat once to call the animate out of the inanimate— once and never again. In those days there were wonders. From one of these wonders we have our breath—from the other our faith by a long descent."

Continuing from these preliminary notes, he apparently waited for images which would enable him to imply analogies between one working hypothesis of science and one axiom of religion. By definition, an axiom is a statement universally accepted as true, while an hypothesis is an unproved theory, proposition, supposition, accepted to explain certain facts or to provide a basis for further investigation. For a believer like RF, an axiom concerning the existence of God may be found in the biblical evidence that God, although now silent, once talked directly with Moses and others. For the Darwinian scientist, by contrast, a working hypothesis is that the heat of the sun once called the animate out of the inanimate—and some scientists have claimed that this hypothesis of spontaneous generation makes the concept of a Creator-God superfluous. RF, starting from his preliminary notations, went on to correlate these two notions in the following first-draft pair of couplets (ASCL):

> As God once declared he was true
> And then took the veil and withdrew
> So the sun once quickened the earth
> And left all that followed to birth.

Apparently dissatisfied with such assertive analogizing of these implicitly contrary hypotheses, he may have waited for images which might serve to separate the analogous elements before combining them. Autumn foliage, in Franconia, probably reminded him of a biblical correlation which other poets had used. Whittier, remembering Moses and the burning bush, had seen God in the miracle of autumn ("The Chapel of the Hermits"):

> We lack but open eye and ear
> To find the Orient's marvels here;
> The still small voice in autumn's hush,
> Yon maple wood the burning bush.

Elizabeth Barrett Browning had made her own analogy out of the same associations (Book VII of "Aurora Leigh"):

> Earth's crammed with heaven,
> And every common bush afire with God;
> But only he who sees takes off his shoes.

RF, preferring to be more subtle in conveying his own piety, chose to begin with fall imagery which might indicate doubts caused by the lack of heat in the autumn sun:

> When I spread out my hand here today,
> I catch no more than a ray
> To feel of between thumb and fingers;
> No lasting effect of it lingers.

[628]

There was one time and only the one
When dust really took in the sun;
And from that one intake of fire
All creatures still warmly suspire.

And if men have watched a long time
And never seen sun-smitten slime
Again come to life and crawl off,
We must not be too ready to scoff.

If RF had chosen to end his poem entitled "Sitting by a Bush in Broad Sunlight" with this third stanza, the poem might have been interpreted as a defense of the scientific theory concerning the beginning of life through spontaneous generation. In full context, however, the third stanza is ambiguous. Those who scoff might be inclined to ask, If dust really did take in the sun at one time, why shouldn't such a miracle recur? If, by contrast, this event is viewed as a God-inspired miracle, analogous to God's giving life to dust when he created Adam and breathed into his nostrils the breath of life so that he became a living soul, the latter miracle could be associated with the "one time" when "dust really took in the sun." Then these two miracles could be correlated with God's speaking to Moses from the burning bush. RF, continuing the poem toward the latter analogizing, introduced a reminder of God's pledge to Moses from the burning bush:

God once declared He was true
And then took the veil and withdrew,
And remember how final a hush
Then descended of old on the bush.

Having established these analogies, Frost concluded with a further extension:

God once spoke to people by name.
The sun once imparted its flame.
One impulse persists as our breath;
The other persists as our faith.

Through these analogizings, Frost thus seemed to resolve the ambiguities to his own satisfaction by reconciling the scientific hypothesis with a Christian axiom. Many other Victorian poets made similar gestures in their attempts to reconcile science and religion.

Further light is thrown on RF's attitude toward this poem by Wilbert Snow, in "The Robert Frost I Knew" (op. cit., pp. 22–23): "I tried to spoof him once about a poem of his entitled 'Sitting by a Bush in Broad Sunlight' and quickly found that I had made a mistake and touched a tender chord. Only later did I learn of his superlative sensitivity. He even told me that he considered the account of man's creation as recorded in the first chapter of Genesis as no more miraculous than the combined factors of air, heat, light, moisture, climate, and other conditions brought into exact harmony to make life upon this planet possible. . . . When he read in the paper that there was a professor of biology in one of our ivy colleges who was not completely convinced of the exactitude of Darwin's theory of Evolution, that he wanted first to see the missing link, Frost was immensely delighted. In our conversation about the Scopes trial, which everybody was talking about during those years, his sympathies were all on the side of Bryan and the old Southern farmers who carried their Bibles to the courthouse during the trial. Over and over he kept saying that Clarence Darrow lacked imagination, that he depended too much on rationality to solve the problem of human existence." (For supporting evidence, see Note 14 of Chapter 20.)

24. RF to LU, 31 Aug. 1925; *Letters to Untermeyer,* p. 176.

25. Some other elements of similarity involve contrarieties here. Compare, for example, contrarieties in the last twenty-two lines of "The Bear" with those in the following passage from the second epistle in Pope's "Essay on Man":

> *Know then thyself, presume not God to scan,*
> *The proper study of mankind is Man.*
> *Placed on this isthmus of a middle state,*
> *A being darkly wise and rudely great:*
> *With too much knowledge for the Sceptic side,*
> *With too much weakness for the Stoic's pride,*
> *He hangs between, in doubt to act or rest;*
> *In doubt to deem himself a God or Beast;*
> *In doubt his mind or body to prefer;*
> *Born but to die, and reasoning but to err;*
> *Alike in ignorance, his reason such,*
> *Whether he think too little or too much;*
> *Chaos of thought and passion, all confused;*
> *Still by himself abused and disabused;*
> *Created half to rise, and half to fall,*
> *Great lord of all things, yet a prey to all;*
> *Sole judge of truth, in endless error hurl'd;*
> *The glory, jest, and riddle of the world!*

26. "The Bear" was first published in the *Nation,* Vol. 126, No. 3276 (18 April 1928), p. 447.

27. In the Table of Contents for *West-Running Brook,* RF gave five notations on dates of early poems. After the title, "A Peck of Gold," he added the italicized notation, *"As of about 1880."* He added the identical notation after the title, "Once by the Pacific." Because RF was only six years old in 1880, both uses of this date must obviously refer to the time of the experiences retrospectively evoked in these poems. After the title, "Bereft," he added this italicized notation: *"As of about 1893."* (For background on the experience which inspired "Bereft" see *The Early Years,* pp. 152–

153.) After the title, "The Flower Boat," the italicized notation is "*Very early.*" (See *Selected Letters,* p. 355, for RF's statement that it was written "in about 1894 or 5." It was published in *Youth's Companion* in 1909.) After the title, "The Thatch," the italicized notation is "*As of 1914.*" This date refers to the experience, not to the date of writing; it was actually written not long before its first published appearance, in *West-Running Brook.* (For background on "The Thatch," see *The Early Years,* pp. 464–465, 602.)

28. For background concerning the excitement and enthusiasm with which RF read and talked about Bergson's *Creative Evolution* in 1912, see *The Early Years,* pp. 381–382, 579–581.

29. See Chapter 20, pp. 291–293, for a summary of RF's talk at Bryn Mawr on 15 Jan. 1926.

30. Quoted from the Buffalo (N. Y.) *Evening News,* 11 Nov. 1927, p. 27, in a report of a reading given by RF at the Grosvenor Library, Buffalo, 10 Nov. 1927. Earlier that year, on 31 March 1927, RF gave a public reading of his poems at the University of Michigan, and on that same day Alfred Adler lectured at the same campus on the "inferiority complex." Both occasions were reported on the front page of the Michigan *Daily,* 1 April 1927.

31. Frederic G. Melcher to RF, 10 March 1927; DCL.

32. In a letter dated 27 May 1928 (DCL), R. H. Thornton informed RF that he would reach South Shaftsbury on Tuesday, 29 May 1928; that he would spend the afternoon and evening with RF, and would return to New York city on the night train. The schedule was carried out, and this meeting represents one of RF's shrewdest financial triumphs.

33. R. H. Thornton to RF, 5 June 1928 (DCL): "I am enclosing to you copies of the contract for your new book of lyrics. I need not tell you how happy I am that you are going to publish this volume with us; my visit to you must already have made that evident." In this letter, Thornton reviewed the terms they had discussed.

34. R. H. Thornton to RF, 6 July 1928 (DCL), making the Holt promise of "a definite guarantee of $250.00 a month in royalty from the sales of your several books for the next five years," and adding, "We hope, of course, that the royalties may return to you a great deal more than this." The advance of $2,000 on *West-Running Brook* was mailed in a letter from Thornton to RF dated 26 July 1928.

22. HELPING TO SHAPE AN IMAGE

1. RF to Gorham B. Munson [c. 16 June 1927]; WUL. Gratitude is here expressed to Mr. Munson for his many different forms of assistance in clarifying details concerning his complicated friendship with RF.

2. Edward Davison to LT, in conversation, 11 Sept. 1967. Gratitude is here expressed to Mr. Davison for his many different

forms of assistance in clarifying details concerning his complicated friendship with RF.

3. Gorham B. Munson, "Robert Frost," *Saturday Review of Literature*, Vol. 1, No. 35 (28 March 1925), p. 625. One reason why RF may have fluctuated between wanting to be a "good Greek" and wanting to defend his New England heritage by posing as a "good Puritan" was his awareness that, since the days of Shakespeare, many poets, critics, and historians had used "Puritan" as a dirty word. Back in 1869, Matthew Arnold had continued this trend by insisting that the tug-of-war between Hebraism and Hellenism could be viewed as a conflict between anarchy and culture; that the Puritans (ancient and modern) had warped one side of their humanity at the expense of other sides until they became "incomplete and mutilated men." (Matthew Arnold, *Culture and Anarchy* [Cambridge, 1932], p. 11.) Part of RF's bitterness toward Arnold, as expressed in "New Hampshire," may have been caused by the harshness of Arnold's attitude toward puritanism. In fact, a careful tabulation of RF's various attitudes will show that he was usually more inclined to defend puritanism than Hellenism. See Chapter 33, pp. 482–485, for an account of a particularly outspoken defense, made in the commencement address entitled "What Became of New England?" which he delivered at Oberlin College on 8 June 1937.

4. RF to LU, 6 June 1918; *Letters to Untermeyer*, pp. 67–68.

5. Louis Untermeyer, *Modern American Poetry* (New York, 1921), p. 176.

6. Another remarkable example of RF's spoon-feeding may be found in the statements and documents (BMCL) he gave to Elizabeth Shepley Sergeant to guide her in writing her article, "Robert Frost, A Good Greek Out of New England," *New Republic*, Vol. 44, No. 565 (30 Sept. 1925), pp. 144–148.

7. Quoted in Munson's detailed account, "The Classicism of Robert Frost: Reminiscences of a Biographer," *Modern Age*, Summer 1964, pp. 291–305.

8. Munson to RF, 19 Dec. 1926; DCL.

9. Munson, "A Comedy of Exiles," Fairleigh Dickinson University *Literary Review*, Vol. 12, No. 1 (Autumn 1968), p. 44.

10. Ibid., p. 49.

11. For source, see Note 7 of this chapter.

12. John Farrar to RF, 27 Dec. 1926; DCL.

13. Edward Davison, in conversation with LT on 11 Sept. 1967, said he still possessed the biographical notes he made from his various sessions with RF. The Amherst *Student* for 3 Feb. 1927, p. 1, carried an article, "Frost Sponsors Poet Lecturing in Chapel." Excerpts: "Edward Davison, one of the outsanding young Englishmen produced by the war, will lecture in Johnson chapel next Monday [7 Feb. 1927] at 8:30 P. M. His rise to prominence has been very sudden, as at the end of the war he was unknown, and is now distinguished in England and this country for his book of verse, 'The Harvest of Youth.' . . . Professor Frost speaks very

highly of 'The Harvest of Youth.' " A lengthy report on the lecture ("An Approach to Poetry") was given on p. 1 of the Amherst *Student* for 11 Feb. 1927.

14. The Amherst *Student*, 14 March 1927, carried an announcement of Munson's lecture, the article beginning, "Gorham Munson, critic, writer and editor in the field of modern literature, will speak Friday, March 18, on 'New Movements in American Letters.' Mr. Munson has just completed a work on the authors of the Nineteenth Century, and is now engaged in writing a critical biography of Mr. Frost and his works."

15. Munson to RF, 30 March 1927; DCL.

16. Munson to RF, 1 June 1927; DCL.

17. For details concerning the many generous forms of financial assistance given RF by his grandfather, see *The Early Years*, pp. xvii–xviii, 260–264, 275–276, 573–575.

18. RF's apparent goal, at this point in his letter, is to heighten the myth of isolation on the Derry farm, but the facts do not support the claim. Among the visitors who came to the Frost farm and stayed longer than overnight were Frost's sister Jeanie (on several occasions), Mrs. Frost's father (Edwin White), Mrs. Frost's sister Leona (Mrs. Nathaniel Harvey) and her three children. For an account of two visitors (Carl Burell and Jonathan Eastman) who moved to the farm in Derry and stayed with the Frosts for several months, see *The Early Years*, pp. 263–278.

19. Again, the facts do not support the claim. Among the neighborhood visitors who called at the Frost farm were members of the following families: Bricault, Clark, Guay, Miltimore, Newell, Osgood, Palmer, Patterson, Perkins. References to these visitors may be found in *New Hampshire Girlhood: The Derry Journals of Lesley Frost*, with Notes and Index by Lawrance Thompson and Arnold Grade (New York, 1969).

20. RF's statement to Munson about poverty gives no hint of extravagances already mentioned in Chapter 10, pp. 135–136: that RF grew bored with the farm during mud-season of 1903, took his wife and two children to New York City, and rented a furnished apartment in which they lived for a month, going and coming (part way) on the Fall River Line night boat; that, during at least five of the eight summers on that farm, he spent at least a month vacationing with his family in Bethlehem, N. H., a hay-fever retreat; that in August of 1909 he took his family to Willoughby Lake in Vermont and (during part of this vacation) rented a cottage on the shore. This long letter to Munson gives no indication of such gallivantings, nor of the already mentioned annuity from his grandfather's estate which enabled him to afford these modest luxuries.

21. According to Lesley Frost's journals, in *New Hampshire Girlhood*, there were three stoves on the ground floor of the Derry farmhouse: one in the kitchen, one in the living room, one in the parlor. The farm contained plenty of firewood free for the cutting, but the winters were long and RF was lazy, as he frequently con-

fessed. If, then, there were times when the Derry farm had only "one warm room in winter," such a predicament was not a sign of poverty.

22. Arthur Stanley Pease.

23. For source, see Note 1 of this chapter.

24. Arthur James Balfour, *Theism and Humanism* (London, 1915), p. 248. When Sidney Cox visited RF in Franconia during the summer of 1915, RF lent him a copy of *Theism and Humanism.* Cox, in his first letter to RF after this visit, mentions the book by author and title, promising to return it soon. It is now in the Frost collection, NYUL.

25. Irving Babbitt, *Rousseau and Romanticism* (New York, 1957), pp. 276–277.

26. Ibid., p. 290.

27. Munson, "Robert Frost and the Humanistic Temper," *The Bookman*, Vol. LXXI, No. 4 (July 1930), p. 422. Even prior to the appearance of this article, RF had passed hostile judgment on Munson's book. On 7 Jan. 1930, he wrote to Melcher (*Selected Letters*, pp. 363–364), concerning a check list of articles which Melcher was compiling, "You seem to have most of the articles about me. Garnett, Sergeant, Elliott, Van Doren, Lowell and Untermeyer's. . . . Let's leave Gorham B. Munson's book out of it . . ."

28. Quoted in Munson's answer, 17 Feb. 1931 (DCL), which begins, "I really owe you a reply to your letter of last fall, which contained the wittiest dialogue and repartee the Humanist controversy produced. I have intended to answer all along, but found it embarrassing to do so . . ." (According to Munson, RF's letter, thus answered, has disappeared.)

29. RF to Edward Davison, 27 June 1930; DCL.

30. RF to Edward Davison, 20 Oct. 1927; DCL.

23. TO EUROPE FOR HEALTH

1. RF to Otto Manthey-Zorn, from Bellevue, France, [18] Aug. 1928; ACL. The final decision to take Marjorie to Europe for her health was arrived at only after elaborate medical consultation and tests. Some of these were foreshadowed in a letter from EWF to Mrs. Von Moschzisker, 21 Sept. 1927 (ACL): ". . . it is almost impossible for me to leave Marjorie now. She is still a great anxiety. Last winter she was in bed a good deal of the time with a nervous prostration following a bad attack of grippe. She gained some strength through the spring and early summer, and began to do things and see people, but she did too much, for now she is down again—seems completely exhausted and has lost the six or eight pounds she had added so slowly and laboriously to her weight. I am feeling a good deal discouraged, and Robert and I have lately decided to take her to Florida for the winter. If a winter in an easier climate doesn't do her some permanent good, I shall feel inclined to have her go into a sanitarium for a while, and find

out what other nurses can do for her. We are thinking of going down [to Florida] about the middle of November, and we could stop a couple of days with you then . . ."

Marjorie and her parents did start for Florida in mid-November, as planned, and they accepted the invitation of their friend Miss Mary E. Goodwillie to stop off in Baltimore for a visit, en route. In Baltimore, Miss Goodwillie persuaded them to consult a specialist at Johns Hopkins University Hospital. As a result, Marjorie's parents left her there for several days. During this Baltimore visit, RF made fair copies of three poems ("Spring Pools," "Sand Dunes," and "Atmosphere") on the endpapers of *A Boy's Will, North of Boston,* and *Mountain Interval,* respectively, in Miss Goodwillie's library, and dated each fair copy "November 22 1927" (JHUL).

Instead of continuing the trip to Florida, after this Baltimore visit, Marjorie and her parents returned to South Shaftsbury and stayed there until after Christmas. RF, writing to George F. Whicher on 10 Dec. 1927 (ACL) about plans for returning to Amherst early in January, explained the next phase: "We'll be coming up [to Amherst] from Baltimore when we come. We are taking Marj to Johns Hopkins for another examination before sending her south with a friend." This second stay of Marjorie's, in the Johns Hopkins University Hospital, lasted for ten weeks. Miss Goodwillie kept in close touch with her, and Mrs. Frost went down to visit her briefly in February of 1928. Again it was found necessary to cancel the plan for taking or sending Marjorie to Florida. On 10 July 1928, EWF wrote Mrs. Von Moschzisker: "You have heard news from us, I know, through Miss Goodwillie. She was the greatest help in the world to us, last winter and spring. I shall never cease being grateful to her. Marjorie and Robert and I are going abroad the 4th of August . . ."

2. Walter de la Mare to RF, 4 July 1928; DCL.
3. RF to John W. Haines, 29 July 1928; DCL.
4. For source, see Note 1 of this chapter.
5. Idem.
6. Idem. This summary of RF's views of Wilson is a paraphrase of RF's statements on the subject in this letter to Manthey-Zorn.
7. Idem.
8. RF to John W. Haines, 25 Aug. 1928; copy DCL.
9. RF to Charles A. Monroe, 5 Sept. 1928; PJMC. While RF was abroad, Monroe kept him informed about doings in South Shaftsbury. In a letter dated 9 Nov. 1928 (MCL), Monroe wrote to RF, "Wales Hawkins died on the morning of Election Day. He was conscious and took an interest in things up till the night before he died. I think he would have liked to live another day so as to get the election returns. He was a strong Hoover man. I shall miss him very much. He was my literary adviser. Whenever he would tell me that a book was good I would read it and find it so."
10. John W. Haines, "Home Places. III. England," in *Recognition of Robert Frost,* edited by Richard Thornton (New York, 1937), p. 96.

11. Puritanism is immediately under consideration by RF, here, and in his statement, "But my work was still all before me," he seems to echo, deliberately, the familiar start of the final passage in *Paradise Lost*, beginning, "The world was all before them . . ."

12. Unwonted severity in argument and in punishment was often shown by RF when anyone opposed him—and thus offended him. He had hinted as much in a letter to John Bartlett, written while Munson was gathering materials for his biography of RF:

"It was an inspiration of mine to give Munson direct access to my past through two or three of my independent friends. I thought it would be fun to take the risk of his hearing something to my discredit. The worst you could [reveal] was my Indian vindictiveness. Really I am awful there. I am worse than you know. I can never seem to forgive people that scare me within an inch of my life. I am going to try to be good and cease from strife." (RF to Bartlett, 1 Nov. 1927; *Selected Letters*, p. 346.)

13. RF to Haines, London, 11 Oct. 1928; copy, DCL.

14. Helen Thomas to EWF [c. 15 Oct. 1928]; DCL: "I would like to tell you how very much I appreciated your & Robert's frankness about my work. It showed true friendship & interest, but I felt a bit sad with your feeling about it. I was happy and grateful that you spoke as you did. After all I can't have it all ways. I had the comfort of writing & the satisfaction of publishing the book, & if I have not pleased each of the special people I must face that, to be content, or try to be, with the pleasure the book seems to have given a lot of people. And this is a real satisfaction to me that the book has definitely helped Edward in all sorts of ways . . . it has hastened a wider acknowledgment of him & interest in his work."

15. RF to Haines, London, 11 Oct. 1928; copy, DCL. RF never seemed to relinquish his feeling that this meeting with Helen Thomas did indeed end "one passage" in his life. Five years earlier, in 1923, he had dedicated his *Selected Poems*: "To / Helen Thomas / In Memory of / Edward Thomas /." An enlarged edition of *Selected Poems* was scheduled for publication late in the autumn of 1928, with the same dedication. RF wrote from England trying to have the dedication cancelled, but his request was received too late. When the third edition was issued in December of 1934, a copy of it was sent to him in Key West. Acknowledging receipt of it, in a letter dated 26 Dec. 1934, he wrote to Richard H. Thornton (DCL):

"I must say of the Selected that I like the form you have given it better than ever. But there is one very very disappointing thing about it. That dedication to Mrs. Thomas has got in again. How could it have after all I have said? Mrs. Thomas ceased to be a friend of ours some years ago. I'm deeply humiliated to be put in the position of trying to keep it up with her after it is over. I hope not too many copies of the book have been bound up and that something can be done to discontinue the mistake. I hope also that this can be entirely between you and me—I mean kept from the public and the collectors. Let's see if they will find out the change for themselves and let's not help them in the least to surmise the reasons. I dont want a story made of it."

Thornton answered in a letter dated 4 Jan. 1935 (DCL): "I am very sorry that the dedication to Mrs. Thomas was left in the new edition of *Selected Poems*. I was not here when the proofs were going through, and therefore I know little of how it happened. Not over three hundred copies of the book have gone out so far, and we shall take this page out of all the books on hand. This can easily be done, without disfiguring the bound copies. We shall say nothing whatever about the change."

16. These articles were subsequently gathered into Helen Thomas's second book entitled *World Without End* (London and New York, 1931), which contained her sincere tribute to RF for his having helped Edward Thomas realize his potential as a poet. (See *The Early Years*, pp. 468, 602.)

17. RF to Cox, 11 Oct. 1928; *Selected Letters*, p. 351. The Schnitzler reference is to *Fräulein Else*. RF gives, as his reason for telling Cox these details, his decision that he will not permit Cox to continue his work on a volume of reminiscences about RF. Initially, RF had given Cox permission to proceed. At various times during 1927–1928 Cox had submitted portions of his MS to EWF, asking her to advise him. She apparently encouraged him, for he did continue. RF, writing for the first time about this project, in this letter from London dated 11 Oct. 1928, very solidly tried to discourage him; but Cox persisted. A few years later (c. 19 April 1932), RF again tried to discourage him:
"Honestly, Sidney,

"You are getting out of hand. I'm afraid you aren't going to let yourself be unduly influenced by me any more.

"I grow surer I don't want to search the poet's mind too seriously. I might enjoy threatening to for the fun of it just as I might to frisk his person. I have written to keep the over curious out of the secret places of my mind both in my verse and in my letters to such as you. A subject has to be held clear outside of me with struts and as it were set up for an object. A subject must be an object. There's no use in laboring this further years. My objection to your larger book about me was that it came thrusting in where I did not want you. . . ." (*Selected Letters*, p. 385.)

Cox still persisted, and nearly five years later (1 Jan. 1937) RF tried to use another way of discouraging him:

"You and I are not the kind that can be described as either wild or tame: I always maintain that I would be the same in a society of one as in a society of one hundred and thirty million. My conditioning is all internal. My appetites are checked by each other rather than by anything in my surroundings. Or do I deceive myself? I dont care if I do in this respect. . . . Look out I don't spoof you. About five years ago I resolved to spoil my correspondence with you by throwing it into confusion the way God threw the speech of the builders of the tower of Babel into confusion. My reason is too long to go into tonight . . ." (*Selected Letters*, p. 435.)

RF never did succeed in persuading Cox to abandon work on the volume of reminiscences. Although it underwent various revisions, it was posthumously published with a compassionate introduction by RF, and was entitled *A Swinger of Birches: A Portrait of Robert Frost* (New York, 1957).

18. W. W. Gibson to RF, 3 Oct. 1928; DCL.

19. RF to Haines, 11 Oct. 1928; copy, DCL. The poem, "Reunion: To Robert Frost," was published in Gibson's next volume entitled *Hazards* (London, 1930). The offending passage:

> *Disastrous years have had their way with us:*
> *Terrors and desolations and distresses,*
> *That put a sudden period to our youth*
> *Just when our powers were ripening, left us aged*
> *Before our time . . .*

20. RF to Edward Davison, 11 Oct. 1928; DCL.

21. "This Russian Jew, four years older than I, with his long, lean, melancholy face, wearing an expression equally compounded of aesthetic yearning and of Mephistophelian irony, fascinated me no less with his knowledge of Russian life and literature than with his smouldering Hebraic mysticism, his air of perpetual exile, and his queer combination of active mentality and of fatalistic resignation. A man of many careers, who had registered a splendid and unworldly failure in them all. . . ." (John Gould Fletcher, *Life Is My Song*, p. 243.)

22. John Cournos to RF, 17 Oct. 1928; DCL. In later years, Cournos gave to LT and others different versions of how and when he saw RF in England in 1928. See, for one example, his *Autobiography* (New York, 1935), p. 272. The version here used is based on the letters from RF to JC and from JC to RF, which confirm RF's account as told to LT.

23. RF to Padraic Colum, 18 Sept. 1928; *Selected Letters*, pp. 349–350. Years later, Colum published one anecdote about his being RF's guide in Dublin: "We were in Dublin, Robert Frost and I. As the car swung into a court-yard, 'Where are we now,' he asked. 'In Dublin Castle.' 'What does one do in Dublin Castle?' 'If one is an American,' I said, 'one goes into that office and asks for a genealogy.' It was the office of the Ulster King-at-Arms. 'I'll do it,' Robert said. 'What name, sir?' asked the genealogical expert. 'Frost.' 'Lincolnshire Frosts or Somersetshire Frosts?' Robert did not know. 'What Christian name is usual in the family?' 'Robert.' 'Lincolnshire Frosts. . . .' 'Then I want the genealogy of the Lincolnshire Frosts. . . . Will you tell me what arms I get?' 'A grey squirrel and a pine tree, sir.' " (Padraic Colum, "Frost in Dublin," *Mark Twain Quarterly*, Vol. III, No. 4 [Spring 1940], p. 11.)

RF, in his own version of this anecdote, enjoyed the association with a "grey squirrel and a pine tree." Frost genealogies repeatedly state, however, that the Nicholas Frost family originated in Cornbre Hill, Cornwall, and came to America from Tiverton in Devonshire.

RF, writing to Edward Davison from London on 11 Oct. 1928 (DCL), makes this reference to the question: "Squier [J. C. Squire] and I havent been able as yet to agree on a time together. We plan a motor trip to Tiverton where my ancestors came from. I dont know what struck him this way, but he seemed to like the idea of my having originated in Devon. He says we must make the most of it—celebrate it by going down there and looking up the family records in the regulation American fashion. Maybe I'll find I have a coat of arms. Then it wont matter what I do to earn a living any more." (The planned motor trip to Tiverton with Squire was apparently canceled.)

24. When RF revisited Ireland in 1957, Curran was among those waiting at the Dublin airport to greet him. LT, traveling with RF during the 1957 visit, was there told for the first time that RF had stayed with Curran during the 1928 visit. Curran, in subsequent conversations with LT, confirmed.

25. For background on RF's early admiration for the poetry of Yeats, and on his first meeting with Yeats, see *The Early Years*, pp. 361–362, 412–414. RF, writing to Edward Davison from London, 11 Oct. 1928 (DCL), refers to Yeats in a sarcastic manner which reflects his disappointment:

"I talked four days and nights on end with A. E. That was a real bout. It was like the late war—you couldnt tell who was to blame for it or who was most exhausted by it. Anyway there's another man I like to think of. . . .

"If I have forgotten anything or anyone it is not invidiously. Oh yes there was Yates. He was the best I ever saw him & quite seemed to see me in the room. I had been scared by stories I had heard about his senatorial greatness."

26. Conrad Aiken is thus quoted in Joy Grant, *Harold Monro and the Poetry Bookshop* (Berkeley, 1967), p. 101.

27. Ezra Pound to Harriet Monroe, 30 Sept. 1914; D. D. Paige (ed.), *The Letters of Ezra Pound*, pp. 40ff.

28. Joy Grant, op. cit., p. 143.

29. Ibid., p. 105.

30. RF to LT, 24 Jan. 1943.

31. J. C. Smith to RF, 26 Oct. 1928; DCL.

32. Mrs. Jessy Philips Mair to RF, 16 Oct. 1928; DCL.

33. RF to LT, 27 July 1941.

34. RF to LT, 28 June 1951. Also, F. S. Flint to RF, 1 Nov. 1928 (DCL), in which Flint asks RF to meet him "tomorrow" at the post-office entrance "by the Washington statue in Trafalgar Square."

35. RF to LT, 28 June 1951.

36. Mrs. Grace O'Conor to RF and EWF, 7 Nov. 1928; DCL. Mrs. O'Conor, after commiserating, adds, "You have been most generous to us, and it has been a great joy to have seen you so often. Do let us be of any help we can to you or to your daughter before you sail."

37. Mrs. Grace O'Conor to EWF, "Wednesday" [14 Nov. 1928]; DCL.

38. RF to LT, 31 Oct. 1946.

39. RF to Haines [undated, but received 2 Nov. 1928]; DCL. This guilty confession occurs in the following context: "This may as well end the expedition. It has been too much of a strain anyway. I wish I could promise to see you again. But it wouldnt be honest as things are. I've made Elinor unhappier keeping her on than I think I ever made her before. She's too sick for a jaunting party and I shouldnt have dragged her out of her home."

40. Retrospectively, RF tried to joke about the return voyage. In a letter to J. J. Lankes, from South Shaftsbury, on 22 Dec. 1928, he wrote to his socialistic friend (TUL): "The captain or admiral on the bridge stopped the boat on us right in the middle of a 120 mile gale while he thought what to do with us (we were only second class anyway). Would he sink the ship and make the first class suffer for the class deficiencies of the second class? There we swung in the biggest conradly waves one thousand miles from France and England while he considered whether the British merchant marine could stand the reproach and what proportion of us were American nationals. The nobler nature within him stirred and after mending the prow of the ship a little (she was the Olympic) he proceeded on his way to Quarantine N. Y. I'm practising to write some sea tales: so pay no attention to me. I mean dont try to separate truth from fiction. I may say in confidence, however, that that about the Olympic (45000 tons) stopping in the big storm was too true for comfort."

24. GOOD OLD FOLKWAYS

1. RF to LU, 24 Oct. 1928; *Letters to Untermeyer*, p. 193.

2. RF talked before the National Council of Teachers of English, in Baltimore, on 30 Nov. 1928; three days later, he gave a reading at the North Carolina College for Women, at Greensboro. On 16 Dec. 1928, RF wrote to Stringfellow Barr (VaUL), "I am just home from France England North Carolina Maryland and New York. Till a day or two ago I hadn't seen Vermont since July."

3. See Note 1 of Chapter 23 for an account of the circumstances under which Marjorie Frost first went to the Johns Hopkins Hospital.

4. RF, in a letter to Wade Van Dore, 21 May 1928 (PWES), mentions Irma's return and explains it euphemistically: "My daughter has come home sick from Kansas and she will be all my son and his wife ought to have on their hands and minds while we are away. It is serious or I shouldnt find it in my heart to ask you to change your plans. We are a very mixed-up family just at this minute and I know you wouldnt want to add to our confusion."

5. RF, responding to Lesley's announcement of her marriage, wrote to her, in a letter dated 18 Sept. 1928 (PLFB), "I celebrated your news by intending a song, and I should have sung it if my harp hadnt been hanging in a willow tree in a strange land. As it

was I could not be kept from smiling. So I smiled for a day in honor of the occasion—not because I rejoice more over marriage than over any other step in love, but because it is about the only step in anybody else's love that is any of my business."

6. In LU's autobiographical *Bygones* (New York, 1965), an early chapter is entitled "Taking Marriage Lightly."

7. RF to LU, 23 Jan. 1922; *Letters to Untermeyer*, pp. 141–142.

8. RF to LU, 1 Feb. 1922; ibid., p. 143.

9. Ibid., p. 143. RF, having written "The Nose-Ring" apparently for this particular use, never chose to publish it.

10. RF to LU, 20 June 1925; ibid., p. 175.

11. RF to LU, 31 Aug. 1925; ibid., p. 176.

12. RF to LU, 14 March 1926; ibid., p. 180.

13. *Bygones*, pp. 102–105.

14. LU's published account of the circumstances surrounding the suicide (*Bygones*, pp. 101, 107–108) includes his claim that he had won Richard's sympathies.

15. RF to LU, 3 May 1927; *Letters to Untermeyer*, pp. 186–187.

16. RF to LU, 11 Oct. 1928; ibid., pp. 190–191.

17. RF to Edward Davison, undated, but written during the summer of 1927; DCL.

18. RF to LU, 24 Oct. 1928; *Letters to Untermeyer*, pp. 192–193.

19. Ibid., p. 193.

20. RF, particularly fond of this witticism, told it to LT on many occasions. Long before LU's second divorce from Jean Starr, RF's sympathies were decidedly with LU. RF wrote to LU (6 Jan. 1929, ibid., p. 194), "I can't help thinking at this moment that if Jean only had the self-respect to act out in good faith her independence of you you might, left to your own freedom of movement, find that she was the only girl you wanted to live with. She drains you insensible with her desperate demands on you. I told her that. I ought not to be telling it to you: it might make the remedy less effective for you to know about it."

25. ENCOURAGING YOUNGER POETS

1. Quoted by Harry Salpeter in an interview-article "Poet Frost, Non-Professional," New York *Evening Sun*, 4 Dec. 1928, p. 14.

2. Idem.

3. Idem.

4. Idem.

5. "Robert Frost Will Give Reading Thursday Night," Amherst *Student*, 11 March 1929, p. 1.

6. "Frost Interprets J. M. March's Poem," Amherst *Student*, 18 March 1929, p. 1. The article begins, "Professor Robert Frost's reading, previously announced as from the works of 'an Amherst poet,' drew to a close the annual series of faculty readings in Williston Hall, at 7:30 Thursday evening, March 14. The largest group which has turned out for any of this year's series was in

attendance." J. M. March disappointed RF by abandoning poetry and by making a career of scriptwriting in Hollywood. In 1932, when RF was in Los Angeles, he telephoned March and said he would like to call on him. March put him off with excuses, and RF took these excuses as evidence that March was ashamed of his having settled for a relatively easy way out of those difficulties involved in making a career as a poet. The phone-call marked the end of the friendship between RF and his former student.

7. RF, "Introduction," *The Arts Anthology, Dartmouth Verse 1925* (Portland, Maine, 1925), pp. v–viii.

8. RF to Kimball Flaccus, 26 Oct. 1930; *Selected Letters*, p. 369.

9. RF, "The Manumitted Student," *The New Student*, Vol. VI, No. 1 (12 Jan. 1927), p. 5.

10. RF to Clifford Bragdon, 7 March 1929; ACL. Bragdon surrendered his literary ambitions and became a professor of education and child study at Smith College.

11. RF to B. F. Skinner, 7 April 1926; *Selected Letters*, pp. 326–327. Instead of going on immediately with the writing of fiction, Skinner next devoted himself to earning a Ph.D. degree in psychology, at Harvard. Thereafter he became a distinguished figure in the field of psychology, with an international reputation. Unable to turn his back completely on his literary inclinations, he did make at least one return. In 1948, he published a novel which had a profound effect on some of the behaviorists throughout the next twenty years: *Walden Two*.

12. RF to Wade Van Dore, 30 May 1927; PWES.

13. RF to Wade Van Dore, 21 May 1928; PWES.

14. Wade Van Dore, "The Echo," provided by him and gratefully used here with his permission.

15. Wade Van Dore, "Man Alone," *Far Lake* (New York, 1930), p. 44.

16. RF's "The Most of It" was first published in *A Witness Tree* (1942); collected in *The Poetry*, p. 338.

17. RF to Lawrence H. Conrad, 10 July 1926; PLHC. Gratitude is here expressed to Lawrence H. Conrad for making available to LT all thirteen of the letters he received from RF. *Temper* was the last novel published by Conrad, who made a successful career as a professor of English at Upper Montclair Teachers College, in New Jersey.

18. For a summary of this important Bryn Mawr talk, see Chapter 20, pp. 291–293.

19. RF's talk, "Education by Poetry," delivered before the Alumni Council, at Amherst, on 15 Nov. 1930, and stenographically recorded, was revised by RF before it was published in the Amherst *Graduates' Quarterly*, Vol. 20, No. 2 (Feb. 1931), pp. 75–85; reprinted in *Selected Prose of Robert Frost*, op. cit., pp. 33–46.

RF's way of correlating his belief in art with his belief in God becomes even more important to an understanding of the man and the poet when it is used to illuminate some of his other statements.

His claim that "the height of poetry, the height of all thinking" is achieved in the "attempt to say matter in terms of spirit and spirit in terms of matter" should help to explain his cryptic self-epithet, "Synecdochist," discussed in Note 23 of Chapter 33. It also foreshadows the central theme in the longest (and, to RF, the most important) of the final poems: "Kitty Hawk" (*The Poetry*, pp. 428–442).

In "Education by Poetry," RF's particular way of talking about "belief" is closely related to the impetus he derived from William James at a crucial time; particularly from the essays in *The Will to Believe*. (In John Bartlett's "Robert Frost Visit Notes" made on 28 June 1932 [VaUL], RF is quoted as saying, "The most valuable teacher I had at Harvard, I never had. . . . He was William James. His books meant a great deal to me.") See *The Early Years*, pp. 231–232, 536–538, for the context of the following statement by James:

"Not a victory is gained, not a deed of faithfulness or courage is done, except upon a maybe; not a service . . . that may not be a mistake. It is only by risking our persons from one hour to another that we live at all. And often enough our faith beforehand in an uncertified result is the only thing that makes the result come true."

Compare this with RF's saying, ". . . these three beliefs that I speak of, the self-belief, the love-belief, and the art-belief, are all closely related to the God-belief . . . the belief in God is a relationship you enter into with Him to bring about the future. . . ." Compare both of these passages with RF's saying in 1961 (Lathem, *Interviews*, p. 271): "The Founding Fathers didn't believe in the future. . . . They believed it *in*. You're always believing ahead of your evidence. . . . The most creative thing in us is to believe a thing in, in love, in all else. You believe yourself into existence. You believe your marriage into existence, you believe in each other, you believe that it's worthwhile going on, or you'd commit suicide, wouldn't you?" (For another Jamesian use of these ideas and images, by RF, see Note 27 of Chapter 28.)

20. Frederick S. Allis to RF, 17 Nov. 1930; DCL.

26. A FARM FOR MYSELF

1. RF to LU, 6 Jan. 1929; *Letters to Untermeyer*, p. 194.
2. Idem.
3. RF to Wade Van Dore, 3 April 1929; PWES.
4. RF to J. J. Lankes, undated, c. May 1929; TUL. One appeal for help, made previously by Lankes to RF, occurs in a letter which contains this: "I am kicking *ALL* the time at *EVERYTHING*. I make not only myself miserable but everyone near me. I am the only guy in step—all the rest of the world is out of step. Why, as a matter of fact, I am determined not to pass away here because I do not want any of the pukey parsons to say the last word over my poor helpless

leg bones. Tell me how to calm this soul-destroying kickiness of mine if you would do me a kindness. . . ." (J. J. Lankes to RF, 27 Dec. 1928; DCL.) A good example of the "kickiness" in Lankes occurs in the following passage from a later letter he wrote to RF from Hilton Village, Virginia:

"The people next door keep a radio going pretty much all the time. When the goddamned thing is not wailing out 'Springtime in the Rockies'—an art-work contributed by some insufferable infant prodigy—the red-headed boy is drowning it out with his screeching induced by his mother. When she isn't knocking hell out of him, her horse laugh retches the atmosphere. Quarreling, snarling, dogs barking, hucksters bawling their wares, planes making the damndest din, Red-head and his sister shrieking at each other, the mother shrieking at both . . ." (J. J. Lankes to RF, 1 Aug. 1931; DCL. Grateful acknowledgment is made to Junius Bartlett Lankes, son of J. J. Lankes, for permission to make quotations from various Lankes letters used here and elsewhere in this volume.)

5. EWF to J. J. Lankes, 11 June 1929 (TUL): "I will just outline the situation here in a few words, so you can judge for yourself. Our new farm is 1 1/2 miles from Carol's house, where you visited us. . . . Robert and I are renting a house [the Shingled Cottage] which is 3 or 4 miles from Carol's and 4 or 5 miles from the new place. . . . A young friend from Detroit, 29 years old, whom we knew at Ann Arbor, is now living in one of the rooms, and helping with the cleaning up and repairs a part of each day. He is a young poet of some promise, and wants to have considerable free time, but he has to earn his own living and wants to work with his hands a part of the time, in order to do so. He is quite shy and idealistic, though very vigorous, physically. His name is Wade Van Dore. He has his belongings, a cot bed, etc in one of the rooms in the house. There are seven rooms. Do you think you would like to occupy one or two of the other rooms, and either get your own meals, or combine with Wade? We shall not move over before the 1st of October. . . . We are having quite extensive repairs made, but the worst of that will be over by the 1st of July. It is a very quiet picturesque place. Of course you would have some meals with us. We would take over necessary furniture . . . and I am sure you could find the right kind of light in the house. . . ."

6. J. J. Lankes to his wife, Mrs. Edee Bartlett Lankes, 9 July 1929; copy, DCL; original, PJBL.

7. RF to LU, 12 Aug. 1929; *Letters to Untermeyer*, pp. 195–196.

8. J. J. Lankes to Mrs. Edee Bartlett Lankes, 13 July 1929; copy, DCL; original, PJBL. Other excerpts from letters which Lankes wrote to his wife during this summer are here grouped because they cast light on the personality of RF:

July 6: "I must get stocked up on material for future books on Frost or his poetry. He spent all afternoon with us yesterday. It was raining and he couldn't get out until in the evening. We had supper together—boiled potatoes, sardines and strawberries. Mighty frugal meal for many persons. Then we started out for a walk up in the hills to a birch grove. . . . Frost seems to have no use at all for the English. He spoke of the lack of literature English colonies produce. He thinks in the next line-up Germany will fight on the side of America against the enemy [England]."

July 17: "Frost grandpere says very goodnaturedly to Prescott grandchild something like this if Prescott says 'Look grandpa, I found my rake.' 'What the Hell was the rake doing there, Prescott.' Or in the car he says 'Where the Hell do you think you are going, Prescott.' And Mrs. Frost looks at me and at Robert after the question has been repeated 4 or 5 times—'Must you talk like that to him, Robert?' You can't help liking her."

July 23: "Frost, Wade and myself wandered around the farm last Sunday. . . . Afterwards, sitting under some trees at the edge of a hill overlooking the valley, discussed all sorts of things—the muddle scientists are in—all theories being considered wrong now and everybody up a tree. I think it pleases Frost especially that science is in a hole. . . ."

"Frost is certainly well read on all sorts of things and is interested in almost everything. He is reading the "Chemistry in Medicine" which we have, and finds it very good. He is well posted on wild flowers, geology, and especially interested in the work of glaciers that crushed this part of the country. . . . He says the State of Maine is bouncing up out of the ocean at the rate of one inch a year; that is supposed to be the resiliency of it—like rubber after having been pressed down and being released (by the glacier some 15,000 to 30,000 years ago), resuming its former shape."

July 25: "Frost made a lance [out of a sapling] and began to throw it. Presently a contest was started—each of us four [RF, his son-in-law John Cone, Van Dore, Lankes] took turns in throwing. Frost threw furthest and truest by a good margin. I did not shine. Frost is always throwing something anyway. . . . Then he started another stunt—throwing a [good-sized] stone [backward] over the head to see how far it can be thrown. He was first until the last round, when his son-in-law took the lead. . . . Back to North Bennington where we had 2 ice creams and ginger ales, it being rather late in the day. Then in time back here [the Gully house] with refreshments of weak lemonade, and muskmelons. There was considerable bantering all the time. Frost talks like his poetry all the time."

July 28: "The happenings here concern Frost mostly—seeing that he is our only visitor. He came about three during a slight rain and talk was in order—on Art. . . . The talk drifted to poetry—leaders and followers—geniuses and good craftsmen. He expressed admiration for Longfellow, and stressed his fine carftsmanship and dry sense of humor, a quality very little known apparently. It seems Untermeyer is boosting Longfellow now just because Frost has pointed out to him this quality."

July 31: "This evening, Wade and I started for Frost's place [Shingled Cottage] by way of Carol's [Stone Cottage]. When we got to Carol's found Frost was there with company. . . . Percy MacKaye. . . . We hardly got around the corner of the house when he [RF] said [to me], 'I've run away on you fellows. I've been to Middlebury [Bread Loaf School of English]. Don't tell Wade. I couldn't stand to have him around. But I've had 15 hours of Percy and I'm bored to death.' I expressed surprise. 'O, Percy has the reputation of having bored more people than any man alive.' And he was boresome—for a man of his reputation fearfully dull. . . ."

Aug. 2: "Percy MacKaye was here this a. m. with Frost. He is a pleasant enough chap but fussy. . . . He worries about his artistic appearance. . . . Gosh, it does one good . . . to see Frost utterly disinterested in the tricks. Just human."

"A lot of the poets who made a stir ten years ago are having tough sledding. Lindsay is almost a goner economically—past 50, a young wife and baby and no demand for his act and darn little for his work. Kreymborg having downright difficulty getting along. . . . Frost appears to be the best fixed of the lot. He can get $200 a lecture any time. . . ."

"[Now it is] Saturday, almost 5 o'clock—the Frost party has just left. [The Lincoln] MacVeaghs were with them."

Aug. 6: "Frost and MacVeagh were here this noon for a while. . . ."

Aug. 7: "I am going to the 'Shingle House' the last two weeks in August. . . . Poor Frost blames himself for having got me into 'this mess' [of trying to live with Wade Van Dore]. I keep insisting I am still the debtor, that I've done a lot of work and his offer of this working place has helped me out of a hole. In spite of my abusive language I'm not so het up as it seems. I marvel that any person can be so frightfully dull, stupid and insensitive [as Van Dore] and yet claim to be a poet."

Aug. 11: "The English poet who was 'wished' on Frost—[Edward] Davison—lives in Arlington for the summer. He came back yesterday to this place for supper—since we would not eat at his place. Met a Mrs. [Halley P.] Gilchrist who has charge of reading activities [for the Poetry Society of Southern Vermont]. She engages poets to lecture or read there. Frost has the distinction of always making more for the organization than they pay out. He is an asset whereas most people they engage are liabilities.

"Frost has suffered terribly [in the past] with hay fever. Bleeding throat and tongue caused by cracked membrane . . . coughs well past Christmas. It rather scares me."

Aug. 22: "From the looks of things he [RF] has lived down his hay fever, for he plans not to go away for (or from) it this season—the first in 20 years that he has deliberately planned not to go away. . . . The Frosts sup here tomorrow and then away to Franconia for several weeks—to pay promises made when he thought he had to go there for relief. Didn't have a flick of hay fever trouble while [at the Shingled Cottage] in Bennington."

9. RF to James R. Wells, 27 June 1930; *Selected Letters*, p. 365.

10. RF to J. J. Lankes, 7 June 1930; TUL. RF's best expression

of gratitude to Van Dore is worth quoting as a corrective to RF's earlier misrepresentation in telling LU that Van Dore "has a principled objection to work and the courage and ingenuity to dodge it." Writing to Van Dore from the Gully Farm in the summer of 1936, he reviewed some of the hard work Van Dore had done:

"The elm you planted east of the house is a fine growing tree five or six inches in diameter, breast high. The road you built with Olin has needed hardly any repairs in the seven years we have ridden it. The ditches you dug on the side hill have protected the house and yard from wash and flood like a Government flood control project. I think of you often in connection with these works. There are the maples you planted on the bump above the barn too. One of them is quite a tree now. There's quite a grove of red pine where you made the nursery. I took some of the [red pine] trees out to scatter round but a lot got left where they were." (RF to Van Dore, undated; PWES.)

11. RF to Warren R. Brown, 12 Sept. 1933; *Selected Letters*, p. 398.

27. FRIENDSHIP MEANS FAVOR

1. RF to Lawrence H. Conrad, 24 Aug. 1926; PLHC.
2. RF to LU, 6 Jan. 1929; *Letters to Untermeyer*, p. 194.
3. RF to Richard Thornton, 31 Oct. 1930; DCL.
4. RF to LU, 12 Oct. 1921; *Letters to Untermeyer*, p. 137.
5. RF to H. L. Mencken, 22 Aug. 1930; *Selected Letters*, pp. 366–367. Several years earlier, in another obsequious letter to Mencken, RF made a revealing statement on the subject of freethinking. The circumstances involved the attempt of the New York Society for the Suppression of Vice to obliterate Theodore Dreiser's novel, *The "Genius."* In a countermove, made by the Authors' League of America on 24 Aug. 1916, a resolution was drawn up which began as follows:

"We, the undersigned, American writers, observe with deep regret the efforts now being made to destroy the work of Theodore Dreiser. . . . we believe that an attack by irresponsible and arbitrary persons upon the writing of an author of such manifest sincerity and such high accomplishments must inevitably do great damage to the freedom of letters in the United States, and bring down upon the American people the ridicule and contempt of other nations. . . ."

Mencken, one of the leaders in appealing to authors for signatures to this resolution, wrote to scores of them, including RF. In his answer, RF wrote:

"With all my heart—on general principles—though I don't know much about Dreiser's books beyond that they are honest, and though I don't care a hang for 'the ridicule and contempt of other nations' . . . I had not heard that the Comstockians were after

[647]

Dreiser. . . . These fools should consider where H. G. Wells has come safely out in his latest by being left entirely alone to think things out for himself. The way our wildest attempts to think free always end in the same conclusion is the saddest proof that no other conclusions are possible." (Quoted in Dorothy Dudley, *Forgotten Frontiers: Dreiser and the Land of the Free* [New York, 1932], p. 367.)

RF's reference to H. G. Wells, here, may help to illuminate what is particularly revealing in the sentence about "our wildest attempts to think free." Wells, in the various phases of his prolific literary career, first expressed the extraordinary freedom of his own imagination in his scientific romances, and then expressed another variety of freedom in his sociological novels. Early in his career he revealed his belief in one view which RF hated: the theory that the Darwinian concept of the evolution of species provided a vision of a society which was evolving more or less inevitably toward Utopia. But Wells's belief underwent a radical change after the start of the First World War. Renouncing his optimistic reliance on the evolutionary doctrine, he turned (for a relatively short time) to a more or less optimistic belief in God as the organizing intelligence controlling the destiny of man. He first explained this change of viewpoint in a book which RF apparently refers to as "his latest": *God: the Invisible King* (1917).

To RF, all truth had to center on the belief in God as the invisible King and as the organizing intelligence controlling the destiny of man. Therefore he could invoke Wells's act of turning away from evolutionary materialism to some form of Christian doctrine, and could use this act as evidence to support the statement, "The way our wildest attempts to think free always end in the same conclusion is the saddest proof that no other conclusions are possible." He admits that he does not "know much about Dreiser's books." If he had known them well, he might have cited Dreiser's naturalism as being, for RF, merely another example of "our wildest attempts to think free." Or if he had known Mencken's irreligious attitude (as later expressed in his *Treatise on the Gods*), RF would have been more careful about revealing his own puritanical views to Mencken. (For another oblique revelation of RF's pleasure in carrying on the warfare between science and religion, see the quotations in Note 8 of this chapter.)

6. RF to LT, repeatedly.

7. Genevieve Taggard to RF, 19 Aug. 1928; DCL.

8. RF went so far as to write out for Genevieve Taggard a list of "Approximations" concerning year-dates for the writing of each poem which appeared in his first four volumes. This list is now in JLA. Among the notes which Miss Taggard made during this conversation with RF in 1928—or perhaps during a later conversation, prior to 1932—were two direct quotations given by her to Dorothy Dudley and used in *Forgotten Frontiers*, op. cit., p. 423, as follows: "Frost when confronted in conversation with new marvels of science . . . said: 'Isn't science just an extended metaphor; its aim

to describe the unknown in terms of the known? [See RF's description of Synecdochist in Note 23 of Chapter 33.] Isn't it a kind of poetry, to be treated as plausible material, not as cold fact?' When reminded of Einstein's theory of relativity he is quoted as saying: 'Wonderful, yes, wonderful but no better as a metaphor than you or I might make for ourselves before five oclock.'" (In *Forgotten Frontiers*, the source cited for these quotations is as follows: "Reported by Genevieve Taggard.") RF never tired of making remarks like these for the purpose of trying to denigrate modern science.

9. RF to LT, repeatedly. Mary Austin's version of the incident occurs in her autobiographical *Earth Horizon* (Boston, 1932), p. 334:

"I remember a talk I had with Robert Frost . . . I thought he would catch what I was driving at in the rhythms of the local speech. And after we had finished, he went away, and Madame Bianchi asked me what I thought of him, and I told her that he came nearer getting the local rhythm than anybody else. She was quite vexed with me. She said nobody in his own country thought much of him; they thought him merely a clod-hopper. Madame Bianchi was thinking of Emily Dickinson; she had no consenting for any other New England poet. Not even for Edwin Arlington Robinson."

10. When John Erskine first taught at Amherst (1903–1909) he became well acquainted with the unmarried Martha and her widowed mother, Mrs. Austin (Susan Gilbert) Dickinson. An excellent account of the scandal caused by Martha's marriage occurs in Erskine's autobiographical reminiscences, *The Memory of Certain Persons* (New York, 1947), pp. 128ff.

11. RF to LT, repeatedly.

12. An account of RF's first acquaintance with the poetry of Emily Dickinson may be found in *The Early Years*, pp. 124, 509–510.

13. Theodore Morrison to RF, 22 Nov. 1928; DCL.

14. RF to J. J. Lankes, 22 Dec. 1928; TUL.

15. RF to Frederic G. Melcher, 1 Sept. 1930; *Selected Letters*, p. 367.

16. Carl Van Doren, *Three Worlds* (New York, 1936), pp. 202ff.

17. RF to LU, 6 June 1930; *Letters to Untermeyer*, pp. 199–200.

18. RF to LT, repeatedly. One public account of this incident was recorded and printed. It occurs in "Poverty and Poetry," *Biblia*, op. cit., p. [14].

19. Before the London publisher, William Heinemann, decided to bring out an English edition of RF's *Selected Poems,* he hesitated long enough to complain that he did not like the ways in which RF made unacknowledged borrowings from other poets. In a letter to Henry Holt and Co., dated 10 April 1919 (DCL), he said with tantalizing vagueness that one of RF's poems contained two lines from a celebrated British ballad, and that another poem contained a striking image borrowed from one of Shakespeare's most famous sonnets.

Presumably, Heinemann was first referring to RF's early poem entitled "Love and a Question," in which these four lines occur:

> *The bridegroom looked at the weary road,*
> *Yet saw but her within,*
> *And wished her heart in a case of gold*
> *And pinned with a silver pin.*

An anonymous Scottish ballad, first published in Allan Ramsay's *Tea-Table Miscellany,* in 1724, and reprinted in William Allingham, *A Selection of the Choicest British Ballads* (Cambridge, 1865), pp. 42–43, is there entitled "Waly, Waly." In it, the first four lines of the eight-line fifth stanza are as follows:

> *But had I wist before I kissed*
> *That love had been so ill to win,*
> *I'd locked my heart in a case o' goud,*
> *And pinned it wi' a siller pin.*

RF owned a copy of Allingham's *Ballad Book;* he may have inherited it from his mother. This copy is now in the RF collection, NYUL.

One of Shakespeare's most famous sonnets, and a favorite of RF's, is Number 116, which ends:

> *Love alters not with his brief hours and weeks,*
> *But bears it out even to the edge of doom.*
> *If this be error and upon me proved,*
> *I never writ, nor no man ever loved.*

RF does seem to have borrowed something from the second of these four lines, in his own sonnet entitled "Into My Own" (*The Poetry,* p. 5), which begins:

> *One of my wishes is that those dark trees,*
> *So old and firm they scarcely show the breeze,*
> *Were not, as 'twere, the merest mask of gloom,*
> *But stretched away unto the edge of doom.*

Against Heinemann's complaint, RF might have defended himself for these early borrowings in much the same way he later defended those Dartmouth undergraduates who published a volume of poems for which he wrote the introductory essay. See the first paragraph of that essay, quoted on pp. 355–356 of Chapter 25.

20. Untitled MS; VaUL.

21. RF to James A. Notopoulos, 26 Aug. 1930; ACL.

22. RF to Richard Thornton, c. 1 Oct. 1930; *Selected Letters,* pp. 368–369.

23. Unsigned review of *West-Running Brook*: "Robert Frost's Poems and Outlook on Life," Springfield *Union-Republican,* 30 Dec. 1928, p. 7–E. Similarities between elements in this unsigned

review of *West-Running Brook* and elements in the signed review of *Collected Poems* (cited in Note 25 of this chapter) caused LT to write Granville Hicks and ask if he wrote the unsigned review. (Hicks was an instructor in the Department of English at Smith College in Northampton, not far from Springfield, from 1925 to 1928.) In his helpful reply (4 Jan. 1970; PUL), he presented circumstantial evidences and then concluded, ". . . the chances are one hundred to one that I wrote the [unsigned] piece."

24. Quoted from Emerson's "Considerations by the Way" in *Conduct of Life*.

25. Granville Hicks, "The World of Robert Frost," *New Republic*, Vol. 65, No. 835 (3 Dec. 1930), pp. 77–78. Hicks was correct in suggesting that RF lacked sympathy for the theories of Sigmund Freud; in fact, the entire subject of modern psychoanalysis was anathema to RF.

26. "Robert Frost on Sixtieth Birthday Talks of Joys of Living," Amherst *Student*, 25 March 1935, pp. 1–2; reprinted in full in *Selected Letters*, pp. 417–419. In this letter, RF again reveals his kinship with one element in Emerson's puritan heritage. Compare RF's way of ending this letter with the following passage from Emerson's essay entitled "Experience" (*Essays, Second Series*):

"The fine young people despise life but . . . I am thankful for small mercies. I compared notes with one of my friends who expects everything of the universe, and is disappointed when anything is less than the best, and I found that I begin at the other extreme, expecting nothing, and am always full of thanks for moderate good."

Closely related is one of RF's remarks recorded in paraphrase by Elizabeth S. Sergeant while she was visiting one of his Amherst classes in 1925:

"The day I saw him on an Amherst platform he was steering his class towards the reading of Emerson by asking it to define an 'idealist.' Is he a man who measures up from nothing, or one who measures down from everything? Might he be, especially if an artist, somewhere between the two?" (*Fire Under the Andes* [New York, 1927], pp. 287–288.)

27. Genevieve Taggard, "Robert Frost, Poet," New York *Herald Tribune Books*, Vol. 7, No. 12 (30 Nov. 1930), p. 9.

28. Hugh Walpole, "London Letter, November," New York *Herald Tribune Books*, Vol. 7, No. 12 (30 Nov. 1930), p. 9.

29. The other nominators were George Pierce Baker, Wilbur L. Cross, Bliss Perry, and Henry Van Dyke. Of these, RF was best acquainted with Wilbur L. Cross. RF said he derived an "evil pleasure" from his being elected to membership in the Academy ahead of Edna St. Vincent Millay. She was perhaps his most serious platform-competitor at this time and, he said, he dreaded the possibility that she might be thus honored by the Academy before he was. (RF to LT, 21 Feb. 1940.) Such a confession provides merely one more example of RF's desire to triumph over those who had hurt his pride, unintentionally. This particular

example is more easily understood when it is considered within the context provided by more than twenty other examples listed in the Index, under the FROST topical subhead, VINDICTIVE.

28. NO ARTIST SHOULD HAVE A FAMILY

1. RF to LU, 6 Sept. 1930; *Letters to Untermeyer*, p. 204. The full paragraph containing these sentences may reward meditation in the light of Genevieve Taggard's already quoted remarks: "Frost is too cussedly non-conformist to trust even his own words as texts five minutes after he has uttered them. His mind is too seasoned, too humorous, to relish the owlish solemnity of dicta and dictations." Although she is there paraphrasing what he repeatedly said, he was never as objective in this regard as he claimed. Consider as evidence the full paragraph:

"I found your letter waiting for me when we got here [Franconia] tuckered at the end of the month. This is the latest we ever fled the plague [hay fever] since we began to be flees, in 1906 to be historic. One sickness and another in the family kept us till I could have cried out with the romantics that no artist should have a family. I could have, if the idea hadn't been so stale and unoriginal. I have been thinking about art lately (not with a capital A but with a capital F) and the conclusion I have reached is that it is the bodiless child of a perversion not necessarily but preferably major, such as embracery or godamee, but at least not getting married or not having children if married. Art is nothing but to get ashore out of the stream of animal perpetuations. It is systematically to get some fun out of sex without having to work for it. Hell, yes that must be so, so many fools seem to think so. If there's an ideal that lends itself to facile spieling in our day equally well with that of evolution it is that of detachment (sic-K!)."

This ironic-sarcastic blast, aimed at certain so-called fools, is more solemn than humorous. RF begins it by implying that although his own artistic endeavors have been interfered with, recently, by family illnesses, he has realistically managed to curb his impatience. If his art came first, he further implies, or if he placed his art in a position of primary importance, then he might join the romantics in saying that no artist should have a family.

But his art did come first, most of the time, and all else came second—including his wife and children. The day would come when one of these children would accuse him of having killed his wife after mutilating his children, and then would say that he never should have married. (See Chapter 34, pp. 495–496.) For the moment, however, his family problems are causing him to suffer through a passing mood of ugliness. Needing a target against which to vent his curbed impatience and rage, he conveniently fashions it out of a romantic concept of art.

(Remember previous evidences that the all-pervading elements in RF's puritanism sometimes caused him to admire and defend an extremely austere concept of art. A good example occurs in a previously quoted letter to LU which contains this: "I'm in earnest. Just as the only great art is inesthetic so the only morality is completely ascetic. I have been bad and a bad artist." See Note 15 of Chapter 11.)

His immediate target for attack is, he implies, a concept of art so flatulent and perverted that it is suitable only for those Lesbians and Sodomites who seek escape from the procreative consequences of love.

As previously shown, however, many of RF's critics claimed that he used his own so-called realistic art for purposes of achieving escape from realities, an obvious example being the first poem in his first book: "Into My Own." In response to his repeated counterclaims that his apparent motions of escape and detachment were, in actuality, forms of pursuit and aspiration, his critics answered that such claims were not convincing. These critics further insisted that his rationalized and strategic retreats were romantic in the sense that they blinked many facts of human experience which he found unpleasant.

In conclusion, RF's blast against a romantic concept of art, in the passage under consideration, lends no support to Genevieve Taggard's claim. His mood is so dark that he apparently does relish the owlish solemnity of his ironic-sarcastic statements, and he apparently does not notice any self-contradictory elements in these dicta.

2. Gorham B. Munson, who attended each of these lectures, quoted excerpts from them in his contribution to the "Readers and Writers" column of the *New English Weekly*, 21 July 1932, pp. 330–331. These excerpts (and even Munson's original notes, preserved in the Munson papers, WUL) indicate that none of these talks was as good as RF's Bryn Mawr talk on "Metaphor" or his Amherst talk on "Education by Poetry."

3. EWF to Mrs. Edith H. Fobes, 5 May 1931; *Selected Letters*, pp. 371–372.

4. RF to John Bartlett, c. 7 May 1931; *Selected Letters*, pp. 373–374.

5. Irma's husband, John Paine Cone, had grown tired of poultry farming on the eight-acre farm which RF had bought and given to the Cones in North Bennington. He enrolled in the Massachusetts Agricultural College in Amherst, entering as a sophomore in the fall of 1930, and specializing in landscape gardening. From there he went on to Yale, to do graduate work in architecture. He was graduated with honors, first in his class, and became a successful architect.

6. RF to LU, 12 June 1931; *Letters to Untermeyer*, pp. 207–208.

7. EWF to Mrs. Edith H. Fobes, c. 25 July 1931; *Selected Letters*, p. 376.

8. RF to LU, 1 Aug. 1931; *Letters to Untermeyer*, pp. 212–214.

9. EWF to Mrs. Edith H. Fobes, 2 Aug. 1931; *Selected Letters*, pp. 378–379.

NOTES

10. Among the many sources of information concerning this visit of the Frosts in Boulder, Colorado, in 1931, the best is the unpublished diary of Thomas Hornsby Ferril, to whom gratitude is here expressed for permission to quote the following excerpts:

"July 17, Friday. Joe Hare [Librarian, University of Denver] calls me this a. m. to advise that Robert Frost will attend a Cactus Club picnic in the mountains next Monday night.

"July 20, Monday. Tonight Robert Frost was at the Cactus Club, reading his poems, reminiscing about Ezra Pound, Wilfrid Gibson, Rupert Brooke, Lascelles Abercrombie, Amy Lowell . . . and kicking the central American poet [T. S. Eliot] in the hind end. Also talked about Skipwith Cannel and how Harriet Monroe fell for the damned stuff. . . . After that evening, Joe [Hare] and I took him to Evergreen where we spent the night in the Douglas tents, Joe and I in one tent and RF in the other.

"August 1, Saturday. Helen [Ferril] and I at George and Jean Cranmer's [in Evergreen], picking up the three Frosts en route. Arriving there, Frost and I went for a walk up the beautiful canyon as far as the gorge. Henry Goddard Leach . . . fishing without any luck. Frost caught one on the back throw, not knowing he had one. Bear Creek Canyon above the Cranmer place. After dinner RF read some poems.

"August 2, Sunday: Brought Frosts to dinner here [Denver] tonight. George and Jean Cranmer, Kurt Richter, and Henry Goddard Leach of the *Forum*.

"August 4, Tuesday: This afternoon Hellie and I went up to Ann Evans' mountain house [in Evergreen]. Frost and his wife were there for dinner. Also Joe Hare. Frost told me of his early life in San Francisco. How they used to catch cats under some hotel and sell them for a dime apiece. Now and then they hanged one, they didn't know why.

"August 11, Tuesday: [Frost reading, University of Colorado] . . . I introduced Frost. Frost read many things including 'Home Burial' and 'The Witch of Coos.' He has been very kind to me. . . . As RF came out of the theater [after the extremely successful reading] he hummed, 'I wish my mother could see me now, with a fence-post under my arm.' He loves Kipling . . .

"August 12, Wednesday: At Blanchard's in Boulder Canyon, where RF and about thirty others were guests of John Bartlett. After dinner, RF said his so-called Irish play ["The Cow's in the Corn"] and 'Birches' and 'Stopping by Woods.'

"August 16, Sunday: Blanche Rose McNeil called Helen today . . . to say that RF had praised me to the skies with all manner of superlatives during his last lecture. Poor Robert. He's affected by the altitude, I guess.

"August 19, Wednesday: Frost came down from Boulder tonight to speak at the Women's Press Club. Poor devil, he was all in. He read among others 'The Mountain' which is the poem he should prefer to have in anthologies.

"August 22, Saturday: In Boulder, picked up Robert and Mrs.

Frost, brought them here for dinner. We ate on the boards. . . . Frost talked about the small increment any poet can add to the form that has come down to him. . . . He and I went down to get his tickets to California, then came home, walked in the rain from the garage, and sat up until midnight discussing his and my poems."

"August 23, Sunday: In the morning mother had breakfast for us all in the back porch. All he has for breakfast is a glass of milk of which about one third is hot water. Sliced cucumbers. We bundled them off on a train for Salt Lake at 8:15. Helen was amused the way Elinor bundled Robbie off to bed [the night before]: 'Robbie, it's time to go to bed.' He had previously complained to me he didn't want to go to bed."

RF's genuine admiration for Thomas Hornsby Ferril was given expression in a pleasant snatch of rhyming. When RF next visited the Ferrils, in Denver, during the summer of 1932, he wrote on the flyleaf of Ferril's copy of RF's *Collected Poems* the following lines:

> *A man is as tall as his height*
> *Plus the height of his home town.*
> *I know a Denverite*
> *Who measured from sea to crown*
> *Is one mile five foot ten*
> *And he swings a commensurate pen.*

These lines were used by Yale University Press, in 1934, to advertise Ferril's book of poems entitled *Westering*.

11. EWF to Mrs. Fobes, 26 Aug. 1931; *Selected Letters*, p. 379. The address of the house which the Frosts rented in Monrovia was 261 North Canyon Boulevard—only a half-mile from the entrance to the Canyon.

12. RF to LT, 25 Feb. 1940.

13. According to John Bartlett (for source, see Note 26 of this chapter), RF said this poem "from memory" at a public performance in Boulder, Colorado, on 11 Oct. 1932. In talking to Bartlett about the details, RF said he "really wet the second shoe at Long Beach, California, but that he wasn't going to give Long Beach a place in any poem because he didn't like it well enough; that, on the other hand, he did like the beach at the Cliff House." Also, according to Bartlett, RF was undecided whether to call it "A Record Stride" or "My Record Stride." There was a particular reason why he entitled it "My Olympic Record Stride" when he sent a copy of it to LU in Dec. 1932 (*Letters to Untermeyer*, pp. 232–233). The Olympic Games were actually held in Los Angeles, in 1932, and RF attended them on three days: the third, the tenth, and the thirteenth of August. When the poem was first published, in the *Atlantic* for May, 1936, it bore the title which became permanent: "A Record Stride." The text here used follows that of the earlier version, sent to LU; for the revised version, see *The Poetry*, pp. 294–295.

14. RF's remarks about the relation of injustice to tragedy may raise the question as to what concept of tragedy he has in mind. When he says "we have to take" earthly injustice "like a spear-point in both hands to our breast," he is using a vivid analogy to describe, quite accurately, the Christian concept of accepting and submitting to the divine will, no matter how mysterious its workings may be. But the Christian concept of tragedy involves justice: the just consequences of actions motivated by sinful pride and disobedience. RF's remarks under consideration seem therefore to confuse two opposed categories: the Christian concept of acceptance versus the Christian concept of tragedy.

His frequent return to the pair of opposites, justice and mercy (ultimately dramatized by him in "A Masque of Mercy," *The Poetry*, pp. 493–521), reflects theological notions he could have derived in part from Milton's *Paradise Lost*. On one occasion when his conservative attitude toward the merciful New Deal caused him to argue politics with his liberal friend, Wilbert Snow, RF invoked Milton in a way which threw much light on his theological roots. Snow, in his essay entitled "The Robert Frost I Knew" (op. cit., p. 23), provides a context for the Milton reference:

"The entire problem of justice versus mercy intrigued him. In the 1930s he sat up until well past midnight many times in our home denouncing mercy and lauding justice. My wife and I pled the cause of mercy and pointed out the mercies which filled the pages of the New Testament. He retorted that he was an 'Old Testament Christian' who feared the softening effects of mercy. Justice as laid down in Deuteronomy delighted him and once when he was coming to our house he wrote ahead and warned me to read Deuteronomy before he arrived. His case against the New Deal was that it was putting mercy too much above justice, and was in danger of wrecking all we have achieved in our American experiment."

The letter which RF "wrote ahead," in Jan. 1938 (ibid., pp. 33–34), to warn Snow to read Deuteronomy on the subject of divine justice, contains RF's interpretation of the famous passage in *Paradise Lost* (Book III, lines 80 through 134) where Milton represents God as explaining to his "onely Son" the relationship between justice and mercy; the passage which contains these lines:

> . . . *in Mercy and Justice both,*
> *Through Heav'n and Earth, so shall my glorie excel,*
> *But Mercy first and last shall brightest shine.*

RF, continuing his perennial argument with Snow, begins this letter reproachfully:

"Bill Bill

"Use your brains a moment while we brush up your vocabulary. You simply must not quibble in a serious matter like a win-at-any-cost public debater. Don't pretend you don't know what Milton meant when he said mercy was always first. You know your Milton and your Puritanism. He used it in the sense of first aid to what? To the deserving? No, to the totally depraved and undeserving. That's what we are and have been since the day Eve ate the rotten apple. . . . 'In Adam's fall We sinned all.' Mercy ensued. There could be nothing for us but mercy first last and all the time from the point of view of the religious pessimist. . . . There is the pre-supposition of a whole setup of sin, failure, judgment, and con-demnation. Mercy comes in rather late to prevent execution—sometimes only to delay it. It is too easy to understand Milton. He faced and liked the harshness of our trial. He was no mere New Testament saphead. (I should like to think Christ was none; but have him your own way for the time being. You'd better have read up on your Deuteronomy before I see you again.) Milton loved Cromwell for his Ironsides and Michael for licking the Devil. He had a human weakness for success; he wanted the right to pre-vail and was fairly sure he knew what right was. Within certain limits he believed in the rewards of merit. But after all was said for the best of us he was willing to admit that before God our whole enterprise from the day we put on fig leaves and went to work had been no better than pitiful. I'm like that . . ." (See Note 30 of Chapter 17 for some other quotations which throw additional light on RF's view of our "pitiful" enterprise.)

15. RF to LU, 23 Feb. 1932; *Letters to Untermeyer*, pp. 219–220.

16. Marjorie Frost to RF and EWF, 22 March 1932; *Selected Letters*, p. 384. It should be obvious that Marjorie's father had helped her endow the word "Victorian" with exceptionally ideal-istic significance.

17. Idem.

18. RF to Marjorie Frost, dated 26 March 1932 (RF's birthday, which he superstitiously regarded as his good-luck day); *Selected Letters*, p. 384.

19. RF to Willard E. Fraser, 18 April 1932; *Selected Letters*, pp. 384–385.

20. During this visit, Fraser took the elder Frosts to meet Pro-fessor Earl H. Morris, the distinguished archaeologist. Morris, learning that RF was genuinely interested in Mayan culture, pre-sented to him an inscribed copy of Morris's book entitled *The Temple of the Warriors*.

21. See Louis Mertins, *Robert Frost: Life and Talks-Walking*, op. cit., p. 180–182. Apparently forgetting that RF was in Monrovia in 1931, Mertins tries to compress into one year, 1932, events involving RF which occurred in 1931 and 1932.

22. RF's appearance at Occidental College on the evening of 27 Sept. 1932 is touched on in an interview entitled "Frost at Occidental College" by Lee Shippey, in his column, "The Lee Side of L. A.," Los Angeles *Times*, 29 Sept. 1932, p. 4. The interview is largely a cluster of straight quotations from RF, giving an auto-biographical summary of his early years.

23. When RF completed the reading at the University of Cali-

fornia on the evening of 29 Sept. 1932, a young lady held out to him copies of *North of Boston* and *New Hampshire*, saying, "Would you autograph these for a Monrovia cure-chaser?" She was Miss Helen Browning Lawrie, and after RF talked with her he asked if she would call on Lillian Frost. Miss Lawrie was given the address, and the next day she carried to Lillian a bouquet of flowers. Marjorie met her at the door and said that Lillian was not seeing anyone; then Marjorie added, "You could come in and call on me." Thus began a friendship which became important for all three of these cure-chasers. This meeting is mentioned here because Miss Lawrie subsequently received scores of letters from Marjorie and Lillian Frost; letters which report the doings of the Frost family in considerable detail. Gratitude is here expressed to Miss Lawrie for her assistance to LT when he called on her in Monrovia in June 1956. For understandable reasons, she did not make available to LT all the letters in her possession, but she planned provision for their permanent preservation.

24. John Bartlett's "Notes from Conversations with Robert Frost" (see Note 26 of this chapter) contains a glimpse of RF's visit to the California Institute of Technology on the occasion of his reading there, 30 Sept. 1932.

"He told of conversing at dinner with Robert Millikan, the scientist, and J. B. S. Haldane, the biologist . . . and of making the statement—baiting his two companions—that science, mathematics, poetry—all were [languages involving] metaphors—and of being agreed with immediately by both; of Haldane's remarking, 'We are all wallowing about in metaphors with no bottom.' Of Haldane inquiring if he had read Haldane's book *Daedalus*. RF had started it, had been terribly annoyed by certain poor metaphors in it. He referred to one in particular which was terrible; came back to it two or three times—finally [said] it was about 'milk.' E. F. leaned toward him, 'Don't Robert!' There were smiles and chuckles in the gathering; RF did not. Haldane declared his conception of science was [that of] 'the great confuser' [and] said that was the whole point of *Daedalus*."

Bartlett seems to be reporting accurately, here, an incident which may serve as another example of RF's pleasure in putting words into the mouth of an opponent for the purpose of retrospectively triumphing over him. As he carried on his own private warfare against scientists, he repeatedly played the game of "baiting" them by claiming that their thinking was merely metaphor-making—and poor metaphor-making. (For other examples, see Note 8 of Chapter 27, and the full text of RF's "Education by Poetry," *Selected Prose*, pp. 33–46.) But he certainly misrepresented Haldane in claiming that Haldane agreed with RF; further misrepresented him in asserting that the whole point of *Daedalus* was to describe science as the "great confuser." Moreover, as can easily be shown, RF misrepresented himself when he implied that his primary reason for disliking *Daedalus* was that he was "terribly annoyed" by the "poor metaphors" in it.

The full title for Haldane's booklet is *Daedalus, or, Science and the Future: A Paper Read to the Heretics, Cambridge* [England], *on February 4th, 1923* (New York, 1924). Therein, Haldane asserts that science is continuously forcing alterations in human attitudes toward seemingly stable beliefs. RF apparently concealed from Bartlett and the other listeners the fact that one of Haldane's primary concerns, throughout *Daedalus*, is to review some of the conflicts between science and religion, and then to prophesy that science will gradually cause the "last eclipse" of the gods. Even the brief glance at the Darwinian controversy must have annoyed RF:

"Darwin's results are beginning to be appreciated, with alarming effects on certain types of religion. . . . We may expect, moreover, as time goes on, that a series of shocks of the type of Darwinism will be given to established opinions on all sorts of subjects. . . ." (Ibid., p. 52.)

Haldane, selecting different ways to illustrate his central point, does indeed imply that science is the great confuser, but only in the sense that all the innovative discoveries of science are confusing to believers in dogma: "Science is as yet in its infancy, and we can foretell little of the future save that the thing that has not been is the thing that shall be; that no beliefs, no values, no institutions are safe." (Ibid., p. 87.) RF must have been annoyed by such an assertion, and even more annoyed by Haldane's critical attitude toward a certain ignorance which Haldane finds reflected in the metaphors of poets:

". . . the blame for the decay of certain arts rests primarily on the defective education of the artists. . . . Now if we want poets to interpret physical science as Milton and Shelley did . . . we must see that our possible poets are instructed, as their masters were, in science and economics. I am absolutely convinced that science is vastly more stimulating to the imagination than are the classics. . . ." (Ibid., pp. 27–29 passim.)

The so-called metaphor which RF found "terrible" in *Daedalus* occurs during Haldane's observation that all great biological innovations which have improved relationships between man and other animals have at least potentially offended the religious beliefs of some people. Having broached this point, he continues:

"There is no great invention, from fire to flying, which has not been hailed as an insult to some god. But if every physical and chemical invention is a blasphemy, every biological invention is a perversion. There is hardly one which, on first being brought to the notice of an observer from any nation which has not previously heard of their existence, would not appear to him as indecent and unnatural.

"Consider so simple and time-honoured a process as the milking of a cow. The milk which should have been an intimate and almost sacramental bond between mother and child is elicited by the deft fingers of a milkmaid, and drunk, cooked, or even allowed to rot into cheese. We have only to imagine ourselves as drinking any of its other secretions, in order to realise the radical indecency of our relation to the cow." (Ibid., pp. 44–45.)

This passage must have been offensive to RF for reasons which had less to do with implied analogies or metaphors than with Haldane's central theme about the series of shocks given to established beliefs—particularly religious beliefs—by scientifically valid and useful innovations. Haldane, continuing, explains his reason for identifying the scientific worker with *Daedalus:*

"It is with infinite relief that amidst a welter of heroes armed with gorgon's heads or protected by Stygian baptisms the student of Greek mythology comes across the first modern man [Daedalus] . . . He was the first to demonstrate that the scientific worker is not concerned with gods." (Ibid., pp. 46–48 passim.)

Although RF was so obsessively concerned with his own God that he always resented any opposed view, advanced by any scientist, he nevertheless seems to have given Bartlett no hint of Haldane's central thesis in *Daedalus.* The point of this note is that RF's way of mocking Haldane illustrates once again RF's willingness to misrepresent scientists for purposes of denigrating and of thus triumphing over them—at least to his own satisfaction.

25. Before the Frosts left Monrovia, they visited the Henry E. Huntington Library in nearby San Marino to examine some of RF's early manuscripts acquired by that library. For details, see the letters exchanged prior to this visit (*Selected Letters*, pp. 354–356) and a speculative discussion of problems raised by two of those manuscripts (*The Early Years*, pp. 530–532).

26. The best source of information about RF's two visits to Boulder, Colorado, in the summer of 1932, may be found in the thirty-four typewritten pages of unpublished "Notes from Conversations with Robert Frost" made by John Bartlett (VaUL). The first entry is entitled "Robert Frost Visit Notes, Saturday, June 25 to Wednesday, June 29, 1932." Some of these notes summarize and quote from RF's reminiscences about his San Francisco boyhood, his high-school days in Lawrence, his years on the farm in Derry, his teaching at Pinkerton Academy, and his experiences at Amherst College. Others give his reactions to current literary and political events. Many of the notes describe the immediate events at Boulder. Bartlett's sixteen typewritten pages of notes concerning RF's visit to Boulder, 10–13 Oct. 1932 (VaUL) are entitled "Robert Frost Material—Dictated Thursday Evening, Oct. 13, 1932."

27. RF's visit in Ann Arbor in October 1932 was well reported in the Michigan *Daily*. The first announcement appeared in the issue for Friday, 14 Oct. 1932, p. 1, under the heading, "Robert Frost to Arrive in City Monday [17 Oct. 1932]," and began, "Mr. Frost will arrive in Ann Arbor Monday. He will speak before a meeting of graduate students in English and members of the English Department at 8 P. M. in the Union. Tuesday Mr. Frost will give readings of his poetry at 4:15 P. M. in Lydia Mendelssohn Theatre. Wednesday he will hold a meeting with students interested in writing. . . ." The *Daily* for Tuesday, 18 Oct. 1932, p. 1,

carried a report of RF's talk to the graduate students, under the heading, "Robert Frost Calls Writing of Poem Performance in Belief." From the excerpts given, it is clear that RF here drew heavily on the talk entitled "Education by Poetry" he had previously given at Amherst. Here follow a few of the direct quotations from the *Daily* article: "Writing a great poem is largely a 'performance in belief.' . . . 'Poems are not worried into shape,' Mr. Frost said, 'but believed in. A poem, like a game, is played when it is played and should not become definite until the last word is written. That is what you judge by. The writing of a poem depends on the performer's condition. Everything must be just right.' Mr. Frost commented on contemporary poets [T. S. Eliot et al.] and the current tendency to avoid obviousness. 'The easiest way not to be obvious is to be obscure, to have expression without conveyance. But the only unobviousness I want to achieve is to keep the definite thought in suspension until the last word.' Continuing his idea that the success of things depends on belief in them, Mr. Frost said: 'The United States is being believed into existence. It will be a long time before it is completed. It is not yet time to talk of "scrapping" it in favor of a new government.' " (On "believing ahead of your evidence," see Note 19 of Chapter 25.) The same issue of the *Daily* for 18 Oct. 1932, p. 5, carried a "Campus Society" note to the effect that Mr. and Mrs. Frost were being entertained in the home of Dean Bursley. The *Daily* for Sunday, 23 Oct. 1932, p. 1, carried an article, " 'Writing Has to Be Casual' Is Frost's Advice to Young Poets." This article was based on an interview which provided this direct quotation: " 'As a writer, I have only one regularity, and that is that I never write in the afternoon, often in the morning and often in the evening . . . but I can remember no time in my life when I have written poetry during the hours from noon until dinner time.' "

28. RF to LT, 21 Aug. 1946. Several versions of this anecdote have been circulated; one is in *The Trial by Existence,* pp. 313–315. RF's earliest printed account of it occurs in a letter to LU, 12 Dec. 1932 (*Letters to Untermeyer,* p. 231), as follows:

"I larked the same way at a party where I met T. S. Eliot a month ago. He offered to read a poem if I would read one. I made him a counter-offer to *write* one while he was reading his. Then I fussed around with place-cards and a borrowed pencil, pretending an inspiration. When my time came I said I hadn't finished on paper but would try to fake the tail part in talk when I got to it. I did nine four-line stanzas on the subject 'My Olympic Record Stride.' (I might write it out and enclose it for you.) Several said 'Quite a feat.' All were so solemn I hadn't the courage to tell them that I of course was lying. I had composed the piece for my family when torn between Montauk, Long Island, and Long Beach, California, the summer before. So be cautioned. They must never know the truth. I'm much to blame, but I just couldn't be serious when Eliot was taking himself so seriously. There is much to give an old man the fan-tods."

RF's performance on this occasion may serve as a reminder of his half-playful and half-serious claim,

I only go
When I'm the show.

The dinner was arranged, in fact, with an eye to a date which would be convenient for RF. On 21 Oct. 1932, Ferris Greenslet had written him (DCL): "I am hoping sometime in the course of the next two or three weeks to arrange a small poetic party for T. S. Eliot, now at Harvard, who has been made a temporary member of the St. Botolph [Club] as you have been made an honorary member [through the auspices of David McCord]. I should like to have it on some date that would make it possible for you to be with us. I understand from Dave McCord that you are coming down to lecture at Wellesley between now and election. If you will let me know what evening you could be in Boston to join in the above symposium, I will try to arrange it for that evening."

(See Note 13 of this chapter for the record of RF's having quoted from memory "My Olympic Record Stride" during a public performance approximately one month prior to the party at the St. Botolph Club.)

29. EWF to Mrs. Fobes, 10 Jan. 1933; DCL.

30. For the itinerary of the visit to Texas, 18–29 April 1933, the best sources of information may be found in the Baylor *Lariat*, April 11, 14, 18, 19, 20 and 26.

31. EWF to Richard H. Thornton, 31 May 1933; *Selected Letters*, pp. 394–395.

32. RF to Willard E. Fraser, 26 Feb. 1934; *Selected Letters*, p. 405.

33. RF to G. R. Elliott, 20 April 1934; *Selected Letters*, p. 407.

34. RF to LU, 29 April 1934; *Letters to Untermeyer*, p. 240.

35. RF to LU, 15 May 1934; *Letters to Untermeyer*, pp. 241–242. RF, admiring Arnold's "Cadmus and Harmonia," also knew Ovid's version of the myth in the *Metamorphoses*. According to Arnold's version, Cadmus, living under a curse, marries Harmonia, and they have four children. One by one, the children are overtaken by terrible misfortunes. The parents, crushed with grief, finally entreat the gods to relieve them of misery by changing them into unfeeling serpents. The gods grant their entreaty.

RF had previously mentioned the myth of Cadmus and Harmonia, in a letter written shortly after his return from Colorado and California, in the fall of 1932: "People ask us if we had a pleasant trip. We did have like Cadmus and Harmonia. Some day we are expecting the reward of being placed safely in changed forms where forgetting all this Theban woe we can stray a couple of old snakes forever placid and dumb. Don't let me excite your sympathy. I'm really indomitable." (RF to C. L. Young, 1 Nov. 1932; WCL.)

36. EWF to Mrs. Fobes, 12 June 1934; *Selected Letters,* p. 409.
37. EWF to Mrs. Fobes, 15 July 1934; *Selected Letters,* p. 412.

29. THINGS IN PAIRS ORDAINED

1. The source of the motto is cited in Note 11 of this chapter.
2. The family correspondence indicates that the Frosts arrived in Rockford, Illinois, on or about 4 Oct. 1934; that they left there for South Shaftsbury on or about 11 Oct. 1934. EWF, writing to Willard Fraser from South Shaftsbury on 14 Oct. 1934 (PWEF), expressed the reluctance with which she had taken leave of her grandchild: "After you left [Rockford], last Tuesday, I sort of gave out, and went to bed for two days. . . . How I do miss precious Robin! . . . My arms feel empty without her."
3. There are various references to this particular heart attack. EWF, writing to Mrs. Fobes on 31 Dec. 1934 (*Selected Letters,* p. 415), places it in the immediate context: "We went to Amherst [from South Shaftsbury] the 15th of October, and I tried to fulfill some of my obligations there, but I was not at all well. In November I had a severe attack of angina. So that is added to the other heart complications, and I am following a strict routine prescribed by our Amherst doctor [Nelson Haskell]." Lesley Frost Francis, writing to her mother in Dec. 1934 (DCL), suggests a broader context: "It doesn't seem as though I could talk—or even think— about your attack of angina. . . . It's too frightening. But there is a lot of comfort in knowing that lots of people have a few attacks of it after just such a strain as you have been through, and then never have any more. . . . No more stairs, cellar stairs or other stairs. . . . And no more carrying weights around, as you carried Robin."
4. RF, writing to Harold G. Rugg from Key West on or about 20 Dec. 1934 (*Selected Letters,* p. 414), mentioned the double reason for the long journey: "Look where I am. I say it is for Mrs Frost's health and she says it is for mine."
5. RF to LU, 10 Jan. 1935; *Letters to Untermeyer,* pp. 250–251.
6. "I have [been] in a state of nervous exhaustion for seven or eight months, and I have had angina. I am following strict doctor's orders now, and have improved a little." (EWF to Mrs. L. W. Payne, Jr., 24 March 1935; *Selected Letters,* p. 419.)
7. These and other details were told to LT by Mrs. Jessie Porter Kirke Newton in Key West on 18 Feb. 1940. She added that RF, enjoying the discovery that she was well informed concerning the history of Key West, invited her to call on the Frosts in their rented house near the Casa Marina; that she did visit them there on several occasions, and that during these visits EWF showed very little interest in anything.
8. RF to LU, 10 Jan. 1935; *Letters to Untermeyer,* p. 251.
9. RF is apparently quoting from memory his favorite passage in Emerson's twelve-line poem, "Berrying." As has been explained

(see Note 13 of Chapter 17), RF's view of nature was variable and inconsistent. At many times, however, he was completely sympathetic with Emerson's view of nature as being emblematic of the divine plan. Like Emerson, he had a fondness for building poems around opposed ways of looking at a particular phenomenon in nature, always favoring the more optimistic of the two views, even when the optimistic view required shutting at least one eye. Because the first eight lines of Emerson's "Berrying" suggests an important kinship, in this regard, between RF and Emerson, they are here quoted:

> *"May be true, what I had heard,—*
> *Earth's a howling wilderness,*
> *Truculent with fraud and force,"*
> *Said I, strolling through the pastures,*
> *And along the river-side.*
> *Caught among the blackberry vines,*
> *Feeding on the Ethiops sweet,*
> *Pleasant fancies overtook me. . . .*

RF's admiration for Emerson was acknowledged in another self-revealing statement he wrote at Key West under date of 18 Dec. 1934 (JLA). The Massachusetts Library Association asked several authors to make up lists of their ten favorite books, with brief comments. RF's list, eventually published in *Books We Like* (Boston, 1936, pp. 141–142), is quoted in *The Early Years*, pp. 549–550.

10. Notice that RF's reference to "pairs ordained to everlasting opposition" occurs in the same sentence with "trying to decide between God and Devil." It should be obvious that RF's philosophical delight in opposites was firmly built on a foundation of "either . . . or," where all the fundamental oppositions are allegorically viewed as extensions of the warfare between God and the Devil.

11. RF, "Introduction," *Threescore: The Autobiography of Sarah N. Cleghorn* (New York, 1936), pp. vii–ix. This "Introduction" contains internal evidence that it was written in Florida during RF's first visit there, in 1935. See Note 13 of this chapter for reference to a talk he gave at the University of Miami on 1 March 1935. He stayed for two days as the guest of Professor Orton Lowe in Coral Gables, and the "Introduction" contains a passage which suggests that during the stay his host took him sightseeing at least to the edge of the Everglades, roughly an hour's drive west of Coral Gables:

"I have just come indoors from boasting among the egrets of the Everglades of Florida that I was acquainted with the lady up north who by writing to the papers . . . had done more than anyone else to get them free of the terrible Minoan tax on the flower of their youth and beauty. . . ."

In his "Introduction," RF also mentions Sarah Cleghorn's famous "poem about the children working in the mill . . ." This beautifully

sardonic quatrain entitled "The Golf Links" first appeared in
F. P. A.'s column in the New York *Tribune* in 1915:

> *The golf links lie so near the mill*
> *That almost every day*
> *The laboring children can look out*
> *And see the men at play.*

12. RF, "On the Heart's Beginning to Cloud the Mind," first
published in *Scribner's*, April 1934. When RF sent the first-draft
MS of this poem to Otto Manthey-Zorn, in a letter dated 10 Aug.
1937 (TCL), he said the text of it was "just as I wrote it out, in a
hotel bedroom in Wilkesbarre, Pennsylvania, one midnight about
five years ago. It was one of those nice impulses I can't have too
many of."

13. RF, "Before the Beginning and after the End of a Poem,"
a talk given at the fourth annual Winter Institute of Literature,
at the University of Miami, on 1 March 1935; published entire in
*The Carrell: Journal of the Friends of the University of Miami
Library*, Vol. 6, No. 2 (Dec. 1965), pp. 6–9. This talk begins with
a veiled reference to Wallace Stevens, as follows:

"Tonight, I am going to read some of the time and talk some
of the time. I have just been thrown with a distinguished poet
visiting here [in Florida, more specifically, in Key West] from New
England; distinguished, but not as well known as he might be.
We spent an evening on a modern theme. We were playing with it
all of the time. He had had three drinks and they brought out
what underlay his mind about me. He was afraid that I had
written too much. I supposed English poets could have gotten
together and tried to outbrag each other as to who had written most.
I claimed that I had written as little as he. 'You have written on
subjects that were assigned,' is what he meant."

Wallace Stevens was staying at the Casa Marina in Key West
during part of the time the Frosts were staying in a nearby apartment. Apparently Stevens invited RF to have dinner with him at
the Casa Marina, for when RF visited in Colorado during the summer of 1935, Bartlett made the following entry in his "Notes"
(VaUL):

"RF told a story of an evening, much of a night, spent in Florida
with a New Englander, vice-president of a big Connecticut insurance company, but also a poet—kept the two lives absolutely
separate—and a judge, friend of the man in his capacity as insurance vice-president (around the country the company had many
aides of this sort). The vice-president–poet drank heavily at dinner, offended by making passes at the waitresses, and in the hotel
room was very drunk. He would order the judge to tell the same
story over and over again. It was interesting to watch his brain
begin to clear, as he stopped drinking and applied himself maud-
linly to the task of becoming sober. The next day he remembered
nothing whatever of what had happened. The judge was the master

of an incredible stock of off-color jokes. Seen in Connecticut at a later date, the vice-president rather shamefacedly had referred to the Florida episode. Down there he drank—never at home; but his countenance belied his statement. RF rather liked the man in some ways."

Some further insights concerning RF's fondness for gossip may be derived from these two utterances concerning Stevens. As has been shown in Note 3 of Chapter 16, RF was inclined to distort facts in order to retaliate against any individual who had hurt him. His denigration of Stevens is particularly obvious in the gossip Bartlett recorded: Stevens "drank heavily at dinner" and "offended by making passes at the waitress" and "in the hotel room was very drunk" and was apparently delighted by his friend's "incredible stock of off-color jokes" and later apparently lied about his drinking habits.

Nearly five years later, in Feb. 1940, Stevens and RF met again in a seemingly friendly evening of discussion at the Casa Marina in Key West, and LT was there with RF. On this occasion, Stevens teased RF by saying, "Your trouble, Robert, is that you write poems about—*things*." RF replied, "Your trouble, Wallace, is that you write poems about—*bric-a-brac*." It is possible that Stevens teased RF in 1940 by using the same charge he had made in 1935. RF, in his talk at Miami on 1 March 1935, at least seems to misrepresent Stevens by claiming he "meant" that RF wrote on "subjects that were assigned." Such a claim by RF may have been convenient for purposes of mockery, but it simply does not make sense, and it does not match up with any of the half-playful, half-serious complaints against RF's poetry which LT heard Stevens make.

14. L. D. Wickenden '35, "Frost's Second Talk Stresses Originality," the Amherst *Student*, 27 May 1935, p. 1.

15. Donald W. Craig, "Frost Delivers Lectures on Poetry," the Amherst *Record*, 29 May 1935, p. 2.

16. [Unsigned], "Amherst Seniors Have Last Chapel; Frost Is Speaker," Springfield *Republican*, 15 June 1935, p. 1.

17. This anecdote, told by Merrill Moore to LT and recorded on 18 April 1947, seems accurate. Moore added that Robinson resolved RF's hostilities as gently and tactfully as a grownup sometimes resolves a child's petulance.

18. The news that Robinson might be dying may have aroused in RF a strong sense of guilt over the jealous ways he had reacted against the Maine poet during the previous twenty years. Characteristically, RF might have tried to assuage that guilt by creating a mythic story which would imply that he finally made adequate amends. At least, he did tell such a story, repeatedly. Louis Mertins writes that "long after Robinson died," RF made the following statement:

"I never stopped admiring Robinson, nor did my regard for much of his poetry wane. It wasn't all great—I'll not grant that. But you'll have to admit he never quit. He just sawed wood to the last log. I wrote him a letter, a long letter for me, not a great while before he died, and told him how I appreciated his work. He was a lonely soul and lived much inside himself. His poetry is proof of that, unmistakable proof. I have no way of knowing if my letter pleased him, but I'm glad I wrote it. Before I had published a book I was never conscious of the existence of any contemporary poet. But as soon as my first book came out I became jealous of all of them—all but Robinson. Somehow I never felt jealous of him at any time." (Louis Mertins, *Robert Frost: Life and Talks-Walking* [Norman, Oklahoma, 1965], p. 251.)

One mythic element in that passage is obvious: RF's claim that he never felt jealous of Robinson. But there is evidence that RF did write to Robinson "not a great while before he died." Early in January 1935, Robinson entered a New York hospital for an examination; he died there of cancer on 5 April 1935. In December of 1934, shortly before he entered the hospital, he was visited by Chard Powers Smith, one of his friends and biographers, who gives the following account of this visit:

"One day I came into his room in New York and found him sitting as usual beside the round table with his back to the door, and he failed to greet me. Something important. I sat down as usual in the second rocker between the guest bed and the second window. E. A. had a letter in his hand, one page. He seemed to be reading it over and over. I don't think he rocked any. Perhaps his rocking days were over. He laid the letter on the table, didn't look at me, and presently said. 'I'm afraid Frost is a jealous man.' There was pain on E. A.'s face which may have been physical, but also may not have been. He could not understand a poet being small. . . . Now he was only hurt and confused. He did not tell me the contents of the letter. Frost, of course was notoriously a sly one. . . ." (Chard Powers Smith, *Where the Light Falls: A Portrait of Edwin Arlington Robinson* [New York, 1965], p. 361.)

Wilbert Snow, who heard RF tell another version of how he made adequate amends to Robinson before he died, gave the following account (op. cit., p. 21):

"He told me a few years later that when he heard Robinson was in the hospital he had a hunch he might not come out alive. Frost believed in hunches far more than most men. He said, 'I sat down and wrote him a long letter telling him that few if any had made a contribution comparable to his. I told him he had given this country a great number of lyrics that would be cherished as long as we had a country. And I told him much more.' Somehow Frost's letter made me feel that it was written in part at least as an atonement for the way he had acted toward a brother poet he really admired. I wish that letter could be found. It may be yet. . . ."

Probably that letter was the same one RF described to Mertins; the same one Chard Powers Smith saw Robinson reading just prior to his entering the hospital. It is also probable that Robinson, more hurt that comforted by it, therefore destroyed it. None of

Robinson's other close friends and relatives with whom LT talked and corresponded in the late thirties and in the forties knew of the existence of such a letter.

19. This first version of RF's "Introduction" to *King Jasper* was sent to LU by RF with a letter dated 21 Aug. 1935; the complete text of it is printed in *Letters to Untermeyer*, pp. 261–264.

20. RF to R. P. T. Coffin, 24 Feb. 1938; *Selected Letters*, p. 461.

21. RF, Introduction to *King Jasper*, op. cit., p. xiii. RF, soon given another opportunity to make amends for his jealous treatment of Robinson, rejected it. On 5 Dec. 1935, Mrs. William Vanamee, Assistant to the President of the American Academy of Arts and Letters, wrote to RF (copy, AAAL) and said that Mr. Charles Dana Gibson, Chairman of the Committee on Commemorative Tributes, had requested her to invite RF to write, for presentation to the Academy, the tribute for Robinson as former member. RF did not answer the letter. On 23 December 1935, he and Mrs. Frost arrived in Miami, Florida, for their winter vacation, and they celebrated Christmas there with their children. During the next few weeks, he seemed to be in good health, enjoying the Florida sunshine. On 8 Jan. 1936, Mrs. Vanamee wrote to him again (copy, AAAL). On 21 Jan. 1936 RF replied (*Selected Letters*, p. 425):

"I have been sick in bed most of the time for a month or so, and no secretary to answer my letters for me.

"Will you be so kind as to tell Mr. Charles Dana Gibson that I have already said my say about Robinson in my preface to King Jasper. I am not a practiced prose writer and prose costs me a great deal. I went far far out of my way to do honor to Robinson there. What I wrote may not seem enough to his friends, but it was my best and I am sure any attempt on my part to add to it would only take away from it. You must see the beauty of my having learned to let well enough alone. I am told it is one of an artist's most valuable acquirements."

22. RF to LU, 8 July 1935; *Letters to Untermeyer*, p. 260.

30. A FURTHER RANGE

1. RF's dedication, in *A Further Range* (New York, 1936).

2. EWF to J. J. Lankes, 11 Sept. 1935; TUL.

3. This couplet occurs in John Bartlett's typewritten notes entitled "Robert Frost's Visit, C. U. Writers Conference, 1935" (35 pp., VaUL). When not otherwise indicated, the information used in this chapter concerning the 1935 visit of RF to Colorado is taken from this Bartlett document.

4. The direct quotations, in this summary of RF's talk on "What Poetry Thinks of Our Age," are taken from two Colorado newspaper reports: "Crowd Overflows C. U. Theater for Frost's Lecture" (Boulder *Daily Camera*, 31 July 1935, p. 1) and "Frost Talks on

'What Poetry Thinks' " (undergraduate newspaper, *The Silver and Gold*, 1 Aug. 1935, p. 1).

5. "Two Tramps in Mud-Time" (*The Poetry*, pp. 275–277) was first published in the *Saturday Review*, 6 Oct. 1934.

6. The source is cited in Note 23 of Chapter 27.

7. Almost identical versions of this incident involving Florence Eldridge March were told to LT, in Colorado, 1960, by Thomas Hornsby Ferril and by Professor Francis Wolle. Much the same type of challenge was made by Gamaliel Bradford in a letter to RF dated 5 March 1924 (*Selected Letters*, pp. 298–299):

"I reflected a great deal upon your suggestions as to the fundamental quality of style and the importance of the acted element, that is, of the element of utterance. When, however, you come to applying all this to the art of the writer, I am not so sure that I quite follow you. It is probable that every writer hears his own composition as well as he sees it. But the subtle possibilities of variation in the matter are so wide, that I can hardly feel that you are right in feeling that any one interpretation out of many can possibly be imperatively indicated. Take the *Hamlet* line you instance: 'So I have heard, and do in part believe it'—a line, by the way, constantly quoted in my family. I can imagine half a dozen ways of reading that, and I am not at all sure which would satisfy Hamlet or Shakespeare. . . ."

RF himself provided the best disproof of his own dogmatic claims that he could rigorously control meanings by poetically arranging words so that there could be only one convincing way to hear them. His own changes of mood and attitude often caused him to read his poems in different ways, and thus give them different meanings. Moreover, according to his own confession, his entire formal arrangement of the poems in *A Boy's Will* deliberately assigned a retrospectively ambiguous meaning to some of his initially unambiguous early lyrics. (See *The Early Years*, pp. 396–400.)

8. RF was being mischievous when he said he hesitated to put in print his poem first entitled "To a Thinker." He actually sharpened the political insinuations when he changed the title and published it under the title, "To a Thinker in Office."

9. RF's reasons for gradually increasing his uses of wit, humor, whimsicality—and even his occasionally comic onstage manner—were so complicated that no safe generalization can be made. It is probable, however, that the major reason was the self-protective one already considered in Note 12 of Chapter 18.

10. A more detailed account of this expedition is given in *The Trial by Existence*, pp. 342–345.

11. There are several recorded accounts of this incident involving Witter Bynner. Of these, the earliest occurs in John Bartlett's notes, cited in Note 3 of this chapter. Another was told by RF to LT, and recorded, on 25 March 1940. Bynner's own retrospective account is here quoted with his permission. It was sent to LT by

him in a letter 9 Oct. 1961 (PUL) which explained that he was copying the account from his carbon of a letter he wrote to Elizabeth Shepley Sergeant on 28 March 1955:

"Do you remember that day when Robert Frost was . . . here and when discussing Horatio Colony, author of *A Book of Leaves* (a remarkable collection of poems which Frost himself had brought to my attention) [RF convincingly denied this to LT] because I was at a pitch of ardor over them and R. F. said he disliked a flavor of 'bestiality' which ran through them, I suddenly lost my temper and declaring, 'Colony is a better poet than either of us!' emptied my mug of beer over the Frosty head. You and the company were properly shocked—as was I when I realized what I had done. He only murmured, 'You must be drunk,' which I guess I was— and you wiped him off. The first time I saw him after the episode was I think about a decade ago at Hanover, New Hampshire. Learning that he was in the [Hanover Inn] dining room with a Dartmouth professor, I went to their table and asked, 'Do you remember me?' hoping that his quickest memory would not be the beer episode. R. F. looked me straight in the eye for almost half a minute, then proceeded to recite with ease and accuracy two of my poems. It was a pretty incident and relieved me much."

12. Ralph Waldo Emerson, "New England Reformers."

13. The quoted passage is taken from Benson Y. Landis, "Poetry and Rural Life: An Interview with Robert Frost," *Rural America*, June 1931; reprinted in Lathem, *Interviews*, pp. 75–78. The article begins, "I received my inspiration to seek an interview with Robert Frost from George Russell. AE had suggested in many of his addresses on his tour of America [in 1931] that we should enlist the poets in our efforts to build a worthy country life in America. He had said: 'It ought not to be hard to interest a man like Robert Frost.'"

14. RF to LU, 13 May 1932; *Letters to Untermeyer*, pp. 222–223.

15. RF to LU, 15 Oct. 1935; *Letters to Untermeyer*, p. 265. Although RF here mentions his already completed poem about "proposing to supply the sorrow felt if the storm will supply the tears," he never used it. Entitled "The Offer," it is in ibid., p. 228.

16. The direct quotations are taken from the newspaper article, "American Poet to Lecture in Institute of Literature," *Miami Herald*, 27 Jan. 1936, p. 5a.

17. One of the curtain raisers arranged at Harvard by Robert Hillyer was a reading by RF in the Morris Gray series at Harvard College on 17 April 1935. Answering the invitation, RF wrote to Hillyer on 22 March 1935, from Key West (VaUL): "It is good of you not to let Harvard forget the old regular poet whom she taught Latin and Greek. I was just thinking I might have to resort to eccentricities if I hoped to attract her attention. That put me in too hard a place for my age—sixty by the time you get this letter. Yes I should like you to come. The time, four-thirty on April 17th, seems all right. You see where we are in all humility. I mean you see what we have come to. It has done me more good than it has

Elinor. You are a large part of what I shall be looking forward to."
18. RF to J. L. Lowes, c. 18 Dec. 1935; *Selected Letters*, p. 423.
19. RF to G. R. Elliott, 20 Jan. 1936; *Selected Letters*, p. 424.
20. President Stanley King is thus directly quoted in a newspaper article, "Robert Frost Status Declared Unchanged," Springfield *Republican*, 18 Feb. 1936, p. 2. The article describes RF's position on the Amherst faculty as unique: "He holds no regular classes or seminars, but while in residence he is accessible to any student seeking his counsel and instruction, and his 'conversations' on a wide range of literary and philosophical subjects are considered to be contributions of great value to the educational program of the college. Johnson chapel is invariably packed to capacity when he gives his rare lectures before the student body."
The Harvard announcement, made on 20 Jan. 1936, appeared in the Boston *Herald*, 21 Jan. 1936, p. 3: "Pulitzer Prize Poet Gets Harvard Post." The article described the lectureship as follows: "The lectureship under which he will speak was established under a gift of $200,000 made in 1925 by Charles Chauncey Stillman, '98, in memory of Charles Eliot Norton, '46, professor of the history of art at Harvard. Under the terms of the gift, the holder of the chair must be a man of high distinction and international reputation and must deliver at least six public lectures on poetry."
21. RF to G. Whicher, 20 Jan. 1936; ACL.
22. RF told LT that he was particularly pleased by DeVoto's insistence, in the article entitled "New England: There She Stands" (*Harper's*, Vol. CLXIV, No. 3 [March 1932]), that any enterprising and yet unemployed victim of the depression could rent a small farm in New England and support himself through his own raising of meat, fruit, vegetables; that he would need to earn no more than $300, annually, from outside sources, to be self-sustaining.
23. This visit with DeVoto occurred on 17 Jan. 1936; some of the autobiographical details which RF told DeVoto during this visit were recorded under that date by DeVoto, on three small looseleaf notebook sheets (SUL). RF's account of the visit was told to and recorded by LT on 10 Jan. 1947.
24. "Provide, Provide" (*The Poetry*, p. 307) was first published in *New Frontier*, Sept. 1934. The first-draft manuscript of it is preserved in AAAL.
25. "A Roadside Stand" (*The Poetry*, pp. 286–287) was first published in *Atlantic Monthly*, June 1936.
26. See *The Early Years*, pp. 39–40.
27. Ibid., pp. 224–227.
28. Ibid., p. 277.
29. See RF on "my rage," in Note 14 of Chapter 4.
30. See *The Early Years*, p. 576, for details on this event.
31. RF to LU, 15 Feb. 1936; *Letters to Untermeyer*, p. 271.
32. "Latest Poem by Robert Frost Versifies New Deal As Lost," Baltimore *Sun*, 26 Feb. 1936, p. 1. This article contains the earliest-known publication of RF's unrhymed couplet beginning, "I never dared be radical . . ."

33. RF to H. G. Leach, 15 March 1936; *Selected Letters*, p. 428. The full texts of the *Sun* and *Times* editorials on "To a Thinker in Office" are reprinted in Lathem, *Interviews*, pp. 85–87.

31. A HARVARD YEAR

1. EWF to Mrs. Fobes, 21 Jan. 1936; *Selected Letters*, p. 425.
2. John Holmes, "Robert Frost as He Talks to Multitudes," Boston *Evening Transcript*, 21 March 1936, Book Section, p. 1; revised and then reprinted in *Recognition of Robert Frost*, pp. 114–119, under the title, "Harvard: Robert Frost and the Charles Eliot Norton Lectures on Poetry."
3. For references to RF's Bryn Mawr writing course, see Chapter 11, pp. 154–155.
4. "I was laid low by a severe attack of grippe immediately on our arrival in Cambridge, and am only just beginning to regain my strength. We had an unsatisfactory winter in Florida this year. Robert took a cold in New York just before we went south, and we had such cold, changeable weather down there, that he didn't shake it off for a whole month. Then the rest of the time it was cloudy and lots of rain, and he didn't thrive and store up energy as he did during the preceding winter in Florida. Then there was the question of this Charles Eliot Norton lectureship at Harvard. At first they insisted that he come to Cambridge February 1st. He was *very* reluctant to do that, of course, on account of his health, but, because of the importance of the lectureship, he wanted very much to accept the invitation, and they finally consented to postpone the beginning of residence here until March 1st. We are to stay until May 19th." (EWF to Miss Emma May Laney, 29 March 1936; ASCL.)
5. Several corroborations of elements in RF's religious belief are provided by his saying: "The surest thing you know is that we'll never understand. And we'll never lack resources to stay here, to hang onto this globe. We'll never be shaken off. The two things go together. Well, you know, God can count on me never to be disappointed in him. That means I am not an idealist. Of course I have wished for things at times; for instance, an extra moon. But I haven't committed suicide about it—yet."
For the believer, the surest thing one knows is indeed that one will never understand God's purposes, even though they may be reflected cryptically in nature and in human nature. The biblical echoes in RF's remarks, here, should be obvious. "Touching the Almighty, we cannot find him out . . ." (Job 37:23) ". . . how unsearchable are his judgments, and his ways past finding out!" (Romans 11:33). The same implied attitude of acceptance and submission underlies RF's saying, "God can count on me never to be disappointed in him." Other approaches to this aspect of RF's belief may be found in Note 14 of Chapter 8, and in Note 24 of Chapter 17.

When he goes on to say, "That means I am not an idealist," he is using the word "idealist" in a sarcastic sense which is hinted by his adding, "Of course I have wished for things at times; for instance, an extra moon." The believer's attitude, here, may be defined in terms of this opposite: impatiently wishing for a more perfect or more ideal condition in this world, instead of waiting patiently for the perfect condition in the next world, the Earthly Paradise. The attitude of patient waiting thus enables the believer to transcend many griefs and grievances in this world. And only a nonbeliever would view such pious acceptance as a fantastic means of escape from reality.

Another possible means of escape, appealing strongly to RF's imagination since childhood, is hinted in his humorous remark, "But I haven't committed suicide . . . yet." His recurrent and self-indulgent play with fantasies of killing himself is described at length in *The Early Years*. (His last elaborate indulgence of those fantasies occurred immediately after he made a sympathetic interpretation of Hemingway's reasons for suicide, in July 1961, and insisted that he was going to follow Hemingway's example.) After the death of Amy Lowell, in 1925, there was more than humor in his confiding to LU, "Ever since childhood I have wanted my death to come in as effectively and affectingly." (See p. 278 of Chapter 19.) It was also to LU that RF made another playfully serious confession about a closely related form of escape from unpleasantness: "I hate so to be crossed I have come to think not being crossed is the one thing that matters in life. I can think of no blissfuller state than being treated as if I was always right." (*Selected Letters*, p. xvii.) All of these spoiled-child attitudes were accidentally encouraged during RF's boyhood by his mother's well-intended ways of dealing with him.

But it was through no accident that his mother had also taught him the more acceptable form of escape from unpleasantness provided through those religious beliefs she had inculcated so deeply, and supporting evidence for those elements of belief which are here quoted in the text from his Harvard statements may be found in many of his poems and letters. When considered within this framework, even the subtitle of his poem "At Woodward's Gardens, or, Resourcefulness is More Than Understanding" is pertinent. Also closely related is the full text of his poem entitled "Riders," and the full text of "Our Hold on the Planet." A more subtle acceptance-poem, written about 1920, according to RF, but not published until 1962, is "The Draft Horse."

From Harvard, on 15 March 1936 (PEMR), RF shared with his friend Charles Monroe in South Shaftsbury some amusing and yet serious ways of looking at those who ask too much of God instead of patiently submitting to his will: "No denying the snow went off too fast and it rained too hard [this year] for human contrivances. Maybe too impatient praying precipitated it. People should be careful how they pray. I've seen about as much harm as good come from prayer. It is highly doubtful if man is equipped for judicious prayer. We dont know the Lord well enough to know how he will take our petitions and suggestions. His psychology may not be exactly human. We are certainly in a hard place. I believe it has been remarked before. Still I dont believe we can be shaken off. We are apparently here to stay as a race if not as individuals."

6. RF, brought up in a political atmosphere as a result of his father's ambitions, never outgrew his own wish that he might be elected to office as a United States Senator. The wistful hint, here, that he would enjoy entering into a political campaign, was given elaboration in a letter from RF to Lankes, 3 Dec. 1936 (TUL): "Last year the only thing I thought I was up to was being a U. S. Senator." The desire was not merely to achieve glory through prominence in the public eye but also to achieve power. His fantasies concerning the success with which he might wield extraordinary power, if he had it, took curious forms. One example of such dreaming occurs in the same half-serious and half-playful letter to Lankes, which continues:

"Now I would be satisfied if I could be a farm manager. I'd like to own a big farm—about as big as Rhode Island with ten or fifteen villages of workmen (Chinese by preference) [i.e., to RF, slave labor] scattered over it and a narrowgage railroad all my own. I bet I could run that whatever else I cant do. I'm getting ready to bust loose in some new direction. The sun is very spotted and I feel it in my pituitary."

7. RF, in referring to "the evil search for synonyms," was expressing his prejudice in favor of using images which imply (rather than state) analogies, images and actions which merely hint at metaphoric and symbolic extensions of meaning. A convenient example is the familiar poem "Stopping by Woods."

8. Lawrence C. Dame, "1,000 Hear Robert Frost, Poet, Give Views on Life in Harvard Lecture," Boston *Herald*, 19 March 1936, p. 29.

9. RF to LU, 1 Jan. 1916; *Letters to Untermeyer*, p. 22.

10. An editorial in the Harvard *Alumni Bulletin*, 20 March 1936, pleased RF: "The audiences at Mr. Frost's lectures on the Norton foundation must have gratified the poet, and should also gratify the University. . . . It is at least a question whether any such audiences as Mr. Frost has attracted have before gathered since the inauguration of the Norton chair. . . . Americans have an insatiable and exclusive craving for European lectures. Perhaps we are now accumulating a little evidence on the other side. Mr. Frost seems to prove that there is at least one American whom his countrymen delight to hear."

Reference has been made to the fact that RF's contract with Harvard required him to prepare for publication a manuscript of the six lectures he gave. At his request, stenographic records were taken of the lectures, and a typewritten transcript of these records was sent to him by the Harvard University Press. LT, calling on RF in Amherst in June of 1936, was shown the unopened package, and was told by RF that he had no desire to revise the transcripts for publication. The package mysteriously disappeared—it was probably burned by RF—and the lectures were never printed. Presumably there was a carbon copy of the stenographic transcripts. LT made repeated enquiries concerning this point, at the Harvard University Press, and was repeatedly told that no carbon copy could be found. Although there were various reasons why RF deliberately avoided preparing the manuscript for publication, perhaps the strongest was his self-confessed laziness.

There are at least four sources of fragmentary information concerning what RF said in these lectures. For the first of these, see Note 2 of this chapter; for the second, see Note 8 of this chapter; for the third, see Eric W. Carlson, "Robert Frost on 'Vocal Imagination, the Merger of Form and Content.'" *American Literature,* Vol. XXXII, No. 4 (Jan. 1962), pp. [519]–522; for the fourth, see Daniel Smythe, *Robert Frost Speaks* (New York, 1964), pp. 27–33.

11. This incident, with the quotations as given, was told by RF to LT, and recorded, on 19 March 1962.

12. The Bernard DeVoto Papers (SUL) contain, in the file of undated letters, a formal summary which DeVoto made of the circumstances under which he served at Harvard up to the time his appointment was terminated in the spring of 1936. The summary also contains a copy of President Conant's letter to DeVoto, dated 6 May 1936.

13. "I have just sent you a telegram announcing that the Book-of-the-Month Club has chosen *A Further Range* as [half of] a dual choice along with Andre Maurois' new book. The choice means delaying publication of the book a bit, as they are unable to take it for the month of May. There seems a strong probability that it will be sent out the first of June. . . . The minimum guarantee is for 50,000 copies, for which they will pay us $7,000, to be divided [equally] according to the contract between yourself and us. On all sales over 50,000 they are to pay us 20¢ a copy royalty. Mr. Scherman, the president of the Club, told me over the telephone that he felt sure it would yield us around $8,000. . . ." (R. H. Thornton to RF, 16 March 1936; carbon copy, Holt file, PUL.)

The limited edition of *A Further Range* was published on 20 May 1936, by Holt; the trade edition on 1 June 1936; the Book-of-the-Month Club edition, June 1936.

14. EWF to Mrs. Nina Thornton, 23 March 1936; *Selected Letters,* p. 429.

15. David McCord, in conversation with LT, 3 Sept. 1941, said that RF's machinations in winning support from individual members of the Pulitzer Prize Committee, for the award to *A Further Range,* surpassed any of RF's other "wiley" strategies and tactics. RF learned from LU the names of the two other members of the Pulitzer Prize Committee for Poetry, and went out of his way to ingratiate himself with them.

16. RF to LU, 9 May 1936; *Letters to Untermeyer,* pp. 276–277. RF's meaning, here, is somewhat clarified if his quotation from

Southey's "My Days Among the Dead Are Passed" is considered within its original context:

> *My days among the Dead are passed,*
> *Around me I behold,*
> *Where'er these casual eyes are cast,*
> *The mighty minds of old:*
> *My never-failing friends are they,*
> *With whom I converse day by day.*

17. Ibid., p. 277.
18. RF to M. A. deWolfe Howe, 6 Jan. 1936; HUL.
19. RF to J. J. Lankes, 8 Feb. 1936; PJBL. Other parts of this letter provide some extraordinary insights. A brief context is needed. In 1932, RF helped Lankes obtain a position at Wells College as artist in residence; R. P. T. Coffin was already there as poet in residence. On 21 Nov. 1935, RF gave a reading at Wells College, and Lankes was hurt because RF was given more publicity than Lankes. RF, annoyed by this latest demonstration of habitual complaining, and suspecting Lankes's motives in sending information concerning the attack on RF in the *New Republic*, began this letter to Lankes, 8 Feb. 1936 (TUL):

"I am offended as you are offended that the publicity person at Wells should have failed to make me chiefly your guest when I was in Aurora. Such is justice and truth in the newspapers and magazines. . . ." Then, after scolding Lankes for bothering about such matters, RF continued, "I was pretty cross with you for that bad letter about The New Republic. You felt it would be good for my ego to know I wasnt thought as well of by everybody as I was by my friends. You didnt want it to escape me. You were bent on punishing me for having left behind in Aurora when I came away the best of the woodcuts you gave me. Well I shouldnt have left it behind. But you have to remember I was tired with what I had been through and I was thinking more of your health than of your pictures. You should have made allowances and sent the picture along after me. I'm not much good in a lot of ways, but I'm a good friend, I know, I know. You're merely irratable at times. And I dont mind your being toward other people. But please go easy on me."

Lankes continued to complain, and within a few months he was blaming RF for having helped to secure for him permanent tenure at Wells College, as artist in residence, with the rank of associate professor. RF answered, in an undated letter received 3 Dec. 1936 (TUL):

"Blame me for your position all you like, but give me a chance to succeed with you in it. That is to say make the position so you can be yourself in it and continue to be what you are. I've done my part; you do yours. . . . You needat talk your constitutional arty rot to me. For God's sake take a little comfort in the realities. You're all fixed up to go. Put your own production first where it belongs and where the college will always be proud to see it. Remember what the college gets most from you is your reputation for woodcuts out in the world. Dont let the petty teachers false sense of duty fool you out of that. What you perform in real art and what comes to the college notice round about from the public field will do more to teach those girls than anything you say to them in a class. Not that what you say to them in a class wont count too. It will count considerably and considerably more than what most teachers say, because you are art at first hand. There is nothing second hand about you. . . . The only marvel is (you are such a cuss) that they can see their advantage in you. I shall end by admiring them almost as much as I admire you.

"No rest for me, but it is something if I can be the means [of] bringing others to anything like rest. We can think of you as having a home you can eat in without nervous constipation of the stomach. It will be like the Robinson Crusoe story for us. We'll come out to you and warm your house. You disgusted me last year with your forlornness. Gee let me have a little pleasure in the last go down. Let's help each other get something more done."

20. Newton Arvin, [review of Robinson's *King Jasper*], *New Republic*, Vol. LXXXV, No. 1101 (8 Jan. 1936), p. 262. One sentence in Arvin's criticism, as quoted, deserves further consideration: "There is a cant of skepticism, a complacency of the pessimist, as well as their opposites, and it is profoundly disappointing to see distinguished minds succumbing to them." Arvin implies that the complacency of the pessimist is as unattractive as the complacency of the optimist; that the cant of the skeptic is as unattractive as the cant of the believer. Although these four postures may seem to exist separately, they were all closely bound together in RF's consciousness. Each of them has been scrutinized in previous notes. See, for example, Note 14 of Chapter 8 for a consideration of the close relationship between RF's religious belief and his skepticism—and the convenience he derived from using both factors to buttress his conservatism when preaching his version of laissez faire through piously saying, "Let what will be, be." See also Note 24 of Chapter 17, where RF's skepticism is further analyzed to show how it enabled him to assert his superiority over others by taking a scornful view of almost any idea he did not advance as his own. The two edges of his complacency—the pessimistic and the optimistic—are best examined in his continuous play with the terms "mercy" and "justice." See particularly Note 14 of Chapter 28, where RF is invoking Milton for the purpose of defending his own puritan views, and where he tries to protect or rationalize the complacency of the viewpoint of "the religious pessimist."

21. Newton Arvin, "A Letter on Proletarian Literature" [a review of *Proletarian Literature in the United States: An Anthology*], *Partisan Review*, Vol. III, No. 4 (Feb. 1936), pp. 17–18. The *Partisan Review* for April 1936 contained a "Symposium on Marxism and the American Tradition" (pp. 3–16), and the preliminary

statement explained, "In the belief that the problem of defining Americanism in relation to Marxism and revolutionary literature is of the greatest importance for the understanding of all these forces, the editors have asked a number of writers of diverse shades of opinion to reply to a questionnaire on the subject." The answer nearest to RF's prejudices was by William Carlos Williams, as follows:

"The essential democracy upon which an attempt was made to found the United States has been the central shaft about which all the other movements and trends of thought have revolved—without changing it in any way. This deeply embedded feeling for a democracy has defeated the more radical thought of each era, such as that of Tom Paine, Gene Debs, Bill Haywood, making their movements and thoughts seem foreign to the environment. It is this same democracy of feeling which will defeat Marxism in America and all other attempts at regimentation of thought and action. . . ."

22. Ruth Lechlitner [in a review of Muriel Rukeyser's *Theory of Flight*], *Partisan Review*, Vol. III, No. 2 (March 1936), pp. 29–30.

23. Newton Arvin, "A Minor Strain," *Partisan Review*, Vol. III, No. 5 (June 1936), pp. 27–28.

24. Horace Gregory [review of *A Further Range*], *New Republic*, Vol. LXXXVII, No. 1125 (24 June 1936), p. 214.

25. R. P. Blackmur, "The Instincts of a Bard," *Nation*, Vol. 142, No. 3703 (24 June 1936), pp. 817–819.

26. Rolfe Humphries, "A Further Shrinking," *New Masses*, Vol. XX, No. 7 (11 Aug. 1936), pp. 41–42.

27. Ferner Nuhn to RF, undated [c. 5 Aug. 1936]; DCL; quoted with permission. Gratitude is here expressed to Ferner Nuhn for his generous assistance in providing information concerning the long friendship between RF and the Nuhns, starting in the spring of 1930.

28. The Frosts stayed in Washington, D.C., for a few days in early Dec. 1934: RF gave a talk before the National Council of Teachers of English, in Washington, on 1 Dec. 1934. During this visit, the Nuhns introduced RF to the Wallaces and to several other prominent New Dealers including Rexford Guy Tugwell, who was then Under Secretary of Agriculture and a member of the "Brain Trust" which drew up the Agricultural Adjustment Act, 1933.

29. RF to LU, 12 March 1920; *Letters to Untermeyer*, pp. 97–99.

30. When RF writes, "I argued in a monologue lately," he may be referring to his talk given at Harvard on 17 March 1936 (see Note 5 of this chapter) or to several other talks in which he frequently elaborated on "the fact of our race's having survived" as evidence that "those for us must be more than those against us." As so often happened when he kept playing with an idea in talk after talk, the idea finally was shaped into a poem; this time, into

"Our Hold on the Planet" which was first published in RF's Christmas booklet for 1940. Part of the inspiration, this time, may have come from RF's reading the following passage in John Burroughs's *Accepting the Universe* (New York, 1920), p. 45:

". . . to feel at home on this planet . . . I look upon as the supreme felicity of life. . . . In spite of . . . short-comings and delays and roundabout methods, here we are, and here we wish to remain. . . . Whatever has failed, we have succeeded, and the beneficent forces are still coming our way. . . . Some power other than ourselves . . . is more positive than negative, more for us than against us, else we should not be here."

If RF did read *Accepting the Universe* (and there are many other strong circumstantial evidences that he did), he was forced to forgive or at least overlook certain passages which would have offended him. Burroughs preaches a religious doctrine concerning what he calls "radical optimism." He describes it, however, as "an attempt to justify the ways of God to man on natural grounds," after dismissing the orthodox concept of a personal God:

"What I am trying to get rid of is the pitying and meddling Providence which our feeble faith and half-knowledge have enthroned above us. We need stronger meat than the old theology affords us. . . . we need encouragement in our attitude of heroic courage and faith toward an impersonal universe; we need to have our petty anthropomorphic views of things shaken up and hung out in the wind to air. . . .

"Our fathers had a complete and consistent explanation of the problem of evil that so perplexes us. They invented or postulated two opposing and contending principles in the world—one divine, the other diabolical. One they named God, the other, Satan. Their conception of God would not allow them to saddle all the evil and misery of the world upon him; they had to look for a scapegoat, and they found him in the Devil. One is just as necessary to a consistent cosmogony as the other. If we must have an all-wise, all-merciful, all-powerful, all-loving God—the author of all good and the contemner of all evil—we must also have a god of the opposite type, the great mischief-maker and enemy of human happiness. . . .

"Wrestle with the problem as we may, we are impaled on one or the other horn of the dilemma. Our traditional God is more cruel and more indifferent to human suffering than any tyrant that ever gloated over human blood and agony, or else he is fearfully limited in his power for good. . . .

"In an equal measure the old Hebraic conception of God as a much magnified man, the king and ruler of heaven and earth, with heaven as his throne, has gone out. God is now little more than a name for that tendency or power in the universe which makes for righteousness, and which has brought evolution thus far on its course." (Ibid., pp. 18, 38–40.)

RF could have had no sympathy for Burroughs' notion of an impersonal God within or behind a universe which is acceptable because it is constantly improving through the gradual working-out of evolution. Nor would RF have enjoyed the ways in which Burroughs mocked and dismissed the view of "Nature" which he found in three of RF's favorite poets: Wordsworth, Milton, and Emerson:

"The Nature that to Wordsworth never betrays us, and to Milton was 'wise and frugal,' is a humanized, man-made Nature. The Nature we know and wrest our living from . . . is of quite a different order. It is no more constant than inconstant, no more wise and frugal than foolish and dissipated. . . . When we infuse into it our own idealism, or recreate it in our own image, then we have the Nature of the poets, the Nature that consciously ministers to us and makes the world beautiful for our sake. When in his first book, 'Nature,' Emerson says that the aspect of Nature is devout . . . we see what a subjective and humanized Nature, a Nature of his own creation, he is considering. . . ." (Ibid., p. 22. For a brief glance at RF's fluctuating attitude toward Nature, see Note 13 of Chapter 17.)

31. RF's pun, involving the relation of the Old Deil to the New Deal, is based on the Scottish way of pronouncing Devil, and of spelling it De'il.

32. This particular passage, in this letter, should be of extra interest to anyone who is trying sympathetically to understand RF's psychological peculiarities. The suggestion has been made repeatedly, in this biography, that RF cherished many ideals which he tried to live up to; that in certain cases when he failed to live up to them, he claimed he had succeeded, even though such a claim sometimes forced him to deceive himself or others—or both. As a student of William James, and as a former teacher of psychology, he was familiar with what James refers to as the internal "rivalry and conflict of the different mes." In the passage under consideration, RF is perhaps deceiving himself, or perhaps trying to deceive Ferner Nuhn, by asserting (at a surprisingly late moment in this letter), "Both those people in the dialogue are me." He is further suspect when he adds, "I enjoyed having one part of me impose on the other." He is also suspect when he goes on to claim, "The fun of the imposition was what kept me writing." He might have been more accurate if he had admitted that, for him, the fun was always great when he could triumph in argument by successfully imposing his conservative views on a liberal opponent such as Nuhn. "Show yourself up to yourself now and then for health, say I." Viewed as an ideal, this exhortation is familiar; but in the remainder of this passage this exhortation is being inverted in a way which is not convincing. RF is claiming that Nuhn has misinterpreted RF's meanings in "Build Soil," and that if the poem is seen in the new light provided by this passage, Nuhn will be more sympathetic. But by the time RF wrote "Build Soil" his inner sympathy for any form of socialistic idealism had become so weak as to be practically nonexistent. In fact there is no evidence that he ever possessed any strong sympathy for such idealism.

An entirely different example of an attempt, on RF's part, to protect one of his ideals, through deliberately deceptive postures, is at least timely here. On 9 Aug. 1936—the day after RF wrote to Nuhn about "Build Soil"—Professor Robert S. Newdick of Ohio State University wrote to RF (DCL) about another poem by RF. Newdick had begun gathering materials for a biography of RF, with the poet's permission, and had just found in the Pinkerton Academy Library a file of the literary magazine, the Pinkerton *Critic.* In the issue for March 1907, Newdick discovered a five-quatrain poem entitled "The Later Minstrel," which RF had written in connection with the Pinkerton celebration of the centennial of Longfellow's birth. (See *The Early Years,* pp. 562–563, for the text of this poem, and for reference to an article by LT concerning a separate broadside-printing of this poem in 1907, an article written with RF's aid and published with his permission in 1948.) Newdick, in his 1936 letter to RF, copied the full text of the poem and asked, "Do you recall it?" Instead of answering in a separate letter, RF wrote on Newdick's letter and returned it to him. In the wide margin beside the text of "The Later Minstrel," RF wrote,

"I didn't write this. I wondered at the time where it had crept in from. Of course it is no high school child's work—you know I just begin to wonder if Margaret Bartlett of Boulder Colorado wasn't capable of writing it. John was the editor and could have published it for her without telling me. My advisorship was purely nominal. You have my permission to ask them."

RF did write "The Later Minstrel." The academic year 1906–1907 was his first full year at Pinkerton and he was not yet the advisor to the undergraduate editorial board of the *Critic.* Furthermore, John Bartlett and Margaret Abbott, Class of 1911, were not even freshmen at Pinkerton when "The Later Minstrel" was published in the *Critic.* Newdick wrote again to RF, reminding him of other details which implied that he was the author of "The Later Minstrel." Newdick even quoted from the *Critic* for March 1907 an account of the Longfellow centennial observance, including this: "Mr. Frost wrote a poem for the occasion . . . you may find it printed in another part of the 'Critic' if you wish to read it." Newdick added, "Won't you therefore give the matter another thought . . ." RF replied, at the foot of this undated request (DCL), which he returned to Newdick,

"I still fail to recognize the poem about Longfellow as mine. Dont the quotation from The Critic make you suspicious? It sounds to me as if someone was ascribing the poem to me to give it authority or to involve me for my good in the school affairs."

Any speculation about RF's motives for thus trying to deceive Newdick, concerning the authorship of this poem, might start from RF's question and warning to Sidney Cox (*Selected Letters,* p. 435): "Or do I deceive myself? I don't care if I do in this respect. . . . Look out I don't spoof you." RF could have derived pleasure from a decision to "spoof" Newdick, but it would seem that RF may have had another motive. He may have established a practical ideal concerning the minimum level of quality which any poem of his should measure up to before he would choose to preserve it. Perhaps this early piece did not measure up to that minimum level. Perhaps he therefore wanted to disown it, even if he was required to deceive Newdick (and others) in the process.

33. RF to Ferner Nuhn, 8 Aug. 1936; first draft, DCL. LT learned through correspondence with Nuhn in 1969 that RF did not send to Nuhn any version of this letter. But in his next conversation with Nuhn, RF did say that Nuhn's letter was so good that it did deserve a reply, LT also learned from Nuhn. As is repeatedly implied in Nuhn's letter to RF, "Build Soil" contains numerous hints that RF shaped some of his own political views around his own version of the laissez-faire doctrine. Perhaps the most overt statement, on this point, occurs in the following playfully serious lines from "Build Soil" (*The Poetry*, p. 320, lines 127–130):

> *Were I dictator, I'll tell you what I'd do.*
> *What should you do?*
> > *I'd let things take their course*
> *And then I'd claim the credit for the outcome.*

34. Theodore Morrison to RF, 22 Nov. 1928; DCL.
35. Theodore Morrison to RF, 27 May 1933; DCL.
36. To understand RF's battle with John Farrar at the Bread Loaf Writers' Conference in 1929 and the various reasons why RF attended the Conference rarely during the first nine years of its existence, a considerable background of information is needed. Such background is worth giving here because it throws light on RF's temperament.

Literary jealousies complicated RF's relations with Bread Loaf from the start. Just before he returned to America from England in 1915, he had begun to dream of inviting to his own farm, each summer, a group of writers. In these dreams he always saw himself as the central image. From England he wrote to Sidney Cox on 2 Jan. 1915 (*Selected Letters*, pp. 148–149),

"I should like now to go to a small college with the chance of teaching a few ideas or barring that I shall get me a farm where between milking one cow and another I shall write Books III IV & V and perhaps draw a few people about me in time in a sort of summer literary camp. We will talk of this some day."

In May of 1915, writing to Cox from Bethlehem, N.H., RF again mentioned his dream: "We hope to be settled on a farm of our own before long. We have found what we want in Franconia. The summer-camp scheme will have to wait a while." Six years later, after he had moved from Franconia to South Shaftsbury and had heard about the ideal setting for the Bread Loaf School of English (which had completed its first session in the summer of 1920), RF wrote to the director, Professor Wilfred Davison, inviting him to South Shaftsbury to discuss some additional plans for creating what amounted to a variant of RF's ideal of a "summer literary camp." (See Chapter 12, p. 161.)

The invitation, followed by Davison's visit, resulted in RF's first appearance at the Bread Loaf School of English, for a brief stay, in the summer of 1921, but because his feelings were hurt during that brief stay he refused to appear at Bread Loaf in 1922. In the summer of 1923, he went to Bread Loaf for one evening of reading. When he summoned Davison to Amherst, in December of 1923, for additional discussions of the Bread Loaf plan, he gave his own ideas on how the art of writing could and could not be taught.

When some of his proposals and suggestions were tried at Bread Loaf, in the summer of 1926, with the establishment of the additional "Conferences on Writing," in a two-week session which followed immediately after the six-week School of English, RF was hurt because he was not asked to take charge of these "Conferences." He was at least invited to give an evening reading at that first session, in 1926. He went, gave the reading as requested, and lingered there for several days.

Wilfrid Davison wrote to RF on 6 Dec. 1926 (carbon copy, MCL), inviting him to give a reading at the Bread Loaf School of English in the summer of 1927, and adding, "Both sessions at Bread Loaf last summer were considered successful by the students, I think. The Conferences on Writing, under Mr. [John] Farrar's direction, proved even more helpful and interesting than I had dared hope. We are expecting to repeat them this coming summer."

At this time, RF was on friendly terms with John Farrar, and yet jealous because Farrar had obtained the position which RF wanted. Bitterness was added to jealousy when RF was not even invited to participate in the "Conferences on Writing" at Bread Loaf in 1927. Davison did ask him to give a reading of his poems at the 1927 School of English, but RF initially refused, giving as his excuse the possibility that he might go abroad. He added that if his travel plans changed he would be glad to give a reading. Davison wrote to him again on 29 Jan. 1927 (carbon copy, MCL):

"We certainly do want to put you down as a visitor even if only on an 'off chance.' If you should go to Europe this summer, we will present our regrets to the School and tell them we shall hope you will come some other summer."

Davison wrote a follow-up letter on 2 March 1927. He wrote again on 5 July 1927 (carbon copy, MCL): "Just a note to inquire whether you can tell yet when we may expect you at Bread Loaf." Apparently receiving no answer, he wrote once more, on 28 July 1927 (carbon copy, MCL): "Could you tell me soon when we may expect you at Bread Loaf. I am trying to arrange the program for the remaining days of the session, and want to be sure that we reserve for you the date that will best suit your convenience. . . . Classes are over August 10th. . . ."

RF apparently arrived for a three-day stay during the last week of the School of English: on 3 Aug. 1927, Mrs. Frost wrote to Mrs. Madison C. Bates (PMCB): "Robert has had an agreement to go to Middlebury [Bread Loaf] for three days' conferences during the summer school. He has been putting it off until the last minute, but as this is the last week of the session, he simply *must* go." (If he had gone one week later, he would have been at Bread Loaf during part of the "Conferences on Writing," but Farrar had charge of that session, and Farrar still had not invited him.)

In July of 1928—shortly before he sailed for France—RF gave a reading before the School of English, and he apparently discovered that neither Wilfred Davison nor his assistant Robert M. Gay (a professor of English literature at Simmons College) liked the way in which Farrar had been running the (now so-called) "Conference." When both Davison and Gay expressed eagerness to find a replacement for Farrar, RF apparently confided that he would be willing to take the place of Farrar. On 16 Jan. 1929, Gay wrote to RF (DCL):

"I meant to have written you long since to tell you how delighted I was when Davy wrote me that you were to take charge of the Conference next summer. . . . The main thing seems to be to get rid of the commercial flavor of the Conference, and I do not think that will be hard. . . . The morning meetings of the Conference have as a rule been profitable, I am sure, but the afternoon 'discussions' have not. The latter too often became merely one more lecture . . . and the subject 'discussed' was trivial or commercial. . . . To sit there for hours, as we did, and discuss how to sell MSS, the 'taboos' of editors, and so forth, seemed quite literally a desecration. . . . Your presence and influence alone will do much. . . ."

Although Davison and Gay seemed to agree that RF should take charge of the Writers' Conference at Bread Loaf in the summer of 1929—and although the catalogue actually listed RF as "Director" —Dr. Paul D. Moody, President of Middlebury College, apparently refused to sanction the arrangement thus made. John Farrar remained the director of the Conference, and RF was invited merely as a member of the staff. The jealousy caused by this disappointing arrangement set the stage for an unpleasant verbal battle between RF and Farrar during one of the public sessions. RF's complaint was that Farrar was trying to run the conference as a commercial literary agency, that Farrar was merely shopping for manuscripts. There was more than jealousy behind RF's quarreling: he also took pleasure in being vindictive because Lesley Frost had complained to her father that she had been mistreated by Farrar while she worked for him in the newly established publishing firm of Doubleday Doran in New York City.

Nevertheless, RF was unable to oust Farrar from the directorship of the Writers' Conference. Instead, Farrar apparently arranged that RF would not be invited back for the 1930 session of the Conference. President Moody, apparently on Farrar's side, tactfully shunted the troublemaking RF away from the Conference, and some other shuntings occurred after the unexpected death of Davison on 22 Sept. 1929. Moody appointed Professor Gay to serve as director (or dean) of both the Bread Loaf sessions, with Professor Harry G. Owen (of the Department of English at Middlebury College) as assistant dean, and with Farrar still the director of the

Writers' Conference. RF was invited to be the main speaker at the Broad Loaf service for the dedication of the Wilfred Davison Memorial Library, on 21 July 1930—during the School of English session. As instructed, Gay wrote a follow-up letter to RF on 9 June 1930 (DCL):

"President Moody has just telephoned to me that you have agreed to come up on the 21st and 22nd [of July], and I am delighted. And also grateful. He also told me that he had suggested that you might like to give your evening reading or talk at the same time, instead of August 8, as previously arranged. This we can arrange without trouble, and I suggested that, since you will speak at the dedication of the library on Monday, July 21, you might like to read the following night. . . ."

RF, thus manipulated, felt that he was being punished for his open quarreling with John Farrar at the 1929 session. On 14 July 1930—one week before he gave his memorial talk—he wrote to LU (*Letters to Untermeyer*, pp. 201–202):

"I am left out of the Two Week Manuscript Sales Fair as I had reason to suppose I would be. I thought perhaps it would be less embarrassing all round if I simply forgot to go to the earlier educational session at Bread Loaf. But I have been come after by Pres. Moody and flatteringly written after by our friend Gay to be present and help them dedicate the Memorial Library to Wilfred Davison on Monday July 21st. . . . I agreed to go on the understanding that they would give you your choice of sessions. I knew you said you came [in 1929] a good deal to be there when I was. But of course we are going to see each other here right off anyway, and maybe it would be too ostentatious for you to desert the Farrow session because I was left out of it. You may be sure I don't mind your being with that gang for a visit if only as a spy and agent provocateur. You can't imagine how cleanly I have forgiven the Johnnie. The explanation is that I am at heart secretly tickled if I offended him unintentionally. I suppose it to have been unintentionally, because to this hour I don't know what my offense was. I am too cowardly to offend anybody intentionally and usually too skillfull to do it unintentionally. So I am stuck. I can't hurt anybody no matter how much he deserves it. When I do it is a triumph of the divinity that shapes our ends. It gives me a funny feeling I must say I like. I suppose it's a manly feeling, but I'm such a stranger to it I hardly know. Yes I came off so well with the Johnnie that I shan't care if you do treat him as if nothing had ever happened. I even evened the score between him and Lesley."

In spite of RF's boast that he had triumphed over Farrar, he was deeply hurt at being "left out of" the 1930 Writers' Conference at Bread Loaf. For various reasons, he did not appear at the Conference during 1931 or 1932. In the spring of 1933, when the newly appointed director, Theodore Morrison, wrote RF and offered to pay him $50 for a single reading at the Writers' Conference session in 1933, RF did not answer the letter. But when Dean Owen invited him to give a reading at the School of English session in

1933, RF refused, using as his excuse some disparaging reference to the low honorarium offered by Morrison.

In a letter dated 27 March 1933 (DCL), Morrison tried to explain: "I hope I haven't been guilty of a blunder. Harry Owen seems to think that I have said or written something to you that led you to have qualms about coming to Bread Loaf on account of the fee. . . ." After describing at length the budget reduction for Bread Loaf, because of the depression, he continued, "This long explanation is due partly in justice to Harry [Owen]. I have nothing whatever to do now with the School [of English] session, and if anything I have said on behalf of the Conference has led you to feel qualms about visiting the School, you are making the innocent suffer with the guilty!" In the same letter, Morrison wrote, "Mrs. Fisher has usually come free, and undertook to do so again. I asked Farrar to come free." RF answered (in a letter apparently slightly misdated 27 May 1933, the date of Morrison's letter; DCL):

"Now what have I done? I simply assumed the Bread Loaf money was all in one reservoir and I would be saving embarrassment all round if, taking the hint from you and using a little frankness, I offered to relieve the school of my expense this summer. Please don't let it worry you. My philosophy is to take reasonable money for my reading as the only way to make the job the least bit important in my own eyes, and when what I ask eliminates me and I am out, to count myself well out. Reading in public never improves my health. I have been sick in bed with a temperature for two weeks and am still shut in from an overdose of reading in the middle and south. John Farrer and Dorothy Fisher are different from me. They probably feel themselves beyond price anyway. Then again they are both Vermonters and glad to do anything free for the institutions of Vermont. I'm not a Vermonter. I belong to one of the Original Thirteen Colonies that made the Union and will lay down my life for the principle that the western boundary of New Hampshire is the western bank of the Connecticut at high water and takes in for taxation all the wharves on the western bank. What you say about the two dropped office assistants and the half-dropped librarian makes me all the surer I am right in getting myself dropped too. Better that I lost a hundred jobs out of a possible two hundred than that the least of these underlings lost only one. Such has been my doctrine and policy ever since the New Deal came in. And when you stop to consider, it's not so terribly unselfish at that."

This pleasant badinage, used as a verbal smokescreen, may have concealed RF's hurt feelings, but he did not again appear at the Bread Loaf Writers' Conference until the summer of 1936. In summary, his only known appearances at it during the first nine years of its existence were in 1926 and 1929. (Some glimpses of RF's far more numerous appearances at the School of English may be found in George K. Anderson, *Bread Loaf School of English: The First Fifty Years* [Middlebury, 1969], pp. 30–34, 87, 90, 121, 142, and 164.)

37. RF to LU, 7 Aug. 1936; *Letters to Untermeyer,* p. 283.
38. EWF to Mrs. E. W. Fobes [Aug. 1936]; DCL.
39. EWF to Richard Thornton, 13 Sept. 1936; DCL.
40. The "Ode" was written by the Poet Laureate, John Masefield, and RF was not impressed with it. He mentioned it in a letter to Harold G. Rugg at Dartmouth (4 Dec. 1936; DCL), while refusing to write another occasional poem:

"After long long consideration (you should say so—and one long more), I have reluctantly come to the conclusion that I dont see how I can ever again promise you or anyone else a poem for an occasion. Look at the way I failed them with not only one poem but two at Harvard. And look at the sad way Masefield didn't fail them. I'm modest. I often say Who am I that I should hold myself above doing things badly. . . . I have kept poetry free thus far, and I have been punished for the mere thought of making it a duty or a business. . . . I made myself wretched and even sick last summer with the dread of what I had let myself in for at Harvard. I now think I was very foolish to try anything at my age so against my lifelong habits. Poetry has been a self indulgence with me and theres no use trying to put a better face on it."

41. The American Academy had asked RF to give a prose lecture in connection with the annual meeting on 12 Nov. 1936, the honorarium to be $250. On 5 June 1936 (AAAL), RF wrote accepting the invitation. On 18 Sept. 1936, EWF wrote to the American Academy, saying RF was recovering from his attack of shingles and was not certain he would be able to keep his promise. On 7 Oct. 1936, she wrote again saying he could not attend the annual meeting.

42. RF to LU, 25 Nov. 1936; *Letters to Untermeyer,* p. 284.
43. RF's best account of this incident occurs in his recorded talk, "Poverty and Poetry," *Biblia,* op. cit., pp. [14]–[15].

32. PRIDE OF ANCESTRY

1. RF to Edward Morgan Lewis, 1 July 1930; JLA. The entire letter is quoted in an unpublished doctoral dissertation by Hobart Lewis Morris, Jr.: *Edward Morgan Lewis—A Biography* (Syracuse University, 1968), p. 732. Gratitude is here expressed to Dr. Morris for his generosity in making his dissertation available as background for this chapter, and for his other acts of assistance in providing information about the friendship between RF and Lewis.

2. This anecdote, and the entire story of RF's friendship with Lewis as given in this chapter, are based in part on RF's various accounts as told by him to LT. The essentials of the immediate anecdote occur in Morris, p. 554, but are there drawn from another source.

3. For an account of RF's youthful exploits as a baseball player, see *The Early Years,* pp. 58–59, 74–75, 78–79.

4. Details on the career of Lewis as a major league baseball

player are here taken from the chapter entitled "Professional Baseball (1896–1901)" in Morris, pp. 180–207.

5. For source, see Note 24 of this chapter.

6. This anecdote was told by Lewis to his daughter, Gwendolyn (Mrs. Samuel W. Hoitt), who told it to LT during an interview in Durham, N. H., 8 July 1969. Gratitude is here expressed to Mrs. Hoitt for her many acts of assistance in gathering information concerning the friendship between RF and her father.

7. RF to Lewis, 18 March 1930; JLA.

8. RF, "Perfect Day—A Day of Prowess," *Sports Illustrated*, Vol. 5, No. 4 (23 July 1956), p. 51.

9. The entire citation is quoted in Morris, pp. 556–557.

10. RF to Lewis, 23 June 1930; JLA.

11. RF to Lewis, undated, but c. May 1932; JLA.

12. The entire citation is quoted in Morris, p. 739.

13. RF to Lewis, 2 Aug. 1934; JLA.

14. Quoted from "Relicts" in Shirley Barker, *The Dark Hills Under* (New Haven, 1933), p. 30.

15. "Old Voices," ibid., p. 13.

16. "I sing misunderstanding," RF wrote to Harcourt in 1917 (see p. 110 of Chapter 8). Even as RF stubbornly misunderstood and misinterpreted Robinson's sonnet entitled "New England" (see Notes 13 and 15 of Chapter 18), so he misunderstood and misinterpreted Shirley Barker's "Portrait"—for his own convenience. In 1938, when RF offered LT a paraphrase of "Portrait" in explaining how it had inspired the retort entitled "Pride of Ancestry" (cited in Note 17 of this chapter), RF insisted that "Portrait" explicitly revealed Shirley Barker's romantic and sentimental belief that she had gained her poetic gifts through her descent from an illegitimate offspring born to her ancestor described in "Portrait." Such an interpretation is completely irresponsible: neither explicitly nor implicitly does the poem convey this notion. The central point of it is that even as this once-vivid ancestor is now only a faded picture on the wall, so the speaker will some day be, and the concluding lines are as follows:

> *Rise where I can, by fame, or fight, or love,*
> *The time will come when I shall only be*
> *A calm gray face behind a walnut frame,*
> *To which a child will lift appraising eyes*
> *And lightly ask, "Which grandmother is that?"*

17. "Pride of Ancestry" is here quoted with the permission of Alfred C. Edwards, sole executor of the estate of RF. The source is a MS copy (PUL), given by RF to LT in 1938. An oblique reference to another MS copy of this poem, given elsewhere in 1938, occurs in *Selected Letters*, pp. 482–483:

"Anyone who would drag in Freud to explain my having failed to autograph a solitary check would naturally prefer my sexiest poem The Bearer of Evil Tidings to anything else of mine he ever saw. But if he likes that one best I think I can show him one he will like better. I wrote it once a year or two ago in impatience with the family of nobodies it celebrates."

The undated letter from which this passage is quoted was written early in Nov. 1938, and if RF is correct in saying "Pride of Ancestry" was written "a year or two ago," it could not have been written earlier than Nov. 1936. The assumption is made by LT, however, that RF wrote at least the first draft of "Pride of Ancestry" in the heat of his vindictive rage, soon after he received and read *The Dark Hills Under*—in Aug. 1934.

18. Quoted from "Relicts" in *The Dark Hills Under*, p. 35.

19. Quoted from "Girl in the Mirror," ibid., p. 18.

20. "Not All There" (*The Poetry*, p. 309) was first published in *Poetry* magazine, Vol. 48, No. 1 (April 1936). An early draft—probably the first—is in the H. B. Collamore collection of Frost books and manuscripts, TCL, and is entitled "Don't Anybody Laugh."

RF's twofold retaliation against the poetry of Shirley Barker, in writing "Not All There" and "Pride of Ancestry," further reveals the hypersensitivity of his responses whenever his beliefs or prejudices were offended. Perhaps even more revealing, in the latter poem, is the strange intermingling of revulsion, moral earnestness, and prurience evoked by his responses to sexual elements in *The Dark Hills Under*. These responses, which are also intermingled with his puritanical distaste for Catholicism, are not completely hidden beneath the ribald surface. Similar self-revelations occur in several other snatches of poetic ribaldry which he wrote—and never published. A glimpse of them is available in *Letters to Untermeyer*, pp. 373–374.

21. RF to Lewis, 19 Sept. 1935; JLA.

22. "This Man My Friend" is quoted in Morris, op. cit., 549–550. Shirley Frances Barker (1911–1965) achieved a considerable literary reputation as the author of historical novels, most of which have New England settings. Her first novel, *Peace, My Daughters*, was published in 1949. Her second novel, *Rivers Parting*, appeared in 1952 and was a Literary Guild selection. *Swear by Apollo*, one of her later novels (1959), was also a Literary Guild selection. Of her fifteen books, only two were poetry: *The Dark Hills Under* (1933) and *A Land and a People* (1952). Born in Farmington, N.H., she was graduated from the University of New Hampshire, with honors, Phi Beta Kappa, in 1934. She received a Master of Arts degree in English from Radcliffe College in 1940. After gaining a degree in library science from the Pratt Institute Library School in 1941, she served until 1954 as a librarian in the New York Public Library's department of American history and genealogy. In 1954 she moved from New York City to Concord, N.H., where she supported herself as a professional writer. Near the end of her life she served for some time as a librarian in the State Library in Concord. Her death, caused by asphyxiation, in Penacook, N.H., on 18 Nov. 1965, was ruled a suicide. (An attempt by

LT to determine whether her papers contained any letters from RF, brought word from her executor, Mr. Wallace Kimball of Derry, N.H., that all of her letter-files and papers had disappeared under mysterious circumstances.)

Gratitude is here expressed to Miss Mildred E. Morrison, the librarian of the Dover (N.H.) Public Library, for much assistance in gathering information about Shirley Barker and Edward Morgan Lewis.

23. "Poems Read by Robert Frost," *Services of the University of New Hampshire in Memory of Edward Morgan Lewis . . . May 25, 1936* (Durham, N. H., 1936), pp. [17]–[19]. With the poems, in this brochure, are the opening remarks made by RF, including the anecdote of the Eisteddfod in Utica. These opening remarks also include a neutral reference to Shirley Barker:

"My last correspondence with him, strangely enough, was concerning another new poet. His teachings were mainly of the older poets—Browning, Tennyson—but his interest was alive and of the moment. This new poet, I might name. Some of you know her— Shirley Barker of this state."

33. STRIKE THAT BLOW FOR ME

1. RF to DeVoto, c. 1 Jan. 1937; *Selected Letters*, p. 436.
2. Lillian Frost to Helen B. Lawrie, c. 3 Jan. 1937; PHBL.
3. RF to DeVoto, c. 5 Nov. 1936; *Selected Letters*, p. 430.
4. Idem.
5. Ibid., p. 431.
6. Granville Hicks, "A Letter to Robert Hillyer," *New Republic*, Vol. 92, No. 1194 (20 Oct. 1937), p. 308. The parody is there published as a review of Hillyer's book entitled *A Letter to Robert Frost and Others* (New York, 1937). The two excerpts are here quoted with the permission of Granville Hicks and of the *New Republic*.
7. RF had previously encouraged DeVoto to write a biography of RF, and for a time DeVoto planned to do so. He made notes for such a biography. A quarrel between RF and DeVoto, beginning in 1938 and continuing until 1943, caused DeVoto to abandon this plan. (See *Selected Letters*, pp. 481–482, 508–510.)
8. *Selected Poems*, by Robert Frost. With Introductory Essays by W. H. Auden, C. Day Lewis, Paul Engle, and Edwin Muir (London, 1936).
9. RF to DeVoto, c. 1 Jan. 1937; *Selected Letters*, pp. 436–437.
10. Edmund Wilson, "Complaints; II. Bernard DeVoto," *New Republic*, Vol. 91, No. 1157 (3 Feb. 1937), p. 405.
11. Bernard DeVoto, "My Dear Edmund Wilson," *Saturday Review*, Vol. 15, No. 8 (13 Feb. 1937), p. 8.
12. RF to DeVoto, 16 Feb. 1937; *Selected Letters*, p. 440.
13. RF to DeVoto, 26 March 1937; *Selected Letters*, p. 441.
14. RF's influence on President Paul D. Moody, in behalf of

DeVoto, actually began in May 1936. On 2 June 1936, President Moody wrote to DeVoto (SUL), "I have been seething with indignation ever since Robert Frost was here a week ago and told me that you were leaving Harvard to take up the work on the *Saturday Review*. That you are taking over that potentiality pleased me immensely; but that you are leaving Harvard I consider a great misfortune to them and to education. There are some of us who think of you increasingly as the white hope of American Letters and that any institution should let you escape its grasp seems to me utterly unthinkable. It is a reflection on American education."

15. RF to DeVoto, May 1937; *Selected Letters*, pp. 444–445.

16. RF's constant defense of theism against humanism is reflected in his quietly sarcastic statement, "One might forget God, and talk about the highest in himself."

17. An early foreshadowing of a central theme in RF's "Masque of Mercy" (see *Selected Letters*, p. 555) may be found explicitly stated in the sentences, "I can't imagine any honest man without the fear of finding himself unworthy in the sight of someone else. It might be something you didn't care to call by name." Compare this with the following passage in RF's "Introduction" to *King Jasper* (p. vi):

"Two fears should follow us through life. There is the fear that we shan't prove worthy in the eyes of someone who knows us at least as well as we know ourselves. That is the fear of God. And there is the fear of Man—the fear that men won't understand us and we shall be cut off from them."

18. RF is here paraphrasing part of his poem, "The Gift Outright," written a year earlier.

19. RF's tirade against Santayana, here, deserves more than passing notice. "Santayana is the enemy of my spirit," RF said repeatedly to LT and others. His obsessive hatred of Santayana was bound up with his obsessive admiration for William James— the two professors who had the most profound influence on RF at Harvard College from the fall of 1897 to the spring of 1899. (These opposed responses, during this period, are described and interpreted in *The Early Years*, pp. 238–246.) In his commencement address at Oberlin, RF suggests that Santayana was indeed the enemy of RF's spirit, partly because of the way in which the philosopher played with the word, "illusion," in discussing that aspect of religious belief—immortality—to which RF clung with a desperation born of fear. RF's paraphrase (and parody) of Santayana, here, is better understood if it is compared with the following pasage in Santayana's *Reason in Religion* (New York, 1905), pp. 51–52:

"Illusions incident to mythology are not dangerous in the end, because illusion finds in experience a natural though painful cure. . . . Nor is the illusion involved in fabulous thinking always so complete and opaque as convention would represent it. In taking fable for fact, good sense and practice seldom keep pace with dogma. There is always a race of pedants whose function it is to materialize every ideal, but the great world, half shrewdly, half doggedly, manages to escape their contagion. . . . All the doctrines that have flourished in the world about immortality have hardly affected men's natural sentiment in the face of death, a sentiment which those doctrines, if taken seriously, ought wholly to reverse. Men almost universally have acknowledged a Providence, but that fact has no force to destroy natural aversions and fears in the presence of events; and yet, if Providence had ever really been trusted, those preferences would have lapsed, being seen to be blind, rebellious, and blasphemous. Prayer, among sane people, has never superseded practical efforts to secure the desired end; a proof that the sphere of expression was never really confused with that of reality. Indeed, such a confusion, if it had passed from theory to practice, would have changed mythology into madness."

Reference is made, in Note 13 of Chapter 10, to the possibility that Mrs. Frost's irreligious taunts may have caused RF to develop the self-protective habit of joking about religious matters when in the presence of a nonbeliever: ". . . to disarm him," as RF wrote, "by seeming to have heard and done justice to his side of the standing argument." Santayana's witty and ironic ways of presenting one side of the "standing argument," in the lectures at Harvard, may have had much to do with RF's manner of developing self-protective uses of wit and irony. But RF's serious continuation of his own arguments against Santayana, at Oberlin, approximately forty years after he heard those lectures, helps to reveal the intensity of his hatred for Santayana.

20. RF's Oberlin talk entitled "What Became of New England?" was stenographically recorded. It was subsequently edited by Robert S. Newdick and was published in the Oberlin *Alumni Magazine,* May 1938. The lines quoted from Christopher Smart's "A Song to David" are stanzas 76 and 77.

21. Cox is correct in pointing out that RF used the word "superstitious" in a nonpejorative sense. The roots of the word permit and justify such usage: *super + stare.* Taken etymologically, a superstition is an opinion or notion or belief which stands above reason, in that it is not dependent on either reason or knowledge. Support for Cox's interpretation may be found in one of RF's notebooks (DCL) which he kept in 1956 and 1957. On the first page of this notebook, the following entry occurs:

"The God Question. Religion is superstition or it is nothing. It is still there after philosophy has done its best."

On the same page, RF defines philosophy as "nothing but" an "attempt to rationalize religion."

22. Sidney Cox, *Robert Frost, Original "Ordinary Man"* (New York, 1929), pp. 36–37. Notice in particular, here, the statement "God, he said, is that which a man is sure cares, and will save him, no matter how many times or how completely he has failed." That statement contains the essence of Universalist doctrine. RF's paternal grandparents were members of the Universalist Church, in Lawrence, Mass. He lived with them and attended church with

them for several months, immediately after his arrival in New England from San Francisco in 1885. (See *The Early Years*, pp. 51–52.)

Among the many corroborations of Cox's claim that RF believed in a benevolent personal God, one other may be worth citing here. In the early 1920s, RF visited at the home of Madison C. Bates, then president of the Poetry Society of Southern Vermont, and headmaster of Burr and Burton Seminary in Manchester, Vt. During this visit, Bates asked RF if he felt drawn toward or influenced by the pantheistic concept. RF replied that he did not; that he held the commonly accepted Christian belief concerning the nature of God and of his relationship to man. Then RF, raising his arm and pointing aloft as though for emphasis, said, "I think there is an Old Fellow up there who takes a benevolent hand in human affairs." (Madison C. Bates, letter to LT, 7 Feb. 1947.) For another closely related statement by RF, see *The Early Years*, pp. 491–492. See also, RF's poem entitled "The Fear of God" (*The Poetry*, p. 385).

23. Louis Untermeyer, *From Another World* (New York, 1939), p. 208. LU there states that he is quoting from "one of the first letters I received from him [RF] when we were lightly arguing about labels and the emphasis of understatement." The quoted passage does not occur, however, in *Letters to Untermeyer*.

RF repeatedly made related uses of the words, "Synecdochist" and "synecdoche." In 1931 he said, "I started calling myself a Synecdochist when others called themselves Imagists or Vorticists. Always, always a larger significance. A little thing touches a larger thing." (*Trial by Existence*, p. 325.) Six years earlier he had said, "Imagery and after-imagery are about all there is to poetry. Synecdoche and synecdoche. My motto is that something has to be left to God." (Sergeant, "Robert Frost, A Good Greek out of New England," op. cit., p. 147.) Again: "I believe in what the Greeks called synecdoche: the philosophy of the part for the whole; skirting the hem of the goddess. All that an artist needs is samples." (Ibid., p. 148.)

Repeatedly, RF made his poems synecdochic by endowing physical facts, or images in nature, with implicit metaphysical extensions of meaning, as for example in "I Will Sing You One-O." Such a procedure is traditional in religious poetry: Christian doctrine is drenched with poetic references to the ways in which nature and human nature give partial reflections of the whole. But there are many places outside Christian doctrine where RF could have found additional inspiration for endowing the word, synecdoche, with meanings which correlate physical parts with the spiritual whole. Emerson's essay entitled "The Poet" deals primarily with this relationship, as the following passage suggests:

". . . the world is a temple whose walls are covered with emblems, pictures and commandments of the Deity—in this, that there is no fact in nature which does not carry the whole sense of nature. . . ."

Emerson, in concluding the same essay, uses an even more

vivid pair of metaphors to convey the same ideal. The poet, he says, draws his images from

". . . wherever are forms with transparent boundaries, wherever are outlets into celestial space . . ."

Going further, in his essay entitled "Poetry and Imagination," Emerson states that even as the poet reveals partial glimpses of God, so God poetically reveals himself to man:

"God himself does not speak prose, but communicates with us by hints, omens, inferences and dark resemblances in objects lying all around us."

In his essay on Plato, Emerson implies that Plato used a synecdochic method of teaching us how metaphysical truths are knowable through the physical:

"They are knowable, because being from one, things correspond. There is a scale; and the correspondence of heaven to earth, of matter to mind, of the part to the whole, is our guide."

Similar to Emerson's statement, there, is RF's in his "Education by Poetry" essay: "Greatest of all attempts to say one thing in terms of another is the philosophical attempt to say matter in terms of spirit, or spirit in terms of matter, to make the final unity." Also closely related is RF's saying, "I was brought up a Swedenborgian. I am not a Swedenborgian now. But there's a good deal of it that's left with me. I am a mystic. I believe in symbols. I believe in change and in changing symbols." (*Interviews*, p. 49.)

In either the Emersonian or the Frostian sense, these synecdochic procedures of the poets might be traced back to the following celebrated passage in "The Symposium" where Plato obliquely elaborates the ascent through the physical to the metaphysical, as though up a flight of stairs:

"He who has been instructed thus far in the things of love, and who has learned to see the beautiful in due order and succession, when he comes towards the end will suddenly perceive a nature of wondrous beauty. . . . He who from these ascending under the influence of true love, begins to perceive that beauty, is not far from the end. And the true order of going, or being led by another, to the things of love, is to begin from the beauties of earth and mount upwards for the sake of that other beauty, using these as steps only, and from one going on to two, and from two to all fair forms, and from fair forms to fair practices, and from fair practices to fair notions, until from fair notions he arrives at the notion of absolute beauty, and at last knows what the essence of beauty is." (Jowett translation.)

24. *Selected Letters*, p. 225. In his reference to the "Scotch symbolist" convention, RF is apparently suggesting the lyrics and narratives of the following poets who made elaborate uses of symbolism, metaphor, synecdoche, and allegory: Robert Henryson (1425–1500), William Dunbar (1460?–1520?), and Gavin Douglas (1475?–1522?).

25. RF to LU, 4 Oct. 1937; *Letters to Untermeyer*, pp. 295–296.

26. RF to LU, 5 Oct. 1937; ibid., p. 296: "Say I hate or have come to hate the thought of all the letters I ever wrote. I never intended them to be kept. I cant ask people to destroy them I suppose. But in a particular one like the last about Elinors peril I wish I could make an exception. I cant bear that it should ever become a public matter whether I am dead or alive. Please burn it. Be easy on me for what I did too emotionally and personally. It spoils letters when it gets so they're undeniably collectors items or biographers material. Gee there are some eventualities we didnt bargain for, and I'm going to have them different if I can."

27. EWF to Mrs. Nina Thornton, 1 Nov. 1937; DCL.

28. EWF to Mrs. Nina Thornton, 30 Dec. 1937; *Selected Letters*, pp. 453–454.

29. RF to DeVoto, 29 Dec. 1937; *Selected Letters*, pp. 452–453. In the passage quoted from this letter, RF's account of two closely related situations deserves special attention. First, "I said to Sidney Cox years ago that I was non-elatable. While I wasn't actually fishing I suppose I hoped he might see I wanted to be contradicted." Intermittently, throughout the poetry and prose of RF, reflections may be found of this posture, this act of making a remark which invites the reader or listener to challenge it for purposes of noticing what is and is not implied. (Some aspects of this highly protean posture are examined in the notes to Chapter 17 which are devoted to different parts of the poem entitled "New Hampshire.") RF goes on to say that when he told his wife that he was "non-elatable," she answered, "What a lie." She obviously knew that he either wanted or deserved to be contradicted on this point.

Closely related to these two situations—and to RF's pleasure in challenging his listeners or readers intermittently through striking postures—is the artistic game he played in writing "The Road Not Taken," as described in Note 6 of Chapter 7. Repeatedly, he gave hints of his fondness for challenging listeners or readers in similar ways. One such hint occurs in his writing to John Bartlett about the latter's children, whom RF had not seen for some time: ". . . how those youngsters of yours are coming up. . . . I'd like to tease them. They look as if they could take care of themselves. I probably couldnt baffle them very much at my crypticest. Never mind I can baffle some people." (1 Nov. 1927; *Selected Letters*, p. 346.)

Among the many aspects of RF's poetry and prose which deserve more attention than has yet been given them, none is more tantalizingly difficult than his intermittent ways of baffling and teasing his readers. Although his motives for playing this artistic game were complicated, some of them are taken under consideration in Note 12 of Chapter 18 ("I own any form of humor shows fear and inferiority") and in Note 13 of Chapter 10 (on RF's shamefaced ways of protecting his religious belief).

30. *Recognition of Robert Frost* (previously cited in Note 10

of Chapter 23) was a labor of love on the part of Richard Thornton. He had risen to the rank of president in the firm of Henry Holt and Company before he volunteered to supervise the editing and publishing of this volume as a gesture of friendliness to RF at a time when RF was threatening—once again—to leave the firm. *Recognition of Robert Frost* was almost ready for publication, in 1937, when RF caused another crisis. While visiting Thornton in the president's office, he was shown galley sheets of an anthology of essays edited with an introduction by Morton D. Zabel— *Literary Opinion in America: Essays Illustrating the Status, Methods, and Problems of Criticism in the United States Since the War.* RF, examining the table of contents, was enraged to discover that none of the essays was devoted to him. He began his protest with the reprimand that Holt, as RF's publisher, should not publish any such book which omitted reference to Holt's most distinguished author. Thornton did his best to persuade RF that *Recognition of Robert Frost* would make amends for the omission in Zabel's book. Instead of being mollified, RF became adamant. He insisted that if Holt did publish Zabel's book, RF would find a new publisher. Charles Madison, who was then editor in the College Department at Holt, tells how the crisis was resolved:

"For all his devotion to Frost, Thornton's position as president of Holt made the request that he break the contract with an author doubly difficult. Painfully aware that Frost's objection was an ultimatum and that the firm could not afford to lose its leading author, the Holt executives—lacking the founder's ethical firmness and independence of action—abjectly submitted. The college editor [Charles Madison], who had originally arranged for the book's publication, managed to sell the plates to a friendly publisher [Harper] slightly below cost and kept the outraged critic [Zabel] from suing the firm by absorbing the permission fees amounting to several hundred dollars. The distressing incident was never again mentioned by either side, but some members of the firm and the critic believed that Holt had lost something precious as a consequence." (Madison, *The Owl Among Colophons*, op. cit., pp. 175–176. RF proudly told LT all the details of this incident, in 1941.)

31. Bernard DeVoto, "The Critics and Robert Frost," *Saturday Review*, Vol. XVII, No. 10 (1 Jan. 1938), pp. 3–4. One counterattack was made by F. O. Matthiessen, in a letter to the *Saturday Review*, Vol. XVII. No. 15 (5 Feb. 1938), p. 9. He defended Blackmur's article as a "thoroughly serious, if constricted and somewhat fumbling effort to define some of Frost's limitations in his further range into political and social poetry," and concluded by insisting that Blackmur's observations were far better than DeVoto's "tub-thumping and windy declarations."

32. Sidney Cox to DeVoto, 6 Jan. 1938, SUL.

33. Quoted by RF in a letter to DeVoto, 20 Jan. 1938; *Selected Letters*, p. 456.

34. RF to Theodore Morrison, 12 Feb. 1938; DCL.

35. RF to R. P. T. Coffin, 24 Feb. 1938; *Selected Letters*, pp.

461–462. In this letter and elsewhere, RF almost too eagerly dis-associates himself from Plato and Platonism; indeed, he protests too much. His letter to the Amherst *Student* (partially quoted in Chapter 27, pp. 386–388) ends with this differentiation: "To me any little form I assert upon it [upon chaos] is velvet, as the saying is, and to be considered for how much more it is than nothing. If I were a Platonist I should have to consider it, I suppose, for how much less it is than everything." In a sense, however, RF be-gan and ended as a Christian Platonist, and his repeated disavow-als merely help to illustrate the basic conflict between the idealizing and the realizing sides of his being.

Platonism, like Christianity, assigns primary importance to the perfection in the all-controlling Form of Forms. As shown in Note 24 of this chapter, Platonism urges that human beings should "begin from the beauties of earth and mount upwards for the sake of that other beauty . . . the notion of absolute beauty." Christianity adapted these notions from Platonism, and RF liked to say that his mother taught him to be guided by this difficult exhortation: "Be ye therefore perfect, even as your Father in Heaven is perfect." The older he grew, however, the more easily he accommodated himself to the imperfections of this world, as he confessed to DeVoto (*Selected Letters*, p. 482):

"One of the greatest changes my nature has undergone is of record in 'To Earthward' and indeed elsewhere for the discerning. In my school days I simply could not go on and do the best I could with a copy book I had once blotted. I began life wanting perfec-tion and determined to have it. I got so I ceased to expect it and could do without it. Now I find I actually crave the flaws of human handwork. I gloat over imperfection."

Such a statement obviously oversimplifies the facts and again gives unintentional hints concerning the conflicts between RF's instinctive drives, his idealizing drives, and his unsuccessful at-tempts to reconcile them. His fear of death caused him to cling desperately to his childhood belief in his chance to achieve, through divine grace, that ultimate perfection-redemption-salva-tion: eternal life-after-death. To that extent, then, his views re-mained Christian and Platonic, to the end of his life, in spite of his intermittent denials.

36. These remarks by RF, on crudity as raw materials from which the human artist creates forms, are closely related to cer-tain statements in his letter to the Amherst *Student* (cited in Note 26 of Chapter 27) about chaos as raw materials:

"The background is hugeness and confusion shading away from where we stand into black and utter chaos; and against the back-ground any small man-made figure of order and concentration. What pleasanter than that this should be so? . . . But it is more because we like it, we were born to it, born used to it and have practical reasons for wanting it there. . . ."

37. RF's "drag the unbedded beauty out of bed" seems to be a playful modification of the Platonistic passage in the "Defence of

Poetry" where Shelley says that poetry "lays bare the naked and sleeping beauty" of the world "which is the spirit of its forms."

38. RF to R. P. T. Coffin [c. 7 March 1938]; *Selected Letters,* pp. 464–465.

34. AND I THE LAST . . .

1. In the motto for this chapter, the first sentence is quoted from a letter, RF to G. R. Elliott [10 May 1926], ACL; the second and third sentences are quoted from a letter, RF to Wade Van Dore, 14 April 1932 (PLFB).

2. This summary of RF's experiences and thoughts during the two days in which Elinor Frost lingered, before her death, are based on RF's account, told to LT (and recorded) on 19 Feb. 1940.

3. The friend who accompanied Lesley Frost to Jacksonville for the formalities of the cremation was Clifford B. Lyons who was then an instructor at Florida University in Gainesville. Lyons told LT that he saw the envelope placed in the casket, and that Lesley said she did not know what was in the envelope. She later made the same statement to LT, in corroboration. RF never mentioned to LT either the envelope or the contents, and the incident became one of the many subjects LT therefore considered too delicate and private to ask about, in conversations with RF.

4. RF to LT, 19 Feb. 1940. Subsequently, Lesley Frost corroborated this version of the exchange between herself and her father. In addition, however, she did make very careful discriminations between what she felt was and was not admirable in RF's treatment of his children. Her most incisive tribute to both her parents occurs in her "Introduction" to *New Hampshire's Child.*

5. RF to LT, repeatedly, usually ending with some such assertive statement as this one, directly quoted from RF: "That's the way it has to be, with the artist." In Cellini's *Autobiography,* the description of the casting of "Perseus" extends from Chapter 74 through Chapter 78. For reference to the time when RF used this text at Amherst College, see Note 7 of Chapter 18. RF's poem "The Bonfire" will reward study by anyone trying to understand his ways of trying to help his children cope with fear, its many forms and causes.

6. Hervey Allen was almost accurate in saying that RF "has been lecturing" at the University of Florida. He had been scheduled to lecture. In a letter to Charles Monroe, 17 March 1938 (PEMR), RF had written, "We'll be heading north next week, though you may not see us in South Shaftsbury for some time yet. I have been perfectly quiet except for one lecture at Stetson University a few days ago. In parting I shall do one each at the two State Universities here and at Tallahassee. My first one north will be at a Catholic womans college at Washington. . . ." (All these projected talks and readings were canceled.)

7. Hervey Allen to John Farrar and Stanley Rinehart, 22 March 1938; *Selected Letters*, pp. 468–469.

8. RF to Hervey Allen, 12 April 1938; *Selected Letters*, p. 470.

9. RF to Carol Frost, 15 April 1938; VaUL.

10. RF to Bernard DeVoto, 12 April 1938; *Selected Letters*, pp. 470–471.

11. RF to Mr. and Mrs. G. R. Elliott, 13 April 1938; *Selected Letters*, pp. 471–472.

12. The honorary bearers were Fred S. Allis, Reginald Cook, Sidney Cox, Bernard DeVoto, George R. Elliott, Donald Fisher [husband of Dorothy Canfield Fisher], Dr. Nelson Haskell, Robert Hillyer, Stanley King, Otto Manthey-Zorn, David McCord, Frederic G. Melcher, Paul E. Moody, Theodore Morrison, Wilbert Snow, Lawrance Thompson, Richard Thornton, Louis Untermeyer, and George F. Whicher.

13. Elinor Frost's closest friend in Amherst did protest. When told of the plan for the funeral service, Mrs. G. R. Elliott insisted that no such plan should have been considered; that it was exactly what Elinor Frost would have hated. (G. R. Elliott to LT, 29 March, 1947.)

14. Plans for this ritual had been published. The Springfield *Republican* for 11 April 1938 carried in its "Amherst" column the following notice: "Services for Mrs. Robert Frost, who died March 20 in the South, will be held the 22nd at Amherst College Chapel. Following the service, her ashes will be scattered at Derry, N.H." On the day after the services, the Springfield *Union* for 23 April 1938 carried a short article, "Rites Are Held for Mrs. Frost." This article listed the honorary bearers and concluded with this statement: "Her ashes will be scattered at Derry, N.H., the former home of Mr. and Mrs. Frost." They were not scattered. See Note 26 of this chapter.

15. RF's poem "On the Sale of My Farm" is quoted in *The Early Years*, pp. 367–368.

16. RF to DeVoto, 6 March 1938; *Selected Letters*, p. 464. After the Untermeyer incident at Amherst, and even after RF reached Gainesville in Dec. 1937, another complication involving RF at Amherst seems to have developed. George F. Whicher apparently wrote to RF about it, and he answered from Gainesville on 3 Jan. 1938 (ACL):

"Well all I can say under the circumstances is I'll be damned! I have no reason in philosophy or religion to suppose I shan't be. Still I dont mean it as surrendering or in any way compromising my chances up to the last minute of keeping out of Hell. I want both parties contending to understand that I have yet hopes of myself proving the deciding factor in the dispute for my soul. —Nonsense aside I'm sorry people will behave some ways. Maybe your solution is the best possible. I wonder what Stanley [King] thinks of us."

17. RF to Dorothy Canfield Fisher, 2 June 1938; VtUL.

18. RF to Richard Thornton, 14 May 1938; DCL.

19. RF paid $6,200 for the Sunset Avenue property in Amherst; he sold it to Amherst College for $9,000, but from that amount Amherst College deducted $115.71 to cover taxes and the costs of transfer. (Record of sale, PLLF.)

20. This is RF's often-repeated statement concerning the influence of the writings of William James on him. For a more explicit statement of his, on this point, see Note 19 of Chapter 25.

21. Again, this is RF's often repeated reference to the influence of *The Vision Concerning Piers Plowman,* as title alone, on his own poetry.

22. There is a story connected with RF's reference to the "Desert Fellowship." On 14 June 1935, immediately after RF had given his successful Last Chapel Address to the Amherst Seniors on "Our Darkest Concern," President King was so pleased with it that he said he would like to do something special for RF. Previously, RF had been talking about the need for a special fellowship for poets among seniors at Amherst, and in response to King's offer, RF said he wished that such a fellowship could be set up immediately: the first award should be made to an Amherst senior named James Hayford, who would be reading the Class Poem at the graduation exercises, the next day. King asked for further details, and RF gave them. He wanted Amherst to award $1,000 to Hayford, under certain conditions. First, Hayford must promise to disappear for twenty years and not be heard from, as a poet. He must also promise not to go to graduate school and get sullied in that way. He was a Vermonter, and RF wanted him to go to a small town of his choice to do nothing except write. This would be comparable to those acts of religious men who retired into the desert for ascetic purposes, or to those Orientals who sat under a Bo Tree, contemplating the navel. President King humored RF by granting the wish. During the commencement ceremony, when awards were being made, he presented to the astonished James Hayford the Desert Fellowship check for $1,000.

A few months later, King told RF that the boy had violated the contract by getting married. That was no violation, said RF: according to the terms of the contract, marriage was one of the few things he had left to do. The Desert Fellowship award was never made again, and RF assumed that King considered the one award a waste of (his own personal) money. RF considered it a practical joke, perpetrated to express his disgust for graduate study in literature. Hayford subsequently became a teacher at the Burr and Burton Seminary in Manchester, Vermont. (RF to LT, 21 Aug. 1946.)

23. RF to President Stanley King, 4 June 1938; quoted from the first draft, PLLF.

24. President Stanley King to RF, 7 June 1938; PLLF. RF's deep (and justifiable) sense of guilt in having disappointed President King and others at Amherst College apparently caused him to build an extraordinary self-protective myth around the facts concerning how it happened that he resigned in 1938. The docu-

mentary evidence offered in the text of this chapter shows, however, that RF initially and persistently made the moves for "closing
myself out of Amherst," and that he was motivated at least in part
by his knowledge of complaints against the various ways in which
he had reportedly failed to fulfill his contractual obligations. One
of his frankest statements occurs in a letter, RF to J. J. Lankes,
2 Aug. 1938 (TUL):

"You're not coming to see me at Amherst because in the excitement I have kicked Amherst from under me. I dont know just what
happened there. I've been intending to get free for several years.
It was a delicate position and I needed constant reassurances as
to my value in it. I didnt get them unmistakably enough last year."

A far more important motive for his resignation from Amherst
was his expectation of a permanent appointment at Harvard.
Priding himself on his power to manipulate his friends, he continued to exert influence on those who had power at Harvard;
continued, that is, from the time he reached Harvard as the
Charles Eliot Norton Professor in the spring of 1936 until he was
elected to the Board of Overseers at Harvard College on 23 June
1938; indeed, until his Harvard friends raised funds to pay his
salary in a specially created Harvard post, the Ralph Waldo Emerson Fellowship in Poetry, on 10 May 1939—less than a year after
his resignation from Amherst.

Starting in June of 1938, however, he began to create a myth
which was apparently designed to serve several purposes, including
that of assuaging his guilt. He whispered confidentially that he
had been forced out of Amherst by President King for reasons
which were so dark and mysterious that he could not understand
them.

He was just beginning to formulate this myth when Amherst
College made the public announcement of his resignation. The
Amherst *Student* asked him for an "exclusive statement" concerning his reasons for resigning, and published that statement on
page 1 of its issue for 17 June 1938 as follows: "I resigned because
of misgivings as to my value to the college as a 'no-time' teacher."
In the context already supplied, the insinuative ambiguity of this
explanation should be obvious: the "misgivings" could have been
operative in others (including President King) as well as in himself.

As the myth grew, RF became libelous in statements he made
about how President King had forced him to resign. Soon after he
made his "exclusive statement" to the *Student*, he was in Boston
and Cambridge, visiting influential friends and doing his best to
obtain some kind of a teaching offer in the Classics Department
at Harvard. During this visit, he saw Felix Frankfurter and said
he had been forced out of Amherst by King. When Frankfurter
asked why, RF said he didn't know. When Frankfurter said that
"we" must find out why, RF was encouraged. On 28 June 1938, he
wrote to Frankfurter, enclosing a copy of Stanley King's letter of
7 June 1938, and making these extraordinary statements:

"Here is a true copy of Stanley's false reasons for wanting to get rid of me. He is understood by the trustees to be sparing me his real reasons out of consideration for my extreme youth (I am still young enough, he hopes, to be looking for another job and he wouldn't for the world hurt me with other employers of college labor) or out of consideration for my old age (I have no future, but he can't in mercy bring himself to at this time say so). I don't believe the trustees or I will ever get the real reasons. One leak from the trustees' star chamber would suggest he may have jettisoned me for luck like Polycrates' ring. Another has it he threw me away as the sailors threw Jonah overboard for luck. I am told that the member of the board most on Stanley's side against me was the Wordsworthian item-collector who has long resented the coupling of my name with that of his fetish and may well have said (this is biography latterly written) the only thing Wordsworthian he could conceive me capable of would be having an illegitimate child in France during the French Revolution. Which brings me down to the possibility of turpitude. And we cant let it rest there can we? I was never so surrounded with business tact since I was a horse trader in the fairs of Ferghana. I cant expect Stanley or anyone else to come perfectly clean. No motive is perfectly pure. Nobody buys potatoes of me merely for need of potatoes. He must like me as well as my potatoes. So inevitable and so insidious is corruption. Your great kindness of the other day emboldens me to hope we needn't let it rest there." (First draft, PLLF.)

Frankfurter did let the matter rest, almost there. But RF kept improving the story, and Stanley King soon became a monster of such hideous mien that to be hated he needed only to be seen through the eyes of RF. Although King had formally told RF (King to RF, 29 Sept. 1933; DCL) that part of RF's salary was drawn from the John Woodruff Simpson Fund, RF jumped to the conclusion that his total salary had been paid out of King's own pocket. He mentioned this as a supposition, in a letter which presumably tried to set the record straight for his biographer, Robert S. Newdick, on 20 July 1938 (VaUL):

"Did I fail to speak to you of my resignation from Amherst? I had been on the verge of getting out for two or three years. I got rather a jolt when I discovered that the president was only too anxious for the chance to get me out the minute I should give him an opening. There has been a bad misunderstanding about my relationship to the college this last twelve year term. I thought I was a regular professor with all the rights and privileges of a professor, among them the pensional. But it turns out I wasn't. My salary was never budgeted by the trustees as I was promised by Pres. Olds it would be when I came back to Amherst from Michigan. I was simply kept in a fancy way out of the pocket of some rich alumnus. I should have suspected as much from the talk that has been going round about my lack of gratitude. To whom? For what? I had assumed from the pressure put on me to bring me back that I was wanted for value I could confer. The relationship has become something disgustingly personal and patronageous without my realizing it in time. Pres. King has been so mysterious both in his determination to get me out and in refusing to give his reasons that I have arrived at him as my guess as to what rich alumnus was my keeper. I have been through a lot of hard thinking for this result. He has been having a grand pose of magnanimity before the trustees in not having let me know of my obligations to him. He is done with me partly because I havent shown my appreciation by coming to hear him talk in Chapel and faculty meeting and perhaps just a little because he is spending much of his own personal wealth on doubling the Amherst plant in his administration. No bitterness about the plant be it understood. I am a good deal displeased with myself in having been such a fool as to have been so cheated about my standing."

RF, in his conversations with LT, always represented King as heinous. In 1949, RF explained to LT that the newly announced life-appointment given him, as Simpson Lecturer in Literature at Amherst College, was arranged by President Cole to make amends for the so-called shabby treatment which President King had given RF in 1938. Apparently RF had convinced himself, by 1949, that the myth was the actual truth. It was far from the truth, but the confusion thus achieved had presumably assuaged his guilt.

25. RF told LT, repeatedly, about this visit to the farm, but the passages quoted from RF's poems are LT's choices.

26. Mrs. Lillian LaBatt Frost (widow of Carol Frost) told LT that RF did not take the urn to Derry when he made his visit to the Derry farm; that she and Carol were sympathetic with RF's reasons for choosing not to scatter the ashes. Mrs. Lesley Frost Ballantine also told LT that she had agreed with her father's decision.

Nevertheless, the published announcements (described in Note 14 of this chapter) caused some confusion, and may have caused Louis Mertins to make the mistaken statement (in *Robert Frost: Life and Talks-Walking*, p. 228) that RF did scatter the ashes in Derry. (For the circumstances which determined the final resting place of the ashes, in Old Bennington, Vt., see *Selected Letters*, pp. 445, 470.)

27. There were at least two seemingly separate clusters of reasons why RF "refused to be bowed down as much as she was by other deaths." The first of these is implied in his way of ending his poem, " 'Out, Out—[brief candle]' ": ". . . And they, since they / Were not the one dead, turned to their own affairs." Although such a statement may seem cold and unfeeling—and may even seem to be an implicit criticism of those who thus responded—it contains a hint of RF's sensible belief that the primary concern of the living must be with life, and that there is something psychologically unhealthy about even well-intended brooding over the dead. (See "Home Burial," which dramatizes this theme.) Remember also that RF, knowing his attitude in this regard might be challenged

by sentimentalists, once represented himself as thus viewed, shortly after his sister was placed in the mental hospital where she died (RF to LU, 12 April 1920; *Letters to Untermeyer,* p. 103): "And I suppose I am a brute in that my nature refuses to carry sympathy to the point of going crazy just because someone else goes crazy, or of dying just because someone else dies."

The other seemingly separate cluster of reasons why RF refused to be bowed down as much as EWF by the death of someone else is at least suggested by his confession: "I'm a mere selfish artist most of the time." His acknowledged self-centeredness caused him to develop a dread concerning the prospect of only one death: his own. To some degree, then, he may have been trying to rationalize and justify his own egoism when he advanced psychological reasons for refusing to be bowed down by the death of his sister, whom he actually disliked. Later, he was not bowed down for long by the death of his favorite daughter, Marjorie. It was apparently his own dread of his own death which caused him to cling to his inherited religious belief, in an understandably restrictive way. For him, the essential factor in that belief was the promise of a life after death, and the older he became, the more often he made specific references to his belief in "salvation." (As final evidence on this point, see the passage quoted from his last letter, in Note 15 of Chapter 11.)

28. RF to J. J. Lankes, 2 Aug. 1938; TUL.

29. Mrs. Lillian LaBatt Frost told LT that she accidentally saw the showy orchis in the vase beside the urn in the cupboard when she went there to place some ironed shirts of RF's on the shelf where he usually kept them, and she was embarrassed by her awareness that she had thus intruded.

During the first few months after the death of Elinor Frost, RF told many of his friends that he died when she died, at least that he wished he had died with her.

INDEX

NAMES, PLACES, DATES are correlated with topics, interpretations, and conclusions—all previously deployed on three separate levels: Introduction, Central Narrative, Notes. Because this Index makes available some configurations and summaries which are not explicitly given elsewhere, it provides a fourth level of ordering.

Readers are particularly invited to browse through the Robert Frost entries under the sixty-three topical subheads which help to illuminate the complicated and contradictory responses of Frost as man and as artist. To expedite reference and cross-reference, the topical subheads are grouped here with page numbers:

ANTI-INTELLECTUAL 716
ATHEISM 716
BAFFLER-TEASER-DECEIVER 716
BELIEVING 717
BOOKS OF POETRY 717
BRUTE 718
CAMPAIGNER 718
CHANGE 718
CHARLATAN 718
CLASSICIST 718
COWARDICE 719
DEATH 719
DEPRESSION, MOODS OF ... 719
DESIGN 719
ENEMIES 719
ESCAPIST 719
FARMER 720
FEAR 720
FRIENDSHIP 720
GOD 720
GOSSIP 721
HATE 721
INSANITY 721
JEALOUSY 722
JUSTICE VS MERCY 722
LAISSEZ FAIRE 722
MISUNDERSTANDING 722
MURDERER 722
MYSTIC 722
MYTH-MAKER 722
NATURE 723
OPPOSITES 723

POEMS 723
POETIC THEORY 725
PREACHER 725
PRETENDER 725
PROGRESS 725
PROPHET 725
PROSE 726
PUNISHMENT 726
PURITAN 726
RAGE 727
REBEL 727
RELIGIOUS BELIEF 728
RETALIATIONS, POETIC 728
REVENGE 728
SCIENCE, DELIGHT IN 728
SCIENCE VS RELIGION 729
SELF-CENTEREDNESS 729
SKEPTIC 729
SPOILED CHILD 730
STYLE 730
SUPERSTITION 730
SYMBOLIST 730
SYNECDOCHIST 730
TALKS, TITLES OF 730
TEACHER 731
THEISM VS HUMANISM ... 731
UTOPIA 731
VENTRILOQUIST 731
VICTORIAN 731
VINDICTIVE 731
WAR, ATTITUDE TOWARD .. 732

[705]

INDEX

A

Abbot Academy
  RF reads at, in 1916, 73, 536-537
Abercrombie, Lascelles
  RF writes to, in 1915, 63-64; RF
  visits, at Leeds in 1928, 339
Adams, Franklin P., 59, 534
Aiken, Conrad, 337, 639
Aldington, Richard, 19
Allegheny College
  RF pursues a bat with a broom
  at, 262, 607
Allen, Hervey
  RF becomes well-acquainted with,
  in Miami in 1936, 436; RF men-
  tions, 440; RF is visited by, in
  1938, 498-500
Allis, Frederick S.
  letter from, to RF, 365, 643; is
  an honorary bearer at memorial
  service for EWF in 1938, 699
American Academy of Arts and Letters
  RF is elected to membership in,
  in 1930, 389, 651; RF is asked to
  give a talk at, in 1936, 468, 687;
  RF is asked by, to write a memorial
  tribute to Robinson, but declines,
  668
American Drama Society
  presents two of RF's dramatic
  dialogues in 1915, 60, 534-535
Amherst College
  RF gives his first reading at, in
  1916, 78, 97; RF receives offer
  from, 82ff; RF begins teaching at,
  in Jan. 1917, 97ff; first courses
  taught by RF at, 98, 99, 100, 544,
  551; RF resigns from, in Jan. 1920,
  120-122
  RF returns to, in Sept. 1923, 228-
  229, 249ff; again resigns from, in
  June 1925, 263, 269-270
  RF again returns to, on a part-
  time basis, starting Jan. through
  March 1927, 295-296, 306; resigns
  from, in June 1938, 503ff, 700ff
Amherst College *Student*
  important letter from RF to, published in, 386-388, 651
Amherst, Massachusetts
  RF's places of residence in:
  1917, Jan. to June: Godwin house
    on Dana St., 98ff
  1917, Sept. to 1918, June: Frank
    Wood house on Pelham
    Road, 111ff, 553
  1918, Sept. to 1920, Feb.: 19 Main
    St., 119ff
  1923, Sept. to 1925, June: 10 Dana
    St., 252ff

  1927, Jan., Feb., March, through
    1930, Jan., Feb., March:
    Tyler house, 34 Amity St.,
    306ff
  1931, Jan. Feb., March, through
    1932, Jan.: 21 Lincoln
    Ave. [no reference]
  1932, Feb., to 1938, June: 15 Sun-
    set Ave., 398ff, 505-506,
    700
Anderson, George K.
  *Bread Loaf School of English:
  The First Fifty Years*, 686
Anderson, Margaret Bartlett
  Robert Frost and John Bartlett,
  532
Armstrong, A. Joseph
  persuades RF to talk and read in
  Texas, during Nov. 1922, 208ff;
  helps bring RF to Texas again in
  April 1933, 404, 662; again, winter
  1936-1937, 476ff
  *Through Heaven's Back Door: A
  Biography of A. Joseph Armstrong*,
  quoted, 209, 588; cited, 588
Arnold, Matthew
  RF quotes from "In Harmony
  with Nature" by, 235; full text, 595
  RF quotes from "Sohrab and
  Rustum" and "The Scholar Gipsy"
  by, 235; context, 596
  RF, in 1932: "People ask us if
  we had a pleasant trip. We did
  have like Cadmus and Harmonia."
  662
  RF, in 1934: "My favorite poem
  long before I knew what it was
  going to mean to us was Arnold's
  'Cadmus and Harmonia.'" 407
  RF, in 1934: "And here we are
  Cadmus and Harmonia not yet
  placed safely in changed forms."
  408
  RF, in "New Hampshire," may
  have mocked, who represented
  Puritans as "incomplete and mutilated men," in *Culture and Anarchy*, 632
Arvin, Newton
  criticizes RF, in a review of *King
  Jasper*, 452; "A Letter on Proletarian Literature" by, 452; again
  attacks RF, in a review of *A
  Further Range*, 453-454
Austin, Mary
  in *Earth Horizon*, tells of her
  talk with RF on speech rhythms,
  649
Authors' League of America
  RF in 1917, supports, by resisting censorship of Dreiser's *The
  "Genius,"* 647-648

INDEX

B

Babbitt, Irving
RF resents being called a disciple of, 324ff; *Rousseau and Romanticism* by, is quoted, 325; cited, 634

Balfour, Arthur James
Theism and Humanism by, is lent to Cox by RF in 1915, 634; is quoted, 324-325; cited, 634

Bancroft, William Markus
RF meets, anonymously, 209-210, 588

Barker, Shirley
biographical sketch of, 689; sends copy of *The Dark Hills Under* to RF in 1934, 471; RF's unfavorable response to, 471ff; writes poetic tribute to Edward Morgan Lewis, 475

Barnard College
Lesley Frost attends, briefly, 154

Bartlett, John T.
RF writes to, in 1915, on "the winning subject of the fortunes of my book," 24; RF writes to, in 1915, on "my speech before the Authors' Club," 41; RF visits, in Derry, in 1915, 47-48
moves to Colorado in 1917, 287, 390; with wife, assists Marjorie Frost in Colorado in 1931, 391; RF sends thanks to, 392
welcomes RF and EWF to Boulder, summer 1931, 393ff; welcomes them again, summer 1932, 400ff, 660; again welcomes them to Boulder, summer 1935, 423ff, 668
"Notes from Conversations with Robert Frost" (1932, 1934, 1935) by, quoted, 133-134, 648, 655, 658, 660, 665-666; cited, 660, 665, 668

Baseball
RF's passion for the game of, 466ff; reference to a *Sports Illustrated* article by RF, on a World Series game of, in 1956, 688

Batal, James A.
"Poet Robert Frost Tells of His High School Days in Lawrence," quoted, 268-269; cited, 611

Bates, Katharine Lee
on RF in 1915: "I only wonder that so sensitive a poet can bring himself to face an audience at all." 72
RF gives a reading for, in Boston, in 1916, 72-73; gives readings for, at Wellesley College, in 1919 and 1922, 204

Bates, Madison C.
meets the Frosts in Vermont in 1919, 147-148; takes EWF house-hunting, 564; on RF's fondness for bees, 572-573; quotes RF: "I think there is an Old Fellow up there who takes a benevolent hand in human affairs." 693

Battell, Joseph, 161, 194

Baxter, Sylvester
RF meets, in March 1915, 14-15; RF is guest of, in 1915, 39-40; presides at first meeting of the New England Poetry Club, 42; RF to, on "Stopping by Woods," 596
"Talk of the Town" by, quoted, 20-21; cited, 523
"New England's New Poet" by, 524-525

Beach, Joseph Warren
friendship begins between RF and, in 1916, 216; RF participates in the wedding ceremony of, 216-217; friendship ends after RF gossips about, 218
mistakenly represents RF as "a refined agnostic" in *The Concept of Nature in Nineteenth-Century Poetry*, 590

Benét, Stephen Vincent, 353

Bennington College
RF, in 1926: "The only thing that worries me is . . . Bennington College coming in on our pastoral serenity." 297
RF, in 1927, lives in the Shingled Cottage near the campus of, 307

Bergson, Henri
RF reads and admires *Creative Evolution* by, in 1911, 624
RF, in 1917: "What I like about Bergson and Fabre is that they have bothered our evolutionism so much . . ." 300
RF, in 1926, apparently praises the metaphors of, 624
RF, in writing "West-Running Brook," borrows and adapts some metaphors from, 300-304
RF is annoyed by Babbitt's attack on, 325

Beveridge, William Henry
RF, in 1928, gives a reading for, at the London School of Economics and Political Science, 339

Bianchi, Martha Dickinson
is quoted as saying RF is "merely a clod-hopper." 649
RF describes his visit in the home of, 377-378

Biblia
"Poverty and Poetry" by RF, published in, first cited, 534

[707]

Blackmur, Richard
attacks RF in a review of *A Further Range*, 454-455; is answered by DeVoto, 488; RF: "This Blackamur you seem to fear. . . . Who is Blackamur anyway?" 490
Bo Tree Fellowship
RF, in June 1935, persuades President King of Amherst to establish, 700
Bohr, Neils
RF meets, and discusses scientific problems with, at Amherst in 1923, 617
Bonner, Sue Grundy
see Walcutt, Sue Bonner
Book-of-the-Month Club
selects *A Further Range* in 1936, 449, 675
Books We Like (1936)
contains RF's listing of (and his comments on) his ten favorite books, 664
Borrow, George Henry
RF uses *Lavengro* by, in an Amherst course, 251
Bourne, Randolph
RF mentions, in a limerick, 113
Bowdoin College
RF visits G. R. Elliott at, in 1921, 569-570; RF talks on "Vocal Imagination" at, in 1925, 293
Brace, Donald, 155
Bradford, Gamaliel
RF meets, at Wellesley, through Katharine Lee Bates, in 1919, 204; RF is shown part of MS for *Damaged Souls* by, 204; RF urges Holt to publish a novel by, 584; RF urges LU to publish poems by, 584-585; RF's theory of the sound of sense is challenged by, 669
writes a letter about RF's Parker House incident, 256-257, 606
is annoyed by the rumor that he is author of *A Critical Fable*, 319
The Letters of Gamaliel Bradford quoted and cited, 584
Bragdon, Clifford, 357, 642
Braithwaite, William Stanley
RF meets, in March 1915, 15; two articles on RF written by, 525; long quotation from the second of these articles, 34-36
introduces RF to Robinson, 44; is invited to visit RF in Franconia in Aug. 1915, 57; reprints three of RF's poems in the *Anthology of Magazine Verse for 1915*, 57
RF begins to disparage, 62-63, 64, 353; contrast between RF's earlier and later attitudes toward,

542-543; RF writes reproachfully to, 569
biographical sketch of, 523; "The House Under Arcturus" by, cited, 523; MS "Reminiscences" by, first cited, 523
Bread Loaf School of English
Middlebury College conducts the first session of, summer 1920, 161
RF offers to teach at, 161-162; RF is visited by the dean of, 162; RF's first performance at, in 1921, 171-172, 574-575
RF narrowly avoids the campus of, in 1922, 194
summary sketch of RF's relationship with, from 1920 to 1936, 683-685
Bread Loaf School of English: The First Fifty Years, 686
Bread Loaf Writers' Conference
summary sketch of RF's relations with, from 1926 to 1936, 682-686
Bridges, Robert
RF mentions, in 1915, 35; again mentions, in 1917, 118; RF briefly sees, in Michigan, in 1924, 608; RF visits, in England, in 1928, 349
Bristol, Edward N.
is chief director of all departments at Henry Holt & Co. in 1915, 155; overcomes RF's desire to leave the firm of Holt in 1919, 155-156; is president of the firm when RF again threatens to leave, in 1928, 314-315
Brooke, Rupert
RF's polite response to the death of, 37, 527
Brooks, Cleanth
and Warren, eds., *Understanding Poetry*, letter by RF in, quoted, 597-598
Brooks, Van Wyck
ed., *The Letters of Gamaliel Bradford*, cited, 584
Brown, Abbie Farwell
The New England Poetry Club, quoted and cited, 586
Brown, Alice, 3, 21, 58
Brown, Warren R.
attends RF's first reading at Amherst College in 1916, 111; serves as real-estate agent for RF in Amherst, 111-112, 252, 398; explains the source of his middle initial, 112; tells RF about Stephen Burroughs, 585; helps RF find a registered Newfoundland puppy, 373; RF writes to, 374, 647; gets for RF an evaluation of "Good-by and Keep Cold," 560

INDEX

Browne, George H.
RF meets, in 1915, and makes a business arrangement with, 37; RF gets from, the story used in "Browne's Descent," 537
makes notes on a talk given by RF in 1916, 538; argues against RF's use of "interval" in *Mountain Interval*, 539
Browning, Robert
RF reproaches Amy Lowell for echoing, 56; RF quotes from "A Serenade at the Villa" by, 79, 538-539; RF reads aloud "Love among the Ruins" by, 106; RF and E. M. Lewis exchange quotations from, 468
Bryan, William Jennings
RF sympathizes with, during the Scopes trial, 618, 290-291
Snow: ". . . his [RF's] sympathies were all on the side of Bryan and the old Southern farmers who carried their Bibles to the courthouse during the trial." 630
Bryn Mawr College
RF gives first reading at, in 1920, 154; RF gives a private seminar for members of The Reeling and Writhing Club at, in 1920-1921, 154-155, 156, 570; RF talks on "Metaphors" at, in 1926, 291-293
Burlingham, Charles, 5, 518
Burns Robert, 402
Burroughs, John
Accepting the Universe by, quoted, 678ff; cited, 678
Burroughs, Stephen
RF persuades MacVeagh to reprint *Memoirs of the Notorious Stephen Burroughs*, in 1924, 585
Bursley, Dean Joseph A., 176, 283
Burton, Marion LeRoy
President of the University of Michigan, offers Fellowship to RF in 1921, 175; RF writes to, accepting the offer, 175-176; awards RF an honorary degree, 184
in 1922, invites RF to continue at Michigan, 188, 200-201; RF attends reception given by, 202
in 1924, persuades RF to accept a life-appointment at Michigan, starting in Sept. 1925, 263; dies, 18 Feb. 1925, 279; RF speaks at memorial service for, 279-280; RF's "In Memoriam: Marion LeRoy Burton" cited, 615; RF compares, with President Little, 288-289, 618
Bush, Douglas
Paradise Lost in Our Time by, cited 553

Butler, Dean Pierce
President of Sophie Newcombe College, is host to RF in New Orleans in 1922, 210
Bynner, Witter
in 1921, visits RF at Ann Arbor, 179, 577; in 1925, RF promises to write an introduction for, and later reneges, 622-623; in 1935, RF visits, in Santa Fe, 429-430; Bynner's version of RF's visit, 669-670

C

Cabell, James Branch, 472
Cady, Daniel L., 315
California
RF visits, in 1931, 395-396; again visits, in 1932, 401; attends Olympic Games in Los Angeles, 655
California Institute of Technology
RF meets Millikan and Haldane at, in 1932, 658ff
California, University of, Los Angeles
RF gives a reading at, in 1932, 401, 657
Calvin, John
passage from the *Institutes* of, quoted and cited, 517
Cameron, William J., 621
Canby, Henry Seidel, 162
Canfield, Dorothy
see Fisher, Dorothy Canfield
Cardarette Cottage
the Fobes guest house, bought from Louis M. Cadarette in 1924, is made available to the Frosts, 1925-1936, 616
Carlyle, Thomas
RF: "Carlyle's way of taking himself [stylistically,] infuriates me." 254
Carrell, The
a public talk by RF is printed in, 665
Castiglione, Baldassare
The Book of the Courtier by, quoted, 230; cited, 592
Cather, Willa, 614
Cellini, Benvenuto
RF uses the *Autobiography* of, in an Amherst course, 252; RF cites, to justify artistic self-centeredness, 498, 698
Chalmers, Gordon K., 409
Chaucer, Geoffrey, 223
Churchill, George B., 82, 99
Ciardi, John
Dialogues with an Audience by, quoted and cited, 597
Clark, Helen Archibald, 42, 534

Cleghorn, Sarah N.
  praises *North of Boston* in 1914,
  519; helps to organize a poetry so-
  ciety, 146; writes in defense of
  RF, 203
  RF writes an introduction to
  Threescore by, 411-414, 664; *Three-
  score* quoted and cited, 519
  "The Golf Links" by, quoted, 665
Clymer, W. B. Shubrick
  and Green, eds., *Robert Frost:
  A Bibliography*, cited, 587
Coates, Walter J., 383
Coffin, R. P. T.
  is poet in residence at Wells Col-
  lege in 1932, 676; is winner of
  Pulitzer Prize in 1935, 449; RF de-
  fines himself for, in 1936: 490-491
Colony, Horatio, 429-430, 669-670
Colorado
  RF's interest in, begins when the
  Bartletts move to, in 1917, 390;
  Marjorie Frost is sent to, in 1931,
  390ff; RF and EWF go to, in 1931,
  393-395; RF and EWF return to, in
  1932, 400-401; they return to, from
  California, in Sept. 1932, 401;
  again return to, in 1935, 423
Colum, Padraic
  RF apparently meets, in 1917,
  165; RF again sees, in 1919, 159;
  RF brings, to Michigan in 1922,
  179; RF brings, to Amherst in 1923,
  609; RF is guided around Dublin
  by, in 1928, 336-337, 638
Communism
  RF, in 1915, learns about some
  young American radicals who lean
  toward, 40, 535; RF, in Aug. 1917,
  prophesies that there will be no
  Bolshevik revolution in Russia, 555-
  556
  RF, in 1923: "If well it is with
  Russia, then feel free / To say so
  or be stood against the wall /
  And shot. It's Pollyanna now or
  death." 234
  RF, in 1926: "I've just read . . .
  Max Eastman's *Since Lenin Died*
  (in hopes of getting the truth at
  last from our fiercest American
  Communist)." 289-290
  RF's responses to literary attacks
  made against him by Communist
  critics, 451-455, 463-464
Conant, James Bryant
  President of Harvard University,
  meets RF and differs with him, in
  1936, 448; encourages DeVoto to
  resign from Harvard, 448-449, 675
Cone, Irma Frost
  (Mrs. John Paine Cone), marriage of, in Franconia, Oct. 1926,
  304; is en route to Kansas, 305; son
  is born to, 345; leaves her husband
  in Kansas, and returns to Vermont,
  345; is reunited with her husband,
  345-346; visits RF and EWF at
  Christmas 1932, 403; is living with
  son and husband in Hanover, N.
  H., in Dec. 1936, 476; does not go
  to Florida when her mother dies
  there, 496; attends memorial service in Amherst, 502-503
  see Frost, Irma
Cone, John Paine
  meets and becomes engaged to
  Irma Frost, 295; is married to
  Irma and returns to Kansas with
  his bride, 305; moves to Vermont
  and becomes a poultryman, 345-
  346; completes formal education
  and becomes an architect, 476, 653
Conkling, Grace Hazard, 261, 579
Conkling, Hilda, 579
Conrad, Lawrence
  meets RF at Michigan in 1921,
  224, 380; praises RF, 225-227; helps
  RF prepare MS of *New Hampshire*
  in 1923, 245; is advised by RF on
  novel-writing, 362
Cook, Reginald L.
  is an honorary bearer at the
  memorial service for EWF, 699
Cooley, Charles Horton, 284
Cooley, Mary, 284, 620
Coolidge, Calvin
  associates RF with Denis Mc-
  Carthy, 257-258; RF guesses at
  what Coolidge may have said about
  RF, 607
Cooper, Charles W.
  and Holmes, *Preface to Poetry*,
  cited, 597
Cournos, John, 336, 578, 638
Cowden, Roy, 176-177, 284, 579-580
Cox, Hyde
  and Lathem, eds., *Selected Prose
  of Robert Frost*, cited 585
Cox, Sidney
  hears from RF in 1915, 21, 523;
  visits RF in 1915, 634; in 1927, is
  planning to write a biography of
  RF, 321; is encouraged by EWF, in
  1928, and is discouraged by RF,
  637; is again discouraged by RF, in
  1932, 637; is an honorary bearer at
  the memorial service for EWF, in
  1938, 699
  *Robert Frost, Original "Ordinary
  Man"* by, quoted, 485; cited, 692
  *A Swinger of Birches: A Portrait
  of Robert Frost* by, 638
Craig, Donald W.
  "Frost Delivers Lectures on
  Poetry" by, quoted, 417; cited, 666

INDEX

Cross, Wilbur
  as editor of the *Yale Review*, accepts RF's proposals for publishing tributes to Edward Thomas, in 1917, 548-549; RF to, about resigning from Amherst in 1920, 121-122, 557
Cumberland, Robert W.
  meets RF at Queens University in Kingston, Ontario, in 1921, 571-572
Curran, Constantine P., 337, 639

D

Dame, Lawrence C.
  newspaper article on RF by, quoted, 446-447; cited, 674
Damon, S. Foster
  RF is present at a talk given by, in 1922, 586; *Amy Lowell* by, first cited, 520
Darling, David, 255
Darrow, Clarence, 290-291, 618, 630
Darwin, Charles Robert
  RF admires the account of the voyage of the *Beagle* by, 284; RF is given a first edition of *Journal of Researches* by, 284, 617; RF variously expresses hostility to the Darwinian theory of evolution, 296-297, 300ff, 618, 630
Davids, Corinne Tennyson, 572
Davies, William Henry, 335-336
Davison, Edward
  from England, in 1925, brings to RF letters of introduction, 317; is invited by RF to write a biography of RF, 317ff; offends RF, and is given ambiguous treatment, 320ff; abandons writing biography of RF, 327
  RF sees, in Florida in 1935, 422; RF sees, in Colorado in 1935, 423
Davison, Wilfred E.
  first dean of Bread Loaf School of English, 1920, 161; RF offers aid to, 161; RF is visited by, in Jan. 1921, 162; RF is offended by, at Bread Loaf, summer 1921, 171-172; RF is again visited by, in Dec. 1923, 259; RF is characterized in a journal entry by, 259-262
  in 1926, is said to have been "planning for years" to write a biography of RF, 321; death of, Sept. 1929, 684; RF speaks at memorial service for, 685
Dearborn *Independent*
  RF's contributions to, 621; RF is invited to solicit MSS for, 621

De la Mare, Walter, 118, 328-329, 339
DeVoto, Bernard
  RF admires "New England: There She Stands" by, in 1932, 671; RF befriends, in Miami in 1936, 436-437
  makes notes for a biography of RF, in 1936, 671, 690; befriends RF at Harvard, 445; is advised by RF to resign from Harvard, 448
  as editor-in-chief of the *Saturday Review*, offers to slaughter leftist critics of RF, 463; RF praises *Forays and Rebuttals* by, 477-479
  is satirized by Granville Hicks, 479; is asked by RF to postpone the slaughter, 480-481
  sends RF "The Critics and Robert Frost," 487; RF praises the article, 487-488; article summarized, 487-489; cited, 696
  RF writes to, soon after the death of EWF, 501-502; RF invites, to be an honorary bearer at memorial service for EWF, 699
Dodd, Loring Holmes
  shows RF a Lankes woodcut made to illustrate a poem by RF, 598-599
  Celebrities at Our Hearthside by, quoted and cited, 599
Dole, Margaret, 36, 524
Dole, Nathan Haskell
  RF meets, in March 1915, and is the guest of, 14ff; RF's letter of thanks to, quoted, 24; cited, 524; arranges RF's first two public appearances, 30, 33, 36-37; introduces RF at an early reading, 72-73
  "A Migration of Poets" by, cited, 524
D'Ooge, Martin L.
  mentioned 174; the widow of, enrages RF by accusing him of being an inconsiderate tenant, 186-187
Dostoievski, Feodor Mikhailovic
  RF: "It makes the guild of novel writers sick / To be expected to be Dostoievskis / On nothing worse than too much luck and comfort." 234
Dreiser, Theodore
  RF, in 1917, signs a resolution condemning censorship of *The "Genius"* by, 647-648
du Chêne, Aroldo
  makes a sculptured head of RF in 1920, 562-563
Dudley, Dorothy
  Forgotten Frontiers: Dreiser and the Land of the Free by, quoted

Dudley, Dorothy (*cont.*)
and cited, 647-648; again quoted, 648-649
Dunbar, William, 402

E

Early Years, The, first cited, 515
Eaton, Walter Prichard, 602
Edwards, Alfred C., 574, 688
Einstein, Albert, 649
Eliot, T. S.
on Vachel Lindsay, quoted, 182; cited, 578-579
RF: "I like to read Eliot because it is fun seeing the way he does things, but I am always glad it is his way and not mine." 220
RF meets, for the first time, in London in 1928, 333, 337-338
RF is reported as verbally kicking at, in 1931, 654
RF attends a dinner in honor of, in 1932, 402-403, 661-662
Humphries, in 1936: ". . . Frost, who professes to think Eliot a charlatan, has, for a long time, been getting away with a good deal in this regard." 455
Elliott, George Roy
RF is pleased with article written by, in 1919: "The Neighborliness of Robert Frost," 152-153; cited, 565
describes RF's first visit to, at Bowdoin in 1921, 569-570; is persuaded by RF to take a position at Amherst in 1925, 293-294; urges President Olds to invite RF back to Amherst from Michigan in 1926, 662
RF writes to, soon after the death of EWF, 502; is an honorary bearer at memorial service for EWF, 699; the wife of, protests against holding the service for EWF, in a church, 699
RF writes his last letter to, in 1963, 568
The Cycle of Modern Poetry by, cited, 565; quoted, 565-566
Emerson, Ralph Waldo
"Berrying" by, quoted, 412; cited, 663-664
"Considerations by the Way" by, quoted, 385; cited 651
"Experience" by, quoted and cited, 651
"Monadnoc" by, quoted, 34-35
"Nature" by, quoted, 167
"New England Reformers" by, quoted, 430; cited, 670

"Ode Inscribed to W. H. Channing" by, quoted, 233, cited, 592-593
"On the Fugitive Slave Law" by, quoted and cited, 593
"The Poet" by, quoted and cited, 693-694
"Poetry and Imagination" by, quoted and cited, 694
"Swedenborg" by, quoted and cited, 604
"Uriel" by, described by RF as "the greatest Western poem yet" and as "the greatest poem written in America," 543; speculation on RF's reasons for elevating "Uriel," 543-544; RF's way of casting himself in the role of Uriel, 623-624; RF: "I believe I will take example of Uriel and withdraw into a cloud —of whiskers." 187, 581
RF, at Amherst in 1917, preaches the Emersonian doctrine of the dependence of form on soul, 98
RF: "Emerson has one of the noblest [and] least egotistical styles." 243
RF: "I used to try to get up plausible theories about prayer like Emerson." 568
Elliott: "While loving Emerson, he [RF] ALWAYS criticized Emerson's lack of perception of evil and sin." 57)
Engle, Paul, 433-434, 690
Erskine, John
The Moral Obligation to Be Intelligent by, summarized, 103-104; cited, 552
The Memory of Certain Persons by, cited, 649

F

Fabre, J. Henri
RF: "What I like about Bergson and Fabre is that they have bothered our evolutionism so much . . ." 300
The Hunting Wasps by, mentioned, 300
Fahnestock, Zephine Humphrey, 412
Farjeon, Eleanor
Edward Thomas: The Last Four Years by, quoted and cited, 518
Farrar, John
RF meets, at Yale, in 1917, 316
reviews and praises *New Hampshire* in 1923, 230, 247, 592; is praised by RF for being a good Puritan, 305
is appointed first director of the

Farrar, John (*cont.*)
  Bread Loaf Writers' Conference, in 1926, 316
    asks RF to select his own biographer for a monograph to be published in 1927, 316; gets into difficulties with RF over the choice made, 320-321
    the friendship between RF and, is ended by RF's jealousy, 682ff
Faulkner, William
  RF's unfavorable response to the writings of, 424
Fay, Charles Ernest, 36-37
Feld, Rose C.
  "Robert Frost Relieves His Mind" by, quoted and cited, 619
Ferril, Thomas Hornsby
  RF meets, in Denver in 1931, 393; RF again sees, in Denver in 1932, and writes a poem for, 655; RF again sees, in Boulder in 1935, 426ff
    excerpts from the journal of, quoted, 654-655
Firuski, Maurice, 587
Fisher, Donald
  is an honorary bearer at the memorial service for EWF, 699
Fisher, Dorothy Canfield
  (Mrs. Donald Fisher), is a reader of *North of Boston* for Henry Holt & Co., in 1914, 5, 519; RF meets, in Boston, Dec. 1915, 146; helps RF find and purchase a home in Vermont in 1920, 147-149
    gives a talk for RF at Michigan in 1923, 224-225; attends the wedding of Carol Frost and Lillian LaBatt in 1923, 258; is urged by RF to contribute to the Dearborn *Independent*, 621
Fletcher, John Gould
  describes meeting RF in 1915, 18ff, 523; is guest of the Frosts in England in 1928, 333
  Life Is My Song by, first cited, 518
Flint, F. S.
  RF spends an evening with, in London in 1928, 339-340
Fobes, Edith Hazard
  (Mrs. J. Warner Fobes), befriends the Frosts in Franconia in June 1915, 81; hostess to RF and EWF in Franconia during hay-fever season, 1924, 616; makes guest house available to the Frosts, each summer, 1925-1936, 616
Francis, Lesley Frost
  (Mrs. James Dwight Francis), marriage of, in 1928, 345, 640-641; soon wants a divorce, 345; gets

divorce in June 1931, 392
  in Dec. 1936, visits RF and EWF in San Antonio, while en route to Mexico, 476-477
  in Dec. 1937, joins parents in Gainesville, 487; is there when her mother dies, 495; upbraids her father for his inconsiderateness, 495-496; later, pays tribute to both parents, 698
  see Frost, Lesley
Fraser, Marjorie Frost
  (Mrs. Willard E. Fraser), marriage of, 404-405; birth of daughter to, 406; illness and death of, 406-407; burial of, in Billings, Montana, 407
  see Frost, Marjorie
Fraser, Willard
  meets Marjorie and becomes engaged to marry her, 399-400; marriage of, 404-405; birth of daughter and death of wife, 406-407; takes daughter to Vermont, 409; takes daughter to Montana, 409, 603; takes daughter to visit her grandparents in Texas, 476
Freud, Sigmund
  RF, in 1926, on, as metaphormaker: "Freud's metaphor is that life is nothing but appetite, alimentary or sexual." 624
  Hicks on RF in 1930: "He cannot give us the sense of belonging in the industrial, scientific, Freudian world in which we find ourselves." 386, 651
  RF, in 1938: "Anyone who would drag in Freud to explain my having failed to autograph a solitary check would naturally prefer my sexiest poem The Bearer of Evil Tidings . . ." 688
Frost, Carol
  mentioned, 1, 26, 49, 67, 149, 167, 174
  illness of, in 1916, is feared to be tuberculosis, 85-86
  writes poetry, but is not encouraged by his father, 560
  runs away from home, after being reprimanded for wanting to buy an expensive rooster, 185-186; buys the rooster, 581
  goes on Long Trail hike, 189ff; announces his engagement to Lillian LaBatt, 198
  RF, in Jan. 1923: "Yesterday Carol froze an ear and a toe sawing with a cross-cut out in a zero wind." 591
  marriage of, 258; is given the

INDEX

Frost, Carol (*cont.*)

South Shaftsbury farm as a wedding present, 367-368

illnesses of, continue to perplex his parents, 282, 287; is urged by his father to move to Colorado for health, 287

takes his family to Pittsfield for Christmas 1925, 289; father helps, in selling flowers, 371

rents his Vermont farm and goes West in 1931, because of wife's illness, 391-392; with his family, stays in Monrovia, California, 395; is visited by his parents, in Monrovia, summer 1931, 395-396; is again visited there by his parents, summer 1932, 401; drives East with his son, summer 1933, and returns to California, 405; after wife's recovery, spring 1934, returns with his family to Vermont, 409

drives to Key West with wife and son, Dec. 1934, 409ff; drives to Miami with wife and son, Dec. 1935, 433ff; drives to San Antonio with wife and son, Dec. 1936, 476ff

drives to Gainesville, Florida, with wife and son, Dec. 1937, 486ff; helps his parents select a house for purchase in Gainesville in March 1938, 493; quickly leaves Gainesville after the death of his mother, 496; his father writes to, from Gainesville, 500-501; goes with wife to memorial service in Amherst, 502-503; provides a room for his father in the Stone Cottage, 507; plans to build an ell on the Stone Cottage for his father, 512

FROST, ELINOR WHITE

(MRS. ROBERT LEE FROST), takes children from New York to Bethlehem, New Hampshire, in 1915, 4-5; attitude of, toward teaching her children at home, 26-27; RF had considered divorce from, 30; attitude of, toward RF's neglect of his poetry while campaigning, 31, 79, 526

illness of, and miscarriage, Nov. 1915, 63-64; RF: "It is the old story: what she has gone through so many times. . . . The doctor frightens me about her heart." 63

reproaches RF with silences, 79; says RF would not dare to be a soldier, 108

RF's dedication to, in *Mountain Interval*, quoted, 539

RF in 1917: "Elinor has never been of any earthly use to me." 115

RF in 1920: "Elinor has just come out flat-footed against God . . ." 140; background on atheistic views of, 140, 560ff

quarrels with RF, 138-139; criticizes RF for not sufficiently helping their children with writing, 560

reaction of, to plans for going to Michigan in 1921, 174; from Michigan, in 1923, writes her own praise of RF's poems, 245-246

becomes impatient with Amherst students, 269; serving as amanuensis for RF, invites Amy Lowell to Amherst, 272-273; describes Amy Lowell's visit, 273; again writing to Amy Lowell for RF, explains why RF will not attend gala dinner in 1925, 275-276; is shocked by death of Amy Lowell, 276-277

with RF, visits Jeanie Frost in Maine hospital, in 1925, and gives an account of the visit, 131-132

is worried over the illnesses of her children, in 1925, 282

is ill after a miscarriage in June 1925, 281, 282, 617

is wearied by the move to Michigan in the fall of 1925, 282-283; is described by Van Dore as "pale in complexion," 286; hastens to Pittsfield because of Marjorie's illness, in Dec. 1925, 289; writes about Marjorie's condition in 1925-1926, 618-619

RF, in 1926: "Elinor stands being separated from the children worse than I do." 289

arranges early departure for Franconia in Aug. 1926, 299; describes the Fobes guest house, 616; in Feb. 1927, writes at length about family illnesses, 306-307

is intermittently ill throughout the European trip, in 1928, 328ff; RF, in 1928: "I've made Elinor unhappier keeping her on than I think I ever made her before. She's too sick for a jaunting party and I shouldnt have dragged her out of her home." 342, 640

in Dec. 1930, goes to Baltimore with RF because of Marjorie's illness, 390; is upset by news that Lillian also has tuberculosis, 391

in June 1931, is worried over the tardy arrival of Lesley's second child, 392-393; in June 1931, goes with RF to Colorado to see Marjorie, 393-395; goes on to California to see Lillian, Carol, and Prescott, 395-396

FROST, ELINOR WHITE (*cont.*)

in Nov. 1931, chooses Victorian décor for new Amherst home, 398

in summer 1932, again goes West with RF, 400-402; in spring 1933, goes to Texas to be with RF, 404; is unable to attend Marjorie's wedding in Montana in June 1933, 405; goes alone to be with Marjorie during confinement in March 1934, 406ff; is embittered by Marjorie's death, 408; cares for baby Robin, 409; has heart attack, 409, 663

with RF, goes to Key West, winter 1934-1935, 410ff, 663; with RF, goes to Colorado in July 1935 to see granddaughter, 422, 423; with RF, goes to Miami, winter 1935-1936, 433ff; with RF, goes to Cambridge and is ill there, 445, 672

advises RF not to worry about a possible bomb, 464

with RF, goes to San Antonio, winter 1936-1937, 476ff

in Oct. 1937, undergoes surgery for cancer, 485-486; in Dec. 1937, goes with RF to Gainesville, 486-497; dies in March 1938, 493-494; body of, is cremated, 495

RF plans to carry out wish of, that her ashes be scattered, 495, 501; plan is publicly announced, 699; memorial service for, in Amherst, 502; abandonment of plans to scatter ashes of, 507-510; ashes of, buried in the Old Bennington Cemetery, 703

Frost, Elliott

RF's and EWF's first child, for whose death at the age of four RF blamed himself: ". . . even as I hope to be forgiven a murder I once did." 623

Frost, Irma

mentioned, 1, 26, 49, 67, 149, 174, 185, 190, 201

has pneumonia in Jan. 1922, 221, 590-591; attends Art Students League in New York City, starting Sept. 1924, 282, 612; attends RF's birthday party in New York City, March 1925, 275; is hay-fever victim, 282

goes to Pittsfield for Christmas 1925, 289; gives up study of art in New York and joins parents in Ann Arbor, spring 1926, 295; becomes engaged to marry John Paine Con_, in Ann Arbor, spring 1926, 295; during summer 1926, is busy with plans for wedding, 299

see Cone, Irma Frost

Frost, Isabelle Moodie

(Mrs. William Prescott Frost, Jr.), mother of RF, shapes his religious belief, xiii-xiv, 515, 567, 593, 626, 627-629, 673, 697

RF, in 1931: " 'I wish my mother could see me now . . .' " xiii, 654

Frost, Jeanie Florence

background: early life of, 125-126; is having difficulty when RF returns from England in 1915, 10-11

enters University of Michigan in Feb. 1916, at the age of 39, 127, 522; is graduated, Aug. 1918, 127-128

as a teacher in Mill River, Mass., gets into trouble, 128; appeals to RF for help, 128-129; is arrested in Portland, Maine, for disturbing the peace, and is declared insane, 123, 129, 558

is committed to the State Hospital in Augusta, Maine, by RF, 129; is visited there by RF on several occasions, 130ff; dies there on 7 Sept. 1929, 133; RF makes arrangements for burial of, 559

Frost, Lesley

mentioned, 1, 26, 49, 67, 149, 174; gets into academic difficulties at Wellesley College, and drops out, 115-118; goes to work in an airplane factory, 118, 119; briefly attends Barnard College, 118-119, 154

Raymond Holden tries to dedicate a poem to, 141; works in New York City, summer 1920, 149

briefly attends University of Michigan, 184-185; impatiently returns to Vermont, 186

organizes plan for the Long Trail hike, 189; goes on the hike, 190ff; writes an account of the hike, 199

returns to New York City to learn bookselling, 310; with Marjorie, opens bookstore in Pittsfield, Mass., spring 1924, 272, 612; attends RF's birthday dinner in New York City, March 1925, 275

is happy with work in the Pittsfield bookstore, 282; is helped by RF during Christmas season of 1925, 289; solicits MSS for the Dearborn *Independent*, 621; becomes engaged to be married, 345

New Hampshire's Child: The Derry Journals of Lesley Frost, cited, 633

see Francis, Lesley Frost

Frost, Lillian LaBatt

(Mrs. Carol Frost), marriage of, in 1923, 258-259; RF's characteriza-

INDEX

Frost, Lillian LaBatt (*cont.*)

tion of, as bride, 258-259; gives birth to son, in 1924, 289, 298; undergoes major surgery, July 1926, 299

in 1931, is found to have tuberculosis, 391; goes with husband and son to California, 392, 394-395; makes slow recovery, 401, 405; after recovery, returns to Vermont, 624

goes with husband and son to Key West in Dec. 1934, 409ff; to Miami in Dec. 1935, 433ff; to San Antonio in Dec. 1936, 476ff; to Gainesville in Dec. 1937, 486ff; returns to Vermont in March 1938, 496; attends memorial service for EWF in Amherst, 502-503

see LaBatt, Lillian

Frost, Marjorie

mentioned, 1, 26, 49, 67, 145; attends North Bennington High School, 1921-1922, while her parents are in Michigan, 174; lonesome and discouraged, is visited by her mother, 185; is informed that Carol has disappeared, and reports his return to Vermont, 186; goes on the Long Trail hike, 189ff

continues high school while parents spend academic year 1922-1923 in Michigan, 201

with Lesley, opens bookstore in Pittsfield, Mass., spring 1924, 272, 612; is hospitalized in Pittsfield, 289, 618-619

RF: "Marjorie's long illness (means more than sickness) . . ." 297; RF compares the ailments of, with those of his sister Jeanie, 619

recuperates slowly in Ann Arbor, spring 1926, 295; continues recuperating in South Shaftsbury, summer 1926, 298-299; spends most of the winter of 1926-1927 in bed with nervous prostration, 634; spends part of the winter of 1927-1928 in a Baltimore hospital, 635

summer 1928, goes to France and England, 328ff

in Jan. 1929, begins nurse-training course in Baltimore, 344; in Dec. 1929, is found to have tuberculosis and is sent to Colorado, 390-391; improves slowly, 391-392, 393-394; writes that she is engaged to be married, 399-400; receives blessing of her father, 400

see Fraser, Marjorie Frost

FROST, ROBERT LEE
(26 March 1874–29 Jan. 1963)

ANTI-INTELLECTUAL

RF's religious justification for being an anti-intellectual, 552-553

RF: ". . . [Meiklejohn] detests my dangerous . . . anti-intellectualistic philosophy . . ." 121

Snow: "Over and over [RF] said that Clarence Darrow lacked imagination, that he depended too much on rationality to solve the problem of human existence." 630

RF defines philosophy as "nothing but" an "attempt to rationalize religion." 692

ATHEISM

"I inspected a young Harvard Ph.D. and found him of the opinions that there was no God and that we all ought to commit suicide. . . . I asked him at once if one followed from the other on the ground that it wasn't polite for the creature to exist when God the Creator didn't . . ." 249

"Elinor has just come out flatfooted against [belief in the existence of] God . . ." 140

Thomas to RF: "It all comes of [my] not believing. I will leave nothing to chance knowingly. But, then, I suppose the believers calculate to the best of their ability." 89

RF to Thomas: "All belief is one. And this proves you are a believer." 90

BAFFLER-TEASER-DECEIVER

"Or do I deceive myself? I don't care if I do in this respect. . . . Look out I don't spoof you." 637

"I'd like to tease them. They look as if they could take care of themselves. I probably couldnt baffle them very much at my crypticest. Never mind I can baffle some people." 695

"I have written to keep the over curious out of the secret places of my mind both in my verse and in my letters to such as you." 637

"About five years ago I resolved to spoil my correspondence with you by throwing it into confusion the way God threw the speech of the builders of the tower of Babel into confusion. My reason is too long to go into tonight . . ." 637

[716]

INDEX

FROST, ROBERT LEE (*cont.*)

"I trust my meaning is not too hidden in any of these places. I can't help my way of coming at things." 546

"The best of your parody of me was that it left me in no doubt as to where I was hit. I'll bet not half a dozen people can tell who was hit and where he was hit by my Road Not Taken." 546

RF to Bradford: "Don't spare to be a little wicked yourself over these wicked people. Not that I would have you make the judicious grieve, but you can afford to make the judicious guess. Tease us." 204

"I'm afraid I deceived her a little in pretending for the sake of argument that I didn't think the world as bad a place as she did." 501

"I said to Sidney Cox years ago that I was non-elatable. While I wasn't actually fishing I suppose I hoped he might see I wanted to be contradicted." 487

"After hearing all you said in my favor today, I tried it at the wistfullest I could command on Elinor. 'What a lie,' she answered. 'You can't talk in public or private without getting elated. You never write but from elation.'" 487

"I own any form of humor shows fear and inferiority. Irony is simply a kind of guardedness. So is a twinkle. It keeps the reader from criticism." 254

"Humor is the most engaging cowardice. With it myself I have been able to hold some of my enemy in play far out of gunshot." 254

"I should like to be so subtle at this game as to seem to the casual person altogether obvious." 300

see STYLE and RELIGIOUS BELIEF

BELIEVING

"You're always believing ahead of your evidence." 643

"The Founding Fathers didn't believe in the future. They believed the future in." 643

"The most creative thing in us is to believe a thing in . . . You believe yourself into existence." 643

". . . you believe that it's worthwhile going on, or you'd commit suicide, wouldn't you?" 643

"There are two or three places where we know belief outside of religion. One of them is at the age of fifteen to twenty, in our self-belief.

A young man . . . has something that is going to believe itself into fulfillment, into acceptance." 364

"There is another belief like that, the belief in someone else, a relationship of two that is going to be believed into fulfillment . . . the belief of love." 364

"Every time a poem is written . . . it is written not by cunning, but by belief." 365

". . . those three beliefs that I speak of, the self-belief, the love-belief, and the art-belief, are all closely related to the God-belief . . ." 365

"The United States is being believed into existence. It will be a long time before it is completed. It is not yet time to talk of 'scrapping' it in favor of a new government." 661

"There's no greater mistake than to look on fighting as a form of argument. To *fight* is to leave words and act as if you believed—to *act* as if you believed." 41

RF to a young writer: "Belief, Belief. You've got to augment my belief in life or people mightily or cross it uglily." 359

". . . literature is the next thing to religion in which as you know or believe an ounce of faith is worth all the theology ever written." 85

see RELIGIOUS BELIEF

BOOKS OF POETRY

A Boy's Will (1915)
Henry Holt & Co. makes arrangement for an American edition of, 518; Holt secures copyright for, 573-574; remainder copies of the English edition of, are sold in U. S. A. as rare books, 587

North of Boston (1915)
first English edition of, described, 517; Holt makes arrangement for an American edition of, 5ff, 573-574; becomes a best-seller in Aug. 1915, 56; Holt secures copyright for, 574; remainder copies of the English edition of, are sold in U. S. A. as rare books, 587

Mountain Interval (1916)
first mention of, 80; RF completes MS of, 82; dates and places of writing the poems in, 540-542; special edition of, in 1921, 563

New Hampshire (1923)
RF makes plans for, 224; decides on title and subtitle for, 229; initial inspiration for the title poem in, 230-231; analysis of title poem

INDEX

FROST, ROBERT LEE (*cont.*)
in, 232-236; illustrations for, 246-247; excerpts from reviews of, 247-248; is awarded Pulitzer Prize, 248
Selected Poems (1923)
RF resists the publisher's plan for, 219; EWF praises RF's poems in, 245-246; publication date of, 590; dedication in, is cancelled, 636-637
West-Running Brook (1928)
RF prepares MS of, 299-313; RF drives a hard bargain with his publisher over the contract for, 314-315
Collected Poems (1930)
RF tries to arrange favorable reviews for, 375ff; reviews of, 385-386; is awarded Pulitzer Prize, 389
A Further Range (1936)
growth of MS for, 423ff; is a Book-of-the-Month Club selection, 449, 675; is awarded Pulitzer Prize, 449-450, 675; is attacked by leftist critics, 453ff

BRUTE

"And I suppose I am a brute . . ." 130
"A real artist delights in roughness for what he can do to it. He's the brute who can knock the corners off the marble block and drag the unbedded beauty out of bed." 491
"It is a coarse brutal world, unendurably coarse and brutal, for anyone who hasn't the least dash of coarseness or brutality in his own nature to enjoy it with . . ." 559

CAMPAIGNER

RF's campaign in England on behalf of *A Boy's Will* and *North of Boston*, xi-xii
RF, returning home, begins a new campaign on his own behalf, in New York City and in Boston, xii, 6, 10, 12-32
RF enlists the services of Braithwaite and Untermeyer in his campaigning, 31-33, 34
RF similarly enlists the services of Harcourt, 55-56
RF campaigns on behalf of *New Hampshire*, 218-220, 227-228, 238-239; on behalf of *Collected Poems*, 375ff; on behalf of *A Further Range*, 432ff, 441ff, 449, 675
RF campaigns for a suitable biographer in 1926, 316
RF campaigns to cultivate DeVoto as a defender, 477ff

RF: "Ain't I wiley. You remember Amy Lowell the author and poet? Well they's a life of her out and they tell me it's a caution the wileyness she showed with editors and reviewers." 433

CHANGE

"Most of the change we think we see in life / Is due to truths being in and out of favor." 601
"It has not changed . . ." 244
RF's religious justification for opposing the teleological concept of change, 601
"A poet may be concerned with jails, the poor-houses, the slums, the insane asylums, and wars; or, because he sees no possibility of change, he may try to find what happiness he can for himself and be cruelly happy." 425
"It is not the business of the poet to cry for reform." 425
see PROGRESS

CHARLATAN

RF views Amy Lowell as a charlatan, 274; views Carl Sandburg as a charlatan, 179-180; views T. S. Eliot as a charlatan, 455
Humphries on RF: ". . . his poses and posturings . . . Frost, who professes to think Eliot a charlatan, has, for a long time, been getting away with a good deal in this regard." 455
see BAFFLER-TEASER-DECEIVER

CLASSICIST

Thomas to RF: "I hope people aren't going to crowd to see you milking & find out whether your private life is also like a page from Theocritus. It will spoil the milk." 48
RF models his poem "New Hampshire" after the *Sermones* of Horace, 231
Vergil's "First Eclogue" provides the form for RF's "Build Soil," 432
". . . How about being a good Greek, for instance? / That course, they tell me, isn't offered this year." 318
"The Classicism of Robert Frost," 632; "Robert Frost, A Good Greek Out of New England," 632
RF is pleased to be called "the purest classical poet in America today," 318; is more inclined to defend puritanism than classicism, 632

INDEX

FROST, ROBERT LEE (*cont.*)

COWARDICE

Jeanie to RF: ". . . you coward!"
126

"I am too cowardly to offend anybody intentionally and usually too skillful to do it unintentionally." 685

"Humor is the most engaging cowardice." 561

"One could run away from things in cowardice . . ." 134

"Such is my indolence cowardice or both that I will grant anything you please rather than run the risk of argument." 333

"I might decide that I ought to fight the Germans simply because I know I should be afraid to." 547

EWF tells RF he wouldn't dare to be a soldier, 107

"The doctor was flattering enough to say it would have turned me yellow if there had been any yellow in me to bring to the surface. Little the doctors know us in our true moral inwardness." 151

"My aversion to letter-writing this time is altogether cowardly." 585

EWF to RF on his religious belief: "Nonsense and you know its nonsense Rob Frost, only you're afraid . . ." 140

DEATH

RF's fear of his own death, viewed in relation to his religious belief, 562, 568-569, 703-704

"This is my last, my ultimate vileness, that I cannot make up my mind to go now where I must go sooner or later." 567

death of RF's first child, 623; death of his sister Jeanie, 133; death of his daughter Marjorie, 406-408; death of his wife, 738ff

"I refused to be bowed down as much as she by other deaths. But she has given me a death now that I cant refuse to be bowed down by. Here I am brought up short when in every way you can name I was still going full tilt. I'm not behaving very well." 511

see FEAR and RELIGIOUS BELIEF

DEPRESSION, MOODS OF

"The poet in me died nearly ten years ago. Fortunately he had run through several phases, four to be exact, all well-defined, before he went. The calf I was in the nineties

I merely take to market. I am become my own salesman." 80

"The conviction closes in on me that I was cast for gloom as the sparks fly upward . . . I am of deep shadow all compact like onion within onion and the savor of me is oil of tears." 114

"Laugh no more, gentles, laugh no more. For it is almost too hard . . . I am so deeply smitten through the helm that I am almost sad to see infants young any more." 399

DESIGN

". . . the evident design is a situation here in which it will always be about equally hard to save your soul." 387

RF's poem, "I will Sing You One-O," viewed as reflecting his belief in God's universal design, 601

RF's poem entitled "Design," 600

see RELIGIOUS BELIEF and DELIGHT IN SCIENCE

ENEMIES

"What do you say if we cook up something to bother the enemies we left behind in Derry?" 25

"The Ellery Sedgwick of the piece is mine ancient enemy the editor of The Atlantic." 21

"I am . . . that discouraged it would do my enemies . . . good to see me." 47

"Down with our enemies." 61

"Iron cross for you if you kill more than so many of my enemies at once." 61

". . . I have been able to keep some of my enemy in play far out of gunshot." 254

"There's no sense in helping our enemies reach us: The New Republic might blaze away till its guns jammed . . ." 451

ESCAPIST

"I'm a very artful dodger of unnecessary pains." 451

"Hicks says I'm an escapist." 490

Amy Lowell on RF: ". . . a quite beautiful pose, / (Or escape, or indulgence, or all three, who knows?)," 206

RF on escape vs aspiration, 292

"I have been asked if I consider myself an escapist . . . Well, a man may climb a tree and still not be an escapist. He may go up there to pick something." 425

INDEX

FROST, ROBERT LEE (*cont.*)

"But I wasn't escaping. No escape theory will explain me. I was choosing when to deliver battle." 323

"Me for the hills where I don't have to choose." 235

"Escapist[?]—Never," 594

RF's use of his religious belief as a means of escape, 552-553, 672-674

"My motto is that something has to be left to God." 693

FARMER

"My dream would be to get the thing started in London and then do the rest of it from a farm in New England where I could live cheap and get Yankier and Yankier." 2

"Looked at a little farm yesterday right forninst Lafayette." 27

"You will be glad to hear that my cows and I have composed our differences and I now milk them anchored at one end only." 48

"I doubt if what we have had from our summer's planting has cost us any more than it would have in the market." 49

RF is described by a reporter, in 1916: "He is a Puritan who has fought the soil for sustenance and has fought the world for recognition as a poet." 78

"I see a possibility of my getting south to farm sooner or later. I am not going to be satisfied with just grass-farming. But this place will have to serve for a year or two . . ." 86

RF, after explaining his resignation from Amherst in Jan. 1920: "There was all the excuse I needed to get back to my farming." 121-122

RF, in 1926: "We ought to have gone back farming years ago or we ought to have stayed farming when we knew we were well off." 282

RF, in 1930: "Robinson spoiled farming for me when by doubting my farm he implied a greater claim on my part to being a farmer than I had ever made. . . . What am I then? Not a farmer—never was—never said I was." 381

FEAR

"Two fears should follow us through life. There is the fear that we shan't prove worthy in ourselves. That is the fear of God. And there is the fear of Man—the fear that men won't understand us and we

shall be cut off from them." 420

RF's fear that he would fail as a poet, 79-80

"Sometimes I almost cry I am afraid I am such a bad poet. But tonight I don't care if God doesn't care." 394

RF's fear of standing alone, to talk in public, 31, 33, 72

RF's fear that he is being persecuted, 61ff

RF's fear of having Robinson excel over him, 530-532

"I can never seem to forgive people that scare me within an inch of my life." 636

RF's fear that he may become the victim of nervous troubles such as those which destroyed his sister's life, 123-134, 558

"I made myself wretched and even sick last summer with the dread of what I had let myself in for at Harvard." 687

RF's poem, "The Bonfire," viewed as reflecting his attempt to help his children cope with fear, 698

RF's fear of death, viewed as the primary motivation for his desperate way of clinging to his religious belief, 562, 567, 568-569, 704

RF's poem, "The Fear of God," quoted, 10, cited, 522

see COWARDICE and RAGE and INSANITY

FRIENDSHIP

"Friendship means favor and I believe nothing can flourish without favor . . ." 375

"I don't want to antagonize anyone whose friendship won't hurt us." 82, 542-543

"Just as most friendship is feigning, so is most liking a mere tacit understanding between A and B that A shall like B's work as much and as long as B likes his." 246

GOD

"But something has to be left to God." 139

"My motto is that something has to be left to God." 693

". . . the furthest [heavenly] bodies / To which man sends his / Speculation, / Beyond which God is." 244

"We don't know the Lord well enough to know how he will take our petitions and suggestions." 674

"Well, you know, God can count

INDEX

FROST, ROBERT LEE (*cont.*)
on me never to be disappointed in him." 446

"If there is a universal unfitness and unconformity as of a buttoning so started that every button on the vest is in the wrong button hole and the one empty button hole at the top and the one naked button at the bottom so far apart they have no hope of getting together, I don't care to decide whether God did this for the fun of it or for the devil of it." 490

"You hear that, God? We are saying . . . No disrespect intended. We believe in you. Go in and win. At any rate do the best you can." C14

"Another one: 'a jealous God.' . . . What is jealousy? It's the claim of the object on the lover. The claim of God is that you should be true to Him, and so true to yourself." 483

"One might forget God, and talk about the highest in himself. I can't imagine any honest man without the fear of finding himself unworthy in the sight of someone else. It might be something you didn't care to call by name." 483

a reporter at Ann Arbor, in 1921, comments on RF's belief about "God's way of thinning us out," 1, 7-178

"It is immodest of a man to think of himself as going down before the worst forces ever mobilized by God." 387

"I think there is an Old Fellow up there who takes a benevolent hand in human affairs." 692

Cox on RF: "God, he said, is that which a man is sure cares, and will save him, no matter how many times or how completely he has failed." 485, 692

"I won't do one single thing . . . till I God damn please . . ." 215

"God damn me when he gets around to it." 511

see RELIGIOUS BELIEF and FEAR

GOSSIP

"I like the actuality of gossip, the intimacy of it." 43

Swain: "Frost is an excellent gossip . . . He is humorous and ruthless." 580

Ladd: "Frost revealed to them . . . his fondness for gossip." 99

RF, gossiping about an extramarital love affair: "Ain't that sumpin?" 140

RF gossips about Beach, 215-218; about Braithwaite, 64; about Gibson, 532-533; about T. S. Eliot, 661-662; about Pound, 54-55, 450; about Robinson, 381, 490-491, 531; about Stevens, 665-666

HATE

"I always hold that we get forward as much by hating as by loving." 120, 274-275

"It's only when we hate ourselves and our shortcomings that we can love and need God. All religions are based on that one: 'And thou shalt hate thy neighbor as thyself.'" 516

"I'm sick this morning with hate . . ." 41

"I came back from Michigan University all puffed out with self-hate that would have curdled the ink in my pen if I had tried to write to you at that time." 188

". . . I think I know enough of hate . . ." 152

INSANITY

"You do just right to humor me when I am like that: one of my wife's relatives married into a family in which there was a taint of insanity." 61

"You and I are not clever, Louis: we are cunning, one with the cunning of race[,] the other with the cunning of insanity." 62

Bartlett: "Frost . . . observed how he could look back . . . and see times when it seemed a miracle they had 'come through.' Will had something to do with it. He could contemplate his sister's life . . . and see half a dozen times when by making the right decision she could have saved herself." 134

Bartlett, paraphrasing RF: "One could run away from things in cowardice . . . one could run away from them and retreat into the ego, in the direction of paranoia." 134

Bartlett, paraphrasing RF: "We all have our souls—and minds—to save. And it seems a miracle that we do; not once but several times. He could look back and see his hanging by a thread. His sister wasn't able to save hers. She built the protecting illusion around her-

FROST, ROBERT LEE (*cont.*)
self and went the road of dementia
praecox." 134
  see FEAR and RAGE

JEALOUSY

"Before I had published a book I
was never conscious of the existence
of any contemporary poet. But as
soon as my first book came out I
became jealous of all of them . . ."
667
RF to LU, in 1915: ". . . these
poets . . . I wish you would give
them all Hell and relieve my feeling
without involving me in the odium
of seeming jealous of anybody." 63
"I wonder do you feel as badly
as I do when some other fellow does
a good piece of work?" 536
RF's jealousy of Robinson, 43-46;
of Masters, 61ff; of Sandburg, 179-
180; of Millay, 651; of Wallace
Stevens, 665-666; of all contemporary poets, 535
". . . jealousy is a passion I approve of and attribute to angels.
May I be guarded and watched over
always by the jealousy of a strong
nature. It is better than arms around
the body. Jealousy alone gives me
the sense of being held." 375
"What is jealousy? It's the claim
of the object on the lover. The claim
of God is that you should be true
to Him, and so true to yourself. The
word still lives for me." 483

JUSTICE VS MERCY

Snow: "The entire problem of
justice versus mercy intrigued him.
In the 1930s he sat up until well
past midnight many times in our
home denouncing mercy and lauding justice." 656
RF interprets Milton's line, "But
Mercy first and last shall brightest
shine." 656-657
RF's frequent return to "justice
vs mercy" is ultimately dramatized
by him in "A Masque of Mercy," 656
". . . Christ posed Himself the
whole problem and died for it. How
can we be just in a world that needs
mercy and merciful in a world that
needs justice." 568

LAISSEZ FAIRE

RF's way of correlating his religious doctrine of acceptance with
his social-political doctrine of laissez
faire, 552-553
"Let what will be, be." 453, 553
"Let not man bring together what
God hath put asunder." 553
"Let the rich keep away from the
poor for all of me . . . I need them
in my business." 102
"Were I a dictator . . . I'd let things
take their course / And then I'd
claim the credit for the outcome."
682

MISUNDERSTANDING

"The best of misunderstanding any
one is that it sort of disposes of him
and clears your mind of him and
so leaves you with the one less detail
in life to be bothered with. Of course
it is the same with understanding.
Of what use is either understanding
or misunderstanding unless it simplifies by taking away from the sum and
burden of what you have to consider. . . . I sing misunderstanding."
110

MURDERER

RF, in 1926: "But I forgive you . . .
even as I hope to be forgiven a
murder I once did." 622
RF recalls five people he wanted
to murder, 439-440
RF is accused, by his daughter, of
having killed his wife, 495-496

MYSTIC

"I was brought up a Swedenborgian. I am not a Swedenborgian now.
But there's a good deal of it that's
left with me. I am a mystic. I believe in symbols . . . and in changing symbols." 694
"I'll bet I could tell of spiritual
realizations that for the moment
would overawe the contentious." 561
"For Once, Then, Something," 561
  see SYMBOLIST and SYNECDOCHIST

MYTH-MAKER

RF romantically idealizes his
homecoming by asserting he did not
know he had an American publisher,
517
gives an idealized statement of
why he went to England, 55-56
gives an idealized account of how
he acquired his farm in Franconia,
525

FROST, ROBERT LEE (*cont.*)

in later years, gives an idealized account of how he teased Sedgwick, 528-529

gives an idealized account of how Edward Thomas responded to "The Road Not Taken," 545

gives an idealized account of how he made a living from "nothing but poetry," 157, 570

gives idealized accounts of how many miles he walked during the Long Trail hike, 583

gives an idealized account of how he forced Joseph Warren Beach to marry, 589

gives an idealized account of how "Stopping by Woods" was written "with one stroke of the pen" when it "just came" to him, complete, 596

at the Parker House in Boston, makes the idealized claim that his Amherst home has no street address, 256-257, 606-607

gives an idealized account of how he will be freed from all teaching obligations at Michigan, 268-270, 611-612

makes a convenient claim that he cannot write a preface, as promised, because his daughter is dangerously ill and his wife is prostrated, 622-623

gives Munson an idealized account of life on the Derry farm, 321-322, 633-634

makes an idealized claim about his capacity to be detached and objective, 652-653

retrospectively idealizes his final peace-making gesture toward Robinson, 666-667

in discussing "Build Soil," makes the idealized claim, "Both those people in the dialogue are me." 680

makes the idealized claim that someone else wrote "The Later Minstrel," 681

retrospectively idealizes his claim that President King forced RF to resign from Amherst, 700-703

see VENTRILOQUIST

NATURE

RF, obsessed with the controversy over the theory of natural selection, opposes Darwin and defends the Christian belief that the firmament showeth God's handiwork, 595-596

RF mocks Arnold for saying, "Nature is cruel, man is sick of blood." 235

Amy Lowell satirizes RF's view of Nature: ". . . To whom every grass-blade's a telephone wire / With Heaven as central and electrifier." 206, 586

RF's "Sitting by a Bush" is viewed as an attempt to reconcile the religious and the scientific sides of the Victorian controversy over Nature, 627-630

see SCIENCE VS RELIGION and SYNECDOCHE

OPPOSITES

"In order to know where we are we must know opposites." 425

"Our lives are an attempt to find out where we are standing between extremes of viewpoint . . ." 417

". . . trying to decide between God and the Devil . . . between endless other things in pairs ordained to everlasting opposition." 413, 664

"The philosopher values himself on the inconsistencies he can contain by main force. They are two ends of a strut that keeps his mind from collapsing. He may take too much satisfaction in having once more remarked the two-endedness of things." 413

"Get up there high enough and the differences that make controversy become only two legs of a body the weight of which is on one in one period, on the other in the next. Democracy monarchy; puritanism paganism; form content; conservatism radicalism; systole diastole; rustic urbane; literary colloquial; work play." 290

see PURITAN

POEMS

Acceptance, 308-309, 552
Acquainted with the Night, 309-310, 627
After Apple-Picking, 597
Armful, The, 307-308, 627
At Woodward's Gardens, 447, 673
Ax-Helve, The, 77, 78, 81, 239, 565
Bear, The, 312-313, 630
Bereft, 630
Birches, 30, 37, 57, 541, 598
Black Cottage, The, 59, 601
Blueberries, 59
Bond and Free, 541
Bonfire, The, 81, 541, 698
Brown's Descent, 537, 542
Build Soil, 430ff, 456ff
Census-Taker, The, 239
Code, The, 59, 534

INDEX

FROST, ROBERT LEE (*cont.*)
Cow in Apple Time, The, 541
Cow's in the Corn, The, 275, 614, 621
Death of the Hired Man, 6, 57, 60, 534
Desert Places, 597
Design, 600
Door in the Dark, The, 311
Draft Horse, The, 673
Dust of Snow, 152, 154
Empty Threat, An, 242-243
Encounter, An, 541
Escapist—Never, 595
Evening in a Sugar Orchard, 142-143
Exposed Nest, The, 541
Fear of God, The, 10, 522
Fire and Ice, 151-152, 154
Fish-Leap Fall, 50, 532
Flower Boat, The, 631
Flower-Gathering, 536
For Once, Then, Something, 153, 241, 561
Fountain, A Bottle, A Donkey's Ears, and Some Books, A, 563-564
Fragmentary Blue, 153
Generations of Men, The, 59, 561
Gift Outright, The, 597, 691
Girl's Garden, A, 541
Going for Water, 536
Gold Hesperidee, The, 239
Good-by and Keep Cold, 139, 153, 560
Grindstone, The, 239
Hail First President, 529
Happiness Makes Up, 488
Hill Wife, The, 541
Hillside Thaw, A, 142
Home Burial, 535, 560, 703
House Fear, 541
Hundred Collars, A, 59, 534, 535
Hyla Brook, 541
I Never Dared Be Radical, 442, 671
I Only Go, 424, 662
I Will Sing You One-O, 243-245
Impulse, The, 541
In Neglect, 58, 508
In the Home Stretch, 531, 541
Ingenuities of Debt, The, 598
Into My Own, 650, 653
It Is Almost the Year Two Thousand, 565
Kitty Hawk, 643
Later Minstrel, The, 681-682
Leaf Treader, A, 433
Line-Gang, The, 542
Lines Written in Dejection, 555
Locked Out, 565
Loneliness, 541
Lost in Heaven, 432
Love and a Question, 650
Lovely Shall Be Choosers, The, 597
Lowes Took the Obvious . . . 382
Lucretius Versus the Lake Poets, 581

Man Is As Tall, 655
Masque of Mercy, A, 656
Masque of Reason, A, 552-553, 623
Master Speed, The, 304, 626
Meeting and Passing, 541
Mending Wall, 534, 536
Misgiving, 154
Most of It, The, 361-362
Mountain, The, 534, 597
Mowing, 536
My Olympic Record Stride, 397, 403, 655
Need of Being Versed, 154
Nose-Ring, The, 346, 641
Not All There, 474
Not to Keep, 90, 565
Nothing Gold Can Stay, 565, 598
November, 597
Oft-Repeated Dream, The, 541
Old Man's Winter Night, An, 540
On the Heart's Beginning to Cloud the Mind, 414-416, 665
On the Sale of My Farm, 503, 699
Once by the Pacific, 303, 626, 630
Onset, The, 154
Our Hold on the Planet, 678-679
"Out, Out—", 541
Oven Bird, The, 541
Patch of Old Snow, A, 540
Paul's Wife, 239
Pauper Witch of Grafton, 239, 141-142
Pea Brush, 541
Peck of Gold, A, 630
Perhaps You Think, 116
Place for a Third, 153, 154, 569
Prayer in Spring, A, 552, 601
Pride of Ancestry, 473, 688-689
Provide, Provide, 437-438
Putting in the Seed, 541
Range-Finding, 541
Record Stride, A, 397-398, 403, 625
Reluctance, 536
Riders, 673
Road Not Taken, The, 37, 57, 86, 88ff, 544-548
Roadside Stand, A, 438-439
Runaway, The, 551, 565
Sand Dunes, 310, 627
Servant to Servants, A, 536
Seven Arts, The, 113
Sitting by a Bush, 627-629
Smile, The, 541
Snow, 531, 542
Sound of Trees, The, 37, 527, 542
Spring Pools, 295, 620
Star in a Stoneboat, A, 154, 239-240
Star-Splitter, The, 240-241, 599-600
Stars, 560
Stopping by Woods, 237, 596ff, 599, 609
Telephone, The, 541
Thatch, The, 630

FROST, ROBERT LEE (*cont.*)
Time to Talk, A, 541
To a Thinker, 427-428, 441ff
To Earthward, 697
To E. T., 95-96, 549-550, 569
To Prayer, To Prayer I Go . . . , 566-567
Trial by Existence, The, 601
Tuft of Flowers, The, 31
Two Tramps in Mud Time, 425-426, 491
Valley's Singing Day, 154
Vanishing Red, The, 542
West-Running Brook, 298, 299ff, 624-626
Wild Grapes, 239
Witch of Coös, The, 239
Wood-Pile, The, 25, 597

POETIC THEORY

". . . all the fun's in how you say a thing." 58
"A poem . . . begins as a lump in the throat, a sense of wrong, a homesickness, a lovesickness. It is never a thought to begin with. It is at its best when it is a tantalizing vagueness. It finds its thought and succeeds, or doesn't find it and comes to nothing. . . . A poem . . . must never begin thought first." 65
". . . I call this principle 'sound posturing,' more literally, getting the sound of sense. What we do get in life and miss so often in literature is the sentence sounds that underlie words." 35
". . . every meaning has a particular sound-posture, or to put it another way, the sense of every meaning has a particular sound which every individual is instinctively familiar with." 35
"All poetry is to me first a matter of sound. I hear my things spoken." 68
"What I am most interested in emphasizing in the application of this belief to art, is the sentence of sound, because to me a sentence is not interesting merely in conveying a meaning of words; it must do something more; it must convey a meaning by sound." 35
RF condemns the "evil search for synonyms," 447, 674
RF's theory of controlling meanings in "the sound of sense" is challenged by an actress, 427; is challenged by another poet, 669; is unintentionally disproved by RF himself, in the structural arrangement of *A Boy's Will,* 669

see STYLE and BAFFLER-TEASER-DECEIVER

PREACHER

"Here begins what probably won't end till you see me in the pulpit." 250
". . . the pulpit has been one of my chief speaking places." 501
" 'Let me preach to you, will you, Meliboeus?' 'Preach on. I thought you were already preaching. But preach and see if I can tell the difference.' " 483-485
Ladd: "One evening he surprised a small number of them with his denunciation of Greenwich Village life . . . It was talk which . . . would have delighted the ears of any fundamentalist preacher . . ." 99

PRETENDER

"I'm a good stout pretender when I set out to be." 449
"I have suffered nervous collapse in my time from the strain of conscious competition and learned from it how to pretend . . ." 449

PROGRESS

"Now I get my punishment . . . for letting myself believe . . . that there is such a thing as progress. Mea culpa." 601
"Whatever progress may be taken to mean, it can't mean making the world any easier a place in which to save your soul—or if you dislike hearing your soul mentioned in open meeting, say your decency, your integrity." 387
"The most exciting movement in nature is not progress . . ." 278
RF's religious belief is used to explain in what sense there is never "such a thing as progress." 601
see CHANGE

PROPHET

RF is obsessively fascinated by his belief that he has a gift of prophecy, 555-556
RF is usually coy or shy about confessing his belief in the Romantic-Victorian concept that the poet is a prophet, 626
RF, in June 1915: "I think the war

FROST, ROBERT LEE (*cont.*)
may end in five years in favor of the Germans. In that case Canada will join us to save herself . . . Maybe you don't see it as I do. But the prophecy stands." 556

RF, in Aug. 1917, prophesies there will be no Bolshevik revolution in Russia: "Live in hope or fear of your revolution. You will see no revolution this time . . ." 555

RF, in July 1929: ". . . in the next line-up Germany will fight on the side of America against the enemy [England]." 645

"My prophetic soul told me I was in for it forty five years ago . . . Is it not written in a poem of mine . . ." 304

RF's poem "The Master Speed" viewed as a prophecy which failed, 626

RF's poem "Once by the Pacific" viewed as a safe form of prophecy, 626

PROSE

1919: "A Way Out," 108-109, 554
1924: "Preface" to *Memoirs of the Notorious Stephen Burroughs,* 585
1925: "The Poetry of Amy Lowell," 277-278, 615
1925: "Introduction" to *The Arts Anthology,* 355-356, 642
1926: "The Manumitted Student," 357, 642
1930: "Education by Poetry," 363-365, 642
1935: "Letter to the Amherst *Student,*" 386-388, 651
1935: "Introduction" to Robinson's *King Jasper,* 419-422, 668
1937: "What Became of New England?" 483-485, 692
1937: "Poverty and Poetry," 534, 687
1956: "Perfect Day—A Day of Prowess," 469, 688
1957: "Introduction" to *A Swinger of Birches,* 638

PUNISHMENT

RF is punished harshly by his father, xiv; is taught to believe that God is a harsh punisher, xiv; gradually becomes a harsh punisher, himself, xiv

"Now I get my punishment . . . for letting myself believe . . . that there is any such thing as progress." 116

"I've been punished often enough in the past for pretending not to see what was wrong with the poor."187

"All this sickness and scatteration of the family is our fault . . . It's a result and a judgment on us." 282

"I have kept poetry free thus far, and I have been punished for the mere thought of making it a duty or a business." 687

RF to Lankes: "You were bent on punishing me . . ." 676

"What you need is someone to be severe with you, someone intimate enough to know how much punishment you can take and still live." 357

RF on undergraduate poets who fail: "They can't take the punishment; they don't want to take the punishment." 353

PURITAN

"Yes, I suppose I am a Puritan." 230

"I'm descended from the Puritan who had both his ears cut off twice . . ." 461

"A high churchman says I am the last sweepings of the Puritan latrines." 490

"And I have all the dead New England things held back by one hand as by a dam in the long deep wooded valley of Whippoorwill, where, many as they are, though, they do not flow together by their own weight. . . . I hold them easily—too easily for assurance that they will go with a rush when I let them go." 114

RF sympathetically interprets the Puritan theology of Milton's *Paradise Lost,* 656-657

RF's puritanism, like Milton's, is partly Arminian, 614

RF, in 1920: "I am writing my Puritan Poem so to speak and expect to finish it by—and by." 566; RF's poem of self-abasement, 566-567

"It is only when we hate ourselves and our shortcomings that we can love and need God. All religions are based on that one: 'And thou shalt hate thy neighbor as thyself.' " 516

"That is my last, my ultimate vileness, that I cannot make up my mind to go now where I must go sooner or later." 567

"Leave the evils that can be remedied or even palliated. You are of age now to face essential Hell. Cease from the optimism as much that makes good as that sees good.

FROST, ROBERT LEE (*cont.*)
Come with me into the place of tombs and outer darkness." 567

"Just as the only great art is inesthetic so the only morality is completely ascetic. I have been bad and a bad artist." 567

RF, in 1916, defends the New England Puritans, 76

a reporter on RF: "He is a Puritan who has fought the soil for sustenance and has fought the world for recognition as a poet." 78

"She's not the only Puritan by all I hear. Johnny Farrar has been getting right up and walking right out of the theatre in protest against something said or done in the play . . ." 305

"New England gave most to America . . . a stubborn clinging to meaning—to purify words until they meant again what they should mean. Puritanism has that meaning entirely: a purifying of words and a renewal of words and a renewal of meaning. That's what brought the Puritans to America . . ." 483

see OPPOSITES

RAGE

"I get to railing and I can rail myself into damning my best friends to Hell. Sometimes I think I need holding in." 82

"Sedgwick was teasing me . . . but it has been a long fight with editors, my rage had gathered considerable headway and it's hard to leave off believing the worst of them." 528

rage against the immigration officers at Ellis Island, in 1915, 2, 7

rage against Amy Lowell's portrayal of RF and EWF, 114-115; against Amy Lowell's satirical thrust at RF, 206

rage against his wife for disagreeing with him, 30; against his sister for being a radical, 128; against his son's wish to buy a rooster, 185-186; against his daughter's teachers at Wellesley, 115-118

rage against Braithwaite for placing Robinson above RF, 64-65; against Robinson for being more popular than RF, 379-380; against Robinson for doubting that RF is a genuine farmer, 381

rage against Stark Young at Amherst, 82-83, 108ff; against Meiklejohn for defending Stark Young, 120-122; against Whicher, 266

rage against Raymond Holden in Franconia, 144; against Wilfred Davison at Bread Loaf, 172-173

rage against Carl Sandburg at Michigan, 179-180; against his landlady in Ann Arbor, 186-187; against himself for buying expensive mountain-climbing boots in Ann Arbor, 193

rage against Beach for seeming to play a lascivious trick on RF, 216-217, 589; against Rascoe for allegedly misquoting RF, 221-223; against the clerk at the Parker House in Boston, 256-257

rage against the humanitarian humanists at Amherst, 120-121; against the scientists at Michigan, 296-297

rage against Davison for his wrong way of starting a biography of RF, 317; against Munson for his wrong way of ending a biography of RF, 323ff

rage against Helen Thomas, for her way of describing her husband, 334ff, 636-637

rage against Lowes, for reasons unknown to Lowes, 382-383, 649-650

rage against Coates for allegedly excluding RF from the ranks of Vermont poets, 383-384

rage against T.S. Eliot for finding little or no poetry above the Scottish border, 402-403

rage against the New Deal, 411; against Witter Bynner, 429-430; against Harvard defenders of charwomen, 437-438; against those whom he wanted to murder, 439-440; against Pound's complaints, 450

rage against what he imagined to be the romantic notions of Shirley Barker, 471-474, 688-689

renewal of an old rage against Santayana, 484, 691-692

REBEL

RF to LU: "I thought you and we was going to be rebels together. And being rebels doesn't mean being radical; it means being reckless like Eva Tanguay. It means busting something just when everybody begins to think it's so safe it's safe." 84

"I like a young fellow as says, 'My father's generation thought that, did they? Well that was the Hell of a way to think, wasn't it? Let's think something else for a change.' A disconnective young fellow with a plenty of extrication in his make-up." 84

RF imaginatively identifies his own

FROST, ROBERT LEE (*cont.*)
brand of rebel independence with those values he finds in Emerson's rebel-poem, "Uriel," 543-544

RELIGIOUS BELIEF

evidences that RF derives his religious belief from his mother's curious blending of Scotch-Calvinistic-Presbyterian - Swedenborgian - Unitarian - Universalist beliefs, xiii-xiv, 515, 567, 593, 627-630, 673-674, 697
RF is taught to believe in a punishing God, xiii-xiv; is taught to believe that in Adam's fall we sinned all, 656-657; is taught to believe that suffering is divinely inflicted for purposes of trial, testing, punishment, and purification, 593-594
"One can safely say after from six to thirty thousand years of experience that the evident design is a situation here in which it will always be equally hard to save your soul." 387
". . . before God our whole enterprise from the day we put on fig leaves and went to work has been no better than pitiful." 657
RF is taught to believe in the Christian doctrine of right reason, acceptance, obedience, 552ff; is taught to believe that there is "no connection man can reason out / Between his just deserts and what he gets." 553
from what he is taught to believe, RF draws divine justification for his anti-intellectualism and for his laissez-faire social doctrine, 553
RF's self-protectively humorous and consequently misleading references to his religious belief, 560ff
"Belief is better than anything else, and it is best when rapt, above paying its respects to anybody's doubts whatsoever." 254
"We only joke about it to avoid an issue with someone . . . Humor is the most engaging cowardice. With it myself I have been able to hold some of my enemy far out of gunshot." 254, 560-561
"I'll bet I could tell of spiritual realizations that for the moment would overawe the contentious." 290, 561
". . . the belief in God is a relationship you enter into with Him to bring about the future." 364
Snow: "[RF] even told me that he considered the account of man's creation as recorded in the first chap-

ter of Genesis as no more miraculous than the combined factors of air, heat, light, moisture, climate, and other conditions brought into exact harmony to make life upon this planet possible." 629-630
"God once declared he was true / And then took the veil and withdrew, / And remember how final a hush / Then descended of old on the bush." 629
"I used to try to get up plausible theories about prayer like Emerson. My latest is that it might be an expression of the hope I have that my offering of verse on the altar may be acceptable in His sight . . ." 568
"Why will the quidnuncs always be hoping for a salvation man will never have from anyone but God. I was just saying today how Christ posed himself the whole problem and died for it." 568

RETALIATIONS, POETIC

"Not All There" (against Shirley Barker), 474
"Pride of Ancestry" (against Shirley Barker), 473
"Lucretius Versus the Lake Poets" (against Howard Mumford Jones), 581
"Lowes Took the Obvious" (against John Livingston Lowes), 382
"The Most of It" (against Wade Van Dore), 361-362

REVENGE

"Christ forgive me the sin of vengefulness: from this hour forth I will have no more of it. Perhaps I only say so because for the moment I am sated." 525
"I ought not to give way to thoughts of revenge in the first place . . . [but] I am human enough to want to make them squirm a little before I forgive them." 25
see VINDICTIVE

SCIENCE, DELIGHT IN

". . . science offers just compensation. Think of the great abysses opened up by our study of the atom. Think of the strange and unaccountable actions of the hurrying winds experienced by our travelers of the skies. Think of the marvels of marine life lately brought to us by the explorers of the distant oceans, each more wonderfully wrought than

INDEX

FROST, ROBERT LEE (*cont.*)
ever mermaid or water sprite of which the poet dreamed." 288

"Life has lost none of its mystery and its romance. The more we know of it, the less we know. . . . If science has expelled much of our fear, still there is left a thousand things from which to shape our dreams." 288

"Keats mourned that the rainbow . . . had lost its glory . . . Yet knowledge of its causation could not spoil the rainbow for me. I am so sure that it is not given to man to be omniscient. There will always be something left to know, something left to excite the imagination of the poet . . ." 288

SCIENCE VS RELIGION

"Only in a certain type of small scientific mind can there be cocksureness, a conviction that a solution to the riddle of the universe is just around the corner." 288

". . . Jacques Loeb . . . felt he had within his grasp the secret of vitality. Give him but ten years and he would have it fast. He had the ten and ten more, and in ten more he was dead. Perhaps he knows more of the mystery of life now than ever he did before his passing." 288

in the standing argument between science and religion, RF takes his battle-position on the side of religion, 288ff

"You should have heard me standing off a club of scientists the other night on the subject of evolution. . . . All I had to do was ask them questions for information. The last one led up to was, Did they think it was ever going to be any easier to be good." 296

"If there's an ideal that lends itself to facile spieling in our day equally well with that of evolution . . ." 652

"What I like about Bergson and Fabre is that they have bothered our evolutionism so much . . ." 300

"West-Running Brook" is viewed as RF's Bergsonian way of bothering the scientists by deriving religious parables from evolution imagery, 300-303

RF, during the Dayton "Monkey Trial," sides with the fundamentalists against the evolutionists, 618

Snow: "When [RF] read in the paper that there was a professor of biology . . . who was not completely convinced of the exactitude of Darwin's theory of Evolution, that he wanted first to see the missing link, Frost was immensely delighted." 630

"It will take twenty years for that to penetrate to the Clarence Darrowsians and Daytonians." 291

RF makes a Victorian reconciliation between science and religion in one poem, "Sitting by a Bush," 627-629

"They say time itself is circular and the universe a self-winding clock. Well well just when it reaches the back country . . . the latest science says . . . it isn't a mechanism at all, whatever we fools may be." 291

Lankes: "I think it pleases Frost especially that science is in a hole." 645

RF mocks some scientific uses of metaphor, in "Education by Poetry," 364; again mocks, at Michigan, 288-289; again mocks, in reporting his conversation with Haldane and Milliken, 658ff; again mocks, using Einstein as target, 649

SELF-CENTEREDNESS

"I'm a mere selfish artist most of the time." 356

"I only go / When I'm the show." 424

"Still one can't pretend not to like to win the game. One can't help thinking a little of Number One." 25

RF, citing Cellini's way of damaging his home for the sake of his art, concludes: "That's the way it has to *be*, with the artist." 498, 698

"The rest of me is swallowed up in thoughts of myself. . . . I'll be damned. It shows how far we can get along in our egotism without noticing it." 566

"Forgive me my selfishness . . ." 214

RF is accused by his wife of being too self-centered in his attitude toward his children, 560; is accused by his daughter of being too self-centered in his attitude toward his wife, 495-496

SKEPTIC

RF's various postures and pretenses of being more skeptical than he actually is, 600

RF's ways of invoking skepticism for purposes of concealing his religious belief—and thus protecting it from criticism, 560-562

FROST, ROBERT LEE (*cont.*)
RF's ability to find religious justification for a certain variety of skepticism, 552-553

SPOILED CHILD

"I'm become a spoiled child of fortune." 265
RF's spoiled-child attitudes, accidentally encouraged by his mother, 673
"I hate so to be crossed I have come to think not being crossed is the one thing that matters in life. I can think of no blissfuller state than being treated as if I was always right." 673
"Ever since childhood I have wanted my death to come in as effectively and effectingly." 278
RF's spoiled-child attitude toward fantasies of suicide, 615, 673

STYLE

". . . style in prose or verse is that which indicates how the writer takes himself and what he is saying." 253
"His style is the way he carries himself toward his ideas and deeds." 253
"I own any form of humor shows fear and inferiority. Irony is simply a kind of guardedness. . . . Humor is the most engaging cowardice." 254
possible influence of EWF on RF's style, 560-561; possible influence of Santayana on the same aspect, 691-692
"The style is the man. Rather say the style is the way the man takes himself. . . . If it is with outer seriousness, it must be with inner humor. If it is with outer humor, it must be with inner seriousness. Neither one alone without the other under it will do." 421-422
see BAFFLER-TEASER-DECEIVER

SUPERSTITION

Cox: "Mr. Frost frankly calls himself superstitious; by which he means that he accepts no explanation of mystery. He is religious." 485, 692
RF: "The God Question. Religion is superstition or it is nothing. It is still there after philosophy has done its best. . . . [Philosophy is] nothing but an attempt to rationalize religion." 692
". . . it didn't cure my evil mood because it threw me into a superstitious fear that you would incur for me the jealousy of gods and men." 399

SYMBOLIST

"I wish for a joke I could do myself, shifting the trees entirely from the Yankee realist to the Scotch symbolist." 485
"I am a mystic. I believe in symbols . . . and in changing symbols." 694
"Imagery and after-imagery are about all there is to poetry. Synecdoche and synecdoche. My motto is that something has to be left to God." 693

SYNECDOCHIST

"If I must be classified as a poet, I might be called a Synecdochist, for I prefer the synecdoche in poetry— that figure of speech in which we use a part for the whole." 485
"I started calling myself a Synecdochist when others called themselves Imagists or Vorticists. Always, always a larger significance. A little thing touches a larger thing." 693
"I believe in what the Greeks call synecdoche: the philosophy of the part for the whole; skirting the hem of the goddess. All that an artist needs is samples." 693
Amy Lowell on RF: ". . . To whom every grass-blade's a telephone wire / With Heaven as central and electrifier." 206
RF: ". . . the height of poetry, the height of all thinking, the height of all poetic thinking, [is] that attempt to say matter in terms of spirit and spirit in terms of matter." 364
". . . any poem is most valuable for its ulterior meaning. I have developed an ulteriority complex." 314

TALKS, TITLES OF

All Thinking Is Metaphor, 401
Before the Beginning and After the End of a Poem, 447, 665
Better Part of Imagination, The, 540
Composing in Things, 540
Crudities, 491
Does Wisdom Signify? 445
Education by Poetry, 554ff
Having a Literary Moment, 75, 538, 540
Learning to Have Something to Say, 434
New Sound in Poetry, The, 537
Old Ways to Be New, The, 444

INDEX

FROST, ROBERT LEE (*cont.*)
Originality in Modern Poetry, 416
Our Darkest Concern, 417, 700
Poetry as Prowess, 447
Poetry of Axe Handles, 538
Poverty and Poetry, 534
Renewal of Words, The, 444
Sound of Poetry, The, 537
Tone Quality of Poetry, The, 538
Uses of Ambiguity, The, 433
Vocal Imagination, 445
Waiting Spirit, The, 540
What Became of New England? 482ff
What Poetry Thinks of Our Age, 424
Writing a Poem Is a Performance in Belief, 661

TEACHER

"I'm a good teacher, but it doesn't allow me time to write. I must either teach or write—can't do both together. But I have to live." 67

"I should awfully like a quiet job in a small college where I should be allowed to teach something a little new on the technique of writing and where I should have some honor for what I suppose myself to have done in poetry." 83

RF's teaching methods at Amherst College, in 1917, 97ff

". . . he required no papers. He hardly gave any tests or examinations. His class was the most loosely run and undisciplined class of any . . . I attended in college. . . . the boys in the back row would actually be playing cards together while he was holding forth." 100

"Frost has been trying his hardest to make his own course gutty enough to take the place of all the guts which have recently evaporated. Under the strain of doing as little as possible . . . he fell sick just in time to get out of making the Senior chapel address—the one piece of work he was in danger of doing." 118

RF: "I'm rather blue over my teaching. I don't like the boys as much as I ought to." 256

Mrs. Wolcutt: "I have been asked . . . to describe his teaching methods. They were, of course, non-existent. He merely talked . . ." 620

RF's inconsistent utterances about his theory and practice of teaching, 612ff

THEISM VS HUMANISM

RF, in 1927, is offended by an attempt to represent him as a humanist, in the Babbitt tradition, 324ff

RF is annoyed by Munson's article, "Robert Frost and the Humanistic Temper," 326

RF: "One might forget God in a lull of faith. One might forget God, and talk about the highest in himself." 483, 691

RF, in 1915, lends his copy of Balfour's *Theism and Humanism*, 634

UTOPIA

"Men have always dreamed of Utopia in the past; I suppose Utopia will get us yet." 417

"Life wastes away into death, insanity, poverty and crime: Utopia aims to alleviate and stop these sorrows." 417-418

"All ages of the world are bad—a great deal worse anyway than Heaven. If they weren't, the world might just as well be Heaven at once and have it over with." 387

VENTRILOQUIST

RF apologizes for having put words in the mouth of Joseph Warren Beach, 217-218

RF puts words in the mouth of President Burton, 279-280, 615; of J. B. S. Haldane, 658-660; of President Meiklejohn, 121, 557; of Premier Khrushchev, 616

VICTORIAN

Marjorie Frost to RF about the man she is going to marry: "He is a dear, kind, and considerate man, another real Victorian, papa, with the beautiful ideals that I had feared no longer existed." 400

RF subscribes to the Victorian belief in the poet as prophet, 626

RF makes a Victorian reconciliation between science and religion in one poem, 627-629

RF, in 1931, buys a Victorian house in Amherst and decorates it with Victorian furnishings, 398

VINDICTIVE

"He said he was vindictive, and the comments he made showed it." 260

RF: ". . . my Indian vindictiveness. Really I am awful there. I am worse than you know." 636

FROST, ROBERT LEE (*cont.*)
  RF's vindictive gestures against:
Arnold, Matthew, 235, 595-596, 632
Barker, Shirley, 471-474, 688ff
Beach, J. W., 216-218, 589
Braithwaite, W. S., 44, 542-543
Burell, Carl, 25-26, 525
Davison, Edward, 317ff
Davison, Wilfred, 172-173
Eliot, T. S., 401-403, 661
Farrar, John, 682-686
Frost, Carol, 185-186
Frost, Elinor, 108
Frost, Jeanie, 128
Haldane, J. B. S., 658-660
Holden, Raymond, 141-145
King, Stanley, 700-703
Lowell, Amy, 274-276
Lowes, J. L., 381-383
Millay, Edna St. Vincent, 651
Munson, Gorham, 323-326
Rascoe, Burton, 220-223
Robinson, E. A., 380-381, 418-419
Sandburg, Carl, 179-180
Sedgwick, Ellery, 12ff, 37ff
Stevens, Wallace, 665-666
Thornton, Richard, 695-696
Young, Stark, 105ff
Zabel, Morton D., 695-696

WAR, ATTITUDE TOWARD

"Glorious war, isn't it?" 108
"Write a lot. Enjoy the war. I've made up my mind to do the second anyway. I don't see why the fact that I can't be in a fight should keep me from liking the fight." 107
"Nothing is true except as a man or men adhere to it—and live for it, to spend themselves on it, to die for it. Not to argue for it! There's no greater mistake than to look on fighting as a form of argument. To *fight* is to leave words and act as if you believed—to *act* as if you believed." 411
  throughout RF's poetry, the images involving "things in pairs ordained to everlasting opposition" presuppose the fundamental warfare between God and the Devil, 664

Frost to Untermeyer, first cited, 526
Frost, William Prescott (1823-1901)
  (grandfather of RF), annuity of $800 from the estate of, paid regularly during these crucial years, 11, 28, 522, 526-527
  RF repeatedly conceals the fact of the annuity, 156, 321, 570, 633
Frost, William Prescott, Jr. (1850-1885)
  (father of RF), mentioned, xiii, 2, 318, 450

Frost, William Prescott (1924-   )
  (grandson of RF), 614, 289, 392, 395, 405, 409, 410, 476, 486, 512

G

Garland, Hamlin, 163, 225, 591
Garnett, Edward
  in 1915, offers to the *Atlantic* an article on RF, 38-39, 528; RF sends thanks to, 51; "A New American Poet" by, quoted, 52, 59-60; cited, 533; RF meets, in England in 1928, 340
Gay, Robert M., 684, 685
Gettell, Raymond, 101ff
Gibbon, Edward, 251, 603
Gibson, Charles Dana, 668
Gibson, W. W.
  mentioned, 59, 117-118; RF tells anecdotes about, 532-533; RF sees, in Chicago in 1917, 164-165; RF visits, in England in 1928, 332, 335
  writes a poem to commemorate RF's visit, 335, 638
Gilchrist, Mrs. Halley P., 146ff, 203
Goodell, Henry H., 607
Goodwillie, Mary
  describes meeting RF in 1915, 551; RF tells of a talk he gave for, in 1917, 102
  is visited in Baltimore by the Frosts in Nov. 1927, 635; befriends Marjorie Frost, 635; is visited again by the Frosts in Dec. 1937, 487
Gould, Jean
  Robert Frost: The Aim Was Song, 519
Grade, Arnold
  and Thompson, eds., *New Hampshire's Child,* 633
Grant, Joy
  Harold Monro and the Poetry Bookshop, cited, 639
Graves, Robert, 547
Green, Charles R.
  and Clymer, eds., *Robert Frost: A Bibliography,* cited, 587
  letter to, from W. E. Hocking, 523
Greenslet, Ferris, 402, 662
Gregory, Horace, 454, 481, 488
Grimald, Nicholas, 627
Guest, Edgar A., 182, 197, 582, 578
Gulliver, Harold S., 197, 582

H

Hackett, Francis, 8, 520
Hagedorn, Hermann, 412
Haines, John W.
  in 1921, rescues remainders of

INDEX

Haines, John W. (cont.)
the English editions of *A Boy's Will* and *North of Boston*, 587ff
RF writes to, in 1928, 328, 330; RF and EWF visit, in 1928, 332
Haldane, J. B. S.
RF tells of "baiting," in 1932, 658; *Daedalus* by, quoted and cited, 659-660
Harcourt, Alfred
in 1915, tells RF how Holt became publisher of *North of Boston*, 5ff, 518ff; is appealed to, by RF, for assistance, 55; almost persuades RF to leave Holt in 1919, 155ff; RF writes to, in 1923, 224-225; again, in 1933, 584
Hard, Margaret
(Mrs. Walter Hard), *A Memory of Vermont*, quoted and cited, 583-584
Hard, Walter
RF on the poetry of, 584
Harvard University
RF, in 1916, is Phi Beta Kappa poet at, 78, 80-81
RF, in 1935, gives a reading in the Morris Gray lecture series at, 670
RF, in 1936, is Charles Eliot Norton Professor at, 444-448; fails to fulfill part of contract with, 434, 674, 675
RF is unable to fulfill other obligations at, in 1936, 462-463
Hawkins, Clifford, 168-169
Hawkins, Wales Monroe
RF befriends, 169; RF learns about the death of, 635; Frost Collection at Middlebury College, to commemorate the friendship between RF and, 572
Hawthorne, Nathaniel, 261
Hayford, James, 700
Hazlitt, William, 603
Heinemann, William
the London publisher, disapproves of unacknowledged borrowings in two of RF's early poems, 649-650
Hemingway, Ernest, 410, 673
Henderson, Alice Corbin, 524
Herbert, Willis E., 27ff, 526-527
Heyward, DuBose, 440
Hicks, Granville
attacks RF in an unsigned review, 384-385, 650-651; again attacks RF in a signed review of *Collected Poems*, 385-386; attacks DeVoto and RF in "A Letter to Robert Hillyer," 479, 690
Hillyer, Robert
brings RF to Harvard in 1935,

670; with RF, attends dinner in honor of T. S. Eliot, 402; publishes "A Letter to Robert Frost," 478; inspires "A Letter to Robert Hillyer, 478-479; is an honorary bearer at memorial service for EWF, 699
Hocking, William Ernest
RF meets, in 1915, and visits in the home of, 13-14, 15-16; RF again visits, 249; RF mentions, 122
The Meaning of God in Human Experience, 13, 250; letter from, to C. R. Green, quoted, 16, cited, 523
Holden, Raymond
complicated friendship between RF and, in Franconia, 1915-1920, 136-145; lends to RF the Franconia house bought from RF, 171, 173
is named by RF as one of the promising younger poets, in 1920, 144; again in 1928, 353
"Reminiscences of Robert Frost" by, cited, 562; passages quoted from, 140-141, 144-145, 560, 562-563, 563-564; "Interval Between Felled Trees" by, 562; *The Reminding Salt* by, 562
Holmes, John
and Cooper, *Preface to Poetry*, cited, 597; letter from RF to, quoted, 531-532
Holt, Florence Taber
(Mrs. Henry Holt), RF meets, in New York City in 1915, 9, 521-522
Holt, Henry
RF visits, in Vermont, in 1923, 228
Holt, Henry, & Company
publishes American editions of *A Boy's Will* and *North of Boston* in 1915, 3, 5-9, 518-521; obtains copyrights with difficulty, 573-574; publishes *Mountain Interval* in 1916, 80, 82, 540; refuses to give RF copyrights on first three books when he tries to leave the firm in 1919, 155-156; makes amends, 156-157; publishes *Selected Poems* in March 1923, 219, 590
publishes *New Hampshire* in Nov. 1923, 238, 246-247, 315
persuades RF not to leave the firm as planned, in 1927, 314-315; gives attractive contract for *West-Running Brook*, in 1928, 314-315, 344
publishes *Collected Poems*, in 1930, 315, 384
postpones publication of *A Further Range* when it becomes a selection of the Book-of-the-Month Club, 449, 675
see Brace, Bristol, Harcourt, Mac-

Holt, Henry, & Company (*cont.*)
Veagh, Madison, Thornton
Horace
    RF models "New Hampshire" on
the *Sermones* of, 231
Howe, M. A. de Wolfe, 450-451
Howells, William Dean
    praises *North of Boston*, 57-58;
invites RF to visit, 58
    RF is asked to take part in me-
morial service for, 163; RF writes
a tribute to, 163-164, 571
Humphries, Rolfe, 455, 464

I

Ibsen, Henrik, 247
Interviews with Robert Frost
    ed., Edward Connery Lathem, first
cited, 536

J

Jackson, Gardner
    as an undergraduate at Amherst
College, in 1917, meets RF, 104;
"The Reminiscences of Gardner
Jackson" cited, 551; quoted, 100,
104-105; article on RF by, quoted,
268, 271; cited, 611; asks RF to
review *Letters of Sacco and Van-
zetti*, 379
James, William
    RF: "A teacher who influenced
me most I never had." 506, 700
    RF: "The most valuable teacher
I had at Harvard, I never had. . . .
He was William James. His books
meant a great deal to me." 643
    RF resents Babbitt's attack on,
325; also resents Santayana's at-
tack on, 691
    The Will to Believe by, quoted
and cited, 643
Jeffers, Robinson, 353
Jewell, Ernest, 11-12, 522
Jones, Llewellyn, 526
Jonson, Benjamin, 603
Joyce, James
    RF: "I have heard that Joyce
wrote *Ulysses* as a joke." 220

K

Keats, John, 288
Kerr, W. P. R., 333
Key West, Florida
    RF and EWF spend winter of
1934-1935 in, 410ff

Khrushchev, Nikita Sergeyevich, 616
King, Basil, 526
King, Stanley
    (President of Amherst College),
RF writes to, in April 1934, excus-
ing himself from obligations, 406
    arranges to have RF give three
public lectures at Amherst College,
spring of 1935, 416; defends RF,
and permits him to be absent from
Amherst in 1936, 435-436; a review
of RF's relations with, 503-504
    goes to Florida to see RF, shortly
after the death of EWF, and resists
RF's wish to resign from Amherst,
500, 505; is honorary bearer at memorial service for EWF, 699; arranges to have the College buy RF's
home, 505, 700
    RF sends letter of resignation to,
506ff
    RF fashions a mythic account of
how he was forced out of Amherst
College by, 700-703
King Jasper, by Edwin A. Robinson
    RF's first draft of an introduc-
tion for, quoted, 419-422; source
cited, 668
Kipling, Rudyard, xiii, 515, 609, 654
Kreymborg, Alfred
    Troubadour: An Autobiography,
quoted and cited, 536

L

LaBatt, Lillian
    Marjorie Frost's closest friend in
high school, 174; goes with the
Frosts on the Long Trail hike in
1922, 190ff, 582; becomes engaged
to marry Carol Frost, 198-199
    see Frost, Lillian LaBatt
Ladd, Henry A.
    "Memories of Robert Frost" by,
quoted, 103; cited, 551
Landis, Benson Y.
    "Poetry and Rural Life" by,
quoted, 431-432; cited, 670
Landor, Walter Savage, 187, 296, 581
Lankes, Edee
    (Mrs. J. J. Lankes), letters to,
from her husband, about the Frost
farm in 1929, 644-646
Lankes, Julius John
    background sketch of, 599; RF
asks for, as illustrator of *New
Hampshire*, 238; RF praises the
earlier work of, 246; RF is disappointed in the *New Hampshire*
woodcuts, 247
    illustrates *West-Running Brook*,
315; receives RF's account of the

Lankes, Julius John (*cont.*)
 return voyage from England in
 1928, 261
 lives on RF's farm, summer 1929,
 369-373, 643-646
 in 1932, is helped by RF in obtaining a position as artist-in-resi-
 dence at Wells College, 676; is
 scolded by RF in 1936, 451-452,
 676-677
Latham, Ronald
 translator, Lucretius: *On the
 Nature of the Universe,* quoted and
 cited, 625
Lathem, Edward Connery
 *Robert Frost: His "American
 Send-off"—1915* by, cited, 522, 527-
 528
 ed., *Interviews with Robert Frost,*
 first cited, 536
 ed., *The Poetry of Robert Frost,*
 first cited, 516
 ed., with Cox, *Selected Prose of
 Robert Frost,* first cited, 585
Lawrence, D. H., 29
Lawrie, Helen Browning, 657-658
Lechlitner, Ruth
 (Mrs. Paul Corey), while an
 undergraduate at Michigan, becomes acquainted with RF, 576;
 retrospectively describes a visit to
 the Frost home, 576; a review by,
 quoted, 452-453; cited, 678
Lewis, Edward Morgan
 background sketch of, 466-467;
 meets RF in 1917, 466; views poetry
 as prowess, 467; as President of
 the University of New Hampshire,
 presents an honorary degree to RF,
 in 1934, 469-470; tells RF about the
 poet Shirley Barker, 471; death of,
 465; RF participates in memorial
 service for, 475
Lewis, Sinclair, 170, 572
Lindsay, Vachel
 sends a copy of *The Congo* to
 RF, in 1915, 182; RF meets, in
 Chicago, in 1917, 182; RF meets
 again, in New York City, in 1918,
 182; RF writes a parody of, 183,
 579; RF attends a performance by,
 in 1921, 183, 579; RF brings, to
 Michigan, in 1922, 183; RF mentions, in 1929, as having lost popularity, 646
Lippmann, Walter, 8, 591-592
Little, Clarence Cook
 successor to Burton, as President
 of the University of Michigan, in
 1925, 283-284; RF disapproves of,
 as a scientist, 296
Lloyd, Alfred H., 292, 592
Longfellow, Henry Wadsworth

 RF, in 1923, defends and praises,
 619; RF, in 1924, admires an element in the style of, 254; RF, in
 1925, again defends and praises,
 293
 RF, in 1926, teases the Bryn
 Mawr students for disliking the
 name of, while liking the poetry
 of, 291-292, 619
 RF, in 1936, denies authorship
 of a poem he wrote as tribute to,
 in 1907, 681
Lowe, Orton, 664
Lowell, Amy
 tries to find an American publisher for *North of Boston* in 1914,
 6; reviews *North of Boston* in 1915,
 3-4
 RF visits, in Brookline, in March
 1915, 16-20, 523
 is elected first president of the
 New England Poetry Club in 1915,
 42-43; RF writes a congratulatory
 jingle for, in 1915, 529
 RF reproaches, for imitating
 some of Browning's "intonations,"
 56
 RF is enraged by the portrayal of
 him in *Tendencies in Modern Poetry,*
 114-115; RF, in 1920, considers exposing, "for a fool as well as fraud,"
 274
 in 1922, RF is host to, when she
 gives a reading at the University
 of Michigan, 181-182; later in 1922,
 RF is annoyed by the satirical
 passage aimed at him by, in *A
 Critical Fable,* 205-207; soon thereafter, RF directly mocks, in a public talk, 212; in 1923, RF indirectly
 mocks, in a satirical passage in
 "New Hampshire," 233
 in Feb. 1925, RF is host to, when
 she gives a reading at Amherst College, 272-273; refuses to attend a
 dinner in honor of, 273ff; is made
 uncomfortable by the death of,
 276ff
 "The Poetry of Amy Lowell" by
 RF, quoted, 277-278; cited, 615
Lowes, John Livingston
 in 1923, RF admires, because
 Lowes "snaps his fingers in dismissal of T. S. Eliot," 220
 in 1929, RF is outwitted and annoyed by, 382; RF retaliates
 against, in verse and in prose, 382-
 383
 in 1932, RF and Lowes are
 guests at a dinner in honor of
 Eliot, 402
 in 1936, RF is brought to Harvard by, to serve as Norton lec-

Lowes, John Livingston (*cont.*)
  turer, 434, 444
Lucretius
  RF reveals his familiarity with
  De Rerum Natura by, 624-625
Lynch, John and Margaret
  mentioned, 1-2, 4; RF rents
  rooms in the farmhouse of, in
  1915, 23ff
Lyons, Clifford P., 698

M

Mackall, Lawton, 219
MacKaye, Percy, 160, 162, 531, 646
MacLeish, Archibald, 353, 416-417
MacVeagh, Lincoln
  as a Holt representative, visits
  RF in Franconia in 1919, 156; arranges to have RF serve as a consulting editor for Holt, starting in
  1920, 156-157; receives from RF an
  account of the Long Trail hike, in
  1922, 199; receives from RF news
  that RF is returning to Michigan
  in Oct. 1922, 201; directs publication of *Selected Poems* in 1923,
  213, 218-219, 245-246, 590-591;
  makes arrangements for illustrating and publishing *New Hampshire* in 1923, 238, 245, 247
  resigns from Henry Holt & Co.,
  314; as owner of The Dial Press,
  accepts RF's advice to reprint
  *Memoirs of the Notorious Stephen
  Burroughs*, in 1924, 585
  visits RF in South Shaftsbury, in
  1929, 646
  RF mentions, as U. S. Ambassador to Greece, in 1934, 471
Madison, Charles A.
  as editor of the college department, Henry Holt & Co., is forced
  by RF to break a contract, in 1937,
  695-696
  RF to, on poems written or not
  written with one stroke of the pen,
  597-598
  The Owl among the Colophons
  by, quoted, 155, 696; first cited, 570
Mair, Mrs. Jessy
  in 1928, invites RF to give a reading at the London School of Economics and Political Science, 339
Manthey-Zorn, Otto
  RF writes to, from Paris, in 1928,
  634; RF sends MS of a poem to, in
  1937, 665; RF asks, to serve as
  honorary bearer at memorial service for EWF, 699; RF stays in the
  home of, at the time of the memorial service, 502, 503

March, Florence Eldridge, 427
March, Joseph Moncure, 353-354, 641-
  642
Marks, Jeannette, 75, 538
Marlowe, Christopher, 223, 594
Masefield, John, 21, 59, 687
Masters, Edgar Lee, 61ff
Matthiessen, Francis Otto, 450, 696
McCarthy, Denis Aloysius, 42, 257-258
McCord, David
  is one of the younger poets at the
  dinner for T. S. Eliot in 1932, 402;
  brings RF to Harvard for a reading
  in 1935, 670; helps to bring RF
  back to Harvard in 1936, 434; RF
  mentions, 440; is an honorary
  bearer at the memorial service for
  EWF, 699
Meiklejohn, Alexander
  as President of Amherst College,
  offers RF a teaching position there
  in 1916, 82, 86; introduces RF to
  E. M. Lewis, early in 1917, 465
  RF works well with, for a short
  time, 101; RF begins to find fault
  with, 102-103; RF complains to,
  about Stark Young, 105, 553; RF is
  temporarily soothed by, 110-111;
  RF finally becomes enraged at, and
  resigns, 120-121
  RF seems to put words in the
  mouth of, 121, 557
  is dismissed from Amherst College, 228, 591-592
Melcher, Frederic G.
  editor-in-chief of *Publishers'
  Weekly*, finds work for Lesley Frost
  in New York City, summer 1920,
  149
  arranges so-called fiftieth birthday dinner for RF, in 1925, 273-274
  is consulted by RF in 1930 about
  the status of the New School for
  Social Research, 379-380
  advises RF to leave the firm of
  Henry Holt & Co., in 1928, 314
  is an honorary bearer at the memorial service for EWF, in 1938,
  699
Melville, Herman
  RF uses *Typee* by, in a course
  at Amherst, 251
*Memoirs of the Notorious Stephen
Burroughs*
  RF writes a "Preface" for, 585
Mencken, H. L., 376, 533, 647-648
Mertins, Louis
  *Robert Frost: Life and Talks-
  Walking* by, 542, 666-667, 703
Miami, University of
  RF talks before the Winter In-
  stitute at, in March 1935, 416, 665;
  again talks at, in Jan. 1936, 433-434

Michigan, University of
RF goes to, in Sept. 1921, on a one-year appointment, 174ff
RF returns to, in Sept. 1922, on a second one-year appointment, 200ff
RF and EWF visit, in April 1924, 262; RF is offered a life appointment at, 607-608; accepts, 263, 267, 269-270; RF goes to, in fall of 1925, 436ff; confides that he may not stay at, 293-294; resigns after one year, 295-296
RF returns to, for one week, in March 1927, 307; again returns to, in Oct. 1932, 401-402, 660-661
Millay, Edna St. Vincent, 305, 399, 651
Millikan, Robert Andrews, 658
Milton, John, 223, 552, 565-566, 656-657
Monro, Harold, 333, 337-338
Monroe, Charles A.
becomes a friend of RF's, in South Shaftsbury, 169; RF quotes, on bees, 169-170; RF writes to, from London in 1928, 331-332; helps RF find and buy the Gully Farm in 1928, 366ff; RF writes to, from Harvard in 1938, 673-674; RF writes to, from Gainesville in 1938, 698
Monroe, Harriet, 18-19, 182, 533
Moody, Harriet, 158, 164-165
Moody, Paul D., 684-685, 690-691, 699
Moore, Marianne, 264
Moore, Merrill, 418-419, 441
Moore, Virginia, 347
More, Paul Elmer
is host to RF in March 1921, 165-166; describes RF's visit, 166; *A Century of Indian Epigrams* by, 167, 572; *Paul Elmer More* by A. H. Dakin, 572
Morris, Earl H., 657
Morris, Hobart Lewis, Jr.
Edward Morgan Lewis—A Biography by, cited, 687
Morrison, Kathleen Johnston
(Mrs. Theodore Morrison), is a leader in bringing RF to Bryn Mawr College in 1920-1921, 445; with her husband, gives reception for RF after the first Norton lecture at Harvard in 1936, 445
Morrison, Theodore
in 1928, invites RF to review *Letters of Sacco and Vanzetti* for the *Atlantic*, 461-462; in 1932, is one of the younger poets attending the dinner in honor of T. S. Eliot, 402; in 1933, as director of the Bread Loaf Writers' conference,

invites RF to perform for a fee of $50, and gets no answer, 462, 685; writes again, and gets a refusal, 686; in 1936, with his wife, gives reception for RF after the first Norton lecture at Harvard, 445; in 1936, persuades RF to accept an invitation to give a reading at the Bread Loaf Writers' Conference, 462; in Feb. 1938, exchanges letters with RF about attacks on RF made by leftist critics, 489-490; in April 1938, is an honorary bearer at memorial service for EWF, 699
Morrow, Dwight, 400
Morrow, Dwight, Jr., 400
Munson, Gorham B.
in 1925, describes RF as the "purest classical poet in America today," 318; in 1926, is invited by RF to write a biography of RF, and accepts, 319; in 1927, is invited by RF to lecture at Amherst, 321; submits MS of biography to RF, who sends suggestions for revision, 321-323; publishes biography of RF, 323; annoys RF by representing the poet as a humanist, 324ff; in 1931, attends six lectures given by RF, 653; *Robert Frost: A Study in Sensibility and Good Sense* by, 323-324; quoted and cited, 517; "Robert Frost" by, 632; "Robert Frost and the Humanistic Temper" by, quoted, 326; cited, 634; "The Classicism of Robert Frost: Reminiscences of a Biographer" by, quoted, 319; cited, 632; "A Comedy of Exiles" by, quoted, 319-320; cited, 632

N

New Deal, The
RF writes critically of, in Jan. 1935, 411
RF on, in June 1935: "Personal freedom has always been considered by the world as too remotely unsocial; this personal freedom has now vanished in favor of a new freedom of relationships of social rights and contracts." 417
RF conceals another attack on, behind the title of his talk in Colorado in Aug. 1935: "What Poetry Thinks of Our Age," 424ff
RF associates "Provide, Provide" with, 437-438
RF satirizes the humanitarianism of, in "A Roadside Stand," 438-439

INDEX

New Deal, The (*cont.*)

RF, in 1936, inspires a newspaper article entitled, "Latest Poem by Robert Frost Versifies New Deal As Lost," 441ff

RF, in 1936, on the largesse of: "Every man's home his own poorhouse," 448

New England Poetry Club, The

RF attends the organization meeting of, in 1915, 41ff; congratulates Amy Lowell when she is elected first president of, in 1915, 529; is elected vice-president of, in 1917, and president of, in 1919, 341; summary of RF's rare participations in the meetings of, 586-587; *The New England Poetry Club*, by Abbie Farwell Brown, 586

New Republic, The

reprints "The Death of the Hired Man" in 1915, 6, 521; publishes Amy Lowell's review of *North of Boston* in 1915, 3-4

RF contributes poems to, while Torrence is poetry editor of, 219

RF is told about an attack on him in, 451; excerpts quoted, 452

RF to Lankes in 1936: "The New Republic might blaze away till its guns jammed and I would never know it except through you who are apparently one of the last remaining die-hard readers. Its subscription list has almost touched the vanishing point." 451

RF is again attacked in, 454, 678

New School for Social Research, The

RF, in 1930: "Do you think I would derogate from my dignity or aloofness if I did a series of lectures . . . on poetry this winter at the New School of Social Research. I'm not afraid of the radicals . . ." 379

RF gives six lectures at, in 1931, 380, 391, 653

RF is threatened by a radical at, in 1936, 464

Newdick, Robert S., 681, 692

Newton, Jessie Porter Kirke, 411, 663

Norton Lectureship, Charles Eliot

T. S. Eliot is appointed to, at Harvard in 1932, 401; RF is appointed to, in 1936, 434ff, 444ff

Nuhn, Ferner

takes exception to RF's theme in "Build Soil," 455-458; RF provisionally replies to, 458-460, 682

Nutt, David, and Company

RF's difficulties with, over the American editions of his first two books, 5-6, 518-519, 573-574, 587

O

O'Brien, Edward J., 41ff

Occidental College

RF gives a reading at, in 1932, 401, 657

O'Conor, Grace, 341ff, 639-640

O'Conor, Norreys Jephson, 586, 341ff

Olds, George Daniel

is appointed President of Amherst College after the dismissal of Meiklejohn, in 1923, 228; persuades RF to return to Amherst in 1923, 228-229; invites RF to dinner with Neils Bohr in 1923, 617; visits RF in Ann Arbor in 1926 and again persuades him to return to Amherst, 295-296, 621-622; letter from, to President Pease, on the terms made with RF in 1926, 622

Olympic Games

RF attends, at Los Angeles in 1932, 655

O'Neill, Eugene, 603

O'Reilly, John Boyle, 14, 523

Osborn, Chase Salmon, 175, 575

Owen, Harry G., 684

P

Page, D. D.

ed., *The Letters of Ezra Pound*, quoted, 54, 533; cited, 533

Palmer, George Herbert, 81, 208

Parker House incident, 256-257, 606-607

Peabody, Josephine Preston, 33, 43, 527, 537-538

Pease, Arthur Stanley, 323, 621-622, 634

Peele, George, 264, 610

Perry, Bliss, 531

Perry, Mrs. Margaret, 586-587

Piers Plowman, The Vision Concerning

RF on: "A book that influenced me most I never read." 506, 700

Plato, 251, 694

Platonist, 388, 491, 697

Poetry of Robert Frost, The

first cited, 516

Poetry Society of America, The

the poetry of RF is disparaged at a meeting of, in Dec. 1914, 8, 521

RF first attends a meeting of, in Feb. 1915, 8

RF explains his theory of poetry, at a meeting of, in Jan. 1916, 73, 537

Pope, Alexander, 552, 630
Porter, Charlotte Endymion, 42, 534
Porter, Admiral David Dixon, 411
Pound, Ezra
  in 1915, writes a friendly farewell letter to RF, 533
  in 1915, Amy Lowell tells RF of her experiences with, 18ff
  returns to the controversy over RF's reception in U. S. A., 53ff; replies to Harriet Monroe's reprimand about the manner of his returning, 533
  RF scolds Braithwaite for paying attention to, 55
  RF mocks, in 1935, for trying to achieve originality by "imitating somebody that hasn't been imitated recently," 416; Pound criticizes RF for his "cheap witticisms," 450; RF proposes to send a rough response to, 450
Prescott, William Hickling, 251
Pulitzer Prize
  awarded to: New Hampshire, 248; Collected Poems, 389; A Further Range, 449-450, 675

Q

Queens University, Kingston, Ontario
  RF spends a week at, in March 1921, 165, 571-572
Quiller-Couch, Sir Arthur
  ed., Oxford Book of English Verse, 291-292

R

Rascoe, Burton
  interviews RF, in 1923, 220; writes an article on RF, 220-221; is reprimanded by RF in a letter not sent, 221-223
Rasmussen, Johan Victor, 242
Recognition of Robert Frost
  ed., Richard H. Thornton, 488; cited, 635, 695-696
Reed, John, 40, 113
Reese, Lizette Woodworth, 305-306
Richards, Edward Ames
  in 1920, as an Amherst undergraduate, publishes a poem which stimulates RF, 299-300, 623; in 1922, starts on the Long Trail hike with RF, 190ff; in 1963, writes an account of his friendship with RF, 582
Rittenhouse, Jessie Belle
  in 1915, summarizes the unfavorable view of RF held by some members of the Poetry Society of America, 8, 521; unfavorably reviews North of Boston and arouses RF's displeasure, 53, 533
Robinson, Edwin Arlington
  RF to Mosher in 1913: "I wish sometime if you know Robinson you could put me in the way of knowing him too . . ." 529
  RF meets, through Braithwaite, in 1915, 44; RF goes to a Boston bar with, 44, 529; RF receives from, a copy of The Porcupine, 45; RF's letter to, about The Porcupine, 45-46
  RF sends to, a copy of A Boy's Will, which is praised by, 530
  RF is a speaker at a Poetry Society meeting which is attended by, in 1916, 73, 530; RF admires the response of, to LU, at this meeting, 74; after the meeting, RF receives a letter and a copy of The Man Against the Sky from, 530; when RF fails to acknowledge either the letter or the book, Robinson is hurt, 530-531
  RF sends to, a copy of Mountain Interval, which is acknowledged, 531
  RF refuses to pay tribute to, on Robinson's fiftieth birthday, 531-532
  RF makes slurring remarks about the sonnet "New England" by, in 1923, 254-256, 605-606
  RF, in 1927, is made jealous by the success of Tristram, 380
  RF, in 1930: "Robinson spoiled farming for me when by doubting my farm he implied a greater claim on my part to being a farmer than I had ever made. The whole damn thing became disgusting in his romantic mouth." 381
  RF, in 1930: "How utterly romantic the enervated old soak is. The way he thinks of poets in the Browningese of 'Ben Johnson'! The way he thinks of cucolding lovers and cucold husbands in 'Tristram'!" 381
  RF goes to dinner with Merrill Moore, 418-419
  RF is nominated for membership in the American Academy by four prose-writers and, 389
  RF's letter to, in 1934, causes Robinson to say, "I'm afraid Frost is a jealous man." 667
  RF, after the death of, makes this claim: "Somehow I never felt jealous of him at any time." 667

Robinson, Edwin Arlington (*cont.*)
RF writes an "Introduction" for *King Jasper*, 419-422; RF, on this "Introduction": "The nearest I ever came to getting myself down in prose . . ." 490
RF, invited by the American Academy to write a memorial tribute for, refuses, 668
RF, in 1938: "Then again I am not the Platonist Robinson was. By Platonist I mean one who believes what we have here is an imperfect copy of what is in heaven. The woman you have is an imperfect copy of some woman in heaven or in someone else's bed." 490-491
Romig, Edna Davis, 525
Roosevelt, Franklin Delano
RF, in Key West in Jan. 1935, criticizes, 411
RF satirizes, in "To a Thinker in Office," 427-428, 669; RF publicly confirms the implied association, 441-442; RF privately denies that the initial association was deliberate, 443
Root, Merrill, 143ff
Rossetti, Christina Georgina, 251
Rowell, Wilbur E.
as lawyer handling annuities from the estate of RF's grandfather, is visited by RF in March 1915, and is able to make an advance payment, 11, 522; is again visited by RF, in May 1915, and makes another advance payment, 526; RF receives an $800 annuity payment from, in July 1916, 526
assists RF in handling finances for RF's sister Jeanie, 123ff
Rugg, Harold Goddard, 537
Rukeyser, Muriel, 678
Russell, Ada Dwyer, 18, 276
Russell, George (AE), 337, 670

S

Sacco and Vanzetti
RF's unsympathetic response to, during the trial of, 376-377
RF refuses two invitations to review *Letters of Sacco and Vanzetti*, in 1928, 378-379
Sandburg, Carl
"Met Frost; about the strongest, loneliest, friendliest personality among the poets today; I'm going to write him once a year; and feel the love of him every day." 577

RF dislikes, when they first meet, 179
RF on, in 1922: "He is probably the most artificial and studied ruffian the world has had." 180
encourages RF to give readings in Texas in 1922, 209
Santayana, George
RF: "Santayana is the enemy of my spirit." 691
RF's early hatred for, at Harvard, in the nineties, 691; RF's attack on, forty years later, 484; *The Last Puritan* by, is a bestseller at the time of RF's attack, 484
Sarett, Lew, 286
Schauffler, Robert Haven, 7-8, 521
Schoenfield, Allen
"Science Can't Dishearten Poets, Says Robert Frost," passage quoted from, 288; cited, 618
Scott, Arthur, 4
Scott, Mildred Minturn, 4-5
Scott, Russell, 4-5
Sears, Fred C., 560
Sedgwick, Ellery
RF calls on, and goes to dinner with, in March 1915, 12ff; RF offers three poems to, 37ff; excerpts from letters by, to Edward Garnett, 522, 528
Selected Letters of Robert Frost first cited, 516
Selected Prose of Robert Frost first cited, 585
Selva, Salomon de la, 17
Sergeant, Elizabeth Shepley
Robert Frost: The Trial by Existence first cited, 519; quoted, 693
Fire Under the Andes by, cited, 597
"Robert Frost, A Good Greek out of New England" by, cited, 632, 693
Seven Arts, The, 80, 113, 554
Shakespeare, William
RF quotes from *As You Like It* by, 213, 589; quotes another passage from *As You Like It*, 235, 595; paraphrases a passage in *Macbeth*, 462; responds to a passage quoted from *Henry IV, Part I*, 467-468
RF uses Emerson's essay on, in *Representative Men*, as a text in an Amherst course, 251
RF is asked to write a commemorative poem on, 542
RF is accused of plagiarizing from Sonnet Number 116 by, 650
Shelley, Percy Bysshe, 442, 698
Sheridan, Richard Brinsley, 603
Silver, Ernest L., 81, 440

Sinclair, May, 529
Sitwell, Edith, 341
Skinner, Burrhus Frederic, 358-359, 642
Smart, Christopher, 484-485
Smith, Chard Powers
   Where the Light Falls by, quoted and cited, 667
Smith, James Cruikshank, 338-339
Smith, Lois
   Through Heaven's Back Door by, quoted, 209, quoted and cited, 588
Smythe, Daniel
   Robert Frost Speaks, cited, 675
Snow, Wilbert
   meets RF at the fiftieth birthday dinner, in 1925, 614-615; praises RF in an article, "New England and the New Poetry of America," 1925, 614
   RF is guest of, in Dec. 1926, 305; RF takes, to New York City for a dinner in honor of Lizette Reese, 305
   summarizes RF's hostility to Darwin's theory of evolution, 629-630; angers RF in a reference to "Sitting by a Bush," 629
   is reprimanded by RF for misinterpreting a line in *Paradise Lost*, 656-657
   tells of how RF refused to send a tribute to Robinson on his fiftieth birthday, 531; tells of how RF tried to make amends to Robinson, 667
   is an honorary bearer at the memorial service for EWF, in 1938, 699
   "The Robert Frost I Knew" by, first cited, 531
Southey, Robert, 449, 676
Spitzer, Lyman, 626-627
Squire, J. C., 178, 577, 591, 639
Stevens, Wallace
   RF disparages "Peter Quince at the Claviar" by, in 1915, 63
   RF is displeased to have Munson lecture on, at Amherst in 1927, 321
   RF meets, in Key West in March 1935, 665-666
   RF gossips about, in Colorado, in the summer of 1935, 665; RF's gossip gets back to, 450
Stevenson, Robert Louis, 253
Stowe Notes, by Robert Taber, 521
Strauss, L. A., 578, 612
Suckow, Ruth, 376, 678
Sullivan, Mark
   in 1915, calls RF merely a short-story writer, 59; *National Floodmarks* by, cited, 534; in 1926,

relays to RF a comment made by President Coolidge, 257-258; *Our Times* by, quoted and cited, 607
Swedenborg, Emanuel, 251, 694
Swinburne, Algernon Charles, 620

T

Taber, Robert, 521
Taggard, Genevieve
   sends to RF a copy of *May Day*, which she edited, 377; visits RF in Amherst, in 1929, 377-378
   RF gives to, a list of titles and dates to indicate when he wrote each of the poems in his first four books, 648
   favorably reviews RF's *Collected Poems*, in 1930, 388; quotes RF elsewhere, 648-649
Teasdale, Sara, 183, 521
Tennyson, Alfred, Lord
   RF, in 1926, makes a passing reference to "The Voyage of Maeldune" by, 290
   RF, in 1936, reads a passage from "In Memoriam" by, at the memorial service for Edward Morgan Lewis, 475
   RF, in 1938, quotes another passage from "In Memoriam" and also quotes from "Idylls of the King," 499-500
Texas
   RF first visits, in Nov. 1922, 208ff; RF returns to, in April 1933, 404, 662; RF spends the winter of 1936-1937 in San Antonio, 476ff
Thomas, Edward
   sends his son Mervin to U. S. A. with the Frosts in 1915, 2-3; letter from, to RF, in 1915, quoted, 27; introduces RF's poetry to Edward Garnett, 38, 39
   has a habit which inspires RF to write "The Road Not Taken," and is the first to receive a copy of it, 88-89, 544-548
   RF writes to, shortly after the enlistment of, 89-90; RF receives letters from, in France, 91
   RF seeks an American publisher for the poems of, 87, 91ff
   is killed in action, on Easter Monday 1917, 93; RF writes letter of condolence to the widow of, 93-94; RF writes to Garnett about the death of, 94-95; RF encourages others to write articles on, 95, 549; RF writes his own tribute to, 95-96

Thomas, Helen
(Mrs. Edward Thomas), writes to the Frosts in 1917, 92-93; RF writes to, 93-94; in 1923, RF dedicates *Selected Poems* to, 636; in 1928, RF and EWF visit, in England, 334-335, 636; RF deletes the dedication to, in the next printing of *Selected Poems*, 636
pays genuine tribute to RF in *World Without End*, in 1931, 637
Thomas, Mervyn, 2-3, 4-5, 7, 548
Thomas, R. George
ed., *Letters from Edward Thomas to Gordon Bottomley*, quoted and cited, 548
Thompson, Lawrance
Robert Frost: The Early Years, first cited, 515
ed., *Selected Letters of Robert Frost*, first cited, 516
ed., with Grade, *New Hampshire's Child: The Derry Journals of Lesley Frost*, 633
Thoreau, Henry David
RF on, in 1922: "In one book (Walden) he surpasses everything we have had in America." 285
RF on, in 1915: "I'm . . . glad of all the unversified poetry of Walden—and not merely nature-descriptive, but narrative as in the chapter on the play with the loon on the lake, and character-descriptive as in the beautiful passage about the French-Canadian wood-chopper. That last alone . . . must have had a good deal to do with the making of me." 602
Walden provides a basis for RF's friendship with Warren R. Brown, 111; also provides a basis for RF's friendship with Van Dore, 285; is used as a text in one of RF's Amherst courses, 251
RF on the style of, 253-254
Thornton, Richard H.
successor to MacVeagh as head of the trade department, Henry Holt & Co., is sent to call on RF in Vermont in 1928, 314; in 1936, informs RF that *A Further Range* is a Book-of-the-Month Club choice, 449, 675; in 1937, prepares to publish a book-length tribute to RF, 695-696; is given an ultimatum by RF, 696
ed., *Recognition of Robert Frost*, mentioned, 488, cited, 635, 695-696
is an honorary bearer at the memorial services for EWF, in 1938, 699

Threescore
by Sarah Cleghorn, first cited, 519
Tilley, Morris P.
meets RF in Franconia in 1916, 127, 176; assists RF's sister Jeanie at the University of Michigan in 1916, 127, 557
welcomes the Frosts to Ann Arbor in 1921, 176, 189; writes to, about a planned visit to Ann Arbor in April 1924, 607-608
"Notes from Conversations with Robert Frost" by, 576, 602
Torrence, Ridgely
RF meets, in New York City, in March 1919, 159; RF visits, in Dec. 1920, 159-160
becomes poetry editor of *New Republic* in 1920, 159
RF again visits, in 1923, 219, 591, 599
Townsend, R. C.
"In Defense of Form" by, quoted and cited, 596
Tottel's Miscellany, 627
Trial by Existence, first cited, 519
Trowbridge, John Townsend, 42, 106
Tufts College
RF reads at, as Phi Beta Kappa poet, in 1915, 30, 36-37
Turgenief, Ivan Sergeyevich, 247, 602
Tyler, Dorothy
is a senior at Michigan when she meets RF, in 1925, 284-285; is one of "The Three Graces" editing *The Outlander*, 285; on RF as a teacher, 619-620
"Remembering Robert Frost" by, quoted and cited, 620

U

Untermeyer, Jean Starr
(Mrs. Louis Untermeyer), mentioned, 40; accompanies LU to Ann Arbor in 1922, 180; is divorced from LU, 347; is remarried to LU, 348; is again divorced from LU, 351; RF hopes LU will marry Jean Starr every other time, 351
Untermeyer, Louis
biographical sketch of, 39-40; RF begins to correspond with, in 1915, 31-32; excerpts from first article on RF by, 32; cited, 526; RF's response to *Challenge* by, 32-33
RF meets, in Boston, in May 1915, 39ff; RF encourages, to serve

Untermeyer, Louis (*cont.*)
as a defender of RF, 60-63; RF, in bitter moods, confides his fears to, 64-65, 79-80, 113-114
RF listens to, reading parodies of Robinson, Masters, Amy Lowell, Lindsay, and RF, in 1916, 73-74, 537-538; RF mentions a parody of his own, in a letter to, 546
RF encourages, to write an article on Edward Thomas, 95, 549
RF is placed on the editorial board of *The Seven Arts* by, 80; RF commemorates the demise of *The Seven Arts* with a limerick addressed to, 113
RF, in 1922, brings LU to Michigan to lecture on "Certain American Poets," 180-181
RF and LU try to unmask Amy Lowell as the anonymous author of *A Critical Fable*, 205-208
RF consults LU about sending a letter of rebuke to Burton Rascoe, 221
RF again brings LU to Michigan to lecture, in 1923, 224
RF persuades LU to absent himself from the dinner in honor of Amy Lowell, 273-275; RF writes to, about the death of Amy Lowell, 278-279
RF reveals much about himself in his comments on the marital difficulties of, 344-352
RF is assisted by, immediately following the death of EWF, 501; RF asks, to serve as an honorary bearer at the memorial service for EWF, 699

V

Van Dore, Wade
begins to correspond with RF, in 1922, 285; meets RF in Franconia, summer of 1922, 285-286; visits RF three times in Ann Arbor, 1925-1926, 285-287, 289, 294
RF writes to, in 1927 and 1928, 359-360; RF asks, to serve as hired man on the South Shaftsbury farm in 1929, 368ff, 643ff
dedicates to RF the volume of poems entitled *Far Lake*, in 1930, 360
RF is provoked by, to write "The Most of It," 360-362
Van Doren, Carl
requests interview with RF, 218-219; writes article on RF: "The Soil of the Puritans," 590; is

master of ceremonies at RF's fiftieth birthday dinner, 275; *Three Worlds* by, cited, 649
Van Doren, Mark
attends the dinner in honor of RF, in 1925, 627; as poetry editor of the *Nation*, solicits MSS from RF, 627
Vergil
RF, in writing "Build Soil," adapts his form from the "First Eclogue" of, 432

W

Walcutt, Sue Bonner
on RF's teaching methods at the University of Michigan, 620
Wallace, Henry, 457, 678
Walpole, Hugh, 389
"Waly, Waly"
Scottish ballad from which RF is said to have plagiarized, 650
Warren, Robert Penn, 423, 426, 597-598
Wells, H. G., 648
Wells College
RF gives a reading at, in 1935, 676
Wesleyan University
RF visits, in Dec. 1926, and stays for one week, 305
Weygandt, Cornelius
visits RF in Franconia in 1915, 76; is host to RF in Philadelphia in 1916, 76-77; is host to the Frosts in Wonalancet, N. H., in 1916, 81, 540; passage quoted from a review by, cited, 602
a chapter on RF, in *The White Hills* by, cited, 540, 602
Wheelwright, John Brooks, 402
Whicher, George F.
attends RF's first reading at Amherst and retrospectively describes it, 97, 551; in 1917, under RF's supervision, writes a tribute to Edward Thomas, 95, 549; in 1924, is deprecated by RF, 266; in 1936, is informed by RF about the Norton lectureship, 436; in 1938, is an honorary bearer at the memorial service for EWF, 699
Whitcomb, Lois Elisabeth
writes several articles on the poetry program arranged by RF at the University of Michigan, in 1921-1922, 179-183 *passim*; cited, 577-579 *passim*
White, A. B., 589, 217-218
White, Owen S.
"What the Lizard Learned," cited, 551

INDEX

Whitman, Walt, 39, 54, 253-254, 565-566
Wickenden, L. D., 666
Williams, William Carlos, 321, 678
Wilmore, Carl, 66ff, 536
Wilson, Edmund, 231, 480, 592
Wilson, Woodrow, 330, 635
Wolfe, Humbert, 620
Woodberry, George Edward, 85
Wordsworth, William, 32, 36, 549-550, 602

Y

Yeats, William Butler, 639

Young, Charles Lowell
   background sketch of, 556; helps Lesley Frost at Wellesley College, 115ff; goes hiking with RF, 196; receives reports from RF on the Long Trail hike, 196
Young, Stark, 78-79, 82-83, 105ff, 424

Z

Zabel, Morton D.
   RF causes Henry Holt & Co. to break a contract with, in 1937, 695-696